The New York Times

JEWISH
COOKBOOK

The New York Times
JEWISH
COOKBOOK

MORE THAN 825 TRADITIONAL
AND CONTEMPORARY RECIPES
FROM AROUND THE WORLD

Edited by Linda Amster

Introduction by Mimi Sheraton

ST. MARTIN'S PRESS
NEW YORK

The publishers have generously given permission to use material from
the following copyrighted works:
From *Keep It Simple*, by Marian Burros. Copyright © 1981 by Marian Burros.
Used by permission of William Morrow/HarperCollins.
From *Pure and Simple*, by Marian Burros. Copyright © 1978 by Marian Burros.
Used by permission of William Morrow/HarperCollins.
From *The Foods of Israel Today*, by Joan Nathan. Copyright © 2001 by Joan Nathan.
Used by permission of Alfred A. Knopf, a division of Random House, Inc.
From *Jewish Cooking in America*, by Joan Nathan. Copyright © 1994, 1998 by Joan Nathan.
Used by permission of Alfred A. Knopf, a division of Random House, Inc.
From *The Jewish Holiday Baker*, by Joan Nathan. Copyright © 1997 by Joan Nathan.
Used by permission of Schocken Books, a division of Random House, Inc.
From *The Jewish Holiday Kitchen*, Rev. and Exp., by Joan Nathan. Copyright © 1988 by Joan
Nathan. Used by permission of Schocken Books, a division of Random House, Inc.
From *The Book of Jewish Food: An Odyssey from Samarkand to New York*, by Claudia Roden.
Copyright © 1996 by Claudia Roden. Used by permission of Alfred A. Knopf,
a division of Random House, Inc.
From *Mediterranean Cookery*, by Claudia Roden. Copyright © 1987 by Claudia Roden.
Used by permission of Alfred A. Knopf, a division of Random House, Inc.
From *The New Book of Middle Eastern Food*, by Claudia Roden. Copyright © 1968, 1972,
1985, 2000 by Claudia Roden. Used by permission of Alfred A. Knopf,
a division of Random House, Inc.
The lyrics to the folk song "Ode to Potatoes" are excerpted from *The Complete Idiot's Guide to
Learning Yiddish*, by Rabbi Benjamin Blech. Copyright © 2000. Used by permission of
Alpha Books/Pearson Education.

BOOK DESIGN BY DEBORAH KERNER/DANCING BEARS DESIGN

ISBN 0–312–29093–4

10 9 8 7 6 5 4 3 2

WITH MOST LOVING APPRECIATION TO MY BROTHERS,

STANLEY C. MEYERSON, OF CHERISHED MEMORY,

AND

JAMES I. MEYERSON,

FOR OUR ENDURING BONDS OF FAMILY

AND TO THE DEAR ONES WHO CARRY THOSE BONDS WITHIN AND FORWARD:

RICHARD MEYERSON, WENDY MEYERSON FOX, COLLIER MEYERSON,

JASON LUKE, JARROD LUKE

CONTENTS

ACKNOWLEDGMENTS

MY DEEP THANKS AND APPRECIATION TO THE CHEFS, RESTAURATEURS, COOKBOOK AUTHORS AND OTHER FINE COOKS WHO GRACIOUSLY GRANTED permission for the recipes they have created to be included in this book. I am very indebted also to my *New York Times* colleagues Mark Bittman, Marian Burros, Melissa Clark, Florence Fabricant, Amanda Hesser, Moira Hodgson, Bryan Miller, Molly O'Neill and Regina Schrambling, for their many exceptional recipes, which first appeared under their bylines in *The Times*, and to the late Craig Claiborne, Pierre Franey and Jean Hewitt for their recipes. My gratitude also to Florence Fabricant for her astute guidance regarding the selection of some recipes.

Warm thanks to Mimi Sheraton for the Introduction and the chapter headings that enhance this volume and for her cherished recipes. She was unfailingly generous with her time and expertise, making our association a pleasure and a privilege.

Sincere appreciation to Joan Nathan for her similar invaluable contributions to this volume: the essay "The Foods of Israel Today" and the many recipes from articles about Jewish cooking that have appeared often in *The Times*.

I am grateful to Gilda Angel, the former "Kosher Gourmet" columnist for *The New York Jewish Week* and the author of *Sephardic Holiday Cooking*, for authoritative information about the ingredients in the recipes and other aspects of kosher cooking; and to her husband, Rabbi Marc D. Angel, of the Spanish and Portuguese Synagogue of New York City, and Associate Rabbi Hayyim J. Angel for their assistance. Thanks also to Sarah Rosner, of the Orthodox Union, for additional information about kosher certification.

I am indebted to Rabbi Menachem Genack of the Orthodox Union and to Professor Gary Rendsburg, the Paul and Berte Hendrix Memorial Professor of Jewish Studies at Cornell University, for reviewing the article "The Shoket, and Kosher and Trefa

Dishes—Where to Buy Meats," which was published in the February 23, 1896, edition of *The New York Times,* and for their counsel concerning the accompanying recipes, which are reprinted in the Afterword on page 579.

Grateful appreciation to Toby Nussbaum and to Enid Ship, two exceptional kosher cooks, who generously volunteered to review hundreds of recipes and whose critiques helped to shape the book. Very special thanks to Carol Auerbach for the loan of her collection of favorite kosher recipes from *The Times,* which allowed me immediate access to many recipes that predate the electronic archive. She and other people who are dear to me, including Steven Bazerman, Ethel Christin, Helen Doctorow, Arthur Gelb, Barbara Goldsmith, Maxine Jaffe, Elizabeth Levine, Jane Slotin, Terry Tolk and Laurie Wilson, provided sustaining counsel and encouragement. And especially, of course, Mort Sheinman, whom I cherish beyond measure.

I am deeply indebted to Judith Friedlaender and Yosi Ya'ari and to Meeka Ya'ari for securing reprint permissions in Israel and to Suzanne Daley and Laetitia Contri, of the *Times*'s Paris bureau, for similar assistance in France.

At *The Times,* my gratitude to Julie M. Dunn for downloading and organizing recipes, and to Arthur Bovino for similar assistance. Thanks also to Jeff Roth, who checked *Times* microfilm to clarify details in some recipes, and to Tomi Murata, who expedited the publication of this book in so many ways.

At St. Martin's Press, I am particularly indebted to my editor, Marian Lizzi, for her exceptional efforts on many aspects of this volume, and to Julie Mente, Mark Steven Long, Susan Joseph, Steve Snider, Justine Valenti, Elizabeth Catalano and Amelie Littell.

Most special thanks to Mitchel Levitas, then the editorial director of book development at *The Times,* for his invaluable expertise and guidance. He suggested the book to me, shaped it in innumerable ways and coordinated a myriad of details throughout the long and arduous development of this book, and I am deeply appreciative.

My profound appreciation to Phyllis Yellin Schondorf, a dear friend and an accomplished culinary consultant and copy editor, who voluntarily took on the thankless task of scrutinizing, critiquing and clarifying the details of hundreds of recipes.

And, especially, boundless gratitude and most heartfelt thanks of all to Michael Roos for his technical wizardry and support in so many ways. Without his unstinting and indispensable assistance, this book simply would not have been possible.

PREFACE

◆

by Linda Amster

WHAT BEGAN FOR ME AS A STRAIGHTFORWARD PROCESS OF COMPILING RECIPES FOR THIS BOOK BECAME, INSTEAD, AN UNEXPECTED AND FASCINATing voyage of discovery.

On a personal level, there were the dishes of my youth—the chicken soup, the pot roast smothered in onions, the stuffed cabbage, the sponge cake. Memories of my mother's traditional Ashkenazic cooking endure and can be effortlessly summoned. But her recipes, unfortunately, cannot. Although I had recreated many of them in my own kitchen, there were others—her famous teiglach, for example, those delectable dough balls coated in honey—that I had never dared to duplicate. So a bonus of working on this volume was that, as I culled the archives of *The New York Times,* I found not only the classic recipes for dishes I had savored as a child and some variations, but also others brand new to me—further expanding my knowledge of Ashkenazic food.

But my voyage of discovery in a larger sense was my introduction to kosher cuisines with which I had not been very familiar—dishes from the Mediterranean, the Middle East and from other parts of the world. Before beginning the editing process, I had worried that there might not be enough to give this volume the breadth and balance it required. On the contrary and to my delight, I found a trove of mouth-watering kosher recipes from those regions—such an array and abundance that it was often difficult to choose which to include.

There was another unexpected reward in assembling this collection—the arc of history that is reflected in recipes that span eras from the ancient to the contemporary. The Lentil Levivot recipe on page 304, for example, may actually resemble the one for the first Hanukkah latkes. Those fried pancakes, made from lentils, barley or flour, were prepared throughout the Middle East centuries before potatoes were introduced to

Europe from the New World and transformed into the treat that Ashkenazis traditionally devour as they celebrate the Feast of Lights. In these pages, classic recipes for levivot and latkes are joined by many of their modern descendants—variations of vegetable pancakes based on such diverse ingredients as sugar snap peas, Jerusalem artichokes, mushroom-pecan and curried sweet potatoes.

But innumerable recipes in this book do not fit into a neat category of culinary historical imperatives. Some were chosen because their ingredients are found in dishes typically associated with Jewish cooking. Others are included because they are the traditional fare in places where large established Jewish communities have resided; Jewish families prepared such indigenous dishes in their homes, and many took the recipes with them when they migrated elsewhere, as Joan Nathan documents in "The Foods of Israel Today" on page xxiii, which is an excerpt taken from the Introduction to her book of the same name. While the selection of those recipes was necessarily subjective and consequently may be open to discussion, even dissent, the intent was to present a wide range of dishes all appropriate for a kosher table—dishes that reflect the tastes and the culinary heritage of Ashkenazic, Sephardic and Mizrachi Jews.

Finally, there is a third category of recipes, the contemporary fusion cuisine that Mimi Sheraton discusses in her Introduction on page xv. These innovative presentations of traditional ingredients by today's most gifted chefs and food writers are refreshing additions to the kosher menu—dishes like David Burke's Pastrami Salmon; Alain Ducasse's Rib-Eye Steaks with Peppered Cranberry, Marmalade and Swiss Chard; Wolfgang Puck's Lamb Chops with Lamb's Lettuce; David Bouley's Fava Beans with Honey, Lime and Thyme; Todd English's Tuna Tabbouleh; and Bill Yosses' Bittersweet Chocolate Dacquoise with Halvah Cream. Sometimes, as these pages show, a single dish can inspire variations that cross the spectrum of Jewish cuisine: for example, gravlax, a popular appetizer of salmon fillets that "cook" as they marinate in a crust of seasonings, can be prepared in the Northern European tradition with dill as the predominant flavor. At Fleur de Sel in Manhattan, the fish is coated with citrus rinds for a decidedly Sephardic spin; at Istana, the spices encrusting it evoke the flavors of Morocco. It is the fusion recipes, juxtaposed with those handed down for generations, that broaden the kosher repertoire, giving it a special dimension that I have tried to reflect in this book.

To aid readers, all recipes are labeled *meat, dairy* and/or *pareve* (acceptable with either meat or dairy dishes). Those with more than one designation contain either an optional dairy ingredient (such as butter) or an optional meat ingredient (such as chicken broth) that may be omitted to change the category of the dish. In a few instances, margarine or oil has been substituted for butter in a recipe, or vice versa, and there are some recipes in which balsamic vinegar replaces sherry vinegar, which does not have a kosher certification. In no case did these changes compromise the integrity of the dish. A more serious substitution occurs in a few meat recipes that originally called for Worcestershire sauce, which contains anchovy. Since the Shulchan Aruch, the Code of Jewish Law, prohibits the eating of fish and meat together (see Advisory Note, page 582), I followed the guidance of Gilda Angel, an authority on kosher cuisine, who reviewed the recipes, substituting an equal amount of tamari in the few meat dishes that call for the savory character of Worcestershire sauce.

The salt measurements in the poultry and meat recipes are reprinted as they appeared in *The New York Times*. Since meats and poultry are salted during the koshering process, cooks may wish to either reduce the amount of salt to taste in the recipes or eliminate salt entirely when preparing the dishes.

The name noted at the end of each recipe is the byline of the person who wrote the article in which it appeared in *The New York Times*. To augment recipes from the paper's pages, I have included recipes from cookbooks by the following authors who were formerly affiliated with *The New York Times*: Craig Claiborne, the renowned food editor whose coverage profoundly influenced generations of its readers and food professionals; food and restaurant critic Mimi Sheraton, whose informative and lively Introduction and chapter headings illuminate this volume; two food columnists, Molly O'Neill and Pierre Franey; and food writer Jean Hewitt. All of the recipes in this book were taken from these sources, with the exception of those on pages 199, 201, 202, 262 and 435, which were contributed by the sources to whom they are credited. Chefs and restaurants are credited as they appeared at the time of publication. Since then, some chefs may have moved and some restaurants may have closed. Unless otherwise noted, restaurants cited are located in New York City.

For readers who are not familiar with the flavoring agents of Middle Eastern cuisine, the Explanatory Notes on page 582 contains descriptions of some ingredients that appear in those recipes, as well as a listing of sources where they may be purchased. It also contains a section about koshering liver as well as other entries about the preparation of some ingredients used in many dishes. A chapter called "Suggested Holiday Dishes" (page 587) offers menu suggestions for selected Jewish holidays. The listings are not intended to be comprehensive but simply to present an idea of some recipes that are suitable for those occasions.

Many of the recipes in this book include a separate preparation for a savory or sweet component, such as an onion confit or a honey sauce, that may be used to complement other dishes of your choice. Recipes for these versatile ingredients are identified within the text by a recipe title in capitalized letters that are somewhat smaller than those of the main title.

Because the recipes in this volume come from many sources and were originally published over a long span of time, there are a few inconsistencies in terminology, but they are minor and should not pose a problem in preparation of the dishes. For convenience, the instructions of some older recipes, calling for manual chopping, slicing and pureeing, have been replaced with updated techniques using a food processor. Similarly, in most cases, the professional and personal identifications of recipe contributors appear in this book as they did in the paper, although they may have changed since their original publication.

As I have noted, compiling this collection was an unexpected and rewarding introduction to the rich diversity of dishes that may grace a Jewish table. As you leaf through its pages, I hope you will make similarly gratifying discoveries, through recipes and revelations that enhance your pleasure in kosher cooking.

A TABLE BEFORE ME

by Mimi Sheraton

Thou preparest a table before me in the presence of mine enemies . . .
My cup runneth over.

—PSALMS 23

"WHO IS A JEW?" HAS BEEN A RECURRENT QUESTION IN PHILOSOPHY, POL-
ITICS AND LITERATURE FOR CENTURIES, AND A DEFINITIVE ANSWER HARDLY
seems imminent.

"What is Jewish food?" is a less critical and weighty question, but one that runs
parallel. It too revolves around a history of wandering and settling, of maintaining religious observances in strange and often hostile cultures and of the emotional tugs
between assimilation and memory. It is too easy to say that Jewish food is anything Jews
eat, especially considering their well-demonstrated taste for Chinese dishes.

I submit that Jewish food is the world's oldest fusion cuisine, a currently fashionable
term applied to a multi-ethnic culinary blend devised by chefs in search of enthusiastic
reviews and (with luck) superstar status. By contrast, the Jewish kitchen developed naturally
over centuries, as home cooks migrated with their native dishes, fused them with strange
local products and food customs and with recipes of their new Jewish neighbors from
other countries. Despite the constant change, one food ritual has remained the same:
kosher laws—*kashruth*—are the kitchen commandments, the acknowledged modifiers of
secular influences. My maternal grandmother, who was born in the southern Ukraine,
moved to Cracow in Poland as a young bride and learned to cook from a Hungarian Jewish
neighbor, with the result that many of her dishes had the pungent spicy taste of hot and
sweet paprika. Her Hungarian strudels were legendary. And reflecting her Ukrainian childhood, my grandmother baked big, horseshoe-shaped bread rolls filled with chicken livers,

onions and kasha that she called knishes. Served in slices, they were totally unlike the individual pastry packets we know by that name here. But any authentic Ukrainian cookbook includes recipes for knishes with various fillings, all shaped like my grandmother's.

Such fusion is developing now at an ever-increasing rate, providing much of the inspiration for the remarkable range of recipes in this book. Through travel, mass communication and an increase in food connoisseurship, young and adventurous Jewish home cooks, kosher or not, are adapting a worldwide array of dishes, often making them compatible with health concerns and modern tastes. However elusive a description of such culinary aesthetics may be, it is clear that these days, in even strictly kosher kitchens, just about every cuisine is being cooked up, from Italy, France and Latin America to China and Greece. From prestigious chefs and restaurants come new candidates suited to the Jewish menu (and found in this book) such as David Bouley's Fava Beans with Honey, Lime and Thyme; Mushroom and Eggplant Ratatouille from Wolfgang Puck; Tuna Tabbouleh from Todd English; and Salmon Pastrami from David Burke. And as for humble halvah in a classy soufflé, who knew?

Of course, not all Jews order from the same menu to begin with. The largest and best-known group in the United States—and the one that still defines Jewish cooking in this country—are the Ashkenazim, Jews of Eastern European origins who spoke German-based Yiddish and carried their dishes from Germany, Austria, Poland, Hungary, Romania, Czechoslovakia, Russia, Ukraine, Latvia and Lithuania. Their foods and language differ entirely from those of the Sephardim, who originated in Spain (called Sephard in Hebrew); their lingua franca is the Latin-Spanish–based Ladino. After their expulsion from Spain under the Inquisition, in 1492, Sephardim migrated throughout the Mediterranean into countries such as Greece, Italy, Turkey and North Africa; in other countries such as Syria, Lebanon, Jordan, Morocco, Tunisia, Egypt, Yemen, Iran and Iraq they joined the Oriental or Mizrachi (Eastern) Jews, whose communities had been there for centuries. Nowhere is that cultural blend more apparent these days than in Israel, where a totally new and exciting Jewish cuisine is developing.

There are even further culinary differences within both the Eastern European and Middle Eastern Jewish cuisines. Jews from the south of Poland and Ukraine in the region of Galicia are known as Galitzianas and, just as they spoke a different, more Germanic dialect, they also adopted the softer, subtler seasonings of Germany and Austria for their cooking and baking. Their arch-rivals, the Litvaks of Lithuania and northeastern Poland, preferred earthier, more rustic versions of the same dishes, more Russian in character. There is much teasing between the two as to which group ruins gefilte fish by adding sugar, just as there is teasing about dialect; the Litvaks say *bagel* while the Galitziana pronunciation makes a bagel sound like a *beigel*.

The Yiddish language, based primarily on medieval German, includes food words of other origins. In German, for example, duck is *ente* and noodles, *nudeln*. But Yiddish adopts Eastern European *katchka* for duck, and Lithuanian *lokshen* for noodles.

Foods shape our memories of home and childhood, and I am not sure I ever approach a Friday night without recalling, at least for a moment, the traditional Sabbath dinner—even though I often complained about it as a child. Growing up in a moderately observant family of Ashkenazic background, I knew that if it was Friday night, it must be chicken soup. Even then I hated routine and once rudely demanded to know why we had to eat chicken soup every single Friday night. "Is it part of the religion?" I asked. "Does the Bible say that Jews must have this particular soup every Shabbes?"

My mother was not sure how to answer me. She knew it was not a religious rite, but she also firmly believed that a wonderfully golden, aromatic chicken soup, flecked with parsley and adrift among rice, noodles or matzoh balls, was considered the ultimate Jewish treat and therefore worthy of the week's most important family meal. Born in Brooklyn, she probably had no inkling that in the impoverished backwaters of Eastern Europe, a chicken was a luxury and was served only on the most special occasions. Even though she herself ignored the law that proscribed Jews from cooking on Shabbes—the Sabbath lasting from before sundown Friday to nightfall Saturday—observant Jews prepared food that required no cooking for Saturday lunch. The answer: cold chicken.

None of this explained why we could not have a velvety, verdant split pea soup or a rich mushroom and barley soup, and a beefy pot roast, redolent of garlic, onions and paprika that had slowly simmered away as the meat melted to tenderness. Or—my favorite—roast duck nested on delicious, grainy buckwheat groats, called kasha.

One thing I could be sure of: all of my Jewish friends would be eating the same meal on Friday nights, perhaps differing only in the choice of vegetables and desserts. Similarly, all of us would share gefilte fish and matzoh balls at the Passover Seder; it didn't matter when else we had them. Imagine, then, my astonishment when, as a young adult, I met a Sephardic Jew for the first time and learned that gefilte fish and matzoh balls are not part of their cuisine, to say nothing of chopped chicken livers, noodle pudding—kugel—and not even the braided bread—challah—for which Middle Eastern pita seemed, to me, a flat substitute, literally and figuratively.

To make matters even stranger, Sephardim eat fish cooked with rhubarb, and on Passover some are allowed rice, although it was forbidden to Ashkenazim. And for Hanukkah, the Sephardic treat is big, puffy jelly doughnuts—*soofganiyot*—instead of latkes, the thin, crisp and oniony potato pancakes that I loved. Indeed, probably the only truly universal Jewish food is matzoh, the unleavened flat bread particularly associated with Passover, but eaten throughout the year.

In any event, it didn't take long for me to appreciate what struck me as the exotic Sephardic cuisine with its golden olive and sesame oils, its mellow eggplant and supple bean purees, the juicy grilled lamb, lemony chicken, grainy couscous and succulent rice pilafs heady with the fragrances of cinnamon, cardamom and gildings of saffron. And only when I went to Israel was I able to extend that admiration to culinary wonders of other Jewish kitchens: Uzbekistan's lamb, vegetable and noodle soup; Yemen's heady spice mixes such as *zhug* and *hilbeh*; Moroccan *tagine* with meatballs; and Bukharan flat bread, to name only a few.

To grasp the origins and enduring guidelines of Jewish cuisine, it is necessary to know the basic religious laws that shape it, even if one chooses to bypass them. Most important, to the observant they are permanent spiritual reminders of what it means to be Jewish, even as each day's meals are being planned and prepared.

French cuisine had Escoffier, the Italian cucina, Pellegrino Artusi, but observant Jewish cooks answer to a higher authority: the Almighty by way of Moses who, tradition tells us, received what became interpreted as the rules of kashruth along with the Ten Commandments on Mount Sinai. If there are culinary influences more enduring than that, I have yet to hear about them. While many religions have some dietary prohibitions (Muslims may not eat pork, Hindus are forbidden beef and some sects impose total vegetarianism), I know of none with so wide a range of intricate rules dictating not only what foods may be eaten, but how they must be prepared and served, often with religious rituals performed at various stages.

Observant Jews may eat only meat of animals that chew their cud and have cloven hooves, which eliminates pigs, horses and rabbits, whose meat is considered *trayf*—forbidden. Also forbidden are the hindquarters of any four-footed animal, which rules out, for example, sirloin steak, rump roasts and legs of lamb or veal. (In some countries, the removal of a certain nerve renders hindquarters edible, but that is not permitted by the rabbinate in the United States.) Forequarter cuts such as chuck or shoulder, breast or brisket, rib steaks and the tender band known as skirt steak or Romanian tenderloin are often adapted to recipes based on hindquarter cuts, with adjustments that compensate for differences in tenderness, texture and the amount of fat.

Poultry may be eaten in its entirety, but may consist only of chicken, duck, goose, turkey, quail, squab and Cornish hens; as with meat, no wild game is permitted because it must be killed to be caught and so cannot be slaughtered according to ritual. For the same reason, no animal found dead may be eaten. All meat and poultry must be slaughtered by a professional known as a *shochet*, who says a prayer as he slashes the jugular vein and trachea with a razor-sharp knife in a single swipe, causing instant, painless death and allowing the blood to quickly drain from the body.

To make sure the animal is not diseased, it must be examined by an official inspector, a *mashgiach*, in addition to whatever government inspection is required. *Glatt kosher* is a term now broadly applied to mean the strictest observance, including that restaurants and food shops be *shomer shabbes*, closed for the twenty-four hours of the Sabbath. But the most basic meaning of *glatt kosher* refers to the condition of an animal's organs when inspected after slaughter. Lungs are examined closely, and if they have no lesions are pronounced *glatt*, or smooth.

Once the animal is bled and butchered, the remaining blood must be eliminated by several soakings and washings in cold water and applications of kosher coarse salt for specified periods of time. The koshering may be done by a butcher or at home with poultry. Liver is the one organ that must be broiled by direct flame. I believe that the admonition to remove every vestige of blood accounts for the common preference among many older Jews for well-done meat, although younger, secular Jews have learned to like beef and even lamb done medium or rare.

Laws of kashruth also include the separation of meat or poultry (in Yiddish, *flayshedig* from the German *fleisch* for meat) and dairy (*milchedig* from the German *milch* for milk). Instead of those terms, Sephardim designate the division as "of meat" and "of cheese"—*de viande* and *de fromage* in French; Ladino or Spanish-speaking Sephardim use *de carne* and *de queso*. Meat and dairy products may not be kept, cooked or eaten together; each requires its own set of cooking and eating utensils and in the strictest homes, different dish towels and sinks (or sink liners). Although permissible times vary, dairy foods may not be eaten sooner than three to six hours after meat, but meat may be eaten almost immediately after dairy if the mouth has been rinsed and a piece of bread chewed. That explains the prohibition against serving cream-based desserts after meat main courses, leading to the ersatz nondairy cream substitutes, none of which are used in recipes in this book. Far better to have a perfect apple pie in a crust made with vegetable shortening, or a luscious, wine-poached fruit than a chalky, fake, whipped cream cake that is a better choice when it can be made authentically to follow a dairy meal.

Kosher laws also account for fundamental changes in dishes borrowed from other cuisines, a perfect case in point being that much-loved favorite chicken fricassee. It is based on the Hungarian chicken *paprikash*, originally sautéed in lard and finished with sour cream to achieve a rich, pink sauce. Eliminating pork and dairy products, Jews make it with either chicken fat, vegetable oil or margarine; by leaving out the sour cream, you wind up with a clear, roseate paprika sauce and a very different dish. I have no idea how tiny meatballs came to be added to the Jewish version, but I'm glad that they did.

Foods that may be eaten with either meat or dairy are considered neutral, or pareve. Among those foods are eggs (kosher only if there are no blood spots in the yolks and if they were laid by healthy, well-fed hens), and all grains, fruits and vegetables not prepared with meat or dairy products. Leafy vegetables must be assiduously washed to eliminate any insects that are classified as *trayf*.

Fresh and saltwater fish are also pareve, but to be kosher, must have fins and over-lapping scales that can be removed while leaving the skin intact. That eliminates all shell-fish as well as eels, skate, shark, swordfish and sturgeon and its precious roe, caviar. Permissible "caviars" are prepared with the roe of kosher fish, most especially salmon and whitefish.

Packaged foods, cured meats and the like, and even kitchen soaps are marked as being kosher and also as pareve, if they are.

Contemporary Jewish cuisine thus represents old and new. Few want to give up the traditional, defining dishes that form a bond among Jews all over the world, almost as strong as ties of religion and what remains of Yiddish and Ladino. In my travels to places as distant from each other as Australia and Argentina, Denmark and Mexico, I felt a strong sense of community with Ashkenazim I met, especially when conversation inevitably turned to recipes—for sweet-and-sour stuffed cabbage; blintzes enfolding fluffy, creamy cheese; and the delights (and risks) of nibbling on *gribenes*, those crunchy, high-cholesterol cracklings that remain when chicken fat is rendered.

Sephardic Jews enjoy the same reassuring sense of familiarity in their travels, espe-cially at holidays when traditional foods are most evocative, symbolizing continuity with the past, both personal and historical. To celebrate Purim, for example, Sephardim would feel at home abroad as they share a dessert of small, syrupy fritters known as

Haman's ears, a different form of the Israeli soofganiyot included in this book. To the Ashkenazim, the same holiday would seem incomplete without hamantaschen, tri-cornered pastries filled with prune or apricot jams or poppy seeds, to recall the pockets of Haman, the Persian court official whose destruction of the Jews was averted by the wiles of the beautiful Queen Esther.

Although the oldest surviving cookbook was probably one written by the Roman Apicius, and is dated between the second and fourth centuries C.E., the Old Testament, although hardly a cookbook, is a much older guide to precise culinary fundamentals. As we are reminded by Gillian Feeley-Harnik in her inspired and insightful book *The Lord's Table: The Meaning of Food in Early Judaism and Christianity* (Smithsonian): "The power and authority of the Lord is manifested in his ability to control food: to feed is to bless."

With such entwined promises of spiritual and bodily nourishment, is it any wonder that food has played so important a role in the celebration of Jewish life?

THE FOODS OF ISRAEL TODAY

by Joan Nathan

STARTING AT THE IMPRESSIONABLE AGE OF TWENTY-SIX, I LIVED IN ISRAEL FOR TWO YEARS AND HAVE RETURNED OFTEN THROUGHOUT THE YEARS. IN 1992 I went with a Maryland Public Television crew to film segments for my documentary, *Passover: Traditions of Freedom*. I returned from this trip with a determination to tell more of the stories that make Israeli culture and cuisine so compelling. Over the years, from the clear perspective of an affectionate outsider, I have been able to observe the changes Israel has undergone with a clarity that only distance can provide.

Someone once told me that even if you don't live in Israel, Israel can teach you how to live. It's true: the intensity of the political atmosphere reminds us of the preciousness of life and the importance of seizing the moment. This extreme sense of the present interacts with the rich ancient history of the land, the biblical birthplace of the Western world, to bring a certain energy and dynamism to every aspect of life there, whether religious or secular.

But an Israeli cuisine? A *cuisine* is usually defined as cooking that derives from a particular culture. Since the Jewish population has essentially been dispersed throughout the world, Jewish food, and by extension the food of Israel, while centered in the Jewish dietary laws expounded in the Book of Leviticus, subsumes the cuisines of countries throughout most of the world. Unlike in France and Italy, for example, where cooking has been grounded in the same soil for thousands of years, in Israel, the "new food" is a hybrid, inspired by every corner of the world, but with an increasing emphasis on native ingredients.

The original ingredients used by cooks in the land of Israel included the seven biblical foods mentioned in Deuteronomy—barley, wheat, figs, dates, pomegranates, olives and grapes. *Mizrachi* or "Oriental" Jews— those who left Palestine for Babylonia at the time of the destruction of the First Temple and have always remained in the Middle

East—have always maintained a cuisine more rooted in the original biblical ingredients. The Jews who migrated to Spain and Portugal after the destruction of the Second Temple in 70 C.E. adapted the new local foods to their dietary laws. Following the Inquisition and their expulsion from the Iberian peninsula, these people became known as Sephardic Jews, and their cuisine took on the tone of their new homelands of Greece, Morocco and Turkey. So, too, Ashkenazic cooking developed as other Jews made their journeys to Central and Eastern Europe. Today, all these foods are being embraced by many of the Jews returning from afar to the "land of milk and honey." Christian and Moslem cultures of the region have also contributed their own customs to Israeli cooking, so today Israel's emerging cuisine is truly global in scope.

I love discovering the connections between people and food, and nowhere more so than in Israel. Through culinary haunts one can uncover the enormously exciting story of how these pioneers transformed a harsh land to one bursting with new produce and culture. Some of their recipes are as old as the land; others are quite modern. Every recipe has a story that reflects not only the varied influences of a Jewish population coming from ninety different countries, but also the Christian and Muslim traditions from throughout the Middle East. Israel is a land that transcends ethnic identity, where an immigrant's native tongue might be Russian or Farsi, Polish or Ladino, where some Jews came knowing how to bless bread in classical Hebrew but could not use modern Hebrew to buy bread and cheese.

During a visit to Massada, one of Herod's hilltop fortresses, an archaeologist might pull out of his pocket a two-thousand-year-old olive or date pit which he found in an ancient garbage pile. On that same day, a new Israeli chef at Jerusalem's King David Hotel might prepare a modern *amuse gueule* of sushi made from seaweed filled with pine nuts and cured olives with a quail cooked in a date syrup. At the Levinsky market in Tel Aviv, a Greek deli run by Holocaust survivors from Salonika stands across the street from a Turkish *burek* baker and a Persian market where the prices are written in Farsi, Hebrew and Arabic. Meanwhile, every Friday grandmothers all over the country prepare traditional Libyan, Persian, Italian and German Jewish meals for their families. The Sabbath, even in secular Israel, is the centerpiece of the week, with all meals leading up to it.

A typical Israeli main meal, as codified in the *Israel Defense Force Cook Book*, includes a Middle Eastern hummus or tahina, a central European turkey schnitzel with a Turkish eggplant salad, or a Hungarian goulash-type stew with fresh native fruit for dessert. Over the years I have noticed that most tourists in Israel, when asked to name a local dish, usually mentioned only street food—hummus, *schwarma* (spicy rotisserie-grilled meat in a pita) and falafel, or the addictive sunflower and pumpkin seeds whose shells carpet some city sidewalks. But few of these dishes can be identified solely as "Israeli"; hummus and falafel, for example, are certainly not Israeli—they are adapted from local Arab foods. While these street foods are indeed popular, it is important to consider also the multinational dishes that are so common in Israeli homes.

While Sabbath and holiday recipes increasingly reflect the diverse heritage of Jews from many parts of the world, there is a noticeable gap between generations: A Czech survivor of the Holocaust, for example, may make for her children a stuffed chicken from Prague as a tribute to a community that exists now only in her memory. But her children, who have grown up in Israel, have less of an emotional connection to their Czech heritage and more of a willingness to cook and eat foods native to Israel. Thus, traditional food is yielding both to the more modern everyday convenience food— frozen schnitzel, packaged hummus and prepared soup—and to today's sophisticated restaurant cuisine, which increasingly plays with the bounty of the global market, resulting in a distinctly cross-cultural eating experience.

When I lived in Jerusalem in the early 1970s, only tourists, diplomats or foreign journalists ate in restaurants. Grabbing hummus and falafel at a fast-food stand or dropping into a café for coffee and cake was the Israeli idea of "dining out." Food was scarce, and wasting time on such a bourgeois matter seemed contrary to the pioneering spirit of the country. In fact, the restaurants were so bad in those days that Henry Kissinger, engaging in his Middle East "shuttle diplomacy," once moaned, "Why can't a country with two and a half million Jewish mothers have better food?" Today, even Henry Kissinger might agree that that lament is a thing of the past.

The founding fathers and mothers of modern Israel had an idea of a melting-pot culinary style. David Ben-Gurion, Israel's first prime minister, envisioned that the country would have a distinct "Israeli food," like an "Israeli dance." But twenty years ago during the country's adolescence, they realized that the melting-pot idea wasn't going to work. Dov Noy, professor of folklore at the Hebrew University of Jerusalem, says, "As the Oriental and Sephardic intelligentsia emerged in Israel, the idea of a kind of multiculturalism developed, and Israelis became aware that the Jewish people and other peoples in Israel have many languages and cultural ways. Then the melting-pot idea was given up. Now we think of Israeli food as a mosaic within the frame of the nation, where each dish is a different color and stands by itself."

For the past thirty or so years, excitement inspired by this multiculturalism has been building in Israel's culinary community. The country has become an increasing presence in the international food world, contributing new and unusual products made from native ingredients. When I lived in Israel we ate kohlrabi and cauliflower but certainly not the blueberries and broccoli people eat there today. Israel—known globally in the past almost solely for its Carmel tomatoes and Jaffa oranges—is now second to France for excellent foie gras. With boutique cheeses being made throughout the country, kosher wines from the Golan Heights winning first-class competitions worldwide and more cookbooks being written per capita than in almost any other country, Israel is bursting with culinary creativity. The interplay of cultures and cuisines has made eating an art such as it has never been in Israel before.

Despite their global lifestyles, the new Israeli chefs still cultivate a link to the foods of the Old Testament. Grapes, dates, lentils and chickpeas are but a few of the ancient ingredients that have captured their imaginations in producing signature dishes. With constant waves of immigration, Israel is rapidly incorporating the native cuisines of its new populations. The story of Israeli food is not just a Jewish story—its recipes cross borders more easily than people do. It is also the story of a land that has overcome harsh natural deprivation to bring forth new agricultural produce. Because it constantly incorporates so much from the rest of the world, Israel may never boast of one "cuisine," but it will always retain a rich mixture of fine tastes. It reflects the modern mosaic of the country, embracing the culinary influences of its Arab neighbors and accommodating the varied tastes of the world's Jews.

APPETIZERS

The Yiddish word *forshpeiz*, "before food," is the key here, for appetizers on the Jewish menu, as on all others, are meant to whet the appetite, but not to satiate it. Served in small portions, they are usually savory and salty enough to titillate the palate. They may be of luxurious ingredients such as caviar or smoked salmon, or as plebeian as briny herring in a sour cream or wine sauce, or the smoky eggplant mousse that is the lemony, Middle Eastern *baba ghanouj*.

So important is this category of foods, especially to the Ashkenazim, that in Jewish neighborhoods of large cities there are specialty shops known as appetizer stores, much like dairy delicatessens. They offer an array of nonmeat foods that are generally preserved with salt, including smoked and pickled fish of all kinds and appropriate accompanying salads.

Some of the most typical and best-loved Jewish dishes are, in fact, appetizers: gefilte fish, chopped liver, smoked whitefish salad, pickled herring and, from Roman Jews, the famed *carciofi alla Giudia,* the artichokes that are flattened and fried to resemble crisp sunflowers.

Sephardic Jews generally refer to appetizers as *mezze* and incorporate much of what we know as Greek and Middle Eastern first courses, including versions of stuffed grape leaves, the crunchy bean croquettes falafel and hummus, the velvety puree of sesame paste and chick peas. Add contemporary innovations on traditional tastes such as salmon and beet tartare, mushroom ceviche and Middle Eastern "wontons" stuffed with lamb, and you begin to see how the Jewish fusion cuisine continues to develop. In addition to the appetizers that follow, there are many other candidates in chapters on fish, vegetables and salads.

Those who observe kosher law have to plan accordingly, omitting meat-based appetizers before dairy main courses, and vice versa. Fortunately, that poses few problems as there are so many delectable choices in each category.

CHOPPED LIVER

meat

ADAPTED FROM *The Second Avenue Deli Cookbook*

1½ pounds beef liver, koshered and cut into
    1-inch pieces (see Note, page 582)
1 pound chicken livers, trimmed of fat and membrane
    and koshered (see Note page 582)
3 tablespoons plus 2 teaspoons corn oil
2 tablespoons plus 2 teaspoons Schmaltz
    (page 413)
4 cups coarsely chopped onions
4 large hard-boiled eggs, peeled
2 teaspoons salt
¼ teaspoon freshly ground black
    pepper

1. Preheat broiler. Rinse beef and chicken livers and drain well. Place livers in a large baking pan and drizzle with 2 tablespoons corn oil. Toss livers to coat with oil. Broil 8–10 minutes, then turn livers over. Broil another 5 minutes, until livers are fully cooked and lightly browned on both sides. Transfer to a covered container and refrigerate until chilled.

2. While livers are chilling, prepare onions. In a large skillet over medium heat, combine 1 tablespoon plus 2 teaspoons schmaltz and remaining tablespoon plus 2 teaspoons corn oil. Add onions and sauté until golden and browned at edges, about 20 minutes. Transfer to a covered container and refrigerate until chilled.

3. In a food processor, combine beef and chicken livers, onions, hard-boiled eggs, remaining tablespoon schmaltz, salt and pepper. Blend until smooth. Transfer to a covered container and chill thoroughly.

Yield: 3 cups

—ALEX WITCHEL

MIMI SHERATON'S CHOPPED MUSHROOMS, EGGS AND ONIONS · (VEGETARIAN CHOPPED LIVER)

dairy, pareve

ADAPTED FROM *From My Mother's Kitchen*

2 tablespoons butter or margarine
1 tablespoon minced onion
4 medium mushrooms, cleaned and coarsely chopped
4 eggs, hard cooked and coarsely chopped
Salt and freshly ground white pepper to taste

1. Heat the butter or margarine in a small skillet over moderate heat, and when hot and bubbly add the onion. Sauté until it begins to wilt. Add the mushrooms and continue to sauté, stirring frequently, until the mushroom liquid evaporates and they begin to soften, 5–7 minutes. Do not brown the mushrooms or onion.

2. Turn the mixture onto a chopping board or into a

wooden bowl. Add the coarsely chopped eggs and continue to mix by chopping until evenly combined. Be sure to scrape in all the fat and any liquid left from the sautéing. Season to taste. Chill several hours before serving.

Yield: About ¾ cup

—MIMI SHERATON

CLASSIC GEFILTE FISH

pareve

ADAPTED FROM Ruth Messinger

> *10 pounds whole fish (a combination of whitefish, pike and carp—but no more than one-third carp), cut into fillets (reserve bones, skin and heads)*
> *8 medium onions, quartered*
> *8 medium carrots, roughly chopped*
> *6 stalks of celery with leaves, roughly chopped*
> *3–4 whole matzohs*
> *2 cups plain seltzer*
> *6 whole eggs*
> *3 large egg yolks*
> *2 tablespoons salt or to taste*
> *1 teaspoon pepper*
> *1 cup matzoh meal as needed*
> *¼ cup lemon juice*

1. Combine the fish bones, skin and heads in a 10-quart or larger stockpot. Add half of the onions and carrots and all the celery.

2. Place the fish fillets in a food processor and pulse until coarsely ground (you may have to do this in batches). Set aside.

3. Put the remaining onions and carrots in the food processor and chop medium-fine. Mix with the ground fish by hand.

4. Soak the matzohs in the seltzer for 5 minutes, then squeeze dry and crumble. Add the matzohs, whole eggs, egg yolks and half the salt and all the pepper to the ground fish mixture.

5. Lightly shape the fish mixture into balls 2–2½ inches in diameter. If the balls will not hold their shape or if mixture feels too sticky, add matzo meal until it is the consistency of meatballs.

6. Place the balls in the pot on top of the bones and vegetables. They can be in a double layer. Add cold water to cover the fish balls almost completely. Add lemon juice and remaining salt. Bring to a boil; reduce heat and simmer uncovered for 1½–2 hours, or until the balls are solid and the liquid has been reduced by half. Frequently baste any uncovered balls as they cook.

7. Remove fish balls with slotted spoon. Place on a platter and wrap with plastic wrap and refrigerate.

8. Let broth simmer to reduce again by half. Cool; strain and pour a light layer over the fish balls. Chill. Broth will gel. Serve with Fresh Horseradish (page 413).

Yield: 40 pieces

NOTE: *Recipe may be halved.*

—MARIAN BURROS

SIMPLIFIED ODESSA-STYLE GEFILTE FISH

pareve

<small>ADAPTED FROM</small> Primorski, Brighton Beach, Brooklyn

4 large onions, peeled
¼ cup oil
2 matzohs
2 medium carrots, peeled
2 beets, peeled
2 pounds ground fresh carp
2 pounds ground fresh whitefish
4 large eggs
1 tablespoon salt, or to taste
1 teaspoon freshly ground pepper, or to taste
Red or white horseradish for garnish

1. Chop 3 onions and sauté until soft in the oil in a frying pan; then pulse in a food processor until chopped but not mushy.
2. Soak matzohs in cold water until moistened. Drain and squeeze dry.
3. Put carrots, beets and fourth onion in a fish poacher or wide pot. Add 8 cups water and bring to boil; reduce to simmer.
4. To the ground fish, add ground onions, matzohs, eggs, salt and pepper and mix well with your hands to a tacky consistency.
5. Lay two large sheets of foil on a counter. Carefully spoon the fish mixture on top, fold sides of foil up around fish and tightly seal. Gently place in pot, adding water if necessary to almost cover the fish. Simmer 1 hour. Remove from heat, cool in broth and serve or refrigerate.
6. To serve, carefully remove foil, place fish on a platter, decorate with the cooked vegetables and garnish with horseradish.

Yield: 15–20 servings

<small>NOTE:</small> *In Odessa, the skins of the fish traditionally were sewn together to encase the stuffing. As a shortcut, simply place a few long sheets of skin, slightly overlaying, on a piece of aluminum foil, fill them with the chopped fish mixture, then cover it with more skin and enclose the whole "fish" in the foil before simmering it in a broth colored red with beets. The result will have the look of a whole fish without the mess. While many Russians insist that the gefilte fish mix should be at least 75 percent carp, others prefer at least 50 percent whitefish.*

—JOAN NATHAN

BAKED GEFILTE FISH LOAF

pareve

<small>ADAPTED FROM</small> *The New York Times Heritage Cookbook*

2 pounds whitefish, filleted
2 pounds pike, filleted
2 pounds carp, filleted
1 onion
3 eggs
¾ cup ice water
½ teaspoon sugar
3 tablespoons matzoh meal
2 teaspoons salt
¾ teaspoon freshly ground black pepper
Toasted almonds
Grated horseradish or horseradish-filled beets

1. Preheat the oven to 350 degrees.

2. Grind the fish fillets with the onion and place in a chopping bowl. Chop until very fine. Add the eggs, ice water, sugar, meal, salt and pepper and beat until thoroughly blended.

3. Turn mixture into a narrow loaf pan and cover lightly with aluminum foil. Bake 1 hour.

4. Serve hot or cold. To serve, slice the loaf and garnish slices with toasted almonds. Serve with grated horseradish or small beets hollowed out and filled with horseradish.

Yield: 6–8 servings

CARPE À LA JUIVE

pareve

ADAPTED FROM *Jewish Cooking in America*

> ½ *cup chopped parsley*
> 3 *small onions, sliced in rounds*
> 2 *cups water*
> 1 *teaspoon freshly ground white pepper*
> ½ *teaspoon grated nutmeg*
> 1 *tablespoon matzoh meal*
> 1 *sprig saffron*
> *Juice of 3 lemons*
> 1 *(3-pound) carp, pike or salmon, cut into 1-inch*
>   *steaks (reserve head and tail)*
> 3 *egg yolks*

1. In a large pot over high heat, bring parsley, onions and water to a boil, then reduce the heat to medium and simmer until tender, about 5 minutes. Add the white pepper, nutmeg, matzoh meal, saffron and lemon juice.

2. Put all the fish pieces (the head and tail, as well as the steaks) into the water, adding more water to cover, if necessary. Cover and poach over medium heat for 10–15 minutes or until the fish is cooked. Remove the steaks to a platter, arranging them in the original form of the fish. Leave the head and tail in the broth and cook over medium-high heat until the broth is reduced by half, about 15 minutes. Adjust the seasoning and strain broth into a bowl, reserving the head, tail and parsley mixture. Return the broth to the pot, add the 3 yolks, whisking well, bring just to a boil and remove from the heat. Bring to room temperature.

3. Add the head and tail to the steaks, re-forming the entire shape of the fish. Cover with the onions and the parsley and some of the reduced broth. Cover and refrigerate overnight with the remaining broth refrigerated separately. Serve the fish at room temperature with any remaining broth poured over it or in a separate bowl.

Yield: 6 servings

NOTE: *This is possibly the first recipe for a Jewish dish to appear in the pages of* The New York Times. *It was published in 1879 in a Household Hints column about the preparation of carp, a then unfamiliar fish to most readers. Carpe à la Juive is both a classic and a contemporary dish, particularly among Jews of Alsatian heritage, who serve it at Seder in place of gefilte fish. For a variation, substitute 2 cloves minced garlic, 2 teaspoons grated fresh ginger, salt to taste and, if desired, 1 cup of sliced mushrooms for the nutmeg, saffron and lemon juice in Step 1. Omit egg yolks.*

—JOAN NATHAN

HUMMUS

pareve

ADAPTED FROM *The New York Times International Cookbook*

2 cups cooked or canned chickpeas, drained
⅔ cup tahini
¾ cup lemon juice
2 cloves garlic
1 teaspoon salt
Italian parsley leaves

1. Place the chickpeas, tahini, lemon juice, garlic and salt in a blender and blend until smooth. Alternatively, the chickpeas may be sieved and mashed along with the remaining ingredients.

2. Pile into small bowl and garnish with parsley leaves. Serve as an appetizer with pita, Sesame Pita Chips (page 45) or as a dip for raw vegetables.

Yield: About 3 cups, or 8–10 servings

WARM HUMMUS

dairy

ADAPTED FROM Develi, Istanbul

4 cloves garlic
1 teaspoon cumin seeds
Coarse salt
2 cans chickpeas (15½ ounces each), drained
3 tablespoons tahini
5 tablespoons extra-virgin olive oil
3 tablespoons fresh lemon juice
2 tablespoons unsalted butter
2 tablespoons pine nuts
½ teaspoon kirmizi biber or Aleppo pepper (see Note)
Flat bread for serving

1. Preheat oven to 400 degrees. With food processor running, drop garlic, cumin seeds and large pinch of salt through feed tube and process until minced. Add chickpeas, 2 tablespoons hot water, tahini, oil and lemon juice and process until smooth. Transfer mixture to shallow casserole, preferably earthenware.

2. Heat butter in small skillet. Add pine nuts and kirmizi biber, stirring briefly, and pour over chickpea mixture. Bake for 20 minutes and serve hummus warm with wedges of flat bread or with Sesame Pita Chips (page 45).

Yield: 8–10 appetizer servings

NOTE: *A mixture of equal portions sweet paprika and cayenne pepper rubbed with a few drops of olive oil can be substituted.*

—FLORENCE FABRICANT

SPICED GINGERED HUMMUS

pareve

2 garlic cloves

1 tablespoon coarsely chopped fresh ginger

Juice of 2 lemons

1¼ cups cooked chickpeas

¼ cup smooth unseasoned peanut butter

½ teaspoon crushed hot red pepper flakes,
   or to taste

Salt to taste

Chips or Sesame Pita Chips (page 45) or raw
   vegetables for dipping

1. With the machine running, drop the garlic and ginger through the feed tube of a food processor and process until minced. Scrape the sides of the bowl, then add the lemon juice. Process briefly, then add the chickpeas and process until the mixture is smooth.

2. Add the peanut butter a little at a time and process until the mixture is smooth and has a creamy consistency. If it is too stiff, add a little water.

3. Add the hot red pepper flakes and salt to taste. Transfer to a dish and serve with chips or pitas or Sesame Pita Chips or with vegetables for dipping.

Yield: 1½ cups, or about 6 servings

—FLORENCE FABRICANT

BABA GHANOUJ

pareve

ADAPTED FROM *The New York Times
International Cookbook*

2 large eggplants

Juice of 2 lemons

2 tablespoons tahini

Salt

1 large clove garlic

¼ chopped parsley or pomegranate seeds

2 tablespoons olive oil

1. Cook the eggplants until soft over charcoal or on top of gas flame. If gas unit is used, line the metal around the burner with aluminum foil. Place the whole, unpeeled eggplants over charcoal or over slow-to-medium gas flame. Cook the eggplants on all sides, turning as necessary, until soft throughout and the skin is charred. Eventually the eggplants will "collapse." Set them aside for about 1 hour to cool.

2. Peel the eggplants and discard the skin. Put the flesh into a mixing bowl and immediately add the lemon juice. Mash well. Add the tahini and blend well. Add salt to taste.

3. Place the garlic clove between sheets of waxed paper and mash and pound gently with a mallet or the bottom of a skillet. The garlic should be mashed as fine as possible. Add to the eggplant mixture, stir well and chill. Place in a flat serving dish and garnish with parsley or pomegranate seeds. Pour olive oil over the dish and serve as an appetizer.

Yield: 8 servings

BABA GHANOUJ WITH TOMATOES AND PEPPERS

pareve

ADAPTED FROM The Soho Charcuterie

2 pounds eggplant

1 or 2 cloves of garlic, pressed

¼ cup tahini

¼ cup lemon juice

6 ounces peeled, chopped tomatoes (about 1 cup)

½ pound green and/or red peppers, diced

8 scallions, sliced, or about 1 cup

¼ cup chopped parsley

2 teaspoons salt

1. Preheat oven to 400 degrees.

2. Spear the eggplants several times with a knife, so that they will not explode in the oven. Bake them for 25–35 minutes or until a knife goes into them with no resistance.

3. Slice the eggplants in half. With a spoon, remove the eggplant flesh from the skin. (It is easiest to do while the eggplant is still hot; wear a rubber glove.) Puree the eggplant.

4. When the puree has cooled, add all the remaining ingredients, reserving a little parsley and diced peppers for garnishing.

5. Taste for salt; add more if necessary.

6. Serve with fresh or toasted wedges of pita bread and leaves of curly lettuce or chicory or with Sesame Pita Chips (page 45).

Yield: Hors d'oeuvres for 15–20 or a first course for 8–10

—CRAIG CLAIBORNE

DRIED CHICKPEAS • (ARBES)

pareve

1 can chickpeas

Freshly ground black pepper

1. Drain chickpeas, rinse under cold water, then spread them on a towel and dry thoroughly. Season with black pepper and serve in small bowls as a nosh.

NOTE: *Arbes, or nahit, a snack food, are traditionally served at Purim. They are also nibbled at a bris, the ceremony of* circumcision and naming of a baby boy and, in some Jewish cultures, are also served on the first Sabbath a week after the birth. Coarse salt is often used instead of, or with, the black pepper. For variety, season lightly with ground cumin and/or flakes of Aleppo or Turkish red pepper, which has both a sweet and fiery flavor (see Note, page 7). If you wish, you can substitute raw chickpeas for the canned version: Soak them in water to cover overnight, then drain and boil them in water to just cover about 20 minutes, until al dente.

—ARTHUR SCHWARTZ

MOSHE'S FALAFEL AS A CANAPÉ

pareve

ADAPTED FROM *New York Cookbook*

1 pound dried chickpeas, soaked overnight in cold
    water, drained and rinsed
3 cloves garlic, crushed
1 large onion, finely chopped
⅓ cup finely chopped fresh parsley
1 teaspoon ground coriander seeds
1 teaspoon ground cumin
1 teaspoon salt
1 teaspoon baking soda dissolved in ½ cup
    water
Vegetable oil for deep-fat frying

1. In a food processor or blender, grind the soaked chickpeas. Add the garlic, onion, parsley, coriander, cumin, salt and baking soda mixture. Process until smooth.
2. In a large, wide pot, heat the oil, making sure that it is at least 3 inches deep. Heat until the oil is hot but not smoking. Using a 1-inch ice-cream scoop, form the chickpea mixture into balls that are slightly smaller than golf balls.

3. Carefully slide the falafel into the oil. Do not crowd the pot. Cook each until golden brown, about 3 minutes on both sides. Use a slotted spoon to remove the balls and drain on paper towels. The falafel can be made up to 2 hours ahead of time and served barely warm, with toothpicks and Sesame Sauce (see recipe).

Yield: 35 falafel

◆ SESAME SAUCE ◆

pareve

1 cup tahini paste
1 clove garlic, crushed
Juice of 1 lemon
¼ cup cold water
¼ teaspoon salt
Dash of freshly ground black pepper

1. Combine all the ingredients in a bowl and whisk until smooth. Refrigerate until ready to serve.

Yield: 1½ cups

—MOLLY O'NEILL

YOGURT CHEESE · (LABAN)

dairy

ADAPTED FROM *The New York Times International Cookbook*

4 cups yogurt
½ teaspoon salt
⅓ cup olive oil

2 tablespoons chopped fresh mint leaves
Mint leaves for garnish

1. Mix the yogurt and the salt and put in a bag made of several layers of cheesecloth. Tie the bag and suspend it over a bowl to catch the drips. Leave overnight.

2. Remove the solid cheeselike mixture from the bag and either form into balls or make a mound with a depression in the middle. Place in serving dish. Pour the olive oil over the balls or into the depression and sprinkle with chopped mint. Garnish with the mint leaves and serve as an appetizer.

Yield: About 1½ cups, or 6 servings

RICE-STUFFED GRAPE LEAVES • (DOLMADAKIA)

pareve

ADAPTED FROM *The New York Times Large-Type Cookbook*

1 cup olive oil
3 large onions, chopped
1 clove garlic, finely chopped
1 teaspoon salt
¼ teaspoon black pepper
1 cup rice
2 tablespoons snipped fresh dill
¼ cup finely chopped Italian parsley
2 tablespoons pine nuts
6 scallions, finely chopped
1 cup lemon juice
3 cups water
1 jar (8 ounces) grape leaves
Lemon wedges

1. Heat ½ cup oil in a skillet and sauté onion and garlic until tender.
2. Add salt, pepper and rice and cook slowly 10 minutes, stirring frequently. Add dill, parsley, nuts, scallions, ½ cup lemon juice and 1 cup water; stir. Cover and simmer gently until liquid has been absorbed, about 15 minutes.
3. Rinse grape leaves under running water, separate and place shiny side down on a board. If leaves are small, put 2 together.
4. Place 1 teaspoon rice filling near stem end of each leaf and roll up jelly-roll fashion toward tip, tucking in edges to make a neat roll.
5. Place remaining oil, lemon juice and 1 cup water in a large skillet. Arrange rolls in a pan, separating layers with parsley stems if more than one layer is made. Place a heavy plate or weight on top and simmer 25 minutes. Add 1 cup water and cook about 10 minutes longer. Cool. Serve with lemon wedges.

Yield: About 24 rolls

BEEF-STUFFED GRAPE LEAVES
WITH APRICOTS • (YERBA)

meat

ADAPTED FROM Valerie Mishaan

2 dozen (approximate) grape leaves (half a
   12-ounce jar)
½ cup raw rice
1 pound ground beef chuck
Salt
Allspice
1 tablespoon tamarind sauce (temerhindy)
1 teaspoon dried mint leaves
1 clove garlic, minced
½ pound dried apricots

1. Drain grape leaves. Store half of the leaves in the refrigerator for another use. Place the other leaves in a bowl and wash them thoroughly under running water to remove any brine taste.

2. Wash and strain rice thoroughly.

3. Combine rice with ground beef and mix well. Season to taste with salt and allspice.

4. Open leaves flat and place a heaping teaspoon of the rice-and-beef mixture on each leaf. Fold sides over filling. Starting from stem end, roll leaf up into a tight package.

5. Prepare a sauce by mixing together the tamarind sauce, 1 cup of water, the mint leaves and the garlic.

6. Line the bottom of a 1½- to 2-quart ovenproof pan with a layer of dried apricots. For a layered effect, place a layer of stuffed leaves, seam side down, on top of the apricots. Continue alternating like this, if more than 1 layer is made, finishing with a layer of apricots. Or you may wish to place all the grape leaves in a single layer in a large pan and tuck the apricot halves among them.

7. Pour sauce over the apricots and add more water if necessary until the water level rises to cover the grape leaves.

8. Cook, covered, over low heat for 90 minutes.

9. Preheat the oven to 375 degrees.

10. Bake yerba for 1 hour. Serve immediately or cool in the liquid.

*Yield: 8 servings as an appetizer;
4 servings as a main dish*

NOTE: *Yerba may be refrigerated or frozen after Step 8. When ready to serve, defrost frozen yerba and bake at 375 degrees for 1 hour.*

—RAYMOND SOKOLOV

GRAPE LEAVES STUFFED WITH LAMB AND FIGS

meat

ADAPTED FROM Matthew Kenney

8 cups chicken stock
¾ cup basmati rice

3 tablespoons olive oil
½ pound lean ground lamb
1 tablespoon chopped garlic
1 tablespoon Aleppo pepper
½ teaspoon ground cumin

Salt and freshly ground black pepper
¾ cup diced dried figs
½ cup toasted pine nuts
½ bunch scallions, chopped
3 tablespoons fresh chopped mint
1 tablespoon dried mint
3 tablespoons chopped parsley
36 grape leaves
Extra-virgin olive oil, for garnish
Lemon wedges, for garnish

1. Bring 1½ cup chicken stock to a boil in a small saucepan. Add rice and reduce heat. Simmer rice, covered, until tender, about 20 minutes. Cool.

2. Preheat oven to 350 degrees. In large skillet, heat olive oil over medium-high heat. Cook lamb and garlic, stirring, until lamb is browned. Stir in Aleppo pepper, cumin, salt and black pepper and cook a few seconds more. Transfer to large bowl. Add rice, figs, pine nuts, scallions, mint and parsley and combine well. Season with salt and pepper.

3. To stuff leaves, place one on a work surface, shiny side down. Place a heaping teaspoon of filling in center of leaf near the base. Fold bottom of leaf over filling, then fold sides over toward center. Roll toward tip of leaf. Repeat for each leaf.

4. Bring remaining 6½ cups stock to a simmer in a saucepan. In a 9-by-13-inch pan, arrange stuffed leaves, packing them close together, seam side down (you can make a second layer if they don't all fit in one layer). Pour hot stock over. Cover pan with foil and bake until leaves are tender, about 1 hour. Let leaves cool in cooking liquid.

5. To serve, drizzle with olive oil and garnish with lemon for squeezing over tops.

Yield: 36 pieces

—MARIALISA CALTA

ARTICHOKES JEWISH-STYLE · (CARCIOFI ALLA GIUDIA)

pareve

4 medium to large artichokes
Vegetable oil for deep frying
1 lemon

1. Trim the stalks and tough outer leaves from the artichokes. Cut off the top third of the leaves. Press the remaining leaves back carefully, spreading them out like the petals of a flower, taking care not to break them. Place the artichokes in a large bowl of cold water with the juice of the lemon to prevent them from turning brown.

2. Meanwhile, heat the oil in a large pot. When you add the artichokes, 1 or 2 at a time, wear gloves and hold the lid of the pan tilted over the oil. The oil will spatter at first because of any water clinging to the leaves of the artichokes. Be very careful because the oil can catch fire if it spatters too much.

3. Once the pot has calmed down, leave the lid off and allow the artichokes to cook until golden and tender. Keep a steady watch in case of any spattering. When the artichokes are cooked, drain them upside down on paper towels and serve at once with the lemon, cut into quarters.

Yield: 4 servings

—MOIRA HODGSON

ARTICHOKES WITH WINE
AND OLIVES • (PROVENÇALE)

pareve

4 large artichokes

Juice of ½ lemon

½ cup extra-virgin olive oil

6 baby onions, peeled

4 cloves garlic, minced

1 cup dry white wine

1 bay leaf

½ teaspoon fennel seed

1 teaspoon coriander seeds, crushed

Coarse salt and freshly ground pepper to taste

¼ pound niçoise olives

1. Remove the outer leaves of the artichokes. Cut the chokes into quarters. Scrape out the hairy leaves from the chokes, and using a knife, pare away any tough outer green parts. Place the quarters in a bowl of cold water, to which you have added the juice of ½ lemon.

2. Pour 1 cup water into a large sauté pan and add the remaining ingredients except for the olives. Bring to boil, then add the artichokes. Simmer, covered, stirring frequently for 15 minutes. Uncover and cook until the artichokes and onions are tender (about 5–10 minutes). Add more water or wine if necessary.

3. Arrange the artichokes on a serving dish and spoon the sauce over them. Garnish with olives and serve hot or cold.

Yield: 4 servings

—MOIRA HODGSON

ASPARAGUS MIMOSA

pareve

ADAPTED FROM *Asparagus, All Ways*

2 large hard-cooked eggs, shelled

¼ cup chopped fresh chives

1 tablespoon chopped fresh dill

1 tablespoon minced parsley

Salt

2 pounds asparagus, stem ends trimmed and peeled

1 tablespoon Dijon mustard

2 tablespoons fresh lemon juice

6 tablespoons grapeseed or peanut oil

Freshly ground white pepper to taste

1. Bring a large pot of water to a rolling boil. Prepare a large bowl of ice water and set aside.

2. Rub eggs through a coarse sieve into a mixing bowl. Add chives, dill and parsley, and toss with a fork to distribute evenly. Season with salt to taste. Set aside.

3. Working in batches, add asparagus to boiling water, and blanch 2–3 minutes, until tender but crisp. Using tongs, transfer to ice water to chill, then drain well. Pat completely dry and transfer to a clean dry bowl.

4. In a small bowl, whisk together mustard and lemon juice, then whisk in oil. Season with salt and pepper to taste. Pour over asparagus and toss to coat. Lift asparagus out of dressing and arrange on platter, all tips facing in the same direction. Spoon egg mixture over stem ends. Serve remaining dressing on the side.

Yield: 4–6 servings

NOTE: *A variation for a dairy meal is Asparagus Polonaise. Cook 2 pounds of asparagus as above and transfer to a* platter. *Sprinkle spears with ¼ cup fine bread crumbs that have been sautéed in 6 tablespoons of unsalted butter, melted, and then sprinkle with one sieved hard-cooked egg and 1 tablespoon minced parsley.*

—REGINA SCHRAMBLING

GRILLED ASPARAGUS WITH VINAIGRETTE

pareve

16 jumbo asparagus
1 small bunch chives
⅓ cup Italian parsley
⅓ cup basil leaves
1 clove garlic, green part removed
⅓ cup olive oil
Coarse sea salt and freshly ground pepper to taste
Lemon juice to taste

1. Preheat grill or broiler. Snap off the tough ends of the asparagus and trim the stalks with a vegetable peeler. Parboil for a minute and drain. Cool to room temperature, then spread out on a plate.

2. Combine the chives, parsley, basil, garlic and olive oil in a blender. Puree and season to taste with salt, pepper and lemon juice.

3. Sprinkle the asparagus with olive oil, salt and pepper and grill over medium heat, turning frequently, for about 6 minutes or until tender. Put on a warm serving dish. Pour the mixture over the asparagus and serve.

Yield: 4 servings

—MOIRA HODGSON

EGGPLANT CAVIAR

dairy

2 medium-size eggplants, about 1½ pounds total
    weight
¼ cup finely minced onions
1 teaspoon finely minced garlic
⅓ cup finely chopped parsley
1 tablespoon lemon juice
¼ cup yogurt
2 tablespoons olive oil
Salt and freshly ground pepper to taste
¼ cup finely chopped green pepper
2 tablespoons seeded tomato, cut into small cubes

1. Preheat the oven to 400 degrees.

2. Prick the eggplants in several places with a two-pronged fork.

3. Place a sheet of heavy-duty foil in the oven. Put in the eggplant and bake 1 hour or less until eggplants are collapsed. Let cool.

4. Split the eggplants and scrape out the pulp. Put pulp through a food mill or food processor or chop it. There should be about 2 cups. Put in a bowl.

5. Add remaining ingredients. Mix well and chill. Serve with buttered toast.

Yield: 6 servings

NOTE: *This dish lends itself to many variations. Some cooks prefer to use 3–4 tablespoons of lemon juice instead of yogurt; others may wish to omit the green pepper and/or the tomato. Or you might want to try a Persian version, adding dried mint and a little cinnamon to the eggplant mixture; or a Yemenite version with tomato puree and Yemenite Zhug (page 423).*

—CRAIG CLAIBORNE

EGGPLANT CAVIAR WITH INDIAN FLAVORS • (BRINJAL BHURTA)

pareve

ADAPTED FROM *The Varied Kitchens of India*

2 eggplants, about 1/2 pound each
1/2 cup finely chopped onion
1/2 cup finely chopped tomato
1/2 teaspoon finely chopped fresh hot chili
1/2 teaspoon salt, or to taste
1 teaspoon corn or peanut oil
1 tablespoon fresh lemon or lime juice
1 tablespoon finely chopped fresh coriander
Toast, crackers or papadums (crisp Indian flat breads) for serving

1. Preheat oven to 375 degrees.

2. Hold the eggplants over an open flame or place under a broiler, turning them to char the skin.

3. Wrap the charred eggplants in foil, place in oven and bake about 25 minutes, until they are soft. Remove from oven, peel and discard the skin and allow the eggplants to cool.

4. Chop the eggplant pulp and mix it with the onion, tomato, chili, salt, oil, lemon or lime juice and coriander. Refrigerate. Serve cool or at room temperature, with toast, crackers or papadums.

Yield: 6 servings

—FLORENCE FABRICANT

CAPONATA

pareve

ADAPTED FROM *Cooking with Herbs & Spices*

1 medium eggplant
6 tablespoons olive oil
1 clove garlic, minced
1 onion, thinly sliced
3 tablespoons fresh or canned tomato sauce
¾ cup chopped celery stalks
2 tablespoons capers
12 stuffed green olives, cut into halves
2 tablespoons wine vinegar
1 tablespoon sugar
Freshly ground black pepper to taste

1. Peel the eggplant and cut it into slices. Sauté in 5 tablespoons of the oil.
2. Remove the eggplant from the skillet and add the remaining tablespoon of olive oil. Cook the garlic and onion in it until the onion is brown.
3. Add the tomato sauce and celery and simmer until the celery is tender. If necessary, add a little water to the skillet.
4. Return the eggplant to the skillet and add the capers and olives. Heat the vinegar with the sugar and pour it over the eggplant. Add pepper to taste and simmer the mixture 10–15 minutes longer, stirring frequently.
5. Serve hot or cold with lemon wedges. Cold caponata may be served on lettuce leaves.

Yield: 6–8 appetizer servings

NOTE: *Caponata is said to have been developed before the Spanish Inquisition as an eggplant salad prepared by Sicilian Jews for the Sabbath lunch.*

MUSHROOM CEVICHE

pareve

ADAPTED FROM *The Art of South American Cooking*

1 pound small white button mushrooms, cleaned, with stems trimmed
¼ cup extra-virgin olive oil
1½ cups fresh lemon juice
2 cloves garlic, peeled and crushed
½-inch piece fresh ginger, minced
1 jalapeño pepper, seeded and finely chopped
Coarse salt to taste
¼ cup finely chopped scallions
2 tablespoons chopped fresh dill
¼ cup finely minced red bell pepper

1. Place mushrooms in a bowl and toss with olive oil. In another bowl, combine lemon juice, garlic, ginger, jalapeño pepper and salt to taste. Add mushrooms and marinate 30 minutes at room temperature.
2. Add the scallions and dill and marinate for another 30 minutes. Check the seasonings, sprinkle with diced red pepper and serve.

Yield: 6–8 servings

—FLORENCE FABRICANT

MUSHROOMS IN SAFFRON MARINADE

pareve

3 tablespoons extra-virgin olive oil

¾ pound mushrooms, the whiter the better, sliced

1 tablespoon sliced garlic

Salt to taste

4 pinches saffron threads, crushed

½ cup dry white wine

Freshly ground black pepper to taste

1½ tablespoons fresh lemon juice

1 tablespoon finely chopped flat-leaf parsley

4 slices lightly toasted country bread

1. Heat I tablespoon oil in a large skillet. Add mushrooms and garlic and cook, stirring, over medium-low heat, until mushrooms look moist. Sprinkle with salt and add saffron and wine. Cook slowly about 7 minutes, until mushrooms have wilted and the liquid just films the pan.

2. Remove from heat, season with pepper and add lemon juice and remaining oil. Check seasonings, fold in parsley and allow to cool about 30 minutes before serving with toast.

Yield: 4 appetizer servings

—FLORENCE FABRICANT

COLD VEGETABLE MOUSSE

pareve

2 cups carrots, halved lengthwise and cut on a
    diagonal about ¼ inch thick

4 small zucchini (about 7 inches long), cut into
    ⅛-inch cubes

3 cups small broccoli flowerets

¼ pound string beans, cleaned and halved (1½ cups)

4 tomatoes, skinned, cored, seeded and cut into ½-inch
    cubes

4 scallions, with the green, diced

¼ cup white wine vinegar

3 envelopes unflavored gelatin

2 cups mayonnaise (page 415)

4 scallions, with part of green, chopped

2 tablespoons fresh basil, diced

¼ cup chopped parsley

3 egg whites, whipped to soft peaks

Salt and pepper to taste

Tabasco to taste

1. In large, deep pot bring lightly salted water to boil. Cook carrots until tender but still firm (about IO minutes). Plunge in ice water to refresh them and drain well. Set aside on paper towels to drain further.

2. Repeat this cooking, refreshing and draining with zucchini (cook only about 5 minutes), broccoli (about 3 minutes) and string beans (about 5 minutes).

3. Add diced tomatoes and scallions to drained vegetables. Heat vinegar in small saucepan and add gelatin, stirring until well dissolved. Remove from heat to cool.

4. When vinegar mixture is room temperature, mix with mayonnaise in large bowl. Add carrots, zucchinis, broccoli, string beans, tomatoes, scallions, parsley and basil. Gently fold in egg whites. Add Tabasco, mix well and taste for seasoning.

5. Pour mixture into 10-cup mold, cover and refrigerate until set (at least 2 hours). To unmold, place mold in warm water for several seconds, then invert over platter and shake. Cut mousse gently with serrated knife.

Yield: 10 cups

—BRYAN MILLER

FESTIVE LAYERED FISH MOUSSE · (MOUSSE TRICOLOR)

dairy

1 pound sole fillets, cleaned

½ pound salmon fillets, cleaned and cut into thin slices

6 cups Court Bouillon (see recipe below)

2 tablespoons unflavored gelatin

6 slices truffles (optional)

Sprigs of dill (optional)

1 pound leaf spinach, blanched and squeezed

1 teaspoon salt

½ teaspoon ground white pepper

¼ teaspoon ground nutmeg

Dash of cayenne pepper

½ cup Béchamel Sauce (page 417)

1 cup heavy cream

¾ cup Crème Fraîche (page 431)

2 cups Dill Sauce (see recipe below)

1. Place a 5-cup loaf pan in refrigerator to chill.

2. Poach sole fillets and salmon slices separately in 3 cups of the court bouillon, for about 4 minutes each. Place fish in collander or wire mesh sieve and let cool.

3. In a heavy saucepan combine the remaining 3 cups of court bouillon with the gelatin and heat slowly, stirring constantly, until the gelatin has dissolved completely. Do not allow it to boil. Set aside to cool.

4. When the aspic has thickened enough to coat a spoon, pour it into the chilled loaf pan. Rotate the mold until the entire inside is coated with the aspic. Pour off the excess and reserve. Refrigerate mold until aspic is set. Repeat this process 3 times, continuing to reserve remaining aspic. Decorate the bottom and sides of the mold with the truffles or dill, and refrigerate mold.

5. To make the mousses: Place sole, salmon and spinach each into a separate bowl.

6. Combine salt, pepper, nutmeg and cayenne pepper, and divide evenly among the 3 bowls.

7. Add the béchamel sauce to the spinach.

8. Whip the heavy cream and set aside.

9. Put sole mixture into the bowl of a food processor with 2 tablespoons of the reserved aspic. (If the aspic has thickened, heat lightly before adding it to the sole mixture.) Process mixture until very smooth.

10. Transfer the sole mixture to a bowl, add ¼ cup of crème fraîche and mix well. Fold half of the whipped cream into the mousse and taste for seasoning. Spoon mixture into the prepared mold and refrigerate.

11. Repeat process with salmon, using 2 tablespoons of aspic, ½ cup of crème fraîche and the remaining whipped cream.

12. Spoon salmon mousse on top of the sole mousse and refrigerate again.

13. Put spinach mixture into bowl of food processor, add 2 tablespoons of aspic and process until very smooth. Taste for seasoning, then spoon on top of salmon mousse.

14. Cover top of mold with wax paper and refrigerate for at least 8 hours. To unmold the mousse, dip the mold into hot water for a few seconds and invert it onto a serving platter. Serve with cucumber salad and dill sauce.

Yield: 10 servings

NOTE: *This mousse can be prepared the day before you plan to serve it.*

Court Bouillon

pareve

> 2 sprigs parsley
> 1 bay leaf
> 2 sprigs thyme
> 1 stalk celery
> 1 carrot
> 1 onion, stuck with cloves
> 1 clove garlic
> 5 cups water
> 2 cups white wine
> Salt to taste
> 5 whole peppercorns

Tie together parsley, bay leaf and thyme. Place in a pot with remaining ingredients. Cover and bring to a boil. Simmer, uncovered, for 15 minutes. Strain and set aside until ready to use.

◆ DILL SAUCE ◆

dairy

> 1 cup mayonnaise
> ½ cup Crème Fraîche (page 431)
> ½ cup sour cream
> 2 tablespoons lemon juice
> 1 teaspoon dry white wine
> Salt and pepper, to taste
> Dash of cayenne
> 3 tablespoons chopped fresh dill

Combine all the ingredients and mix well. Refrigerate until ready to use.

Yield: 2 cups

—BRYAN MILLER

COLD SALMON MOUSSE
WITH MUSTARD-DILL SAUCE

dairy

1½ *pounds very fresh salmon fillets (deboned and*
   skinned)
⅛ *teaspoon grated nutmeg*
⅛ *teaspoon cayenne pepper*
1 *teaspoon coarse salt*
Freshly ground pepper to taste
2½ *to 3 cups heavy cream*
2 *egg whites*
3 *tablespoons chopped fresh chives*

1. Preheat oven to 375 degrees.

2. Cut salmon fillets into 1-inch cubes. Place them in bowl of food processor or blender and season with nutmeg, cayenne pepper, salt and black pepper. Puree fish while gradually pouring in cream—the mixture should be smooth but not runny—and turn off machine. Add egg whites and chives and puree again briefly. Taste for seasoning.

3. To test for texture before cooking the mousse, drop a teaspoon of the mixture into simmering water and let it poach for 2 minutes. Remove it. It should be fluffy and slightly resilient, not rubbery. If mousse is too rubbery, add more cream.

4. Scoop mixture into greased 6-cup mold, a little at a time, pressing down firmly to avoid formation of air pockets. Place mold in an ovenproof dish partly filled with boiling water. Cook in oven for about 40 minutes.

5. Remove mold from oven and set aside to cool. When it is room temperature, refrigerate until thoroughly chilled. To unmold, place mold in hot water for several seconds and then invert over platter. Shake mold and mousse should dislodge. Serve with Mustard-Dill Sauce (see recipe).

Yield: 6 cups

NOTE: *It is important that all the ingredients be well chilled before you begin working, as they will be easier to handle. Even the mixing bowl should be cold.*

❖ **MUSTARD-DILL SAUCE** ❖

pareve

¼ *cup mustard (American-style mustard, which is*
   slightly sweeter than French mustard, works well)
2 *tablespoons chopped fresh dill*
1 *teaspoon sugar*
2 *tablespoons vinegar*
Salt and freshly ground pepper to taste
1 *cup vegetable oil*
2 *tablespoons water*

In mixing bowl combine mustard, dill, sugar, vinegar, salt and pepper. Add oil a little at a time while stirring vigorously. Thin out with water.

Yield: About 1 cup

—BRYAN MILLER

SMOKED-SALMON MOUSSE WITH BLACK-BREAD TOAST AND SALMON CAVIAR

dairy

ADAPTED FROM Remember Basil's

6 ounces smoked salmon, cut into small pieces

½ cup softened butter (unsalted)

½ cup Crème Fraîche (page 431)

1 long sprig of dill, finely chopped

3 chives, minced

1 tablespoon freshly squeezed lemon juice

Freshly ground pepper to taste

1 small loaf of sliced black bread

Fresh red salmon caviar

Dill for garnish

1. Puree the salmon in a food processor while slowly adding the softened butter and crème fraîche.

2. When these ingredients are combined, add the herbs and lemon juice and freshly ground black pepper to taste, or about four grinds of the pepper mill. Remove the mixture from the processor, place it in a bowl and refrigerate for 15 minutes before serving. The mousse will harden quickly in the refrigerator, so remove it as soon as it will hold its shape but is still spreadable.

3. Cut the black bread into small triangles, rectangles or circles and toast at 350 degrees until dry on both sides. When the toast is cool, top each piece with a dollop of mousse. Garnish with salmon caviar and a sprig of dill.

Yield: Hors d'oeuvres for 8–10

—CRAIG CLAIBORNE

COLD ZUCCHINI TERRINE WITH RAW TOMATO-BASIL SAUCE

pareve

2 pounds zucchini

½ cup good-quality olive oil

3 to 4 cloves garlic, peeled and chopped fine

2 tablespoons chopped parsley

1½ teaspoons salt

½ teaspoon ground black pepper

1 cup water

3 envelopes unflavored gelatin (about 2½ tablespoons)

Raw Tomato-Basil Sauce (see recipe below)

1. To make terrine, trim and cut zucchini into ¼-inch slices. Heat the olive oil in a large saucepan or two skillets and, when hot, add zucchini in one layer. Sauté over high heat for about 5 minutes, until zucchini begins to wilt but still retains its bright color. Stir in the garlic and parsley, cook for about 10–15 seconds, and place mixture in bowl of a food processor. Process for 30–40 seconds, until pureed. Transfer mixture to a bowl and stir in the salt and the pepper.

2. Put water in a small saucepan and sprinkle gelatin on top. When absorbed, heat mixture, stirring gently, until gelatin is melted and mixture is well combined. Add to zucchini mixture and mix to incorporate. Line a 6-cup loaf pan with plastic wrap and pour mixture into it. Cover with plastic wrap and refrigerate overnight or for 4–5 hours, until well set.

3. Prepare tomato-basil sauce and refrigerate until ready to use.

4. To serve, spoon about 3 or 4 tablespoons of sauce onto each of 6 serving plates. Cut terrine into 1-inch slices and place a slice of terrine on top of sauce on each plate. Serve with crunchy bread.

Yield: 6 servings

◆ **RAW TOMATO-BASIL SAUCE** ◆

pareve

1½ cups cubed ripe tomatoes (about 2 regular tomatoes or 3–4 plum tomatoes)
1 tablespoon red wine vinegar
3 tablespoons olive oil
¼ teaspoon Tabasco sauce
½ teaspoon salt
2–3 tablespoons finely shredded basil

1. Push very ripe tomato pieces through a food mill or, if tomatoes are hard and unripe, puree first in a food processor. The tomato puree can be used unstrained if you do not object to the small pieces of seeds and skin it contains. If you do, strain through a sieve or a food mill fitted with a small screen. You should end up with about 2 cups.

2. To the tomato puree, add vinegar, olive oil, Tabasco and salt and mix well. Stir in the shredded basil and set aside until serving time.

Yield: About 2 cups

NOTE: *A raw tomato-basil sauce is delicious, especially when made with fresh, very ripe tomatoes. When tomatoes are not as ripe or red as they should be, use plum tomatoes, which are fleshy and less watery.*

—JACQUES PEPIN

MULTI-LAYERED VEGETABLE TERRINE ◆ (TERRINE DE LÉGUMES)

dairy

8 medium-size asparagus spears
2 small zucchini, about ½ pound
4 small tomatoes, about 1 pound
3 carrots, about ½ pound
¼ pound mushrooms
1 pound fresh spinach
1½ pounds skinless, boneless fish fillets such as tilefish, flounder or red snapper

1 egg
1½ cups heavy cream
Salt and freshly ground pepper to taste
⅛ teaspoon freshly grated nutmeg
1 teaspoon butter
1½ cups Sauce Verte (page 418)

1. Preheat the oven to 350 degrees.

2. Cut asparagus spears at the base; the prepared spears should be about 6 inches long.

3. Trim the ends of the zucchini. Cut each zucchini lengthwise into 5 or 6 strips, each about 6 inches long.
4. Cut the tomatoes into quarters. Remove seeds; press quarters gently in a clean cloth to extract a little excess liquid. Do not mangle them. Set aside.
5. Trim and scrape the carrots. Cut lengthwise into quarters. Set aside.
6. Cut off stems of mushrooms. Cut caps in half crosswise.
7. Bring enough water to a boil to cover the vegetables when they are added. Add the carrot strips and bring to a boil. Simmer about 2 minutes and add the asparagus. Let cook about 1 minute. Add the zucchini and mushrooms. Cook 1 minute. Drain all. Set aside.
8. Meanwhile, drop the spinach into enough boiling water to cover. When the water returns to a boil, simmer about 1 minute. Drain. Run under cold water and squeeze between the palms to extract most of the moisture.
9. Cut fish into 2-inch cubes. Put cubes into container of a food processor. Add the egg and start processing while gradually adding the cream through the funnel. Add salt and pepper to taste and the nutmeg. Spoon and scrape fish mixture into a mixing bowl.

10. Put spinach into container of a food processor. Process to a fine puree. Add spinach to fish and blend.
11. Grease an 8-by-5-by-3-inch loaf pan with the butter.
12. Spoon in a layer of the fish mousse and smooth it over. Add a third of the carrots, a thin layer of fish mousse, a layer of zucchini strips, a thin layer of mousse and so on. Add layers, including the mushrooms and asparagus, until the vegetables and fish mousse are used, ending with a layer of fish mousse.
13. Cover the pan closely with a sheet of aluminum foil.
14. Set the pan in a basin of hot water. Set this on top of the stove and bring the water to the boil.
15. Put the pan (in the basin) in the oven and bake 45 minutes. Let cool. Cover closely with aluminum foil. Chill overnight. Slice and serve with sauce verte.

Yield: 24 buffet servings

NOTE: *This terrine makes a spectacular visual presentation for a special occasion.*

—CRAIG CLAIBORNE

LUTECE'S SMOKED SALMON TERRINE WITH SPINACH

dairy
ADAPTED FROM *The Lutece Cookbook*

1 pound fresh spinach, stems removed
Salt
½ pound (2 sticks) unsalted butter, at room
    temperature, plus butter for buttering the terrine
1 tablespoon Worcestershire sauce (see Note, page 582)

½ teaspoon Tabasco sauce
1 pound smoked salmon, cut in thin slices

1. Wash the spinach in three changes of cold water and drain it. Put it in 3 quarts of boiling salted water (not in an aluminum pot), and cook vigorously over high heat for 4 minutes. Plunge the spinach into ice water to cool it. Drain. Press the

excess water out of the spinach by forming it into a ball in your hands and squeezing it.

2. Put the spinach, butter, Worcestershire sauce and Tabasco into a food processor. Process until you have a smooth paste.

3. Butter the bottom and sides of a 1½-quart terrine mold. Then line the mold with parchment paper.

4. Fill the mold with layers of thinly sliced salmon, alternating with ¼-inch layers of the spinach. The bottom and top layers should be salmon.

5. Refrigerate at least 3 hours before serving. To remove the terrine from its mold, invert it over a serving plate. If necessary, slip a knife between the parchment paper and the mold, or lower the mold into hot water for a few minutes before inverting it.

6. Cut the terrine in ¼-inch slices with a knife that is dipped in hot water before each cut.

Yield: 6 servings

—MOIRA HODGSON

CHARLES PALMER'S SPRING SALMON, POTATO AND PESTO TERRINE

meat

ADAPTED FROM Charles Palmer, Aureole

4 starchy Maine potatoes, each about fist size

1½ pounds salmon—use center-cut fillet—boneless, skinless

Salt and freshly ground pepper to taste

2 shallots, peeled

2 cups chicken stock

1 tablespoon plus 1½ cups olive oil

¾ cups Pesto (page 419)

⅓ cup red wine vinegar

Zest of 1 lemon

Juice of 1 lemon

1 bunch basil, leaves shredded

1 cup mixed greens, such as arugula, mâche, purslane, etc.

½ cup walnuts, toasted (see Note)

1. Peel the potatoes and place in a large pot. Cover with cold salted water. Cook until the potatoes are tender, or when a knife inserted in the center of the potato slides out easily. Drain and allow to cool only long enough to handle. Slice the potatoes into ¼-inch-thick slices.

2. Cut the salmon into 3 pieces and season both sides with salt and pepper. Slice 1 shallot and place on the bottom of a shallow pan. Put the salmon on top of the shallot and pour in the chicken stock and 1 tablespoon of the olive oil. There should be enough liquid to cover the fish. Brush a piece of wax paper with oil and place over the fish. Cook over medium heat. When the liquid has come to a boil reduce the heat to a simmer. Cook 8 minutes, or until the fish is slightly pink in the center. Remove the salmon from the liquid and cool. Then break the meat with your fingers into small pieces.

3. Line a terrine mold or bread loaf pan, approximately 3½ by 7 by 3 inches, with wax paper, cutting the paper to fit the mold precisely.

4. Place an even layer, about ¼ inch deep, of salmon on the bottom of the mold. Press the salmon evenly into the mold. Using a pastry brush, brush the salmon with pesto.

5. Place a layer of potatoes on top of the salmon-pesto layer. Trim the potatoes to fit the mold precisely. Brush the layer of potatoes with pesto.

6. Repeat the process until there are 3 layers each of salmon and potatoes.

7. Cover the top of the terrine with plastic wrap and weight down with heavy cans that fit within the terrine. Refrigerate overnight.

8. Prepare the vinaigrette by mixing the 1½ cups of olive oil, red wine vinegar, lemon juice and zest, and salt and pepper to taste. Mince the remaining shallot and mix into the vinaigrette. Just before

serving, add the shredded basil and pieces of broken walnuts.

9. Dress the greens, reserving some vinaigrette for saucing the terrine. Divide the greens among 8 plates, placing the greens in the center.

10. Cut the terrine into 8 slices. Place a piece on the greens and drizzle on the remaining vinaigrette.

Yield: 8 servings

NOTE: *To toast walnuts, spread the pieces on a cookie sheet. Cook in a preheated, 350-degree oven. About every 5 minutes, toss the pieces to assure even cooking. Cook until slightly darkened and crisp, about 15 minutes.*

—LINDA WELLS

ROULADES FILLED WITH SMOKED SALMON OR CAVIAR

dairy

Basic Sponge Roll

dairy

¼ cup butter plus 1 teaspoon for greasing foil
½ cup sifted flour
2 cups hot milk
4 eggs, separated
Pinch of salt

1. Preheat the oven to 400 degrees.

2. Select a jelly-roll pan measuring about 10 by 15 inches. Cut a rectangle of heavy-duty aluminum foil to fit inside the pan with an overlapping margin of about 1 inch all around. Place the foil inside the pan,

shiny side up. Carefully fold the overlapping edges of foil around the pan to keep it firmly in place. Put the 1 teaspoon of butter in the pan and place the pan in the oven until butter melts. Brush this melted butter over the foil-lined bottom.

3. Melt the remaining ¼ cup of butter in a saucepan and add the flour, stirring with a wire whisk. Add the milk, stirring rapidly with the whisk, and cook until thickened and smooth. Simmer, stirring, about one minute.

4. Put the egg yolks in a small mixing bowl and beat well. Add a little of the hot sauce to the yolks, beating constantly. Off the heat, add this mixture to the sauce, stirring constantly. Add the salt to the egg whites and beat until they are stiff. Fold them into the sauce.

5. Pour the batter into the pan and smooth over the top. Bake 15–18 minutes, or until the cake rebounds to the touch and is golden brown on top. If the cake splits on top, don't worry. It will seal itself once it cools. After cooling, turn the cake out onto a clean dish towel. Carefully remove and discard the foil. The cake is now ready to be spread with a filling and folded.

Yield: 8–12 servings

Smoked Salmon Roulade

dairy

1 Basic Sponge Roll for roulades (see recipe above)
3 ounces cream cheese at room temperature
1 cup sour cream
¼ pound smoked salmon
¼ cup finely chopped dill
Dill sprigs for garnish

1. Prepare the sponge roll and have it ready.
2. Combine the cream cheese and 3 tablespoons of the sour cream. Blend well and spread this over the sponge roll.
3. Cut the salmon lengthwise into thin, ¼-inch strips. Arrange the strips down the length of the sponge roll in parallel rows, leaving about an inch of space between them. Sprinkle with the chopped dill. Roll the cake like a jellyroll, folding the small end over and over to make a roll about 10 inches long.

4. Using a knife with a serrated blade, carefully slice off the bulky ends of the roll. Cut the remaining roll into neat, ½-inch slices and top each with a spoonful or so of the remaining sour cream. Top each serving with a small sprig of dill. Serve lukewarm or cold.

Yield: 8–10 servings

Caviar Roulade

dairy

1 Basic Sponge Roll for roulades (see recipe above)
3 ounces cream cheese at room temperature
1 cup sour cream
¼ pound salmon caviar

1. Prepare the sponge roll and have it ready.
2. Combine the cream cheese and 3 tablespoons of the sour cream. Blend well and spread this over the sponge roll. Roll the cake like a jellyroll, folding the small end over and over to make a roll about 10 inches long.
3. Using a knife with a serrated blade, carefully slice off the bulky ends of the roll. Cut the remaining roll into neat, ½-inch slices and top each serving with a spoonful or so of the remaining sour cream. Top each serving with a dollop of caviar. Serve lukewarm or cold.

Yield: 8–10 servings

—CRAIG CLAIBORNE AND PIERRE FRANEY

LUDMILA RAITZIN'S PIROJOK

pareve, dairy, meat

Dough

pareve, dairy

1½ ounces fresh yeast mixed with warm water to give
   ¾ cup altogether (or substitute 3 packages of dry yeast)
5 cups flour, sifted
½ stick unsalted margarine or butter
2 tablespoons oil
3 teaspoons sugar
½ teaspoon salt
1 egg yolk
1¼ cups warm water
1½ cups oil

1. Mix yeast and warm water mixture and set aside
for 15 minutes.
2. Put margarine or butter in saucepan and melt on
very low flame.
3. In large bowl, mix flour, melted margarine or butter, 2 tablespoons of oil, sugar, salt, egg yolk and
warm water. Mix thoroughly.
4. Add yeast-water combination to the mixture and,
with your hands, make a dough, mixing and gently
kneading for 10 minutes. Place dough back into the
bowl and cover it with a towel. Set aside for 4 hours.
5. Prepare fillings.
6. Shape dough into small round balls. Press out
with thumbs into a circle about ¼ inch thick and
2½–3 inches in diameter. Place filling on half of the
circle and fold over to make a half-moon. Pinch
edges together and seal with the tines of a fork.
7. Fry in 1½ cups oil.
8. Drain on paper towels.

Yield: 72 pieces, each 2½ by 1¾ inches

Mushroom Filling

pareve

1 medium onion, finely chopped
4 tablespoons oil
1 pound fresh mushrooms, sliced
Salt and pepper to taste

1. Sauté onion in the oil in the skillet until soft.
2. Add mushrooms to the onions and sauté over a
low flame for 30 minutes. Season to taste.

Egg Filling

pareve

4 eggs, hard-cooked
1 bunch dill
1 bunch scallions
Salt and freshly ground pepper to taste.

Chop eggs, dill and scallions finely and mix together.
Salt and pepper to taste.

Chicken Filling

meat

3 pounds chicken pieces, cut up
1½ teaspoon salt
2 medium onions, sliced
3 stalks celery, cut in halves
4 carrots, peeled, cut in halves
5 cups water
¼ cup vegetable oil

1. In large pot, poach chicken for 1 hour in water to
cover, adding to it salt, 1 onion, celery and carrots.

2. Brown remaining onion in skillet until soft and golden.

3. Remove chicken from pot, remove meat from bones, discard bones, skin and cooked vegetables.

4. Grind or chop chicken and browned onion together. Season to taste.

NOTE: *When using this filling, select unsalted margarine for the dough.*

The versatile dough may also be the basis for a sweet filling:

Raisin Filling

pareve

>   8 ounces seedless golden raisins
>   ¼ cup confectioners' sugar (optional)

1. Fill pirojok with raisins.

2. After pastries are fried, sprinkle top with optional sugar.

—LESLIE RUBINSTEIN

MUSHROOM AND KASHA PASTRIES

dairy

>   3 tablespoons butter
>   ¼ cup finely chopped onion
>   ½ pound mushrooms, finely chopped
>   1 cup cooked kasha
>   ½ teaspoon salt
>   Freshly ground black pepper
>   ⅛ teaspoon ground cloves
>   Pinch nutmeg
>   3 tablespoons sour cream
>   1 egg beaten with 1 teaspoon cold water
>   Cream Cheese Pastry (page 502)

1. Preheat oven to 425 degrees.

2. Melt butter in a heavy skillet. Add onion and sauté until the onion just begins to brown. Wrap mushrooms in a cloth napkin or several thicknesses of paper towel and squeeze to extract as much moisture as possible. Add mushrooms to the skillet and sauté, stirring, until the mushroom liquid has evaporated and the mushrooms begin to brown.

3. Add kasha, salt, pepper, cloves and nutmeg and mix well. Off heat, stir in the sour cream.

4. Roll pastry on a floured board to a thickness of ⅛ inch. Using a round pastry cutter or a glass 3 inches in diameter, cut circles of pastry.

5. Place a scant teaspoon of the filling in the center of each pastry circle. Fold pastry over and crimp the rounded edge with tines of a fork to seal, making half-circle turnovers. Brush each with beaten egg. Place on a baking sheet.

6. Bake for 20 minutes, until golden brown.

Yield: About 40 hors d'oeuvre pastries

NOTE: *Cooled turnovers may be frozen and reheated without defrosting in a 425-degree oven for 10–15 minutes.*

—FLORENCE FABRICANT

BEEF-FILLED PASTRIES · (LAHME-EL-GINE)

meat

ADAPTED FROM *The Best of Craig Claiborne*

½ teaspoon active dry yeast
⅓ cup warm water
½ teaspoon sugar
1½ teaspoon salt
¼ cup corn oil
1 cup sifted all-purpose flour
½ pound ground beef
2 onions, finely minced
2 tablespoons tamari sauce (see Note)
2 tablespoons tomato sauce
¼ teaspoon ground cinnamon
¼ teaspoon ground allspice
6 dozen pine nuts

1. Dissolve the yeast in the water. Add the sugar, ½ teaspoon salt and the oil to soften yeast. Gradually add the flour, kneading in the last portion if it is too difficult to stir in with a spoon.

2. Place the dough in a bowl, cover, and let it rise in a warm place free from drafts for about 3 hours, until doubled in bulk.

3. Combine the beef, onions, tamari sauce, tomato sauce, cinnamon, allspice and remaining salt.

4. Preheat oven to 400 degrees.

5. Roll out the raised dough on a lightly floured board to a rectangle ¹⁄₁₆ inch thick. Cut circles from the dough with a glass or cookie cutter 2½ inches in diameter. Repeat process until all dough is used.

6. Place 1 tablespoon filling on each dough round and spread evenly over the surface. Garnish with 3 pine nuts. Bake for 15–20 minutes, or until golden. Serve hot.

Yield: 24 pastries

NOTE: *The tamari sauce is a substitute for Worcestershire sauce in the original recipe (see Note, page 582). These appetizers can be frozen after they are baked and reheated before serving.*

MIDDLE EASTERN LAMB-STUFFED DUMPLING-WONTONS

meat

¾ pound ground lamb
2¼ teaspoons ground coriander
¾ teaspoon ground cinnamon
2¼ teaspoons kosher salt
Freshly ground pepper to taste
3 tablespoons golden raisins

3 tablespoons coarsely chopped pistachios
36 wonton skins (3 by 3¼ inches)
Vegetable oil for deep frying

1. Mix together the lamb, spices, raisins and pistachios until well combined. Brush the edges of 1 of the wonton skins with water. Place 1½ teaspoons of the filling in the center. Bring the corners of the skin together over the filling and press the edges together to seal tight. Repeat with the remaining skins and filling.

2. Working in batches, deep-fry the wontons until nicely browned. Make sure the oil is not too hot or the skins will brown before the filling is cooked through. Drain on paper towels and serve immediately.

Yield: 12 servings

—MOLLY O'NEILL

AQUAVIT'S PICKLED HERRING

pareve

> 12 herring fillets in brine
> 2 cups sugar
> 1 cup white wine vinegar
> 1 carrot, thinly sliced
> 1 red onion, chopped
> ½ leek, white part only, chopped
> 1 bay leaf
> 4 black peppercorns
> 4 white peppercorns

1. In a medium mixing bowl, combine the herring with enough water to cover. Refrigerate overnight.
2. Drain the herring and pat dry with paper towels. Arrange the fillets in a shallow pan and set aside.
3. In a medium saucepan, combine 3 cups water, the sugar and the vinegar. Bring to a boil, stirring to dissolve the sugar. Remove from the heat. Add the carrot, onion, leek, bay leaf and peppercorns. Allow the pickling brine to cool completely, and then pour over the herring. Refrigerate overnight.

Yield: 12 fillets

NOTE: *For a spicier herring, add 5 tablespoons chopped cilantro and 2 lightly crushed dried chilies to the pickling liquid. The basic pickled fillets can be served as an hors d'oeuvre or used in Herring Salad (page 33). Chef Samuelsson also recommends folding the pickled herring into the following dressing:*

Aquavit's Dressing for Pickled Herring

dairy

> 2 tablespoons freshly squeezed lime juice
> Grated zest of ½ lime
> ¼ cup mayonnaise
> ½ cup sour cream
> 1 tablespoon finely chopped cilantro
> Kosher salt to taste
> Freshly ground white pepper to taste

Combine the ingredients. Blend until smooth and refrigerate overnight. Before serving, fold in 4 sliced herring fillets.

Yield: 8 servings

—MARCUS SAMUELSSON

SAVORY HERRING

dairy

2 whole salt herrings
⅓ cup dry bread crumbs
3 tablespoons butter
⅓ cup cream
1 tablespoon chopped chives

1. Soak herrings for 12 hours in several changes of cold water. Remove from water and bone and skin them, producing 4 fillets.
2. Preheat oven to 400 degrees.
3. Coat fillets thoroughly with bread crumbs. Butter a small au gratin dish with 1 tablespoon butter, lay on fillets and dot with remaining butter.
4. Pour cream over and bake 5–10 minutes.
5. Sprinkle with chopped chives before serving.

Yield: 4 servings

NOTE: *This dish is an excellent first course for breaking the Yom Kippur fast. For variety, omit the bread crumbs and the chives. Slice 1 large onion, lightly sauté it in 1–2 tablespoons of butter until soft. Top fillets with onions and proceed with Step 4.*

—ROBERT FARRAR CAPON

MATJES HERRING IN SHERRY SAUCE

pareve

ADAPTED FROM *The New York Times International Cookbook*

1 cup medium-dry sherry
1 medium red onion, cut lengthwise into sixteenths
2 shallots, quartered
2 whole bay leaves
2 tablespoons granulated sugar
3 matjes herring fillets
Bay leaf for garnish
Onion ring for garnish

1. Combine the sherry, onion, shallots, bay leaves and sugar in a saucepan. Bring to a boil and remove from the heat. Cool.
2. Rinse the herring fillets under cold running water and drain. Pat dry on absorbent paper towels. Cut the herring crosswise into halves before mixing with the sauce.

Yield: 6 or more servings

NOTE: *The herring can be served immediately. Or, for a more intense flavor, marinate it in the liquid, refrigerated, for 2–3 hours.*

HERRING SALAD WITH BEETS AND APPLES

dairy

ADAPTED FROM Aquavit, New York City

2 large beets

4 fillets of Pickled Herring (page 31)

2 large Granny Smith apples, peeled, cored and cut
　　into ¼-inch dice

1 yellow onion, cut into ¼-inch dice

2 tablespoons mayonnaise

2 tablespoons sour cream

1 tablespoon chopped parsley

1. Preheat oven to 350 degrees.

2. Place beets in a small roasting pan and bake until tender when pierced with a fork, about 1½ hours. Cool, peel and cut into ¼-inch dice.

3. Cut 4 pickled herring fillets into ¼-inch dice and place in a medium bowl. Add the beets, apples, onion, mayonnaise, sour cream and parsley. Mix gently. Chill thoroughly, 4 hours to overnight, before serving.

Yield: 4 servings

—MARCUS SAMUELSSON

JOYCE GOLDSTEIN'S PICKLED SALMON

pareve

ADAPTED FROM *Back to Square One*

2 cups white vinegar

1½ cups water

6 tablespoons sugar

2 tablespoons kosher salt

2 pounds salmon fillet, skin and bones removed

2 tablespoons mixed pickling spices

6 bay leaves

2 white or yellow onions, sliced ¼ inch thick

1. Bring the vinegar, water, sugar and salt to a boil. Let this mixture cool completely.

2. Cut salmon into pieces that are approximately 1 by 2 inches.

3. In a ceramic crock, glass bowl or plastic container, place a layer of salmon pieces, then a sprinkling of pickling spices and bay leaves, a layer of onions, then salmon, spices and onions—continuing until you have used it all. Pour the cooled marinade over the fish. Cover the container and refrigerate for 3–4 days.

4. Serve the salmon chilled, but not ice cold, along with the marinated onions.

Yield: 10 to 12 servings

NOTE: *The salmon will keep 3–4 days after the pickling is finished.*

—JOAN NATHAN

SALMON MARINATED IN WINE AND HERBS

pareve

4 cups kosher salt or sea salt

1 boneless salmon fillet (2½ pounds) with skin on

2 cups Chablis wine

½ cup olive oil

¾ cup coarsely chopped chervil, parsley, chives and
    cilantro

2 tablespoons crushed white pepper

2 tablespoons coriander seeds

1. Spread 1 cup of salt over the bottom of a flat dish. Put the salmon fillet, skin side down, over the salt. Cover the fish completely with the remaining salt and let stand in a cool place for 6 hours.

2. Rinse the fillet well under cool water and allow to dry in a cool place.

3. Blend the wine and oil in a bowl. Add ½ cup of the herb mixture, the crushed white pepper and the coriander seeds. Pour the mixture into a flat dish. Place the fillet skin side up in the marinade. Cover with plastic wrap. Refrigerate for 8 hours.

4. To serve, slice the salmon into large, thin slices. Place on large plates. Strain and push the marinade through a fine sieve. Check the seasonings for taste. Trickle the marinade lightly over the salmon. Sprinkle the remaining ¼ cup of herbs over all. Serve cold.

Yield: 10 servings

NOTE: *The marinating liquid "cooks" the salmon.*

—BRYAN MILLER

CLASSIC GRAVLAX

pareve

ADAPTED FROM *The Best of Craig Claiborne*

2 large bunches fresh dill

3½–4 pounds center-cut, boned fresh salmon with
    skin on (2 fillets)

¼ cup kosher salt

¼ cup sugar

1 teaspoon coarsely ground white peppercorns

1. Cut off and discard any very tough stems from the dill. Rinse the dill and pat it dry.

2. Pat the fillets dry with paper or kitchen towel, being careful that the fish does not break.

3. Mix together salt, sugar and pepper. Using your hands, rub seasonings carefully into the pink flesh of the fish.

4. Place one-third of dill in bottom of deep flat dish large enough to hold the salmon. Use glass, china, enameled, plastic or stainless steel container, but not an aluminum one. Place one fillet, skin side down, on dill. Place another third of the dill on the flesh side that is facing up. Put the second salmon fillet, skin side up, over the dill. Cover with remaining dill.

5. Cover fish with plastic wrap, place a heavy plate or board on top of it and refrigerate. The fish should marinate in the spice-dill mixture for 24–36 hours, preferably the latter. Turn the "sandwich" every 12 hours, always replacing the weight.

6. When ready to serve, remove salmon from refrigerator and remove the weight. Unwrap fish and drain any liquid that may have accumulated. Scrape off dill and pepper, transfer salmon to a cutting board and slice it thinly on the diagonal, away from the skin. Serve with Mustard-Dill Sauce (page 21), or with lemon wedges and freshly ground black pepper.

Yield: 12–20 servings

NOTE: *Refrigerated gravlax will keep approximately 8 days, but it is best not to slice the fish until you are ready to serve it.*

LA CARAVELLE'S CITRUS GRAVLAX

pareve

ADAPTED FROM Cyril Renaud

> 2 cups salt
> 2 cups sugar
> Grated zest of 2 oranges, 2 lemons, 2 limes,
>   2 grapefruit
> 2 tablespoons juniper berries
> 1 tablespoon cracked coriander seeds
> 1 bunch dill, stems and all, roughly chopped
> 2 tablespoons gin
> 1 fillet of salmon (2–3 pounds), pin bones removed

1. Mix together the salt, sugar, zests, juniper, coriander, dill and gin. Place the salmon, skin side down, on a large sheet of plastic wrap. Cover the flesh side of the salmon with the salt mixture, making sure to coat it completely.

2. Wrap the fish well in the plastic wrap and refrigerate for 12–24 hours.

3. Unwrap salmon and rinse off the cure. Dry fish, then slice on the bias. Serve plain or with lemon wedges, crème fraîche, sour cream or light vinaigrette.

Yield: At least 12 servings

NOTE: *The longer the gravlax sits, the drier and stronger flavored it will become. If you are planning to serve the gravlax unsauced, allow it to ripen in the refrigerator for 24 hours.*

—MARK BITTMAN

MOROCCAN-SPICED GRAVLAX

pareve

ADAPTED FROM Vincent Hodgins

1 tablespoon fennel seeds
1 tablespoon anise seeds
1 tablespoon caraway seeds
1 tablespoon coriander seeds
2 teaspoons cumin seeds
1 clove
1 cardamom pod
1 teaspoon ground cinnamon
¼ cup sugar
¼ cup salt
2 tablespoons fresh cracked black pepper
1 fillet of salmon (2–3 pounds), pin bones removed

1. Place the fennel, anise, caraway, coriander, cumin, clove and cardamom in a dry skillet and toast over medium heat, shaking the pan frequently, until the mixture is aromatic, 1–2 minutes. Grind all the spices together, then mix with the cinnamon, sugar, salt and pepper.

2. Place the salmon, skin side down, on a large sheet of plastic wrap. Cover the flesh side of the salmon with the spice mixture, making sure to coat it completely.

3. Wrap fish well in plastic wrap and refrigerate for 48 hours.

4. Unwrap salmon, and rinse off cure. Dry, then slice on the bias. Serve plain or with lemon wedges, Crème Fraîche (page 431), sour cream or a light vinaigrette.

Yield: Serves at least 12

—MARK BITTMAN

RUSS & DAUGHTERS'S SMOKED SALMON TARTARE

pareve

2½ pounds smoked salmon (preferably a mild variety like Gaspe Atlantic salmon or Western Nova), cut into small pieces
1 medium red onion, peeled and very finely chopped
½ cup finely chopped scallions
1 tablespoon minced fresh parsley
2 tablespoons red wine vinegar
1½ teaspoon olive oil

Combine salmon, red onion, scallions, parsley, vinegar and oil in a large bowl and mix gently.

Yield: About 24 servings

NOTE: *At dairy meals, the tartare is nice served on cocktail-size sliced pumpernickel bread spread with unsalted butter.*

—JASON EPSTEIN

SALMON AND BEET TARTARE

pareve

ADAPTED FROM Esca, New York City

4 medium beets, washed and trimmed

1½ teaspoons finely chopped fresh chives

1½ teaspoons minced tarragon

1 teaspoon Dijon mustard

3 teaspoons finely chopped shallots

6 teaspoons lemon juice

3 drops Tabasco sauce

2½ tablespoons extra-virgin olive oil

Salt and freshly ground black pepper

8 ounces skinned salmon fillet, cut into very small dice

1½ teaspoons finely chopped fresh parsley

Pea shoots for garnish, optional

1. Preheat oven to 400 degrees. Place beets in small roasting pan with ½ cup water. Cover and cook until tender when pierced with a fork about 1 hour. Cool, then peel and cut into very fine dice.

2. In a bowl, combine beets with ¾ teaspoon chives, ¾ teaspoon tarragon, ½ teaspoon mustard and 1½ teaspoons shallots. Add 4½ teaspoons lemon juice, Tabasco and 1½ tablespoons olive oil. Mix well and season with salt and pepper to taste. Cover and refrigerate.

3. In a medium mixing bowl, combine salmon, remaining chives, tarragon and shallots. Add parsley and remaining mustard and lemon. Add remaining oil and season to taste. Mix well, cover and refrigerate until ready to serve.

4. To assemble: On each of 4 serving plates, place one-quarter of the beet tartare in the bottom of a 3-inch ring mold. Top with an even layer of one-quarter of the salmon tartare. Pat gently to compress. Remove ring molds and garnish with pea shoots, if desired.

Yield: 4 servings

—MARK BITTMAN

LE BERNADIN'S FRESH AND SMOKED SALMON SPREAD

pareve

ADAPTED FROM Le Bernadin Cookbook: Four Star Simplicity

1 bottle dry white wine

2 tablespoons chopped shallots

1 tablespoon fine sea salt, plus more to taste

2 pounds fresh salmon fillet, fat trimmed, cut in 1-inch cubes

6 ounces smoked salmon, fat trimmed, cut into tiny dice

2 tablespoons thinly sliced fresh chives

⅓ cup fresh lemon juice

1 cup mayonnaise, homemade or prepared

¼ teaspoon freshly ground white pepper

Toasted baguette slices, for serving

1. Place wine, shallots and I teaspoon of the salt in a large saucepan and bring to a boil. Add the fresh salmon and poach for 40 seconds. Drain in a sieve and run cold water over the fish just to stop the cooking. Drain well and refrigerate until cold, at least 1½ hours. Discard the poaching liquid.

2. Place smoked salmon in a large bowl and stir in the chives. Add the poached salmon and use the side of a wooden spoon to shred the salmon as you mix. Stir in the lemon juice, mayonnaise and pepper. Add sea salt to taste.

3. Refrigerate up to 6 hours, then serve with toasted baguettes.

Yield: 4 cups, 8–12 servings

—FLORENCE FABRICANT

SMOKED FISH SPREAD

dairy

ADAPTED FROM *The New York Times Heritage Cookbook*

¾ pound smoked whitefish or sablefish
1 (8-ounce) package cream cheese, softened
2 tablespoons light cream
2 tablespoons lemon juice
1 tablespoon drained and chopped capers
Freshly ground black pepper to taste
Pumpernickel bread squares or rounds
Thin lemon slices
Fresh dill weed

1. Remove skin and bones from the fish and flake. Combine fish with the cream cheese, cream, lemon juice, capers and pepper. Chill.

2. Serve on pumpernickel bread, garnished with tiny piece of lemon and bit of dill weed.

Yield: 2 cups

RUSSIAN BLINIS WITH CAVIAR

dairy

1½ cups milk
1 package granular yeast
1½ cups unbleached
    white flour
½ cup buckwheat flour
½ teaspoon salt
1 teaspoon sugar
4 eggs, separated
¼ pound unsalted butter, melted
6 ounces red caviar
2 cups sour cream

1. Scald the milk and set aside.

2. Dissolve the yeast in ¼ cup warm water.

3. Sift the white flour into a bowl, add the buckwheat flour, salt and sugar.

4. Beat the egg yolks until thick. When the milk has cooled to lukewarm, add the yolks and 3 tablespoons of the melted butter. Add the yeast. Mix well and pour into the flour. Mix thoroughly, removing any lumps. Set aside in a warm place lightly covered with a towel for about 2 hours, or until doubled in bulk.

5. Whip the egg whites until they stand in stiff peaks and fold them into the batter.

6. Lightly butter a small frying pan. Pour in just enough of the pancake mixture to coat the bottom of the pan. When the mixture begins to bubble, turn the pancake over and cook lightly on the other side. Wrap the pancakes in a napkin and keep them warm in the oven while you cook the others. Serve in a pile, wrapped in a napkin.

7. Serve the caviar, the sour cream and the remaining melted butter in small bowls on the table. Each person puts a pancake on a plate, butters it, adds sour cream and caviar and rolls it like a crepe.

Yield: 6–8 servings

—MOIRA HODGSON

SPINACH CREPES WITH SMOKED SALMON AND CREAM CHEESE

dairy

1 package frozen chopped spinach, defrosted
3 large eggs
1½ cups milk
1 cup flour
1 bunch scallions, trimmed and minced
⅓ cup chopped fresh dill
Pinch of cayenne pepper
Salt and freshly ground black pepper
½ cup water
1–2 tablespoons vegetable oil
1 pound cream cheese, at room temperature
1 tablespoon grated lemon rind
1 tablespoon fresh lemon juice
2 shallots, finely minced
2 tablespoons drained capers
2 teaspoons Hungarian paprika
12 ounces smoked salmon, in thin slices

1. Squeeze the spinach to drain out all excess moisture. Set aside. Place the eggs and milk in a bowl or food processor and beat until well blended. Blend in the flour until smooth. Add the spinach, scallions, half the dill, the cayenne pepper, salt and pepper and blend until very smooth. Stir in the water and allow the batter to rest for 15 minutes.

2. Heat a 7- to 8-inch crepe pan over medium-high heat. Brush with oil. Pour about ⅓ cup of the batter into the pan, tilting the pan to coat the bottom evenly. Fry about 2 minutes, until lightly browned, turn the crepe over and cook about 30 seconds longer. Remove the crepe from the pan and repeat with the remaining batter, making 10–12 crepes.

3. Beat the cream cheese until light and fluffy. Add the lemon peel, juice, shallots, remaining dill, capers and paprika. Spread each crepe with some of this mixture, then cover with a layer of smoked salmon. Roll each crepe jellyroll fashion and wrap in plastic wrap. Refrigerate at least 2 hours.

4. Trim the uneven ends off the rolls and slice each into rounds ½ inch thick. Chill until ready to serve.

Yield: About 60 hors d'oeuvres

—FLORENCE FABRICANT

OVEN-BAKED CHICKEN WINGS WITH HONEY

meat

ADAPTED FROM *The Best of Craig Claiborne*

18 chicken wings
Salt and freshly ground black pepper to taste
2 tablespoons vegetable oil
½ cup soy sauce
2 tablespoons ketchup
1 cup honey
½ clove garlic, chopped

1. Preheat oven to 375 degrees.

2. Cut off and discard the wing tips of the chicken wings. Cut the remaining wings in two parts and sprinkle with salt and pepper.

3. Combine the remaining ingredients and pour over chicken wings in a greased baking dish. Bake for 1 hour, until well done and the sauce is caramelized. If chicken starts to burn, reduce the heat and cover wings with foil.

Yield: 36 pieces, 8–10 hors d'oeuvres servings

SPICY CHICKEN WINGS

meat

18 chicken wings
1 medium onion
2 garlic cloves
3 scallions
½ cup soy sauce
2 teaspoons whole allspice, crushed in a mortar

2 teaspoons crushed hot red pepper flakes, or to taste
¼ teaspoon freshly grated nutmeg
1 tablespoon sesame oil
1 teaspoon dark brown sugar

1. Cut off and discard the wing tips of the chicken wings. Cut the remaining wings in 2 parts and place the pieces in a glass or ceramic bowl.

2. Chop the onion, garlic and scallions. Place in a blender or food processor with the remaining ingredients and process to make a thick sauce. Pour this sauce over the chicken, cover and marinate in the refrigerator at least 4 hours or overnight.

3. Preheat a broiler. Drain the chicken wings and place them on a broiling pan. Pour any remaining marinade into a saucepan and bring it to a simmer.

4. Broil the chicken wings until they are well glazed and cooked through, about 20 minutes. Turn them once during broiling and baste them with the reheated marinade. Serve hot or warm.

Yield: 36 pieces, 8–10 hors d'oeuvres servings

—FLORENCE FABRICANT

CAVIAR PIE

dairy

ADAPTED FROM *The Best of Craig Claiborne*

6 large hard-cooked eggs, peeled
¼ pound butter at room temperature
½ cup finely chopped onion
Tabasco sauce to taste
½ cup sour cream
4 ounces red caviar (salmon roe)
Buttered toast wedges

1. Put half the eggs through a sieve. Chop the remainder on a flat surface until fine and blend the two together. Add the butter, onion and Tabasco. Blend well and shape into a flat round cake. Chill until set.

2. Make a built-up rim of sour cream around the upper rim of the pie. Make a shallower, flat layer of sour cream in the center. Spoon the red caviar over the flat layer. Cut the pie into wedges and serve with buttered toast.

Yield: 6–8 servings

MUSHROOM-STUFFED EGGS

dairy

<small>ADAPTED FROM</small> *The New York Times Menu Cook Book*

6 medium mushrooms
Juice of ½ lemon
¼ cup butter
6 hard-cooked eggs
1 tablespoon finely chopped dill
Salt and freshly ground black pepper to taste

1. Mince mushrooms finely. Sprinkle with lemon juice.

2. Heat one tablespoon of the butter and cook mushrooms in it, stirring, until they give up their liquid. Continue to cook until almost all liquid evaporates. Cool.

3. Peel and halve the eggs. Mash the yolks in a bowl. Add the remaining butter, the mushroom mixture, dill and salt and pepper to taste. Stuff the whites with the mixture. Serve.

Yield: 6 servings

RADISH CANAPES

dairy

12 plump red radishes
6 slices square black bread
2 tablespoons salted butter, softened
Freshly ground black pepper to taste

1. Scrub radishes and slice off tops and tips. Slice radishes paper thin.

2. Spread bread with butter.

3. Arrange radish slices, slightly overlapping, on buttered bread. Grind pepper over radishes. Cut each square in quarters on the diagonal, arrange on plate and serve with cocktails or alongside a salad.

<small>NOTE:</small> *For a favorite variation at meat meals, substitute schmaltz for the butter and sprinkle with salt, if desired. At Passover, serve with matzoh instead of bread.*

Yield: 24 canapes

—FLORENCE FABRICANT

POLISH SOUR CREAM AND MUSHROOM DIP

dairy

ADAPTED FROM Helen Ciesla Covensky in
Jewish Cooking in America

4 tablespoons salted butter

2 medium onions, diced

1 pound mushrooms, coarsely chopped

Salt to taste

Freshly ground pepper to taste

1 cup sour cream

2 tablespoons fresh dill, snipped

Paprika to taste

1. Melt 2 tablespoons of the butter in a frying pan and sauté the onions until golden. Set aside.

2. Place the remaining butter in the pan and add the mushrooms. Sauté about 10 minutes, stirring occasionally, until the water evaporates.

3. Combine the onions and mushrooms in a serving bowl. Season with salt and pepper. Fold in the sour cream and sprinkle with fresh dill and paprika. Serve as a dip with dark rye bread, pita or fresh vegetables.

Yield: 3 cups (about 6 servings)

—JOAN NATHAN

DAVID MINTZ'S TOFU HERB DIP

pareve

1 pound tofu

2 tablespoons soy oil

2 tablespoons apple cider vinegar

3 tablespoons fresh lemon juice

2 scallions, finely chopped

1 teaspoon finely minced garlic

½ cup finely minced parsley

2 tablespoons finely minced fresh mint
   (or 1 tablespoon dried)

Salt and pepper to taste

1. In a food processor, puree the tofu with the oil, vinegar and lemon juice.

2. Add the remaining ingredients and spin until well blended. Adjust seasonings and chill for use.

Yield: 2 cups

NOTE: *This low-calorie dip is refreshing with raw vegetables. It can be thinned with a few tablespoons of water for salad dressing and will keep in the refrigerator for up to 10 days.*

—LORNA J. SASS

ROSEMARY-LEMON BEAN PUREE

pareve

ADAPTED FROM Frico Bar

  *2 cups cooked white beans, such as cannellini, drained
    but moist*
  1–2 cloves garlic, peeled
  Salt to taste
  Freshly ground black pepper to taste
  ¼ cup plus 1 tablespoon extra-virgin olive oil
  2 teaspoons minced fresh rosemary
  Grated rind of 2 lemons

1. Put the beans in the container of a food processor with 1 clove of garlic and a healthy pinch of salt. Turn the machine on, and add the ¼ cup olive oil in a steady stream through the feed tube; process until the mixture is smooth. Taste, and add more garlic if you like and then puree the mixture again.
2. Place the mixture in a bowl and use a wooden spoon to beat in the rosemary, lemon zest and the remaining tablespoon of olive oil. Taste, and add more salt and pepper as needed. Use immediately, or refrigerate for as long as 3 days.

Yield: 2 cups

NOTE: *This puree can be made in about 10 minutes with canned beans but, like most bean dishes, this puree is best made with freshly cooked dried beans. For dried beans: cook the beans in enough unsalted water to cover them (presoaking is unnecessary) with a couple of bay leaves, until very tender. For canned beans: use almost two full 15-ounce cans, drained. This puree is very versatile as a dip for breadsticks, pita or other bread, or for raw vegetables; or as a basis for a sandwich; or as the centerpiece of a plate of lightly and simply cooked vegetables (carrots, green beans, turnips, asparagus, potatoes or cauliflower). Or roll smoked salmon or thinly sliced cooked vegetables around a bit of the puree and serve as hors d'oeuvres.*

—MARK BITTMAN

OLIVE DIP · (OLIVADA)

pareve

ADAPTED FROM Restaurant Associates

  1 red pepper
  1 cup Kalamata olives
  ½ red onion
  1 clove garlic
  1 stalk celery
  2 tablespoons balsamic vinegar
  1 tablespoon oregano
  *½ cup extra-virgin
    olive oil*

1. Prepare the broiler. Char the red pepper, turning to cook on all sides. Let cool slightly, tear off blackened skin and remove seeds and veins.

2. While pepper is roasting, pit the olives. Peel onion and garlic, trim celery and chop in large pieces.
3. Combine all ingredients in food processor. Pulse until mixture is spreadable.

4. Serve with bread, crackers or Sesame Pita Chips (see below).

Yield: 6 servings

—TRISH HALL

SALMON SOUR CREAM DIP

dairy
ADAPTED FROM *The New York Times International Cookbook*

1 can (1 pound) salmon
½ teaspoon salt
4 drops Tabasco sauce, or to taste
1 teaspoon grated onion
1 cup sour cream

1 tablespoon drained red caviar
Fresh vegetable dippers

1. Drain and flake the fish. Blend in salt, Tabasco and onion. Fold in sour cream and chill.
2. Garnish with caviar. Serve with vegetable dippers (cauliflowerets, celery, carrot, green pepper and cucumber sticks) which have been chilled until crisp.

Yield: About 1 pint

SESAME PITA CHIPS

pareve
ADAPTED FROM The Golden Door

Vegetable oil spray
2 whole wheat pita pockets
2 egg whites
¼ teaspoon dark sesame oil
1 tablespoon sesame seeds

1. Spray a baking sheet with vegetable oil. Set aside. Separate the pita pockets into halves. Cut each half into 8 sections. Set aside.

2. Combine egg whites and sesame oil in a glass or ceramic bowl. Brush the egg-white mixture on both sides of the pita. Sprinkle both sides with sesame seeds. Place on the baking sheet and bake until crisp, about 10 minutes. Store in a cookie tin.

Yield: 4 servings

NOTE: *Julie Burks, nutritionist at the health spa in Escondido, California, prepares these delicious pita chips in large quantities. They will keep for up to 2 weeks in a tightly sealed container, when stored in a cool place.*

—MOLLY O'NEILL

SOUPS

THERE ARE SOUPS AND THEN THERE IS CHICKEN SOUP, THE DEFIN-
ING AND ICONIC DISH OF EASTERN EUROPEAN JEWS, WHO ACCORD
it special status, aesthetically, medicinally and emotionally. Based on a large fowl
past egg-laying prime, the soup simmers slowly, extracting all of the flavor from
the tired bones, skin and meat of the played-out bird, magically turning water
into a rich and fragrant broth. Because the chicken is bled as part of ritual
slaughter, it produces a very clear and light soup, ideally, one that is limpid and
not greasy, but with just enough pinpoint globules of fat to cast a sunny glow.
It is easy to get into an argument on the proper ingredients for chicken soup. It
is generally agreed among Eastern Europeans that root vegetables such as carrots, parsnips, *petrouchka* (the root of flat, Italian parsley), knob celery, onions
and stalk celery with leaves are desirable, when available, along with parsley and
dill. More controversial ingredients are garlic, tomato, potato, bay leaf and ginger. Best of all, perhaps, this clear soup is traditionally enhanced with succulent
garnishes of matzoh balls, noodles, meat-filled kreplach, rice and more.
Sephardic and Middle Eastern Jews prize many chicken soups, but generally
accord them no special powers and add exotic flavors as in the Persian version,

gilded with turmeric and scented with cardamom. Many are enriched with rice and a final, silky liaison of egg yolk and lemon.

Soups of all sorts are important on Jewish menus, and the heartier combinations of meat and vegetables—Tunisian lamb *chorba,* mushroom and barley soup with beef flanken, paprika-spiked goulash soup—along with bread, often are the complete meal. This was especially true of poorer Jews in Eastern European countries with long winters, where hot soup was the most warming and economical dish. Lighter soups of vegetables or fish preceded dairy or meat main courses, and, in the spirit of fusion, might even include Genoa's green minestrone, Marseilles's saffron-scented *soupe de poissons,* or an elegant chilled smoked fish consommé created by the master chef Eberhard Mueller.

Summer brings its own collection of well-chilled, restorative soups, such as classic borschts, whether beet-red or the sour cream–based white borscht with gently soured with sorrel (called *schav*); cold sour cherry soup; a restorative, silky gel of cucumbers, herbs and lime juice; a Persian carrot soup with mint; or the cool and beautiful Malagan white gazpacho, garnished with green grapes and toasted almonds.

STOCKS AND BROTHS

◆ ◆

RICH CHICKEN BROTH

meat

ADAPTED FROM *The Best of Craig Claiborne*

5 pounds meaty chicken bones

16 cups cold water

2 cups coarsely chopped onions

½ pound carrots, coarsely chopped (about 2 cups)

1 garlic clove, peeled

10 sprigs of fresh parsley

1 bay leaf

½ teaspoon dried thyme

10 whole black peppercorns

1. Put the chicken bones in a large stockpot and cover with water.

2. Add the remaining ingredients and bring to a boil. Reduce the heat so the liquid simmers slowly.

Cook for 2 hours, skimming fat and scum from the surface every 15–20 minutes.

3. Strain the broth through a fine sieve into a large bowl. Let cool to room temperature and then cover and refrigerate.

4. Remove the fat from the top of the broth with a slotted spoon. Use the clear broth as needed. It can be frozen in convenient-size containers.

Yield: 10 cups

NOTE: *The secret of chicken soup is the bird—the older and fatter, the richer the broth. Be sure to bring the soup to room temperature before refrigeration, to prevent possible souring. Once soup is refrigerated, the fat will congeal and is easily removed.*

CHICKEN STOCK

meat

ADAPTED FROM *The New York Times Menu Cook Book*

6 pounds chicken wings, backs or necks

2½ quarts water

1 small onion, peeled and halved

½ cup chopped celery leaves

¼ cup chopped fresh parsley

1 large bay leaf

6 allspice berries

2 teaspoons salt

⅛ teaspoon freshly ground black pepper

1. Wash the chicken pieces and place them in a saucepan with the water. Add the onion, celery leaves, parsley, bay leaf, allspice, salt and pepper. Simmer, covered, for 2½ hours.

2. Lift chicken and bones from the stock and strain liquid through a fine sieve. The stock may be further reduced if a concentrated flavor is desired. Cool the stock to room temperature and refrigerate. Discard the layer of fat before using.

Yield: 6 cups

NOTE: *While nothing is quite as satisfactory as homemade stock, there are many substitutes available: chicken broth or bouillon in jars, cans, granules or cubes. Remember, however, that the purchased products may be more salty than homemade stock and adjust the seasoning in the recipe accordingly.*

BEEF BROTH

meat

ADAPTED FROM *The Best of Craig Claiborne*

5 pounds meaty neck bones of beef
32 cups (4 quarts) water
1 large carrot, trimmed and scraped
1 turnip, trimmed and scraped
1 large onion, peeled and stuck with 2 cloves
1 large celery rib, cut in half
1 garlic clove, left whole
1 bay leaf
2 fresh thyme sprigs, or ½ teaspoon dried

Salt to taste
24 peppercorns, crushed

1. Place the bones in a kettle and add cold water to cover. Bring to a boil and simmer for about 2 minutes. Rinse well under cold water.
2. Return the bones to a clean kettle and add the 4 quarts of water and remaining ingredients. Simmer for 3 hours. Strain. Discard the solids. May be refrigerated or frozen in convenient-size containers for future use.

Yield: 3 or more quarts

LAMB BROTH

meat

3 pounds lamb with bone
8 cups cold water
1 cup coarsely chopped onions

1 cup coarsely chopped carrots
1 cup coarsely chopped celery ribs
1 clove garlic
½ teaspoon dried thyme
6 sprigs parsley

½ bay leaf

1 teaspoon peppercorns

Salt to taste, if desired

1. Combine all the ingredients in a kettle and bring to a boil over high heat.

2. Reduce heat and let simmer about 1 hour, skimming from time to time. Strain. Discard the solids.

Yield: About 2 quarts

—CRAIG CLAIBORNE AND PIERRE FRANEY

VEAL STOCK

meat

6 pounds veal bones, cut into 2- to 3-inch pieces by the butcher

1 tablespoon vegetable oil

2 onions, halved

2 carrots, sliced into 3 pieces

1 rib celery, sliced into 3 pieces

2 cloves garlic

1½ pounds veal stew meat, cut into 2-inch chunks

6 whole cloves

3 sprigs thyme, or ½ teaspoon dried

1 bay leaf

3 stems parsley

10 peppercorns

1. Preheat the oven to 425 degrees. Rinse the veal bones and pat them dry; toss the bones with the oil. In a deep roasting pan, add the veal bones and roast, turning occasionally, until the bones begin to brown, about 30 minutes. Add the onions, carrots, celery and garlic to the pan, toss well and continue to roast, turning occasionally, until deeply browned, about 40 minutes more.

2. Using tongs, transfer the bones and vegetables to a large stockpot and add the veal meat. Pour off and discard any excess oil from the roasting pan and place the pan over medium heat. When hot, pour in 1½ cups water, scrape up any brown drippings from the bottom of the pan and add the water mixture to the stockpot. Wrap the cloves, thyme, bay leaf, parsley and peppercorns in a small square of cheesecloth and add the bundle to the stockpot. Add 6 quarts (24 cups) cold water.

3. Over medium heat, slowly bring the stock to a simmer; this will take about 45 minutes. Skim off any fat or foam that rises to the surface. Continue to simmer the stock slowly, uncovered, for 6 hours, skimming as needed.

4. Strain the stock through a fine-mesh strainer and discard the solids. To cool, pour the stock into a large kettle and place the kettle in a sink filled with cold water. Stir the stock occasionally. If the water in the sink becomes too warm, drain and refill with cold water. When the stock is completely cooled, pour into individual containers, cover them and refrigerate for at least 24 hours. Before using, remove and discard the layer of congealed fat. Stock will keep refrigerated up to 3 days and frozen up to 6 months.

Yield: About 4 quarts (16 cups)

—MOLLY O'NEILL

FISH STOCK

pareve

ADAPTED FROM *The Best of Craig Claiborne*

3 pounds meaty fish bones, preferably with head and
 tail on but gills removed
8 cups water
1 cup dry white wine
2 cups coarsely chopped onions
4 fresh parsley sprigs
1 cup coarsely chopped celery
1 bay leaf
½ teaspoon dried thyme
6 whole black peppercorns
Salt to taste
½ cup chopped green part of leeks, optional

1. Combine all the ingredients in a kettle or large saucepan.
2. Bring to a boil and simmer for 20 minutes. Strain and discard the solids. Freeze leftover stock in convenient-size containers.

Yield: About 10 cups

ROASTED VEGETABLE STOCK

pareve

6 large yellow onions
6 carrots
1 bunch celery
2 parsnips
4 cloves garlic
2 tablespoons olive oil
6 medium plum tomatoes
1 bay leaf
6 sprigs fresh thyme
10 sprigs parsley
1 tablespoon freshly ground pepper
Water to cover

1. Preheat oven to 450 degrees.
2. Peel onions and cut in chunks. Peel carrots and cut in large rounds. Trim celery and chop in 1-inch pieces. Peel parsnips and cut in large rounds. Peel garlic and mince. Chop tomatoes.
3. Toss vegetables and garlic with oil and spread on a baking pan. Put in oven and roast for about an hour or until nicely browned. Stir occasionally to release steam.
4. Remove vegetables from oven, place in large, deep pot, add water to cover, add herbs and pepper.
5. Simmer over very low heat for 3 hours. Add additional water if necessary. Cool and strain. May be refrigerated or frozen in convenient-size containers for future use.

Yield: About 4 quarts

NOTE: *Roasting the vegetables before simmering in water enhances the flavor of the stock.*

—TRISH HALL

MIMI SHERATON'S CLASSIC CHICKEN SOUP

meat

ADAPTED FROM *The Whole World Loves Chicken Soup*

1 (5- to 6-pound) chicken, with neck and all giblets
  except liver
12 cups water, plus more as needed
2 medium carrots, peeled and quartered
3 stalks celery with leaves, cut in half
1 medium onion, with peel, cut in half
3 sprigs Italian parsley
10 black peppercorns
2 small leeks, green and white parts, split and washed
  well, optional
2 sprigs fresh thyme or ½ teaspoon dried, optional
1 small bay leaf, optional
5 whole cloves, optional
2–3 tablespoons kosher salt
Chopped fresh parsley or dill, for garnish, optional

1. Place the chicken in a 6- to 7-quart soup pot and add the water (it should cover the chicken). Cover the pot and bring to a boil. Uncover, reduce to a bare simmer and skim foam as it rises to the surface. When foam subsides, add remaining ingredients, using only 1 teaspoon of salt.

2. Cook chicken, turning 2 or 3 times, until meat loosens from bone, about 2½ hours. Add more water during cooking if chicken is not seven-eighths covered. Add salt gradually, tasting the soup from time to time.

3. Remove chicken, giblets and bones and set aside. Strain the soup through a fine sieve and discard vegetables. Either skim fat from soup if serving immediately or let it cool thoroughly, then cover, refrigerate and skim fat when the soup is cold. Chicken can be pulled from the bones and reheated in the soup. Garnish with parsley or dill, if desired. Recipes for traditional accompaniments appear on pages 58–60.

Yield: 6–8 first-course servings or 4–6 main-course servings

NOTE: *It is necessary to cool the soup thoroughly before refrigerating to prevent it from going sour. The strained broth can be frozen in small containers for future soups or in ice-cube trays to use in sauces.*

—MOLLY O'NEILL

HANA ELBAUM'S CHICKEN SOUP WITH FLANKEN

meat

4½ pounds chicken pieces
4 pounds flanken
1 beef shinbone with meat
5 carrots, peeled, in large chunks
4 celery stalks in large chunks
1 parsnip, peeled, in chunks
1 turnip, peeled, in chunks
2 parsley roots, peeled and halved
1 onion, peeled and halved
5 garlic cloves, peeled
1 leek, white and light green parts only, halved
  lengthwise and washed
1 zucchini, trimmed, in chunks
1 bunch parsley

1 bunch dill
2 marrow-bone ends
4 thinly sliced, peeled carrots
4 thinly sliced celery stalks
Salt and freshly ground black pepper to taste

1. In a very large pot, combine chicken pieces, flanken and shinbone. Add water to cover, place over high heat and bring to a boil. Reduce heat to medium-low. Carefully remove foam as it forms.

2. When there is no more foam, add vegetables in following order: carrot chunks, celery chunks, parsnip, turnip, parsley roots, onion, garlic, leek and zucchini. As vegetables become tender, remove them.

3. When all vegetables have been removed, add parsley and dill. Simmer until flanken is very tender, about 2 hours. Discard parsley and dill. Remove flanken and chicken and set aside. Strain soup, then return meat, chicken and shinbone to pot.

4. Before serving soup, remove fat from surface. Add marrow-bone ends, sliced carrots and sliced celery. Place over medium heat and simmer until vegetables are tender. Remove and discard marrow bones. Leave shinbone in until the meat is falling off the bone. Remove flanken and chicken; slice and serve separately. Season soup with salt and pepper to taste. Ladle into bowls and serve.

Yield: 6–8 servings

—ALEX WITCHEL

PERSIAN CHICKEN SOUP WITH GUNDI • (CHICKPEA DUMPLINGS)

meat

ADAPTED FROM *Jewish Cooking in America*

1 (3-pound) chicken, cut into 8 pieces
6 medium onions, peeled and quartered
2 green peppers, sliced
Salt to taste
Freshly ground pepper to taste
1/2 teaspoon turmeric
1 clove garlic, crushed
1/2 pound medium chickpea flour, available at
    Middle Eastern markets
1/2 pound ground chicken or turkey
1/2 teaspoon ground cardamom
1/4 cup water
1/2 cup cooked chickpeas

1. Place the chicken pieces in a pot and cover with cold water. Bring to a boil. Remove any froth that accumulates.

2. Add 2 of the onions, the green peppers, salt and pepper, 1/4 teaspoon of the turmeric and the garlic. Simmer, covered, for 45 minutes or until the chicken is tender. When the chicken is cool, remove it and set aside. Skim the fat from the broth and set the broth aside.

3. Remove the skin and bones from the chicken and cut the meat into bite-size pieces. Set aside.

4. To make the dumplings, grate the 4 remaining onions.

5. Add the onions to the chickpea flour and mix well. Add the ground chicken, salt and pepper to taste, the remaining turmeric and the cardamom. Mix well, using your hands. Add enough water to make a sticky dough about the consistency of meat-balls. You should be able to stick your finger through the mixture easily. Cover and refrigerate for a couple of hours so the mixture is easier to handle.

6. Dip your hands in cold water and form the mixture into dumplings about 2 inches in diameter.

7. Pour the reserved chicken broth into a soup pot. Bring to a boil, correct the seasonings and add the dumplings. Cover and reduce the heat. Simmer for 15–20 minutes. Add the chickpeas and the chicken and simmer for another 5 minutes.

8. Serve as a soup, or serve the gundi alone as an appetizer, sprinkled with fresh herbs like basil and mint and accompanied by pickled vegetables and flat bread.

Yield: 8 servings

—JOAN NATHAN

KURDISH CHICKEN SOUP WITH KUBBEH • (BULGUR DUMPLINGS)

meat

ADAPTED FROM Morduch Restaurant, Jerusalem, in *The Foods of Israel Today*

12 cups Rich Chicken Broth (page 48)
2 celery stalks, with leaves, cut into 2-inch chunks
5 small zucchini, cut into 2-inch chunks
Juice of 2 lemons, or to taste
12 Kubbeh Dumplings (see recipe below)
2 tablespoons fresh basil or dill

1. In a large pot, bring the chicken broth to a boil.
2. Add the celery, zucchini, lemon juice and the kubbeh. Cover, and simmer about 25 minutes, until the dumplings are soft.
3. Add the basil or dill, and adjust the amount of lemon juice to taste.
4. Simmer a few minutes more and serve immediately in soup bowls, giving each person 1 large dumpling and lots of zucchini.

Yield: 10–12 servings

◆ **KUBBEH DUMPLINGS** ◆

meat

2 cups fine bulgur
2 cups semolina
Salt to taste
Pepper to taste
½ medium onion, chopped
1 tablespoon olive oil
½ pound chopped beef or lamb
2 tablespoons pine nuts
¼ teaspoon allspice
2 tablespoons chopped parsley

1. Soak the bulgur in warm water to cover for about an hour.
2. Squeeze dry and mix with the semolina and salt. Knead well with your hands, adding water if necessary, to form a malleable dough. For smoother dough, pulse in food processor with metal blade.

3. Sauté the onion in the oil and then add the meat. Cook thoroughly, stirring, for about 5 minutes.

4. Add the pine nuts, allspice, salt, pepper and chopped parsley. Drain and set aside.

5. Divide the dough into 12 balls about 2½ inches across. Dip your hands in water and make an opening, keeping the walls around ¼ inch thick.

6. Insert a heaping teaspoon of the meat mixture into the hole and close up again. Refrigerate about an hour or until ready to cook.

Yield: 12 dumplings

—JOAN NATHAN

GREEK AVGOLEMONO SOUP WITH ORZO

meat

ADAPTED FROM *The Best of Craig Claiborne*

> 8 cups *Rich Chicken Broth (page 48)*
> ½ cup orzo
> Salt to taste
> 3 eggs
> ½ cup lemon juice

1. Bring the chicken broth to the boiling point. Add the orzo and cook until the orzo is tender, about 15 minutes. Add the salt.

2. Beat the eggs until frothy. Add the lemon juice to the beaten eggs and continue beating until the mixture thickens and is tripled or quadrupled in volume.

3. Continue beating while slowly adding 2 cups of hot chicken broth to the egg mixture. Return this mixture to the simmering chicken broth. Turn off the heat and serve immediately. Do not let the soup continue to cook after the egg is added or it is apt to curdle.

Yield: 8 servings

NIGELLA LAWSON'S COLD CURE CHICKEN SOUP

meat

> 3 pounds chicken wings
> 1 carrot, peeled and halved
> 1 onion, peeled and halved
> 1 cinnamon stick
> 1 (3-inch) knob of ginger, peeled

> 1 tablespoon Maldon salt or 1½ teaspoons
>   table salt
> Zest (in strips) and juice of 1 Seville orange, about
>   ¼ cup (see Note below)
> Chopped cilantro, for garnish
> 1 small red chili pepper, seeded and cut into fine
>   rings, for garnish

1. In a large saucepan, combine chicken, carrot, onion, cinnamon, ginger and salt. Add 3 quarts water, orange zest and juice.

2. Place over high heat and bring to a boil, then reduce heat to low. Simmer, uncovered, until liquid has reduced to about half and chicken flavor is strong, 1½ to 2 hours.

3. Pour through a fine mesh strainer into a bowl and discard solids. Allow broth to cool to room temperature, then refrigerate overnight or for up to 3 days. When ready to serve, remove layer of solidified fat from surface and wipe surface of congealed soup with a paper towel to remove traces of grease.

4. To serve, warm soup, ladle into mugs or bowls and garnish with chopped cilantro and chilies.

4 servings (about 6 cups)

NOTE: *A substitute for Seville orange juice may be made by combining 2 parts orange juice to 1 part lime juice. You can make more of a meal of this soup by adding shredded cooked chicken and noodles to the broth.*

—NIGELLA LAWSON

COLETTE ROSSANT'S
CHICKEN SOUP WITH TINY VEAL BALLS

meat

2 tablespoons olive oil

2 garlic cloves, sliced

1 pound veal breast

1½ pounds chicken wings

4 quarts water

1 onion stuck with 2 cloves

2 bay leaves

2 celery stalks, cut into 1-inch pieces

2 carrots, scraped and cut into 1-inch pieces

Salt to taste

10 peppercorns

1 dill sprig

Veal Balls (see recipe below)

¼ pound fresh kosher salmon caviar

1 bunch watercress

1. Heat the olive oil in a 10-quart soup kettle. Add the garlic and sauté for a minute, then add the veal and brown on all sides. Add the chicken wings and 4 quarts of water. Bring to a boil, lower the heat and cook for 20 minutes, skimming the top from time to time.

2. Add the onion, bay leaves, celery, carrots, salt, peppercorns and dill. Bring to a boil, lower the heat and cook for 1 hour or until the veal is tender when pierced with a fork.

3. Remove the veal and save for making the meatballs. Strain the soup through a fine sieve. Cool to room temperature and refrigerate until ready to use.

4. When preparing to serve, skim the fat from the surface of the soup. Bring the soup to a boil, lower the head and gently drop in the tiny veal balls. Cook for 15 minutes.

5. To serve, pour the soup into individual bowls. Place three veal balls in each bowl, garnish each with ½ teaspoon of fresh salmon caviar and watercress leaves.

Yield: 8 servings

◆ VEAL BALLS ◆

meat

1 pound cooked breast of veal
1 egg
Salt and pepper
¼ teaspoon cumin
¼ teaspoon ground or grated fresh ginger
2 tablespoons chopped parsley
3 tablespoons flour

1. Cut off all the meat from the bones.

2. Place the meat in a food processor with the egg, salt, pepper, cumin, ginger and parsley. Process until all the ingredients are very finely ground and mixed.

3. Remove to a bowl. Add the flour and mix well (you may need an extra tablespoon of flour). Make tiny balls the size of an olive. Refrigerate until ready to use in the soup.

Yield: 24 or more veal balls

EGG DROP SOUP

meat

4 cups Chicken Stock, canned or fresh (page 48)
4 eggs
1 tablespoon soy sauce, or to taste
Salt, if necessary, and freshly ground black pepper
   to taste
½ cup chopped scallions, both white and green parts
1 teaspoon sesame oil, or to taste

1. Bring 3 cups stock to a boil over medium-high heat in a 6- to 8-cup saucepan. Beat remaining stock with eggs and soy sauce until well blended.

2. When stock is boiling, adjust heat so it bubbles frequently but not furiously. Add the egg mixture in a steady stream, stirring occasionally, until eggs gather together in small curds, 2–3 minutes.

3. Taste, and add salt if necessary (or more soy sauce). Then add plenty of pepper, the scallions and the sesame oil. Taste again, adjust seasonings and serve.

Yield: 2–4 servings

—MARK BITTMAN

MATZOH BALLS

meat

ADAPTED FROM *The New York Times Heritage Cookbook*

4 teaspoons Schmaltz (page 413)
2 eggs
¼ cup hot chicken soup
Salt and freshly ground white or black pepper to taste
⅔ cup matzoh meal
1 tablespoon finely minced parsley
8 cups rapidly boiling water

1. Beat eggs lightly with the chicken soup. Add the schmaltz, beating continuously, until it is dissolved.

When thoroughly blended, gradually add the salt, pepper, matzoh meal and parsley. The mixture should be as thick as light mashed potatoes. Spoon into a bowl, cover and refrigerate at least 4 hours.
2. With wet hands, shape the mixture into balls and drop into the boiling salted water. Cover, reduce the heat and simmer 35 minutes. When 1 ball tests done (cut it open to see if it is light colored and cooked all the way through), remove balls from pot carefully with a slotted spoon. Drain. Serve in hot chicken soup.

Yield: 12–15 matzoh balls

LOW-FAT MATZOH BALLS

meat

½ cup matzoh meal
4 egg whites, slightly beaten
2 tablespoons polyunsaturated oil
2 tablespoons water
¼ teaspoon salt
Chicken soup, about 3 cups

1. Combine all ingredients, except chicken soup, and place in refrigerator for 20 minutes.
2. Shape into 10 balls.
3. Boil in hot chicken soup to cover for 20 minutes, in covered pot. These may be made ahead and reheated in chicken soup.

Yield: 10 matzoh balls

NOTE: *To prepare firm, dense matzoh balls, add a high proportion of matzoh meal to the mixture and cook for 20 minutes or less. To prepare light matzoh balls, increase the number of eggs and simmer the matzoh balls 30 minutes or longer. The lightest versions usually call for stiffly beaten egg whites folded into the mixture. For a change of pace, try matzoh balls stuffed with ground beef.*

Ultra-Orthodox Jews do not eat matzoh balls during Passover because they believe that if the matzoh meal touches water, it will rise, going against the biblical injunction against eating leavened food. Instead, they eat noodles made from potato starch and eggs.

—DENA KLEIMAN

MARROW MATZOH BALLS

meat
ADAPTED FROM *The New York Times Heritage Cookbook*

2 large marrow bones, cut into 1½-inch pieces
1 cup matzoh meal
Salt to taste
⅛ teaspoon nutmeg
1 cup boiling water
2 eggs
Boiling salted water

1. With a sharp knife, dig out the marrow from the bones (there should be about ½ cup) and place in a small skillet. Heat gently until the marrow is melted.

Remove skillet from heat.

2. Stir the matzoh meal until it is completely coated with fat. Add the salt and nutmeg. Add the 1 cup boiling water and beat until mixture leaves the sides of the skillet.

3. Beat in the eggs, 1 at a time. With wet hands, form the mixture into small balls. Drop into boiling salted water and boil ½ hour.

Yield: 12–15 marrow balls

NOTE: *To remove marrow from bones with a microwave, place the bones on a paper towel or plate and microwave for 40 seconds. Scrape out the marrow with a spoon or table knife.*

KREPLACH

meat
ADAPTED FROM Olga Gurwitz

FOR THE DUMPLINGS:

3 eggs
½ cup safflower oil
½ teaspoon salt
1¾ cups flour
½ cup water

FOR THE FILLING:

½ cooked chicken, 1½ to 2 pounds
1 egg
½ onion

Salt to taste
Freshly ground black pepper to taste

1. To make the dough, gently beat the eggs, oil and salt together in a large bowl. Slowly add the flour and water as needed. Transfer to a floured board and knead until smooth and loose. Cover with a kitchen towel and set aside for 2 hours.

2. To make the filling, remove chicken meat from bones, remove skin and grind meat with the egg, onion, salt and pepper. Taste to correct seasoning.

3. Roll out dough, a portion at a time, to between ⅛ inch and ¼ inch thick. Cut it into rounds 3 inches across. Place a heaping teaspoon of filling in center of dough rounds and fold edges over to make a half-moon. Press to seal. Refrigerate until ready to cook.

4. Bring a large pot of salted water to a boil. Lower to a simmer. Gently place kreplach in the water, one at a time, in batches of 6–8 and cook for 20–25 minutes, or until the dough is cooked through. Drain and serve in chicken soup or plain.

Yield: About 30 kreplach

—MOLLY O'NEILL

LITHUANIAN BLINCHIKI STUFFED WITH MEAT

meat

1 pound chuck or other stewing beef
2 medium-size onions
1 medium-size carrot, peeled
Salt to taste
Ground pepper to taste
3 eggs
1 cup water
3 tablespoons vegetable oil
¾ cup sifted flour
Margarine or vegetable oil for frying
2 tablespoons chopped parsley
2 tablespoons beef broth, if needed
¼ cup bread crumbs

1. Cut beef into 2-inch chunks. Quarter an onion. Simmer beef together with an onion, carrot, salt, pepper and water to cover for 1 hour, or until the meat is tender. Put meat through a grinder or food processor until shredded.

2. Meanwhile, beat together the eggs, 1 cup water, ½ teaspoon salt and 2 tablespoons vegetable oil. Stir in the flour.

3. Heat a little margarine or oil in a nonstick skillet. Pour about 2 tablespoons of batter into it, titling pan to coat bottom. Use just enough batter to make a very thin pancake. Let bottom brown, then carefully turn out onto a plate, browned side up. Make the rest of the pancakes.

4. Dice remaining onion. Heat remaining tablespoon of oil in a skillet and sauté onion until golden. Add shredded meat, parsley, salt, pepper and, if needed to moisten, 2 tablespoons beef broth.

5. Spread a heaping tablespoon of filling in center of the browned side of each pancake. Fold over once to make a semicircle, then fold one of the ends over as you would a crepe, in quarters. Sprinkle pancakes with bread crumbs and fry in additional margarine or oil for a minute or two until brown. You can also place the blinchiki in a greased casserole and bake 10 minutes in a 450-degree oven. Serve as an accompaniment to chicken soup.

Yield: 14 blinchiki

—JOAN NATHAN

BEET BORSCHT

meat, dairy, pareve
ADAPTED FROM *The Best of Craig Claiborne*

2 tablespoons butter or unsalted margarine

1 cup finely chopped onion

1 garlic clove, finely minced

1½ cups finely shredded cabbage

6–8 medium-size beets, about 1½ pounds,
    trimmed and peeled

2 cups tomatoes that are cored, blanched,
    peeled and chopped

¼ cup red wine vinegar

1 teaspoon sugar

Salt to taste

Freshly ground black pepper to taste

3 cups fresh or canned Vegetable Stock (pages 51) or
    Beef Broth (pages 49)

Boiled potatoes

Sour cream, optional at dairy meal

1. Heat the butter or margarine in a large, deep saucepan or a small kettle and add the finely chopped onion. Cook, stirring, until the onion is wilted and add the garlic and cabbage. Continue cooking, stirring the cabbage until wilted.

2. Grate or shred the beets and add them to the cabbage. Add the tomatoes, vinegar, sugar, salt, pepper and stock or broth. Bring to a boil and simmer for about 1 hour. Serve with boiled potatoes and, if desired at a dairy meal, sour cream.

Yield: 4–6 servings

NOTE: *Butter may be an ingredient only at dairy meals, used with vegetable stock; at pareve meals, margarine may be substituted; beef broth may be used at meat meals, but only with margarine.*

CARROT-GINGER SOUP

dairy
ADAPTED FROM *Bill Eichner*

2 cloves garlic, minced

2 large yellow onions, minced

2 teaspoons olive oil

5 cups shredded carrots

2 cups grated potatoes

2 inches fresh ginger root, shredded

1 teaspoon ground cumin

7 cups vegetable broth

Salt and freshly ground pepper to taste

½ cups yogurt, for garnish

1. In a large soup pan, over medium heat, sauté the garlic and onions in the olive oil until softened, about 5 minutes. Add the carrots, potatoes, ginger, cumin and broth, cover and simmer for 20 minutes or until the carrots are tender but not mushy.

2. Remove the pot from the heat. Puree half this mixture in a food processor or blender. Combine the pureed and unpureed parts of the soup together to create one nicely textured whole. Add more broth if necessary to achieve the desired consistency. Taste and adjust seasoning. Serve hot, garnished with a dollop of yogurt.

Yield: 6 servings

NOTE: *At a meat meal, soup may be served without yogurt.*

—MOLLY O'NEILL

EGGPLANT AND TOMATO SOUP

meat

ADAPTED FROM *Cooking with the 60-Minute Gourmet*

1 eggplant (about 1 pound)
¼ cup peanut, corn or vegetable oil
2 tablespoons unsalted margarine
1½ cups chopped onions
1 tablespoon finely minced garlic
Salt to taste
Freshly ground black pepper to taste
1 bay leaf
½ teaspoon dried thyme
3 cups chopped, canned imported tomatoes
¼ cup raw rice
4 cups fresh or canned chicken broth

1. Trim off the stem end of the eggplant. Peel the eggplant and cut it into 1-inch cubes. There should be about 5 cups. Heat the oil in a large, heavy pan, and when it is hot and almost smoking, add the cubed eggplant. Cook, shaking the pan and stirring until the cubes are lightly browned. Drain the eggplant on paper towels. There should be about 2¼ cups.

2. Heat the margarine in a pan and add the onions and garlic. Cook, stirring, until the mixture is wilted and add the eggplant cubes, salt and pepper. Add the bay leaf and thyme. Cook, stirring, about 1 minute and add the tomatoes.

3. Add the rice and broth and bring to a boil, stirring. Cook, covered, about 30 minutes. Remove the bay leaf and pour the mixture into the container of a food processor or electric blender. It may be necessary to do this in 2 batches. Puree until smooth.

4. Return the soup to the pot and bring to a simmer. Serve.

Yield: About 7 cups or 7–8 servings

GARLIC SOUP

meat

ADAPTED FROM Jean-Georges Vongerichten

3 tablespoons extra-virgin olive oil

4 whole garlic bulbs, separated into cloves, peeled and
    thinly sliced

2 teaspoons fresh thyme leaves

6 cups Chicken Stock, preferably homemade (page 48)

Salt to taste

Freshly ground black pepper to taste

2 large eggs

1 tablespoon white wine vinegar

1. In a large saucepan over medium heat, heat the olive oil and add garlic and thyme. Sauté until garlic is soft and translucent, about 6 minutes.

2. Add chicken stock and bring to a boil over high heat. Reduce the heat to medium and simmer until the liquid is reduced by half and the garlic is very tender, about 15 minutes.

3. Season to taste with salt and pepper. In a small bowl, combine eggs and vinegar and beat with a fork until well blended. Whisk into soup and stir until soup has thickened. Serve hot.

Yield: 4 servings

—MARIAN BURROS

DRIED FAVA BEAN SOUP • (BESSARA)

pareve

ADAPTED FROM *The Book of Jewish Food*

1 pound skinless, split, dried fava beans

Salt to taste

5 garlic cloves, chopped

1/4–1/2 cup olive oil

1/2 teaspoon paprika

1 1/2–2 teaspoons cumin

1/4 teaspoon turmeric

Pinch of cayenne pepper

Juice of 2 lemons

1 large bunch of cilantro, chopped, about 1/2 cup

1. Soak the beans in water for 2 hours, drain and put in a pot with 2 quarts of cold water. Bring to a boil, skim and simmer, covered, for 2 hours, until the beans are very soft. Add the salt and mash the beans by hand or, for a smoother texture, puree in a blender and return to the pot.

2. Fry the garlic in 2 tablespoons of the olive oil until golden, about 3 minutes. Add the paprika, cumin, turmeric and cayenne. Add to the soup and simmer for 30 minutes longer, adding water if the soup becomes too thick. Just before serving, stir in the lemon juice and the cilantro. Garnish with a drizzle of olive oil, if desired.

Yield: 6 servings

—MOLLY O'NEILL

JERUSALEM ARTICHOKE SOUP

meat

ADAPTED FROM Eucalyptus Restaurant, Jerusalem, in
The Foods of Israel Today

2 medium onions, peeled and diced in ½-inch pieces
2 tablespoons extra-virgin olive oil
1 clove garlic, minced
1½ pounds Jerusalem artichokes (also known as
    California sunchokes), peeled
4 cups Chicken Broth, canned or homemade
    (page 48)
Salt to taste
Freshly ground pepper to taste
10–12 blanched almonds
2 tablespoons water
Pinch saffron

Juice of ½ lemon
2 tablespoons flat parsley with stems, diced

1. Using a heavy casserole, sweat the onions in the olive oil over low heat, covered, about 20 minutes. Uncover, add the garlic and artichokes and increase heat. Continue sautéing for a few more minutes.
2. Add the chicken broth and salt and pepper to taste. Bring to a boil and cover. Simmer for 30 minutes.
3. Meanwhile, using a spice grinder, grind the almonds and mix with water. Whisk mixture into the soup with the saffron strands and the lemon juice. Reheat, sprinkle with parsley and serve.

Yield: 6–8 servings

—JOAN NATHAN

COLETTE ROSSANT'S MUSHROOM CONSOMMÉ

meat

2 tablespoons dried mushrooms
½ cup boiling water
6 cups rich Beef Broth, preferably homemade
    (page 49)
½ pound fresh mushrooms plus 6 whole fresh
    mushrooms for garnish
Salt to taste
Freshly ground pepper to taste
¼ cup dry sherry

1. Put the dried mushrooms into a small bowl and pour the boiling water over them. Let soak 20 min-

utes. Drain but save the mushrooms and soaking liquid.
2. Put the broth into a saucepan and add the reserved soaking liquid.
3. Put the drained mushrooms into the container of a food processor or blender. Wash and drain the fresh mushrooms. Set aside the 6 mushrooms to be used for garnish. Add the remainder to the container of the food processor or blender. Chop finely, stirring down as necessary. Scrape the chopped mushrooms into the broth. Bring to a boil and simmer 15 minutes.
4. Line a colander or sieve with cheesecloth and pour in the mushroom mixture. Drain well, pushing

the solids down with a heavy spoon to extract additional liquid. Discard the chopped mushrooms.

5. Bring the mushroom liquid to a simmer and add salt and pepper and the sherry.

6. Thinly slice the reserved 6 mushrooms and add the slices to the broth. Serve piping hot.

Yield: 6 servings

—CRAIG CLAIBORNE

WILD MUSHROOM SOUP

meat, pareve
ADAPTED FROM Design Cuisine

 2½ pounds fresh mushroom stems or caps and
   stems (porcini, portobello, shiitake, oyster,
   chanterelle)
 5 tablespoons extra-virgin olive oil
 2 garlic cloves, crushed
 3 large shallots, finely chopped
 2 tablespoons finely chopped parsley leaves
 1 quart Rich Chicken Broth (page 48) or vegetable
   broth, canned or homemade
 1 cup firmly packed pureed cooked white potato
 Salt to taste
 Freshly ground black pepper to taste

1. Rinse mushrooms quickly and drain immediately. Dry and finely chop in food processor, leaving a couple of mushrooms sliced. With hot oil in nonstick pan, sauté the mushrooms, in batches a single layer deep. When all the mushrooms are cooked, including the sliced ones, return them to the pan, add garlic, shallots and parsley and sauté for 2 minutes longer.

2. In a separate pot, bring the broth to a simmer. Add the pureed potato and stir. Add the mushrooms and slices and any juices to broth; season with salt and pepper, allow to steep a couple of minutes and serve.

Yield: 6 servings

—MARIAN BURROS

SORREL AND POTATO SOUP

pareve, dairy

 1 pound sorrel
 2 tablespoons extra-virgin
   olive oil
 2 cups chopped onions

 2 baking potatoes (1 pound total), peeled and cut in
   ½-inch cubes
 4 cups water or Vegetable Stock, canned or homemade
   (page 51)
 ¼ teaspoon fine sea salt or to taste
 Yogurt, optional

1. Discard the stems from the sorrel. Wash the leaves well and squeeze dry. There should be about 10 cups of leaves. Set aside.

2. Heat olive oil in a 10-quart or larger heavy, nonreactive pan. Add onions and cook slowly until soft and sweet. Stir in 8 cups of the sorrel and cook, stirring, until it softens, reduces in volume and turns olive green.

3. Stir in the potato cubes, water or stock and salt. Bring to a boil, reduce heat, cover and simmer for 10–15 minutes, until potatoes are tender. Remove cover, take off heat and let sit 10 minutes. In batches, puree in a food processor.

4. Serve the soup hot or cold. Before serving, cut the remaining 2 cups of sorrel leaves in thin strips and sprinkle on the soup. If serving cold at a dairy meal, a dollop of yogurt can be added as well.

Yield: 6 servings

—SUZANNE HAMLIN

HEARTY VEGETABLE SOUP

dairy, meat, pareve

1 cup chopped onion

1 cup chopped celery

1 cup chopped carrot

3 cups peeled, chopped tomatoes, fresh or canned

Salt and pepper to taste

2 cups diced, peeled potatoes

1 cup green beans, in 1/2-inch lengths

1 1/2 cups corn kernels (fresh, canned or frozen)

1 1/2 cups diced zucchini (or mixture of zucchini and yellow squash)

4 cups Chicken Stock (page 48) beef stock or water

1 teaspoon minced fresh thyme

1 1/2 cups kidney beans or chick peas, rinsed and drained

4 tablespoons freshly grated Italian Parmesan cheese, optional (see Note)

1. Combine onion, celery and carrots in a heavy 5- to 6-quart pot. Cover and cook over low heat until the vegetables are tender, about 10 minutes. Stir them from time to time as they cook.

2. Add the tomatoes with their juice, season to taste with salt and pepper and simmer for 10 minutes. Add the potatoes and simmer 10 minutes longer. Add the beans, corn and zucchini along with the stock or water. Bring to a simmer, check seasonings and add thyme.

3. Simmer about 30 minutes longer, until all the vegetables are tender. Stir in the kidney beans or chickpeas and cook just long enough to heat them through.

4. At dairy meals, serve with some Parmesan cheese dusted on each portion and with whole grain bread or rolls on the side.

Yield: 8 servings

NOTE: *Serve cheese only if water is used as the liquid.*

—FLORENCE FABRICANT

MARK BITTMAN'S VEGETARIAN MUSHROOM BARLEY SOUP

pareve

1 ounce dried porcini mushrooms (about 1 cup)

2 tablespoons olive oil

¼ pound shiitake or button mushrooms, stemmed
   and roughly chopped

3 medium carrots, peeled and sliced

1 cup pearl barley

Salt and pepper to taste

1 bay leaf

1 tablespoon soy sauce

3 cups water

1. Soak porcini in 3 cups very hot water. Put olive oil in a medium saucepan and turn heat to high. Add shiitakes and carrots and cook, stirring occasionally, until they begin to brown. Add barley and continue to cook, stirring frequently, until it begins to brown; sprinkle with a little salt and pepper. Remove the porcini from their soaking liquid and reserve liquid. Sort through porcini and discard any hard bits.

2. Add porcini to pot and cook, stirring, for about a minute. Add bay leaf, mushroom soaking water and 3 cups additional water. Bring to a boil, then lower the heat to a simmer; cook until barley is very tender, 20–30 minutes. Add soy sauce and taste. Add salt if necessary and plenty of pepper. Serve hot.

Yield: 4 servings

NOTE: *According to Mark Bittman, who created this soup, the dried porcini mushrooms, which are widely available and can be reconstituted in less than 10 minutes, are the key ingredient in this richly flavored broth. They impart an intense flavor that rivals beef stock. A touch of soy sauce is another break with the traditional recipe, but it really completes the flavor profile. At meat meals, chicken stock may be used instead of water.*

—MARK BITTMAN

SPLIT PEA AND BARLEY SOUP

dairy, pareve

1 pound green split peas

Water

3 tablespoons butter or cooking oil

1 cup chopped onion

½ cup chopped celery

½ cup chopped carrot

2 bay leaves

½ cup medium barley

Juice of 1 lemon

⅓ cup minced fresh dill

Salt and freshly ground black pepper to taste

Sour cream or plain yogurt, optional

1. Pick over the split peas. Rinse, drain and place them in a saucepan. Cover with water to the depth of one inch, bring to a boil and cook for two minutes. Remove from heat and set aside to soften for one hour.

2. Melt butter or oil in a large, heavy kettle. Add onion, celery and carrot and sauté over medium heat until soft and just barely beginning to color. Drain and rinse the peas and add them. Add 10 cups of water and the bay leaves.

3. Bring to a boil, lower heat to a simmer and cook for one hour. Add the barley and continue cooking one hour longer.

4. Stir the soup, add lemon juice and dill. Season to taste with salt (don't be surprised if you need quite a bit) and pepper. Serve topped with a dollop of sour cream or yogurt if you wish.

Yield: 8–10 servings

—FLORENCE FABRICANT

GREEN MINESTRONE · (MINESTRONE VERDE)

pareve, dairy

½ *medium onion, thinly sliced*
2 *cloves garlic, coarsely chopped*
1 *celery stalk, coarsely chopped*
¼ *cup coarsely chopped flat-leaf parsley*
2 *tablespoons extra-virgin olive oil, plus some for garnishing*
1–2 *small potatoes, cubed (about 1 cup)*
1 *cup cooked beans, such as cannellini, together with the liquid in which they cooked*
1 *bay leaf*
1 *small whole red chili pepper, if desired*
Salt to taste
Freshly ground black pepper to taste
½ *medium zucchini, cubed (about 1 cup), skin on*
3–4 *leaves green chard, finely sliced (about 1 cup)*
¼ *small green cabbage, finely sliced (about 1 cup)*
¼ *cup raw rice*
Extra-virgin olive oil, optional
Freshly grated Parmesan cheese, for garnish, optional

1. Mix together the onion, garlic, celery, parsley and the two tablespoons of olive oil in the bottom of a heavy soup kettle and cook over medium heat. As soon as the vegetables sizzle, turn the heat down and cook slowly, stirring frequently, until the vegetables are soft, about 5 minutes. Do not let them brown.

2. Add the potatoes and beans (drained) and mix well. Measure the bean cooking liquid and add water to make about 4 cups. Add to the kettle, along with the bay leaf, chili pepper, salt and pepper. Cover and cook slowly until the potatoes are soft, 10–15 minutes.

3. Add the zucchini, chard and cabbage and cook, uncovered, until the zucchini cubes are barely tender. Stir in the rice, cover the pan and turn off the heat. Let rest for 30 minutes, allowing the rice to become tender. If necessary, reheat the soup and cook gently until the rice is just done.

4. Garnish with the olive oil or, at a dairy meal, with the cheese or both. (Cheese is typically not offered if the soup is served at room temperature, a summer-time tradition in Milan.) Serve immediately.

Yield: 4–6 servings, depending on what else accompanies the meal

VARIATIONS: *Do not hesitate to use other seasonal vegetables. Pasta, especially a short, tubular shape, can be substituted for the rice. For a richer soup, use a savory chicken stock or veal stock instead of the water and omit cheese.*

—NANCY HARMON JENKINS

MOTHER WOLFF SOUP

pareve

ADAPTED FROM *Sundays at Moosewood Restaurant*

4 quarts water, approximately

½ cup dried lima beans, soaked overnight with water to cover, or brought to a boil and soaked 1 hour

½ cup rice

½ cup barley

3–4 large garlic cloves, peeled and minced

1 tablespoon dried dill weed

1 bay leaf

1 cup diced onions

1 cup chopped celery

2 tablespoons vegetable oil

1 tablespoon sweet Hungarian paprika

1 cup diced potatoes

1 cup diced carrots

½ teaspoon salt

Ground black pepper to taste

1 cup green beans or peas (fresh or frozen)

1 cup chopped tomatoes (fresh or canned)

¼ cup chopped parsley (optional)

1. In a large soup kettle, combine the water, lima beans, rice, barley, garlic, dill and bay leaf and bring to a boil. Lower the heat, cover and simmer for 1½ hours, adding more water if needed as the limas and barley absorb the liquid.

2. When the soup has been simmering for about an hour, prepare the other vegetables. In a large frying pan, sauté the onions and celery in the oil for a few minutes. Sprinkle in the paprika. Add the potatoes, carrots, salt and pepper. Cover and cook a few minutes, stirring frequently, until the vegetables start to soften. Stir in the green beans and continue to cook, covered, a few more minutes until the vegetables are just tender.

3. Stir the soup and remove the bay leaf. Add the sautéed vegetables, tomatoes, parsley if desired and more salt and pepper to taste. Simmer, covered, over very low heat for 1½–2 more hours, stirring occasionally to prevent sticking.

4. Serve immediately. Leftovers can be successfully reheated, although more water may be needed.

Yield: 10–12 servings

—NANCY HARMON JENKINS

TURKISH SPLIT-PEA SOUP WITH MINT AND PAPRIKA

meat, dairy, pareve

ADAPTED FROM *Kitchen Conversation*

8 ounces split peas

2 tablespoons unsalted butter or margarine

1 onion, thinly sliced

1 carrot, peeled and thinly sliced

1 bay leaf

5–6 cups Chicken Stock (page 48) or Vegetable Stock (page 51), canned or homemade

½ pound spinach, washed and chopped

3 teaspoons Hungarian paprika

Milk, water, chicken stock or vegetable stock for thinning

1 teaspoon coarse sea salt

Freshly ground pepper to taste

3 tablespoons chopped mint to garnish

1. Cover the split peas with cold water. Soak for a few hours or overnight. Drain.

2. Melt the butter or margarine in a saucepan over moderate heat. Cook the onion until soft and translucent, about 10 minutes. Add the split peas, carrot, bay leaf and stock to cover and bring to boil. Simmer gently, covered, until the peas are very soft. If the mixture seems dry, add more stock or water as needed.

3. Remove the bay leaf. Add the chopped spinach and 2 teaspoons of the paprika and simmer until the spinach wilts.

4. Puree the soup in a blender or food processor. Add the milk, water or stock to thin. Season to taste with salt and pepper. Serve hot, sprinkle with chopped mint and remaining paprika.

Yield: 4–6 servings

NOTE: *Chicken stock may be used only with margarine.*

—MOIRA HODGSON

TURKISH RED LENTIL SOUP • (EZO GELIN)

pareve, dairy

ADAPTED FROM Sultan's Kitchen, Boston

2 cups red lentils
¼ cup long-grain rice
¼ cup olive oil
1 cup onions, finely chopped
2 tablespoons tomato paste
½ cup peeled, finely diced tomato
2 tablespoons sweet paprika
¼ teaspoon cayenne pepper, or to taste
9 cups Vegetable Stock (page 51) or water
Salt to taste
½ tablespoon finely chopped mint
2 cups plain toasted bread cubes
Lemon wedges
Plain yogurt, optional

1. Place the lentils and rice in a sieve, rinse well and allow to drain.

2. Meanwhile, heat the oil in a heavy 4-quart saucepan. Add the onion and sauté until soft but not brown. Stir in the tomato paste, tomato, paprika and cayenne pepper. Add the lentils, rice and stock. Stir well and simmer, covered, 30 minutes, until the rice is cooked and the lentils have virtually dissolved into a puree. Stir from time to time.

3. Add salt to taste. If the soup is too thick, add a little water.

4. Serve each portion sprinkled with mint leaves and croutons, with lemon wedges. Yogurt may be served on the side at a dairy meal.

Yield: 8 servings

—FLORENCE FABRICANT

RUSS & DAUGHTERS'S
MUSHROOM-BARLEY SOUP

meat

¹/₂ cup dried porcini mushrooms

8 ounces margarine

1 very large onion or 2 medium onions, peeled and
    chopped (about 1 pound)

6 cloves garlic, peeled and finely chopped

1¹/₂ pounds fresh mushrooms, trimmed and thinly sliced

4 stalks of celery with leaves, diced

3 big carrots, peeled and coarsely chopped
    (about 1¹/₂ pounds)

¹/₂ cup chopped parsley

2 tablespoons flour

2 quarts Beef Broth (page 49)

2¹/₂ cups barley, rinsed

2 tablespoons kosher salt or more to taste

Freshly ground black pepper to taste

1. Soak the dried mushrooms in 1 quart hot water
for 1 hour. Strain through a filter or cheesecloth.
Reserve the water. Coarsely chop the dried mushrooms and set aside.

2. Melt the margarine in a large stockpot over
medium-high heat and sauté onions and garlic until
soft, about 10 minutes. Add the fresh mushrooms,
celery, carrots and 4 tablespoons parsley. Cook until
the carrots are tender, about 10 minutes. Add the
flour and stir until blended. Stir in the mushroom
soaking liquid until blended, then stir in the beef
broth and 6 cups water. Stir in the barley, soaked
mushrooms, 2 tablespoons salt and pepper to taste.

3. Heat the soup to boiling, stirring frequently, then
lower the heat, cover the pot and simmer for about
45 minutes or until the barley is tender.

4. Add the remaining parsley, mix thoroughly and
add more water if the soup is too thick. Adjust seasonings if necessary.

Yield: 12–16 servings

—JASON EPSTEIN

FISH SOUP MARSEILLES-STYLE WITH
GARLIC CROUTONS • (SOUPE DE POISSONS)

pareve

2–3 pounds fish bones and heads

1 cup diced celery

1 cup diced onions

1 leek (chop the green part and mince the white part;
    keep them separate)

1 bay leaf

¹/₂ teaspoon thyme

1 teaspoon fennel seeds

1 tablespoon black peppercorns

¹/₂ teaspoon red pepper flakes

1 cup white wine

6 cups water

1 clove garlic, peeled

6 sprigs parsley

2 tablespoons olive oil
¾ cup minced onions
1 tablespoon minced garlic
½ cup celery, chopped fine
1 teaspoon saffron threads
½ teaspoon red pepper flakes
½ teaspoon black pepper
4 tomatoes, peeled, seeded, chopped
¼ cup tomato paste
1 cup white wine
2 pounds firm white fish fillets
Salt to taste

1. Combine in a soup pot all the ingredients up to and including the parsley—except for the leek whites. Bring to a boil, reduce heat and simmer for 10 minutes. Strain the liquid and reserve it (You should have about 8 cups).
2. Pour the olive oil into a soup pot and sauté the onions and minced garlic over medium-high heat just until they are golden. Add the celery and leek whites, saffron, pepper flakes, black pepper, tomatoes and tomato paste. Cook for 3–4 minutes.
3. Add white wine to the pot, bring to a boil and add the reserved fish stock. Bring to a boil, reduce

heat and simmer for about 15 minutes.
4. Cut the fish into ½-inch cubes and add the pieces to the broth. Cook for 5 minutes, taste for seasoning and serve with Garlic Croutons (see recipe).

Yield: 8 servings

◆ **GARLIC CROUTONS** ◆

pareve

1 loaf French or Italian bread
2 cloves garlic, peeled
4 tablespoons olive oil
Black pepper to taste

1. Rub the bread all over with the garlic cloves. Slice the bread into ½-inch pieces and sprinkle one side with olive oil and grate some black pepper over.
2. Place the bread slices on a baking sheet under a broiler until they are golden brown. Turn and broil on the other side.

Yield: 8 servings

—BRYAN MILLER

HUNGARIAN FISHERMAN'S SOUP ◆ (HALASZLE)

pareve
ADAPTED FROM Kalman Kalla

5 pounds whole freshwater fish, such as catfish, pike or
  carp, or 6 cups fish stock and 3 pounds boneless fillet
Salt to taste
2 medium-size onions, peeled and sliced
3 tablespoons hot Hungarian paprika

1 tablespoon sweet Hungarian paprika
4 medium-size Italian-style green peppers, about
  ¼ pound, seeded and sliced
2 large ripe tomatoes, peeled, seeded and chopped, or
  1½ cups canned Italian plum tomatoes, drained
  and chopped
2 sweet green peppers or 3 hot peppers, sliced into
  thin rings (optional garnish)

1. If using whole fish, have your fish shop fillet them but reserve heads and racks or bones. Cut fillets into bite-size pieces, sprinkle with salt and set aside in the refrigerator.

2. Put the fish heads and racks in a kettle with the onions. Cover with water and sprinkle with the hot and sweet paprika. Place over medium heat, bring to a boil, cover and reduce the heat. Cook 45 minutes at a low, steady simmer. (If using prepared stock, place in kettle with onions and paprikas and simmer 25 minutes.) Strain the liquid, discarding the fish pieces and onion. Rinse out kettle.

3. Place the salted fish in the kettle. Add the green pepper and tomatoes. Pour the fish broth over the fish. Return to a low simmer over medium heat and cook, covered, 20 more minutes. Do not stir the soup while cooking. Add more salt if desired.

4. Serve immediately, garnished with raw green pepper, if desired.

Yield: 8 servings

NOTE: *The soup can also be made using only fresh salmon.*

—NANCY HARMON JENKINS

HOT-AND-SOUR FISH SOUP

pareve

ADAPTED FROM *The Best of Craig Claiborne*

3–4 pounds very fresh fish bones, preferably with head but with gills removed

Water

1 fresh ginger, 1½-inch length

4 scallions

20 sprigs of cilantro

3–4 tablespoons white vinegar

⅛–¼ teaspoon ground white pepper

½ teaspoon sesame oil

Salt

½ pound skinless, boneless nonoily fish, such as flounder, sole, striped bass, etc.

1. Place the fish bones in a kettle and let cold running water flow over them to remove all traces of blood. When the water runs clear, drain. Then add enough cold water to barely cover the bones. Do not add salt. Bring to a boil and let simmer over very gentle heat for about 20 minutes. Strain. Reserve the broth and discard the bones. Add 6–7 cups of the broth to a saucepan and bring to a boil.

2. Meanwhile, scrape the ginger. Cut the ginger into the thinnest possible slices. Stack the slices and cut them into the finest possible shreds. Set aside. Add the scrapings to the soup. Trim the scallions and cut into 2-inch lengths. Cut the lengths into very fine shreds. Set aside. Pluck or cut off the cilantro leaves from the stems. Set leaves aside. Crush the stems and add to the soup.

3. Strain soup into another saucepan and add the shredded ginger, scallions, cilantro leaves, vinegar, white pepper, sesame oil and salt. Stir to blend flavors but do not cook. Cut the fish into ½-inch cubes and add it to the soup. Bring just to a boil and simmer just until the fish loses its raw look. Spoon into individual soup bowls and serve piping hot.

Yield: 6 servings

SWEET AND SOUR
CABBAGE SOUP • (SAUERKRAUT SOUP)

meat

ADAPTED FROM *The New York Times*
International Cookbook

2 pounds short ribs of beef

2 pounds beef bones

1 cup chopped onion

3 carrots, coarsely chopped

2 cloves garlic, peeled

1 teaspoon dried thyme

1 bay leaf

2 quarts water

2½ cups (20-ounce can) tomatoes

8 cups shredded cabbage

Salt to taste

Freshly ground black pepper to taste

3 tablespoons lemon juice

3 tablespoons granulated sugar

1 pound sauerkraut, washed and squeezed dry

1. Preheat the oven to 450 degrees.

2. Place the short ribs, beef bones, onion, carrots, garlic, thyme and bay leaf in a roasting pan. Bake for about 20 minutes, until the meat is brown.

3. Transfer the mixture to a kettle. Place the roasting pan over heat and add a little of the water. Stir to dissolve the brown particles, then pour this into the kettle. Add the remaining water, tomatoes, cabbage, salt and pepper to taste.

4. Bring the mixture to a boil and skim the fat from the top. Simmer for 1½ hours. Add the lemon juice, sugar and sauerkraut; add more water, if necessary. Cook for 1 hour longer.

Yield: 8–10 servings

HEARTY MEAT SOUPS

WALLSÉ'S GOULASH SOUP

meat

ADAPTED FROM Kurt Gutenbrunner

2 tablespoons duck fat or vegetable oil

2 cups finely diced onions

3 cloves garlic, minced

3 tablespoons Hungarian sweet paprika

1 tablespoon tomato paste

1 tablespoon ground caraway seeds

1 teaspoon dried marjoram

½ teaspoon dried thyme

1 bay leaf

1 tablespoon red wine vinegar

¾ pound lean beef chuck, in ½-inch cubes

½ pound Yukon Gold or German butterball potatoes, peeled and cut in ½-inch dice

Sea salt to taste

2 teaspoons fresh lemon juice

1. Heat fat or oil in heavy broad saucepan or deep sauté pan. Add onions and garlic and cook, stirring slowly and frequently, over medium heat until onions are fragrant and nut-brown.

2. Add the paprika and cook, stirring, about 2 minutes. Stir in the tomato paste, cook about a minute longer, and then stir in caraway, marjoram, thyme and bay leaf. Add vinegar, stir, and add 4 cups water. Stir in beef, bring to a slow simmer and cook 30 minutes.

3. Add potatoes and 2 more cups water, and cook 20 minutes longer, until potatoes and meat are tender. Season to taste with salt, add lemon juice, adjust sea-soning and serve, or set aside and reheat before serving. If soup becomes too thick, add a little more water.

Yield: 3–4 servings

NOTE: *This soup is even better the day after it is made. The paprika should be sweet Hungarian, not Spanish, and it must be cooked so that it doesn't taste raw, but not too long because it will burn and become bitter. Unless you use paprika all the time, you should buy it fresh for the soup. For variety, you can add cranberry beans or flageolets, shredded cabbage and even sauerkraut to the soup. And, for a dairy meal, a fish like carp is a good substitute for the meat. Goulash soup is traditionally served with hefty slices of rye bread.*

—KURT GUTENBRUNNER

YEMENITE HIGH HOLIDAY SOUP STEW

meat

ADAPTED FROM the Zadok family, in *The Jewish Holiday Kitchen*

3 pieces marrow bone, about 2 pounds

1 (3-pound) chicken, cleaned and quartered

3 pounds beef shoulder ribs or stew meat (fat removed), left whole or cut into large pieces

Up to 5 quarts water

10–12 cloves garlic, separated but unpeeled

2 large onions, peeled and quartered, or 9 small white onions, peeled

1 large white turnip, unpeeled but quartered

4 leeks or green onions, coarsely cut

3 celery stalks, cut into 2-inch pieces

1 medium zucchini or acorn squash, cubed

3 medium unpeeled carrots, cut into 3-inch pieces

1 large tomato, almost quartered but not cut apart at bottom

3 medium potatoes, peeled and diced

1 small bunch parsley or cilantro, woody stems trimmed

Salt to taste

1 tablespoon Hawayij spice combination or to taste (see recipe below)

Helbeh as garnish (page 423)

1. In a soup kettle, place the beef marrow bones and chicken with water to cover. Bring to a boil, then simmer until a froth forms. Remove the meat and bones and discard the water.

2. Clean the kettle, add the beef and bones and cover with water, adding as much as 5 quarts. Bring to a boil again, lower the heat and add the unpeeled garlic cloves. Add the onion, turnip and leeks or green onion. Cover and cook about 1½ hours or until meat seems relatively tender.

3. Remove the marrow bones, add the chicken, cover and simmer another 20 minutes. Cool and refrigerate overnight.

4. Before serving, skim off the fat and add the celery, the zucchini or acorn squash, carrots, tomato and potato. Cover and simmer another 20 minutes.

5. Just before serving, add the parsley or cilantro, salt and Hawayij and cook for final 10 minutes. Remove garlic cloves. Adjust seasonings.

6. Place a bowl of soup at each table setting. Serve with pita or a pita-type bread and Helbeh dipping sauce. Dip the bread into the Helbeh and then into the soup, scooping up the meat and vegetables.

Yield: 10–12 servings

◆ **HAWAYIJ** ◆

(Yemenite Spice Combination)

pareve

  2 tablespoons whole black peppercorns
  1 tablespoon black caraway seed
  1 teaspoon whole cumin
  1 teaspoon cardamom seeds
  1 teaspoon saffron
  2 teaspoons turmeric

Pound all ingredients together in a mortar and pestle, or use a coffee grinder or a standard blender.

Yield: About 4 tablespoons

—JOAN NATHAN

VEGETABLE BEEF SOUP

meat

ADAPTED FROM *The New York Times Heritage Cookbook*

  3 pounds brisket
  3 quarts water
  1 tablespoon salt
  ½ teaspoon freshly ground
     black pepper
  2 carrots, quartered
  3 onions, chopped
  ½ head cabbage, coarsely shredded
  4 stalks celery, chopped
  3 tablespoons tomato paste
  1 cup diced potatoes
  1½ cups fresh peas

  2 teaspoons uncooked rice, soaked for 1 hour in cold
     water and drained, optional

1. Place the beef in a heavy kettle and add the water, salt and pepper. Bring to a boil and simmer, covered, 1½ hours.

2. Add the carrots, onions, cabbage and celery and simmer ½ hour. Add the tomato paste, potatoes and peas. For a thick soup, add rice. Simmer until vegetables and rice, if desired, are tender. Shred meat and serve in soup, or serve separately.

Yield: 8 servings

NOTE: *You can add any vegetables at hand and make the soup as thick and varied as you wish.*

BEEF AND BARLEY SOUP

meat

ADAPTED FROM *Pure and Simple*

4 cups canned tomatoes

¾ pound boneless chuck, cut in 1½-inch cubes

Salt and pepper to taste

Tops from ½ bunch celery

2 sprigs parsley

¼ cup pearl barley

1 cup tomato juice

½ pound green beans, tips cut off, washed and cut in
    half

½ cup coarsely chopped rutabaga

1½ cups coarsely chopped cabbage

½ cup sliced carrots

½ cup sliced celery

½ cup thinly sliced onion

1. Drain the liquid from the tomatoes and reserve.
Add enough water to liquid to make one quart.

2. Place in large kettle with beef, salt and pepper to
taste, celery tops and parsley. Cover and cook slowly
for 1 hour.

3. Add barley. Cook one hour longer.

4. Remove and discard celery tops and parsley. Add
tomato juice, reserved tomatoes and remaining ingredients.

5. Bring to a boil. Reduce heat and cook about 45
minutes.

6. Serve immediately. Or refrigerate or freeze and
reheat before serving.

Yield: 2½ quarts

—MARIAN BURROS

CHORBA SOUP WITH LAMB

meat

ADAPTED FROM *Cuisine et Pâtisserie Tunisiennes*

3 tablespoons extra-virgin olive oil

1 pound boneless lamb shoulder, well trimmed of fat
    and diced fine

Salt to taste

Freshly ground black pepper

2½ cups canned tomato puree

3–4 tablespoons Harissa (page 421)

¼ cup finely chopped onion

¼ cup finely chopped celery

2 tablespoons chopped flat-leaf parsley

¾ cup fine pearl barley, millet or orzo

1 lemon, in 6 wedges

1. Heat oil in a large heavy saucepan. Season lamb
with salt and pepper and add to pan. Sauté over
medium-high heat, stirring, until it has browned.

2. Mix ½ cup of the tomato puree with ½ cup water
and add it to the pan along with 3 tablespoons of
the harissa. Cook for a couple of minutes; add the
onion, celery, parsley and the remaining tomato
puree. Stir in 3 cups water. Bring to a simmer and

cook over low heat, covered, until the lamb is very tender, about 20 minutes.

3. Add another 3 cups water and bring to a boil. Slowly add the barley, millet or orzo in a thin stream, stirring. Cook about 10 minutes. Taste for seasoning, adding more salt and harissa if desired. Serve with lemon wedges.

Yield: 6 servings

—FLORENCE FABRICANT

POMEGRANATE SOUP

meat

8 cups water or Vegetable Stock (page 51),
    canned or fresh
1–2 lamb shanks, cracked and rinsed
½ cup yellow split peas
1 cup chopped onion
3 large beets with greens
¼ cup short-grain white rice
1 bunch scallions, trimmed and sliced into thin rings
    (include most of the green)
2–3 tablespoons sugar
2–3 tablespoons lime juice
½ cup chopped parsley
1 cup pomegranate juice or 2 tablespoons
    pomegranate molasses (see Note, page 583)
2 cups chopped spinach leaves
½ cup chopped cilantro, optional
1 tablespoon dried crushed mint
¼ teaspoon cinnamon
¼ teaspoon black pepper

1. In a large, heavy pot bring 7 cups of the water or stock to a boil. Add the lamb shanks, split peas and onion. Bring to a boil again, then reduce the heat and skim the surface. Cover and simmer for 40–50 minutes, until the meat and peas are tender. Peel and chop the beets; reserve the greens. Add the beets and rice to the pot; cover and cook for 25 minutes more.

2. Remove the lamb shanks with tongs, pull the meat from the bones and shred or chop, discarding the bones and fat. Return to the pot, then add the scallions, sugar, 2 tablespoons of the lime juice, the chopped parsley and the pomegranate juice. Rinse and chop the beet greens and add, along with the chopped spinach. Cook, stirring, for a minute or two, until the greens have wilted.

3. Taste and adjust the seasonings, adding another tablespoon of sugar and lime juice, if desired. Add the remaining cup of water or stock to thin, if necessary. Add cilantro, if desired. Heat briefly and ladle into bowls. Mix together the dried mint, cinnamon and black pepper, and sprinkle a little on each serving.

Yield: 6 servings

—SUZANNE HAMLIN

SPAGO'S LENTIL SOUP WITH LAMB MEATBALLS

meat

ADAPTED FROM François Kwaku-Dongo

FOR THE SOUP:

2 tablespoons olive oil

1 medium onion, minced

1 carrot, chopped

5 garlic gloves, minced

½ rib celery

1 sprig fresh parsley

1 sprig thyme

1 tablespoon turmeric powder

2 teaspoons cumin powder

1 pound lentils

10 cups Chicken Broth (page 48)

Salt to taste

Freshly ground pepper to taste

Juice of ½ lemon

1 tablespoon chopped fresh mint, for garnish

½ teaspoon minced lemon peel, for garnish

FOR THE MEATBALLS:

1 pound ground lamb

½ cup bread crumbs

1 cup blanched almonds, toasted and ground
  (see Note, page 582)

½ cup chopped onion

⅓ cup raisins, chopped

1 egg, lightly beaten

3 cloves garlic, minced

2 tablespoons chopped parsley

2 tablespoons chopped fresh cilantro

¼ teaspoon chili flakes

Salt and freshly ground pepper to taste

1. To make the soup, place the olive oil in a large saucepan over medium heat. Add the onion, carrot, garlic, celery, parsley and thyme and sauté until soft. Add the turmeric and cumin and continue to cook for 5 minutes. Add the lentils and chicken broth and season lightly with salt and pepper. Reduce the heat and simmer until the lentils are tender, 30–45 minutes, skimming as necessary. Discard the parsley and thyme, transfer two-thirds of the soup to a blender and blend until smooth. Return the blended liquid to the saucepan and add the lemon juice and more salt and pepper to taste. Set aside.

2. Preheat the oven to 400 degrees.

3. To make the meatballs, combine the lamb, bread crumbs, almonds, onion, raisins, egg, garlic, parsley, cilantro and chili flakes. Season lightly with salt and pepper. Use a teaspoon to shape the mixture into 40 small meatballs, placing them on a baking sheet. Bake until lightly browned, about 10 minutes.

4. Combine the mint and minced lemon peel. Warm the soup and ladle into 4 bowls. Divide the meatballs among the bowls, sprinkle with mint and lemon peel and serve immediately.

Yield: 4 servings

—MOLLY O'NEILL

LAMB, VEGETABLE AND NOODLE SOUP

meat

ADAPTED FROM Isak Bayarev, in *Jewish Cooking in America*

2 tablespoons vegetable oil

1 pound boneless lamb or beef shoulder, cut into
    ½-inch cubes

3 medium yellow onions, chopped

1 red pepper, diced

6 celery stalks, diced

3 cloves garlic, peeled and minced

2 large carrots, peeled and diced

1 cup peeled, seeded and chopped tomatoes, fresh or
    canned

1 tablespoon tomato paste

½ teaspoon ground cumin

½ teaspoon cayenne pepper or to taste

Salt to taste

Freshly ground black pepper to taste

½ pound medium spaghetti or egg noodles, cooked

¼ cup chopped fresh cilantro for garnish

¼ cup chopped fresh dill for garnish

1. Heat oil in a large heavy pot over medium heat. Add meat and brown on all sides, stirring occasionally. Remove with a slotted spoon and set aside.

2. Add onions and sauté until translucent, about 10 minutes. Add peppers, celery and garlic, and sauté for 10–15 minutes.

3. Add 8 cups of water, carrots, tomato paste, cumin, cayenne pepper, and salt and pepper to taste. Simmer for 20 minutes, covered. Skim off any fat that might accumulate.

4. Place a heaping portion of spaghetti or noodles in each of 6 large serving bowls. Ladle soup over top and sprinkle with fresh cilantro and dill.

Yield: 6 servings

—JOAN NATHAN

COLD SOUPS

♦ ♦

ALMOND BUTTERMILK SOUP

dairy

1 cup blanched slivered almonds, toasted

1½ cups crustless bread cubes, toasted

2 large cloves garlic, peeled and coarsely chopped

1½ teaspoons grated orange zest

6 cups buttermilk

2½ tablespoons fresh lemon juice

3 tablespoons fresh orange juice

2 teaspoons kosher salt, plus more to taste

Freshly ground pepper to taste

¼ cup whole cilantro leaves

1. Place the almonds, bread, garlic, orange zest and I cup of buttermilk in a blender. Process until smooth. Pour into a bowl and stir in the remaining buttermilk, lemon juice, orange juice, salt and pepper. Refrigerate until cold.

2. Taste and adjust seasoning with additional salt and pepper if needed. Ladle soup into bowls and float several cilantro leaves in each one.

Yield: 6 servings

—MOLLY O'NEILL

MIMI SHERATON'S COLD BEET BORSCHT

pareve, dairy

ADAPTED FROM *From My Mother's Kitchen*

> *4 large fresh raw beets (see Note below)*
> *Juice of 2 lemons*
> *5 cups water*
> *Pinch of salt, optional*
> *Pinch of sour salt (also called citric acid), optional*
> *4 large egg yolks*
> *Pinch of sugar, if needed*
> *Salt to taste*
> *Freshly ground white pepper to taste*
> *Boiled potatoes, garnish, optional*
> *Sour cream, garnish, optional*

1. Wash and peel the beets and grate on the coarse side of the grater. Place in a saucepan with the lemon juice, 5 cups water, and, if desired, salt and sour salt. Bring to a boil, reduce the heat, cover and simmer until beets are tender, about 30 minutes. Remove from the heat.

2. In a bowl, beat the egg yolks with a fork until they are thin and watery. Slowly ladle some of the hot borscht into the eggs, beating constantly. When about half the soup has been added, pour the egg mixture back into the pot with the remaining soup, again pouring slowly and beating constantly.

3. When all the egg mixture has been added, pour the soup back and forth between the pot and a bowl or pitcher about 10–15 times, until the mixture is smooth, airy and creamy. Add more lemon juice to produce a winey effect; add a tiny pinch of sugar, salt and white pepper as needed. Pour back and forth several more times. Chill thoroughly.

4. Garnish each serving with a boiled potato. Sour cream is another traditional garnish for this soup, unless it is being served at a meal that includes meat and rules of kashrut are being observed.

Yield: 1–1½ quarts

NOTE: *Canned beets may be used for this soup, with excellent if slightly less flavorful results. Use whole beets, even though you will grate them, as they have more taste and better color. For the above recipe, use a 1-pound can of whole beets and grate them. Cook for 10 minutes in a combination of their own canning liquid plus 1½ cans of water to make a total of about 5 cups of liquid. Proceed with the recipe as described above.*

PERSIAN CARROT SOUP WITH MINT

pareve

2 teaspoons vegetable oil

4 onions, chopped

3 cloves garlic, minced

1 eggplant, peeled, seeded and diced

2 tablespoons chopped parsley

1 rib celery, chopped

8 large carrots, peeled and chopped

2 potatoes, peeled and chopped

1½ teaspoons salt, plus more to taste

2 teaspoons freshly ground pepper, plus more to taste

2 teaspoons chopped fresh mint

1. Heat oil in a large, heavy nonreactive pot over medium heat. Cook onion and garlic for 5 minutes. Stir in eggplant and parsley and cook until softened, about 10 minutes. Add 8 cups water, celery, carrots and potatoes. Simmer for 15 minutes. Stir in salt and pepper and cook over low heat for 30 minutes. Let cool.

2. In batches, puree the soup in a food processor. Refrigerate until cold. Season with salt and pepper to taste, divide among 4 bowls, garnish with mint and serve immediately.

Yield: 4 servings

—MOLLY O'NEILL

COLD SOUR CHERRY SOUP

dairy

ADAPTED FROM *The New York Times Large-Type Cookbook*

2 cans (1 pound each) pitted sour cherries

1½ tablespoons cornstarch

⅓ cup sugar or to taste (see Note below)

½ cup dry red wine

1¾ cups water

1 cinnamon stick (2 inches long)

⅓ cup farina

2 cups milk

2 egg yolks

¼–½ cup sugar (see Note below)

1. Place cherries and their liquid in saucepan. Mix cornstarch and sugar together and gradually stir in wine. Add to cherries.

2. Add water and cinnamon stick; bring to a boil and simmer 5 minutes. Cool and chill.

3. Mix remaining ingredients in a saucepan and bring to a boil, stirring constantly. Reduce heat and simmer 2 minutes. Pour into a shallow dish; cool and chill.

4. Just before serving, remove cinnamon stick and spoon farina mixture into soup.

Yield: 4 servings

NOTE: *This may be served as soup or as dessert. The amount of sugar depends on which course of the meal the soup will be.*

KOLODNIK · (LITTLE COLD THING)

dairy

ADAPTED FROM Sidney Mintz

4 radishes, cut wafer-thin

2 small cucumbers (pickling variety if possible),
    cut wafer-thin

5 scallions, finely chopped

½ bunch watercress, minced

8 leaves Boston lettuce, minced

1 cup minced fresh dill

4 medium-size new potatoes, peeled

2 cups whole milk

¾ teaspoon citric acid (sold as sour salt in grocery
    stores)

2 tablespoons butter

Kosher salt to taste

Freshly ground black pepper to taste

1. Place 2 earthenware bowls in the refrigerator and chill completely. After preparing the radishes, immediately place them into 1 chilled bowl and return to the refrigerator. Then, in order, prepare the cucumbers, scallions, watercress and Boston lettuce. Toss this mixture with ½ cup of the dill and refrigerate.

2. Boil the potatoes until they are tender. Meanwhile, place the milk in the second earthenware bowl. Add the citric acid (or sour salt), whisk and return to the refrigerator for 10 minutes. Combine this curdled milk with the chilled vegetables, toss well and return it all to the refrigerator.

3. When the potatoes are tender, drain, toss with the butter, the remaining dill and salt and pepper to taste. Serve the soup very cold with a very hot potato on the side. Alternate eating the hot potato with the tart soup. Small portions of the soup are recommended, since it is quite filling.

Yield: 4 servings

—MOLLY O'NEILL

GREEN GAZPACHO

pareve

2½-inch-long section of day-old Italian bread,
    crusts removed

1 medium-to-large cucumber, peeled, seeded and
    coarsely chopped

½ small green pepper, seeded and chopped

2 scallions, chopped

2 tablespoons chopped parsley

1 clove garlic, peeled and chopped

4 tablespoons olive oil

2 tablespoons tarragon vinegar

1½ cups cold water

Salt to taste

Freshly ground black pepper to taste

1 tablespoon snipped chives

1. Place bread in food processor and process until well crumbled.

2. Add half the cucumber with pepper, scallions,

parsley, garlic, oil and vinegar to processor and process until pureed. Add a little water if necessary.

3. Add rest of cucumber and water and process with rapid on-off (pulse) motion only until cucumber is uniformly chopped fairly fine; do not allow it to become a puree. Season to taste with salt and pepper and process for another second or two.

4. Chill soup, preferably for several hours. Serve garnished with chives.

Yield: 2–4 servings

—FLORENCE FABRICANT

JELLIED CUCUMBER, HERB AND LIME SOUP

meat

ADAPTED FROM *A Feast of Fruits*

1¼-ounce envelope unflavored gelatin
¼ cup cool water
2 cups Chicken Stock (page 48), canned or fresh
1 large cucumber, peeled, seeded and coarsely
   chopped
3 scallions, green and white parts sliced thin
⅓ cup fresh lime juice, or to taste
3 tablespoons chopped fresh dill
2 tablespoons snipped fresh chives
Salt to taste
Freshly ground black pepper to taste
Lime slices for garnish

1. In a cup, soften the gelatin in the water for 5 minutes. Pour it and the stock into a small saucepan and stir over low heat until dissolved.

2. Put the mixture into a food processor, along with the cucumber, scallions and lime juice. Process until mixture is smooth, with a little texture (not a fine puree).

3. Season with dill, chives, salt and pepper. Add more lime juice, if desired. Pour into a bowl, cover and refrigerate 3 hours or overnight.

4. When ready to serve, use a large spoon to stir the solids throughout the jellied soup. Scoop it into cups or stemmed glasses and garnish each with a thin slice of lime.

Yield: 6 servings

—SUZANNE HAMLIN

MALAGAN WHITE GAZPACHO WITH ALMONDS AND GRAPES

pareve

4 ounces blanched almonds (see Note, page 582)

1 large clove garlic, peeled and chopped

1 teaspoon salt

1 (4-inch) section fresh Italian bread, crust removed

2½ cups ice water

⅓ cup olive oil

2 tablespoons tarragon vinegar

1 tablespoon sliced blanched almonds, lightly toasted
    (see Note, page 582)

1 cup seedless green grapes, halved

1. Place almonds, garlic and salt in blender or food processor and process until finely ground (a blender will produce finer results).

2. Soak bread in cold water, squeeze out well and add to blender in small pieces with ½ cup ice water. Process until smooth.

3. With machine running, add oil in thin stream. Add vinegar and transfer mixture to bowl.

4. Add 1 cup of water to blender or food processor and process long enough to clean sides of container fairly well, then pour this into bowl along with remaining cup of ice water. Stir and refrigerate until ready to serve. If possible, chill several hours.

5. Check seasoning and serve soup garnished with slivered, toasted almonds and grapes.

Yield: 4 servings

—FLORENCE FABRICANT

SCHAV · (COLD SORREL SOUP)

dairy

1 pound sorrel, sour grass or schav

7 cups water

½ cup sour cream

2 tablespoons flour

¾ cup milk

Salt to taste

White pepper to taste

5 large egg yolks

Pinch of salt, if needed

Lemon juice, optional and to taste

Garnishes: sour cream, minced scallions, cucumbers,
    radishes and hard-cooked eggs

1. It is very important that stems and any hard ribs be pulled from the leaves of the schav and cooked separately; otherwise they will impart an unpleasant hairy texture to the finished soup. Tear off stems and any hairlike particles adhering to them. Wash both stems and leaves thoroughly to remove sand.

2. Place leaves and 6 cups of water in a 2½- to 3-quart saucepan (not made of iron or aluminum). Add stems with one cup of water to another small saucepan. Bring both to a boil, and, after 15 minutes, strain liquid from stems into the larger soup pot. Continue cooking for about 15 minutes longer, or until leaves are completely soft and begin to disintegrate.

3. Blend sour cream and flour, then beat into milk. Bring soup to a rapid boil, then add cream mixture, stirring constantly with a wooden spoon or beating with a whisk. Add about 1½ teaspoons white pepper. Let boil rapidly for about 5 minutes, or until cream mixture is blended with soup stock and all traces of flour disappear.

4. Beat egg yolks with a fork until thin. Remove soup from heat and, using a ladle, slowly trickle some hot soup into the yolks, beating constantly as you do so. Continue this until about three cups of soup have been added to the yolks. Now slowly trickle egg yolk mixture back into soup, again beating steadily as you do so.

5. Using the pot in which the soup is cooked and another bowl or pot with a good long handle, pour the soup back and forth from one receptacle to another, about 15–20 times. It is a good idea to do this over the sink, as it can get messy, and to do it carefully, so little soup will be wasted.

6. Adjust seasonings, adding sugar if too sour, or lemon if you want an even more piquant result. The juice of ½ lemon should be enough. As the soup will be served cold, it is a good idea to taste it again after it has chilled.

7. To serve, ladle soup into chilled cream-soup bowls or cups. Serve whipped sour cream on the side, or add a dollop to each serving. Any or all of the chopped garnishes can be passed around in relish dishes, along with the sour cream.

Yield: About 2 quarts

—MIMI SHERATON

COLD SPINACH SOUP

dairy

1½ *pounds spinach*
6 *cups water*
¾ *cup milk*
½ *cup sour cream*
2 *tablespoons flour*
1½ *teaspoons salt, or to taste*
¼ *teaspoon white pepper, or to taste*
Juice of ½ lemon, or to taste
5 *large egg yolks*
Pinch of sugar, optional
Garnishes: sour cream, chopped scallions, cucumbers, radishes and hard-cooked eggs

1. Wash spinach thoroughly to remove all sand. Cook about 10 minutes or until soft in 6 cups of water in a 2½- to 3-quart saucepan, not made of iron or aluminum.

2. Combine the milk, sour cream and flour, and beat well until the flour is smoothly blended in. Bring the spinach to a rapid boil, then add the cream mixture, stirring constantly with a wooden spoon or beating with a whisk. Add about 1½ teaspoons salt, ¼ teaspoon white pepper and enough lemon juice to give it a winey edge. Boil rapidly for about 5 minutes, or until the cream has blended with the soup stock and all traces of flour disappear.

3. Beat the egg yolks with a fork until thin. Remove the soup from the heat and, using a ladle, slowly trickle some hot soup into the yolks, beating constantly as you do so. Continue this until 3 cups of soup have been added to the yolks. Now, slowly trickle the egg yolk mixture back into the soup, again beating steadily as you do so.

4. Using the pot in which the soup cooked and another pot or bowl with a good long handle, pour the soup back and forth from one receptacle to the other; repeat about 12 times until soup is smooth and well blended.

5. Adjust seasonings, adding a pinch of sugar if necessary, and chill thoroughly.

6. Ladle the soup into chilled cream-soup bowls or cups. Serve whipped sour cream on the side, or add a dollop to each serving. Pass garnishes in individual relish dishes.

Yield: About 2 quarts

—MIMI SHERATON

BARBARA KAFKA'S MOROCCAN TOMATO SOUP

pareve

5 medium cloves garlic, smashed, peeled and minced

2½ teaspoons sweet paprika

1½ teaspoons ground cumin

Large pinch cayenne pepper

4 teaspoons olive oil

2¼ pounds tomatoes, cored and cut in 1-inch pieces

¼ cup packed cilantro leaves, chopped, plus additional leaves for garnish

1 tablespoon white wine vinegar

2 tablespoons plus 2 teaspoons fresh lemon juice

2 tablespoons water

5 teaspoons kosher salt

4 stalks celery, diced

1. Stir together garlic, paprika, cumin, cayenne and olive oil in a small saucepan. Place over low heat and cook, stirring constantly, for 2 minutes. Remove from heat and set aside.

2. Pass tomatoes through a food mill fitted with a large disk. Stir in cooked spice mixture and remaining ingredients. Refrigerate until cold. Serve garnished with cilantro leaves.

Yield: 4 servings

—BARBARA KAFKA

TOMATO BROTH WITH ORANGE PEEL AND CORIANDER

meat, pareve

6 very ripe tomatoes, cut into ½-inch chunks

½ cup Chicken Broth (page 48) or vegetable broth, canned or fresh

Zest and juice of 1 orange

2 tablespoons coriander seed, crushed well in a mortar

1 bay leaf

1 clove garlic, crushed

1 tablespoon extra-virgin olive oil

Kosher salt

Freshly ground black pepper

½ cup finely (⅛ inch) diced cucumber

¼ cup whole Italian parsley leaves

1. In a large saucepan, combine tomatoes, broth, orange zest and juice, coriander, bay leaf, garlic and olive oil. Season with salt and pepper to taste. Bring to a simmer and cook until tomatoes soften, 5–7 minutes. Turn off heat and let cool completely.

2. Strain through a fine sieve, using the back of a large spoon to press as much juice as possible out of the tomatoes. Adjust seasoning. Divide among 4 bowls and garnish with diced cucumber and parsley leaves. Serve at room temperature or chilled.

Yield: 4 servings

—AMANDA HESSER

CHILLED SMOKED-FISH CONSOMMÉ

dairy

ADAPTED FROM Eberhard Müller

FOR THE BROTH:

1 medium carrot

1 small leek

1 small onion

1 stalk celery

1 tablespoon unsalted butter

4 smoked chubs or other small smoked fish

2 quarts Fish Stock (page 51)

4 ounces button mushrooms

½ bay leaf

3 sprigs parsley

1 plum tomato

15 whole black peppercorns

4 large egg whites

1 pound firm, white-fleshed fish scraps or fillet

½ teaspoon gelatin

FOR THE GARNISH:

4 slices smoked salmon, cut into strips

4 finely sliced scallions

4 shiitake mushrooms, thinly sliced

1. To make a broth, finely chop half the carrot, half the leek, half the onion and half the celery. Place in a large pot with the butter and sauté over medium heat, stirring, until softened, 3–4 minutes.

2. Pick the meat from the chubs and set aside for

another use. Add the stock and fish carcasses to the pot and bring to a simmer. Adjust the heat and simmer, skimming any foam that forms on the top, for 45 minutes without stirring.

3. Meanwhile, coarsely chop the remaining carrot, leek, onion and celery and place in a food processor. Add the mushrooms, bay leaf, parsley, tomato, peppercorns, egg whites and fish scraps. Process until finely chopped. Set aside.

4. Strain the fish broth through a fine-mesh sieve and discard the solids. Transfer to a bowl and chill thoroughly. When chilled, remove any fat that has solidified on the top of the stock. Pour the broth into a large saucepan and add the chopped fish and vegetable mix. Place over medium-low heat and stir occasion-ally, until the solids coagulate and float to the top. Adjust the heat so that the mixture is at a bare simmer and simmer without stirring for 30 minutes.

5. Line a strainer with a triple layer of cheesecloth and slowly pour the broth through it. (Do not press the solids.) Allow to drain for 10 minutes. Discard the solids. Dissolve the gelatin in 2 tablespoons of the hot broth. Stir the gelatin back into the broth and refrigerate for several hours, until cold and slightly thickened.

6. Divide the garnishes into 4 chilled soup bowls. Pour the broth over them and serve.

Yield: 4 servings

—MOLLY O'NEILL

FISH

BEING PAREVE, OR NEUTRAL IN KOSHER LAW, AND THEREFORE PER-
MISSIBLE WITH DAIRY OR MEAT DISHES (AND ALSO FORMERLY INEX-
pensive), fish became a vital element in the Jewish diet, as can be seen in the
main courses here and among appetizers. With the current wisdom on the
healthful advantages of fish, it has gained even greater favor. But though pareve,
fish may not share the same plate with meat, and the same utensils may be used
for both only if they are washed in between, a desirable practice aesthetically as
well as philosophically.

Remember that only fish with both scales and fins are kosher, eliminating all
shellfish and many other varieties noted in the introductory text on kashruth. Those
laws, plus the types of fish available in the countries where Jews lived, shaped the
seafood diet, with many freshwater types such as pike, whitefish and carp favored
by Ashkenazim. Carp, in fact, is said to have been introduced to Europe by Jewish
merchants who plied their trade along the Silk Route, bringing carp with them
from China. Even today one sees specific preparations referred to as Jewish carp on
menus in Poland, Hungary, Germany, Alsace and the former Czechoslovakia, often
flavored sweet-and-sour, or in a black sauce based on prunes.

Fried fish, most especially whiting and flounder, are savory standards of the Ashkenazic kitchen and are as often served at room temperature, a special treat on hot summer evenings. Loving both whiting and poached fish, Jews should appreciate the Italian *merluzzo in bianco*, whiting in a cold garlic, parsley and olive oil dressing. Similarly, their passion for Chinese food should make Cantonese steamed fish with ginger and scallions a natural adoptee.

Sephardic and Middle Eastern Jews tend to use lush, enveloping flavors with their fish, such as rich Yemenite and Moroccan spice mixes, pistachios and almonds and the savory sesame sauce tahini.

In addition to those that follow, other delectable fish recipes appear among appetizers and salads.

WHOLE FISH ON A BED OF FENNEL, WITH MASHED JERUSALEM ARTICHOKE-POTATOES

dairy

4 tablespoons olive oil

2 heads fennel, sliced thin

1 clove garlic, minced

1 tablespoon fresh thyme leaves

Coarse sea salt to taste

Freshly ground pepper to taste

2 lemons

1 whole sea bass or red snapper, about 4 pounds,
  head on, scaled and gutted

½ cup chopped fresh tarragon

2 tablespoons parsley

2 pounds Yukon Gold potatoes

1 pound Jerusalem artichokes

2 tablespoons unsalted butter

Tarragon leaves to garnish

1. Preheat the oven to 450 degrees.

2. Heat 2 tablespoons olive oil in a frying pan and cook the fennel with the garlic and thyme leaves until it is soft. Season to taste with salt and pepper.

3. Squeeze the juice of one of the lemons over the skin and in the cavity of the fish. Season it inside and out with salt and pepper. Stuff the tarragon and parsley in the cavity, reserving a tablespoon to sprinkle on top. Slice the remaining lemon thinly.

4. Put a double layer of foil large enough to wrap the whole fish flat on a baking tray. Spoon the fennel from the pan onto the foil. Put the fish on top. Sprinkle it with the remaining olive oil and lemon slices and fold the foil over the fish, sealing it tightly. Bake for 30–40 minutes, or until the fish flakes when tested with a fork.

5. Meanwhile, peel and cut the potatoes and the Jerusalem artichokes into 1½-inch pieces. Steam or boil them separately and then mash together with salt, pepper and butter.

6. Remove the fish from the oven and allow it to rest for 5 minutes. Open the foil, slide the fish onto a platter and serve with the fennel and lemon slices, garnished with tarragon. Serve the mashed potatoes and Jerusalem artichokes on the side.

Yield: 4 servings

—MOIRA HODGSON

BAKED FISH WITH ALMOND STUFFING

dairy

ADAPTED FROM *The New York Times Menu Cook Book*

½ cup plus 2 tablespoons butter

¼ cup chopped onion

3 cups soft fresh bread crumbs

½ cup chopped celery stalks

½ cup chopped green pepper

2 tablespoons chopped parsley

3 eggs, lightly beaten

1 teaspoon salt

Freshly ground black pepper to taste

1 teaspoon dried tarragon or thyme
½ cup chopped toasted almonds (see Note, page 582)
1 striped bass, sea bass or red snapper
    (5–7 pounds), cleaned, washed and dried well

1. Preheat oven to 400 degrees.
2. Melt 2 tablespoons of butter and cook the onion until tender but not browned. Add the bread crumbs, celery, green pepper, parsley, eggs, salt, pepper, tarragon and almonds. Mix well and use the mixture to stuff the fish. Sew up the cavity with kitchen twine.

3. Melt the remaining butter. Line a large baking dish with aluminum foil and pour a little of the butter over the foil. Lay the fish on the foil and sprinkle with additional salt and pepper.
4. Bake the fish for about 1 hour and 15 minutes, basting frequently with the remaining butter. The fish is done when it flakes easily when tested with a fork.

Yield: 6 generous servings

LEMON-SAFFRON FISH WITH FRESH HERBS

pareve

1½ pounds fresh, firm-textured fish fillets
Sea salt to taste
1 pound yellow onions, very thinly sliced
5 cloves garlic, thinly sliced
¼ cup extra-virgin olive oil
Juice of 2–3 medium lemons, ½–¾ cup
Freshly ground pepper
Pinch of saffron threads, crumbled
¼ cup rice
2 tablespoons cornstarch
2 tablespoons minced fresh herbs (flat-leaf parsley,
    tarragon, basil, chervil, chives or dill are all good
    choices)

1. Set the fish fillets on a wire rack. Sprinkle lightly on both sides with a little salt and set aside.
2. For the sauce, add the onion, garlic and oil to a saucepan large enough to hold the fish in one layer. Cover and cook over low heat, stirring occasionally, until the onions are meltingly soft and almost golden, about 20 minutes. Do not let them brown.
3. Add enough hot water to the lemon juice to make 2 cups. Add the lemon water to the onions, along with the pepper and saffron, and let simmer about 5 minutes. Stir in the rice, cover and cook about 10 minutes.
4. Dry the fillets and cut them into serving pieces, then lightly dredge in cornstarch. Add the fish to the pan and cook about 3–5 minutes, spooning the sauce over the fish. Taste for seasoning and add sea salt if necessary. Cover the pan and cook about 10 minutes longer, or until the rice and fish are cooked through. Right before serving, stir in the herbs. Serve hot with additional rice on the side if you wish.

Yield: 4–6 servings

NOTE: *Chicken breasts may be substituted for fish, but do not salt them.*

—NANCY HARMON JENKINS

FISH BAKED WITH RATATOUILLE

pareve

2 tablespoons olive oil
2 tablespoons bread crumbs
2 pounds striped bass, fluke, flounder or scrod fillets
Juice of 1 lemon
Salt and freshly ground black pepper to taste
4 cups of Ratatouille (see recipe below)
2 tablespoons drained capers
Lemon wedges

1. Preheat oven to 400 degrees.

2. Select a baking dish that will hold the fish in a single layer. Oil the dish with a little of the olive oil. Sprinkle 1 tablespoon of the bread crumbs in the bottom of the dish.

3. Arrange fillets in the baking dish, sprinkle with lemon juice and season with salt and pepper.

4. Coarsely chop the ratatouille and mix it with the capers. (If you are using ratatouille that has been frozen without garlic (see Note below), add a clove or two of finely minced garlic and adjust other seasonings such as salt and pepper if necessary.) Spread the ratatouille over the fish, sprinkle with remaining bread crumbs and drizzle with the rest of the olive oil.

5. Bake for 25 minutes. Serve at once or allow to cool and serve at room temperature. Decorate with lemon wedges before serving.

Yield: 6 servings

◆ RATATOUILLE ◆

pareve

1½ pounds eggplant, the smaller the better
1 tablespoon salt, plus to taste

2 medium-large onions
1 large green pepper
1 sweet red pepper
2 large cloves garlic
2½ pounds ripe tomatoes
1½ pounds small zucchini
9 tablespoons olive oil
Freshly ground black pepper to taste
1 teaspoon minced fresh thyme or ½ teaspoon dried
1 teaspoon minced fresh oregano or ½ teaspoon dried
2 teaspoons minced fresh basil
2 tablespoons minced fresh parsley

1. Remove stems from the eggplants and cut, unpeeled, into ¾-inch dice. Place diced eggplant in a bowl, sprinkle with 1 tablespoon salt, weight with a plate that fits into the bowl and set aside for 30 minutes.

2. Meanwhile, prepare remaining vegetables. Peel and thickly slice the onions. Core the peppers, removing all seeds and fleshy white pith, and cut peppers into slices about 2 inches long and ¼-inch wide. Finely mince the garlic. Peel, seed and coarsely chop the tomatoes.

3. Cut the stems from the zucchini, cut the zucchini in half lengthwise and then horizontally into half-inch slices. Set aside.

4. Heat 3 tablespoons of the oil in a large heavy skillet or a shallow casserole. Sauté the onions and peppers over medium heat until the onions become translucent. Add the garlic, stirring it in the pan for a few seconds, and then add the tomatoes. Cook, stirring for about three minutes. Transfer the contents of the pan to a bowl and wipe out the pan.

5. Add 2 tablespoons of oil to the pan and sauté the zucchini over medium-high heat for about 10 minutes, until tender and lightly browned. Add the zucchini to the other cooked vegetables, leaving as much of the oil as possible in the pan.

6. Drain and rinse the eggplant and pat the pieces dry on paper towels. Add 4 tablespoons of oil to the pan, and sauté the eggplant over medium-high heat for about 10 minutes, until tender and lightly browned. Return the other vegetables to the pan and mix with the eggplant.

7. Reheat the ratatouille and cook for 5 minutes. Season to taste with salt, freshly ground pepper, thyme, oregano and basil. Stir in the parsley.

Yield: About 10 cups (2½ quarts)

NOTE: *Ratatouille packed into plastic containers can be stored in the freezer for up to eight months. Be sure to leave at least ½ inch of space at the top of the container for expansion. The flavor will be better if the garlic is omitted and the mixture is underseasoned. Thawed ratatouille may be reseasoned with minced garlic briefly sautéed in a little olive oil and with salt, pepper and fresh parsley.*

—FLORENCE FABRICANT

BAKED WHOLE FISH WITH TAHINI MARINADE

pareve

1 (3-pound) whole white-fleshed fish (such as sea bass or red snapper)
3 tablespoons tahini (see Glossary, page 586)
2 cloves garlic, peeled
2 tablespoons peanut or safflower oil
1 tablespoon soy sauce
2 tablespoons fresh ginger, minced
Juice of ½ lemon or to taste
Freshly ground pepper to taste
2 tablespoons fresh thyme leaves
6 scallions, sliced
2 tablespoons toasted sesame seeds

1. Preheat oven to the 375 degrees. Wipe the fish dry with paper towels.

2. Place the tahini, garlic, vegetable oil, soy sauce, ginger, lemon juice and pepper in a food processor and puree until smooth. Mix in the thyme and spread the mixture over the fish, inside and out. Sprinkle with scallions and bake for 45 minutes to 1 hour, or until the fish is cooked. Sprinkle with toasted sesame seeds and serve.

Yield: 4 servings

—MOIRA HODGSON

ROAST WHOLE FISH WITH CHIVE OIL

pareve

1 bunch chives
½ cup peanut or vegetable oil
1 (1½- to 2-pound) whole fish (Icelandic char,
    bass or snapper)
Coarse salt to taste
Freshly ground pepper to taste
Lemon to garnish

1. Cut one-third from the bunch of chives and reserve. Coarsely chop the remainder and put in a blender with the oil. Puree until smooth. Set aside.

2. Preheat oven to 375 degrees. Season the fish with salt and pepper and sprinkle with oil on both sides. Place on an oiled baking tray and roast 15–20 minutes, or until it is cooked.

3. Remove to a serving dish and sprinkle on the chive oil. Garnish with chives and slices of lemon.

Yield: 2 servings

NOTE: *This is good served with boiled potatoes. The chive oil will keep in a sealed container in the refrigerator for two weeks.*

—MOIRA HODGSON

SIMPLE STEAMED FISH CHINESE-STYLE

pareve

ADAPTED FROM *Every Grain of Rice*

1½ pounds whole, scaled fish like red snapper, rock
    cod, large flounder or black bass; or a thick chunk
    of striped or black bass
1½-inch piece of ginger, peeled and cut in fine slivers
1 scallion, trimmed and sliced in thin strands
    lengthwise
2 cilantro sprigs, leaves only, optional
3 tablespoons peanut oil
4½ teaspoons soy sauce

1. Rinse the fish. Pat dry, then place in a heat-proof dish.

2. Set a rack in a pot and add water to a depth of 1½–2 inches. (If you use a steamer, fill half the lower tier with water.) Bring to a boil. Set dish on rack (or on upper tier of steamer) and steam over high heat for 15–20 minutes, depending on the thickness of the fish.

3. Test for doneness by poking a chopstick or sharp knife through the thickest part of the fish. It should flake easily and look opaque all the way to the bone.

4. When fish is done, use a turkey baster or spoon to discard any accumulated liquid.

5. Sprinkle ginger, scallion and optional cilantro over fish. Heat oil in a small skillet. Add soy sauce and heat for few seconds. Pour mixture over fish. Serve immediately.

Yield: 4–6 servings

—SUZANNE HAMLIN

FISH FILLETS WITH ASPARAGUS
IN LEMON TURMERIC SAUCE

dairy

4 fish fillets (turbot, sole, flounder or
   red snapper)

16 asparagus spears

2 shallots

2 tablespoons unsalted butter

¾–1 cup heavy cream

1 teaspoon turmeric

Juice of ½ lemon

Coarse salt to taste

Freshly ground white pepper to taste

2 tablespoons blanched chopped lemon rind

1. Slice the fish fillets into pieces about 2½ inches by 1½ inches (4 pieces per fillet).

2. Steam the asparagus spears until crisp-tender, not limp. While it is cooking, soften the shallots in the butter. Sauté the fillets, a few at a time, so that they are barely cooked. Do not break when you remove them with a slotted spoon. Keep warm in a very low oven.

3. Drain the asparagus spears and keep warm.

4. Add the cream, turmeric and lemon juice to the pan in which you have sautéed the fish fillets. Bring to a boil. Add any juices that have collected under the fish fillets. Simmer until thickened, stirring, season with salt and pepper and add the lemon peel. Arrange the fillets on individual plates. Pour the sauce on top, garnish with asparagus and serve.

Yield: 4 servings

NOTE: *Boiled new potatoes sprinkled with fresh thyme are an excellent accompaniment.*

—MOIRA HODGSON

FISH STEAKS WITH OLIVES, WALNUTS AND CAPERS

pareve

2 large or 4 small fish steaks

2 tablespoons plus ½ cup olive oil

½ pound black oil-cured olives, pitted

2 tablespoons capers (preferably salted), drained

1 small clove garlic, peeled

6 walnut halves, coarsely chopped

Freshly ground pepper to taste

1 teaspoon fresh rosemary leaves

1. Preheat broiler or coals. Wipe the fish steaks dry with paper towels and coat with 2 tablespoons olive oil. Set aside.

2. Place the olives in the jar of a food processor. Drain the capers and rinse them thoroughly. Add to the olives with the garlic and walnut halves. Add the remaining olive oil and blend until the olives are coarsely chopped. Add more oil if necessary and season with salt and pepper.

3. Broil the fish steaks for 5–7 minutes on each side, or until they are cooked. Spread the olive mixture on top of the steaks and sprinkle them with rosemary.

Yield: 4 servings

—MOIRA HODGSON

FISH IN HAZELNUT CRUST WITH RED PEPPER RELISH

dairy

ADAPTED FROM Tropica

¾ cup shelled hazelnuts

¼ cup dry bread crumbs

½ teaspoon ground coriander

¼ teaspoon ground cumin

2 eggs, beaten

1 cup flour

1 teaspoon cayenne pepper

Salt to taste

1¼ pound fresh mahimahi or red snapper, sliced into 8 equal-size scaloppine, about ½ inch thick

1 tablespoon butter

Red Pepper Relish (see recipe below)

1. Place the nuts in a dry skillet and cook over medium heat, stirring, for about 15 minutes, until they are toasted. Do not allow them to burn.

2. Wrap the hot, toasted nuts in a clean cloth and rub them in the cloth to remove the skins. Chop them fairly fine in a food processor or by hand. Mix the chopped nuts with the bread crumbs, coriander and cumin and spread this mixture on a plate.

3. Place the eggs in a bowl.

4. Combine flour, pepper and salt and spread on another plate.

5. Dip the pieces of fish first in the flour mixture, shaking off any excess, then in the eggs, allowing the excess to run off. Press the fish into the crumbs. Place the fish, as it is coated, on a plate and refrigerate until ready to cook, up to ½ hour.

6. To cook, heat the butter in a large, nonstick skillet. Place the coated fish in the skillet and cook over medium-high heat until the pieces are lightly browned, turning them once until they are browned on both sides, 2–3 minutes on each side. If all the pieces do not fit in the pan, remove those that are cooked to a warm plate and repeat with the rest. It should not be necessary to add additional butter or oil.

7. Serve at once with red pepper relish on the side.

Yield: 4 servings

◆ **RED PEPPER RELISH** ◆

pareve

2 medium-size sweet red peppers
1 tablespoon ground cumin
2 tablespoons crushed coriander seeds
¼ teaspoon pepper
2 teaspoons olive oil
1 teaspoon minced fresh ginger
2 cloves garlic, minced
¼ cup dry white wine
2 heaping tablespoons chopped cilantro leaves

1. Char the skins of the peppers over an open flame or under the broiler until they are completely blackened. Rub off the blackened skin, then split, seed and core the peppers. Chop them fine.

2. Heat a dry, heavy skillet over medium-high heat, add the cumin, coriander and pepper and cook until they begin to become fragrant, 2–3 minutes.

3. Lower the heat and add the oil, ginger and garlic to the skillet. Cook a minute or so, then add the wine and chopped peppers.

4. Increase the heat and cook another few minutes, until there is no excess moisture in the skillet.

5. Remove from heat, stir in the chopped cilantro and set aside until ready to serve.

Yield: About 1 cup

—FLORENCE FABRICANT

RED SNAPPER CRUSTED IN SESAME SEEDS

dairy

4 skinless, boneless red snapper fillets (or blackfish or any other nonoily fish)
¼ cup freshly squeezed lemon or lime juice
2 tablespoons Worcestershire sauce (see Note, page 582)
1 egg, lightly beaten
1 tablespoon milk
Salt to taste, if desired
Freshly ground pepper to taste
¾ cup sesame seeds
¾ cup freshly grated Parmesan cheese
⅓ cup flour
¼ cup olive oil
1 tablespoon butter
Lemon wedges for garnish

1. Put the fish fillets in a dish and add the lemon juice and Worcestershire sauce. Turn the fillets in the mixture and let stand until ready to cook.

2. Put the beaten egg, milk, salt and pepper in a flat

dish and stir to blend. Put the sesame seeds and cheese in a separate dish and blend. Put the flour in a third dish.

3. Lift the fillets one at a time and, using the fingers, wipe off much, but not all, of the marinating liquid. Dip the fillets one at a time in flour to coat well. Dip the pieces into the egg mixture to coat on both sides. Dip in the sesame seed mixture to coat well.

4. Heat the oil and butter in a skillet and add the fish fillets (it may be necessary to cook the fish in two steps if the skillet is not large enough, but the amount of oil and butter indicated should be sufficient). Cook 2 minutes and turn carefully with a pancake turner or spatula. Cook about two minutes on the second side. If all the fillets have not been cooked, add a second batch to the skillet and continue cooking in the same manner. Transfer the fillets to a warm platter. Pour the pan fat over all. Garnish with lemon wedges.

Yield: 4 servings

—PIERRE FRANEY

MEDITERRANEAN FISH

pareve

ADAPTED FROM *The New York Times International Cookbook*

¼ cup olive oil

1 cup finely chopped onion

1 green pepper, cored, seeded and chopped

4 individual fish steaks such as salmon, small fish fillets such as flounder, or small whole fish

Salt to taste

Freshly ground pepper to taste

Cayenne pepper to taste

Juice of 1 lemon

2 tomatoes, cored, seeded, peeled and chopped (about 1½ cups)

½ cup Fish Stock (page 51 or see below)

3 tablespoons tahini

¼ cup dry white wine

2 egg yolks, lightly beaten

2 tablespoons finely chopped parsley

8 stuffed olives

4 slices bread

Vegetable oil for frying

1 clove garlic, cut

1. Heat half the oil in a large aluminum or enamelware skillet and cook the onion and green pepper until wilted.

2. In another skillet heat the remaining oil and cook the fish, first on one side and then on the other, until lightly browned. Transfer the fish in one layer to the skillet containing the onion mixture. Sprinkle with salt, pepper and the cayenne to taste and half the lemon juice. Spoon the tomatoes over the fish and add the fish stock. Cover with aluminum foil or parchment and cook over very low heat 10–15 minutes. Do not overcook.

3. Combine the tahini and remaining lemon juice in a small mixing bowl. Start beating with a whisk and add salt and pepper to taste. Beat in the wine. Carefully pour the liquid from the cooked fish into the tahini mixture and beat well. Beat in the egg yolks and parsley and spoon the mixture over the fish. Run the fish under the broiler until a brown glaze appears. Scatter the olives over the fish.

4. Meanwhile, fry the bread in oil and rub lightly with garlic. Serve the fish and toast while hot.

Yield: 4 servings

This is the simplest of stocks to make. Simply cover a few very fresh, broken fish bones with water. Add I small chopped onion, salt, pepper, half a bay leaf and 3 parsley sprigs and simmer 20 minutes. Strain.

—SUZANNE HAMLIN

FISH IN RHUBARB SAUCE · (PESHE EN SALTSA)

pareve

ADAPTED FROM *Cookbook of the Jews of Greece*

1 pound rhubarb
3 cups water
2 pounds tomatoes, peeled and chopped
2 tablespoons olive oil
1 cup red wine
1 tablespoon honey
Salt to taste
Pepper to taste
2 pounds fish steaks
Juice of 2 lemons

1. Clean rhubarb, stripping off heavy filaments and leaves, and cut into 1-inch sections. Bring the water to a simmer, add rhubarb and cook over low heat until tender.

2. Simmer tomatoes with olive oil in frying pan until reduced to a thick sauce. Add red wine and stir in honey and a little additional olive oil. Sprinkle in salt and pepper to taste. Add tomato mixture to the rhubarb and water and mix well. Simmer over low heat until it thickens enough to evenly coat the back of a wooden spoon, about 20–30 minutes.

3. Heat a little olive oil in a large frying pan, add fish steaks and lightly brown on both sides. Pour the sauce over them and simmer, tightly covered, for 15–20 minutes.

4. Carefully remove steaks to a serving platter. Pour the sauce and then the juice of the lemons over them and cool. Peshe en saltsa is traditionally served cold.

Yield: 4–6 servings

—HENRY KAMM

BLACK SEA BASS WITH TAPENADE

pareve

ADAPTED FROM Gotham Bar and Grill

20 large cloves garlic

Salt to taste

Freshly ground white pepper to taste

½ cup top-quality extra-virgin olive oil

1 pound potatoes, preferably fingerling, Ruby
    Crescent or Yellow Finn

1 medium Spanish onion, peeled and cut into
    ⅛-inch-thick slices

1 small bunch rosemary

1 small bunch thyme

4 (6-ounce) black sea bass fillets, or a 4- to 6-
    pound whole fish

1 lemon, thinly sliced

2 tomatoes, peeled, seeded and chopped

1½ cups dry white wine

2 cups Fish Stock (page 51), canned or fresh

4 (2-inch) slices baguette

¼ cup parsley, coarsely chopped

Tapenade (see recipe below)

1. Preheat oven to 325 degrees. Place the garlic in a medium casserole with a lid. Season with salt and pepper. Drizzle with 1 tablespoon of the olive oil. Cover and roast for 45 minutes to 1 hour, until soft. Set aside.

2. Peel the potatoes and slice into ⅛-inch-thick rounds. Heat 3 tablespoons of the olive oil in a large casserole or sauté pan with a lid. Add the potatoes and season with salt and pepper. Cook, uncovered, over low heat for 10 minutes, stirring occasionally. Add the onions, cover and cook for 5 minutes.

3. Once the garlic is done, raise the oven temperature to 450 degrees.

4. Remove the potato-onion mixture from the heat and pour in the remaining ¼ cup olive oil. Add rosemary and thyme sprigs and cover with the fish fillets. Season with salt and pepper and scatter the roasted garlic, lemon slices and tomatoes over the fish.

5. Place the uncovered casserole over high heat. When the potatoes begin to sizzle, add the wine. Reduce the heat and simmer for 2 minutes. Pour in the fish stock and cover. Bring to a boil. Then place the casserole in the hot oven and roast until fish is done, about 8 minutes.

6. Meanwhile, toast the slices of baguette and rub them with olive oil.

7. Use one or two large spatulas to transfer the fish and vegetables to a serving platter, discarding the rosemary and thyme. Pour sauce over the fish and sprinkle with parsley.

8. Serve garnished with croutons topped with tapenade.

Yield: 4 servings

♦   **TAPENADE**   ♦

pareve

½ cup pitted niçoise olives

½ cup pitted calamata olives

3 anchovy fillets, finely minced (see Note, page 582)

2 teaspoons drained capers

½ clove garlic, peeled and minced

Freshly ground black pepper to taste

1 tablespoon fresh lemon juice

Place olives in a food processor. Pulse until coarsely chopped. Stir remaining ingredients into olives.

Yield: About 1 cup

NOTE: *Tapenade can also be used as a dip for raw vegetables or as a spread for French bread, pita or small pieces of toast. It also works as a topping for a quick bruschetta or even as an uncooked sauce for pasta.*

—BRYAN MILLER

AQUAVIT'S OVEN-STEAMED CHILEAN OR BLACK SEA BASS WITH WARM CITRUS-BEET JUICE

dairy

3 shallots
2 tablespoons extra-virgin olive oil
2 medium red beets, peeled and cut into
    ¼-inch dice
Juice of 2 oranges
Juice of 1 lime
Kosher salt to taste
Freshly ground black pepper
2 sprigs fresh thyme
5 white peppercorns
4 fillets black sea bass or Chilean sea bass,
    5 ounces each
¼ cup white wine
2 cloves garlic, chopped
12 ounces fresh Swiss chard
1 sprig fresh mint
4 tablespoons butter

1. Preheat the oven to 400 degrees. Finely chop one of the shallots. In a small saucepan over medium heat, combine 1 tablespoon of the oil with the chopped shallot and the beets. Cover the pan and simmer until the beets begin to soften at the edges, 2–3 minutes. Add the orange and lime

juices and season to taste with salt and pepper. Simmer until the beets are soft, about 6–8 minutes. Using a slotted spoon, remove the beets and shallots to a small bowl, reserving the cooking liquid in the pan.

2. Roughly chop the remaining shallots; spread them over the bottom of a large cast-iron skillet along with the thyme sprigs and peppercorns. Season the fish fillets with salt and pepper to taste and place them flesh side down over the shallot mixture. Sprinkle the wine over the fish. Cover the pan loosely with a sheet of aluminum foil.

3. Place the skillet over high heat, and cook until wine begins to boil. Transfer skillet, still covered with foil, to oven. Steam fish until the flesh is opaque and flakes when pressed with a fork, about 5–7 minutes.

4. While the fish is steaming, place a large sauté pan over medium-high heat. Heat the remaining oil and add the garlic. Sauté until lightly browned, about 1 minute. Add the Swiss chard, mint and 3 tablespoons of the beet cooking liquid. Toss until the chard is wilted, about 1 minute. Add the reserved beets and shallots to the chard and toss to mix. Season to taste with salt and pepper.

5. Warm the remaining beet cooking liquid over

medium heat. Whisk in butter a tablespoon at a time. Sauce should thicken slightly. Season to taste with salt.

6. To serve, make a bed of chard on each of 4 plates.

Place a fillet on top and pour sauce around the chard. Serve immediately.

Yield: 4 servings

—MARCUS SAMUELSSON

ALGERIAN SPICED STRIPED BASS TAGINE

pareve

ADAPTED FROM Joseph Savino

7 tablespoons extra-virgin olive oil
1/2 cup packed cilantro, heavy stems removed
4 cloves garlic
1 (3-inch) piece ginger, peeled and chopped
2 teaspoons ground cumin
1 teaspoon ground coriander
1/2 teaspoon anise seeds
1/4 teaspoon cayenne pepper
Salt to taste
Juice of 1 lemon
2 pounds wild striped bass fillets, with skin
Freshly ground black pepper to taste
4 ripe plum tomatoes, halved lengthwise
1 medium onion, diced
1 red bell pepper, diced
1 green bell pepper, diced
2 cups diced eggplant
1/4 cup pitted black Moroccan olives
Cilantro leaves for garnish

1. Place 4 tablespoons olive oil in blender with cilantro, garlic, ginger, cumin, coriander, anise, cayenne pepper, 1/4 teaspoon salt and lemon juice. Process until smooth.

2. Cut fish in 4–6 portions. Season with salt and pepper. Place skin side down in dish and coat with mixture. Marinate 2 hours.

3. Meanwhile, heat oven to 300 degrees. Place tomato halves in tagine or in baking dish. Brush with 1 tablespoon olive oil, season with salt and bake 1 1/2 hours, then chop coarsely.

4. Heat remaining oil in skillet. Add onions and peppers and sauté about 5 minutes. Add eggplant and sauté 5 minutes longer. Add tomatoes and olives. Season to taste.

5. Place mixture in tagine or in baking dish, or leave in skillet if it is ovenproof and has a cover. Place fish on top of vegetables, skin side down. Cover tagine, baking dish or skillet. Place in oven to bake for 20–30 minutes, or simmer on top of stove over low heat, about 15 minutes. Garnish with cilantro and serve.

Yield: 4–6 servings

—FLORENCE FABRICANT

STRIPED BASS IN GRAPE LEAVES

dairy

ADAPTED FROM Susan Spicer

1 (16-ounce) jar grape leaves

1 lemon to yield 1 tablespoon lemon zest
(juice squeezed out and reserved)

1 cup instant couscous

4 red peppers

4 tablespoons olive oil for cooking and ½ cup
for vinaigrette

1 tablespoon chopped garlic

1 tablespoon chopped cilantro

1 tablespoon chopped mint

1 tablespoon chopped parsley

2 large scallions, chopped on diagonal
(½ cup)

Zest from ½ orange, minced
(juice squeezed out and reserved)

Salt to taste

Freshly ground pepper to taste

1 (2-pound) striped bass fillet, or black bass,
grouper or snapper

¾ cup dry white wine

2 bay leaves

3 tablespoons chopped shallots

½ cup pitted calamata olives

¼ cup red wine vinegar

1 sprig rosemary leaves, chopped

4 ounces feta cheese

1. Preheat oven to 375 degrees.

2. Blanch grape leaves in boiling water with half the lemon juice. Remove and drain.

3. Place the couscous in a bowl and pour 1 cup boiling water over it. Set aside, covered, for about 5 min-utes. Stir the grains, breaking up any lumps with your fingers.

4. Meanwhile, char the peppers over a barbecue grill or under a broiler. When they are warm enough to handle, run under cold water and remove the blackened skin with a paring knife. Halve and scrape out seeds. Cut each pepper half into 2 large triangles.

5. Heat 1 tablespoon olive oil and garlic in a sauté pan over medium heat. Place the peppers, skin side down, in the pan and cook gently for 15 minutes, or until tender.

6. Add to the couscous bowl the lemon zest, cilantro, mint, parsley, scallions, orange zest, 1 table-spoon olive oil and salt to taste.

7. Arrange the grape leaves, vein side up, in 1 layer, overlapping slightly to form a single sheet large enough to encase the fish. Spoon the couscous down the center of the grape leaves. Salt and pepper the fillet. Lay the fillet, skin side up, over the couscous. Gently encase the fillet and couscous with the grape leaves. The leaves are wet, so they should stick together when you wrap the fillet.

8. Brush 2 tablespoons of olive oil over a roasting pan large enough to hold the fish. Gently turn the fish over and, with your fingers covering the grape-leaf seams, transfer it into the pan. Pour the wine over the fish and add the 2 bay leaves to the pan. Cover with foil. Cook for 15 minutes and baste under the foil with pan liquids. Remove foil and cook another 10 minutes.

9. While fish is baking, make vinaigrette by combin-ing in a bowl the shallots, olives, vinegar, rosemary, orange juice and remaining lemon juice. Whisk in ½ cup olive oil. Season to taste.

10. Remove fish to a platter. The fish is firm but you may wish to use a 3-inch spatula, like a pancake or hamburger turner. Let rest for 5 minutes. To serve, cut 8 portions crosswise with a sharp knife. Arrange each portion in the center of a plate. Garnish with pepper triangles. Spoon vinaigrette over and crumble some feta cheese over the top.

Yield: 8 servings

—BRYAN MILLER AND PIERRE FRANEY

STRIPED BASS, MOROCCAN-STYLE

pareve

ADAPTED FROM *The New York Times International Cookbook*

1 striped bass (5–6 pounds)
Salt to taste
½ cup vegetable oil
3 tablespoons crushed cumin seed
1 tablespoon paprika
1 clove garlic, finely minced
½ cup chopped parsley
Fresh ground pepper to taste
1 lemon, thinly sliced and seeded

1. Preheat the oven to 350 degrees.
2. Rub the fish generously inside and out with salt and let stand 15 minutes.
3. Rinse the fish thoroughly.
4. Combine the oil, cumin seed, paprika, garlic, parsley and pepper and salt to taste.
5. Lay the fish on a sheet of heavy-duty aluminum foil large enough to enclose the fish. Rub the fish inside and out with the oil mixture and wrap tightly in the foil. Bake the fish for 1½ hours, or until the fish is tender when tested with a fork. Open the foil during the last 15 minutes of baking.
6. Garnish with lemon slices and serve.

Yield: 8 or more servings

BROILED BLUEFISH WITH GREEN OLIVE RELISH

pareve

½ cup pitted, brine-cured green olives
1 teaspoon minced garlic
½ medium red onion, peeled and diced
¼ cup roughly chopped fresh parsley

¼ cup extra-virgin olive oil
¼ cup fresh lemon juice
Salt to taste
Freshly ground black pepper to taste
4 bluefish fillets, 8 ounces each and about
  1½ inches thick

3 tablespoons vegetable oil

2 tablespoons ground cumin

1. In a bowl, combine olives, garlic, red onion, parsley, olive oil, lemon juice and salt and pepper to taste. Mix well and set aside. (Relish may be refrigerated up to 4 days; bring to room temperature before using.)

2. Preheat broiler. Rub bluefish lightly with vegetable oil and sprinkle with cumin and salt and pepper to taste.

3. Place the fish on a broiler pan and broil until the flesh is completely opaque throughout, about 5–8 minutes a side, depending on thickness. To check for doneness, slide a sharp, thin knife into one piece and peek inside.

4. Put several tablespoons of relish on each plate place fish on top and serve.

Yield: 4 servings

—JOHN WILLOUGHBY AND
CHRIS SCHLESINGER

CUMIN-CRUSTED BRAISED BLUEFISH

pareve

¼ cup whole cumin seeds

2 tablespoons paprika

1 tablespoon kosher salt

1 tablespoon freshly cracked black pepper

4 (8-ounce) bluefish fillets, skin on (or substitute
  fillets of striped bass, mahi-mahi or mackerel)

3 tablespoons vegetable oil for frying

1 onion, peeled and thinly sliced

2 tablespoons minced garlic

1 cup orange juice

¼ cup fresh lime juice (about 2 limes)

1 tablespoon minced chipotle pepper

1 tablespoon cinnamon

¼ cup roughly chopped fresh oregano

¼ cup raisins

1. Preheat the oven to 350 degrees.

2. In a small bowl, combine cumin seeds, paprika, salt and pepper, and mix well. Rub bluefish fillets

well with this mixture on the flesh side, pressing gently to make sure the rub adheres.

3. In a large sauté pan heat vegetable oil over medium heat until hot but not smoking. Add bluefish, skin side up, and sauté until the seeds just begin to brown, about 2–3 minutes. Remove fish and set aside.

4. Add the onion to the pan and sauté, stirring occasionally, until transparent, about 5–7 minutes. Add the garlic and cook, stirring occasionally, 1 minute more. Add the orange and lime juices, chipotle, cinnamon, oregano, raisins and browned fish (skin side down), and bring to a simmer.

5. Cover the pan and place in preheated oven for 10–15 minutes, or until a peek inside one of the fillets reveals no translucence. Serve immediately.

Yield: 4 servings

—JOHN WILLOUGHBY AND
CHRIS SCHLESINGER

CZECH CARP WITH BLACK PRUNE-RAISIN SAUCE

dairy, pareve

ADAPTED FROM Nika Hazelton

  2 cups wine vinegar or any other vinegar
  1 quart water
  2 medium-size onions, sliced
  2 stalks celery, diced
  1 small carrot, sliced
  1 clove garlic
  2 bay leaves
  6 whole cloves
  6 whole allspice
  1 teaspoon ground cumin
  1 (4-pound) carp, cut in serving pieces

1. In a deep kettle, combine all ingredients except carp and bring to a boil. Simmer for 30 minutes.
2. Add carp, cover and simmer about 30 minutes, or until fish separates from the bones.
3. While fish is cooking, assemble and mix ingredients for Black Prune-Raisin Sauce (see recipe below).
4. Drain carp and reserve liquid.
5. Place carp in a soup tureen or deep serving dish and keep hot while preparing sauce.

◆ **BLACK PRUNE-RAISIN SAUCE** ◆

dairy, pareve

  2 cups cooked prunes, pitted and chopped
  Juice of 1 lemon
  Grated rind of 1 lemon
  1 tablespoon butter or margarine
  ⅓ cup raisins
  ½ cup chopped walnuts or other nuts
  ¼ cup sugar
  Liquid from cooked fish

1. Combine all ingredients except liquid and mix thoroughly.
2. Add to liquid in which fish was cooked. Simmer for 5 minutes and pour over fish. Serve immediately.

Yield: 6–8 servings

NOTE: *This is a kind of stew that can also be made with cod and bass. Boiled potatoes sprinkled with dill or parsley and Cucumber Salad (page 358) are recommended accompaniments.*

—CRAIG CLAIBORNE

ARCTIC CHAR WITH CARROTS AND HONEY

dairy

ADAPTED FROM *Fou de Saveurs*

  12 tablespoons unsalted butter
  1 (3-pound) arctic char, cleaned, head and tail removed
  16 baby carrots, peeled, with stems trimmed
  1½ tablespoons evergreen, acacia or other strong honey

  Sea salt to taste
  Freshly ground black pepper to taste
  ¼ cup vegetable broth
  1 teaspoon lemon juice
  20 white peppercorns, crushed

1. Preheat oven to 300 degrees. Place a skillet or flameproof baking pan large enough to hold fish over medium heat. Add 5 tablespoons butter. When foamy, add fish. Cook 4 minutes on each side, adjusting heat so butter does not brown.

2. Place a large sheet of heavy-duty foil on a work surface. Transfer fish to foil and wrap it, sealing tightly. Set foil-wrapped fish on a baking sheet and place in oven for 5 minutes. Remove from oven and set aside; fish will continue to cook in foil.

3. Fill a small saucepan with 3 cups water and bring to a boil. Add carrots, 1 tablespoon honey and ½ teaspoon salt. Reduce heat and simmer until carrots are tender, about 6 minutes. Drain, set aside and keep warm.

4. In a small saucepan, combine vegetable broth, lemon juice, remaining 7 tablespoons butter and salt and pepper to taste. Bring to a boil, remove from heat and whisk briefly. Sauce should be syrupy; if not, return to heat for a minute or two.

5. Check fish by opening foil and making a small cut into thickest part. It should be slightly rare in center. If additional cooking is needed, return to oven for a few more minutes.

6. To serve, remove fish from foil and place on serving platter. Spoon butter sauce on and around fish and sprinkle with crushed white peppercorns. Arrange carrots on platter, drizzle with remaining ½ tablespoon honey and serve.

Yield: 4 servings

—FRANK PRIAL

CHILLED WHOLE COD IN
TUNA-MAYONNAISE • (COD TONNATO)

pareve

◆ TUNA MAYONNAISE ◆

pareve

⅓ cup mayonnaise, preferably thick and homemade
 with a fruity olive oil or a combination of olive
 and vegetable oils
1 (6-ounce) can imported tuna packed in olive oil, drained
1 ounce anchovy fillets, rinsed and patted dry (see
 Note below)
¼ cup small capers
¼ cup fresh lemon juice
¾ cup fruity olive oil

Poached Cod

pareve

1 whole 8-pound cod, with head on, cleaned, gilled
 and gutted
12 cups water
1 bottle dry white wine
¾ cup white wine vinegar
3 large onions stuck with 3 whole cloves each
4 carrots, chopped
2 ribs celery with leaves, chopped
1 bay leaf
1 teaspoon dried thyme
6 parsley sprigs
6 peppercorns
1 tablespoon salt, or to taste
2 large cucumbers, washed

1. To prepare the tuna mayonnaise, place the mayonnaise in a medium bowl. In the bowl of a food processor fitted with a steel blade, combine the tuna, anchovies, capers and lemon juice, and process until a smooth paste is formed. With the processor on, pour the olive oil through the feed tube in a slow, steady stream. (If doing this by hand, mash the tuna, anchovies, capers and lemon juice with a fork. Slowly whisk in the oil.) Fold the tuna mixture into the mayonnaise and blend well. Cover and refrigerate until needed.

2. In a large pot, make a court bouillon by combining the water, white wine, vinegar, onions, carrots, celery, bay leaf, thyme, parsley sprigs, peppercorns and salt. Bring just to a boil and simmer 1 hour. To poach the cod, place the fish on its side and measure the height at its thickest point. Figure 8–9 minutes poaching time per inch of thickness once the poaching liquid returns to a boil. Wrap the fish in a couple of layers of cheesecloth.

3. Fill a fish poacher or shallow pan large enough to accommodate the fish with enough court bouillon to cover the fish. Bring the liquid to a boil, then lower the fish into the pot. Once the liquid returns to a boil, adjust the heat down so the liquid barely simmers. Time as directed in Step 2.

4. Once cooked, remove the fish from the liquid to a large platter and let it cool for a few minutes. Carefully cut open the cheesecloth with scissors. Remove the top layer of skin and the head, if it has fallen apart or if you do not wish to serve it. Leave the tail intact. Slide the cheesecloth out from under the cod, using a wide spatula to help. Drain off and blot any liquid on the platter with paper towels, cover loosely with foil and refrigerate until cold.

5. Make sure all liquid is removed from the platter. Spoon enough tuna mayonnaise over and around the cod to cover generously. Leave the tail uncovered. Re-cover the platter and refrigerate for at least 4–6 hours, or preferably overnight.

6. To assemble the fish, remove the fish from the refrigerator no more than 2 hours before serving. Smooth the mayonnaise, adding more if needed to fill in any cracks.

7. Run the tines of a fork along the length of the cucumbers to score them. Cut them in half lengthwise and scrape out the seeds with a spoon. Cut the cucumbers into very thin slices. Beginning at the tail end, overlap the slices to create a scale pattern. Serve the top half of the fish, then remove the bones before serving the bottom. Pass the extra mayonnaise at the table.

Yield: 8–10 servings

NOTE: *Because of the anchovies, this dish may not be served with meat (see Explanatory Note, page 582).*

—JOANNA PRUESS

BAKED FRESH COD WITH ONIONS IN A POTATO CRUST

dairy

3 tablespoons sweet butter, melted
1½ pounds of fresh cod fillets, skinless and boneless

Salt to taste
Freshly ground pepper to taste
3 medium-size onions (about ¾ pound), thinly sliced
2 teaspoons minced garlic

4 sprigs fresh thyme, chopped, or ½ teaspoon dried

2 tablespoons olive oil

2 tablespoons chopped parsley

2 pounds new potatoes, peeled and sliced into ⅛-inch rounds

1. Preheat the oven to 450 degrees.

2. Use a third of the melted butter to grease an oval or rectangular baking dish (it should be about 12 by 9 inches). Lay the fish fillets inside. Salt and pepper well.

3. In a bowl, blend the onions, garlic, thyme, salt and pepper. Heat 1 tablespoon of olive oil in a large nonstick skillet and cook the onions for about 3–4 minutes. Stir often, but do not brown the onions. Remove the onions from the heat, stir in the parsley and scatter the onions around the fish fillets.

4. Add the remaining 1 tablespoon of olive oil to the same skillet over medium-high heat. Add the sliced potatoes. Cook the potatoes for about 10 minutes, shaking the pan and stirring regularly to cook them evenly. The potatoes will be cooked only partially after 10 minutes.

5. Spoon the potatoes over the fish fillets to cover completely. Smooth over the top with a spatula. Pour the remaining 2 tablespoons of butter over the potatoes. Bake for 25 minutes, basting two or three times with the juices, until the potatoes are well browned.

Yield: 4–6 servings

—BRYAN MILLER AND PIERRE FRANEY

COD WITH SWEET-AND-SOUR TOMATO SAUCE

pareve

1 teaspoon olive oil

2 small onions, halved and thinly sliced

2 cans plum tomatoes, 1 pound each, drained (liquid reserved) and finely chopped

½ teaspoon grated orange zest

3 tablespoons fresh orange juice

2 tablespoons dry sherry

¼ cup raisins

2 tablespoons balsamic vinegar

1 tablespoon honey

¼ teaspoon ground cinnamon

2 teaspoons salt

Freshly ground pepper to taste

2 tablespoons toasted slivered almonds

4 (4-ounce) cod fillets

2 tablespoons minced scallions

1. Heat the olive oil in a large nonstick skillet over medium heat. Add the onions and turn the heat to medium-low. Cook until completely wilted and browned, about 10 minutes. Add the tomatoes, ½ cup of the reserved liquid, orange zest and juice, dry sherry, raisins, vinegar, honey, cinnamon, salt and pepper. Simmer for 25 minutes.

2. Stir in the almonds. Place the cod in the skillet and cover with the sauce. Simmer until just cooked through, about 10 minutes. Carefully transfer the fillets to plates using a wide spatula. Spoon some of the sauce over the fish, sprinkle with the scallions and serve immediately.

Yield: 4 servings

—MOLLY O'NEILL

FLOUNDER FLORENTINE WITH PISTACHIOS

dairy

4 skinless, boneless fillets of flounder or fluke,
    about 1¼ pounds
1½ pounds fresh spinach
1 tablespoon olive oil
5 tablespoons butter
Salt to taste if desired
Freshly ground pepper to taste
¼ teaspoon freshly grated nutmeg
3 tablespoons milk
⅓ cup flour
2 tablespoons corn, peanut or vegetable oil
¼ cup shelled pistachio nuts
1 tablespoon freshly squeezed lemon juice

1. Pick over the fillets to remove small bones.

2. Remove and discard tough stems or blemished leaves of the spinach. Rinse thoroughly and drain well.

3. Heat olive oil and 1 tablespoon of the butter in a casserole and add spinach. Sprinkle with salt, pepper and nutmeg and stir. Cook about 1 minute or until wilted. Remove from the heat.

4. Put milk in a flat dish and add flounder pieces. Sprinkle with salt and pepper and turn the pieces in the milk. Shake off excess.

5. Blend flour with salt and pepper. Add fish pieces and coat on all sides. Shake off excess.

6. Heat corn oil in a nonstick skillet and add fish fillets. Cook about 1 minute or less, until golden brown on one side. Turn the pieces and cook about 1 minute or less. As the fish pieces are cooked, transfer them immediately to individual plates, rather than to a platter. The fish is delicate and must not be overhandled. Surround each serving of fish with a portion of spinach.

7. Pour off the fat from the skillet and add the remaining 4 tablespoons of butter and pistachios. Heat until bubbling and sprinkle with lemon juice. Pour the sauce over fish.

Yield: 4 servings

—PIERRE FRANEY

BAKED FLOUNDER WITH MOROCCAN SPICES

pareve

1 tablespoon chopped fresh cilantro
1 tablespoon chopped fresh parsley
2 cloves garlic, minced
¼ teaspoon hot Hungarian paprika or large pinch
    cayenne pepper
2 teaspoons ground cumin
1 teaspoon ground coriander
¼ teaspoon cinnamon

Salt to taste
Freshly ground black pepper to taste
2 pounds small flounder fillets
2 large carrots, peeled
3 medium potatoes
8 plum tomatoes
1 Italian frying pepper, seeded and sliced
1 small hot green chili, seeded and chopped
⅓ cup extra-virgin olive oil

1. Combine the cilantro, parsley, garlic, paprika, cumin, ground coriander, cinnamon, salt and pepper. Rub the fish fillets with this mixture. Place them in a glass or ceramic dish, cover with plastic wrap, refrigerate and allow to marinate 2–3 hours.

2. While the fish is marinating, thickly slice the carrots and quarter the potatoes. Place them in a saucepan, cover with water and boil for 15 minutes to parcook them. Allow to cool. Peel and slice the potatoes. Set the vegetables aside.

3. Slice four of the tomatoes and puree the rest.

4. Preheat oven to 450 degrees. Place oven rack in the highest position.

5. Scatter the frying pepper, chili pepper and carrot slices in a baking dish. Place the fish fillets on top, then scatter the potato and tomato slices over them.

6. Mix the pureed tomatoes with the olive oil and season to taste with salt and pepper. Pour over the fish. Cover loosely with foil. Place in the oven and bake about 20 minutes. Serve at once.

Yield: 4–6 servings

—FLORENCE FABRICANT

FRONTIÈRE'S GROUPER WITH ZA'ATAR AND TOMATO

pareve

ADAPTED FROM Frontière

10 large plum tomatoes
2 tablespoons olive oil
4 large cloves garlic, sliced
1¼ cups finely diced onion
1½ tablespoons Za'atar (page 423)
¼ teaspoon salt
¼ teaspoon black pepper
1½ tablespoons fresh lemon juice
4 (6-ounce) grouper fillets
Salt to taste
Pepper to taste
20 asparagus spears, lightly steamed
¼ cup fresh lemon juice

1. Cut tomatoes in large pieces.

2. In medium nonstick skillet, heat 1 tablespoon of the olive oil.

3. Sauté garlic and onion until soft. Add tomatoes and cook 10–15 minutes, until very soft but still chunky. Stir in za'atar, salt, pepper and lemon juice. Cook 1 minute. Keep warm.

4. Sprinkle fish with salt and pepper. Heat 1 tablespoon olive oil in large nonstick skillet. Sauté fish over high heat for 3–4 minutes on each side.

5. To serve, spoon sauce on bottom of 4 plates. Put fish on top. Garnish with asparagus arranged like spokes of a wheel and sprinkle with lemon juice.

Yield: 4 servings

—ROZANNE GOLD

DAVID BOULEY'S BROILED HALIBUT
WITH TOMATO COMPOTE AND GARLIC TAPENADE

dairy

FOR THE HALIBUT:

pareve

2 tablespoons quick-mixing flour
1 teaspoon chopped fresh lemon thyme
4 halibut steaks, 8 ounces each

1. Prepare Tomato Compote and Garlic Tapenade.
2. Preheat broiler.
3. Combine flour and thyme. Dust steaks.
4. Broil 3 minutes on each side. Top with compote.

Yield: 4 servings

◆ TOMATO COMPOTE ◆

dairy

4 large tomatoes
1 tablespoon olive oil
1 teaspoon fresh oregano leaves
1 teaspoon fresh marjoram leaves
1 tablespoon Garlic Tapenade (see recipe below)
1 tablespoon balsamic vinegar
Salt to taste
Pepper to taste

1. Blanch tomatoes 2 seconds in boiling water.
2. Peel, core and seed, and cut into ¼-inch strips.
3. Heat oil in saucepan. Add oregano, marjoram, tapenade and tomatoes. Mix in vinegar, salt and pepper. Keep warm.

Yield: 4 servings

◆ GARLIC TAPENADE ◆

dairy

1 tablespoon plus 1 teaspoon olive oil
1 teaspoon butter
1 medium-size bulb garlic, broken into cloves
1 twig rosemary
1 teaspoon finely chopped fresh marjoram
1 teaspoon finely chopped fresh lemon thyme (or any other kind of thyme)
1 teaspoon finely chopped fresh tarragon
½ teaspoon lemon juice
Salt to taste
Pepper to taste
1 teaspoon finely chopped fresh chives, for garnish, optional
1 teaspoon finely chopped fresh chervil, for garnish, optional

1. Preheat oven to 350 degrees.
2. Mix 1 teaspoon of the oil and the butter. By hand, coat the garlic cloves with this mixture. Place on baking sheet with rosemary twig. Bake until soft, 10–15 minutes. Discard rosemary. Let garlic cool. While still warm, peel and remove stem portion.
3. Place peeled garlic in a blender or food processor with remaining 1 tablespoon oil and other remaining ingredients except the garnishes. Blend until smooth. Garnish, if desired, with chives and chervil.

Yield: 2–3 tablespoons

NOTE: *May be made up to two weeks in advance if kept in refrigerator, and several months if kept in freezer. The tapenade is excellent in soups and may also be used as a spread for small pieces of toast or pita or as a topping for pasta.*

—DENA KLEIMAN

LE BERNADIN'S HALIBUT IN BORSCHT
WITH WARM CHIVE-HORSERADISH SAUCE

meat, dairy, pareve

ADAPTED FROM Eric Ripert

2 tablespoons olive oil or corn oil

1 medium onion, julienned

1 cup julienned fennel

2 tablespoons sliced garlic

2 sprigs fresh thyme

2 sprigs flat-leaf parsley

1 cup chopped savoy cabbage, plus 3 of the darker
    outer leaves, finely julienned

1 quart well-seasoned Chicken Stock (page 48) or
    Vegetable Stock (page 51), canned or fresh

4 cups peeled and julienned fresh beets
    (about 1½ bunches)

Salt to taste

Freshly ground white pepper to taste

1 cup Crème Fraîche (page 431), sour cream or
    mayonnaise

¼ cup prepared white horseradish

½ teaspoon sugar

1 tablespoon minced chives

8 halibut steaks or fillets, each 4–6 ounces, or
    8 portions chilled Classic Gefilte Fish (page 4)

1. Heat oil in a heavy 3-quart saucepan. Add onions and fennel and cook slowly about 5 minutes, until softened. Tie garlic, thyme, parsley and chopped cabbage in a double thickness of cheesecloth and add it to saucepan along with stock and beets. Simmer 15 minutes. Season to taste with salt and pepper. Remove from heat. Discard cheesecloth and its contents. To serve the dish chilled, refrigerate beet mixture at least 4 hours or overnight.

2. Bring 3 cups water to a boil in a small saucepan. Add julienned cabbage leaves, cook just until bright green, then drain. Set leaves aside, covered, to keep warm; for a cold dish, refrigerate.

3. Mix crème fraîche, sour cream or, if using chicken stock, mayonnaise, with horseradish, sugar and chives. If using mayonnaise, thin it beforehand with 2 tablespoons water. This sauce can be gently warmed in a small saucepan or chilled to serve cold.

4. To serve, steam halibut until fully cooked outside and just warm inside, 6–8 minutes. Keep warm. Reheat beet mixture, spoon into warmed shallow soup plates, sprinkle with julienned cabbage and top with fish. As an alternative, spoon chilled beet mixture into shallow soup plates, add cabbage and top with gefilte fish. Serve horseradish sauce, warm or chilled, on the side with either the halibut or the gefilte fish.

Yield: 8 servings

NOTE: *If using chicken stock in the sauce, select the mayonnaise alternative.*

Gefilte fish may be substituted for the halibut. Served in this manner, it combines the fish with classic accompaniments in a novel presentation.

—FLORENCE FABRICANT

SPICED HALIBUT AND TURNIPS

pareve, meat

ADAPTED FROM Hamersley's Bistro, Boston

7 tablespoons olive oil

Ground black pepper to taste

¼ teaspoon cardamom

¼ teaspoon turmeric

½ teaspoon salt, optional

½ teaspoon cilantro

Juice of ½ lemon

4 halibut fillets, 6 ounces each

2 leeks, thinly sliced

2 medium-size turnips, peeled and cut into the size of
   walnut halves

2 shallots, thinly sliced

2 cloves garlic, thinly sliced

1 teaspoon dried thyme

2 tablespoons raisins

½ cup dry white wine

½ cup Fish Stock (page 51) or Chicken Stock
   (page 48), canned or fresh

¼ teaspoon Dijon-style mustard

1. Combine 6 tablespoons olive oil, pepper, cardamon, turmeric, salt, cilantro and juice of ½ lemon and marinate fish in this mixture for 10 minutes.

2. Heat pan for fish and add remaining 1 tablespoon of olive oil.

3. Sauté leeks, turnips, shallots, garlic, thyme and raisins. Toss and cook over high heat for about 5 minutes to soften.

4. Drain marinade from fish and reserve. Add fish, wine and stock to turnip mixture; cover and bring to a boil. Reduce heat and simmer fish 8–10 minutes, depending on thickness of fish.

5. Remove fish and vegetables and keep warm.

6. Reduce liquid in pan to ½ cup. Whisk in mustard. Remove from heat and vigorously whisk in 4 tablespoons of reserved marinade mixture until thickened. Adjust seasoning and serve over fish and vegetables.

Yield: 4 servings

— MARIAN BURROS

SIMPLE BROILED MACKEREL
WITH LEMON AND CINNAMON

pareve

4 (8-ounce) mackerel fillets (or substitute pompano,
   bluefish, mahi-mahi, striped bass or tuna)

2 tablespoons vegetable oil

Juice of ½ lemon

1 clove garlic, minced

1 teaspoon ground cinnamon

1 teaspoon ground cumin

Salt to taste

Freshly ground black pepper to taste

2 tablespoons roughly chopped fresh cilantro (or parsley)

1 lemon, quartered

1. Place the mackerel in a shallow baking dish that is large enough for fillets to lie flat without overlapping. In a small bowl, thoroughly mix the vegetable oil, lemon juice, garlic, cinnamon, cumin and salt and pepper to taste. Pour this mixture over the fish and refrigerate, covered, for 1 hour, turning once after 30 minutes.

2. Remove the fish from the marinade and broil in a heated broiler for 5–6 minutes or until the fish is opaque all the way through. Remove from the broiler, sprinkle with cilantro, garnish with lemon quarters and serve.

Yield: 4 servings

—JOHN WILLOUGHBY AND
CHRIS SCHLESINGER

BAKED MACKEREL IN MUSTARD-SCALLION SAUCE

dairy
ADAPTED FROM *Ann Clark's Fabulous Fish*

2½–2¾-pound whole mackerel, cleaned and gutted
½ lemon
½ teaspoon freshly ground black pepper
½ cup Crème Fraîche (page 431)
2 tablespoons prepared whole-grain mustard
2 teaspoons lemon juice
4 scallions, finely chopped, including the green tops
Salt, if desired

1. Score the mackerel on both sides, making 2–3 large X's ½ inch deep with a small sharp knife. Squeeze the half lemon over the fish.

2. Combine and stir the remaining ingredients. Coat the mackerel with this mixture and allow to marinate ½ hour. Turn once during the marinating so the cuts in the fish are well coated with the sauce.

3. Preheat oven to 375 degrees.

4. Place mackerel in a small buttered oval baking dish and bake until the fish is opaque. Serve at once.

Yield: 2 servings

—FLORENCE FABRICANT

VENETIAN-STYLE POMPANO WITH GOLDEN RAISINS AND PINE NUTS

pareve
ADAPTED FROM *Fish & Shellfish*

1½ pounds pompano fillets (about 4), skin removed
Kosher salt to taste

Freshly ground black pepper to taste
½ cup all-purpose flour
¾ cup extra-virgin olive oil
1 red onion, thinly sliced
1 teaspoon grated fresh ginger

¼ teaspoon ground cinnamon

⅛ teaspoon ground cloves

1 teaspoon ground coriander

½ cup sherry vinegar or balsamic vinegar

2 sprigs fresh thyme

*⅓ cup pomegranate juice or 3 tablespoons
    pomegranate molasses diluted with 3 tablespoons
    water (see Note, page 583)*

2 bay leaves

3 tablespoons golden raisins

3 tablespoons toasted pine nuts

1. Cut the fillets in half crosswise or on a diagonal. Season the fillets with salt and pepper and dredge them in the flour, shaking off any excess. Heat ¼ cup of the oil in a large nonstick skillet set over high heat. Working in two batches, brown the fillets on both sides, removing them from the pan when they are just slightly underdone. Drain the fillets on paper towels.

2. Wipe out the skillet and add the remaining ½ cup of olive oil and the onion. Cook over medium heat, stirring occasionally, until the onion is wilted but not brown, about 10 minutes. Stir in the ginger, cinnamon, cloves and coriander and cook for 1 more minute. Add the rest of the ingredients except the pine nuts and cook for an additional 5 minutes. Let the mixture cool for 5 minutes, then season to taste with salt and pepper.

3. Transfer the fillets to a serving dish and spoon onion mixture over them. Sprinkle with pine nuts, cover the dish with plastic wrap and refrigerate for 8–48 hours. Remove from the refrigerator about 1 hour before serving.

Yield: 8 first-course or 4 main-course servings

—MOLLY O'NEILL

RED SNAPPER FILLETS
WITH THYME AND YELLOW PEPPER

dairy

6 red snapper fillets

2 tablespoons balsamic vinegar

2 tablespoons peanut or vegetable oil

2 tablespoons unsalted butter

6 scallions, cut on the bias

3 shallots, minced

3 tablespoons fresh thyme leaves

1 teaspoon red pepper flakes

1 cup Fish Stock (page 51)

½ cup dry white wine or vermouth

Coarse salt to taste

Freshly ground pepper to taste

FOR THE YELLOW PEPPER SAUCE:

1 clove garlic, coarsely chopped

2 shallots, coarsely chopped

2 yellow peppers, seeded and coarsely chopped

¾ cup Fish Stock (page 51), canned or fresh

½ cup dry white wine or vermouth

1. Preheat oven to 400 degrees

2. Wipe the fillets dry and sprinkle with vinegar and oil. Set aside.

3. Make the yellow pepper sauce. Combine garlic, shallots, yellow peppers, fish stock and wine in a saucepan and simmer 10–15 minutes, or until the peppers are soft. Puree in food processor, season and set aside.

4. Butter a shallow baking pan large enough to hold the fillets comfortably in overlapping layers. Sprinkle with the scallions, shallots, I tablespoon thyme and red pepper flakes. Place the fish on top and add the stock, wine, salt and pepper. Bake 10–15 minutes, or until fish is cooked.

5. Remove snapper fillets from baking pan and place on a heated serving dish. Add cooking juices to the yellow pepper sauce and reduce until thickened. Correct seasoning and pour into a heated sauceboat.

6. Sprinkle the fish fillets with the remaining thyme and serve.

Yield: 4–6 servings

—MOIRA HODGSON

NIGELLA LAWSON'S SNAPPER WITH SEVILLE ORANGE JUICE, PINE NUTS AND OLIVES

pareve

1 teaspoon olive oil
2½- to 3-pound whole snapper, cleaned and scaled
1 teaspoon black peppercorns
5 bay leaves
1 large strip Seville orange zest or 1 strip orange zest and 1 strip lime zest
½ teaspoon salt
1 cup Seville orange juice or ¾ cup orange juice and ¼ cup lime juice
½ cup pitted calamata olives, halved lengthwise
¼ cup pine nuts
¼ cup chopped parsley leaves

1. Heat oven to 400 degrees. Oil a piece of foil large enough to wrap fish in. Place fish in middle of foil and fill its cavity with peppercorns, 4 bay leaves and Seville orange zest (or orange and lime zest).

2. Sprinkle fish with salt and fold two sides of foil together, sealing with a pleat. Fold other two sides in to enclose fish; place on a baking sheet with folds up. Bake 45 minutes.

3. About 15 minutes before fish is ready, place Seville orange juice (or orange and lime juice) in a small saucepan. Add remaining bay leaf, olives and pine nuts. Place over high heat to bring to a boil, then reduce heat to low. Simmer uncovered for 5 minutes. Remove from heat, cover and keep warm.

4. To serve, open foil and peel away skin from top of fish. Carefully remove top fillets and place on warm serving plates. Lift bone from tail end and place bottom fillets on plates, leaving skin behind. Top each serving with a spoonful of orange sauce and a sprinkling of parsley. Pass remaining sauce at table.

Yield: 2–3 servings

—NIGELLA LAWSON

GRILLED RED SNAPPER
WITH TAMARI AND AVOCADO

pareve

ADAPTED FROM Cafe News

4 tablespoons lemon juice

1 tablespoon grated fresh ginger

1 tablespoon fresh minced garlic

1 minced shallot

1 teaspoon honey

1 teaspoon tamari

1 tablespoon tahini

2 pounds red snapper fillets

1 large avocado, skinned and cut into fine dice

1/4 cup fresh minced cilantro

1. In a heavy-bottom skillet, combine the lemon juice, ginger, garlic and shallot and reduce by half over medium heat. In a small bowl, combine the honey, tamari, 1/2 cup water and tahini and whisk into the lemon mixture. Set aside in a warm place.

2. Lay the fish in a broiler pan and broil for about 3 minutes on each side, or until the center of the fish is no longer translucent. To serve, drizzle with the warm sauce and garnish with the avocado and cilantro.

Yield: 6 servings

NOTE: *In this recipe, the tahini, tamari and honey are a counterpoint to the pungent grated ginger, garlic and shallots. For a thinner sauce, simply dilute with additional water. Lightly steamed vegetables and brown rice are recommended accompaniments.*

—MOLLY O'NEILL

BAKED "POACHED" WHOLE SALMON WITH TWO SAUCES

pareve

1 (6- to 8-pound) cleaned, whole salmon, preferably with head left on (see Note below)

1 cup thinly sliced carrot

1 cup thinly sliced onion

1/4 cup thinly sliced shallots

1 cup thinly sliced celery

1/2 teaspoon dried thyme

Salt to taste

8 peppercorns, crushed

1 clove garlic, unpeeled and crushed

1 bay leaf

2 cups dry white wine

1. Preheat oven to 400 degrees.

2. Select a baking sheet large enough to accommodate the fish.

3. Lay out a long double length of heavy-duty aluminum foil on top of the baking sheet. Place the cleaned salmon in the center of the foil and add the carrot, onion, shallots, celery, thyme, salt to taste, peppercorns, garlic, bay leaf and wine. Bring up the edges of the foil and seal as compactly and tightly as possible.

4. Place the fish in the oven and bake 50 minutes to 1 hour. At the end of 50 minutes, loosen the foil and test for doneness. The fish is cooked when the back center fin can be easily removed when pulled with the fingers. Remove from the oven. Serve hot, if desired, with White Wine Sauce or cold with Dill-and-Cucumber Mayonnaise (see recipes below).

Yield: 8–12 servings

NOTE: *Although the salmon is not technically poached or steamed, the result of foil-baking is similar enough to seem almost interchangeable with that of the more proper method. Before baking the fish, measure it to make certain it will fit in the oven. It may be placed diagonally to obtain more space. If the fish will not fit with the head left on, it will be necessary to cut it off. The head may be used for soup or discarded. The meat from a poached fish head also may be used cold in salads.*

◆ WHITE WINE SAUCE ◆ (SAUCE VIN BLANC)

dairy

2 cups of the liquid in which the salmon was baked
   (see recipe above)
Vegetables and seasonings with which the salmon
   was baked
1 cup heavy cream
2 tablespoons butter at room temperature
2 tablespoons flour
4 tablespoons cold butter
Juice of ½ lemon
Salt to taste
Cayenne pepper to taste

1. Pour the liquid from the foil in which the salmon baked into a saucepan. Add the chopped or sliced vegetables with which the salmon was baked. Bring this mixture to a boil and let it simmer about 15 minutes, or until it is reduced to 1½ cups when strained.

2. Strain the sauce and return it to the saucepan. Add the cream.

3. Prepare a beurre manié by blending the room-temperature butter and flour until they form a smooth paste. Bring the sauce to a simmer and gradually add the butter-flour mixture, stirring constantly. When the blend is thick and smooth, add the cold butter, bit by bit, stirring. Add the lemon juice, salt and cayenne to taste. Remove from the heat.

Yield: 3 cups

◆ DILL-AND-CUCUMBER ◆ MAYONNAISE

pareve

1 cup peeled, seeded and diced cucumbers
Salt to taste
2 egg yolks
Freshly ground pepper to taste
2 teaspoons imported mustard, such as Dijon or
   Dusseldorf
2 teaspoons vinegar or lemon juice
2 cups peanut, vegetable or olive oil
¼ cup finely chopped, fresh dill

1. Put the cucumbers in a bowl and sprinkle with salt to taste. Refrigerate 30 minutes.

2. Meanwhile, place the yolks in a mixing bowl and add salt and pepper to taste, mustard and vinegar or lemon juice. Beat vigorously for a second or two with a wire whisk or electric beater.

3. Start adding the oil gradually, beating continuously with the whisk or electric beater. Continue beating and adding oil until all of it is used.

4. Drain the cucumbers. Add the cucumbers and dill and blend well.

Yield: 3 cups

—CRAIG CLAIBORNE AND PIERRE FRANEY

SEARED SALMON WITH BEET SAUCE

pareve

4 medium-size beets

¼ cup balsamic vinegar

Coarse salt to taste

Freshly ground pepper to taste

½ teaspoon sugar

1¼ pounds salmon fillet, skin on

1½ tablespoons Dijon mustard

2 tablespoons peanut or vegetable oil

¼ cup olive oil

About 10 fried sage leaves or 1 tablespoon
    minced fresh sage

Lemon quarters

1. Preheat the oven to 375 degrees. Put the beets in their skins on a rack. Bake for 45 minutes or until the beets are tender when pierced with the tip of a sharp knife.

2. Peel and chop the beets. Put half of them in a small saucepan with the vinegar, sugar, salt and pepper. Add barely enough water to cover and let them simmer for 20–30 minutes over high heat until only 4 tablespoons of liquid remain. Put the remaining chopped beets in a dish and keep warm.

3. Meanwhile, spread the salmon on both sides with mustard and season with salt and pepper. Heat the peanut oil in a nonstick pan, sear the fish on both sides and put it in the oven. Bake for about 20 minutes for medium rare.

4. While the salmon is baking, put the vinegared beets into a blender and add the oil at high speed. Blend until smooth and season to taste with salt and pepper.

5. Put the salmon on a heated serving platter. Spoon the sauce around it. Sprinkle with the remaining chopped beets and fresh or fried sage leaves and garnish with lemon quarters.

Yield: 3–4 servings

—MOIRA HODGSON

SALMON WITH SORREL SAUCE

dairy

4 tablespoons finely minced shallots

1 cup dry white wine, preferably chardonnay

⅓ cup dry vermouth

1 cup heavy cream

4 cups fresh sorrel, washed, stemmed and center veins
    removed

1 tablespoon fresh lemon juice

Salt to taste

Freshly ground black pepper to taste

1 (12-ounce) center-cut salmon fillet, boneless

1. In a saucepan over high heat combine shallots, wine and vermouth. Cook until mixture is almost evaporated. It should have a syrupy consistency. Add cream and bring mixture to a simmer. Cook, stirring frequently, for 30 minutes. Remove from heat and strain sauce through a fine sieve into a clean saucepan.

2. Tear sorrel into thumb-size pieces and drop into

sauce. Add lemon juice, salt and pepper to taste, and cook briefly, stirring. Remove from heat and keep warm.

3. Cut salmon in half widthwise. Then halve each piece, leaving four portions. Pound each piece lightly with the back of a saucepan to make surface even.

4. Season salmon on skin side with salt and pepper. Cook fillets in a nonstick pan over medium-high heat for 30 seconds. Flip and cook another 30 seconds.

5. Distribute sorrel sauce evenly over center of 4 warm serving plates. Place a salmon fillet over each, arranging some sorrel strands around them Serve immediately.

Yield: 4 servings

—BRYAN MILLER AND PIERRE FRANEY

PICHOLINE'S SALMON FILLETS WITH HORSERADISH CRUST, CUCUMBERS AND SALMON CAVIAR

dairy

ADAPTED FROM Terrance Brennan

3 medium cucumbers, peeled

2 tablespoons plus 1 teaspoon sea salt

8 ounces smoked salmon, cut crosswise into 3-inch
    sections

1 cup finely grated fresh horseradish (see Note,
    page 414)

½ pound unsalted butter at room temperature, cut
    into chunks

4 cups freshly grated bread crumbs

3 tablespoons Dijon-style mustard

½ tablespoon cayenne

6 salmon fillets, skinless, about 8 ounces each

Salt to taste

Freshly ground pepper to taste

1 tablespoon olive oil

6 tablespoons Crème Fraîche (page 431)
    or sour cream

3 tablespoons chopped parsley

2 tablespoons chopped dill

2 tablespoons chopped chives

6 tablespoons salmon roe

1. Slice the cucumbers on a bias about ¼ inch thick. In a bowl, toss the cucumbers with 1 teaspoon of sea salt; then transfer to a colander. Let drain for 2 hours.

2. Place the smoked salmon and horseradish in the bowl of a food processor and blend until smooth. Add the butter, bread crumbs, the remaining sea salt, mustard and cayenne. Blend well.

3. Season the salmon fillets with salt and pepper.

4. Turn on broiler. Place 1 tablespoon olive oil in a nonstick sauté pan over medium-high heat. Cook the salmon for about 45 seconds a side. Remove pan from heat. Carefully cover the fillets with the smoked salmon and horseradish mixture.

5. Place the fillets in the broiler and cook until nicely browned. Remove from the oven and keep warm.

6. Quickly heat the cucumbers in the crème fraîche. Distribute the cucumbers evenly over 6 plates. Sprinkle with parsley, dill and chives. Sprinkle some salmon roe around the cucumbers. Arrange salmon over the cucumbers and serve immediately.

Yield: 6 servings

—BRYAN MILLER

PASTRAMI SALMON

pareve
ADAPTED FROM David Burke

1 side of fresh salmon, about 2–2½ pounds, skin
    and bones removed
1 cup coarse kosher salt
½ cup sugar
3 tablespoons cracked pepper
2 bunches fresh cilantro
1 bunch fresh Italian parsley
½ pound shallots, peeled
½ cup molasses
2 tablespoons cayenne pepper
5 bay leaves
2 tablespoons paprika
2 tablespoons ground coriander
3 tablespoons freshly ground black pepper
8 teaspoons mustard oil (See Note, page 583)
1 slice rye toast per serving

1. Place salmon on a platter. In a bowl, combine salt, sugar and I tablespoon of the cracked pepper. Mix well and coat both sides of the salmon with mixture.
2. In a food processor combine cilantro, parsley and shallots. Puree until smooth but not watery. Coat both sides of salmon with mixture.
3. Cover and refrigerate salmon for 2–3 days.
4. Scrape marinade from fish and discard. Dry fish with paper towels.
5. In a saucepan, combine molasses, cayenne and bay leaves. Bring to a boil and simmer for I minute. Allow molasses mixture to cool slightly. Using a brush, paint fish on both sides with the mixture.
6. Sprinkle paprika, coriander, 2 tablespoons of the ground black pepper and the cracked pepper on both sides of fish. Refrigerate salmon overnight.
7. Cut salmon widthwise on a bias into thin slices. Serve with mustard oil and rye toast.

Yield: 8 servings

—BRYAN MILLER

SALMON IN PHYLLO WITH SPINACH AND CHEESE

dairy
ADAPTED FROM Periyali

FOR THE SALMON AND MARINADE:

8 skinless, boneless pieces of salmon fillet, about
    4 ounces each
1 tablespoon coarsely chopped parsley
1 tablespoon coarsely chopped fresh chives
1 teaspoon dried oregano leaves

1 teaspoon dried thyme leaves
½ cup extra-virgin olive oil

FOR THE FILLING:

¼ cup plus 1 tablespoon extra-virgin olive oil
1 small onion, peeled and shredded
1 small leek, cleaned and chopped
1 (10-ounce) package frozen chopped spinach,
    defrosted and squeezed of most of its liquid

1 tablespoon chopped fresh dill

½ teaspoon salt

¼ teaspoon freshly ground white pepper

1 large egg

⅓ cup crumbled feta cheese

½ cup whole-milk cottage cheese

1½ teaspoons grated Parmesan cheese

1½ teaspoons dry bread crumbs

3 tablespoons lemon juice

18 sheets phyllo (see Note, page 583)

1½ cups melted clarified butter

1. Rinse salmon fillets and pat dry on paper towels.

2. Put parsley, chives, oregano and thyme on a cutting surface and chop together until very fine and well combined. Sprinkle in a shallow pan and stir in the olive oil.

3. Coat salmon fillets on both sides with the marinade and set aside about 30 minutes at room temperature, or for 1–2 hours in the refrigerator.

4. To make the filling, heat 1 tablespoon olive oil in a large sauté pan. Add the onion and leek and cook over medium heat, stirring frequently, until lightly browned, about 8 minutes. Stir in the spinach and the remaining ¼ cup olive oil. Cook 4 minutes. Stir

in dill, salt and pepper. Turn the mixture into a bowl and refrigerate until cool. Stir in the egg, cheese and bread crumbs.

5. Preheat oven to 375 degrees. Sprinkle lemon juice over the salmon.

6. Put 2 sheets of phyllo, one on top of the other, on a work surface, keeping the unused pastry covered with a damp towel. Cut sheets in half lengthwise. Cut across into 4 pieces and brush with butter. (These will be used as patches to reinforce phyllo packets).

7. Put 1 sheet of phyllo on a work surface. Brush with butter. Top with another sheet of phyllo. Brush with butter. Put 1 of the patches on top of the phyllo, about 2 inches from the edge. Put 1 piece of salmon over the patch. Cover with ¼ cup of the filling. Fold bottom of phyllo over salmon. Brush the folded portion with butter. Fold in the sides of the phyllo and brush with butter. Roll up the salmon in the phyllo to make a neat packet. Brush the top with butter and seal the end of the roll onto the packet with butter.

8. Repeat Step 7 with remaining ingredients to make 8 packets, putting packets on 2 ungreased baking sheets.

9. Bake until golden brown, about 15 minutes. Serve immediately.

Yield: 8 servings

— BRYAN MILLER

MARCELLA HAZAN'S BAKED TOMATOES STUFFED WITH SALMON, GARLIC AND CAPERS

pareve

ADAPTED FROM *Marcella Cucina*

1 tablespoon large capers, preferably packed in salt

3½ tablespoons extra-virgin olive oil

1 pound fresh salmon

1 tablespoon chopped Italian flat-leaf parsley

1 teaspoon very finely chopped garlic

2 tablespoons fine, dry, unflavored bread crumbs

Salt to taste

Freshly ground black pepper to taste
2 large, firm tomatoes, each about ¾ pound

1. Preheat oven to 400 degrees. Use a little of the olive oil to grease a medium-size baking dish.
2. Drain capers if they are packed in vinegar; soak, rinse and drain them if packed in salt. Chop fine.
3. Remove all skin and membrane from salmon and pick out any bones. Finely dice fish and mix in bowl with 2½ tablespoons olive oil, plus parsley, garlic, capers, I tablespoon bread crumbs and salt and pepper to taste. Toss.
4. Wash tomatoes, cut them in half horizontally and scoop out seeds and centers. (You can reserve what you remove to use in another recipe.) Pat insides of tomatoes with paper towels; stuff with salmon mixture, pressing it down lightly and allowing it to form a mound. Sprinkle with remaining bread crumbs and drizzle with remaining olive oil.
5. Place tomatoes in baking dish and bake on upper level of oven for 35 minutes, until there is a golden crust on stuffing. Allow to cool to lukewarm and then serve, or prepare in advance and serve at room temperature.

Yield: 4 servings

—FLORENCE FABRICANT

SALMON CROQUETTES

pareve
ADAPTED FROM The Pink Teacup

> *2 pounds of salmon fillets, poached in Court Bouillon*
>   *(see recipe below), or 2 cans of salmon*
>   *(15½ ounces each)*
> *1 large onion, finely chopped*
> *3 eggs*
> *1 cup cooked rice*
> *Salt to taste*
> *Black pepper to taste*
> *Flour for coating*
> *2 cups vegetable oil for pan-frying*

1. Drain the salmon and reserve court bouillon (or juice from cans). Place salmon in a bowl and add onion, eggs, rice, salt and black pepper to taste. Stir well and mash salmon with a hand masher. Add a little court bouillon (or juice) so that the mixture is moist but not soupy.
2. Make oblong patties with an ice-cream scoop. Roll patties in flour and pan-fry in 350-degree oil. Brown on both sides. Drain on paper towels.

Yield: 12 croquettes

Court Bouillon

pareve

> *2 pounds of bones from any white-flesh fish*
>   *(halibut or whiting, for example)*
> *1 onion, whole*
> *6 peppercorns*
> *Pinch of thyme*
> *2 quarts water*

1. Place fish bones, onion, peppercorns and thyme in the water and boil for ½ hour. Drain.

2. Wrap salmon in cheesecloth. In a pan large enough to hold the salmon, bring court bouillon almost to a boil. Place the salmon in it and cook, at just below the boil, for 10 minutes for each inch of the salmon's thickness.

—BRYAN MILLER

MARK BITTMAN'S SALMON BURGERS

dairy, pareve

1½ pounds skinless, boneless salmon
2 teaspoons Dijon mustard
2 shallots, peeled and cut into chunks
½ cup coarse bread crumbs
1 tablespoon capers, drained
Salt to taste
Freshly ground black pepper to taste
2 tablespoons butter or olive oil
Lemon wedges
Tabasco sauce

1. Cut the salmon into large chunks and put about a quarter of it into the container of a food processor along with the mustard. Turn the machine on and let it run—stopping to scrape down the sides if necessary—until the mixture becomes pasty.

2. Add the shallots and the remaining salmon and pulse the machine on and off until the fish is chopped and well combined with the puree. No piece should be larger than a quarter inch or so; be careful not make the mixture too fine.

3. Scrape the mixture into a bowl, and by hand, stir in the bread crumbs, capers and some salt and pepper. Shape into 4 burgers. (You can cover and refrigerate the burgers for a few hours at this point.)

4. Place the butter or oil in a 12-inch nonstick skillet and turn the heat to medium-high. When the butter foam subsides or the oil is hot, cook the burgers for 2–3 minutes a side, turning once. Alternatively, you can grill them: let them firm up on the first side, grilling about 4 minutes before turning over and finishing for just another minute or two. To check for doneness, make a small cut and peek inside. Be careful not to overcook. Serve on a bed of greens or on buns or by themselves, with lemon wedges and Tabasco or any dressing you like.

Yield: 4 servings

A Variety of Approaches to Seasoning

The recipe's mustard, shallots and capers are not the only approaches to consider for seasoning the 4 salmon burgers.

While pureeing the first batch of salmon, you can:

- *Use a combination of soy sauce (about 1 tablespoon), sesame oil (1 teaspoon) and ginger (1 teaspoon). Use peanut oil for sautéing if you have it.*
- *Add a small clove of garlic (don't overdo it, because the garlic will remain nearly raw and strong-tasting).*

For the coarser, second batch, you can:

- *Use ½ cup onion or scallions, in addition to or instead of the shallots.*

- Add spice mixtures like curry or chili powder, using 1 teaspoon to 1 tablespoon, depending on your spice capacity.
- Add 1 tablespoon or more of fresh herbs, such as parsley, chervil, dill or cilantro.
- Add red or yellow bell pepper (½ cup), cored, seeded and roughly chopped.

With the bread crumbs, try mixing in lightly toasted pignoli (¼ cup or more) or sesame seeds (about a tablespoon).

—MARK BITTMAN

FILLET OF SOLE PONTE VECCHIO-STYLE

dairy

ADAPTED FROM *I Sapori Mediterraneo (Mediterranean Flavors)*

4 fillets of sole or flounder, weighing 8–10 ounces each

2 cups fresh mushrooms (portobello, crimini, shiitake or white domestic)

2 tablespoons butter

1 small onion, minced

Kosher salt to taste

Freshly ground black pepper to taste

1 cup dry white wine

8 plum tomatoes (fresh or high-quality canned), cut into small dice

Additional kosher salt and freshly ground black pepper to taste

1 scallion, minced

¼ cup fresh minced flat-leaf parsley

1. Cut each fish fillet into 4 pieces lengthwise and set aside. Rinse and dry the mushrooms and chop coarsely. Over medium heat, melt 1 tablespoon of the butter, add the onion and cook, stirring frequently, until soft, about 5 minutes. Sprinkle with salt and pepper. Add the mushrooms, reduce the heat and continue to cook, stirring constantly until the mushrooms are soft, about 8 minutes. Add the wine and continue cooking for 2 more minutes.

2. Preheat the oven to 350 degrees. Add the tomatoes (and up to ½ cup of their juice if using canned tomatoes) to this mixture. Stir and season the mixture with salt and pepper to taste. Add the scallions, stir, cover and simmer for 10 minutes. The mixture may require some water, additional wine or tomato juice to keep it thick but not dry; add what you need to suit your taste. After 10 minutes, stir in the parsley and remove from the heat.

3. Use the remaining tablespoon of butter to grease an overproof pan large enough for the 16 small fish fillets. Season them lightly with salt and pepper and pour the sauce over the fillets. Cover the pan with foil and place in the oven for 15 minutes. Serve with buttered potatoes or steamed white rice.

Yield: 4 servings

—MOLLY O'NEILL

SAUTÉED FILLET OF SOLE WITH FRESH TOMATO AND GINGER SAUCE

dairy

4 ripe tomatoes, about 1 pound

1 tablespoon olive oil

2 tablespoons chopped shallots

1 teaspoon finely chopped garlic

2 tablespoons grated fresh ginger

1 teaspoon ground cumin

Salt to taste

Ground pepper to taste

4 tablespoons butter

4 skinless fillets of lemon sole, about 1 pound

4 tablespoons milk

½ cup flour

2 tablespoons vegetable oil

1 tablespoon fresh lemon juice

4 sprigs fresh basil or parsley

1. Place tomatoes in boiling water for about 10 seconds. Drain and pull away skins; remove cores. Cut tomatoes crosswise and into ¼-inch cubes.

2. Heat olive oil in saucepan and add shallots and garlic. Cook briefly. Do not brown. Add tomatoes, ginger, cumin, and salt and pepper to taste. Bring to a boil and simmer 5 minutes.

3. Place tomato mixture in a blender. Add I tablespoon butter and blend quickly to a fine texture. Check seasoning; transfer to small saucepan and keep warm.

4. Meanwhile, sprinkle fillets with salt and pepper to taste. Pour milk into a shallow bowl; put the flour on a dish. Dip each fillet in milk and dredge with flour, patting so flour adheres and shaking to remove excess.

5. Heat vegetable oil in a large nonstick skillet over medium-high heat. Place as many fillets in the pan as will fit in one layer without crowding.

6. Brown fillets thoroughly on one side; turn, and brown on other side. Cooking will take about 2 minutes on each side, depending on the thickness of the fillets. Do not overcook.

7. Divide tomato mixture equally among warm serving plates. Place fillets over tomatoes and keep warm.

8. While the pan is still warm, wipe it out with a paper towel and return it to medium-high heat. Add the remaining butter and cook until hazelnut brown. Add lemon juice and pour equally over each serving. Top with basil or parsley.

Yield: 4 servings

—PIERRE FRANEY

SOLE MEUNIÈRE WITH LIMES

dairy

4 tablespoons unsalted butter at room temperature

Coarse salt to taste

Freshly ground pepper to taste

2 limes

2 tablespoons chopped chives

½ teaspoon fresh ginger, grated

4 fillets sole (or other white fish)

Flour for dredging

3–4 tablespoons clarified butter

1. Mash the unsalted butter with the salt and pepper in a small bowl. Work in the juice of 1 lime. Grate 1 teaspoon of the peel and add with the chives and grated ginger. Mix thoroughly, shape into a roll about an inch in diameter and refrigerate.

2. Pat the fish fillets dry with paper towels. Dredge lightly with flour. Heat the clarified butter and fry the fillets, turning once, until golden brown.

3. Arrange the fish on a heated serving dish and garnish with the remaining lime, cut into quarters, and the lime butter, sliced and placed on top of the fillets.

Yield: 4 servings

—MOIRA HODGSON

TROUT FILLED WITH SPINACH, MUSHROOMS, PRUNES AND NUTS · (TRUITES FARCIES GRILLÉS)

dairy

ADAPTED FROM L'Ecole de Cuisine Française S. de Mirbeck, East Sussex, England

4 brook or rainbow trout (about 10–12 ounces each), gutted and boned
Salt to taste
Freshly ground black pepper to taste

FOR THE STUFFING:

1 pound fresh spinach, thoroughly washed and patted dry
1 teaspoon safflower oil
1 large onion, peeled and finely chopped
2 ounces small white mushrooms, cleaned and thinly sliced
2 ounces pitted prunes, finely chopped
2 ounces sliced almonds, toasted until light brown

FOR THE SAUCE:

⅔ cup plain yogurt
2 tablespoons olive oil

2 tablespoons freshly snipped chives
Salt to taste
Freshly ground black pepper to taste

1. Rinse the trout under cold water and blot dry. Remove any remaining bones with tweezers. Generously season with salt and pepper.

2. For the stuffing, remove the stems of the spinach, pat dry and cut into chiffonade. Pour the oil into a large skillet and heat. Add the chopped onions, cover and let sweat over gentle heat for 1 minute. Add the spinach, raise the heat to high, add mushrooms and sweat for 1 minute. Remove lid and cook down liquid. Stir in the prunes and cook another minute. Transfer to a flat dish to cool. When cold, combine with the almonds and season to taste.

3. Turn on the broiler and place the rack about 5–6 inches from the flame. Stuff the trout with the spinach mixture, packing it well, and place the fish on lightly oiled foil on a cookie sheet or broiler pan. Broil for 4 minutes on each side. Turn off broiler and leave in trout 4 minutes longer.

4. Meanwhile, prepare the sauce. Put the yogurt in a

small bowl and whisk in the olive oil. Season well to taste, then add the chives. Pour into a gravy boat and pass at the table.

5. Before serving the trout, remove the top skin from each fish. Arrange on individual warmed serving plates with some steamed vegetables, such as new potatoes or broccoli florets.

Yield: 4 servings

—JOANNA PREUSS

GRILLED TROUT WITH CUCUMBER-TOMATO RELISH

dairy

ADAPTED FROM Home

1 large cucumber, seeded and diced
2 cups seeded, chopped tomatoes
¼ cup diced red onion
2 tablespoons fresh mint, cut into ribbons
½ teaspoon red pepper flakes
1 tablespoon lemon juice
Salt to taste
Freshly ground black pepper to taste
1 cup plain yogurt
1 tablespoon lemon juice
Grated zest of 1 lemon
1 teaspoon toasted cumin seeds
1 teaspoon toasted coriander seeds

4 whole brook trout, about 10 ounces each
Olive oil for basting trout

1. To make the cucumber-tomato relish, combine in a bowl the cucumber, tomatoes, onions, mint, red pepper flakes, lemon juice, salt and pepper. Keep cool until served.

2. To make the yogurt sauce, combine in a bowl the yogurt, lemon juice, lemon zest, cumin seeds, coriander seeds, salt and pepper. Keep cool until served.

3. Brush the trout with olive oil. Season with salt and pepper. Grill the trout over charcoal (or broil) for 4 minutes each side. Serve each trout with relish on the side and the yogurt sauce.

Yield: 4 servings

—BRYAN MILLER

NIKA HAZELTON'S SPANISH TROUT

pareve

ADAPTED FROM *The New York Times Menu Cook Book*

4 whole trout, cleaned
½ lemon
Salt to taste
Freshly ground black pepper to taste
2 tablespoons olive oil
½ cup soft fresh bread crumbs
1 garlic clove, minced
2 tablespoons finely chopped flat parsley
½ cup dry sherry

1. Preheat oven to 350 degrees.
2. Rub the trout with the lemon, then squeeze the

lemon and reserve the juice. Season the fish with salt and pepper.

3. Heat the oil over moderate heat. Remove it from the heat and stir in the bread crumbs, garlic and parsley. Sprinkle half of this mixture over the bottom of a greased shallow baking dish. Place the trout on top of the crumbs. Sprinkle the fish with the remaining bread-crumb mixture. Sprinkle with the reserved lemon juice.

4. Bake the fish for 10 minutes, then add sherry. Continue to bake for 10–15 minutes, basting occasionally with the sherry. When the fish is done, it should flake easily when tested with a fork.

Yield: 4 servings

UNION SQUARE CAFE'S MARINATED
FILET MIGNON OF TUNA

pareve

ADAPTED FROM *The Union Square Cafe Cookbook*

FOR THE MARINADE:

2 cups teriyaki sauce
½ cup dry sherry
4 tablespoons finely chopped ginger
½ cup chopped scallions
2 cloves garlic, peeled and thinly sliced
½ teaspoon cayenne
2 teaspoons freshly ground black pepper
Juice of 2 lemons

FOR THE TUNA:

4 yellowfin tuna steaks each weighing 8–10 ounces and each trimmed into a large cube
2 tablespoons olive oil
¼ cup pickled ginger

1. Combine all the marinade ingredients in a bowl and place the tuna steaks in it. Refrigerate for 3 hours, turning the tuna every hour.

2. About ½ hour before cooking, remove the tuna from the marinade to a plate and let it reach room temperature. Preheat a grill, barbecue or pan to very hot.

3. Brush the tuna steaks with olive oil. Grill for 1–2 minutes on each side. The outside should be well seared; the center should be just warm and very rare.

4. Garnish each tuna steak with pickled ginger and serve.

Yield: 4 servings

—BRYAN MILLER

MARIO BATALI'S TUNA AL TAROCCO

pareve

ADAPTED FROM Babbo

½ cup blood-orange juice

½ teaspoon Dijon mustard

1 tablespoon red wine vinegar

Kosher salt

½ cup plus 3 tablespoons extra-virgin olive oil

1 orange

2 scallions, thinly sliced

½ pound wild mushrooms (or a mixture of flavorful cultivated mushrooms), cut into ¼-inch slices

Freshly ground black pepper to taste

1 medium head radicchio, cut into 2-inch chunks and the leaves separated

2 tablespoons toasted pine nuts

½ cup chopped fennel fronds, or a mixture of parsley and mint leaves

4 tuna steaks, 6–8 ounces each

1. First make the vinaigrette. In a small pan over high heat, bring the blood-orange juice to a boil and reduce by half. Remove from the heat and allow to cool.

2. In a small mixing bowl, combine the reduced orange juice, mustard, vinegar and salt to taste. Whisk to blend, and slowly whisk in ½ cup of the olive oil until emulsified. Set aside. Grate and reserve the zest from the orange. Cut any remaining peel and pith from the orange. Over a bowl, cut the orange into segments, reserving the segments and juices released into the bowl.

3. In a 10- to 12-inch sauté pan over high heat, heat 1 tablespoon olive oil and add the scallions. Sauté until the scallions are softened, 30–45 seconds. Add the mushrooms and season with salt and pepper to taste. Sauté until the mushrooms are softened, 2–3 minutes. Add the radicchio, orange segments and any juice. Toss to wilt, 30–45 seconds. Transfer to a platter and keep warm.

4. In a small bowl, combine the orange zest, pine nuts and fennel fronds; set aside. In a 12-inch sauté pan over high heat, heat the remaining 2 tablespoons olive oil until smoking. Season the tuna steaks with salt and pepper to taste. and add to the pan. Sauté for 4–5 minutes, then turn the steaks and sauté for another 2–3 minutes, for medium-rare. Transfer to the serving platter, laying the steaks on top of the radicchio mixture. Sprinkle the blood-orange vinaigrette over the steaks and top with the orange zest mixture. Serve immediately.

Yield: 4 servings

—AMANDA HESSER

BROILED TUNA STEAKS WITH RED-ONION COMPOTE

pareve

FOR THE FISH:

4 center-cut tuna steaks, about 6 ounces each
Salt to taste
4 tablespoons olive oil
4 sprigs fresh thyme or 1 teaspoon dried
1/4 teaspoon red pepper flakes
2 teaspoons coarsely cracked black peppercorns
2 tablespoons chopped fresh basil

1. Preheat a charcoal grill or broiler.
2. Place the tuna steaks on a flat surface and cut out the dark streak of meat, if any. Brush with olive oil on both sides and sprinkle with salt, thyme and pepper flakes. Cover with plastic wrap and let stand for 15 minutes before broiling.
3. Meanwhile, prepare Red-Onion Compote.
4. Sprinkle the tuna on both sides with the cracked peppercorns.
5. If you are using a grill, rub the rack lightly with oil. Place the fish on the grill. If you are using a broiler, place the fish on a rack about 4 inches from the heat. Cook for 3 minutes, and turn. For rare, cook for another 3 minutes or to desired doneness.
6. To serve, place equal portions of onion compote on the side of 4 warmed plates. Place a tuna steak on each plate and sprinkle with basil.

Yield: 4 servings

◆ **RED-ONION COMPOTE** ◆

pareve

Remaining olive oil (*see recipe*)
4 red onions, about 1 1/4 pounds, peeled and thinly sliced
2 tablespoons red wine vinegar
1 whole clove
1/4 teaspoon Tabasco sauce
Salt to taste
2 tablespoons drained capers
2 tablespoons honey

1. Heat the remaining olive oil in a heavy casserole and add the onions. Cover. Cook over medium-high heat for 15 minutes, stirring occasionally.
2. When the onions start to brown, uncover and add the vinegar, clove and Tabasco. Add salt to taste. Cook briefly, stirring, until the vinegar has almost evaporated.
3. Stir in the capers and honey. Cover tightly and simmer for 15 minutes more.

Yield: 2 cups

NOTE: *This compote is also a tasty accompaniment for grilled or roasted meats.*

— PIERRE FRANEY

WHITEFISH WITH
BREAD-MUSHROOM STUFFING

dairy

ADAPTED FROM *The New York Times Heritage Cookbook*

2 pounds whitefish fillets
Salt to taste
Freshly ground black pepper to taste
2 cups soft bread crumbs
1/3 cup melted butter
2 tablespoons parsley, chopped
1/2 teaspoon dried thyme
1/2 teaspoon grated lemon rind
1 tablespoon onion, finely grated
1/4 cup celery, finely chopped
1/3 cup finely chopped mushrooms
Lemon wedges

1. Preheat oven to 350 degrees.
2. Place half the fillets in a single layer in a shallow baking dish. Season with salt and pepper to taste.
3. Mix together the bread crumbs, butter, parsley, lemon rind, onion, celery and mushrooms. Season with salt and pepper. Spread over the fillets in the dish.
4. Top with remaining fillets and bake about 25 minutes, or until fish flakes easily. Serve with lemon wedges.

Yield: 4–6 servings

FRIED WHITINGS

pareve

3 pounds whitings, preferably large fish
Coarse salt
1/2 teaspoon white pepper
1/2 teaspoon powdered cinnamon
1 cup flour
2 or 3 eggs, beaten with 2–3 teaspoons cold water
2 cups fine, dry breadcrumbs
1 tablespoon sweet paprika
Corn oil for frying
1 bunch fresh dill
Lemons, cut in quarters for garnish

1. Rinse fish, remove heads and cut in 2-inch-thick slices. Place in bowl, sprinkle lightly with salt and chill in refrigerator for 1–2 hours. Remove, rinse lightly and dry thoroughly with paper towels.
2. Add white pepper and cinnamon to flour and blend well. Place on a sheet of waxed paper. Beat eggs in a wide flat bowl with water. Combine breadcrumbs with paprika, blend well and place on a another sheet of waxed paper.
3. Dredge each piece of fish lightly in flour. Dip in beaten egg and let excess drip off. Dredge well with breadcrumbs. Place breaded fish slices on a rack and let dry at room temperature for 20–30 minutes.

4. Using a deep skillet, preferably black iron, heat a 1½-inch depth of corn oil to 365 degrees. Fry fish in a single layer at a time; avoid overcrowding in the pan. When first side is golden brown, turn and brown second side. Total frying time should be about 10 minutes. Drain fried pieces on paper towels.

5. Arrange dill branches in a single layer on as many platters as you will need to hold fish. Place hot, drained fish slices on a dill and strew a few branches of dill over top of fish. Let stand 1–2 hours before serving. Garnish with lemon quarters.

Yield: 2–4 servings

NOTE: *Flounder or fluke, cut in slices 1½–2 inches thick, can be fried in the same way.*

—MIMI SHERATON

POACHED WHITING · (MERLUZZO IN BIANCO)

pareve

> 3 pounds whitings, preferably large fish
> Water
> Salt
> Juice of ½ lemon
> ½–¾ cup light Italian olive oil
> Freshly ground black pepper
> About 4 cloves garlic, sliced thin
> ½–⅔ cup finely minced Italian parsley

1. Fish may be poached whole or in large pieces. If anyone likes to pick meat out of the heads, cook with heads; otherwise discard before cooking. Place fish in saucepan or deep skillet and barely cover with water, adding ½ teaspoon salt. Bring to a boil, cover and simmer gently for 8–10 minutes, or until meat flakes when tested with a fork. Do not overcook to a point where fish falls apart.

2. Remove fish with a slotted spoon and drain. As soon as it is cool enough to handle, scrape off skin and lift fish off bones in the largest possible chunks. Try to remove all bones if possible. Place chunks of fish on a platter. Sprinkle with pepper, scatter garlic on top and drizzle with oil. Top with parsley. Let stand at room temperature 2–3 hours before serving. Spoon olive oil over fish once or twice while marinating. Serve at room temperature, either as a first course or an entrée.

Yield: 3–4 servings

NOTE: *This is best if it stands at room temperature for 2–3 hours. If you are preparing the fish ahead of time, refrigerate it and remove it from refrigerator 30 minutes before serving.*

—MIMI SHERATON

POULTRY

If not a chicken in every pot, then try a duck, a goose, a turkey, Cornish hens, quail or the much-loved squab. All of these birds are regarded as special-occasion treats, and in Eastern European cooking, Jewish or otherwise, several are valued for their flavorful schmaltz— rendered fat that is used in other cooking. Even if one generally substitutes more healthful vegetable oils, it's a good idea, at least occasionally, to combine it with a small amount of rendered chicken, duck, or goose fat to enrich the flavor of certain dishes, especially those made with potatoes or members of the cabbage family, such as sauerkraut.

Commonplace in Jewish neighborhoods about fifty years ago, live poultry markets have virtually disappeared. Observant housewives would inspect the live birds, blowing on breast feathers to reveal the color of the skin underneath, thereby determining the fat content; then they checked feet and beaks to determine age and tenderness. After the proper ritual slaughter by the *schochet*, feathers were plucked and the bird was taken home to be koshered with salt and soaking and kept in the refrigerator overnight so rigor mortis would subside and the flesh would not be tough.

Duck and goose, so popular with all groups in Eastern Europe, are roasted or braised to lean succulence, always with plenty of salt and pepper, and possibly with garlic, onions, thyme or sage, and garnishes that might range from sour cherries to caraway seeds or apples. Squab, the most prized and costly of the birds, is reserved for major events like weddings, and along with the newer Cornish hens, is convenient for entertaining because the tiny birds cook quickly and require no carving, one bird being a perfect portion.

For sheer versatility, no meat compares to chicken, as the recipes that follow prove. This ecumenical bird tastes as fine atop Moroccan couscous or tagine with olives and preserved lemons, as with a Yemenite fruit stuffing, an Indian curry sauce, a Chinese sesame chicken with garlic sauce, or as the Ashkenazic chicken fricassee with tiny meatballs, all mellowed with onions and paprika.

SIMPLE ROAST CHICKEN

meat

1 (4- to 5-pound) chicken

1 teaspoon dried thyme

2 whole garlic cloves, peeled

1 bay leaf, crumbled

2 onions, peeled and cut in half

2 tomatoes, cut into quarters

4 ounces margarine, cut into small pieces

Salt to taste

Freshly ground black pepper to taste

4 potatoes, peeled and cut in two

1. Preheat oven to 400 degrees.

2. Stuff the cavity of the chicken with the thyme, garlic and bay leaf. Do not truss the chicken. Place the chicken in a Pyrex baking dish, breast side up. Distribute onions, tomatoes and margarine around and on top of the chicken. Add salt and freshly ground black pepper to taste.

3. Roast the chicken for 45 minutes or so, basting every now and then.

4. Turn the bird breast side down. Add the potatoes and mix well with the juices in the pan. Add more margarine—1 or 2 ounces, if necessary. Lower the heat to 350 degrees. Cook another 45 minutes, basting occasionally. Serve. The skin should be very, very crisp. The chicken may be garnished with the potatoes.

Yield: 4 servings

—NANCY HARMON JENKINS

ROAST CHICKEN BRUSHED WITH HONEY AND CUMIN

meat

ADAPTED FROM *The Foods and Wines of Spain*

¼ cup olive oil

1½ tablespoons sherry vinegar

2 teaspoons ground cumin

2 cloves garlic, crushed

2 tablespoons honey

1 teaspoon salt, or to taste

1 chicken, 3–3½ pounds, trussed

1. Mix the oil, vinegar, cumin, garlic, honey and salt together in a small bowl.

2. Place the chicken in a shallow bowl and brush with the mixture. Marinate at least 2 hours in the refrigerator, rebrushing with the mixture from time to time.

3. Preheat oven to 350 degrees.

4. Roast the chicken on a rack in a roasting pan or, if available, on a spit, until it is done, about 1 hour. Continue brushing the chicken with the marinade as it roasts.

Yield: 4 servings

—FLORENCE FABRICANT

ROAST CHICKEN
WITH LEMON AND ROSEMARY

meat

1 (4-pound) chicken
Half a lemon
2 tablespoons rosemary leaves
Coarse sea salt to taste
Freshly ground pepper to taste
2–3 tablespoons olive oil
¾ cup dry white wine

1. Preheat the oven to 375 degrees. Wipe the chicken dry with paper towels. Squeeze the juice of the lemon all over and inside the chicken. Season the cavity with salt and pepper and put the squeezed lemon half inside. Using your fingers, lift up the breast skin and put rosemary leaves under it on both sides of the chicken.

2. Truss the chicken and put it on a rack on a roasting pan. Sprinkle the skin with olive oil. Roast for about an hour, or until the juices run clear.

3. Put the chicken on a serving dish and keep warm in the turned-off oven. Pour the fat off the cooking juices. Deglaze them with the white wine and season to taste with salt and pepper. Pour the juices over the chicken, garnish with rosemary sprigs and serve. Spoon a little of the sauce onto each portion of carved meat.

Yield: 4 servings

—MOIRA HODGSON

ROAST CHICKEN WITH GREEN OLIVES AND CILANTRO

meat

ADAPTED FROM JO JO

2 tablespoons plus 1 teaspoon extra-virgin
   olive oil
¼ cup minced onion
2 teaspoons minced ginger
2-inch piece cinnamon stick
Pinch saffron or ½ teaspoon turmeric
Kosher salt to taste
2 cups rich chicken stock
2 tablespoons peanut oil
1 (3- to 4-pound) chicken, cut into 4 pieces
Freshly ground black pepper to taste

2 tablespoons minced green olives
2 teaspoons lemon juice
1 tablespoon coarsely chopped cilantro

1. Heat oven to 500 degrees. Place 2 tablespoons olive oil in a small saucepan over medium heat. Add the onion, ginger, cinnamon, saffron and a pinch of salt and cook, stirring occasionally, for about 5 minutes. Add the stock and increase the heat to high. Cook, stirring occasionally, while you prepare the chicken. When the liquid has reduced by about three-quarters and become syrupy, turn off the heat.

2. Heat peanut oil in a large, ovenproof skillet, preferably nonstick, over medium-high heat for a minute or two. Season chicken on both sides with salt and pepper. Place it in the skillet, skin side down, and cook undisturbed until lightly browned, 5–8 minutes. Turn it over and cook the other side for about 2 minutes. Turn it over, skin side down again, and place the skillet in the oven. Check chicken after 15 minutes, and remove pieces as they are cooked through. (Breasts will finish cooking before legs; keep them warm.)

3. To finish the sauce, whisk in the remaining teaspoon olive oil and olives and season to taste with salt and pepper. Cook about 2 minutes over medium-high heat, stirring once or twice. Turn off the heat and add the lemon juice and cilantro. Remove the cinnamon stick.

4. To serve, arrange chicken on 4 plates. Spoon sauce around it, not over it, so that the chicken stays crunchy.

Yield: 4 servings

—AMANDA HESSER

ROAST CHICKEN WITH
POMEGRANATE GLAZE AND FRESH MINT

meat

> 1 bunch (1 ounce) fresh mint
> 1 (5- to 6-pound) chicken, excess fat trimmed; wing
>   tips, neck and giblets reserved for stock
> 2–3 teaspoons kosher salt
> Freshly ground black pepper to taste
> 4 whole cloves garlic, unpeeled
> Seeds from 1 large or 2 small pomegranates
>   (1½ cups) (see Note, page 583)
> Juice from 1 large or 2 small ripe pomegranates
>   (½ cup) (see Note, page 583)
> ½ cup Chicken Stock (page 48)

1. Place rack on second level from bottom of oven. Preheat oven to 500 degrees. Remove leaves from half the mint, reserving stems. Stack the leaves, roll and cut them across into thin strips and set aside.

2. Place the chicken, breast side up, in a 12-by-8-by-1½-inch heavy roasting pan. Sprinkle chicken cavity with some of the salt and pepper and stuff it with garlic, ½ cup pomegranate seeds, the reserved mint stems and the remaining half bunch of mint with leaves attached. Pour ¼ cup pomegranate juice over chicken. Sprinkle with 1 teaspoon salt.

3. Place chicken in oven, legs first. Roast for 50 minutes. Move chicken once after the first 10 minutes with wooden spatula to keep it from sticking. The chicken should not burn. (If chicken smells as if it is burning, reduce heat to 400 degrees and open oven door for a minute to lower the temperature quickly. Continue roasting at lower temperature.)

4. The chicken will be a beautiful mahogany brown. Tilt chicken over pan to drain juices and then remove chicken to a platter.

5. Tilt roasting pan and spoon out fat, leaving any juices. Place pan over medium-high heat. Pour in chicken stock and remaining ¼ cup pomegranate juice. Bring liquid to a boil, scraping up any browned bits from bottom of pan with a wooden spoon. Stir in remaining mint leaves. Lower heat and simmer for 1 minute. Season with salt and pepper. Add any juices that have collected on the platter. Simmer for 30 seconds.

6. Pour about half the pan juices over the bird, taking care that the platter does not overflow. Top with a few remaining seeds. Combine the rest of the juices into a sauce boat with remaining seeds and serve with chicken.

Yield: 3–4 servings

—BARBARA KAFKA

ROAST CHICKEN WITH SPICED APPLES AND ONIONS

meat

ADAPTED FROM Aquavit

1 (3½-pound) chicken
1 medium sweet potato, cut into ½-inch cubes
1 onion, cut into ½-inch cubes
2 Granny Smith apples, peeled, cored and cut into
    ½-inch cubes
2 shallots, cut into ½-inch pieces
1 clove garlic, chopped
Leaves from 2 sprigs fresh thyme
Leaves from 2 sprigs fresh mint, chopped
1 tablespoon olive oil
½ teaspoon ground cinnamon
2 cardamom pods or ¼ teaspoon ground cardamom
2 whole star anise
2 whole cloves or ⅛ teaspoon ground cloves
4 white peppercorns
2 black peppercorns
Kosher salt to taste

1. Preheat oven to 350 degrees. Rinse chicken with cool water and pat dry with paper towels. Fill a medium saucepan half full of water and bring to a boil. Add cubed sweet potato and blanch 2 minutes. Drain, rinse with cold water and drain again. In a mixing bowl, combine blanched sweet potato, onion, apples, shallots and garlic. Add thyme and chopped mint leaves. In a small bowl combine olive oil with 2 tablespoons water and add to vegetable mixture.

2. Using a mortar and pestle, or with the base of a heavy pot on a cutting board, lightly crush together the cinnamon, cardamom, star anise, cloves, white peppercorns and black peppercorns, along with salt to taste. Add half the spice mixture to the vegetables and reserve the rest.

3. Place chicken on a rack in a medium roasting pan. Lightly stuff the cavity with half the vegetable mixture, placing the rest in the bottom of the pan. Truss bird with kitchen string and rub with remaining spices.

4. Place pan in oven and roast about 1½ hours, or until the internal temperature of the meat reaches 160 degrees. Check pan occasionally, adding a bit of water if it becomes completely dry. When vegetables in base of pan are tender, remove and reserve.

5. When chicken is cooked, remove vegetables from cavity and add to the reserved pan vegetables. Carve chicken, cover securely and keep warm. Add enough water to pan juices to make 1 cup, stirring well to deglaze the pan.

Yield: 4 servings

—MARCUS SAMUELSSON

ARGENTINE ROAST CHICKEN WITH VEGETABLES AND CHIMICHURRI SAUCE

meat

ADAPTED FROM Naomi Sisson, in
The Foods of Israel Today

¼ cup vinegar

1 tablespoon ground cumin

1 teaspoon sweet paprika

¼ teaspoon hot pepper flakes

1 head garlic, cloves peeled and crushed

2 teaspoons chopped fresh oregano

½ cup vegetable or olive oil

Salt to taste

Freshly ground black pepper to taste

1 (3-pound) roasting chicken, cut up

2 large bell peppers, diced

3 large tomatoes, sliced

5 large potatoes, peeled and each cut into 6 large chunks

1. Combine vinegar, cumin, paprika, hot pepper flakes, crushed garlic and oregano in a small bowl. Whisk in oil. Season to taste with salt and pepper. Pour sauce over chicken, rubbing skin well. Cover with plastic wrap and refrigerate overnight.

2. When ready to roast, preheat oven to 400 degrees. Grease a large baking pan. Add peppers, then tomatoes. Place chicken, skin side down, on top, pouring half the marinade over. Scatter potatoes around chicken.

3. Roast 20 minutes, then turn chicken pieces over and continue roasting until the chicken is crispy on top, about 30 minutes more.

Yield: 6 servings

—JOAN NATHAN

CZECH STUFFED CHICKEN

meat

ADAPTED FROM Hana Lustigova Greenfield, in
The Foods of Israel Today

½ loaf challah or other soft white bread
   (about 8 ounces)

1 medium onion, diced (1 cup)

2 tablespoons vegetable oil

1 (6-pound) roasting chicken with its liver
   koshered (see Note, page 582)

½ cup mushrooms, finely chopped

¼ cup parsley, finely chopped

¼ teaspoon dried oregano

Salt to taste

Freshly ground pepper to taste

¼ cup pine nuts, roasted, or ¼ cup chopped
   walnuts

1 Granny Smith or other tart apple, peeled and chopped

Juice of 3 oranges (about 1 cup)

1. Preheat oven to 350 degrees.

2. Soak the bread briefly in lukewarm water and squeeze until dry.

3. Sauté the onion in the oil until soft.

4. Dice the liver and add to the onions along with the mushrooms, parsley, oregano, and salt and pepper to taste. Sauté until the mushrooms are soft. Add the bread, pine nuts or walnuts and apples and mix well. Let cool.

5. Stuff filling into the neck and cavity of the chicken; sew or truss closed. Lightly sprinkle outside of the chicken with salt.

6. Place in a roasting pan and bake for 1½ hours, or until the chicken is almost completely cooked. Pour the orange juice over the chicken and continue cooking for another ½ hour or until done.

Yield: 8 servings

NOTE: *Traditionally, Czech Jews made this with duck or goose.*

—JOAN NATHAN

YEMENITE CHICKEN WITH SUMAC-FLAVORED FRUIT STUFFING

meat

ADAPTED FROM *The Yemenite Cookbook*

1 tablespoon vegetable oil
½ cup uncooked rice
1 cup boiling water
Salt to taste
6 dried figs, chopped small
½ cup coarsely chopped walnut halves
½ cup coarsely chopped almonds
½ cup raisins
2 teaspoons powdered sumac (see Glossary, page 586)
1 teaspoon salt
Freshly ground black pepper to taste
1 chicken, 5–6 pounds
2 tablespoons margarine at room temperature
2 cups orange juice, approximately

1. Preheat oven to 350 degrees.

2. In a small saucepan heat the oil. Pour in rice and cook over low heat, stirring, until golden. Pour in 1 cup boiling water and salt to taste. Cover pan and simmer until all water is absorbed.

3. When rice is cooked, remove from heat and mix with figs, walnuts, almonds, raisins, sumac, 1 teaspoon salt and pepper. Let cool.

4. Sprinkle chicken with salt and pepper. Stuff chicken with the fruit mixture and truss. Rub chicken with the margarine and place in a roasting pan. Put any leftover stuffing around chicken and pour 2 cups orange juice over.

5. Bake 1½ hours, basting every 20 minutes and adding orange juice if necessary.

Yield: 8 servings

NOTE: *Sumac imparts a subtle and delicate tang to the stuffing.*

—JOAN NATHAN

RICE STUFFING FOR CHICKEN

meat

ADAPTED FROM *The New York Times Menu Cook Book*

1 cup uncooked rice

2 cups Chicken Broth (page 48), fresh or canned

Salt to taste

1 bay leaf

3 tablespoons margarine

½ cup finely chopped onion

½ cup finely chopped celery

¼ cup finely chopped green pepper

1–2 cloves garlic, finely minced

1 chicken liver, koshered and coarsely chopped
 (see Note, page 582)

3 tablespoons finely chopped parsley

1. Combine the rice, broth, salt and bay leaf. Bring to a boil, cover and simmer exactly 20 minutes. Let cool slightly.

2. Heat the margarine and cook the onion, celery, green pepper and garlic in it until onion is wilted. Add the liver and cook, stirring, until thoroughly browned. Stir the liver mixture and parsley into the rice.

Yield: Enough for a 3- to 4-pound chicken

CHICKEN IN THE POT

meat

1 (3½-pound) chicken cut in half

Water

1 large onion, trimmed of roots but left unpeeled

1 large carrot, scraped

1 stalk celery with leaves

1 sprig parsley and 1 sprig dill, tied together

2 cloves garlic, peeled and crushed

Salt to taste

¼ pound narrow egg noodles

1 tablespoon finely minced parsley

1. Pull off as much of the yellow fat as possible from the chicken. Place chicken halves in a 5- to 6-quart pot along with the gizzard, neck and heart. Reserve the liver for another purpose. Cover with cold water, bring to a boil and allow to boil for 5 minutes, skimming off all the foam and scum that accumulates on the surface.

2. Lower heat to simmer and add the vegetables, herbs and garlic. Stir in salt to taste—you may need as much as 1 tablespoon.

3. Simmer gently for 1 hour 15 minutes, until the chicken is done. At no time should the liquid boil, which would cause the finished soup to be cloudy.

4. When the chicken is done, remove it from the pot and set it aside, covered, to keep warm. Strain the soup through a fine strainer or through a clean linen napkin set into a strainer. Rinse out the soup pot and return the soup to the pot. The soup should be clear, golden and with very little fat on the surface. Chilling it overnight will allow all the fat to be removed, if you wish.

5. Finally, dice the carrot, half the onion without the peel and half of the celery. Discard the rest of the vegetables and herbs.

6. Boil the noodles in a separate pot of water until tender, then set aside, covered, to keep warm.

7. Remove the skin from the chicken and cut the chicken into serving pieces.

8. To serve, reheat the soup to a simmer and return the chicken to the pot. Simmer for 5 minutes. Place a couple of pieces of chicken in each of 4 deep bowls along with some of the noodles and diced vegetables. Ladle hot soup over each serving. Sprinkle with minced parsley and serve.

Yield: 4 servings

—FLORENCE FABRICANT

MIRAVAL'S CHICKEN IN A PUMPKIN "POT"

meat

1 small pumpkin (or 4 acorn squashes)
Olive-oil spray
1 clove garlic, peeled and cut in half
8 cups vegetable broth or Chicken Broth (page 48)
2 teaspoons kosher salt
2 teaspoons freshly ground black pepper
2 skinless chicken breasts, cut into rounds that will fit neatly into the bottom of the pumpkin
1 cup cooked couscous
1 cup diced zucchini
1 cup diced carrots
1 cup mushrooms, quartered
½ cup diced turnip
16 green beans, cut into 1-inch lengths
15 asparagus, cut into 1-inch pieces
1 tablespoon chopped fresh oregano
2 tablespoons chopped fresh basil

1. Preheat the oven to 450 degrees. Cut the base of the pumpkin so that it will sit steadily. Cut off the top to create a lid and set aside. Scrape out the pulp and seeds. Spray the cavity with olive oil and rub it with the garlic. Place the lid back on the pumpkin, wrap in aluminum foil and bake on a sheet for 20 minutes.

2. Meanwhile, season the vegetable or chicken broth with salt and pepper and warm. Remove the pumpkin from the oven and when cool enough to handle, gently peel back the foil on top and remove the lid. Place a layer of chicken in the bottom of the pumpkin. Top with the steamed couscous.

3. Combine all the vegetables, stir in the oregano and basil and divide the mixture evenly over the chicken. Ladle the broth into the pumpkin, replace the lid, rewrap with the foil and bake for 20 more minutes. Serve immediately.

Yield: 4 servings

—MOLLY O'NEILL

GARLIC CHICKEN IN A POT

meat

ADAPTED FROM Antoine Westermann

½ salt-preserved lemon (page 429), rinsed well

¼ cup sugar

⅓ cup olive oil

16 small peeled potatoes (white or sweet) or 2 large
  peeled potatoes, each cut into 8 pieces

16 small onions or shallots, peeled and trimmed

8 carrots, peeled and quartered

4 stalks celery, trimmed and quartered

4 heads garlic, cloves separated but not peeled

Salt to taste

Freshly ground pepper to taste

3 sprigs fresh thyme

3 sprigs Italian parsley

2 sprigs rosemary

1 chicken, whole or cut up

1 cup Chicken Broth (page 48)

½ cup white wine

About 1½ cups flour

1. Preheat oven to 450 degrees. Remove zest from preserved lemon and cut zest into small squares; save pulp for another use. Bring 1 cup water and the sugar to a boil, drop in zest and cook 1 minute; drain and set aside.

2. Heat 2 tablespoons olive oil in a large skillet over high heat. Add vegetables and garlic, season with salt and pepper and sauté until brown on all sides. (If necessary, do this in 2 batches.) Spoon vegetables into a 4½- to 5-quart lidded Dutch oven and stir in herbs and lemon zest.

3. Return skillet to heat, add another tablespoon of oil and brown chicken on all sides, seasoning it with salt and pepper as it cooks. Tuck chicken into casserole, surrounding it with vegetables. Mix together the broth, wine and remaining olive oil and pour it over chicken and vegetables.

4. Mix flour with enough hot water (about ¾ cup) to make a malleable dough. On a floured surface, work dough into a sausage; place dough on rim of casserole. Press lid onto dough to seal casserole. Bake 55 minutes. To break seal, work the point of a screwdriver between pot and lid. If chicken is whole, quarter it. Chicken may be served in the pot or arranged with vegetables on a serving platter.

Yield: 4 servings

—DORIE GREENSPAN

Cooked 4/09 Pesach

MIMI SHERATON'S
CHICKEN FRICASSEE WITH MEATBALLS

meat

ADAPTED FROM *From My Mother's Kitchen*

FOR THE MEATBALLS:

1 pound chopped lean beef
2 small eggs
1 clove garlic, crushed, or 4 teaspoons grated onion
1–2 teaspoons salt (adjust to taste)
½ teaspoon black pepper (adjust to taste)
2 tablespoons fine, dry bread crumbs, as needed

1. Mix the chopped beef with the egg, crushed garlic (or grated onion), salt and black pepper (or adjust to taste).

2. Add just enough bread crumbs to make the mixture firm enough to mold into balls.

3. Toss the ingredients lightly with a fork or the mixture will become too compacted and the meatballs will be hard. Shape into tiny meatballs, each about the size of a hazelnut.

4. Set aside until Step 5 in the recipe below.

FOR THE CHICKEN:

1 broiling or frying chicken (3–3½ pounds), cut into pieces (see Note below) with all giblets except liver
4–5 tablespoons margarine or Schmaltz (page 413), in that order of preference
2 medium onions, peeled and finely chopped
Salt and black pepper to taste
1 tablespoon sweet paprika
1 small (individual size) can tomato juice (see Note below)
1–2 cups water, as needed
2 cloves garlic, peeled

1. Prepare the meatballs.

2. In a 2½-quart Dutch oven, slowly sauté the chopped onion in 3 tablespoons of the fat until the onion is soft and yellow; do not let it brown. Remove and reserve. Add more fat to the pot if needed and brown the chicken pieces lightly until all sides are pale golden brown. Do this in several batches, as the chicken will not brown if crammed into the pan. Remove the chicken, sprinkle with salt and pepper and reserve.

3. Return the onions to the pot and sprinkle with paprika. Sauté for a minute or two, until the paprika loses its raw smell. Add the tomato juice and 1 cup water.

4. Return the chicken to the pot and add the garlic cloves. The liquid should come about halfway up the chicken. Cover and simmer gently but steadily for 10 minutes.

5. Gently and carefully add the meatballs to the pot, moving the chicken aside to make room and shaking the pot intermittently to separate the meatballs. These will be fragile while raw, but once cooked they will become firm and will not crumble or stick together.

6. Add more liquid to the pot if needed. Simmer, loosely covered, for another 20–30 minutes, or until the chicken and meatballs are done. Remove the chicken and meatballs and skim the fat from the gravy.

7. Return the chicken and meatballs and reheat, checking the seasoning as you do so. Serve the chicken and meatballs with rice or noodles. If you plan to make this in advance, add a little water before reheating.

Yield: 4 servings

NOTE: *The chicken should be cut and disjointed into 8 pieces. The breast and thighs can also be cut in half again, if you prefer small pieces. If you prefer, water or chicken stock may be substituted for the tomato juice. Strangely, the* *flavor is more intense and interesting when water is used, with or without tomato juice.*

—MIMI SHERATON

CIRCASSIAN CHICKEN
WITH WALNUT SAUCE

meat

ADAPTED FROM *The New York Times Menu Cook Book*

1 roasting chicken (4–5 pounds)
1 onion, peeled
1 carrot, scraped
1 celery stalk with leaves
3 parsley sprigs
½ bay leaf
Salt
12 peppercorns
3 quarts water
2 cups walnut halves
3 slices of day-old white bread,
  with crusts trimmed
1–2 tablespoons paprika
Cayenne pepper

1. Place the chicken in a large kettle and add the onion, carrot, celery, parsley, bay leaf, salt to taste, peppercorns and water. Bring to a boil and simmer for 1–1½ hours, or until chicken is tender.
2. Remove the chicken, bring the stock to a boil and

cook over high heat until it is reduced by half. Strain the stock and let it cool to lukewarm.
3. Place walnuts in food processor or blender and grind fine. Soak the bread with a little chicken stock, then squeeze it dry. Add the bread to the walnuts. Add the paprika and cayenne to taste and process with walnuts until mixture forms a smooth paste. Place in a mixing bowl.
4. Beat the mixture well with a wire whisk, adding the lukewarm chicken stock gradually. Add 2 cups or more, until the mixture has the consistency of thin mayonnaise.
5. Remove chicken meat from the skin and bones. Cut meat into bite-size pieces and mix with a little of the walnut sauce. Place the chicken in a serving dish and cover it evenly with the remaining sauce. Sprinkle with paprika and serve.

Yield: 6 servings

NOTE: *For a variation, cut cooled chicken into slices and spread with the walnut paste. Wrap and chill. When ready to serve, arrange chicken on serving dish and garnish with ¼ cup chopped parsley.*

CHICKEN IN POMEGRANATE-WALNUT
SAUCE • (FESENJAN)

meat

ADAPTED FROM *The New York Times Large-Type Cookbook*

5 whole chicken breasts

1 stalk celery

½ teaspoon dried thyme

2 sprigs flat-leafed parsley

1 bay leaf

5 tablespoons pareve unsalted margarine

2 large onions, chopped

3 tablespoons tomato sauce

3 cups finely ground walnuts

2½ cups water

3 tablespoons fresh lemon juice

1 teaspoon salt

1 teaspoon cinnamon

¾ cup pomegranate juice (see Note, page 583)

⅓ cup sugar

1. Place the chicken breasts in a large skillet and barely cover with water. Sprinkle the center of the celery stalk with thyme; tie it in cheesecloth with the parsley and bay leaf and add to the skillet. Simmer the chicken over medium heat until tender, about 10 minutes. Cool.

2. Bone the chicken, discard the skin, and divide each breast into 5–8 pieces.

3. Heat the margarine in a large saucepan over medium heat. Sauté the onions until golden. Add the tomato sauce and cook for 5 minutes. Add the walnuts, lower the heat and cook very slowly 5 minutes or longer, stirring continuously to avoid sticking. Add the remaining ingredients and stir until well mixed. Cover and simmer for 40 minutes. Add more sugar or salt to taste.

4. Add the chicken to the sauce and cook slowly for 20 minutes. When ready to serve, place the chicken on a serving dish and pour the sauce over it.

Yield: 10 servings

CHICKEN BREASTS
WITH FRESH FIGS

meat

1½ pounds skinless and boneless chicken breasts

3 tablespoons flour

1½ tablespoons extra-virgin olive oil

½ cup dry Marsala wine

6 fresh green Calimyrna figs, sliced

Juice of ½ lemon

Salt and freshly ground black pepper to taste

½ tablespoon finely shredded basil leaves

1. Cut the chicken into about 12 pieces of uniform size. Dry them and toss them in the flour.

2. Heat the oil in a large skillet and cook the chicken over medium heat until it is lightly browned and cooked through, about 12 minutes. Remove the chicken from the pan.

3. Stir in the Marsala, bring it to a simmer and add the figs. Heat the figs briefly, then stir in the lemon juice and season the sauce with salt and pepper. Return the chicken to the pan, stir gently to mix the ingredients and serve. Sprinkle each serving with some basil.

Yield: 4 servings

—FLORENCE FABRICANT

PERSIAN-FLAVORED ROAST CHICKEN BREASTS

meat

¼ cup toasted sesame seeds
¼ cup ground toasted almonds
2 tablespoons ground cumin
2 tablespoons ground coriander
3 tablespoons ground sumac (see Glossary, page 586)
¼ cup fresh oregano (or 2 tablespoons dried)
4 chicken breasts, bone in, each 12–14 ounces
Salt and freshly ground black pepper to taste

1. Preheat oven to 425 degrees.
2. In a small bowl, combine sesame seeds, almonds, cumin, coriander, sumac and oregano and mix well.
3. Sprinkle chicken with salt and pepper to taste, and rub generously with spice rub. Place in a baking dish, skin side up; roast for 30–40 minutes, or until flesh is completely opaque and juices run clear when a fork is plunged into chicken at thickest part. Serve with Pomegranate-Eggplant Relish (below).

Yield: 4 servings

◆ **POMEGRANATE-EGGPLANT RELISH** ◆

pareve

⅓ cup olive oil
1 medium eggplant, diced medium

1 medium red onion, diced small
2 tablespoons minced garlic
1 cup tomato juice
⅓ cup pomegranate molasses (see Note, page 583)
Salt and freshly ground black pepper to taste
¼ cup roughly chopped fresh mint
Seeds from 1 pomegranate (see Note, page 583)

1. In a large sauté pan, heat oil over high heat until hot but not smoking. Add eggplant and cook, stirring, until well seared and quite soft, about 5–7 minutes.
2. Reduce heat to medium, add onion and cook, stirring, for 2–3 minutes. Add garlic and cook, stirring, for 1 minute.
3. Add tomato juice and pomegranate molasses, bring just to a boil, reduce heat to low and simmer, stirring occasionally, for 5 minutes.
4. Remove from heat. Season with salt and pepper to taste, stir in the mint and pomegranate seeds and serve hot or cold. This relish will keep, covered and refrigerated, for about 6 days.

Yield: About 4 cups

—JOHN WILLOUGHBY AND
CHRIS SCHLESINGER

GRILLED SUMAC CHICKEN

meat

1 medium chicken, quartered, or 3 pounds mixed
    thighs and breasts

1 onion, peeled and minced

3 cloves garlic, crushed

⅓ cup extra-virgin olive oil

1 tablespoon ground dried sumac (see Glossary,
    page 586)

1 teaspoon cinnamon

Salt to taste

Freshly ground black pepper to taste

1. Place chicken in a glass or ceramic dish. In a small bowl, mix onion, garlic, olive oil, sumac and cinnamon together.

2. Pour mixture over chicken; turn pieces several times to make sure they are completely covered. Marinate, refrigerated, overnight.

3. Remove chicken from refrigerator 1 hour before cooking. Grill until done, basting with marinade each time you turn the pieces. Season with salt and pepper to taste and serve.

Yield: 4–6 servings

—RICHARD W. LANGER

ROAST CHICKEN THIGHS
WITH NORTH AFRICAN FLAVORS

meat

12 chicken thighs with bone in, skin removed

Salt and freshly ground black pepper to taste

2 tablespoons olive oil

1 onion, peeled and thinly sliced

1 tablespoon minced garlic

1 tablespoon ground cumin

1 tablespoon minced fresh ginger

1 tablespoon ground cinnamon

1 tablespoon ground coriander

1 teaspoon paprika

1 teaspoon red pepper flakes, optional

1 teaspoon salt

4 cups Chicken Stock (page 48)

2 medium sweet potatoes, peeled and cut into bite-size
    chunks

2 tablespoons lemon juice (about ½ lemon)

¼ cup roughly chopped dried apricots

¼ cup dark raisins

¼ cup chopped blanched almonds

1. Heat the oven to 350 degrees, and sprinkle the chicken thighs with salt and pepper to taste.

2. In a large sauté pan, heat the oil over medium-high heat until hot but not smoking. Add the chicken thighs and brown well (in 2 batches if your sauté pan is not large enough), about 3–4 minutes a side. Remove and set aside in a Dutch oven or small roasting pan.

3. Add the onion slices to the sauté pan and sauté over medium heat, stirring frequently, until they begin to brown, about 5–7 minutes. Add the garlic and cook, stirring frequently, 1 additional minute.

Add the cumin, ginger, cinnamon, coriander, paprika, red pepper flakes and salt, and cook, still stirring frequently, for 1 more minute. Add the stock, sweet potatoes, lemon juice, apricots, raisins, almonds and reserved chicken thighs, and bring the mixture just to a boil.

4. Add the chicken thighs and the mixture to Dutch oven or roasting pan, cover and place in the heated oven. Cook until chicken thighs are tender and cooked through, about 45 minutes. Season with salt and pepper to taste and serve, accompanied by couscous, rice or just crusty bread.

Yield: 6–8 servings

—JOHN WILLOUGHBY AND
CHRIS SCHLESINGER

BRAISED CHICKEN THIGHS WITH POTATOES AND GREEN OLIVES

meat

2 tablespoons olive oil
6 small (4–5 ounces) bone-in chicken thighs
Salt and freshly ground black pepper to taste
2 medium onions, thinly sliced
2 tablespoons minced garlic
⅓ cup white wine
1¼ cups Chicken Stock (page 48)
2 medium potatoes, diced medium
½ cup pitted green olives
½ cup roughly chopped fresh parsley

1. Preheat oven to 200 degrees.

2. In a 10-inch cast-iron skillet, heat oil over medium-high heat until hot but not smoking. Sprinkle thighs with salt and pepper to taste, then place in pan skin side down and sear until well browned, 3–5 minutes. Flip over and brown other side, 2–3 minutes. Remove and set aside.

3. Pour all but about 2 tablespoons of fat out of pan. Add onions and sauté, stirring frequently, until translucent, about 5 minutes. Add garlic and continue to sauté, stirring frequently, for another 2 minutes. Add wine and cook until slightly reduced, about 2 minutes.

4. Add chicken stock, potatoes and olives. Simmer for 5 minutes, adjust seasoning, then place in oven and cook, covered, for 30 minutes or until chicken shows no trace of red near the bone. Remove from oven, stir in parsley and serve at once.

Yield: 2–3 servings

—JOHN WILLOUGHBY AND
CHRIS SCHLESINGER

CHICKEN TAGINE IN FLAT BREAD

meat

3 tablespoons olive oil

2 cups boneless chicken dark meat (about 4 large
   boneless thighs), cut into ½-inch cubes

1 teaspoon ground cumin

Salt and freshly ground black pepper to taste

1 medium onion, chopped

3 cloves garlic, chopped

1 tablespoon minced fresh ginger

⅛ teaspoon saffron threads crushed into ½ cup
   Chicken Stock (page 48)

½ cup small pitted green olives, halved

½ teaspoon grated lemon rind

⅓ cup toasted sliced almonds

4 pieces pocketless pita bread or similar flat bread,
   each about 5–7 inches in diameter

½ cup cilantro leaves

1. Put 2 tablespoons of the oil in a large skillet over
medium-high heat. Season the chicken with cumin
and salt and pepper. Cook the chicken for 5 minutes, stirring so that it browns evenly.

2. Add the onion, garlic and ginger and cook for
3–4 minutes, until the onion softens and turns light
brown. Add the saffron stock, olives and lemon rind
and bring to a simmer. Cook for 10 minutes.

3. Preheat the broiler.

4. Adjust the salt and pepper for the tagine if needed,
stir in the almonds and reduce further so only a few
tablespoons of liquid remain. Remove from the heat.

5. Brush one side of the bread with the remaining
olive oil. Broil for a few minutes until it is lightly
browned and slightly crisp.

6. Put each pita, crisp side down, on a 12-by-12-
inch sheet of foil. Divide the chicken tagine among
the 4 pieces of bread and sprinkle with cilantro
leaves. Roll into a cone and secure the bottom by
twisting the foil. Fold the top back to expose the top
of the roll.

Yield: 4 servings

—SAM GUGINO

GRILLED CHICKEN DRUMSTICKS, ETHIOPIAN-STYLE

meat

2 teaspoons coriander seeds

1 tablespoon star anise, broken into small bits

1 teaspoon fenugreek seeds, optional

1 teaspoon ground ginger

2 teaspoons red pepper flakes

1 teaspoon ground cardamom

1 teaspoon turmeric

1 tablespoon dried mustard

1 teaspoon ground nutmeg

1 teaspoon ground cinnamon

1 teaspoon ground allspice

1 tablespoon cayenne pepper

1 tablespoon freshly ground black pepper

2 tablespoons salt

¼ cup paprika

½ cup dry red wine

¼ cup peanut oil

¼ cup fresh orange juice

16 chicken drumsticks

2 lemons, quartered

1. In a large sauté pan, combine the coriander, anise, fenugreek, ginger, red pepper flakes, cardamom, turmeric, mustard, nutmeg, cinnamon, allspice, cayenne, black pepper, salt and paprika. Toast over medium heat, shaking constantly to avoid burning, until the mixture is heated through and the first tiny wisp of smoke appears, about 3 minutes. The mixture will become very aromatic.

2. Add the red wine to the mixture and cook, stirring constantly, for 2–3 minutes, until a uniform paste is formed.

3. Remove the paste from the heat and allow to cool to room temperature. Add the peanut oil and orange juice and mix well. The paste should be about the thickness of wet sand. Rub the drumsticks all over with the paste and allow to stand, covered and refrigerated, for 2 hours.

4. Remove the drumsticks from the refrigerator and grill over a medium-low for 10–12 minutes, rolling around to ensure even cooking and watching carefully to be sure the paste does not burn. Check for doneness by nicking the largest thigh at the thickest point; it should be completely opaque.

5. Remove from heat and serve at once, accompanied by lemon quarters for squeezing.

Yield: 6 servings

—JOHN WILLOUGHBY AND
CHRIS SCHLESINGER

JAMES BEARD'S CHICKEN WITH 40 CLOVES OF GARLIC

meat

4 stalks of celery, cut into long strips

2 medium-size onions, coarsely chopped

6 sprigs parsley

1 tablespoon chopped fresh tarragon

⅔ cup vegetable oil

16 chicken legs, any mix of drumsticks and thighs

½ cup dry vermouth

2½ teaspoons salt

½ teaspoon freshly ground black pepper

Freshly grated nutmeg

40 cloves garlic, unpeeled

French bread for serving

1. Preheat the oven to 375 degrees. Cover the bottom of a heavy 6-quart casserole with the celery and onions and add the parsley and tarragon. Place the oil in a shallow dish. Dip the chicken pieces into the oil, coat all sides evenly and place in the casserole. Pour the vermouth over the chicken and sprinkle with the salt, pepper and a few gratings of nutmeg.

Tuck the garlic around and between the chicken pieces.

2. Cover the top of the casserole tightly with aluminum foil and fit the lid over the foil to create an airtight seal. Bake for 1⅓ hours without removing the cover. Check for doneness; return casserole to the oven if the chicken seems underdone. Serve the chicken along with the pan juices, the garlic and thin slices of heated French bread with garlic squeezed from the root end of the clove.

Yield: 8 servings

—MOLLY O'NEILL

CHICKEN PAPRIKASH

meat

ADAPTED FROM *The New York Times International Cookbook*

2 large onions, chopped
¼ cup melted chicken fat
1 roasting chicken (4 pounds), cut into serving pieces
2 tablespoons sweet paprika
Salt to taste
Water
1 medium green pepper, sliced
1 medium tomato, peeled and sliced
1 teaspoon tomato paste

1. Sauté the onions in the chicken fat until golden brown.

2. Add the chicken, paprika and 1 teaspoon salt. Cover and simmer for 10 minutes. During the simmering, stir twice and add a little water if needed.

3. Add the green pepper, tomato, tomato paste and 1 cup water. Cover the skillet and cook over low heat for about 50 minutes, stirring and adding water as needed to prevent sticking. Add additional salt to taste. Serve with rice, noodles or dumplings.

Yield: 4 servings

CHICKEN TAGINE WITH OLIVES AND PRESERVED LEMONS

meat

ADAPTED FROM Shallots

5 cloves garlic, finely chopped
¼ teaspoon saffron threads, pulverized
½ teaspoon ground ginger

1 teaspoon sweet paprika
½ teaspoon ground cumin
½ teaspoon turmeric
Salt and freshly ground black pepper to taste
1 chicken, cut in 8 pieces
2 tablespoons extra-virgin olive oil

3 medium onions, sliced thin

1 cinnamon stick

8 calamata olives, pitted and halved

8 cracked green olives, pitted and halved

*1 large or 3 small Preserved Lemons
    (page 429)*

1 cup Chicken Stock (page 48)

Juice of ½ lemon

1 tablespoon chopped flat-leaf parsley

1. Mix garlic, saffron, ginger, paprika, cumin and turmeric together. Add pepper to taste. Rub chicken with mixture, cover and refrigerate and marinate 3–4 hours.

2. Heat oil in heavy skillet. Add chicken and brown on all sides. Remove to platter. Add onions to skillet and cook over medium-low heat about 15 minutes, until lightly browned. Transfer to tagine, if you are using one, or leave in skillet. Add cinnamon stick.

3. Put chicken on onions. Scatter with olives. Quarter the lemons, remove pulp and cut skin in strips. Scatter over chicken. Mix stock and lemon juice. Pour over chicken.

4. Cover tagine or skillet. Place over low heat and cook about 30 minutes, until chicken is done. Scatter parsley on top and serve.

Yield: 4 servings

—FLORENCE FABRICANT

CARDAMOM CHICKEN STEW

meat

*1 tablespoon each: cumin seeds, coriander seeds and
    chili powder*

1 teaspoon ground turmeric

2 tablespoons cardamom seeds

1 tablespoon salt

1 tablespoon freshly ground black pepper

12 chicken thighs

¼ cup vegetable oil

2 onions, peeled and thinly sliced

2 sticks cinnamon or 2 teaspoons ground cinnamon

15 whole cloves

2 tablespoons minced garlic

2 tablespoons minced ginger

2 tablespoons minced red or green chili pepper

2 white potatoes, peeled and cut into quarters

2 cups Chicken Stock (page 48)

2 cups canned coconut milk

⅓ cup chopped cilantro

¼ cup fresh lime juice

Salt and freshly ground black pepper to taste

1. Preheat oven to 350 degrees. In a small sauté pan, toast the cumin, coriander, chili powder and turmeric over medium heat, stirring or shaking frequently, until the first wisp of smoke appears, about 3–4 minutes. Be careful not to burn the spices. Cool to room temperature, grind in a coffee grinder or with mortar and pestle and set aside.

2. Grind the cardamom seeds in a coffee grinder or with mortar and pestle. In a small bowl, combine the ground cardamom with the salt and pepper and mix well. Sprinkle the chicken thighs generously with this mixture. In a large sauté pan, heat the oil over medium-high heat until hot but not smoking. Add the chicken, skin side down, and cook until skin is well browned about 4–6 minutes. Flip over and cook an additional 2 minutes. Remove chicken from the sauté pan and place in a large ovenproof casserole.

3. Add the onions, cinnamon, cloves, garlic, ginger, and chilies to the sauté pan and cook, stirring frequently, until the onions are transparent, about 5–7 minutes. Remove to the casserole.

4. Add the potatoes, chicken stock and coconut milk to the casserole, stir well, place in oven and bake for 40 minutes to 1 hour, or until the chicken thighs are cooked through. To check for doneness, cut into one of the thighs; when the juices run clear, the chicken is done.

5. Remove the casserole from the oven, mix in the toasted spice mixture, cilantro and lime juice, season to taste with salt and pepper and serve.

Yield: 6 servings

—JOHN WILLOUGHBY AND
CHRIS SCHLESINGER

BRAISED CHICKEN WITH SWEET PEPPERS

meat

1 small frying chicken, cut in 6 serving pieces
   (or use 2 pounds of chicken parts)
1/4 cup extra-virgin olive oil
2 tablespoons fresh lemon juice
   (juice from 1/2 lemon)
1 tablespoons finely chopped fresh rosemary
1/2 medium yellow onion, thinly sliced
2 cloves garlic, thinly sliced
1/4–1/2 cup dry white wine
2 red or yellow (or both) sweet peppers, sliced in strips
1 tablespoon capers
2 tablespoons chopped black olives, Greek or niçoise
2 tablespoons finely chopped flat-leaf parsley

1. Put the chicken in a deep bowl and add the oil, lemon juice and rosemary. Turn to coat well. Cover and set aside to marinate for 1 hour or refrigerate 10 hours or overnight.

2. To cook, remove about 2 tablespoons of the flavored oil from the marinade. Place the oil in a heavy saucepan large enough to hold the chicken pieces and set over medium-low heat. Add the onion and garlic and cook, stirring occasionally, until the vegetables are soft. Push the vegetables to the edges of the pan and put the chicken in the middle. Raise the heat to medium and brown the chicken lightly on all sides. Add the wine and peppers. Lower the heat again, cover and continue cooking, stirring occasionally and turning the chicken parts over, for about 30 minutes, or until the chicken is thoroughly cooked and the juices run clear yellow when the meat is pricked with a fork. If necessary, add more marinade.

3. When the chicken is done, stir in the capers, olives and parsley. Let the sauce come to a boil, remove from the heat and serve immediately.

Yield: 4–6 servings

NOTE: *Chicken skin adds a lot of flavor, but you may remove the skin or prepare this dish with skinless, boneless breasts.*

—NANCY HARMON JENKINS

ONION-SMOTHERED CHICKEN

meat

<small>ADAPTED FROM</small> *1,000 Jewish Recipes*

1 (3-pound) chicken, cut in serving pieces
Salt and freshly ground black pepper
2 tablespoons extra-virgin olive oil
3 large onions, halved and thinly sliced
1 teaspoon ground cumin
1 teaspoon ground coriander
1 teaspoon paprika
4 large cloves garlic, chopped
¾ cup Chicken Stock (page 48)
Juice of ½ lemon
1 teaspoon minced flat-leaf parsley

1. Season chicken pieces liberally with pepper.

2. Heat oil in large, deep sauté pan. Lightly brown chicken pieces in two shifts over medium heat. Remove. Add onions, and cook over medium-low heat until softened, about 10 minutes. Return chicken and any juices to sauté pan. Add cumin, coriander, paprika, garlic and stock. Cover and simmer, turning chicken once or twice, about 30 minutes, until cooked through.

3. Remove chicken from pan, leaving onion. Skim excess fat. Add lemon and bring to a simmer. Season with salt and pepper to taste. Return chicken to pan, baste with sauce and reheat a few minutes. Serve sprinkled with parsley.

Yield: 4 servings

—FLORENCE FABRICANT

CHICKEN CURRY

meat

<small>ADAPTED FROM</small> *The New York Times Large-Type Cookbook*

2 chickens (2½–3 pounds each), cut into serving pieces
¾ teaspoon turmeric
½ cup shortening or vegetable oil
2 large onions, sliced
2 stalks celery, diced
2 carrots, sliced
1 green pepper, diced
2 teaspoons curry powder

¼ teaspoon cinnamon
¼ teaspoons cloves
½ teaspoons ginger
1 tablespoon flour
1 bay leaf
2 cups Chicken Broth (page 48)
2 tomatoes, skinned and chopped
Salt to taste

1. Rub chicken pieces with ¼ teaspoon turmeric.

2. In a large heavy skillet, brown chicken pieces in shortening or oil, turning to brown evenly. Remove chicken; reserve.

3. Add onions, celery, carrots and green pepper to the fat remaining in skillet. Sauté until onions are barely tender. Sprinkle with curry powder and remaining turmeric and cook 2 minutes.

4. Sprinkle vegetables with cinnamon, cloves, ginger and flour and cook, stirring, a few seconds. Add remaining ingredients, including salt to taste, and bring to a boil, stirring.

5. Return chicken to skillet and cook, covered, over low heat until chicken is tender, about 30 minutes.

Yield: 8 servings

CHICKEN WITH OKRA • (KOTA ME BAMYES)

meat

ADAPTED FROM Vasiliki Johnides

> 2 pounds tender, fresh okra or 3 (10-ounce) packages
>   frozen okra, defrosted
> 2½ cups white wine vinegar
> 1 chicken, 4–4½ pounds, cut into serving pieces
> Salt to taste, if desired
> Freshly ground pepper to taste
> 6 tablespoons olive oil
> 2 cups finely chopped onions
> 1½ cups finely crushed tomatoes
> ⅔ cup Chicken Broth (page 48) or water

1. If fresh okra is used, wash and then trim off any tough stems. Put the fresh or thawed frozen okra in a mixing bowl and add 2 cups of the vinegar. Refrigerate overnight. Drain thoroughly while preparing the chicken.

2. Sprinkle the chicken with salt and pepper and set aside.

3. Heat 4 tablespoons of oil in a kettle and add the onions. Cook, stirring, until the onions are wilted, about 5 minutes or until the onions barely start to take on color. Add remaining 2 tablespoons of oil and the chicken pieces in 1 or 2 layers. Cook about 3 minutes, turning the pieces occasionally.

4. Add the tomatoes and broth or water and bring to a boil. Cover and let simmer 40 minutes. Add the okra, salt and pepper and stir. Pour the remaining ½ cup of vinegar over all. Do not stir. Cover closely and continue cooking about 30 minutes, or until the chicken is thoroughly tender.

Yield 4–6 servings

—CRAIG CLAIBORNE AND PIERRE FRANEY

GEORGIAN CHICKEN IN
GARLICKY WALNUT SAUCE • (SATSIVI)

meat

ADAPTED FROM *A La Russe*

1 small chicken (2½ pounds)

1 bay leaf

1 large carrot

2 sprigs parsley

6 cups cold water

Salt to taste

4 tablespoons Schmaltz (page 413)

3 large onions

10 small heads of garlic (whole heads, not cloves)

1 generous cup walnuts, ground

2 tablespoons dried coriander seed

1 teaspoon ground black pepper

Cayenne pepper to taste

¼ teaspoon cinnamon

2 tablespoons minced fresh parsley

2 tablespoons minced fresh dill

2 teaspoons vinegar

Minced cilantro for garnish, optional

1. Place the chicken, bay leaf, carrot, parsley sprigs, water and salt to taste in a large stockpot. Bring to a boil, skimming any froth that rises to the surface. Simmer, covered, for 1 hour, then remove the chicken to a large strainer and let it drain. Reserve the broth, measuring out 4 cups.

2. Preheat the oven to 425 degrees. Place the chicken on a cookie sheet and roast it at 425 degrees just until the skin is glazed. Set aside to cool, then bone and separate the meat into good-sized chunks.

3. In a large, heavy skillet melt the schmaltz. Chop the onions and sauté them in the fat until soft and transparent.

4. Meanwhile, peel the garlic (note that 10 entire heads—not cloves—are used) and grind it in a meat grinder or food processor. Grind the walnuts. Finely crush the coriander seed.

5. When the onions are cooked, stir in the garlic, nuts and coriander, then add the remaining spices and herbs. Stir in the vinegar, blending well. Then, in a steady stream, add the 4 cups of reserved chicken broth. Simmer the mixture for 10 minutes, then add the chicken pieces and simmer for 5 minutes more.

6. Remove the satsivi from the heat and transfer to a serving dish. Chill well before serving. Garnish with minced cilantro, if desired.

Yield 8 servings

—DARRA GOLDSTEIN

SESAME CHICKEN WITH GARLIC SAUCE

meat

ADAPTED FROM *The Best of Craig Claiborne*

FOR THE CHICKEN:

6 chicken thighs

1 egg yolk

1 tablespoon soy sauce

1 garlic clove, finely minced

4 cups peanut, vegetable or corn oil

FOR THE BATTER:

1 cup plus 2 tablespoons flour

3 tablespoons cornstarch

1¼ teaspoons baking powder

¾ cup cold water

2 eggs, lightly beaten

2 teaspoons peanut, vegetable or corn oil

1 tablespoon sesame seeds

FOR THE GARLIC SAUCE:

1 tablespoon peanut, vegetable or corn oil

4 garlic cloves, finely minced

1 teaspoon finely chopped ginger

½ cup Chicken Broth (page 48), canned or fresh

1½ teaspoons sugar

2 tablespoons dark soy sauce

¼ teaspoon freshly ground pepper

¾ cup chopped scallions, green part and all

1 tablespoon sesame seeds

1. Bone the thighs or have them boned. Slice the thighs into 4–6 squares of approximately the same size. Place the pieces in a bowl and add the egg yolk, 1 tablespoon soy sauce and minced garlic. Let stand.

2. Sift the flour, cornstarch and baking powder into a bowl. Stir in the water, eggs, 2 teaspoons of oil and sesame seeds.

3. To prepare the sauce, heat 1 tablespoon of oil and add the garlic and ginger. Cook briefly and add the chicken broth, sugar, soy sauce and ground pepper. Simmer for about 5 minutes.

4. Coat the chicken in batter.

5. Heat 4 cups of oil in a wok or skillet and add the batter-coated chicken pieces, one at a time. Do not add all the chicken pieces at once. Cook, stirring to separate the pieces, for about 1 minute, or until golden brown. Drain each batch as they cook. Pour out the oil after cooking the chicken pieces. Return the chicken pieces to the wok.

6. Add the garlic sauce and blend well. Stir in the chopped scallions and sesame seeds and heat through.

Yield: 4 servings

CHICKEN WITH COUSCOUS

meat

ADAPTED FROM *The Best of Craig Claiborne*

½ cup dried chickpeas

2 tablespoons vegetable oil

1 (2½-pound) chicken, cut into serving pieces

½ teaspoon ground cumin

1 tablespoon finely grated fresh ginger

½ teaspoon ground turmeric

¼ teaspoon saffron threads, optional

2 teaspoons finely chopped garlic

Salt and freshly ground pepper to taste

1 leek, trimmed, rinsed and cut into small cubes,
    about ¾ cup

1 cup tomatoes, cut into quarters

6 very small white onions, quartered

4 cups Chicken Broth (page 48)

2 celery stalks, trimmed and cut into 1½-inch
    lengths, optional

3 small carrots, peeled, trimmed and cut into
    1-inch lengths

1 red or green sweet pepper, cored, seeded and cut into
    2-inch cubes

3 very small turnips, cut into quarters

2 small zucchini, trimmed and cut into 1-inch cubes

Couscous (see recipe below)

Hot pepper sauce

1. Soak the chickpeas for at least 6 hours in water to cover. Drain and cook in water to cover about 2 inches above the peas for about 15 minutes, or until tender.

2. Heat the oil over low heat in a casserole and add the chicken. Turn the pieces in the oil and sprinkle with the cumin, ginger, turmeric, saffron, if used, garlic, salt and a generous grinding of pepper. Cook, stirring, until the chicken starts to lose its raw color.

3. Add the leek, tomatoes, onions, and chicken broth and bring to a boil. Simmer for 20 minutes.

4. Add the celery, if used, carrots and sweet pepper and continue cooking for about 5 minutes. Add the zucchini and drained chickpeas and cook for 5 minutes.

5. Press a sieve into the broth and scoop out 3 cups of broth for the couscous.

6. To serve, spoon a generous amount of couscous into individual soup bowls. Serve the chicken and vegetables on top. Ladle a generous amount of broth over each serving. Take a spoonful of the hot broth and add as much hot sauce as you desire. Stir to dissolve. Spoon this over each serving.

Yield: 6 servings

♦ **COUSCOUS** ♦

meat

1½ cups quick-cooking couscous (see Note below)

3 cups strained liquid from the chicken
    (see recipe above)

1. Put the couscous in a saucepan. Pour hot broth over it. Cook over low heat, stirring, for about 2 minutes. Cover and remove from the heat.

2. Let stand for 10 minutes, or until ready to serve. Before serving, fluff the couscous with a fork.

Yield: 6 serving

NOTE: *For this recipe, do not use long-cooking couscous. For dairy meals or if otherwise desired, water or vegetable stock may be substituted for the strained chicken liquid.*

DAISY INY'S IRAQI CHICKEN
WITH RICE AND EGGS · (TABYEET)

meat

2 cups basmati rice

1 (4-pound) broiler

Few dashes turmeric

Freshly ground black pepper to taste

4 tablespoons vegetable oil

Few dashes cinnamon

Pinch cloves

1/4 teaspoon plus of ground cardamom

Dash nutmeg

1 teaspoon tomato paste

Salt to taste

3 cups water

Eggs in the shell, as many as desired

1. Soak rice overnight in water to cover.

2. Rub turmeric into chicken and sprinkle with pepper. Sauté chicken in hot oil for about 10 minutes. Add cinnamon, cloves, cardamom, nutmeg, tomato paste, salt and water. Partially cover and boil chicken for 30 minutes.

3. Remove chicken. Drain rice and add to chicken cooking liquid. Bring to boil and cook 3–4 minutes. Return chicken to pot. Continue boiling until liquid has evaporated almost completely.

4. Place enough foil over chicken and rice to hold the number of eggs you wish to cook. Place eggs in their shells on top of the foil and put casserole in 400-degree oven for 30 minutes. Reduce heat to 300 degrees and bake 30 minutes longer. Reduce heat to 250 degrees and bake for 2–3 hours, until rice forms golden crust on bottom and sides. Remove eggs. To help with removal of crust, place pan in cold water in the sink for a minute or two. Serve chicken on platter surrounded by rice and, if desired, topped with peeled eggs, halved.

Yield: 6 servings

NOTE: *You may wish to prepare the casserole before the Sabbath sundown and serve the eggs at Saturday morning breakfast.*

—MARIAN BURROS

SWEET RICE WITH ORANGE PEEL, CHICKEN, SAFFRON
AND CARROTS · (SHIRIN POLO)

meat

ADAPTED FROM *New Food of Life*

3 cups basmati rice

2 pounds chicken breasts

Salt and freshly ground pepper to taste

1/2 cup vegetable oil

2 cups orange peel in matchstick strips, about 6 oranges (see Note below)

2 cups sugar

6 carrots, cut into strips 1 inch long and about 1/8 inch wide

½ cup slivered blanched almonds

2 tablespoons salt

½ teaspoon ground saffron

2 tablespoons hot water

½ teaspoon cinnamon

¼ teaspoon ground ginger

¼ teaspoon ground cardamom

⅛ teaspoon ground cloves

2 tablespoons chopped pistachio nuts

1. Clean and wash the rice 5 times in cold water, or until the water remains clear.

2. Season the chicken with salt and pepper to taste. Put 2 tablespoons of the oil in a medium frying pan and add the chicken. Cover and cook over low heat for about 25 minutes. Cool, then remove the skin and cut the chicken into small pieces, reserving the chicken juices.

3. In a saucepan, place the orange peel in 3 cups water and boil for 5 minutes. Drain and repeat. Drain the orange peel and place it, the sugar, carrots and 3 cups water in the saucepan and simmer for 15 minutes. Drain, add the almonds and set aside.

4. In a large nonstick pot, add 2 tablespoons salt and bring 8 cups water to a boil. Pour the washed and drained rice into the pot. Boil briskly for 6 minutes, stirring gently twice to loosen any grains that stick to the bottom. Drain the rice in a colander and rinse in lukewarm water.

5. Dissolve the saffron in the 2 tablespoons hot water.

6. In the same pot used for the rice, heat ¼ cup of the oil and a drop of the dissolved saffron.

7. Set aside 4 tablespoons of the carrot mixture for garnish. Cover the saffron-oil mixture with a ½-inch layer of rice, then add a ½-inch layer of chicken and a ½-inch layer of the carrot mixture. Continue layering in this manner until you have used up all the ingredients. End with a large layer of rice, forming it into a pyramid. Sprinkle the cinnamon, ginger, cardamom and cloves over the rice, and pour the remaining oil and saffron over the pyramid. Pour the chicken juices and 1–2 tablespoons water over the pyramid.

8. Place a clean towel over the pot and cover firmly with a lid to prevent any steam from escaping. Cook for 10 minutes over medium heat and another 50 minutes over very low heat. Remove from the heat and allow to cool for 5 minutes. Do not open.

9. Remove the lid and set aside 2 tablespoons of the saffron-colored rice for garnish.

10. Gently spoon the dish onto a platter, shaping it into another pyramid. Garnish with the saffron rice and reserved carrot mixture. Sprinkle with the pistachio nuts.

11. Using a wooden spatula, detach the bottom crusty layer from the pot and serve on the side.

Yield: 6–8 servings

NOTE: *Orange peel already cut into strips is available from Middle Eastern markets.*

—JOAN NATHAN

CHICKEN CROQUETTES •
(KEFTIKES DE POYO)

meat

ADAPTED FROM *Cookbook of the Jews of Greece*

4 large chicken breasts

1 medium onion, finely chopped

½ pound ground beef

½ cup matzoh meal

3 eggs

2 tablespoons finely chopped fresh dill

Salt and pepper to taste

2 tablespoons olive oil

1. Poach the chicken breasts in very little water until the meat is very tender and can be easily removed from the bones.

2. Pass chicken and onion through a coarse grinder and mix with beef, matzoh meal, eggs, dill, salt and pepper in a large bowl.

3. Break off egg-size pieces of the mixture and shape into round, slightly flattened croquettes. Sauté gently in olive oil until well browned on both sides. Serve hot or cold.

Yield: 15–20 croquettes

—HENRY KAMM

ROAST TURKEY WITH WILD RICE, CORN AND
MUSHROOM STUFFING AND GIBLET GRAVY

meat

1 (10- to 12-pound) turkey, with giblets

4 cups water

2 medium-size onions

1 carrot, scraped

1 stalk celery

2 sprigs parsley

Salt and freshly ground black pepper to taste

1 tablespoon vegetable oil

*6 cups Wild Rice, Corn and Mushroom Stuffing
    (page 167)*

2 tablespoons flour

½ cup dry white wine

1. Remove the giblets and neck from the turkey; reserve the liver for another use. Rinse and dry the turkey and allow it to come to room temperature before stuffing and roasting.

2. Place the neck, gizzard and heart of the turkey in a saucepan with the water, 1 onion, the carrot, celery and parsley. Bring to a boil and cook, skimming the surface, for 5 minutes. Reduce heat and simmer about 40 minutes, until the liquid has reduced to 2 cups. Strain and set aside.

3. Mince the gizzard, heart and meat from the neck and reserve.

4. Preheat oven to 425 degrees. Season turkey cavity with salt and pepper; rub skin with oil.

5. Stuff main cavity and neck cavity, then skewer or truss to close. Place extra stuffing in a small casserole, to be heated just before serving.

6. Place turkey on a V-shaped rack and roast, breast side down, for 30 minutes. If you do not have such a rack, roast the turkey breast side up the entire time.

7. Reduce oven temperature to 325 degrees, turn turkey breast side up and continue roasting another 2–2½ hours, until a thermometer inserted in thick part of thigh registers 165 degrees. One-half hour before the turkey is finished, slice the remaining onion and scatter in the pan.

8. Remove turkey from the oven and allow to stand 30 minutes.

9. Drain excess fat from roasting pan. Set the pan on a burner, scatter in flour and cook over medium heat several minutes, stirring and scraping the pan. Whisk in the wine and the giblet stock. Cook a few minutes longer, until sauce has thickened. Strain into a saucepan, forcing most solids through strainer. Add minced giblets and season with salt and pepper.

10. Remove the stuffing from the turkey, carve the turkey, and serve with stuffing and reheated gravy.

Yield: 8–12 servings

—FLORENCE FABRICANT

WILD RICE, CORN AND MUSHROOM STUFFING

pareve

½ cup wild rice (see Note below)
2½ cups water
12 ounces firm-textured white or whole wheat bread
5–6 tablespoons vegetable oil
2 cups chopped onions
12 ounces fresh mushrooms, chopped
2 cups corn kernels, preferably freshly
   cut from the ear
1 teaspoon dried thyme
½ cup chopped parsley
Salt and freshly ground black pepper to taste
Cayenne pepper to taste

1. Bring wild rice and water to a boil in a saucepan. Cover and simmer until tender and water is absorbed, about 30 minutes. Set aside.

2. Place the bread on a baking sheet in a barely warm oven and dry about 30 minutes. Remove crusts and cut into ½-inch cubes.

3. Heat oil in a heavy skillet. Sauté onions until golden. Add mushrooms and increase heat to high. Sauté, stirring, until mushrooms are tender and beginning to brown and most of the liquid has evaporated.

4. Stir in corn, thyme, wild rice and bread. Cook over medium heat until the bread is moistened. The mixture should be barely damp, not soggy. Stir in parsley, season with salt, pepper and cayenne and set aside.

Yield: 8 servings

NOTE: *If wild rice is unavailable, use 8 cups of the bread (a full pound).*

—FLORENCE FABRICANT

BROWN RICE AND PECAN STUFFING

meat

1 cup chopped pecans
2 tablespoons vegetable oil
1½ cups chopped onion
1 cup chopped celery
1 teaspoon dried thyme
2 teaspoons dried sage
2 cups raw brown rice
3⅓ cups turkey stock or Chicken Stock (page 48)
2 tablespoons chopped parsley
1 teaspoon lemon juice
Salt and freshly ground black pepper to taste

1. Toast the pecans by tossing them over medium-high heat in a heavy, dry skillet or baking them in a toaster oven until golden brown. Do not allow them to burn. Remove from the pan and set aside.

2. Heat the oil in a heavy saucepan. Add the onion and celery and sauté over low heat until soft and just beginning to brown. Stir in the thyme, sage and rice. Add the pecans. Add the stock, bring to a boil and boil for 2 minutes. Lower heat, cover and cook until the liquid is absorbed, about 20 minutes. The rice will still be a little firm, but it will continue cooking when it is stuffed into the poultry.

3. Season the mixture with parsley, lemon juice and salt and pepper. Set aside or refrigerate until ready to use to stuff the turkey. When stuffing, do not pack the mixture tightly because the rice will continue to expand.

*Yield: About 8 cups,
enough for a 12-pound turkey*

—FLORENCE FABRICANT

MARIAN BURROS'S FRUIT
AND BREAD STUFFING

meat

1 tablespoon olive oil
4 onions (about 1 pound), coarsely chopped
4 ribs celery, finely chopped
½ pound fresh mushrooms, cultivated or wild,
    trimmed and cut coarse
4 large apples, coarsely chopped
1 cup chopped parsley
½ cup dried cherries

½ cup dried apples, diced
2 tablespoons chopped fresh sage, or ¾ teaspoon dried
2 tablespoons chopped fresh thyme, or ¾ teaspoon dried
10 slices stale bread, broken into bite-size pieces
1½ cups Chicken Stock (page 48)
½ teaspoon salt
Freshly ground black pepper to taste

1. Heat oil in a nonstick skillet. Sauté onion and celery until onion begins to brown.

2. Add mushrooms, apples and parsley, and continue cooking until apples soften and mushrooms release their liquid.

3. Reduce heat and stir in dried cherries, dried apples, sage and thyme. Continue cooking until mixture is well blended.

4. Add bread and stock, and mix well. Season with salt and pepper, then stuff the mixture into a 12- to 14-pound turkey just before cooking. Stuffing may be made ahead and frozen for a week or two. Or it may be refrigerated for two days.

Yield: 10 cups stuffing (about 10 servings)

—MARIAN BURROS

TURKEY AND APRICOT TAGINE

meat

ADAPTED FROM *The Working Cook*

1⅓ cups chopped onion

1 tablespoon coarsely grated fresh or frozen ginger

½ teaspoon cinnamon

⅛ teaspoon turmeric

2 teaspoons olive oil

1 clove garlic, minced

½ pound skinless, raw boneless turkey breast,
　 cut in large chunks

Freshly ground black pepper to taste

12 dried apricots, cut in half

2 tablespoons honey

3 tablespoons fresh lime juice

½ cup Chicken Stock (page 48), no salt added

2 tablespoons pistachios or toasted almonds

Cooked couscous, optional

1. Sauté onion, ginger, cinnamon and turmeric in 1 teaspoon hot oil in large nonstick skillet until onion softens and begins to brown.

2. Push mixture to one side. Add remaining oil and sauté garlic and turkey in the hot oil until turkey browns on both sides.

3. Season with pepper. Add apricots, honey, lime juice and stock and cook until mixture begins to thicken. Add nuts and serve.

Yield: 2 servings

NOTE: *Couscous sprinkled with chopped cilantro is an excellent accompaniment.*

—MARIAN BURROS

TURKEY PILAF IN A PHYLLO "TURBAN"

meat

3 tablespoons olive oil

1 large onion, finely chopped

1 cup rice

½ teaspoon turmeric

1 teaspoon ground cumin

2 cups chicken or turkey stock or broth

½ cup raisins

1½ cups frozen peas

⅓ cup toasted slivered almonds (see Note, page 582)

1½ cups cooked turkey, cut in small cubes

8 sheets phyllo (see Note, page 583)

Freshly ground black pepper and salt to taste, optional

1. Heat the oven to 400 degrees.

2. Sauté the onion in 1 tablespoon of hot oil until it begins to soften. Stir in the rice, turmeric and cumin and cook, stirring, until rice is coated.

3. Add the chicken or turkey stock and raisins; bring to boil, reduce heat and cover. Cook rice for 17 minutes, until liquid has been absorbed and rice is tender. Stir in peas and almonds. Season with pepper

and, if desired, salt. Set aside.

4. Lightly grease a 3-quart casserole with olive oil. Lay 1 sheet of phyllo in casserole so that the dough overhangs edge of casserole. Lightly brush with some of remaining oil. Top with second sheet, at right angle of first sheet, and oil. Continue until 5 sheets have been layered.

5. Place half the rice mixture on the phyllo; top with turkey and then top with remaining rice.

6. Arrange 1 sheet of phyllo over rice and brush lightly with oil; repeat with remaining 2 sheets. Trim edges so that only enough dough hangs over to tuck into sides of casserole. Brush top with oil and bake for 30 minutes, until top is golden brown and sides are beginning to brown. Cool about 10 minutes and serve.

Yield: 6 servings

NOTE: *This recipe works equally well with leftover duck, chicken or any other fowl. The turbans should be put together quickly after the rice is cooked because the phyllo is in whole sheets. The dish must be eaten as soon as it is baked, or the phyllo will become soggy.*

—MARIAN BURROS

MARIAN BURROS'S PICADILLO

meat

ADAPTED FROM *Keep It Simple*

1¼ pounds ground turkey

¾ pound extra-lean ground beef

1 tablespoon corn or canola oil

2 large onions, chopped coarsely

1 cup water

½ cup raw rice

½ cup raisins

1 (6-ounce) can tomato paste

½ cup toasted almonds

½–1 whole jalapeño or Serrano chili, minced

¼ teaspoon ground cinnamon

⅛ teaspoon ground cloves

8–10 canned plum tomatoes

¼ cup or more juice from tomato can

1. Brown turkey and beef in heavy-bottomed hot skillet. Set aside and drain off all fat.

2. Heat oil in skillet and add onions. Sauté until onions soften and begin to turn golden.

3. Place water and rice in small pot, and bring to a boil. Reduce heat, cover and simmer until rice is done and water has been absorbed, a total of 17 minutes.

4. Meanwhile, return beef and turkey to pan with onions, along with raisins, tomato paste, almonds,

chili, cinnamon, cloves, tomatoes and tomato juice and simmer while rice cooks. Mixture should be thick, but not dry.

5. When rice is cooked, stir into meat mixture.

6. Serve wrapped in large flat bread or with flat bread on the side.

Yield: 4 servings

NOTE: *The substitution of ground turkey for most of the ground beef reduces the fat content of the dish significantly without changing the taste. If extra-lean ground beef is unavailable, buy a lean piece of beef and grind it in the food processor at home.*

—MARIAN BURROS

HONEY-GLAZED DUCK

meat

2 ducks (about 5 pounds each)

Coarse sea salt and freshly ground pepper to taste

½ cup celery leaves, chopped

2 small carrots, chopped

1 small onion, quartered

2 cloves garlic, peeled and halved

1 small bunch fresh thyme

1 cup dry white wine

2 tablespoons balsamic vinegar

2 tablespoons honey

3 teaspoons chopped fresh thyme leaves

Sprigs of thyme to garnish the ducks

1. Remove the fat from the ducks' cavities and cut off the extra skin on the tail end. Put the fat and skin in a small saucepan and render it.

2. Meanwhile, prick the ducks all over with the prongs of a fork. Season the cavities and the skin with salt and pepper to taste, rubbing it evenly all over. Put the celery leaves, carrots, onion, garlic and thyme in each cavity. Put the ducks breast side up on racks in large baking pans. Pour about an inch of water in each pan and cover them tightly, first with kitchen parchment, then foil, making sure very little steam can escape. The foil should puff up as the ducks steam. The skin of the duck will be very soft and tender.

3. Preheat the oven to 425 degrees. Combine the wine, vinegar, honey and thyme leaves in a small saucepan and cook over low heat to dissolve the honey. Put the ducks on racks set in baking pans (you can use the same pans used for steaming) and roast for 30 minutes. Brush with the warm wine and honey mixture and reduce heat to 375 degrees.

Brush the ducks repeatedly for the next 15 minutes until they are the color of dark mahogany. You should be left with half the basting liquid.

4. When the ducks are browned, let them rest in a warm place for 5 minutes. Cut them up and arrange the pieces on a warm serving platter. Bring the remaining basting liquid to a boil and pour it over the duck pieces. Garnish with sprigs of thyme and serve.

Yield: 4–6 servings

—MOIRA HODGSON

DUCK WITH OLIVES IN SHERRY SAUCE • (PATO A LA SEVILLANA)

meat

1 duck, 4½–5 pounds, cleaned weight
2 onion slices
2 whole garlic cloves, peeled
½ cup coarsely chopped or thinly sliced pitted Spanish olives (without pimiento)
½ cup dry white wine
2 tablespoons olive oil
½ cup finely chopped onion
1 tablespoon finely minced garlic
½ cup sherry
½ cup plus 3–4 tablespoons Rich Chicken Broth (page 48), fresh or canned
1 cup scraped, thinly sliced carrots
1 sprig fresh parsley
¼ teaspoon dried thyme
1 bay leaf
4 peppercorns
Salt to taste, if desired

1. Preheat oven to 350 degrees.

2. Prick the duck all over the skin with a two-pronged fork. Insert the onion slices and garlic cloves inside the duck. Truss the duck. Place it breast side up in a shallow baking or roasting pan and arrange the neck, if available, around it.

3. Place the duck in the oven and bake 1 hour.

4. Meanwhile, put the olives in a small saucepan and add half of the white wine. Let simmer 5 minutes. Drain.

5. Heat the oil in a shallow ovenproof casserole. Add the chopped onion and minced garlic and cook, stirring, until onion is wilted. Add the sherry, ½ cup chicken broth, carrots, parsley, thyme, bay leaf, peppercorns and salt. Set aside.

6. When the duck has baked for 1 hour, remove it from the oven.

7. Transfer the duck to a flat surface and cut it into quarters.

8. Pour the fat from the roasting pan. Add the remaining white wine and cook over moderate heat, stirring to dissolve the juices that cling to the bottom and sides of the pan. Pour the pan liquid into the casserole containing the vegetable mixture. Let simmer 5 minutes.

9. Arrange the duck pieces skin side up over the vegetables, spooning some of the sauce over the pieces. Return to the oven and bake 1 hour.

10. Transfer the duck pieces to a serving dish.

11. Place a sieve inside a saucepan. Skim off any more fat from the duck. Pour and scrape the vegetables and nonfat pan juices into the sieve and strain. Press the solids with the back of a heavy spoon to extract as much liquid as possible. Discard the solids. Add 3–4 additional tablespoons of chicken broth if desired and add the olives. Heat the sauce and pour it over the duck.

Yield: 4 servings

—CRAIG CLAIBORNE AND PIERRE FRANEY

MRS. JOSEPH AMICO'S ROAST DUCK WITH SOUR CHERRIES

meat

ADAPTED FROM *The New York Times Large-Type Cookbook*

1 duck, 5–6 pounds
½ teaspoon salt
⅛ teaspoon black pepper
Pinch of thyme
2 small onions, sliced
1 medium-size carrot, sliced
1 can (No. 2) sour pitted cherries
½ cup port wine
1 teaspoon cornstarch

1. Preheat oven to 425 degrees.
2. Season inside of duck with salt, pepper, thyme and half the onion slices. Prick skin around thighs, back and lower breast.

3. Place duck, breast side up, in a roasting pan and add the remaining sliced onion and carrot around it. Roast 15 minutes to brown lightly. Reduce heat to 350 degrees and turn duck on its side.
4. After 30 minutes, turn duck on other side. Thirty minutes later, turn breast side up and salt lightly. Cook 15–30 minutes longer, depending on desired degree of doneness. Each time duck is turned, the fat in the pan should be drained off.
5. Remove duck to a warm platter. Remove all but 1 tablespoon fat from pan; add juice drained from cherries and wine. Bring to a boil, stirring well. Strain into a small saucepan; add cornstarch dissolved in a little cold water and heat until thickened. Add cherries, heat through. Serve with duck.

Yield: 4 servings

DUCK STEW WITH BLACK FIGS

meat

2 (4-pound) ducks, each cut into 16 serving pieces
    (have the butcher do this), reserve necks, gizzards
    and wings for stock
8 medium cloves garlic, smashed, peeled and cut in
    half lengthwise
5 whole leaves sage
1 bay leaf
1½ cups medium-bodied red wine
32 small or 24 medium fresh black figs
    (1½ pounds), stems removed
1 tablespoon kosher salt, plus additional to taste
Freshly ground black pepper to taste

1. Place a rack in bottom third of oven and another in top third. Heat oven to 500 degrees.

2. With a pair of kitchen scissors, trim excess fat from duck pieces. In 2 large heavy roasting pans, place duck, skin side down, in one layer. Put one pan on each rack and roast for 15 minutes. Carefully remove pans from oven and pour off fat. Turn duck, meat side down, and return to oven, placing pan from bottom rack on top rack, and vice versa. Roast for 15 minutes. Remove duck pieces to a bowl. Pour or spoon fat from pan, reserving 2 tablespoons.

3. Place one pan on top of stove. Pour ½ cup water into pan. Bring liquid to boil, scraping any browned bits from bottom and sides of pan with wooden spoon. Pour this liquid over the duck in the bowl. Repeat with second pan.

4. In large wide pot, heat the 2 tablespoons of reserved fat over medium heat. Stir in garlic and cook, stirring, until golden, about 4 minutes. With slotted spoon, remove garlic and add to browned duck. Pour off fat and discard.

5. Return duck with its liquid and garlic to the pot. Add sage, bay leaf and 1 cup wine. Cover. Bring to boil. Lower heat and simmer gently for 45 minutes, turning duck every 15 minutes.

6. Stir in figs, salt, pepper and remaining ½ cup wine. Cover. Return to boil. Lower heat and simmer for 10 minutes for small figs, or 10–15 minutes for medium. The figs should maintain their shape.

7. Remove duck and figs to serving platter. Pour sauce into measuring cup, let sit for 1–2 minutes and then skim fat. Season sauce with salt and pepper, pour some over duck and serve.

Yield: 6–8 servings

—BARBARA KAFKA

STEAM-ROASTED GOOSE

meat

ADAPTED FROM *The Way to Cook*

1 fresh goose, 9½–11 pounds
Juice of 1 lemon

Salt and freshly ground black pepper to taste
Handful of mixed celery leaves, sage and thyme
1 large carrot, roughly chopped
1 large onion, roughly chopped
1 celery stalk, roughly chopped

2 cups red wine

½ cup port

1½ tablespoons cornstarch

1. Remove wing tips at the joint and set aside with neck, heart and gizzard. Rub lemon juice inside and outside goose and sprinkle cavity with salt. With kitchen twine, tie drumsticks together. With a skewer or a needle, prick skin (but not flesh) around lower breast and thighs.

2. Place goose, breast up, on a rack in a roasting pan. Add just enough water to sit below rack. Place on top of stove and bring water to a boil. Cover tightly with a lid or aluminum foil. Reduce heat to medium-low and steam for 45 minutes to 1 hour, depending on size of goose. Check water occasionally, adding more if necessary.

3. Preheat oven to 325 degrees. Remove steamed goose from pan and allow to cool for 20 minutes. Pour liquid from pan; strain and reserve fat for another purpose. Return rack to pan and cover with a double sheet of foil. Place celery leaves, sage and thyme inside goose, and place goose breast side down on foil. Add carrot, onion and celery to pan and pour red wine over goose. Cover tightly and place in oven. Braise, basting occasionally, until legs are almost tender when pressed, about 1–1½ hours. While the goose is braising, make stock by combining neck, wing tips, heart and gizzard in a pan with lightly salted water to cover. Simmer for 2 hours, adding more water if necessary.

4. Uncover goose and turn it breast side up. Baste with juices in pan. Roast uncovered, until drumsticks feel quite tender when pressed, about ½ hour. If goose is browned, roast partly covered.

5. Transfer goose to a carving board and keep warm. Pour fat and juices from pan, leaving vegetables in pan. Add goose stock to pan. In a small bowl, blend port and cornstarch. Add to pan and stir well. Strain mixture into a saucepan, pressing vegetables to extract juices. Add salt and pepper to taste.

6. To serve, carve goose and arrange meat on a warm serving platter. Drizzle with gravy; pass remaining gravy separately.

Yield: 8 servings

—R.W. APPLE, JR.

ROASTED CORNISH HENS WITH GRAPES

meat

4 Cornish hens, with necks and gizzards, each about
    1¼ pounds

2 tablespoons vegetable or corn oil

Salt and freshly ground pepper to taste

1 large onion, peeled

¼ cup dry sherry

1 tablespoon red wine vinegar

1 tablespoon honey

1 cup Chicken Broth (page 48),
    fresh or canned

1 tablespoon tomato paste

2 cups green seedless grapes

1 tablespoon margarine

1. Preheat oven to 450 degrees.

2. Place the hens in a shallow baking dish without crowding. Rub hens with oil and sprinkle inside and out with salt and pepper. Cut onion in half. Place

the halves cut side down around the hens. Arrange gizzards and necks around the hens.

3. Place baking dish on top of stove over medium-high heat. Turn the hens over in the dish to coat them with the oil. Brown them for a few minutes. Arrange hens on their sides, place in the oven and bake 15 minutes, basting often.

4. Turn the hens on the other side and continue baking 15 minutes, basting often.

5. Turn the hens breast side up. Bake about 10 minutes, basting often.

6. Transfer the hens to a heated serving platter. Cover with foil to keep warm.

7. Skim off the fat from the pan liquid. Place the dish on top of stove and bring the liquid to a boil. Add the sherry and vinegar and stir to dissolve any brown particles that may cling to the bottom of pan. Strain sauce into a saucepan and bring to a boil. Cook down by half. Add the honey, broth and tomato paste. Stir and add any liquid that may have accumulated inside or around the birds. Add the grapes and bring to a boil.

8. Cook about 1 minute, stirring. Swirl in the margarine and add salt and pepper, if necessary. Pour the sauce over the hens and serve.

Yield: 4 servings

—PIERRE FRANEY

CORNISH HENS WITH FRESH CRANBERRIES

meat

4 Cornish hens with giblets, each about
    1¼ pounds
2 tablespoons corn, peanut or vegetable oil
Salt to taste, if desired
Freshly ground pepper to taste
1 onion, peeled
¼ cup dry white wine
1 tablespoon honey
⅓ cup Chicken Broth (page 48), canned or fresh
1 tablespoon tomato paste
2 cups fresh cranberries

1. Preheat the oven to 450 degrees.

2. Put the hens in a shallow, flameproof baking dish without crowding. Rub the hens all over with oil and sprinkle with salt and pepper. Cut the onion in half and place the halves, cut side down, around the hens. Arrange the gizzards and livers around the hens.

3. Place the baking dish with hens on top of the stove over low heat. Turn the hens around in the dish to coat with the oil. Arrange the hens on their sides. Place in the oven and bake 15 minutes, basting often.

4. Turn the hens on the other side and continue baking 15 minutes, basting often.

5. Turn the hens breast side up and continue baking about 10 minutes, basting often.

6. Transfer the hens to a heated serving platter and cover with foil to keep warm.

7. Skim off most of the fat from the pan liquid in the baking dish. Put the baking dish on top of the stove and bring the pan liquid to a boil. Add the wine and stir to dissolve any brown particles that may cling to the bottom of the pan. Strain the sauce into a saucepan and bring to a boil. Cook down to about half and add the honey, chicken broth and tomato paste. Stir. Add any liquid that has accumulated inside or around the hens. Add the cranberries and bring to a boil.

8. Cook until the cranberries pop, about 3 minutes, stirring often. Add salt and pepper. Pour the sauce over the hens and serve.

Yield: 4 servings

—PIERRE FRANEY

ROASTED CORNISH HENS WITH BULGUR STUFFING • (FARAKH BADARI)

meat

ADAPTED FROM Linda and Saleh Makar

> *4 Cornish hens, about 1 pound each*
> *Salt to taste if desired*
> *Freshly ground pepper to taste*
> *3 cups Bulgur Stuffing (see recipe below) at room*
> *   temperature*
> *3 tablespoons finely chopped parsley*
> *¼ cup corn, peanut or vegetable oil*
> *1 tablespoon freshly squeezed lime or lemon juice*
> *½ teaspoon poultry seasoning or finely chopped sage*
> *1 clove garlic, peeled and crushed*

1. Preheat the oven to 350 degrees.
2. Sprinkle the hens inside and out with salt and pepper. Blend the bulgur and parsley in a mixing bowl.
3. Stuff each game hen with an equal portion of the bulgur mixture. Truss the hens.
4. Place a rack in a shallow roasting pan. Arrange the hens breast side up on the rack. To prepare a basting sauce, blend the remaining ingredients, salt and pepper.

5. Brush the hens with the basting sauce. Place in the oven and roast 1 hour, basting often with the sauce. Remove the trussing string and serve.

Yield: 4 servings

◆ BULGUR STUFFING ◆

meat, pareve

> *1 cup large-grain (No. 3) bulgur*
> *2 tablespoons margarine*
> *½ cup finely chopped onion*
> *1 teaspoon finely minced garlic*
> *1½ cups Chicken Broth (page 48) or water*
> *Salt to taste if desired*
> *Freshly ground pepper to taste*

1. Rinse the bulgur in cold water and drain well.
2. Put the margarine in a small saucepan and add the onion and garlic. Cook, stirring briefly, until onion is wilted.
3. Add the bulgur and blend well. Add the broth, salt and pepper and bring to a boil. Cover closely

and let simmer 20–25 minutes, stirring occasionally from the bottom to prevent sticking. Cook just until all the liquid is absorbed.

Yield: About 3 cups

NOTE: *Stuffing may also be used to fill the cavity of a 3½- to 4-pound roasting chicken.*

—CRAIG CLAIBORNE

SQUAB WITH MUSHROOMS AND TOMATOES

meat

ADAPTED FROM *The Best of Craig Claiborne*

8–10 pieces dried black mushrooms, preferably imported Italian mushrooms
4 fresh, cleaned squabs, split in half
Salt and freshly ground pepper to taste
½ cup olive oil
1 garlic clove, thinly sliced
1 cup finely chopped onion
1 teaspoon dried rosemary
½ cup dry red wine
2 cups crushed fresh or canned tomatoes
1 cup thinly sliced fresh mushrooms
¼ cup tomato paste
⅓ cup water

1. Soak the mushrooms in cold water to cover for 1 hour or longer.

2. Sprinkle the squab halves with salt and pepper. Set aside and reserve the squab livers.

3. Heat all but 2 tablespoons of the oil in a large heavy skillet and add the squab split side down. Brown over high heat, turning, and add the garlic, onion and rosemary. Add the wine, tomatoes and salt and pepper to taste. Squeeze the black mushrooms to extract most of the moisture and add them.

4. In another skillet, heat the remaining 2 tablespoons of oil and cook the fresh mushrooms until wilted. Add them to the squab and cook for 5 minutes.

5. Blend the tomato paste with the water and add it. Cover closely and cook for 30 minutes. Add the squab livers and continue cooking for another 30 minutes. Serve with hot polenta.

Yield: 8 servings

HONEY-MUSTARD QUAIL

meat

18 quail

5 tablespoons honey (approximately)

½ cup Dijon mustard

Salt and freshly ground black pepper to taste

1 tablespoon vegetable oil

½ cup finely chopped shallots

1⅓ cups unsweetened applesauce, preferably freshly made

1. If the quail have not been deboned, butterfly the quail by snipping up the backbone with shears, then flattening them. Put in a large dish. Boned quail, with the breastbones and backbones removed but with the drumsticks intact, can simply be split.

2. Mix 3 tablespoons of the honey with ⅓ cup of the mustard. Season the quail with salt and pepper and coat with the mustard mixture. Set aside to marinate for 45 minutes.

3. Preheat a grill or broiler.

4. Heat the oil in a medium-size saucepan. Add the shallots and sauté until lightly browned. Add the applesauce and the remaining mustard and stir to combine. Heat gently, season with salt and pepper and sweeten to taste with 2 or more tablespoons of honey. Keep warm.

5. Grill or broil the quail until nicely seared and cooked to the desired degree of doneness. Serve with the warm seasoned applesauce.

Yield: 6 servings

—FLORENCE FABRICANT

MEAT

Using forequarter cuts that have been koshered, inventive observant cooks have co-opted many dishes from other cuisines. Much favored are grilled or broiled chops and steaks such as the succulent rib steak and the plump belt of beef known as skirt steak or Romanian tenderloin, especially good if served rare.

Boiling and braising for pot roasts and stews are especially favored as the liquids, fats and seasonings used in their preparation impart moistness and flavor. Those cooking methods are suited to the stringier forequarter cuts, and as a bonus, result in hearty gravies that grace potatoes, dumplings and grains such as rice, bulgur, kasha or cornmeal *mamaliga.* They are also convenient for entertaining, as they the lend themselves to advance cooking and reheating.

Whether beef brisket is simmered in a coffee barbecue sauce, or baked in bean and vegetable Sabbath casserole *cholent,* or sauced with ruby-red pomegranate seeds, it is a standard among Jews everywhere. Lamb shanks braised with prunes or apricots or preserved lemon, or in the biblical Esau's lamb and lentil pottage, reflect a diversity of cultural influences, as do veal dishes such as the Syrian stew with black-eyed peas, or another piquant with capers and sage.

Various innards are traditional favorites on Jewish menus, including pickled or smoked tongue, sweetbreads and liver, although changing tastes are making cuts such as brains, lungs and hearts seem obsolete, alas.

One of the greatest Ashkenazic contributions to mainstream gastronomy are those cured meats sold in what have come to be known as New York Jewish delicatessens, honoring the city where they were introduced to the United States and flourished. Made of beef and highly seasoned, salami, pastrami, corned beef and frankfurters fill the air of food shops and restaurants with mouthwatering aromas. Traditionally store-bought, along with appropriate garnishes such as pickles and potato salad, and usually served in sandwiches, they were one of the earliest prepared, take-out foods. As such, they comprised a traditional Sunday night home supper for Jews two or three generations ago.

CLASSIC BRAISED BRISKET OF BEEF

meat

ADAPTED FROM *The Best of Craig Claiborne*

1 (4½-pound) brisket of beef
Salt and freshly ground pepper to taste
2 tablespoons peanut, vegetable or corn oil
2 cups finely chopped onions
1 cup finely chopped carrots
3 garlic cloves, peeled and left whole
1 bay leaf
6 parsley sprigs
2 thyme sprigs, or ½ teaspoon dried
4 whole cloves
6 crushed peppercorns
1 cup plus 1 tablespoon dry white wine
1 cup chopped, canned tomatoes
1 cup water
1 tablespoon arrowroot or cornstarch

1. Have the butcher trim and slice away almost all the fat from the top and bottom of the beef.
2. Sprinkle the beef with salt and a generous grinding of pepper.
3. Heat the oil in a heavy casserole large enough to accommodate the brisket without crowding.

4. Add the brisket and brown on one side for about 10 minutes. Turn the meat and brown on the second side for about 10 minutes.
5. Pour off the fat from the casserole and add the onions, carrots, garlic, bay leaf, parsley, thyme, cloves and peppercorns. No liquid is added at this point.
6. Cover closely and cook over low heat for 15 minutes. Add 1 cup of wine, the tomatoes and water. Cover and cook for 45 minutes. Uncover and turn the meat. Cover and cook for about 45 minutes.
7. Uncover and turn the meat a third time. Cover and cook for 45 minutes longer. Total cooking time after browning is 2½ hours.
8. Remove the brisket. Skim off all traces of fat from the surface of the sauce. Cook the sauce down for about 5 minutes.
9. Blend the arrowroot or cornstarch with 1 tablespoon of wine and stir it into the boiling sauce. Serve the brisket sliced with the sauce. An excellent accompaniment for this is braised carrots and onions.

Yield: 10 servings

NOTE: *For maximum tenderness, always slice brisket thinly against the grain of the meat.*

ROSH HA SHANA POT ROAST WITH ONION CONFIT

meat

ADAPTED FROM Brendan Walsh,
    French Culinary Institute

1 (3-pound) brisket or eye round, fat removed
Peanut oil

Salt to taste, if desired
Pepper to taste
8 cups beef stock
12 (2-inch) new potatoes
12 baby carrots
18 (5-inch) batons of celery

12 baby turnips

3 leeks

12 cherry tomatoes

11 tablespoons (¾ cup minus 1 tablespoon) softened pareve margarine

1 cup flour

Onion Confit (see recipe below)

1. Rub beef with peanut oil, salt and pepper.

2. Add about 2 tablespoons oil to a pot large enough to hold the beef, stock and vegetables. Brown beef on all sides. Add stock to cover; bring to boil, reduce heat, cover and simmer. Eye round should simmer 2–2½ hours; brisket must cook longer.

3. While beef is cooking, prepare vegetables. Scrub potatoes; trim and scrub carrots; cut celery and trim and scrub turnips. Cut green part from leeks. Trim the root, leaving just a little so leek will hold together. Rinse thoroughly.

4. Turn on broiler; rinse and stem tomatoes and arrange on broiler pan.

5. Blend margarine with flour to a paste and set aside.

6. Twenty minutes before beef is ready, add potatoes, carrots, celery, turnips and leeks. Raise heat to return liquid to simmer; cover and finish cooking.

7. Remove beef and set aside. Remove 8 cups of stock and bring to boil in separate pot. Keep vegetables warm in remaining stock.

8. Gradually beat margarine-flour paste into boiling stock until it has thickened to gravy consistency.

9. Broil tomatoes 3–5 minutes. Do not let them burst.

10. Slice beef against the grain. Spoon thin layer of gravy on a platter and top with sliced beef. Arrange vegetables around the meat, using tomatoes to provide spots of color. Place spoonfuls of onion confit down center of meat and pass additional gravy.

Yield: 6 servings

NOTE: *The beef can be cooked for 1½–2 hours in advance and reheated before adding the vegetables. Sweet dishes are the mainstay of Rosh Ha Shana. The sweetness in this pot roast comes from the onion confit that tops the meat and from baby carrots and baby turnips.*

◆ **ONION CONFIT** ◆

pareve

3 large white onions

2 tablespoons peanut oil

⅓ bunch fresh sage leaves, chopped

2 ounces white wine vinegar

1. Peel onions and slice into thin strips.

2. Heat peanut oil in a large skillet and sauté onions over medium heat, stirring often. After about 30 minutes of cooking it might be necessary to add a little water to prevent them from sticking.

3. After 1 hour add the sage leaves and vinegar and continue cooking, stirring often, 30 minutes more. Set aside until beef is done.

Yield: Enough for 6 servings of beef

NOTE: *The confit can be made a day ahead and refrigerated. Warm slowly to serve.*

—MARIAN BURROS

SWEET-AND-SOUR POT ROAST

meat

ADAPTED FROM *Spice and Spirit: The Complete Kosher Jewish Cookbook*

1 (3-pound) rolled roast or brisket, most fat trimmed off
Salt and freshly ground pepper to taste
Pinch of nutmeg
1 tablespoon flour
2 tablespoons vegetable oil
4 large onions, sliced
1 clove garlic, minced
1 cup dry red wine
2 tablespoons tomato paste
2 tablespoons honey
1 tablespoon thyme
1 tablespoon vinegar

4 sprigs parsley
2 celery tops
1 bay leaf

1. Preheat oven to 325 degrees. Dust roast with salt, pepper, nutmeg and flour. In a 5-quart Dutch oven, heat oil, brown the roast and remove.

2. Brown onions and garlic in remaining oil. Return meat to pot and add remaining ingredients. Cover, place in oven and bake for approximately 2 hours.

3. Remove bay leaf and serve. Or cool dish and remove bay leaf. Refrigerate for several hours, then remove grease on top. Slice meat and cover with sauce. Reheat and serve.

Yield: 6–8 servings

—JOAN NATHAN

BRAISED POT ROAST WITH POMEGRANATES

meat

6 garlic cloves
15 fresh sage leaves or 2 tablespoons dry sage
8 tablespoons olive oil
3 tablespoons red wine vinegar
1 tablespoon lemon juice
1 teaspoon kosher salt
Freshly ground pepper to taste
6 pounds lean brisket of beef
2 garlic cloves, slivered
1 large onion, sliced
4 cups Chicken Stock (page 48), canned or fresh
2 tablespoons soy sauce

Salt and pepper to taste
2 pomegranates or 2 pounds small seedless grapes (see Note below)
Parsley for garnish

1. Place the garlic cloves, sage, 6 tablespoons of oil, the vinegar, lemon juice, kosher salt and freshly ground pepper in a food processor. Process until all the ingredients are finely chopped.

2. Place the meat in a roasting pan. With a knife make several incisions in the meat and insert the slivers of garlic. Then pour the marinade over the meat. Cover the pan with foil and refrigerate overnight.

3. The following day, heat the remaining tablespoons

of oil in a pan large enough to hold the meat. When the oil is hot, add the sliced onion and sauté it until it is lightly golden. Remove the meat from the marinade and brown on all sides over high heat. Then add the marinade, chicken stock, 2 cups of water, soy sauce and salt and pepper to taste. Bring to a boil, lower the heat and simmer for 2½ hours or until the meat is easily pierced with a fork. Remove the meat from the pan and cool.

4. Meanwhile, degrease the sauce. Then cut the pomegranates in two and remove the seeds. Add the seeds to the meat sauce.

5. Slice the meat and return to the saucepan. Reheat gently.

6. With a spatula, remove the meat to a large platter. Pour some sauce with pomegranate over the meat. Garnish with parsley and serve the remaining sauce in a gravy boat.

Yield: 6–8 servings

NOTE: *Pomegranate season begins in early fall. The fruit's slightly bitter taste and deep red color will add zest to the pot roast. Before removing the pomegranate seeds, rub your hands with lemon to prevent the juice from staining your fingers. If pomegranates are unavailable, use small seedless green grapes.*

—COLETTE ROSSANT

POT ROAST WITH CURRIED TOMATO SAUCE

meat

ADAPTED FROM *Cooking with Herbs and Spices*

4 pounds brisket of beef
Salt to taste, if desired
Freshly ground black pepper to taste
1 teaspoon curry powder
1 teaspoon turmeric
1 teaspoon ground ginger
2 tablespoons peanut oil
2 cups chopped onions
2 garlic cloves, finely minced
1 cup peeled and chopped fresh tomatoes or canned Italian plum tomatoes

1 bay leaf
3 fresh thyme sprigs or ½ teaspoon dried thyme
1 cup water or Beef Broth (page 49)

1. Rub meat with salt and pepper to taste, curry powder, turmeric and ginger.

2. Heat oil in a deep casserole or kettle and brown meat well on all sides, about 15 minutes. Pour off fat. Add remaining ingredients and bring to a boil. Cover and simmer until fork tender, 3 hours or longer.

3. Transfer to a platter, slice against the grain and serve.

Yield: 6 servings

BRISKET IN COFFEE-BARBECUE SAUCE

meat

¾ cup vegetable oil

1 large Spanish onion, minced

5 cloves garlic, minced

1 teaspoon crushed red pepper flakes

1 tablespoon tomato paste

7 tablespoons light-brown sugar

5 cups brewed coffee

½ cup cider vinegar

1 (28-ounce can) peeled, chopped tomatoes

Kosher salt and freshly ground black pepper to taste

1 brisket, about 4 pounds

1. In a medium kettle, heat ¼ cup of the oil over medium heat. Add the onion and cook, stirring, until soft and golden brown, about 7 minutes. Add the garlic and cook, stirring, until fragrant, about 30 seconds. Stir in the red pepper. Add the tomato paste and cook, stirring frequently, about 1 minute. Stir in the brown sugar. Pour in the coffee, vinegar and tomatoes, bring to a boil, then lower to a simmer. Simmer 10 minutes. Set aside to cool.

2. Working in small batches, transfer the tomato-coffee mixture to a blender and puree. Season with salt and pepper to taste. Set aside.

3. Preheat the oven to 275 degrees. Season the brisket with salt and pepper. In a Dutch oven with a tight-fitting lid, heat the remaining ½ cup oil. Brown the brisket on both sides. Drain off the oil, leaving the brisket in the Dutch oven. Turn the brisket so that the fat side is facing up and then coat it with the pureed tomato-coffee mixture. Cover the Dutch oven and place it in the oven. Bake for 3 hours, basting frequently.

4. Remove the lid and bake uncovered until the brisket is glazed and very tender, about 1½ hours more. Remove the brisket and set it aside to rest for 10 minutes, covered with foil, before slicing thinly across the grain.

Yield: 10–12 servings

—MOLLY O'NEILL

EASY BRISKET IN SWEET-AND-SOUR SAUCE

meat

ADAPTED FROM *Levana's Table: Kosher Cooking for Everyone*

1 medium onion, quartered

1 (2-inch) piece fresh ginger, peeled

6 large cloves garlic

¼ cup Dijon mustard (omit on Passover)

½ cup dry red wine

½ cup Coca-Cola or ginger ale

1 cup ketchup

¼ cup honey

¼ cup cider vinegar

¼ cup soy sauce (see Note below)

½ cup olive oil

½ teaspoon ground cloves

1 tablespoon coarsely ground pepper
1 first-cut brisket, 6–7 pounds, rinsed and patted
   thoroughly dry

Preheat the oven to 350 degrees.

FOR THE SAUCE:

Process all the ingredients except the meat in a food
processor until smooth.

FOR THE BRISKET:

1. Place the brisket in a pan just big enough to fit it
and pour the sauce over it. Cover tightly with a double layer of foil and bake for 2 hours.
2. Turn the brisket over and bake uncovered for 1
more hour or until very tender. A knife inserted in its
center should go in without any resistance. Transfer
the brisket to a cutting board and let it cool slightly.
3. Transfer the sauce from the roasting pan to a
saucepan. Cook over high heat until it is reduced to
2½ cups. Skim the oil off the top.
4. To serve, cut the brisket into thin slices against the
grain (if the slices look too long, cut the brisket in
half across its whole length before slicing). Pour the
sauce on top and serve hot.

Yield: 12 ample servings

NOTE: *This easy and delicious recipe does not require browning of the meat, as many brisket recipes do. You may omit
   the soy sauce on Passover or if you think your meat might
   be too salty.*

—JOAN NATHAN

CHOLENT BRISKET

meat

1 cup vegetable oil
1 brisket, about 4 pounds
Kosher salt and freshly ground black pepper to taste
2 medium Spanish onions, thinly sliced
1 tablespoon paprika
6 garlic cloves, coarsely chopped
2 tablespoons honey
6 small red bliss potatoes (2 pounds), quartered
3 medium carrots, peeled and cut into 1-inch-thick
   slices
1 cup dried cranberry beans (about 7 ounces), soaked
   in water 1 hour, drained
1 cup dried green lentils (about 7 ounces), soaked in
   water 1 hour, drained
1 cup barley
1 pound beef marrowbones, cut by butcher into
   1-inch pieces

1. Preheat oven to 225 degrees. In a Dutch oven with a
tight-fitting lid, over high heat, heat ½ cup oil. Season
the brisket with salt and pepper. Brown the brisket in
the oil on both sides, then transfer to a platter.
2. Drain the oil from the Dutch oven. Add the
remaining ½ cup oil and reduce the heat to medium.
Add the onions and paprika and cook, stirring, until
the onions are brown and soft, about 6 minutes.
Add the garlic and cook until fragrant, about 30
seconds. Stir in the honey. Remove the Dutch oven
from the heat.
3. Place the brisket on the onion-garlic mixture. Sur-

round the brisket with the potatoes, carrots, beans, lentils and barley and place the marrowbones on top. Cover with cold water by 4 inches. Stir in 1 tablespoon salt and 1 teaspoon pepper. Return the Dutch oven to the heat and bring to a boil. Skim off any scum that forms on the surface of the liquid. Cover and place it in the oven. Bake for 8 hours or overnight.

4. Remove the brisket from the oven. If it seems dry, moisten it with a little water. When ready to serve, reheat, covered, in a 350-degree oven until it is hot. Transfer to a large platter and serve.

Yield: 10–12 servings

—MOLLY O'NEILL

EDITH KLEIN'S CHOLENT WITH PASTRAMI

meat

1 pound dried Great Northern beans
¼ cup chicken fat or vegetable oil
2 large onions, chopped
3 shallots, chopped
3 cloves garlic, chopped
2½ pounds boneless flanken or brisket, in 2-inch chunks
½ pound pastrami, in one piece
1 tablespoon Hungarian paprika
1 tablespoon honey
½ cup pearl barley
Salt and freshly ground black pepper to taste

1. Place beans in a bowl, cover with cold water to a depth of 2 inches and allow to soak at least 4 hours or overnight.

2. Heat fat or oil in a large, heavy casserole. Add onions and shallots and sauté until golden. Stir in garlic and cook for about a minute. Remove the vegetables from the pan with a slotted spoon, draining them well, and set aside.

3. Brown chunks of beef lightly in the fat and remove them.

4. Preheat oven to 400 degrees.

5. Cut pastrami into 1-inch cubes and stir them into the fat; then stir in the paprika and honey. Return onions, shallots, garlic and beef to casserole. Stir in barley. Drain beans and add them.

6. Add 6 cups boiling water to casserole. Cover and place in oven. Bake for 30 minutes.

7. Reduce heat to 250 degrees and bake 30 minutes longer. Remove lid, season to taste with salt and pepper, then cover casserole with a piece of aluminum foil and replace the lid. Place in oven and allow to bake 7–8 hours or overnight.

Yield: 8 servings

—FLORENCE FABRICANT

BOILED BEEF

meat

ADAPTED FROM *The New York Times International Cookbook*

1 brisket of beef, 3–4 pounds

1 shank bone

8 leeks, trimmed and rinsed well

7 carrots

1 onion studded with 4 cloves

2 ribs celery with leaves

12 peppercorns, bruised slightly with a mortar and pestle or the back of a knife

Salt to taste

1 bay leaf

1 teaspoon dried thyme

12 white onions

1. Place the meat and shank bone in a deep kettle or Dutch oven. Cover with boiling water.

2. Add two leeks halved, one carrot quartered, the onion studded with cloves, celery, peppercorns, salt to taste, bay leaf and the thyme. Bring to a boil, cover and simmer 3 hours, or until the meat is tender.

3. During the last 30 minutes of cooking, add the remaining vegetables and cook until tender. Slice beef against the grain and serve on a warm platter surrounded by the vegetables, with any or all of classic accompaniments listed below, or with chutneys or relishes of your choice from pages 413–414, 420 and 426–428.

Yield: 6 servings

Classic accompaniments for Boiled Beef:
   Prepared mustard, preferably Dijon or Dusseldorf
   Cornichon (French gherkins) or other small sour pickles
   Grated fresh horseradish
   Coarse salt, such as kosher or sea salt

NOTE: *For a Beef Salad Vinaigrette: Combine 4 cups of thinly sliced Boiled Beef with 1 cup finely chopped onion, ½ cup finely sliced cornichons or other sour pickles, 1 tablespoon finely chopped chives, 2 tablespoons Dijon or Dusseldorf or other mustard, ⅓ cup wine vinegar, 1½ cups peanut oil, salt and freshly ground black pepper to taste. Serve at room temperature.*

KURT GUTENBRUNNER'S AUSTRIAN BOILED BEEF WITH APPLE-HORSERADISH

meat

1 large onion, halved horizontally but not peeled

3 large carrots, scrubbed

1 large parsnip, scrubbed

1 small celery root, scrubbed

2 celery stalks

1 leek, cut in half

1 pound beef bones

2 pieces beef triangle, each about 1½ pounds

Sea salt to taste

15 black peppercorns

2 bay leaves
4 cloves garlic, peeled
8 branches flat-leaf parsley
4 branches fresh dill
2 sprigs lovage (optional)
Apple Horseradish (recipe below)

1. Char onion on cut side over open flame or by placing cut side down in cast-iron skillet over high heat. Place in 16-quart stockpot with carrots, parsnip, celery root, celery, leek and beef bones. Add 8 quarts cold water. Bring to boil and cook 10 minutes, skimming constantly. Add beef, allow to boil 5 minutes and skim.

2. Reduce heat to simmer and cook, skimming from time to time, 1 hour. Add 1 tablespoon sea salt, peppercorns, bay leaves and garlic. Tie herbs together and add. Continue simmering 1–1½ hours, until meat is very tender.

3. While meat is cooking, prepare Apple Horseradish (below) and set aside.

4. Remove meat from pot and cover with foil. Line large sieve or colander with cheesecloth or linen napkin, and place over very large bowl. Pour in contents of pot. Do not press liquid from vegetables. Transfer strained broth to 6-quart saucepan.

5. Set carrots, parsnip, celery root and celery stalks aside. Discard everything else. Peel and dice carrots, parsnip and celery root. Dice celery stalks. Set aside.

6. Gently simmer the broth to reheat it. Do not boil it or it will turn cloudy. Add salt to taste. Serve some of the broth as a first course, with diced celery root, parsnip and celery stalks.

7. Then serve meat. If it needs to be reheated, steam briefly over remaining broth. Slice meat ½ inch thick across the grain. Place in soup plates with diced carrots, moisten with hot broth and top with apple-horseradish, sea salt and chives.

Yield: 6 servings

NOTE: *The beauty of this dish is that you wind up with two courses, ready in advance, with most of the cooking needing no attention. Chef Gutenbrunner suggests serving the meat with crispy potatoes or boiled potatoes. Red Cabbage (page 258) is also a traditional accompaniment.*

◆ **APPLE HORSERADISH** ◆

pareve
ADAPTED FROM Wallsé

MIX TOGETHER:

½ cup freshly grated horseradish
1 Granny Smith apple, peeled, cored and grated
Juice of 1 lemon
¼ cup minced chives

Yield: Approximately 1¼ cup

NOTE: *This is a superb variation on the grated horseradish that is usually served with Boiled Beef. Other classic accompaniments include small sour pickles (preferably cornichons) or prepared mustards (such as Dijon or Dusseldorf). Chutney (see pages 426–428) offers additional variety.*

—KURT GUTENBRUNNER

CORNED BEEF

meat

8 cups water
1¼ cups kosher salt
1 cup sugar
3 tablespoons pickling spices
1 (4-pound) brisket

1. In a medium pot over high heat, combine the water, salt, sugar and the pickling spices. Boil, uncovered, until the sugar and salt are dissolved, about 1 minute. Transfer the liquid to a container large enough for the liquid and the brisket. Refrigerate the container until the liquid is cool.

2. Place the brisket in the container with the liquid, weighing it down with a heavy object to keep it submerged. Refrigerate the brisket in the liquid for at least 8 days and up to 12 days, turning the brisket each day.

3. Boil the brisket, covered, with its liquid until tender, about 3 hours. Serve as an entrée with horseradish sauce (pages 413–414) or thinly sliced on rye bread with mustard or Russian dressing.

Yield: 1 corned beef, about 6 entrée servings

—MOLLY O'NEILL

CORNED BEEF AND MUSHROOM HASH

meat

ADAPTED FROM Auberge du Soleil, Rutherford, Calif.

2 pounds cooked corned beef, cut into small pieces and shredded
1 cup sliced shiitake mushrooms
6 scallions, white and delicate green parts only
⅓ cup chopped parsley
Salt and freshly ground pepper to taste
2 eggs, beaten
Eggs for poaching, optional

1. Toss the corned beef, mushrooms, scallions, parsley, salt and pepper together in a mixing bowl. Pass through the coarse blade of a meat processor with a steel blade and process until well chopped. Be careful not to overwork the mixture. It should not be a puree. Cover and refrigerate overnight.

2. Form the mixture into small patties. If it seems dry and does not hold together easily (the way hamburger would), add the beaten eggs. The mixture should make 10–12 small patties. Sauté in a nonstick skillet until crispy and brown on both sides. Serve hot. Top each serving with a poached egg, if desired.

Yield: 5–6 servings

—DORRIE GREENSPAN

ALAIN DUCASSE'S RIB-EYE STEAKS WITH PEPPERED CRANBERRY MARMALADE AND SWISS CHARD

meat

2 (24-ounce) boneless rib-eye steaks, each about
    1½ inches thick, at room temperature
Salt to taste
4 tablespoons unsalted margarine
4 large cloves garlic, unpeeled and crushed
Freshly ground black pepper to taste
2 sprigs fresh thyme
Peppered Cranberry Marmalade (recipe below)
Sautéed Swiss Chard (recipe below)

1. Place a heavy sauté pan large enough to hold both steaks comfortably over medium heat. Stand steaks up in pan on fat side and cook until fat has browned and most has been rendered into pan.
2. Use tongs to turn steaks onto a flat side, dust with salt to taste and cook until browned on one side. Turn and cook on second side until somewhat undercooked. Pour off all but a couple of tablespoons of fat and add margarine and crushed garlic. Baste steaks with margarine and remaining fat until cooked almost to desired degree of doneness: for medium rare, it will take about 10 minutes on each side.
3. Remove pan from heat, season steaks with salt and pepper to taste, place a sprig of thyme on each and set pan aside on unlighted burner. Steaks must rest in warm place at least 10–15 minutes. They can rest longer than that if placed in a 150-degree oven after the first 10 minutes.
4. Cut steaks in thick slices, trimming away excess internal fat. Divide among four warm dinner plates and place a generous dollop of cranberry marmalade

alongside. Serve with chard and additional marmalade.

Yield: 4 servings

NOTE: *Chef Ducasse's unusual method of cooking the steak first on its narrow side renders the flavorful fat that is used to brown the meat when it is turned onto its flat sides. You may serve the steaks plain, perhaps with some crispy fried potatoes. But the following original accompaniments create a truly special dish, unique in flavor and presentation.*

◆ PEPPERED CRANBERRY MARMALADE ◆

meat

1 cup cranberry juice
1 cup dried cranberries
½ cup sweet cherry liqueur such as Cherry Heering
    or Cherry Kijafa (not kirschwasser)
6 tablespoons balsamic vinegar
1 tablespoon extra-virgin olive oil
½ cup minced shallots
½ cup minced onion
½ cup minced celery
⅓ cup concentrated beef stock
Salt to taste
Freshly ground black pepper to taste

1. Place cranberry juice in a saucepan, bring to a simmer, add cranberries and remove from heat. Allow to soak 40 minutes.

2. Drain cranberries, reserving juice. Place in a food processor with liqueur and 4 tablespoons vinegar and pulse until chopped.

3. Heat oil in a 3-quart saucepan. Add shallots, onion and celery, and cook over low heat until tender but not colored.

4. Stir in ¼ cup reserved cranberry juice and remaining vinegar, and simmer until most of liquid has evaporated. Stir in cranberry mixture and simmer until thick, about 5 minutes. Stir in concentrated beef stock, salt and a generous amount of pepper. Serve at once, or warm just before serving.

Yield: 2 cups

◆ **SAUTEED SWISS CHARD** ◆

meat

>2 bunches Swiss chard, one red, one white, rinsed
>1½ cups Chicken Stock (page 48)
>2 large cloves garlic, peeled
>2 tablespoons extra-virgin olive oil
>Salt and freshly ground black pepper to taste

1. Trim leaves from stems of chard. Coarsely chop leaves and set aside.

2. Cut stems in pieces ½ inch wide and 2 inches long. Place in a saucepan with chicken stock and simmer 10 minutes, until tender. Drain stems and set aside. (Stock can be reserved for another use.)

3. Impale garlic cloves on a large cooking fork. Heat oil in a large skillet. Add chard leaves and stems. Sauté, stirring with the fork, until leaves have wilted. Season with salt and pepper, and serve.

Yield: 4 servings

—ALAIN DUCASSE

PAN-SEARED CORIANDER-CRUSTED SKIRT STEAK WITH WARM CITRUS RELISH

meat

>2 pieces of skirt steak, 10 ounces each
>¼ cup cracked coriander seed
>1 tablespoon freshly ground black pepper
>1 tablespoon kosher salt
>2 tablespoons vegetable oil
>1 red onion, diced medium
>1 red bell pepper, diced medium

>1 tablespoon minced garlic
>½ cup fresh orange juice
>3–6 dashes Tabasco sauce
>¼ cup fresh lime juice
>¼ cup roughly chopped fresh cilantro
>Salt and freshly ground black pepper to taste

1. Rub steak all over with coriander, pepper and salt, pressing gently to make sure spices adhere.

2. Place a 10-inch cast-iron skillet on a burner and allow to warm over medium-high heat for 5 minutes. Add steak and cook until very well browned, about 4–5 minutes per side. Remove steak from pan and set aside.

3. Add oil to pan and heat until hot but not smoking. Add onion and bell pepper and sauté, stirring frequently, until tender, about 5 minutes. Add garlic and continue to sauté, stirring frequently, for 2 minutes more. Add orange juice and Tabasco and cook, stir-ring occasionally, for 3 minutes. Remove pan from heat and stir in the lime juice, cilantro and salt and pepper.

4. Slice skirt steak thinly on the bias and serve, accompanied by the warm relish.

Yield: 2 servings

—JOHN WILLOUGHBY AND
CHRIS SCHLESINGER

CHINESE ROMANIAN-TENDERLOIN PEPPER STEAK

meat

1 skirt steak, about 1¼–1½ pounds
2 tablespoons corn oil
Pinch salt
1 large garlic clove, minced
2 small green peppers, seeded, trimmed of ribs and
    cut in about ¾-inch squares
1 large onion, peeled and thinly sliced vertically
2 teaspoons cornstarch
2 tablespoons soy sauce
2 tablespoons dry sherry
Pinch sugar
Pinch powdered ginger
Salt to taste
Black pepper to taste

1. Trim all the fat from one side of steak, leaving some on the other side. Cut the meat in half so that it will fit flat in a pan. Heat a large black-iron skillet until it begins to smoke. Place the two pieces of meat in the skillet, fat sides down. Make sure the pieces do not touch. Fry over moderate heat for 5–7 minutes, or until one side is well seared and lifts eas-ily from pan. Turn and fry the other side for about 4–5 minutes, or until it is seared. (The meat should be rare in the center.) Remove the steaks and place them on a platter or a cutting board with a well. Cut the meat in half across the grain, then cut with the grain to make rectangles (about 1 by 1½ inches each). Reserve the juices.

2. Heat the oil in the same skillet, scraping up the coagulated pan juices. Add the salt and garlic and sauté for 1 minute, or until the garlic loses its raw look. Do not let it brown. Add the peppers and onion and sauté, stirring, for 4–5 minutes, or until the vegetables begin to soften.

3. In a small bowl, combine the cornstarch with the soy sauce and sherry. Set aside. Return the meat and the reserved juices to the skillet, cover loosely and simmer for 2–3 minutes. Lower the heat and add the cornstarch mixture. Cook, stirring, for a few seconds until the sauce coats the meat and vegetables. Add the sugar, ginger, salt and a generous amount of black pepper. Serve immediately on heated plates with rice.

Yield: 4 servings

—MIMI SHERATON

BRAISED SHORT RIBS IN PORCINI-PRUNE SAUCE

meat

ADAPTED FROM Laurent Manrique

3 pounds beef short ribs, cut into 3-inch lengths

3 medium carrots, cut into 1-inch pieces

3 stalks celery, cut into 1-inch pieces

1 ounce (about 1 loosely packed cup)
fresh thyme sprigs

2 bay leaves

1 tablespoon black peppercorns

7 medium onions, peeled

3 heads garlic

6 cups hearty red wine

Salt and freshly ground black pepper to taste

4 tablespoons duck fat or vegetable oil

8 cups Veal Stock (page 50) or 6 cups canned beef
broth mixed with 2 cups water

½ pound fresh porcini mushrooms or sliced shiitake
mushrooms

½ pound dried pitted prunes, cut into ⅓-inch
slices

1. In a large nonreactive mixing bowl, combine short ribs, carrots, celery, thyme, bay leaves and peppercorns. Cut 4 of the onions into 1-inch chunks and add to bowl. Cut 2 heads of garlic (with peel) in half crosswise and add to bowl. Pour wine over all and mix well. Cover and refrigerate overnight.

2. Remove short ribs from marinade and drain well. Pat dry with paper towels and season with salt and pepper to taste. Set aside. Strain marinade into a clean bowl, reserving vegetables. Remove thyme, bay leaves and peppercorns and reserve. In a large casserole over high heat, heat 2 tablespoons of duck fat and add short ribs. Sear short ribs until well browned on all sides, about 10 minutes. Remove short ribs and set aside.

3. Preheat oven to 375 degrees. Add 1 tablespoon of duck fat to casserole, then add the reserved vegetables. Sauté, stirring constantly, until lightly browned, about 10 minutes. Add reserved marinade and stir well. Boil marinade until reduced by half, about 15 minutes. Add veal stock, short ribs and reserved thyme, bay leaves and peppercorns. Cover and braise in oven until ribs are very tender, about 2½ hours.

4. Remove short ribs from casserole and set aside. Pour vegetables and liquid through a fine strainer into a large bowl. Discard all solids and return liquid to a clean casserole. Bring the liquid to a boil over high heat and reduce by half, about 10 minutes. Remove from heat and set aside.

5. Cut remaining 3 onions into large dice. Separate the cloves of the remaining head of garlic and peel and thinly slice. In a large sauté pan over medium-low heat, add remaining 1 tablespoon duck fat. Add mushrooms and sauté until lightly browned. Remove from pan and set aside. Add diced onions to pan and sauté until translucent, about 5 minutes. Add sliced garlic to onions and sauté for 1 minute. Add mushrooms and prunes and sauté just until heated.

6. Add sautéed onion, garlic, prunes and mushrooms to the casserole containing the reduced wine mixture. Adjust salt and pepper to taste. Add short ribs and mix gently. Place over medium-low heat and simmer just until thoroughly heated. Serve immediately.

Yield: 4 servings

—ELAINE LOUIE

WINTER SHORT-RIB STEW

meat

3 pounds short ribs, cut across and between the bones
    to form 12 pieces about 2 inches square
    (the butcher will do the cross-cutting)
6 cloves garlic, smashed and peeled
3 cups diced canned or sterile-pack tomatoes
1 bay leaf
4 strips (1-by-4-inch) orange zest
1 strip (1-by-3-inch) lemon zest
¾ cup pearl barley
1 pound green string beans, tips and tails removed
2 tablespoons kosher salt, or to taste
1 large bulb fennel, stalks removed, cut in half, cored
    and cut into thin strips
1 tablespoon coarsely chopped fresh oregano
1 tablespoon coarsely chopped fresh thyme
1 package (10 ounces) frozen baby lima beans,
    defrosted in a sieve under warm running water
Freshly ground black pepper to taste

1. Place a rack in the middle of the oven and heat oven to 500 degrees.

2. Place the short ribs in one layer in a medium roasting pan and roast for 25 minutes. Turn the pieces, add the garlic and roast for 15 minutes more.

3. Remove the ribs to a tall, narrow stockpot. Spoon the fat from the roasting pan and pour any juices over the bones.

4. Place the roasting pan on top of the stove over medium heat and add 1½ cups water. Bring to a boil, scraping any browned bits off the bottom of the pan with a wooden spoon. Pour this liquid over the bones.

5. Add the tomatoes, 2 cups water, the bay leaf, 2 pieces of orange zest and the lemon zest. Cover the stockpot and bring to a boil. Uncover, lower the heat and simmer for 40 minutes.

6. Stir in the barley, the string beans and 2 cups water. Cover and bring to a boil. Uncover, lower the heat and simmer for 30 minutes.

7. Occasionally poke the string beans down into the liquid. Add 2 teaspoons salt and simmer for 10 minutes.

8. Skim the fat. Add the fennel and the herbs. Bring the pot to a boil. Lower the heat and simmer for 5 minutes. Add the remaining salt, the lima beans, two strips of orange zest and 2 cups water.

9. Bring to a boil, lower the heat and simmer for 5 minutes. The meat should be falling off the bones.

10. Remove the meat and the bones from the stockpot. Place two pieces of meat (with or without the bones) in each of six bowls and divide the vegetables and liquid evenly over them.

Yield: 6 hearty servings

—BARBARA KAFKA

CARAWAY SHORT RIBS

meat

ADAPTED FROM *The New York Times Large-Type Cookbook*

4 pound short ribs
1½ teaspoons salt
¼ teaspoon black pepper
1 cup Beef Broth (page 49), canned or fresh
1 cup tomato juice
½ teaspoon oregano
1 teaspoon caraway seeds
1 bay leaf
½ cup chopped onion
3 carrots, sliced
1½ tablespoons flour, optional
Cold water, optional

1. Brown ribs on all sides in a heavy casserole or Dutch oven. Cover tightly and cook slowly 1 hour. Discard drippings.

2. Add salt, pepper, broth, juice, oregano, caraway seeds, bay leaf and onion. Cover and cook 1 hour or until the meat is almost tender.

3. Add carrots; cook 20–30 minutes, until tender. To thicken gravy if desired, mix 1½ tablespoons flour with a little cold water for every cup of liquid. Add to saucepan and cook, stirring.

Yield: 6–8 servings

NOTE: *If desired, 8 ounces of fresh green beans cut into 2-inch lengths may be added to the recipe along with the carrots.*

MOROCCAN TANGIA OF CUMIN-BEEF SHORT RIBS

meat

ADAPTED FROM Julian Clauss-Ehlers

4 beef short ribs (6–7 inches long), separated
½ teaspoon salt
1 teaspoon freshly ground black pepper
4 tablespoons ground cumin
2 Preserved Lemons (page 429), cut in half
8 garlic cloves, peeled and crushed
Steamed couscous

1. Ask your butcher to detach half the meat from top of bone, fold that half back and tie it on itself and around bone, and have him saw off any excess bone. If he won't, do everything yourself. If you can't get long ribs, buy 4 pairs of shorter ribs (2–3 inches) and tie each pair together, meaty sides in.

2. Preheat oven to 325 degrees. Season ribs with salt, pepper and cumin and pack closely in a roasting pan, with lemon halves between ribs. Add garlic and enough water to cover lemons.

3. Cover dish with lid or foil, heat until almost simmering over medium heat and bake for 4 hours (about 3 hours for shorter ribs), keeping liquid barely simmering and turning ribs every hour. (Moroccans often cook at 125 degrees for 8–10 hours; most American ovens don't go that low, so if you want to try the slow-cooking method, it should take about 6 hours at 180 degrees.) When ribs are tender, remove pan from oven and let cool to room temperature. Remove ribs from liquid, cut off strings and set aside. Skim grease from cooking liquid. Return ribs to liquid. Transfer to a clean bowl.

4. Cover and refrigerate for 2–3 days, then warm before serving. Serve with bone in and cooking juice, with freshly steamed couscous.

Yield: 4 servings

—JONATHAN REYNOLDS

GOULASH

meat

ADAPTED FROM *America Eats*

> *2 teaspoons salt, plus more to taste*
> *1 tablespoon sweet Hungarian paprika*
> *½ teaspoon freshly ground pepper, plus more to taste*
> *⅛ teaspoon garlic salt*
> *2 pounds beef chuck, cut into 1-inch cubes*
> *½ cup Schmaltz (page 413)*
> *2 large onions, peeled and chopped fine*
> *1½–2 tablespoons flour*
> *3 cups Beef Broth (page 49) or water*
> *2 tablespoons tomato paste*
> *1 teaspoon caraway seeds*

1. Combine the salt, 1 teaspoon of the paprika, pepper and garlic salt in a small bowl. Season the meat with the spice mixture. Set aside.

2. In a large casserole, heat the schmaltz over high heat until it begins to smoke. Add the pieces of meat in one layer and, while stirring constantly, quickly fry the meat until evenly browned, about 2–3 minutes.

3. Add the onions and cook until wilted, about 3 minutes. Sprinkle the flour over the meat and stir until blended. Add the remaining paprika, reduce the heat to medium low and stir for an additional 2 minutes.

4. Add the broth or water, tomato paste and caraway seeds. Cover and simmer over low heat until meat is tender, about 1–1½ hours. Set aside to cool. Cover and refrigerate overnight.

5. Reheat the goulash over low heat and season with salt and pepper to taste.

Yield: 4–6 servings

—MARIALISA CALTA

CLASSIC BEEF STEW

meat

ADAPTED FROM *The New York Times*
International Cookbook

3 pounds lean beef, cut into 2-inch cubes

1 teaspoon salt

¼ teaspoon freshly ground black pepper

¼ cup salad oil, approximately

1 medium onion, scraped and chopped

2 stalks celery, chopped

2 cloves garlic, minced

½ cup flour

2 cups Beef Broth (page 49), canned or homemade

2 cups dry red wine

2 ripe tomatoes, chopped, or 1 cup canned Italian
    plum tomatoes

4 sprigs parsley

2 bay leaves

¼ teaspoon dried thyme

12 small white onions

6 carrots, scraped and halved

12 small potatoes, peeled

1 tablespoon chopped parsley

1. Sprinkle meat with salt and pepper. Heat oil in a skillet and brown meat on all sides over high heat, adding more oil if necessary.

2. Lower heat to medium. Add chopped onion, chopped carrot, celery and garlic; cook until onion is lightly browned.

3. Stir in flour and cook until flour is blended. Gradually stir in beef broth and wine and bring to a boil. Add tomatoes, parsley sprigs, bay leaves and thyme. Cover and cook over low heat 1½ hours.

4. Add the whole onions, halved carrots and potatoes. Cover again and continue cooking 1 hour longer. Sprinkle with parsley before serving.

Yield: 6 servings

CLAUDIA RODEN'S PRUNE TSIMMES

meat

ADAPTED FROM *The Book of Jewish Food*

2 pounds slightly fat beef brisket, flank or rolled rib

3 tablespoons chicken fat or oil

1½ large onions, coarsely chopped

Salt and pepper to taste

1 teaspoon cinnamon

½ teaspoon allspice

A good pinch of nutmeg

2 pounds new potatoes

1 pound pitted prunes

2 tablespoons sugar, or to taste

1. In a heavy pan over medium heat, turn the meat in the fat or oil to brown it all over, then remove it and fry the onions gently until soft.

2. Return the meat to the pan and cover with water. Season with salt and pepper, add cinnamon, allspice and nutmeg, and simmer for 1½ hours.

3. Add the potatoes, the prunes, the sugar and more water to cover, and simmer ¾ hour longer. You may want to have plenty of black pepper to balance the sweetness. There should be a lot of liquid. Serve hot.

Yield: 8 or more servings

NOTE: *Popular variations of this classic Ashkenazic meat-potato-prune tsimmes include: adding 4 large carrots, cut into pieces, to the recipe; substituting sweet potatoes cut into cubes for the new potatoes; substituting 2 tablespoons of honey for the sugar; adding some red wine to the water.*

SYRIAN SWEET-AND-SOUR BEEF STEW •
(LAHMEH FIL MEHLEH)

meat

ADAPTED FROM Fritzie Abadi

2 pounds moderately lean ground chuck

2 teaspoons allspice

2 teaspoons cinnamon

2 teaspoons kosher salt plus more to taste

⅛ teaspoon freshly ground black pepper
    plus more to taste

3 tablespoons vegetable oil

6 medium onions, peeled and quartered

4 large waxy potatoes, peeled and cut into eighths

12 ounces pitted prunes

1 large eggplant, quartered lengthwise and cut into
    1-inch slices

2 (6-ounce) cans tomato paste

2½ cups water

¼ cup light brown sugar

¾ cup lemon juice

2 tablespoons tamarind paste or 2 tablespoons prune
    butter (lekvar) (see Note below)

Syrian White Rice for serving (page 320)

1. In a large bowl, combine the chuck, allspice, cinnamon, 1¼ teaspoons of the salt and ⅛ teaspoon pepper and use your hands to mix it well.

2. Pour the oil into the bottom of a heavy, 6-quart ovenproof casserole or Dutch oven and place half the onions in the bottom. Place half of the meat over the onions, pressing it down very firmly with your hands. Scatter half the potatoes, prunes and eggplant over the top of the meat. Add the remaining onions to the pot and press the remaining meat over the top of the onions. Scatter the remaining potatoes, prunes and eggplant over the meat.

3. In a large bowl, combine the tomato paste, water, brown sugar, lemon juice, tamarind paste or prune butter, ¾ teaspoon salt and a few grinds of black pepper and mix until smooth. Pour the sauce over the meat and vegetables.

4. Cover the pot and bring it to a boil over medium-high heat. Adjust the heat so that the mixture cooks at a strong simmer. Cook until the sauce is thick and the potatoes are tender but not mushy, about 2 hours. (The dish is often better if prepared a day in advance, refrigerated and reheated in a 350-degree oven before serving.) Season the stew to taste with salt and pepper and serve with Syrian rice.

Yield: 8–10 servings

NOTE: *The original recipe, which called for 1 tablespoon of tamarind paste and 1 tablespoon of Worcestershire sauce, required modification since Worcestershire sauce may not be consumed with meat (see Note, page 582). To approximate the tang that the sauce adds to the dish, Gilda Angel, an authority on kosher cooking who reviewed the recipes in this book, recommends an additional tablespoon of tamarind paste or, for additional sweetness, 2 tablespoons of lekvar.*

—MOLLY O'NEILL

TSIMMES WITH BEEF CHEEKS, DRIED APRICOTS, CRANBERRIES AND ROOT VEGETABLES

meat

ADAPTED FROM Sterling Smith, Le Marais

1 bottle of red wine (Merlot or Cabernet)
3 onions, peeled and cut into ½-inch dice
2 carrots, peeled and cut into ½-inch dice
2 stalks of celery, cut into ½-inch dice
1 bay leaf
2 sprigs fresh thyme
¾ cup honey
4 cloves garlic, crushed
4 pounds trimmed beef cheeks cut into 2-inch cubes
Salt to taste
Pepper to taste
2 tablespoons olive oil
¼ teaspoon of allspice
3 carrots, peeled and cut into 1-inch chunks
3 large turnips, peeled and quartered
8 ounces dried apricots, cut in half
½ cup dried cranberries
2 tablespoons cornstarch
¼ cup warm water

1. Mix the red wine, onions, carrots, celery, bay leaf, thyme, honey and garlic in a large bowl, and add the beef cheeks. Marinate in the refrigerator 24 hours.

2. Remove beef cheeks from the marinade with a slotted spoon, reserving the marinade and vegetables.

3. Preheat oven to 375 degrees.

4. Pat the beef cheeks dry with a paper towel and season with salt and pepper.

5. Place 2 tablespoons of olive oil into a large casserole or Dutch oven. Heat over a medium heat. Add the beef cheeks and brown on both sides over medium-high heat.

6. Add the reserved marinade and ¼ teaspoon of allspice to the meat. Bring to a boil over a medium-high heat. When stew reaches a boil, cover and place casserole in oven.

7. After 1½ hours, remove lid and add the carrot chunks, turnips, apricots and cranberries to the casserole, mixing them into the liquid. Replace lid and return casserole to the oven for 30 minutes.

8. Remove casserole from the oven and place over medium heat burner. Add 2 tablespoons of cornstarch to ¼ cup of warm water. Mix well. Add to stew. Mix well. Cook additional 10–15 minutes over medium heat. Season to taste and serve.

Yield: 5–6 servings

TSIMMES WITH MEATBALLS

meat

ADAPTED FROM *The Second Avenue Deli Cookbook*

1 tablespoon corn oil

1 tablespoon Schmaltz (page 413) or corn oil

3 cups chopped onion

1 tablespoon finely chopped or crushed fresh garlic

2 cups McIntosh apples, peeled and cut into slices ¾ inch long and ¼ inch thick

1 cup carrots, diced into ½-inch pieces

2 cups sweet potatoes, peeled and diced into ¾-inch pieces

2 cups white potatoes, peeled and diced into ¾-inch pieces

1 cup dried, pitted prunes, halved

½ cup fresh pineapple, diced into ¾-inch pieces (or canned, thoroughly drained)

¼ teaspoon cinnamon

2 cups chicken soup or stock

1 teaspoon salt

¼ teaspoon pepper

1. Prepare meatballs first (see recipe below). Heat corn oil and schmaltz in a skillet and sauté onions until browned. Add garlic at the last minute and brown. Remove with a slotted spoon to a large stockpot and set aside. In remaining oil (add a little if necessary), sauté apples until soft and a light, golden hue. Remove to a small bowl and set aside on counter.

2. Add all remaining ingredients except meatballs and apples to stockpot. Stir, bring to a boil, cover, reduce heat and simmer for 20 minutes, stirring halfway through.

3. Add meatballs, cover and simmer another 10 minutes. Add apples and stir.

Yield: 6–8 servings

◆ MEATBALLS ◆

meat

1 pound ground beef

1 pound ground veal

¼ cup matzoh meal

2 teaspoons garlic powder

2 eggs, beaten

¼ cup Chicken Broth or Chicken Stock (page 48)

2 tablespoons ketchup

¼ teaspoon pepper

Flour for dredging

1 tablespoon corn oil

1. Using your hands, thoroughly mix beef, veal and matzoh meal in a large bowl. Add all other ingredients except flour and corn oil, and, still using your hands, mix in thoroughly.

2. Pour about ¾ cup of flour into a separate bowl. Form meatballs about 1½ inches in diameter and dredge them well in flour.

3. Heat corn oil in a large skillet and sauté meatballs until brown and crispy, turning once with a fork (you'll probably have to do this in two batches). Place meatballs on a flat plate covered with aluminum foil and refrigerate until needed.

Yield: About 20 meatballs

FRITZIE ABADI'S SMALL FRIED MEAT PATTIES • (IJEH)

meat

1 pound ground beef, chuck or round

½ cup finely chopped onions

6 tablespoons finely chopped parsley leaves

6 large eggs

¼ cup bread crumbs

1½ teaspoons kosher salt

1 teaspoon ground allspice

½ teaspoon ground cinnamon

¼ teaspoon freshly ground black pepper

Vegetable oil for frying

Pita wedges and Spicy Ketchup (page 420) for
    serving

1. Place the meat in a large bowl and mash with a fork for 2 minutes. Add the onions, parsley, eggs, bread crumbs, salt, allspice, cinnamon and pepper and mix well.

2. Heat a large, heavy skillet over medium heat and cover the bottom with a generous layer of oil. When hot, working in batches, drop the meat mixture by slightly rounded tablespoons into the oil. Fry, turning once, until the patties are lightly browned, about 3 minutes. Transfer them to paper towels to drain. Repeat, adding more oil as needed, until all the meat is cooked.

3. Serve the patties warm with small pita wedges and spicy ketchup.

Yield: About 40 patties

—MOLLY O'NEILL

ISRAELI SWEET-AND-SOUR MEATBALLS

meat

ADAPTED FROM *The New York Times
International Cookbook*

½ pound lean beef, ground

½ pound veal, ground

1 large egg, lightly beaten

1 clove garlic, finely minced

1 onion, finely chopped

6 tablespoons cooking fat

¼ cup finely minced parsley

Salt and freshly ground pepper to taste

1 hard roll

Cold water

3 tablespoons granulated sugar

3 tablespoons vinegar or lemon juice

2 cups boiling beef stock, canned or fresh,
    or consommé

1. Combine the beef and veal in a mixing bowl. Add the egg and set aside.

2. Cook the garlic and onion in 1 tablespoon of fat until the onion is wilted. Add this to the meat. Add parsley and salt and pepper to taste.

3. Soak the roll thoroughly in cold water, then squeeze with the hands to extract most of the moisture. Break up the bread with the fingers and add to the meat. Using the hands, shape the meat into 24 balls.

4. Heat the remaining fat in a skillet and cook the meatballs until browned on all sides. Add the sugar, vinegar and beef stock and pour everything into a saucepan. Simmer 15 minutes and serve hot.

Yield: 24 meatballs

MOROCCAN TAGINE WITH MEATBALLS

meat

2 pounds very lean ground beef
1 medium onion, sliced thin
2 cloves garlic, minced
1 teaspoon ground cumin
1 teaspoon ground coriander
1 teaspoon Hungarian paprika
½ teaspoon ground allspice
Coarse salt and freshly ground pepper to taste
2 tablespoons chopped cilantro

1. Form the beef into walnut-size balls. Arrange them in a single layer in a large, heavy skillet or a casserole with a wide bottom.

2. Arrange the onion slices on top and add all the ingredients except cilantro. Add just enough water to cover.

3. Bring to a simmer and cook gently, uncovered, for 30 minutes, or until the sauce has reduced to a thick gravy.

4. Correct the seasoning and serve sprinkled with cilantro.

Yield: 6 servings

NOTE: *Moroccan tagines are a form of stew, normally cooked in an earthenware pot with a conical lid. A heavy skillet or shallow casserole that goes on top of the stove works equally well for the meatballs. They simmer in a sauce that reduces to a thick gravy and goes well with couscous.*

—MOIRA HODGSON

SWEET MEATBALLS FOR COUSCOUS

meat
ADAPTED FROM *The New York Times International Cookbook*

1½ pounds ground lean meat
1 small onion, peeled and grated

2 tablespoons chopped parsley
1 egg, lightly beaten
½ cup matzoh meal or bread crumbs
½ cup tomato juice
Salt and freshly ground pepper to taste
¼ cup vegetable oil

6 onions, thinly sliced

1 quart water

½ cup raisins, soaked in warm water until plumped

8 dried prunes, pitted, soaked in warm water until softened

1 cup blanched almonds

1 pound peeled, prepared fresh pumpkin, if available, cut into 2-inch pieces

½–1 cup brown sugar, depending on sweetness desired

1 teaspoon ground cinnamon

1. Preheat the oven to 350 degrees.

2. Place the meat in a mixing bowl and add the grated onion, parsley, egg and matzoh meal. Blend, then add the tomato juice, salt and pepper. Knead until smooth. Add 1 tablespoon of the oil and knead again. Shape into small balls.

3. Cook the onions in the remaining oil until tender and brown. Add the water and bring to a boil. Add salt to taste. Drop the meatballs, one at a time, into the simmering liquid; simmer until firm.

4. Pour the meatballs and broth into a baking dish and add the drained raisins and prunes. Add the almonds and pumpkin. Sprinkle with the brown sugar and cinnamon and bake until golden brown and all the liquid disappears. Serve with couscous (page 163).

Yield: 6–8 servings

SYRIAN MEATBALLS • (KOFTE) WITH CHERRIES

meat

ADAPTED FROM Sarina Roffe

2 large onions, thinly sliced

3 tablespoons vegetable oil

1 (15-ounce) can tart dark cherries, pitted

1 pound ground beef

2 tablespoons matzoh meal

1 teaspoon salt, or to taste

¼ teaspoon white pepper

1 teaspoon cumin

½ teaspoon allspice

Juice of ½ lemon

2 tablespoons brown sugar

2 tablespoons tamarind paste (see Glossary, page 586)

½ cup dried apricots

1. In a large frying pan, sauté onions in oil until golden. Add cherry juice, reserving cherries. Simmer for 30 minutes on very low heat.

2. In a bowl combine ground meat with matzoh meal, salt, pepper, cumin and allspice. Form 1-inch balls.

3. Stir lemon juice, brown sugar and tamarind paste into onion and cherry sauce. Add meatballs and cook over very low heat, stirring occasionally, for 30 minutes. Add apricots and reserved cherries, and cook on low heat for another 20 minutes. Serve the meatballs with the sauce.

Yield: 4–6 servings

—JOAN NATHAN

MATZOH MEAT PIE • (MEGINA)

meat

ADAPTED FROM *Sephardic Holiday Cooking*

1 small onion, diced
1 cup chopped parsley
2 tablespoons vegetable oil
2½ pounds lean ground beef
1 teaspoon salt, or to taste
½ teaspoon black pepper, or to taste
12 large eggs
Vegetable oil, for pan
12 matzohs

1. Preheat oven to 350 degrees.
2. Sauté onion and parsley in oil until both are slightly soft. Add meat. Stir and sauté until meat is lightly browned. Add salt and pepper to taste. Let mixture cool. Stir 6 eggs into meat.
3. Pour a ⅛-inch depth of oil into a 10-by-15-inch baking pan.

4. Soak 6 matzohs in warm water until they just begin to soften, but not so long that they fall apart. Beat the remaining 6 eggs with a pinch of salt and slowly and carefully dip matzohs, one by one, into beaten eggs, coating on both sides. Let excess drip off. Arrange first 6 matzohs on the bottom of the baking pan. Turn meat into pan and spread evenly over layer of matzohs. Soak and dip into egg the remaining 6 matzohs and place in an even top layer over the meat.
5. Bake in middle of preheated oven for 45 minutes to 1 hour or until filling is set and top matzohs are golden brown.

Yield: 8–10 servings

NOTE: *It is best to make this dish the day before serving, refrigerate it and reheat it just before it is to be eaten.*

VARIATION: *For added flavor, a little cinnamon or dried herbs, such as thyme, can be added to the meat.*

—MIMI SHERATON

CINCINNATI CHILI

meat

4 cups Beef Broth (page 49), fresh or canned
2 pounds ground beef
1 tablespoon olive oil
3 cups finely chopped onions
1 tablespoon finely minced garlic
¼ cup chili powder or more to taste
1 teaspoon ground cumin
1 teaspoon ground cinnamon
¼ teaspoon allspice

¼ teaspoon ground cloves
⅛ teaspoon hot red pepper or more to taste
1 bay leaf
2 cups fresh or canned tomato sauce
2 tablespoons cider or white vinegar
½ ounce (½ square) unsweetened chocolate

1. Put the broth in a kettle and add the beef a little at a time until it separates into small pieces. Bring to a boil. Cover and let simmer 30 minutes.
2. Heat the oil in a saucepan and add the onions.

Cook, stirring often, until the onions are wilted and start to brown. Set aside. Add the garlic, chili powder, cumin, cinnamon, allspice, cloves, hot red pepper, bay leaf and tomato sauce and bring to a boil.

3. Add the tomato mixture to the meat mixture. Add the vinegar and chocolate. Bring to a boil and cover. Simmer 1 hour. Refrigerate. When ready to serve, skim off the fat, reheat and serve.

Yield: 6 or more servings

—CRAIG CLAIBORNE AND PIERRE FRANEY

SWEET-AND-SOUR STUFFED CABBAGE •
(ASHKENAZIC STYLE)

meat

ADAPTED FROM *The Best of Craig Claiborne*

1 large or 2 small cabbages, about 3 pounds total
1 pound ground chuck
1 teaspoon peanut or vegetable oil
2 cups finely chopped onions
1 garlic clove, finely minced
1 cup fine fresh bread crumbs
1 egg, lightly beaten
¼ cup finely chopped parsley
1 cup drained imported canned tomatoes
Salt and freshly ground pepper to taste
1 (28-ounce) can tomatoes with tomato paste
½ cup white vinegar
¼ cup sugar
1 teaspoon paprika

1. Cut the core from the cabbage and drop the cabbage into a kettle of cold water to cover. Bring to a boil and cook for 5 minutes. Drain well.

2. Put the meat in a mixing bowl and set aside.

3. Heat the oil in a skillet and add the onions and garlic. Cook, stirring, until wilted. Remove from the heat and let cool slightly.

4. Add half the onion mixture to the beef. Add the bread crumbs, egg and parsley. Add the 1 cup of imported tomatoes, the salt and the pepper. Blend thoroughly with the hands.

5. Separate the leaves of the cabbage. Place one large leaf on a flat surface and cover the center with a small leaf. Add about 3 tablespoons of the meat mixture to the center and fold the cabbage leaves over, tucking in the ends. There should be about 18 cabbage rolls in all.

6. Do not drain the tomatoes with tomato paste but crush them.

7. Add half the crushed tomatoes to the bottom of a baking dish large enough to hold the stuffed cabbage rolls close together in one layer.

8. Cover the tomato layer with the stuffed cabbage.

9. Blend the remaining crushed tomatoes with the remaining onion mixture, vinegar and sugar. Spoon this over the stuffed cabbage. Sprinkle with paprika.

10. Preheat the oven to 350 degrees.

11. Cover the dish closely and bring to a boil on top of the stove. Bake for 1 hour and 15 minutes. Uncover and bake for about 20 minutes longer.

Yield: 6–8 servings

STUFFED CABBAGE WITH SPICED BEEF AND APRICOTS (SEPHARDIC STYLE)

meat

1 medium-size green cabbage
1 teaspoon olive oil
1 medium onion, peeled and minced
1 clove garlic, peeled and minced
1 pound lean ground beef
1 cup dried apricots, coarsely chopped
½ cup toasted pine nuts
1 tablespoon grated lemon zest
1 teaspoon ground cumin
2 teaspoons ground cinnamon
1½ teaspoons salt
Freshly ground pepper to taste
1 egg, lightly beaten

1. Bring a large pot of lightly salted water to a boil. Remove the tough outer leaves of the cabbage and slice off the top inch. Place the cabbage in the boiling water and blanch for 10 minutes. Drain and set aside to cool.
2. Heat the olive oil in a large nonstick skillet over medium heat. Add the onion and cook until soft-ened, about 5 minutes. Stir in the garlic and beef and cook until the beef is browned, about 5 minutes more. Stir in the apricots, pine nuts, lemon zest, cumin, cinnamon, salt and pepper. Set aside.
3. Preheat oven to 375 degrees. Remove the center of the cabbage, from the top, to create a "bowl" by cutting into the head with a sharp paring knife to loosen the tightly packed inner leaves, and then scooping them out with a sharp spoon. Finely chop these leaves and stir them into the meat mixture. Add the egg and mix well.
4. Carefully fold back the outer leaves. Fill the cavity with some of the meat mixture and spread the remaining filling between the leaves. Fold the leaves back to re-form the cabbage and tie with the string to secure it. Place the cabbage in a small roasting pan and add ½ cup water. Cover with aluminum foil and bake for 25 minutes. Uncover and bake until the leaves are tender, about 20 minutes more. Place the cabbage on a platter, remove the string and serve.

Yield: 4 servings

—MOLLY O'NEILL

PEPPERS STUFFED WITH SAFFRON RICE AND BEEF

meat

8 medium-small yellow bell peppers
4 tablespoons extra-virgin olive oil
⅔ cup finely chopped red onion
3 cloves garlic, minced
¼ teaspoon saffron threads

½ cup long-grain rice
Salt to taste
10 ounces ground beef
½ teaspoon ground oregano
⅛ teaspoon hot red pepper flakes, or to taste
1 tablespoon finely chopped cilantro

1. Cut any protruding stems from the peppers so they will stand level upside down. Slice about an inch off the rounded end of each pepper to make a wide opening. Using a grapefruit spoon or knife, carefully remove the core, seeds and rib from the peppers, cutting down into the center of each and scooping out the core. Be sure to remove all the seeds. Finely chop the ends of the peppers that were removed.

2. Heat 1½ tablespoons oil in a large skillet. Add chopped peppers, onions and garlic and sauté over medium-low heat until soft.

3. Meanwhile, bring ¾ cup water to a boil in a small saucepan. Add saffron, rice and salt to taste, cover, lower heat and cook 7 minutes, until water is absorbed and rice is just moist but not fully cooked. Transfer rice to a medium-size bowl and mix with contents of skillet. Add beef, oregano and hot pepper flakes and mix thoroughly. Check seasonings and fold in cilantro. Fill peppers with this mixture. If, when scooping out the cores, you acci-dentally split the sides of any of the peppers, tie them with a piece of kitchen string after filling so they keep their shape.

4. Preheat oven to 350 degrees.

5. Put ½ tablespoon of oil in a baking dish large enough to hold the peppers without much room to spare. Arrange peppers standing up in the dish. Add about ½ inch water, cover tops of peppers loosely with a sheet of foil and bake about 1 hour and 15 minutes, until peppers are tender and rice is cooked.

6. Allow to cool in a baking dish, still covered with foil, and serve at room temperature. Drizzle tops with remaining oil before serving.

Yield: 4 servings or 8 appetizer servings

NOTE: *If you are uncertain about the freshness of the beef, you may wish to sauté a small amount of the mixture in olive oil before checking the seasonings.*

—FLORENCE FABRICANT

SPICED BEEF TONGUE

meat

ADAPTED FROM *The New York Times International Cookbook*

1 fresh beef tongue, about 3 pounds
1 tablespoon salt
1 small onion, sliced
Few whole black peppercorns
1 bay leaf
Water to cover
3 strips lemon peel

1 teaspoon cinnamon
2 teaspoons brown sugar
⅛ teaspoon freshly ground black pepper
2 cups dry white wine

1. Place the tongue, salt, onion, peppercorns and bay leaf in a saucepan. Cover with cold water and bring to a boil. Reduce heat, cover the pan and sim-mer until the tongue is fork tender, 2½–3 hours.

2. Remove the tongue from the water and cool slightly. Remove skin and fiber. Cut the meat into thin slices.

3. Place the tongue slices in a casserole and add the remaining ingredients. Bake, covered, in a preheated 375-degree oven until the meat absorbs nearly all the liquid, about 35 minutes. Serve hot or chilled.

Yield: 6 servings

TONGUE DINNER COOKED IN CIDER

meat

12 medium new potatoes, washed

15 white boiling onions (each 1–1½ inches in diameter), peeled

1½ cups dark beer

5 cups apple cider

1 cup apple cider vinegar

½ teaspoon ground cloves

2 teaspoons sugar

1 tablespoon kosher salt

6 small carrots, peeled, cut in half lengthwise and then across into 2-inch pieces

1 large head garlic (about 20 cloves), smashed and peeled

1½-pound piece cooked beef tongue, with skin and fibers removed

1 medium head green cabbage, cut through core into 6 wedges

1. Place the potatoes, onions, beer, cider, cider vinegar, cloves, sugar and salt in a large wide pot over high heat. Cover. Bring to a boil. Lower the heat and cook, covered, at a moderate boil for 10 minutes.

2. Add the carrots, garlic and tongue, pushing the vegetables away as much as possible to allow the tongue to nestle in the liquid. Cover. Return to a boil. Lower the heat and cook, covered, at a moderate boil for 5 minutes.

3. Lay the cabbage wedges on top of the other ingredients. Cover. Return to a boil. Lower the heat and cook, covered, at a moderate boil for 20 minutes, or until the cabbage is tender.

4. Serve slices of tongue, along with a variety of the vegetables, in a large rimmed bowl with a bit of the broth. (The tongue can also be presented on a large platter with the vegetables. The broth can be served on the side.)

Yield: 6 servings

—BARBARA KAFKA

BRAISED CALF'S TONGUE WITH RED WINE AND ONIONS

meat

ADAPTED FROM *Modern French Cooking for the American Kitchen*

2 calf's tongues, about 2 pounds
2 cups red wine
2 cups Chicken Stock (page 48)
2 pounds onions, thinly sliced
1 tablespoon red wine vinegar
3 medium tomatoes, peeled, seeded and diced
1 stalk celery, sliced
1 small bay leaf
Pinch thyme
2 cloves garlic, unpeeled
1 sprig fresh tarragon
Salt and fresh-ground pepper to taste
1 tablespoon minced fresh tarragon

1. In a large saucepan, cook the tongues in boiling, salted water for 45 minutes. Refresh under cold running water and peel if possible. If the tongues do not peel easily, continue with the recipe and peel just before slicing.

2. Preheat oven to 400 degrees.

3. In a saucepan reduce the wine until only 1 cup remains. Add the stock and heat through.

4. Place tongues in an ovenproof casserole. Top with onions, vinegar, tomatoes, celery, bay leaf, thyme, garlic and tarragon sprig. Add wine, stock, salt and pepper. Cover and cook in the oven for about 1 hour, or until tender. As the liquid reduces, add a bit more stock or water, if necessary, to prevent burning.

5. Remove the tongues from the casserole and keep warm. Transfer the vegetables to a food processor or blender and puree. Reheat. Season with salt and pepper to taste.

6. Slice tongues and cover each serving with the vegetable sauce. Sprinkle with minced tarragon.

Yield: 6 servings

—MOIRA HODGSON

CALF'S LIVER WITH CITRUS GLAZE

meat

4 slices calf's liver, about 1¼ pounds, koshered (see Note, page 582)
Flour for dredging
3 tablespoons peanut or vegetable oil
4 shallots, minced
2 leaves fresh sage or 2 sprigs of rosemary, chopped

½ cup freshly squeezed orange juice
1–3 tablespoons red wine vinegar (more or less according to taste)
Coarse salt and freshly ground black pepper to taste

1. Dredge slices of liver lightly on all sides with flour. Shake off excess.

2. Heat the oil in a nonstick skillet large enough to

hold all the pieces of liver in one layer. Add the shallots and gently sauté with the sage or rosemary until soft.

3. Turn up the heat, add the liver and cook over high heat on one side about 2 minutes until browned. Turn and cook about 2 minutes more for medium-rare or longer to desired doneness. Transfer liver to a heated dish and keep warm.

4. Add the orange juice to the skillet, bring to a boil and add a tablespoon of vinegar. Taste for sweetness and add more vinegar if necessary. If the sauce is too dry, moisten with a little water or dry red wine. If it is too liquid, reduce over high heat. Season the sauce with salt and pepper and pour over the liver. Serve immediately.

Yield: 4 servings

—MOIRA HODGSON

SAUTÉED CALF'S LIVER WITH ONIONS AND CAPERS

meat

4 slices calf's liver, about 1¼ pounds, koshered (see
   Note page 582)
Salt and freshly ground black pepper to taste
½ cup flour for dredging
2 tablespoons vegetable or peanut oil
1 cup finely sliced red onion
2 tablespoons unsalted margarine
4 tablespoons drained capers
4 tablespoons finely chopped parsley
2 tablespoons red wine vinegar

1. Sprinkle liver with salt and pepper to taste. Dredge lightly on all sides with flour. Shake off excess.

2. Heat 1 tablespoon of the oil in a skillet. Add onion, salt and pepper. Toss and stir. Cook for about 10 minutes over medium heat until lightly browned.

3. Heat 1 tablespoon oil in a nonstick skillet large enough to hold all the pieces of liver in one layer. Add liver, cook on one side over high heat about 2 minutes until browned. Turn and cook about 2 minutes more for medium-rare or longer to desired doneness. Transfer liver to a heated platter and keep warm.

4. Pour off cooking oil and wipe out skillet. Add margarine, cooked onions and capers. Cook, tossing and stirring over high heat for 1 minute. Add parsley and vinegar and bring to boil. Swirl it around and pour over the liver. Serve immediately.

Yield: 4 servings

—PIERRE FRANEY

CROWN ROAST OF LAMB WITH MUSHROOM-PINE NUT STUFFING

meat

ADAPTED FROM *The Best of Craig Claiborne*

1 crown roast of lamb, 3–4 pounds, ready-to-cook

Salt and freshly ground black pepper to taste

1 tablespoon olive oil

1½ cups finely chopped onions

1 tablespoon finely chopped garlic

¼ pound mushrooms, finely chopped, about 1½ cups

⅓ cup pine nuts

1 pound ground lamb

1 teaspoon finely chopped dried rosemary

½ cup finely chopped parsley

1 cup plus 1 tablespoon fine fresh bread crumbs

1 egg, lightly beaten

¼ cup coarsely chopped onion

¼ cup coarsely chopped carrot

¼ cup coarsely chopped celery

1 bay leaf

2 fresh thyme sprigs, or ½ teaspoon dried thyme

1 cup Chicken Broth (page 48), fresh or canned

1. Preheat the over to 425 degrees.

2. Sprinkle the lamb inside and out with the salt and pepper.

3. Heat the oil in a small skillet and add the finely chopped onions and garlic. Cook over moderate heat, stirring, until the onions are wilted. Add the mushrooms and cook, stirring, until the mushrooms give up their liquid. Cook until liquid evaporates.

4. Meanwhile, put the pine nuts in a small skillet and cook, shaking the skillet, until they are lightly browned. Add the ground lamb, stirring and chopping down with the side of a heavy metal kitchen spoon to break up the lumps. Cook until the meat is lightly browned. Add salt and pepper to taste. Transfer the mixture to a mixing bowl.

5. Add the rosemary, parsley, 1 cup of the bread crumbs and the egg. Add the mushroom mixture and a generous grinding of pepper. Blend well.

6. Place the crown roast on a sheet of aluminum foil. Fill the center with the stuffing, smoothing it over in a rounded fashion with a spatula. Sprinkle with the remaining tablespoon of bread crumbs.

7. Lift up the foil, keeping the roast neatly intact, and transfer it to a shallow roasting pan. Keep the stuffed lamb as neatly intact as possible. If there are any lamb bones, scatter them around the roast.

8. Scatter the coarsely chopped onion, carrot, celery, bay leaf and thyme around the roast. Place in the oven and bake for 1 hour.

9. Transfer the stuffed lamb to a serving dish. Remove and discard the foil.

10. Add the chicken broth to the baking pan with the vegetables and bones. Bring to a boil, stirring. Strain the sauce around the lamb. Carve the lamb, serving 2–4 ribs plus a generous helping of the stuffing for each portion.

Yield: 6 or more servings

NOTE: *This dish makes a spectacular presentation for a festive occasion.*

SYRIAN SPICED RACK OF LAMB

meat

ADAPTED FROM Prime Grill

2 tablespoons cumin seeds

1 tablespoon black peppercorns

1 teaspoon allspice berries

1 teaspoon coriander seeds

1 teaspoon cardamom seeds, removed from the pod

1 cinnamon stick

1 tablespoon paprika

Salt to taste

2 racks of lamb (4 chops each, 1½ pounds total)

2 tablespoons canola oil

1. In a large skillet over medium heat, toast cumin, peppercorns, allspice, coriander, cardamom and cinnamon stick until fragrant, about 3 minutes. Grind spices along with paprika and a pinch of salt in a spice grinder or coffee grinder.

2. Preheat oven to 375 degrees. Salt lamb, then pat spice mixture all over it. Let rest for 15 minutes at room temperature.

3. Heat oil in a large skillet. Brown lamb on all sides. Transfer to a rack set in a roasting pan and roast lamb until done to taste, about 25 minutes for medium-rare (130 degrees on a meat thermometer). Carve lamb into chops and serve.

Yield: 4 servings

—ALEX WITCHEL

HOT AND SPICY RUBBED RACK OF LAMB

meat

ADAPTED FROM Melissa Kelly

1½ teaspoons sea salt or to taste

2 teaspoons dried oregano

1 teaspoon dried rosemary

1 tablespoon caraway seeds

1 teaspoon cumin seeds

½ teaspoon ground turmeric

2 tablespoons extra-virgin olive oil

1 tablespoon roasted garlic (about 2 large roasted cloves, mashed; ½ tablespoon garlic paste may be substituted)

2 tablespoons prepared Harissa (see recipe page 421) or tomato paste seasoned with ground red pepper

2 racks of lamb, frenched

1. Combine the salt, oregano, rosemary, caraway, cumin and turmeric in a mortar, spice grinder or blender and process until fairly well ground. Transfer to a small dish and work in 1½ tablespoons of the olive oil, plus the garlic and the harissa or tomato paste mixture. Rub the lamb with the mixture and set aside to marinate at room temperature at least 3 hours.

2. Preheat oven to 450 degrees.

3. Shortly before serving, heat a heavy ovenproof sauté pan on top of the stove and brush with remaining olive oil. Add the lamb, and sear for a couple of minutes on each side. Turn the lamb so it sits bone side up, and place the pan with the lamb in the oven for about 15 minutes, or until a meat thermometer registers 125 degrees for medium-rare. Carve each rack into 4 double chops.

Yield: 4 servings

—FLORENCE FABRICANT

SPOON LAMB

meat

ADAPTED FROM Antoine Bouterin

½ pound dried navy beans

3 ounces dried porcini mushrooms

2 tablespoons extra-virgin olive oil

1 boned lamb shoulder, about 4½ pounds,
    well trimmed of fat and tied in three places

2 medium onions, coarsely chopped

2 cloves garlic, peeled and smashed

2 tablespoons tomato paste

4 tablespoons flour

2 cups dry white wine

2 carrots, cut in sticks 2 inches long

2 celery stalks, cut in sticks 2 inches long

3 medium zucchini, cut in sticks 2 inches long

3 leeks, chopped

1 white turnip, peeled and diced

1 bouquet garni

1 tablespoon crushed black peppercorns

3 whole cloves

5 cups lamb or Beef Broth (page 49), canned
    or fresh

Salt to taste

1. Place beans in a bowl, cover with water to a depth of 2 inches and set aside to soak at least 4 hours. Place mushrooms in a bowl, cover with warm water and set aside to soak at least 1 hour.

2. Heat oil in a heavy 7- to 8-quart casserole. Add the lamb and brown it on all sides. Remove it from the casserole and remove the string.

3. Preheat oven to 300 degrees.

4. Add onion and garlic to the casserole and cook over medium heat until soft and starting to brown. Blend the tomato paste and flour together and add them to casserole. Cook, stirring, a few minutes, then stir in the wine. Add the remaining ingredients. Drain the beans and mushrooms and add them. Bring to a simmer.

5. Return lamb to casserole, cover and place in oven. Bake for 7 hours.

6. Serve directly from the casserole or transfer to a serving dish and serve with tablespoons. The lamb is so soft it can be pulled apart with a spoon. If desired, serve with mashed potatoes or couscous.

Yield: 6 servings

NOTE: *Seven hours of baking makes the lamb exceptionally tender and succulent.*

—FLORENCE FABRICANT

LEMON ROASTED SHOULDER OF LAMB

meat

ADAPTED FROM *Spoonbread and Strawberry Wine*

1 (9-pound) shoulder of lamb
6 large cloves garlic, minced
1½ cups vinegar
1½ cups water
Juice of 3 lemons
Rind of 1½ lemons, chopped
4½ teaspoons dried mustard
Salt and freshly ground black pepper to taste

1. Prepare lamb by making slices in it, about an inch deep, spaced 1 inch apart. Force minced garlic into openings.
2. In a saucepan combine vinegar, water, lemon juice, rind, mustard, salt and pepper to taste. Bring to a boil and pour over lamb.
3. Bake at 300 degrees for about 3½ hours, basting frequently, until lamb is pink or to desired doneness.
4. To serve, slice thinly and pass pan juices separately.

Yield: 12 servings

—MARIAN BURROS

SHOULDER OF LAMB BRAISED IN CHIANTI

meat

ADAPTED FROM Paul Bertolli

Salt and freshly ground black pepper to taste
3 pounds spring lamb shoulder, cut into ½-inch cubes
3 tablespoons olive oil
1 carrot, peeled and finely diced
1 small stalk celery, finely diced
1 shallot, peeled and diced
1 head garlic, cloves peeled
3 sprigs fresh thyme
2 tablespoons flour
1 bottle Chianti
1 teaspoon red wine vinegar

1. Salt and pepper the lamb. Warm the olive oil in a wide-bottomed pot. When the oil is very hot, add the lamb. Brown the meat well on all sides over medium heat for 10 minutes. Remove it from the pan.
2. Add the carrot, celery, shallot, garlic and thyme and cook over low heat, loosening any brown pan crust with 2 tablespoons of water. Add the meat to the pan and stir in the flour. Cook over medium-low heat for 5–8 minutes.
3. Raise the heat to high, add the Chianti and bring to a boil. Reduce the heat and simmer, covered, 2 hours. Remove the meat from the sauce, discard the thyme and puree the sauce in a food processor. Return the meat to the sauce, stir in the vinegar and serve. Can be made a day in advance and gently rewarmed.

Yield: 8 servings

—MOLLY O'NEILL

BREAST OF LAMB WITH HERBED-BREAD STUFFING • (LYONNAISE)

meat

1 breast of lamb, untrimmed (about 1¾ pounds)

FOR THE STUFFING:

1½ cups lean lamb trimmings (about 6 ounces) or other meat, such as veal or chicken
1 egg
½ cup chopped onion
2 cloves garlic, peeled, crushed and chopped fine (about 1 teaspoon)
¼ cup chopped chives
¼ cup chopped parsley
1 teaspoon thyme
½ teaspoon salt
½ teaspoon freshly ground black pepper
1 cup fresh bread crumbs

TO FINISH THE DISH:

¾ pound onions, peeled and thinly sliced
20 cloves garlic (approximately), peeled
½ cup dry white wine
½ teaspoon salt

1. Place the breast flat on the table and cut with a knife directly on top of the ribs to create a pocket.
2. To make the stuffing, process the meat trimmings with the egg in a food processor for a few seconds. Mix in the onion, garlic, chives, parsley, thyme, salt, pepper and bread crumbs.
3. Push the stuffing into the pocket of the meat and tie it up with string. Don't worry if some of the stuffing is still visible; it will not leak out. In a large aluminum or copper saucepan, brown the meat, fat side down, over medium heat for about 5 minutes. Add ½ cup water, cover, reduce the heat to low and keep cooking slowly for 45 minutes. Discard all the fat that has accumulated in the pan.
4. Add the sliced onions and the garlic and cook, uncovered, for about 5 minutes over medium heat. Add 1½ cups of water, and the wine and salt. Cover and cook for 30–40 minutes longer on low heat until very tender.
5. The meat, when done, should be moist and tender. Slice between the ribs and serve with the natural gravy, onions and garlic mixture.

Yield: 3–4 servings

—JOANNA PRUESS

WOLFGANG PUCK'S LAMB CHOPS WITH LAMB'S LETTUCE

meat

1 very small rack of lamb, 8 tiny well-trimmed chops, about 1 pound
½ cup extra-virgin olive oil

2½ tablespoons sherry wine vinegar
½ teaspoon minced fresh rosemary
½ teaspoon Dijon mustard
Salt and freshly ground black pepper
¼ pound lamb's lettuce (mâche), rinsed and dried

1. Preheat oven to 500 degrees.

2. Brush rack of lamb with a little olive oil and place in shallow baking pan in oven. Roast for 20 minutes for medium rare or to desired doneness.

3. While lamb is roasting, heat vinegar with rosemary in small glass, enamel or stainless-steel saucepan until vinegar is reduced to little more than a tablespoon. Off heat, beat in mustard and gradually whisk in remaining olive oil until well blended. Season to taste with salt and pepper.

4. Place lamb's lettuce in bowl and toss with all but 2 tablespoons of warm dressing. Divide salad onto 4 plates.

5. As soon as rack is cooked, slice into individual chops and place 2 chops on lettuce on each plate. Moisten each chop with a little remaining dressing and serve at once.

Yield: 4 servings

—FLORENCE FABRICANT

GRILLED LAMB CHOPS IN UZBEKI MARINADE

meat

ADAPTED FROM *Back to Square One*

1 large yellow onion, peeled and chopped
10–12 cloves garlic, peeled
3–4 canned plum tomatoes, drained
¼ cup chopped flat-leaf parsley
¼ cup chopped cilantro
1 tablespoon coriander seed, toasted and ground
2 teaspoons cumin seeds, toasted and ground
1 tablespoon Aleppo pepper
½ teaspoon cayenne pepper
½ cup olive oil plus extra for grilling

18 rib lamb chops
Kosher salt and freshly ground black pepper

1. In a blender or food processor, process onion, garlic and tomatoes until liquefied. Mix in parsley, cilantro, coriander, cumin, Aleppo pepper, cayenne and olive oil. Pour over lamb and marinate overnight.

2. Preheat the broiler. Brush chops with oil and season to taste. Broil until rare to medium-rare, about 3–4 minutes on each side, or to desired doneness.

Yield: 6 servings

—AMANDA HESSER

LAMB CHOPS MEDITERRANEAN-STYLE

meat

4 lean rib lamb chops, about 6 ounces each, with most
    of the fat removed

Salt and freshly ground pepper to taste

1 tablespoon olive oil

4 sprigs fresh thyme, or 2 teaspoons dried

1 cup diced eggplant, cut into ¼-inch cubes

1 cup diced zucchini with skin on, cut into
    ¼-inch cubes

¼ cup chopped onions

1 teaspoon chopped garlic

¼ teaspoon ground cumin

2 tablespoons dry white wine

1½ cups fresh tomatoes, peeled and cut into 1¼-inch
    cubes

1 bay leaf

½ cup pitted small black olives

4 tablespoons coarsely chopped fresh basil or parsley

1. Sprinkle the chops with salt and pepper.

2. Heat the oil in a heavy skillet large enough to hold
the chops in one layer. Add the chops and cook over
medium heat until browned on one side, about 5
minutes. Turn, sprinkle with the thyme and cook for
about 5 minutes more for rare, longer for medium or
well done. Remove to a warm platter and keep warm.

3. Pour off the fat from the skillet and add the eggplant and zucchini. Cook, stirring, over high heat
until lightly wilted. Add the onions, garlic and cumin,
and cook 2 minutes, stirring, until wilted. Add the
wine, tomatoes, bay leaf, olives and salt and pepper.
Cook, stirring, and simmer for 5 minutes, adding any
juices that have accumulated on the platter around the
lamb chops. Continue cooking for 1 minute.

4. Remove the bay leaf, sprinkle with the basil and
serve.

Yield: 4 servings

—PIERRE FRANEY

GRILLED SHOULDER LAMB CHOPS
ON ARUGULA AND MINT

meat

2 bunches arugula (or watercress), trimmed, washed
    and dried

1 cup whole fresh mint leaves, cleaned

1 small red onion, peeled and thinly sliced

4 (10- to 12-ounce) shoulder lamb chops, about 1½
    inches thick

Salt and freshly ground black pepper to taste

3 tablespoons vegetable oil

1 tablespoon minced garlic

1 tablespoon red pepper flakes

2 tablespoons roughly chopped fresh rosemary

4 thick slices crusty bread

⅓ cup olive oil

¼ cup fresh lemon juice (about 1 lemon)

12 pickled hot cherry peppers, if desired

1. In large bowl, combine arugula, mint and onion. Toss to mix and then set aside.

2. Sprinkle lamb chops with salt and pepper to taste. In small bowl, combine vegetable oil, garlic, red pepper flakes and rosemary and mix well. Cover chops generously with rub.

3. Grill over medium-hot fire for about 6 minutes a side for medium. To check for doneness, cut into a chop and see whether the center is slightly pinker than you want it to be when you eat it, since it will continue to cook a bit after you remove it from the grill.

4. While lamb is cooking, place bread slices around edge of grill and toast until golden brown, about 2 minutes a side.

5. In small bowl, whisk together olive oil, lemon juice and salt and pepper to taste. Pour over arugula-mint mixture and toss well. Place a portion of this salad mixture on each plate and top with a lamb chop and a slice of grilled bread. Serve warm, garnished with peppers, if desired.

Yield: 4 servings

—JOHN WILLOUGHBY AND
CHRIS SCHLESINGER

BRAISED LAMB RIBS WITH LENTILS

meat

> 2 pounds meaty lamb ribs
> 2 cups (12 ounces) lentils
> 1 large onion, chopped
> 1 large carrot, scraped and diced
> 1 can tomatoes, drained and chopped
> 1 large clove garlic, minced
> 3–4 cups water
> 1 bay leaf
> 1 teaspoon thyme
> 1 teaspoon salt
> ½ teaspoon black pepper
> Vinegar, optional and to taste

1. Cut lamb ribs apart and trim off heavy excess fat. With meat cleaver or sharp knife, cut each rib across into thirds so each piece is about 1½–2 inches long.

2. Wash lentils and pick over but do not soak.

3. Place lamb ribs in cold skillet and gradually heat until they are frying and fat melts. Turn frequently so all sides brown.

4. When lamb is golden brown on all sides, remove to 2-quart casserole or stew pot. Add onion and carrot to hot lamb fat in skillet and sauté over moderate heat until golden brown. Stir in tomatoes and liquid, bring to boil and scrape in coagulated pan juices with wooden spatula. Pour over ribs in casserole. Add garlic, bay leaf, thyme, salt and pepper and 2 cups water.

5. Bring to boil, and then gently stir in lentils. Add enough additional boiling water to come just to level of lentils. Bring to boil, cover, reduce to simmer and cook steadily but gently for about 2 hours or until lentils and lamb are tender. Add boiling water as needed during cooking and stir gently every half-hour or so.

6. Adjust seasonings, adding a few drops of vinegar if you like.

7. This can be served with rice. One cup of raw rice cooked in boiling salted water will be about right.

Yield: 4 servings

—MIMI SHERATON

LAMB WITH QUINCE

meat

1 large onion, sliced

1 green pepper, sliced

2 pounds stewing lamb, cubed

½ teaspoon paprika

½ teaspoon cumin

½ teaspoon ground ginger

Pinch saffron

Coarse salt to taste

Freshly ground black pepper to taste

1 cup water

1 pound quinces, cored and cut in eighths

Cilantro or parsley to garnish

1. Place the onion and the pepper in a heavy casserole. Put the meat on top and sprinkle with the paprika, cumin and ground ginger. Add the saffron, salt and pepper to taste. Pour in one cup water, cover and simmer for one hour.

2. Add the quinces, more water if necessary, and simmer for 30 minutes. Sprinkle with cilantro or parsley and serve.

Yield: 4 servings

—MOIRA HODGSON

LAMB SHANKS BRAISED WITH
APRICOTS AND NORTH AFRICAN SPICES

meat

Lamb shanks have a tenderness, a gelatinous texture that makes them, to some palates, far superior to the more luxurious cuts of meat. Shanks, too, are exceptionally easy to cook. Other than an occasional basting, they require little attention once they are placed in the oven.

1 small cinnamon stick

¼ teaspoon ground nutmeg

¼ teaspoon ground clove

½ teaspoon ground ginger

1½ tablespoons black peppercorns

¼ teaspoon cumin seeds

¼ teaspoon cardamom pods

½ teaspoon coriander seeds

1 teaspoon fennel seeds

3 tablespoons olive oil

4 lamb shanks from young lamb (about 1 pound each), trimmed of excess fat

1 tablespoon kosher salt plus more to taste

12 cloves garlic, peeled

4 small onions, peeled and diced

2 cups Chicken Broth (page 48), homemade or low-sodium canned

20 dried apricots

1 tablespoon chopped fresh thyme

Freshly ground pepper to taste

1. Combine the cinnamon stick, nutmeg, clove, ginger, peppercorns, cumin, cardamom, coriander and fennel in a spice grinder and grind until fine and well mixed. Measure out 3 tablespoons and reserve the rest for another use.

2. Preheat the oven to 350 degrees. Heat 2 tablespoons of olive oil in a large roasting pan over medium-high heat. Season the shanks with the salt, place in the pan and sear on all sides, about 15 minutes. Remove and set aside the shanks. Turn the heat to low. Add 1 tablespoon of oil, the garlic and onions. Cook until browned, stirring often, about

15 minutes. Pour in the chicken broth, raise the heat and deglaze the pan. Stir in the spice mixture and the apricots. Put the shanks back in the pan.

3. Cover with foil and roast until the meat is very soft, turning the shanks frequently and spooning the liquid over them, about 2½ hours. Take out the shanks and degrease the sauce. Stir in the thyme and salt and pepper to taste.

4. Divide the shanks among 4 plates and spoon the sauce over them. Serve with couscous or potatoes.

Yield: 4 servings

—MOLLY O'NEILL

BRAISED LAMB SHANKS WITH PRESERVED LEMONS

meat

ADAPTED FROM Monzu

FOR THE LAMB:

6 lamb shanks, trimmed of fat and membrane
Coarse sea salt and freshly ground pepper
4 tablespoons olive oil
1 cup onion, diced
1 cup shallots, sliced
Bouquet garni (basil, thyme, bay leaf and oregano
   tied in cheesecloth)
4 heads garlic, split
1 cup dry white wine
1 quart Veal Stock (page 50), canned or fresh
1 quart Chicken Stock (page 48), canned or fresh
1¼ cups Preserved Lemons, cut in julienne (reserve
   ¼ cup for garnish) (page 429)

Cannellini Beans

meat

2 cups cannellini beans, soaked overnight in water to
   cover
1 cup onion, chopped in ½-inch pieces
½ cup celery, chopped in ½-inch pieces
5 cloves garlic
½ cup carrots, chopped in ½-inch pieces
4 tablespoons olive oil
1 quart Chicken Stock (page 48)
Coarse sea salt and freshly ground pepper to taste

Garnish

pareve

6 plum tomatoes (halved, seeded and dried in an oven
   at 200 degrees but still moist)
1 bunch arugula, stems removed and leaves washed
   and dried

3 tablespoons chives, chopped, optional

1 tomato, diced, optional

1. Preheat the oven to 350 degrees. Season the lamb shanks well with salt and pepper. In a large roasting pan that can go both on top of the stove and in the oven, heat the oil and brown the shanks on all sides. Remove them to a platter. Add the onion, shallots, bouquet garni and garlic, and cook over moderate heat until the onions are tender.

2. Return the shanks to the pan and deglaze the vegetables with the white wine. Reduce until dry. Add the veal and chicken stocks, and bring to a boil. Add 1 cup preserved lemons. Cover the shanks and bake them in the oven for 1½ to 2 hours, or until tender.

3. Meanwhile, cook the beans. In a heavy casserole, soften the onion, celery, garlic and carrots in the olive oil. Drain and add the beans.

4. Cover the beans with chicken stock and enough water to cover and bring to a boil. Reduce heat to simmer and cook until tender (about 45 minutes). Drain and season to taste with salt and pepper.

5. When ready to serve, add a cup of lamb roasting juices to the beans and combine well. Add the oven-dried tomatoes and the arugula leaves to the beans. Mix well and season to taste with salt and pepper. Keep covered and warm in a low oven.

6. Remove the lamb shanks from the roasting pan, and keep them warm. Reduce the sauce over a moderate flame until it coats the back of a spoon, then strain the sauce. Coat the lamb with the sauce and sprinkle it with the remaining ¼ cup of preserved lemon. If desired, sprinkle with chives and diced tomato. Serve. Pass the beans separately.

Yield: 6 servings

NOTE: *The lamb shanks can be made separately, following Steps 1, 2 and 6, and served with couscous or rice.*

— MOIRA HODGSON

LAMB SHANKS WITH PRUNES

meat

ADAPTED FROM Rose Levy Beranbaum

3 tablespoons flour

1 tablespoon kosher salt

¼ teaspoon freshly ground black pepper

⅛ teaspoon cayenne pepper

4 pounds lamb shanks, cut into 2- to 3-inch pieces

¼ cup vegetable oil

2 cups thinly sliced onions

1 cup thinly sliced celery (about two ribs)

1 clove garlic, minced

½ teaspoon thyme

1 bay leaf

4 cups water

12 small potatoes, scrubbed

2 cups pitted prunes

1. In a plastic or paper bag, combine the flour, salt, black pepper and cayenne and shake to mix. Add a few pieces of lamb at a time and toss to coat with the flour mixture until all the lamb is coated. If any of the flour mixture remains, set aside.

2. Place a large heavy casserole, preferably cast iron, over medium heat. Let it remain until hot. Warm 2 tablespoons of the oil and add only as much lamb as

will fit without crowding. Brown the lamb on all sides, in batches, over medium heat, adding more oil as necessary. Remove the lamb to a bowl and set aside.

3. In the same pan, sauté the onions and celery until the onions are golden brown. Add any remaining flour mixture and the garlic and cook, stirring, for about 30 seconds.

4. Return the lamb to the casserole. Add thyme, bay leaf and water. Bring to a boil, reduce heat and simmer, partly covered, for 1 hour or until the meat is

tender. Add the potatoes and prunes and cook 30 minutes longer, until the potatoes are tender.

5. Using a slotted spoon, remove lamb and vegetables to a serving platter. Increase the heat to high and cook the remaining liquid until it reduces to a thick gravy, about 15 minutes. Remove the bay leaf. Drizzle the gravy over the lamb and prunes, then serve.

Yield: 6–8 servings

—MOLLY O'NEILL

BAKED LAMB SHANKS WITH CHICKPEAS

meat

2 tablespoon olive oil

4 lamb shanks

2 medium onions, sliced

1/2 teaspoon ground allspice

1/4 teaspoon ground nutmeg

1 teaspoon salt, or to taste

1/2 teaspoon pepper

8 ripe tomatoes, peeled, seeded and chopped (or the equivalent, canned)

1 teaspoon oregano

2 cups hot water

1 cup canned chickpeas, drained and rinsed

1. Preheat oven to 450 degrees.

2. Put the oil in a baking dish, add the lamb shanks, turn to coat evenly and bake 30 minutes, turning once.

3. Combine the onions with the allspice, nutmeg, salt and pepper, mix well, and spoon the mixture on top of the lamb shanks. Combine the tomatoes with the oregano and spoon on top of the onion mixture. Carefully pour the water around the shanks.

4. Turn the oven to 400 degrees and bake for 1½ hours, or until meat is tender, basting occasionally. If the dish begins to dry out, add more hot water. Add chickpeas to the juices 10 minutes before the end of the cooking time. Mix everything gently and spoon some sauce over each shank when serving.

Yield: 4 servings

—ROBERT FARRAR CAPON

SPICED LAMB KEBABS

meat

2 pounds shoulder of lamb, trimmed and cut into 1-
    inch cubes

1 tablespoon ground ginger

1 tablespoon ground cinnamon

1 tablespoon ground cardamom

1 tablespoon ground coriander

1 tablespoon honey

1 cup olive oil

Kosher salt to taste

Freshly ground black pepper to taste

Pita or other flat bread

1. In a large bowl, toss the lamb, ginger, cinnamon, coriander, honey and oil. Set aside at room temperature for 1 hour.

2. Prepare a charcoal grill or preheat the broiler. Slide the lamb cubes onto skewers, using 3 cubes per skewer. Season with salt and pepper. Grill or broil, turning often, until browned and cooked to desired doneness. Serve with warm flat breads, wrapping them around the skewers.

Yield: 4 servings

—MOLLY O'NEILL

LAMB BROCHETTES MEDITERRANEAN

meat

FOR THE MARINADE:

¼ cup fresh rosemary leaves, plus 8 full branches for
    the brochettes

2 cloves garlic, coarsely chopped

3 tablespoons grated orange rind

⅓ cup fresh-squeezed orange juice

1 teaspoon coarsely ground black pepper

1 tablespoon olive oil

FOR THE BROCHETTES:

8 lamb chops, about 1 inch thick, bone intact, well
    trimmed

1 small eggplant, cut lengthwise into 3 slabs

1 tablespoon olive oil

Salt and freshly ground black pepper to taste

2 medium white onions, peeled

8 ripe plum tomatoes

1. Combine the marinade ingredients. Add the lamb chops and marinate for 2 hours in the refrigerator, turning and basting frequently.

2. Preheat the oven to 350 degrees. Cut the eggplant slabs crosswise into 8 rectangular strips. Lightly brush the strips with olive oil, place them on a baking sheet, season lightly with salt and pepper and bake until barely tender, about 10–15 minutes. Set aside to cool.

3. Meanwhile, cook the onions in boiling water until tender, about 5–10 minutes. When cool, cut into quarters and set aside.

4. Remove the lamb chops from the marinade and

wipe dry with paper towels. For each brochette, thread on a skewer an onion quarter, a slice of eggplant, a lamb chop, a branch of rosemary, a tomato, a second branch of rosemary, a lamb chop, a slice of eggplant, a tomato and an onion quarter.

5. Grill over charcoal or broil under a broiler, 4 inches from the heat, for 4–6 minutes on each side (4 minutes for medium-rare) or to desired degree of doneness

Yield: 4 servings

NOTE: *Zucchini Couscous (page 318) is an excellent accompaniment for this dish.*

—MOLLY O'NEILL

ESAU'S LAMB

meat

ADAPTED FROM *The New York Times Menu Cook Book*

2 pounds lean lamb, cubed
2 tablespoons vegetable oil
2 cups finely chopped onion
2 garlic cloves, finely chopped
1 cup finely chopped celery
½ teaspoon dried thyme
Salt and freshly ground black pepper
½ bay leaf
3 cups Lamb Broth (page 49)
1 cup dried lentils
¼ cup uncooked rice
½ cup finely chopped parsley

1. Brown the lamb in the oil in a large skillet. Transfer the lamb to a casserole and pour off most of the fat from the skillet.

2. Add the onions, garlic and celery to the skillet and cook, stirring, until onions are wilted. Sprinkle with the thyme and salt and pepper to taste. Add bay leaf and 1 cup of the broth. Bring to a boil, stir the mixture thoroughly and pour it over the lamb.

3. Bring the casserole to a boil, cover and simmer 1 hour.

4. Rinse the lentils and add them to the casserole along with the rice. Add remaining stock and cook, covered, for 1 hour longer, or until lamb and lentils are tender. Pour the stew into a serving dish and sprinkle with parsley.

Yield: 4 servings

LAMB MARRAKECH

meat

<small>ADAPTED FROM</small> *The New York Times*
International Cookbook

1 cup white raisins
Dry sherry
½ cup vegetable oil
3 pounds lean lamb shoulder, cut into 1½-inch
    cubes
2 large onions, finely chopped
3 cloves garlic, finely chopped
Salt and freshly ground pepper to taste
Red pepper flakes to taste
1 teaspoon ground turmeric
3 large, ripe tomatoes, peeled and chopped, or 3 cups
    Italian peeled tomatoes
1 cup Chicken Stock (page 48), canned or fresh,
    approximately
1 cup toasted almonds, optional (see Note, page 582)

1. Soak the raisins in sherry to cover 15 minutes or
longer.
2. Heat the oil in a skillet. Brown the meat in the oil
and transfer it to a Dutch oven. Add the onions and
garlic to the skillet and cook, stirring, until the
onions are wilted. Add the onions to the meat. Add
salt, pepper, red pepper flakes and the turmeric and
stir. Add the raisins, tomatoes and enough chicken
stock to cover. Bring to a boil, then cover and simmer 1½ hours, adding more stock, if necessary.
Serve garnished, if desired, with almonds.

Yield: 6 servings

MOROCCAN BEAN AND LAMB STEW · (DFINA)

meat

½ pound dried chickpeas
½ pound dried baby lima beans
3 tablespoons olive oil
2 large onions, finely chopped
4 large cloves garlic, minced
2 pounds lean boneless lamb shoulder,
    cut in chunks
1 teaspoon ground coriander
1 teaspoon ground cumin
⅛ teaspoon ground saffron
16 medium-size new potatoes, peeled
2 large carrots, peeled and cut in 2-inch chunks
4 eggs in their shells, optional
Juice of 1 lemon
Salt and freshly ground black pepper
2 tablespoons toasted slivered almonds
    (see Note, page 582)
2 tablespoons chopped fresh mint

1. Place chickpeas and beans in a bowl, cover with
water to a depth of 2 inches and soak at least 4
hours or overnight. Drain and rinse the beans.

2. Heat the oil in a heavy casserole. Add onions and sauté until golden. Stir in the garlic, sauté for a minute or so and remove the vegetables from the casserole.

3. Preheat oven to 300 degrees.

4. Add lamb and sauté until lightly browned. Stir in coriander, cumin and saffron. Stir in drained beans and the onion and garlic mixture. Tuck the potatoes, carrots and eggs (if using) among the other ingredients. Add 6 cups water. Bring to simmer.

5. Skim the surface of the casserole, then cover and place in oven. Bake mixture for 1½ hours and add lemon juice and season to taste with salt and pepper. Place a layer of foil over casserole and place the lid back on. Lower temperature to 250 degrees. Bake 6 hours or longer, until liquid has been absorbed but ingredients are still moist.

6. To serve, remove eggs, peel them, cut them in half and arrange them on top of the dfina. Sprinkle the dfina with toasted almonds and chopped mint.

Yield: 8–10 servings

—FLORENCE FABRICANT

LAMB WITH OKRA

meat

2 pounds stewing lamb, cut into 1-inch cubes
Coarse salt and freshly ground pepper to taste
6 tablespoons olive oil
1 onion, chopped
2 cloves garlic, minced
1 green frying pepper, seeded and chopped
1 teaspoon ground cumin
1 teaspoon ground coriander
2 cinnamon sticks
Salt and pepper to taste
½ teaspoon hot pepper flakes
2 cups tomatoes, peeled, seeded and chopped
1½ pounds okra
Lemon juice to taste
2 tablespoons chopped flat-leaf parsley

1. Preheat oven to 375 degrees. Sprinkle the lamb with salt and pepper and sauté the pieces in 2 tablespoons of the olive oil until golden brown on all sides (do this in batches if necessary). Remove the lamb from the skillet and pour off the excess fat.

2. Heat 2 tablespoons of the remaining oil in the skillet and add the onion, garlic and peppers and cook them over moderate heat, stirring, until the onion begins to turn golden brown (about 10 minutes). Add the cumin, coriander, cinnamon sticks, salt, pepper, hot pepper flakes and tomatoes. Cover and bake in the oven for an hour or until the lamb is tender.

3. Meanwhile, trim the cone tops off the okra pods without cutting into the pods. Heat the remaining 2 tablespoons olive oil in a separate skillet and sauté the okra for about 3 minutes. Add the okra to the lamb and bake, covered, for 20 minutes. Sprinkle with lemon juice and parsley and serve.

Yield: 4 servings

NOTE: *Bulgur is an excellent accompaniment.*

—MOIRA HODGSON

NORTH AFRICAN LAMB STEW WITH SWEET POTATOES

meat

2 pounds lamb stew meat, cut into ½-inch cubes

Salt and freshly ground black pepper to taste

2 tablespoons vegetable oil for searing

2 medium onions, peeled and thinly sliced

6 cloves garlic, peeled and cut into thin slivers

¼ cup red wine vinegar

3 quarts Chicken Stock (page 48)

1 (8-ounce) can of chickpeas, drained and rinsed well

¼ cup apricot preserves

1 teaspoon cinnamon

3 medium or 2 large sweet potatoes, peeled and cut into ½-inch cubes

1 tablespoon ground coriander

1 tablespoon ground cumin

10–15 dashes Tabasco or other hot sauce

1 tablespoon ground fenugreek, optional

½ cup raisins

¼ cup chopped cilantro

1 lemon, halved

1. Sprinkle the lamb with salt and freshly ground pepper to taste. In your largest and heaviest sauté pan, heat the oil over medium-high heat until hot but not smoking. Add a single layer of the lamb chunks and sear until browned on all sides, about 3 minutes a side. Remove to a large stock pot. Repeat this process until all the lamb has been browned.

2. Put the onions in the same pan and sauté, stirring occasionally, over medium-high heat until they begin to caramelize, 8–10 minutes. Add the garlic and sauté, stirring, for an additional minute. Add the vinegar and continue to cook for 2–3 minutes, stirring up any browned bits from the bottom of the pan. Remove to the stock pot with the lamb.

3. Add the chicken stock, chickpeas, apricot preserves and cinnamon and bring the mixture to a boil. Reduce heat to low and simmer for 1 hour. Add the sweet potatoes and continue to cook until potatoes are easily pierced with a fork and the stew has thickened slightly, about 30 minutes longer.

4. Add the coriander, cumin, Tabasco, fenugreek, raisins and cilantro. Squeeze the lemon into the stew and stir until well combined. It can be served plain or on top of a mound of couscous.

Yield: 8 servings

—JOHN WILLOUGHBY AND
CHRIS SCHLESINGER

LAMB TAGINE WITH
BABY ARTICHOKES AND MINT

meat

4 cloves garlic, minced

½ cup packed fresh mint leaves, minced

Juice and grated zest of 1 lemon

1 teaspoon ground cumin

¼ teaspoon red pepper flakes

½ teaspoon salt plus to taste

2 pounds well-trimmed boneless lamb shoulder, cut in
   1½-inch cubes

¼ cup raisins

⅓ cup dry sherry

12 baby artichokes

1 tablespoon pine nuts

3 tablespoons extra-virgin olive oil

1 large onion, chopped

2 teaspoons balsamic vinegar

¾ cup cooked or canned chickpeas

Freshly ground black pepper to taste

1 cup well-flavored Chicken Stock (page 48),
   canned or fresh

1. Mix garlic, all but 1 tablespoon mint, lemon juice and zest, cumin, pepper flakes and ½ teaspoon salt in 2-quart bowl. Add lamb, mix well, cover and marinate 2 hours at room temperature. Place raisins and sherry in a small bowl and set aside.

2. When lamb is marinated, trim artichokes, cutting stems flush with bottoms, removing outer leaves and slicing off top ½ inch. Quarter artichokes, place in a bowl and cover with water.

3. Lightly toast pine nuts in 12-inch skillet. Remove. Add 2 tablespoons oil and brown lamb over high heat in 2 shifts to avoid crowding. Remove lamb from pan and lower heat to medium. Add remaining oil and onion and sauté until translucent. Drain artichokes and add, with raisins, sherry, balsamic vinegar and chickpeas. Season with salt and pepper. Transfer to tagine. Place lamb on top. If you are not using a tagine, add lamb to skillet. Add stock.

4. Cover tagine or skillet and cook over low heat until lamb is tender, about 1½ hours.

5. Baste meat with pan juices. If using a tagine, scatter reserved mint and pine nuts on top and serve. Otherwise, transfer to serving dish, garnish and serve.

Yield: 4–6 servings

—FLORENCE FABRICANT

LAMB TAGINE WITH DRIED FIGS AND ALMONDS

meat

¼ cup sesame seeds

½ cup sliced almonds

2 tablespoons olive oil

2½ pounds boned lamb shoulder, trimmed of excess
    fat and cut into ½-inch cubes

Coarse sea salt and freshly ground black pepper
    to taste

2 cloves garlic, minced

1 medium onion, chopped

1 teaspoon ground cumin

1 teaspoon ground cardamom

1 teaspoon turmeric

1 teaspoon ground chili pepper, such as Ancho
    or chili powder

1 cup dried figs, quartered

4 tablespoons chopped cilantro plus 8 sprigs cilantro

1. Preheat oven to 350 degrees. Put sesame seeds on a small sheet pan or pie plate and toast in oven for 6 minutes. Add almonds and toast another 8–10 minutes until golden brown. Set aside.

2. Put olive oil in a large, heavy-bottomed Dutch oven over medium-high heat. Season lamb with salt and pepper. Brown on all sides in two batches, about 10–12 minutes total. Add garlic, onion, cumin, cardamom, turmeric and chili powder to the lamb. Stir well and reduce heat to medium-low. Cook for 5 minutes. Add 2⅔ cups water and bring to boil. Reduce heat, cover and simmer for 1½ hours, or until meat is tender. It should be slightly springy but easy to pull apart with your fingers.

3. Preheat oven to 425 degrees. Strain liquid from the stew into small saucepan or bowl and skim fat. Adjust seasoning and keep warm. Mix meat and figs and spread in a single layer in an ovenproof serving dish. Pour sauce over meat and figs and sprinkle with almonds. Bake 12 minutes, or until crisp and golden. Sprinkle with sesame seeds and chopped cilantro and garnish with cilantro sprigs. Serve from hot dish.

Yield: 4 servings

—MOIRA HODGSON

LAMB AND BARLEY GOULASH

meat

2½ pounds lean lamb, cut into 1½-inch cubes

1 tablespoon corn, peanut or vegetable oil

1½ cups finely chopped onions

2 teaspoons finely minced garlic

2 tablespoons paprika, preferably imported from
    Hungary

4 cups cored, seeded green peppers cut into 1½-inch
    pieces

3 cups crushed, imported canned tomatoes

½ cup medium pearl barley

Salt to taste, it desired

Freshly ground black pepper to taste

3 cups Lamb Broth (page 49)

1½ tablespoons caraway seeds

1. Cut the meat into 1½-inch cubes.

2. Heat the oil in a heavy casserole or kettle and add the cubes. Cook over high heat until the meat is browned, about 5 minutes. The meat may give up a considerable amount of liquid.

3. Add the onions and garlic and cook, stirring, about 1 minute. Add the paprika and stir to coat.

Add the green peppers and tomatoes and stir to blend. Add the barley, salt and pepper.

4. Add the broth and caraway seeds. Bring to a boil and cover. Simmer between 1 hour and 15 minutes and 1 hour and 30 minutes or until the meat is quite tender. Serve immediately.

Yield: 4–6 servings

—CRAIG CLAIBORNE AND PIERRE FRANEY

LAMB AND TOMATOES WITH BULGUR

meat

ADAPTED FROM *The New York Times Menu Cook Book*

1½ pounds lamb, cut into 2-inch cubes
Salt and freshly ground black pepper to taste
1 tablespoon lamb fat or peanut oil
1 cup chopped onions
3 tablespoons margarine
2 cups Italian plum tomatoes, drained
3 cups water
1 cup bulgur

1. Sprinkle the lamb with salt and pepper and brown on all sides in the lamb fat or peanut oil. Add the onions and cook until they are light brown.

2. Add the margarine, tomatoes and water. Season with salt and pepper to taste and bring to a boil. Simmer 40 minutes to 1 hour, until the lamb is almost tender.

3. Rinse the bulgur under cold water and squeeze it to remove excess moisture. Add it to the kettle and cook for 20 minutes longer, or until all the liquid has been absorbed.

Yield: 4 servings

COUSCOUS WITH LAMB AND SEVEN VEGETABLES

meat

ADAPTED FROM *Mediterranean Cookery*

2 pounds lean, boneless stewing lamb

1½ cups chickpeas, soaked for at least 1 hour

2½ quarts water

2 large onions, quartered and thickly sliced

3 cloves garlic, roughly chopped

½ teaspoon saffron or turmeric (see Note below)

2 teaspoons cinnamon

1 teaspoon paprika

1 good pinch of cayenne pepper, or 2 small chili
    peppers, finely chopped

½ teaspoon powdered ginger

Salt to taste

7 or more of the following vegetables: 1 pound
    carrots, cut in half lengthwise; 1 medium white
    cabbage, cut into 8 sections; 6 artichoke hearts; 2
    medium eggplants, quartered; 1 pound small new
    potatoes, halved or quartered; 1 pound baby
    turnips, halved or quartered; 1 pound broad beans,
    shelled; 1 pound pumpkin or any orange-fleshed
    squash, cubed; 1 pound small zucchini, cut in half
    lengthwise; 4 juicy red tomatoes, quartered

2 pounds precooked couscous

1 quart lightly salted water

⅓ cup sunflower oil

½ pound raisins

1 large bunch parsley, chopped

1 large bunch fresh cilantro, chopped

1. Place the meat and chickpeas in a large pot or in the bottom of a couscousier. Cover with 2½ quarts of water, bring to a boil and skim any foam that appears on the surface. Lower the heat and add the onion, garlic, spices and, if you are using them, the chili peppers. Simmer for 1 hour, then add salt to taste.

2. Put in any of the following that you are using: carrots, cabbage, artichoke hearts, eggplants and potatoes. Simmer for 20 minutes, adding a few tablespoons of hot water if the vegetable mixture becomes too dry.

3. Meanwhile, prepare the couscous. Place the couscous in a large bowl, stir in half the salted water and leave for 10 minutes. Add the remaining water and 4 tablespoons of the sunflower oil. Rub the grains between your palms to prevent them from sticking together and forming lumps. After another 10 minutes, the grains should be swollen and tender.

4. Add the raisins and, if you are using them, the turnips and broad beans to the stew. Place the couscous in a steamer or metal colander, set it inside the stew pot, cover and steam—the grains will absorb some of the stew's fragrance. (If you are using a couscousier, put the couscous in the top half and cover.) When the steam begins to rise from the grains, the couscous is done.

5. Ten minutes after adding the turnips and broad beans, put in the pumpkin or squash, zucchini and tomatoes, if you are using them. Five minutes later, add the parsley and cilantro and cook for another 5 minutes.

6. To serve, place the couscous on a large platter, tossing with a fork to separate the grains. Stir in the remaining 4 tablespoons of oil and form the couscous into a mound. Make a well in the mound and place the meat inside. Arrange the vegetables around the couscous and pour the broth into a separate bowl. Serve at once.

Yield: 10 servings

NOTE: *Since the saffron in this dish is there for color rather than flavor, the cheapest grade may be used.*

—NANCY HARMON JENKINS

LAMB AND EGGPLANT BALLS

meat

ADAPTED FROM *The New York Times Menu Cook Book*

1½ pounds lamb, ground
1 tablespoon finely chopped parsley
2 cups peeled, chopped eggplant (1 small eggplant)
⅓ cup soft fresh bread crumbs
1 egg, lightly beaten
1½ teaspoons cornstarch
1¼ teaspoons salt
¼ teaspoon freshly ground black pepper
¾ cup finely chopped onions
3 tablespoons olive oil
1 cup (one 8-ounce can) tomato sauce
⅛ teaspoon dry mustard
½ teaspoon ground cinnamon
¼ teaspoon ground cloves

1. Mix together the lamb, parsley, eggplant, bread crumbs, egg, cornstarch, one teaspoon of the salt, ⅛ teaspoon of the pepper and ½ cup of the onions.

2. Shape the mixture into 20 balls and brown them all on sides in the oil. Pour off the drippings. Combine the remaining ingredients and pour over the lamb balls.

3. Cover and simmer gently for 30 minutes. Uncover and cook for 15 minutes longer. Serve.

Yield: 4–5 servings

LAMB-STUFFED ARTICHOKES,
SYRIAN-STYLE • (ARDISHAWKI MIHSHI)

meat

4 large artichokes prepared for stuffing (see instructions)
1 tablespoon olive oil
1½ cups onions, chopped fine
1 teaspoon finely minced garlic
1 cup mushrooms, chopped fine
½ pound ground lamb
½ cup scallions, chopped fine
¼ cup finely chopped parsley
2 tablespoons finely chopped dill
¼ cup toasted pine nuts
Salt to taste, if desired
Freshly ground pepper to taste
Juice of ½ lemon
1½ cups plus 1 tablespoon water
1 teaspoon cornstarch or arrowroot

1. Prepare artichokes for stuffing and set aside (see below).

2. Heat oil in saucepan and add half the onions and half the garlic. Cook, stirring, until wilted. Add mushrooms and cook until wilted.

3. Put lamb in mixing bowl and add mushroom mixture, scallions, parsley, dill, pine nuts, salt and pepper. Blend well.

4. Stuff artichokes with equal portions of mixture.

5. Select kettle large enough to hold artichokes when placed snugly together. Add remaining onions and garlic, lemon juice and 1½ cups water.

6. Arrange the artichokes close together, stuffed side up, in kettle. Bring to boil. Cover closely and cook over gentle heat about 45 minutes.

7. Remove artichokes to warm serving dish and pour the cooking liquid into saucepan. Bring to simmer.

8. Blend cornstarch with remaining tablespoon cold water. Stir into simmering liquid. When thickened, pour sauce over artichokes and serve.

Yield: 4 servings

—CRAIG CLAIBORNE

How to Prepare
Whole Artichokes for Stuffing

1. Cut off the stems of the artichokes, using a sharp knife, to produce a neat, flat base. Rub any cut surfaces with lemon. Slice off the top "cone" of the artichoke about an inch from the tip. With kitchen scissors, cut off the sharp tips of the leaves about half an inch down.

2. Use a melon-ball scoop to hollow out the choke in the center, pulling and scraping away the tender center leaves above. Turn the artichokes upside down and press down to open the center, facilitating stuffing. Turn right side up and stuff.

—CRAIG CLAIBORNE

SWEET PEPPERS STUFFED
WITH LAMB AND MINTED COUSCOUS

meat

ADAPTED FROM TriBeCa Grill

  6 medium Italian sweet peppers
  1⅓ cups couscous
  2 cups Chicken Broth (page 48), canned or fresh
  1 tablespoon salt
  Pinch turmeric
  5 tablespoons olive oil
  ½ clove garlic, minced
  6 ounces ground lamb
  ½ tablespoon freshly ground black pepper
  2 tablespoons chopped fresh mint
  1 large egg, lightly beaten

1. Preheat the oven to 350 degrees.

2. Remove the stems from the peppers with a paring knife. Remove the seeds, leaving the vegetables whole. Set aside.

3. Place the couscous in a very fine mesh strainer and rinse with cold running water. Rub the couscous between your hands to separate the grains. Spread the couscous in a shallow pan and let it rest for 15 minutes until plumped. Run your fingers through it to keep it from being clumpy.

4. Place 1 cup of the broth, the salt and turmeric in a pot and bring to a boil. Add the couscous and stir. Strain off excess liquid, if any, reserve and return the couscous to the shallow pan to cool quickly.

5. Meanwhile, in a small sauté pan, heat 1 tablespoon of the olive oil over medium heat. Add the garlic and brown slightly. Add the ground lamb and pepper and stir over high heat until the meat is slightly undercooked, about 2–3 minutes. Remove from the heat and let cool.

6. In a mixing bowl, combine the couscous, lamb, chopped mint and egg and mix well. Taste the mixture and add salt and pepper if desired. Stuff the mixture tightly into the peppers, being careful not to break them.

7. Lightly coat a medium-size skillet with 4 tablespoons of olive oil. Place over a high heat and add the peppers. Cook until slightly browned. Measure the reserved broth and, if necessary, add more broth to bring the total to 1 cup. Add this to the peppers. Cover and finish cooking in a preheated oven for 20 minutes, or until the peppers are tender.

8. Serve hot, cold or at room temperature.

Yield: 6 servings

—LINDA WELLS

MIDDLE EASTERN–STYLE LAMB BURGERS WITH DRIED FIG-MINT RELISH

meat

FOR THE LAMB:

> 1½ pounds ground lamb
> ¼ cup roughly chopped fresh parsley
> 2 tablespoons minced garlic
> 2 tablespoons toasted coriander seeds
> 2 teaspoons red pepper flakes
> 1 tablespoon ground cumin
> 2 large pita rounds, halved
> 1 tablespoon olive oil

1. Light a fire in the grill, or heat the broiler.

2. In a large bowl, combine the lamb, parsley, garlic, coriander, red pepper flakes, cumin, salt and pepper. Mix well with your hands until the mixture has an even consistency, then form into 4 patties.

3. Grill the patties over a medium hot fire, or broil, until done the way you like them. Halfway through the cooking time, brush the pita rounds with the olive oil, place them on the grill and cook to desired doneness.

4. Remove the patties from heat; place inside pita halves, along with a tablespoon or two of the relish, and serve, passing any remaining relish separately.

Yield: 4 servings

◆ DRIED FIG-MINT RELISH ◆

pareve

> ½ cup finely chopped dried figs
> ¼ cup roughly chopped fresh mint
> Juice of 1 lemon
> 1 tablespoon honey
> Salt and freshly ground black pepper to taste

Combine the figs, mint, lemon juice, honey and salt and pepper to taste. Mix well and set aside.

Yield: ¾ cup

NOTE: *This relish is an excellent complement to lamb roasts and chops.*

—JOHN WILLOUGHBY AND
CHRIS SCHLESINGER

THE FOUR SEASONS CHOPPED LAMB STEAK WITH PINE NUTS

meat

ADAPTED FROM *The Four Seasons Cook Book*

1 pound ground lean lamb
6 tablespoons pine nuts
1 teaspoon curry powder
¼ teaspoon ground coriander
Salt, if desired
½ teaspoon Hungarian sweet paprika
⅓ cup ice water

1. Combine the lamb, pine nuts, curry powder, coriander, salt to taste and paprika in a mixing bowl.
2. Start blending, gradually adding the ice water. Take care not to overwork the mixture or it will become pastelike and toughen when cooked.

3. Divide the mixture into four portions of equal weight. Shape each portion into a 5-inch-long, egg-shaped patty.
4. Place the patties on a plate. Cover and let chill for 2 hours before cooking. This will bring out the flavor and set the shape.
5. Preheat the broiler to high.
6. Place the patties under the broiler. Cook 5 minutes on one side for rare. Turn and cook 5 minutes on the other side. Cook longer on each side if more well-done meat is desired. Serve with chutney.

Yield: 2–4 servings

NOTE: *If you prefer, you may sauté the patties in olive oil to the desired degree of doneness.*

—CRAIG CLAIBORNE AND PIERRE FRANEY

GRILLED MOROCCAN LAMB SAUSAGE · (MERGUEZ)

meat

ADAPTED FROM *The Mediterranean Kitchen*

2½ pounds lean lamb, ground with ½ pound lamb
* or beef fat*
2 tablespoons water
1½ tablespoons minced garlic
2 tablespoons chopped fresh cilantro
2 tablespoons chopped fresh parsley
2 tablespoons paprika
1½ teaspoons ground cumin
1½ teaspoons ground coriander
1¼ teaspoons cinnamon

¾ teaspoon cayenne pepper or to taste
1¼ teaspoons salt
½ teaspoon freshly ground black pepper
2 tablespoons olive oil

1. Combine all ingredients except the olive oil in a large bowl and mix well. Shape into eight 3-inch-long lozenges, slightly fatter in the middle, or into 8 meat patties.
2. Preheat grill or broiler.
3. Brush lozenges with oil and cook 3–4 minutes on each side. For patties, brush with oil and grill 4–5 minutes on each side.

Yield: 4 servings

NOTE: *The patties may be pan broiled: heat 1 tablespoon of olive oil in a cast-iron skillet or stove-top griddle and add the meat patties. Cook on medium-high heat 3–4*

minutes per side for medium or to desired degree of doneness.

—FLORENCE FABRICANT

PAUL PRUDHOMME'S VEAL ROAST WITH MANGO SAUCE

meat
ADAPTED FROM *The New York Times Passover Cookbook*

1 teaspoon salt
1 teaspoon onion powder
1 teaspoon garlic powder
1 teaspoon cayenne pepper
1 teaspoon freshly ground white pepper
1 teaspoon freshly ground black pepper
1 teaspoon dried basil
1 large mango, peeled and diced
2½ cups veal or beef stock
1 rib-eye veal roast, boned to yield 3–3½ pounds
2 tablespoons olive oil

1. Preheat the oven to 325 degrees.
2. In a small bowl, combine the salt, onion and garlic powders, cayenne, white and black peppers and basil. Set aside.
3. Place the mango and 2 cups of the stock in a saucepan and bring to a boil over high heat. Lower the heat, allowing the mixture to thicken, and cook until the stock is reduced to about 1½ cups, about 20 minutes. Add 1 teaspoon of the seasoning mix and remove from the heat. Puree in a blender or food processor and set aside for a few hours until ready to use.

4. To prepare the roast: cut a series of pockets ¾ inch apart, each pocket about 1 inch wide and 1 inch deep. With your hands, work 5 teaspoons of the seasoning mix into the pockets and along the outside of the roast.
5. In a large nonstick skillet, heat the olive oil over high heat. Sear the meat on all sides.
6. Transfer the meat to a roasting pan. Add the remaining ½ cup of stock to the skillet to deglaze, scraping up any bits from the bottom. Pour the contents of the skillet over the meat. Cover the pan and roast the veal until it is medium-rare, with an internal temperature of 125 degrees, about 45 minutes–1 hour.
7. Serve ½-inch slices of the roast topped with the mango sauce.

Yield: 6 servings

NOTE: *Chef Prudhomme, of K-Paul's Louisiana Kitchen in New Orleans, created this roast veal for a dinner in Jerusalem celebrating the city's three thousandth anniversary. Although the rib-eye roast is expensive, the results are spectacular. It is delicious accompanied by sautéed peppers, eggplant and squash seasoned with the remaining teaspoon of seasoning mixture.*

—JOAN NATHAN

SHOULDER OF VEAL WITH ROOT VEGETABLES

meat

4 tablespoons vegetable oil (canola or peanut)

1 (3½-pound) roast of veal from the shoulder

1½ teaspoons salt

¾ teaspoon freshly ground black pepper

2 white turnips (about ½ pound), peeled and quartered

3 onions (about 1 pound), peeled and quartered

3 carrots (about ½ pound), peeled and cut into
   1-inch pieces on a bias

16 cloves garlic, unpeeled and cut in half crosswise

1 bouquet garni made of 2 bay leaves, 6 sprigs
   parsley and 4 sprigs thyme, tied in cheesecloth

1. Heat the oil in a Dutch oven (cast iron or enamel) and when hot, brown the roast on all sides over moderate heat for about 20 minutes.

2. Remove the meat, sprinkle with 1 teaspoon of the salt and ½ teaspoon of the pepper and set aside.

3. Place the vegetables and bouquet garni in the pan and brown, stirring, over medium heat for about 5 minutes. Mix in the remaining salt and pepper.

4. Return the roast to the pan, arranging it on top of the vegetables. Add a ⅓ cup of water, cover closely with a piece of parchment or waxed paper and put the lid on the pan. Place in a 350-degree oven for 1½ hours, basting or turning the roast in its juices about every 20 minutes.

5. Serve the roast sliced, with the natural juices and surrounded by the cooked vegetables, on a large, warm platter.

Yield: 6 servings

—JONATHAN REYNOLDS

BRAISED VEAL WITH CURRY

meat

ADAPTED FROM *Kosher Cuisine*

3 pounds center-cut, boned shoulder of veal, rolled
   and tied

1¾ teaspoons Madras curry powder

Kosher salt to taste, if desired

Freshly ground pepper to taste

1 pound shallots

3 tablespoons unsalted margarine

2 teaspoons fresh tarragon

1 tablespoon olive oil

6 sprigs fresh parsley

1 bay leaf

1 teaspoon dried thyme

¼ cup flour

1 cup water

1. Rub veal with curry powder, salt, if desired, and pepper.

2. Drop shallots into boiling water to cover. Simmer 1 minute. Drain. When cool enough to handle, peel shallots.

3. Heat 2 tablespoons of margarine in saucepan and add shallots. Sprinkle with 1 teaspoon of the tarragon. Cover closely and cook over low heat 10 minutes.

4. Heat oil and remaining tablespoon of margarine in heavy casserole large enough to hold meat without crowding. Cook meat, turning to cook evenly, until browned on all sides, about 10 minutes.

5. Preheat oven to 325 degrees.

6. Add shallot mixture and remaining teaspoon dried tarragon.

7. Put parsley, bay leaf and thyme in square of cheesecloth. Tie to enclose. Add cheesecloth bag. Cover casserole closely.

8. Make paste of flour and water, stirring to blend. Dip length of cheesecloth, about 2 inches wide, in paste. Arrange it around rim of lid, pressing to seal.

9. Place casserole in oven and bake 1–1¼ hours.

10. Break the seal. Slice the meat, place on a platter, cover and keep warm.

11. Skim surface fat from pan juices. Season with salt and pepper. Bring to a boil. Pour some of the sauce over the meat and serve remainder of sauce on the side.

Yield: 6–8 servings

—CRAIG CLAIBORNE

CHARLES MICHENER'S POTTED VEAL

meat

1 (4- to 5-pound) veal roast, tied
Salt and freshly ground black pepper to taste
All-purpose flour
4 tablespoons olive oil
1½ cups coarsely chopped yellow onion
2 carrots, peeled and coarsely chopped
1 large rib celery, coarsely chopped
2 cups white wine
2 cups veal or beef stock
2 cloves garlic, peeled
2 large sprigs thyme
2 strips lemon peel
½ cup finely chopped onion
½ cup finely chopped carrot
½ cup finely chopped celery
2 ounces dried porcini mushrooms, soaked for
    10 minutes in 1 cup boiling water
1½ teaspoon grated lemon zest
2 tablespoons finely chopped parsley

1. Preheat the oven to 300 degrees. Season the veal with salt and pepper and dust it with flour. In a large, heavy pot or Dutch oven with a tight lid, heat 3 tablespoons of the oil over high heat. Add the veal and brown on all sides. Remove the veal and add the onion, carrots and celery. Lower heat to medium and cook, stirring, until the vegetables are browned, about 10 minutes. Return the veal to the pot and add the wine, stock, garlic, thyme and lemon peel and bring just to a boil. Cover the pot and place it in the oven. Cook until the meat is very tender, about 2½–3 hours.

2. Remove the meat and set aside. Pour the cooking liquid through a fine-mesh strainer. Discard the solids and reserve the cooking liquid. Add the last tablespoon of oil to the pot and place it over medium-high heat. Sauté the finely chopped onion, carrots and celery until tender. Skim any excess fat from the reserved cooking liquid and add it to the pot. Drain the mushrooms, chop them coarsely and add them, along with the soaking liquid, to the pot.

Lower the heat and simmer, partly covered, and cook for 1 hour.

3. When ready to serve, return the meat to the pot with the sauce and place it over medium heat. Combine the zest and parsley and sprinkle it over the meat. Cook, covered, until the meat is thoroughly warmed. Transfer to a platter and serve.

Yield: 10–12 servings

—MOLLY O'NEILL

BRAISED BREAST OF VEAL •
(TENDRONS DE VEAU BRAISÉS)

meat

ADAPTED FROM La Tour de Montlhery, Paris

1 (7-pound) breast of veal (have the butcher cut across the breast to make 6 strips of equal width)
½ cup flour
Salt and freshly ground pepper to taste
¼ cup vegetable oil
½ cup chopped onions
1 tablespoon chopped celery
1 tablespoon chopped garlic
1 cup diced carrots
1 cup dry white wine
1 bay leaf
4 sprigs fresh thyme, or 1 teaspoon dried
3 cups Chicken Stock (page 48)
½ cup canned crushed tomatoes

1. Halve each of the 6 strips of veal crosswise.
2. Dredge the breast sections in flour seasoned with salt and pepper.
3. Heat the oil in a large cast-iron skillet over a medium flame. Add the veal pieces, turning often to brown all over. This should take about 10 minutes.
4. Drain the fat from the skillet and add the onions, celery, garlic and carrots. Cook, stirring, for 2 minutes. Add the wine, bay leaf, thyme, chicken stock and tomatoes. Stir, bringing to a boil. Cover, reduce heat and simmer for 2 hours, or until the meat is well cooked.
5. Remove the excess fat if necessary. Remove the bay leaf. Serve with noodles, rice or mashed potatoes.

Yield: 6–10 servings

—PIERRE FRANEY

VEAL RIB CHOPS WITH BALSAMIC VINEGAR

meat
ADAPTED FROM Paul Bertolli

4 (¾-inch) prime veal rib chops at room temperature
Salt and freshly ground black pepper to taste
2 tablespoons pure olive oil
5 teaspoons good aged balsamic vinegar

1. Season chops on both sides with salt and pepper. Preheat large heavy skillet over high heat.
2. Pour olive oil into skillet, shake to coat bottom evenly and heat over medium-high heat until very hot. Place chops in pan, leaving an inch of space around each, and cook until a nice brown crust has formed, about 4 minutes. Turn chops and cook until desired doneness is reached (medium-rare will take 3 to 4 minutes).
3. Place each chop on a plate, and let it rest for 5 minutes. Drizzle slightly more than a teaspoon of balsamic over each chop and serve immediately.

Yield: 4 servings

NOTE: *The quality of the vinegar makes a great difference in the flavor of this dish. For best results, use the finest aged balsamic vinegar available.*

—MOLLY O'NEILL

VEAL STEW WITH EGGPLANT

meat
ADAPTED FROM *The Best of Craig Claiborne*

3 pounds lean veal, cut into 2-inch cubes
Salt and freshly ground pepper to taste
½ cup peanut, vegetable or corn oil
2 cups diced onions
1 tablespoon finely chopped garlic
¼ cup flour
4 cups diced eggplant
2 cups sliced zucchini
3 cups diced green peppers
3 cups diced tomatoes
1 cup dry white wine
2 cups Chicken Broth (page 48), canned or fresh
3 tablespoon tomato paste
1 fresh thyme sprig, or 1 teaspoon dried
1 cup water

1. Sprinkle the veal with salt and pepper.
2. Heat the oil in a large heavy skillet. It should be large enough to hold the meat in 1 layer. Brown the meat on all sides, turning the pieces as necessary. This will take 15–20 minutes.
3. Add the onions and garlic. Cook briefly, stirring, and sprinkle with the flour. Stir so that meat is coated evenly.
4. Add the eggplant, zucchini and green peppers. Stir and add the tomatoes, wine and chicken broth. Add salt and pepper to taste. Stir in the tomato paste, thyme and water. Bring to a boil. Cover and cook for 1 hour and 15 minutes.

Yield: 8 or more servings

SYRIAN VEAL WITH BLACK-EYED PEAS

meat

ADAPTED FROM Rae Dayan, in
The Jewish Holiday Kitchen

1 medium-size onion, chopped

2 cloves garlic, minced

2 tablespoons vegetable oil

1½ pounds stewing veal, cut into 1-inch cubes

2 cups water

4 cups black-eyed peas, soaked for 6 hours or
   overnight

1 teaspoon salt or to taste

⅛ teaspoon pepper

1 teaspoon allspice

½ teaspoon cinnamon

2 tablespoons tomato paste

1. In a Dutch oven or other heavy frying pan with a cover, sauté the onion and garlic lightly in the oil until translucent.

2. Add the veal and brown briefly. Add ½ cup of the water and cover. Simmer slowly for 20 minutes.

3. Meanwhile, cover the black-eyed peas in water and simmer for 20 minutes. Drain and add the peas, salt, pepper, spices, tomato paste and the remaining 1½ cups of water to the veal mixture. Cover and cook over low heat for 1 hour or until the peas and veal are tender. If the mixture dries out, add a little water. Adjust the spices to taste. Serve warm.

Yield: 8 servings

—JOAN NATHAN

VEAL STEW WITH SPRING VEGETABLES

meat

2 tablespoons peanut or vegetable oil

2 pounds stewing veal, cut into 1½-inch cubes

2 shallots, chopped

1 clove garlic, minced

1 cup white wine

1 cup Chicken Stock (page 48), canned or fresh

1 tablespoon tomato paste

1 tablespoon fresh thyme leaves

1 piece lemon peel

Coarse salt to taste

Freshly ground pepper to taste

8 baby carrots, left whole

8 new potatoes, scrubbed

3 small white turnips, peeled and quartered

½ pound green peas

¼ pound green beans

1. Heat the oil in a heavy casserole. Brown the pieces of veal a few at a time and remove with a slotted spoon. Pour off any excess fat. Add the shallots and garlic and sauté until soft.

2. Add the white wine and stir, scraping up any cooking particles from the bottom of the pan. Add the chicken stock, tomato paste, thyme, lemon peel and salt and pepper and bring to boil. Turn down heat, cover and cook gently for 1 hour.

3. Add the carrots and cook for 20 minutes, or until the vegetables are tender. Meanwhile, in a steamer cook the new potatoes and turnips until tender (about 20 minutes). Cook the green peas and beans until tender (about 5 minutes). Add them to the stew and serve.

Yield: 4 servings

—MOIRA HODGSON

VEAL IN RED WINE SAUCE

meat

4 pounds boneless shoulder of veal, cut into 1½-inch cubes
Salt to taste, if desired
Freshly ground pepper to taste
¼ cup corn, peanut or vegetable oil
3 carrots, trimmed and scraped, cut into ½-inch cubes, about 1¼ cups
1 onion, about ½ pound, peeled and cut into ½-inch dice, about 1½ cups
1 tablespoon garlic, peeled and finely minced
¼ cup flour
4 sprigs fresh thyme
10 sprigs parsley
1 bay leaf
3½ cups (1 bottle) dry red wine
1 teaspoon sugar

1. Sprinkle the veal with salt and pepper.
2. Heat the oil in a large, heavy skillet over high heat, add the veal pieces a few at a time and cook, stirring, until lightly browned on all sides, about 8–10 minutes. Transfer the pieces as they are browned to a large, heavy casserole and continue cooking in the casserole over high heat. Add more pieces to the skillet and continue cooking and browning and transferring the pieces to the casserole until all are browned and added.
3. Add the carrots, onion and garlic to the meat and stir. Cook 10 minutes and sprinkle with flour, salt and pepper, stirring. Tie the thyme, parsley and bay leaf into a bundle and add it. Add the wine and sugar and bring to a boil. Cover and let simmer over low heat about 1½ hours. Remove and discard the herb bundle.

Yield: 6–8 servings

—CRAIG CLAIBORNE AND PIERRE FRANEY

VEAL STEW WITH CAPERS AND FRIED SAGE LEAVES

meat

1 medium onion, chopped
2 cloves garlic, minced (green part removed)

4 carrots, chopped
5 stalks celery, chopped
Approximately 9 tablespoons olive oil
Flour for dredging

4 pounds lean stewing veal, cut into 1½-inch cubes

Coarse sea salt to taste

Freshly ground pepper to taste

1 cup dry white wine

1 can (35 ounces) plum tomatoes, chopped
   with their juice

2 tablespoons flat-leaf parsley, chopped

1 tablespoon fresh thyme leaves

About 30 large sage leaves

3 tablespoons drained capers

1. Preheat the oven to 350 degrees. Soften the onions, garlic, carrots and celery in 3 tablespoons olive oil in a large skillet.

2. Meanwhile, in a large enameled casserole heat 3 tablespoons olive oil. Dredge the veal lightly in the flour, season with salt and pepper to taste and brown the pieces a few at a time. Remove to a plate.

3. Add the white wine to the casserole and scrape up the cooking juices. Return the veal to the casserole along with the vegetables and tomatoes with their juice. Add the parsley and thyme and bring to a simmer.

4. Cover the casserole and put it in the oven. Cook for 2 hours or until the veal is tender. Check halfway through the cooking time to see if it is too liquid or too dry. If it is too liquid, remove the top. If there is still too much liquid at the end of the cooking time, remove the veal with a slotted spoon and put it into a serving dish; keep warm. Boil down the sauce and pour it over the top. If the stew is too dry, moisten it with ½ cup of water or more as needed.

5. While the veal is cooking, fry the sage leaves a few at a time in the remaining oil. Drain them on paper towels and sprinkle them with salt.

6. When the stew is ready to serve, stir in the capers. Sprinkle the sage leaves over the top.

Yield: 8 servings

—MOIRA HODGSON

VEAL STEW WITH SNOW PEAS

meat

4 tablespoons olive oil

½ cup finely chopped onion

½ cup finely chopped carrots

½ cup finely chopped celery

1 large clove garlic, minced

1½ pounds veal shoulder, cut into 1½-inch cubes

¾ cup dry red wine

1 pound plum tomatoes, finely chopped, or 1½ cups
   chopped, drained, canned plum tomatoes

1 bay leaf

½ teaspoon dried thyme

Salt and freshly ground black pepper

1 teaspoon lemon juice

¼ pound fresh snow peas, trimmed

½ tablespoon very finely minced fresh parsley

1 small scallion, very finely minced

1. Heat 2 tablespoons of the olive oil in a heavy casserole. Add the onion, carrots and celery and sauté over low heat until soft but not brown. Add the garlic and continue to sauté for a minute or two. Remove from heat.

2. Dry the veal on paper toweling. Add the remaining oil to a heavy skillet and add as much of the veal as you can at a time without crowding. Brown the veal pieces over medium-high heat. As they are browned, place them over the vegetables in the casserole. When the veal is all browned, add the wine to the skillet and cook, scraping the skillet, until all the particles are dissolved.

3. Pour the contents of the skillet over the meat and vegetables in the casserole, add the tomatoes, bay leaf, thyme and salt and pepper to taste.

4. Bring the casserole to a simmer, cover and simmer for 1½ hours, until the veal is tender. Stir in the lemon juice and recheck the seasonings.

5. Add the snow peas and cook just long enough for the snow peas to turn bright green and become tender, about 5 minutes. Sprinkle with parsley and scallions and serve.

Yield: 4 servings

NOTE: *If you are making this stew in advance, do not add the snow peas. These should be added during the final moments of reheating.*

—FLORENCE FABRICANT

VEAL-ARTICHOKE STEW WITH BULGUR

meat

10 medium artichokes

2–5 cups cool water, enough to cover artichokes

Juice of ½ lemon

1 pound lean, boneless veal, cut into small cubes

½ cup olive oil

3 scallions, chopped

2 medium-size yellow onions, chopped

2 large cloves garlic, chopped

Salt and freshly ground black pepper to taste

2 teaspoons flour

¼ cup freshly squeezed lemon juice

1 small yellow onion, chopped

2 tablespoons olive oil

1½ cups bulgur wheat

3 cups water

2 lemon quarters and chopped cilantro or parsley for garnish

1. Trim artichokes of their stems and tough outer leaves. Use scissors to cut off prickly tips of inner leaves. Cut hearts into quarters, discard the chokes and clean the hearts well with running water. To prevent the artichokes from turning brown, place them in a bowl with the cool water and juice of half a lemon.

2. Over medium heat, brown the meat cubes in ½ cup of olive oil. Add the scallions, onions and garlic and sauté until the onions are translucent. Pour in just enough water to cover the meat, then season with salt and pepper to taste. Cover the pan, lower the heat and cook gently for 20 minutes, or until the meat cubes are tender.

3. Drain the artichokes and put them into the pan with the meat, stirring to mix well. Put the flour into a cup, stir in a little lemon juice to get rid of any lumps and add this mixture along with the remaining lemon juice to the pan. Cook for 20 minutes, or until the artichokes are tender. Remove the lid and simmer for an additional 5–20 minutes to reduce and thicken the sauce. Taste for seasoning—add salt, pepper and lemon juice as desired.

4. In a 1-quart saucepan, sauté the small chopped onion in 2 tablespoons of olive oil over medium heat. Add the bulgur and stir to coat the grains thoroughly with oil. Boil 3 cups of water and pour it over the bulgur. Salt to taste. Cover and cook over low heat until bulgur is fluffy and tender, approximately 10–15 minutes. Remove from the heat and drain if necessary.

5. To serve, place the bulgur on a large platter with a raised edge. Pour the artichoke stew over the grains and garnish with lemon quarters and chopped cilantro or parsley.

Yield: 6–8 servings

—NANCY HARMON JENKINS

ITZHAK PERLMAN'S FAVORITE MEAT LOAF

meat

4 small onions or 2 large ones

1 clove garlic

4½ pounds ground veal

Ketchup to taste

Pepper to taste

Garlic salt to taste

1–2 cups of boiling water

8 ounces, approximately, of flavored bread crumbs

1. Chop the onions and sauté them until translucent, adding garlic clove, minced or put through garlic press, toward the end.

2. Put the meat in a big bowl. Add the onions, garlic, ketchup, pepper and garlic salt. Knead by hand. Add the water and the bread crumbs and mix well by hand.

3. Shape into 2 loaves in baking tins. Cook 30–40 minutes in a preheated 350-degree oven. ("Stick a knife in," Mr. Perlman says. "If it comes out cold, it's not ready; if it's warm, it is.")

Yield: 10–12 servings

—JOHN ROCKWELL

SWEETBREADS DUSTED WITH CLOVES

meat

ADAPTED FROM David Bouley

3 Jerusalem artichokes, peeled

3 large bunches Italian parsley

1 tablespoon honey

¼ cup water

3 tablespoons olive oil

2 tablespoons whole cloves

2 tablespoons instant flour

1½ pounds sweetbreads, soaked overnight in cold water,
    tough outer membrane removed, and patted dry

¼ teaspoon lemon juice

1. Boil the artichokes in water to cover until tender, about 40 minutes. Drain and puree in food processor. Reserve.

2. Wash the parsley and dry well in a salad spinner. Trim off and discard the stems. Heat the honey in a large pan until light in color. Add water and parsley leaves and cook until parsley is wilted.

3. Puree mixture in a blender, then pass through strainer. Combine with artichoke puree. Add 1 tablespoon of the olive oil. Set sauce aside.

4. Grind cloves in a coffee grinder and combine with flour. Dust whole sweetbreads with clove mixture and sauté them in remaining olive oil in a skillet over moderate heat for 5 minutes on each side. Slice sweetbreads into ½-inch-thick slices.

5. When ready to serve, reheat parsley sauce, add lemon juice and spoon onto serving plates. Cover with sweetbreads.

Yield: 4 servings

NOTE: *Roasted celery root, parsnips, turnips and pearl onions are excellent accompaniments.*

—DENA KLEIMAN

VEGETABLES

In many ways, this is the area where the Sephardic and Middle Eastern Jewish cuisines match contemporary tastes more than the Ashkenazic, climate being the main determiner of eating patterns and therefore taste preferences. In the colder countries of Eastern Europe, Jews had few fresh vegetables in winter, relying on roots, tubers and other produce that could be harvested late and stored well. Therefore the vegetable menu relied mostly on potatoes, turnips, parsnips, carrots, onions, leeks, garlic and cabbages, many of which were cooked in meat stews, to emerge hearty and meltingly soft. To preserve some of summer's bounty for winter, they pickled green tomatoes, cucumbers and red peppers, and the grated cabbage they turned into sauerkraut, using salt-brine and sometimes vinegar. Using seasonings of garlic and dill and a variety of spices such as bay leaf, peppercorns, coriander seeds and dried hot chili peppers, they created a category of foods for which they became famous, kosher dill pickles, much-sought-after classics wherever Ashkenazim settled. Similarly, they relied on the extraordinary borovik mushrooms that grew wild in the woods of Poland and Russia, mushrooms so strong that two or three dried caps could flavor a big pot of barley soup, which was fortunate, because they were always extremely expensive.

They did rely on a few famously delicious vegetable preparations, among them strudel filled with red or green cabbage, prune and carrot tsimmes, caraway-scented hot sauerkraut and stuffed cabbage and peppers. If the Eastern European Jews excelled in any area of vegetable cookery, it was with potatoes, a dietary staple so important that they developed many methods of cooking for the sake of variety, and even had a folk song honoring the homely *bulbes*. (See box on page 281.)

Sephardim, on the other hand, drew from the Mediterranean gardens that flourished in the relatively mild climate, and, like others in the area, prepared the lightly cooked vegetable dishes of artichokes, eggplant, tomatoes, zucchini, peppers and onions, stuffed vegetable dolmas and many cold dishes that could be classified as appetizers or salads. Using fresh herbs and olive oil, and celebrating the first greens of springtime, their vegetable cookery is a perfect match for today's tastes.

In contemporary cooking, with its health and fashion emphasis on vegetables, new classics are developing that are well suited to the Jewish palate. Among such are eggplant napoleon, sugar snap peas with sundried tomatoes and mashed yellow turnips with crispy shallots, and David Bouley's braised carrots with Italian parsley.

And anyone who thought that latkes meant only the crisp, classic potato pancakes, should be pleasantly surprised and tempted by richly complex variations based on leeks, mushrooms and pecans, zucchini, lentils, Jerusalem artichokes and curried sweet potatoes.

ARMENIAN ARTICHOKE HEARTS

pareve

6 very large artichokes
2 lemons
4 medium-size onions
4 medium-size potatoes
Salt and white pepper to taste
1 tablespoon sugar
1 tablespoon minced fresh dill
1 cup olive oil
Lemon wedges for garnish

1. Break off outer two or three rows of artichoke leaves. Using a sharp stainless-steel knife, cut off remaining leaves right down to the base or heart.
2. Scoop out choke (the fuzzy substance), peel outer skin from stem and trim base. Keep rubbing artichoke surfaces with lemon as you cut, to prevent blackening.
3. Drop each heart into a bowl of salted water as it is trimmed and add lemon pieces to water as you use them.
4. Peel onions and cut in quarters.
5. Peel potatoes and cut in slices ¼ to ½ inch thick.
6. Cut artichoke hearts in half lengthwise, through the stem.

7. Place in an enamel skillet with a top, cut side down. Fit onion and potato slices around hearts. Sprinkle with salt, white pepper, sugar and dill. Add about ⅓ cup olive oil.
8. Cover artichokes with an inverted dinner plate that fits very snugly inside the rim of the skillet. Pour about 2½ cups of water over the plate. If the plate does not fit tightly enough, the water will run into the skillet and the vegetables will boil instead of steam. Cover pan with its lid.
9. Cook over medium heat for 1 hour. If water evaporates, add more.
10. Add remaining olive oil to artichokes for the last 10 minutes of cooking time. Replace plate and lid and continue cooking.
11. Remove plate and cool vegetables to room temperature. Artichokes look best when served with two halves together, stems up. Potatoes and onions are served around them, along with a wedge of fresh lemon.

Yield: 6 servings

—MIMI SHERATON

STUFFED ARTICHOKES

dairy

6 fresh artichokes
2 cups bread crumbs
1 cup finely shredded Parmesan cheese
½ cup chopped fresh parsley

3 cloves garlic, minced
1 tablespoons oregano
½ teaspoon black pepper
6 cloves garlic, cut in half
Salt, to taste
¼ cup olive oil (or to taste)

1. With one push of a sharp, heavy knife, cut off the upper part of each artichoke at a point about 1–1½ inches from the top. With a pair of scissors, snip off the tips of the remaining outside leaves below that point. Cut the stem off, making a flat base. Using a sharp spoon, dig out the center leaves and the choke, the thistlelike part of the base.

2. Mix the next 6 ingredients in a large bowl.

3. Take each trimmed artichoke and, standing it in the bowl of seasoned crumbs, spread the leaves apart with your fingers and force in as much of the crumb mixture as it will hold.

4. Stand the artichokes in a large pot and sprinkle the garlic pieces around the bottom. Add water to a depth of 1 inch and salt to taste. Drizzle the olive oil over the tops of the artichokes, and simmer, covered, for 30 minutes, or until tender. Serve hot or lukewarm, with the cooking liquid.

Yield: 6 servings

NOTE: *This may be served as a light luncheon dish or as an appetizer.*

—ROBERT FARRAR CAPON

MOROCCAN ARTICHOKES WITH ORANGES AND SAFFRON

pareve

ADAPTED FROM *The New York Times International Cookbook*

Juice of 2 lemons
15 small artichokes
1½ cups water
⅓ cup vegetable oil
2 tablespoons Saffron Water (see recipe below)
1 teaspoon salt
3 oranges, cut into ½-inch-thick slices, seeds removed

1. Place the lemon juice in a glass mixing bowl and add enough water to cover the artichoke bottoms when they are prepared. This is to keep the bottoms from discoloring.

2. Cut off the bottom stem of each artichoke. Cut off the upper quarter of the artichoke leaves, holding the knife parallel to the artichoke bottom. Carefully trim around the perimeter of the artichoke bottom. Using a silver spoon or a melon ball cutter, carefully scrape out the fuzz or "choke" in the center of each bottom. As the bottoms are prepared, drop them into the prepared lemon water. Let stand.

3. Heat the 1½ cups water and the oil in a skillet and add the saffron water. Add the artichoke bottoms and the salt. Cover and simmer 15 minutes.

4. Arrange the orange slices over all and cover again. Simmer 45 minutes to 1 hour.

Yield: 6–8 servings

Saffron Water

pareve

1 teaspoon ground saffron (if whole saffron is used,
  chop it to make 1 teaspoonful)
½ cup cold water

Combine the saffron and water in a small jar with a
screw top. Keep covered in the refrigerator and use
as needed.

Yield: ½ cup

ASPARAGUS AND MUSHROOMS

pareve

1 pound fresh asparagus spears, trimmed of woody
  sections and scraped
2 tablespoons olive oil
½ pound sliced mushrooms (about 2 cups)
2 tablespoons chopped shallots
½ teaspoon salt
Freshly ground black pepper to taste
4 tablespoons chopped cilantro

1. Cut the asparagus spears on the diagonal into 1-
inch pieces.
2. Heat the olive oil in a nonstick frying pan. Add the
mushrooms and sauté over over high heat, tossing,
until the mushrooms are lightly browned. Add the
asparagus pieces. Cook, stirring and tossing, for about
a minute. Add the shallots, salt and pepper. Sprinkle
with the cilantro. Cook for 30 seconds and serve.

Yield: 4–6 servings

—BRYAN MILLER AND PIERRE FRANEY

GRILLED ASPARAGUS WITH VINAIGRETTE

pareve

16 jumbo asparagus
1 small bunch chives
⅓ cup Italian parsley
⅓ cup basil leaves
1 clove garlic, green part removed
⅓ cup plus 1 tablespoon olive oil

Coarse sea salt to taste
Freshly ground pepper to taste
Lemon juice to taste

1. Preheat grill or broiler. Snap off the tough ends
of the asparagus and trim the stalks with a vegetable
peeler. Parboil for a minute and drain. Cool to room
temperature, then spread out on a plate.

2. Combine the chives, parsley, basil, garlic and olive oil in a blender. Puree and season to taste with salt, pepper and lemon juice.

3. Sprinkle the asparagus with olive oil, salt and pepper and grill over medium heat, turning frequently,

for about six minutes or until tender. Put on a warm serving dish. Pour the chive mixture over the asparagus and serve.

Yield: 4 servings

—MOIRA HODGSON

STIR-FRIED ASPARAGUS

pareve

1 pound medium-thick asparagus
2 tablespoons fresh lemon juice
1/2 tablespoon mustard
2 tablespoons extra-virgin olive oil
2 cloves garlic, sliced
Salt and freshly ground black pepper to taste
1/3 cup chopped scallions

1. Snap off the ends of the asparagus where they break naturally and peel the spears. Slant-cut them about 1 inch long.

2. Beat the lemon juice and mustard and set aside.

3. Heat the oil in a wok or skillet. Add the garlic, stir-fry about a minute, then add the asparagus and stir-fry about 5 minutes, until they are crisp-tender, lightly seared but still bright green. Stir in the lemon-mustard.

4. Season to taste with salt and pepper, stir in the scallions and stir-fry another few seconds. Transfer to a serving dish.

Yield: 6 servings

—FLORENCE FABRICANT

SEARED BEETS

pareve
ADAPTED FROM Danube

1 tablespoon hazelnut oil
1 tablespoon walnut oil
1 tablespoon canola oil
4 beets, a little smaller than a tennis ball, sliced less
    than 1/16 inch thick

Salt and pepper to taste
1/4 teaspoon caraway seeds
1/2 teaspoon crushed coriander seeds
1 1/2 teaspoons firmly packed, finely grated
    Fresh Horseradish (page 413)
1 1/2 tablespoons white vinegar

1. In a heavy pan, heat all oils until almost smoking. Stir in beets and cook over high heat, stirring, until coated with oil.

2. Reduce heat to medium. Season with salt and pepper. Stir in caraway and coriander seeds. Continue cooking, stirring occasionally, until beets begin to caramelize and become quite soft, about 20 minutes. If they dry out, add a little more canola oil.

3. Remove from heat and stir in horseradish and vine-gar and at least 2–3 tablespoons water. Stir vigorously to scrape up stickiness on bottom of pan. Mixture should not be dry. Adjust seasonings and cool to room temperature. Serve immediately, or refrigerate and return to room temperature I hour before serving. Serve over mesclun or alongside smoked fish.

Yield: 4 servings

—MARIAN BURROS

BEETS IN ORANGE SAUCE

dairy

ADAPTED FROM *The New York Times Heritage Cookbook*

2 bunches beets
Boiling water
1 tablespoon cider vinegar
¾ cup orange juice
3 tablespoons lemon juice
2 teaspoons grated orange rind
⅛ teaspoon ground allspice
1½ tablespoons cornstarch
1 tablespoon honey
2 tablespoons butter

1. Scrub the beets and cut off the tops, leaving I inch attached. Place in a saucepan and add boiling water to cover. Add the vinegar and cook until tender, about 20 minutes.

2. Drain beets, reserving some liquid. Skin the beets, then slice or dice them and keep warm.

3. Strain enough reserved beet liquid to yield ¼ cup. Combine with the orange juice, lemon juice, orange rind and allspice. Add the cornstarch slowly.

4. Bring to a boil, stirring, and cook until sauce thickens. Stir in the honey and butter and pour over the beets.

Yield: 4–6 servings

GASTON LENOTRE'S BAKED APPLES STUFFED WITH BEETS, PINE NUTS AND CURRANTS

dairy

8 Granny Smith or Golden Delicious apples

3 tablespoons butter

½ cup cooked beets, cubed

Salt and freshly ground pepper to taste

1 teaspoon red wine vinegar

½ cup pine nuts

½ cup dried currants

1 tablespoon brown sugar

1. Preheat oven to 400 degrees.

2. Peel the apples but do not core. If the apples do not stand up on their own, cut a thin slice off the bottom so they will.

3. Cut the top quarter off the apple. This will serve as a lid. Carefully core the apple, being certain not to cut too deeply or widely.

4. Lightly butter inside of each apple, cover with its own "lid" and bake for about 15 minutes. The apples should not become too soft. Cooking time will depend upon the variety of apple and its size. (The apples may be cooked ahead of time, then covered with aluminum foil until just before serving time.)

5. Ten minutes before serving, salt and pepper the beet cubes and sauté lightly in butter. Add vinegar, then 1 minute later, pine nuts and currants.

6. Stuff apples with the mixture and put lid in place. Sprinkle lightly with the brown sugar and place under a grill for 3–4 minutes to caramelize the top.

7. Serve immediately.

Yield: 8 servings as a side dish

—PATRICIA WELLS

CHINESE-STYLE BROCCOLI WITH SESAME SEEDS

pareve

1 bunch broccoli

2 tablespoons peanut or vegetable oil

1 clove garlic, green part removed, chopped fine

3 scallions, chopped

1 tablespoon sesame oil

2 tablespoons toasted sesame seeds

1. Cut off the stalks of the broccoli and discard them. Cut each floweret in half.

2. Heat the oil in a large frying pan or wok. Stir-fry the garlic and the scallions for 1 minute. Add the broccoli and stir-fry until dark green and crisp but tender. Add the sesame oil and seeds and stir-fry for 1 more minute. Serve immediately.

Yield: 4 servings

—MOIRA HODGSON

BRUSSELS SPROUTS WITH WALNUTS

pareve
ADAPTED FROM Ryland Inn, Whitehouse, N. J.

2 cups brussels sprouts
¼ cup walnuts, coarsely chopped
1 tablespoon olive oil or walnut oil
Salt to taste
Freshly ground pepper to taste

1. Bring water in a pot to boil.
2. Slice sprouts thin. Blanch for 1 minute in boiling water; then drain and set aside.
3. Heat oil in skillet on high heat, then add sprouts and walnuts and cook for 1 minute. Season with salt and pepper.

Yield: 4 servings

—TRISH HALL

BRUSSELS SPROUTS AND CARROTS WITH ALMONDS

dairy
ADAPTED FROM The Grange Hall

¼ cup sliced almonds
Kosher salt to taste
3 cups trimmed brussels sprouts (about ¾ pound)
1½ cups julienned carrots (unpeeled)
2 tablespoons butter
Freshly ground black pepper to taste

1. Preheat oven to 350 degrees. Spread almonds evenly on a baking sheet and toast until lightly golden, about 3–5 minutes. Remove from oven and set aside.
2. Bring a large pot of generously salted water to a boil. Add brussels sprouts and cook until slightly tender but still crisp, about 5 minutes. Drain, and when cool enough to touch, cut them into quarters and dry well on a tea towel. Set aside. Meanwhile, bring a medium pot of generously salted water to a boil. Add carrots and cook until slightly tender, about 1 minute. Drain.
3. In a large sauté pan over medium-high heat melt butter. Add almonds and sauté until just slightly darker, about 1 minute. Increase heat to high, add brussels sprouts and carrots and cook, stirring constantly, until vegetables are warmed through and browned on the edges, about 5 minutes. Season with salt and pepper. Serve.

Yield: 4 servings

—AMANDA HESSER

RED CABBAGE ALSATIAN STYLE

dairy, pareve
ADAPTED FROM *The Best of Craig Claiborne*

2 pounds red cabbage
2 tablespoons peanut, vegetable or corn oil
2 whole cloves, crushed
1 tablespoon wine vinegar
2 tablespoons brown sugar
Salt to taste
Freshly ground black pepper to taste
3 tablespoons butter or margarine

1. Pull off and discard any tough or wilted leaves from the cabbage. Trim away and discard the core from the cabbage. Shred the cabbage. There should be about 10 cups.
2. Heat the oil in a heavy skillet and add the cabbage. Cook over moderate heat, stirring, to wilt.
3. Add the cloves, vinegar, sugar, salt and pepper. Cook for 10–15 minutes, stirring often.
4. Stir in the butter or margarine and serve.

Yield: 10 or more servings

RED CABBAGE STEWED WITH FRUITS AND WINE

pareve
ADAPTED FROM Mark Straussman

2 pounds red cabbage, cored and finely shredded
1 medium onion, peeled and grated
2 McIntosh or Granny Smith apples, peeled, cored and grated
1 large Bartlett pear, peeled, cored and grated
4 cloves
8 black peppercorns
½ cup golden raisins
½ cup red currant jelly
1 tablespoon salt, plus more to taste
½ teaspoon freshly ground black pepper
¼ cup plus 2 tablespoons sugar
1 cinnamon stick

1 bay leaf
1 teaspoon ground nutmeg
1 (750-milliliter) bottle dry red wine

1. Place cabbage in a large pot. Add onion, apples and pear. Place cloves and peppercorns on a double layer of cheesecloth and tie with string to make a bag. Add the bag and all the remaining ingredients to the pot. Cover and refrigerate overnight.
2. Place pot, uncovered, over medium-low heat. Bring liquid to a simmer. Simmer, stirring occasionally, until cabbage is tender and liquid has reduced and thickened, about 2 hours. Remove bag, cinnamon stick and bay leaf. Add salt to taste. Serve hot.

Yield: 8 servings

—MARIAN BURROS

CABBAGE STRUDEL

pareve

<small>ADAPTED FROM</small> *The New York Times International Cookbook*

1 head cabbage (2 pounds)
2 teaspoons salt, or to taste
Vegetable oil
Freshly ground black pepper to taste
8 sheets of phyllo (see Note, page 583)
½ cup fine bread crumbs

1. Remove the core from the cabbage and discard it; then grate the cabbage fine. Sprinkle it with 2 teaspoons salt and let stand 15 minutes. Squeeze to remove the moisture.
2. Heat 2 tablespoons oil in a heavy skillet and add the cabbage. Cook, stirring, until the cabbage is lightly browned. Add salt and pepper to taste. Let stand until thoroughly cool.
3. Preheat the oven to 375 degrees.

4. Cover a pastry board with a cloth. Arrange half the phyllo leaves on the board and sprinkle lightly with oil. Sprinkle with half the bread crumbs and lightly with pepper.
5. Spoon a row of the cabbage filling—using half the amount—about 4 inches from the bottom edge of the dough. Fold this bottom edge over the cabbage. Then, using both hands, lift the cloth and let the cabbage roll fall over and over itself until the filling is completely enclosed in the pastry sheet. Repeat with the remaining cabbage filling, phyllo leaves, pepper and bread crumbs.
6. Lightly oil a jelly-roll pan or other shallow baking dish and arrange the strudel on it, seam side down, cutting the rolls in half if necessary to fit them inside the pan. Bake 30 minutes.

Yield: 8–12 servings

SAUERKRAUT WITH CARAWAY

meat

<small>ADAPTED FROM</small> *The Best of Craig Claiborne*

2 pounds sauerkraut
2 tablespoons vegetable oil
1 cup finely chopped onion
1 garlic clove, minced
1 tablespoon sugar
2 teaspoons crushed caraway seeds

2 cups Chicken Broth (page 48), canned or fresh
Salt and freshly ground pepper to taste
1 small raw potato

1. Put the sauerkraut in a colander and squeeze or press to reserve most of the liquid.
2. Heat oil in a heavy casserole and add the onion and garlic. Cook, stirring, until the onion is translucent. Add the sauerkraut sugar, caraway seeds,

chicken broth, salt and pepper. Cover and cook for 45 minutes.

3. Peel and grate potato. There should be about

⅓ cup. Stir this into the sauerkraut. Cover and cook for 15 minutes longer.

Yield: 6 servings

STEAMED BABY CARROTS WITH MINT

pareve

2 bags of baby carrots, about 12 ounces each,
   scraped and washed
3 tablespoons margarine or shortening
1 tablespoon sugar
1 teaspoon lemon juice
Salt and pepper to taste
2 tablespoon chopped fresh mint

1. Steam the carrots for 5 minutes or until barely tender. Melt the margarine in a saucepan. Add the carrots and sprinkle with sugar, lemon juice, salt and pepper. Cook over high heat for 5 minutes, stirring all the time.

2. Remove to a serving bowl.

3. Sprinkle the mint over the carrots and serve.

Yield: 6–8 servings

—COLETTE ROSSANT

HOT AND HONEYED CARROTS

dairy, pareve

2 tablespoons unsalted butter or margarine
1½ pounds carrots, peeled and cut into slices
   1 inch thick
1 small hot green chili, seeded and minced
2 tablespoons honey
3 tablespoons lemon juice
⅓ cup water
Pinch of salt

1. Heat the butter or margarine in a heavy saucepan. Add the carrots and cook, stirring, until they begin to brown. Stir in the chili and sauté another minute or so.

2. Stir in honey, lemon juice, water and salt. Cover tightly and cook 10 minutes, until liquid has evaporated and the carrots are tender.

Yield: 6 servings

—FLORENCE FABRICANT

ROASTED CARROTS WITH GARLIC

pareve

1½ *pounds large carrots (3–4 carrots), peeled*
4 *cloves garlic, sliced*
2 *tablespoons extra-virgin olive oil*
Salt and freshly ground black pepper to taste
1 *tablespoon chopped fresh cilantro*
1 *tablespoon chopped Italian parsley*

1. Preheat oven to 425 degrees.
2. Slice the carrots on an angle about ¾-inch thick. Put the carrots in a baking dish that will hold them snugly in a single layer. Add garlic, oil, salt, pepper, cilantro and parsley and toss all ingredients together to mix well.
3. Rearrange the carrots in a single layer, then put the dish in the oven and roast until the carrots are tender and beginning to brown, which takes about 40 minutes. Turn the carrots once during roasting so they cook evenly. Serve hot or at room temperature.

Yield: 4 servings

—FLORENCE FABRICANT

BRAISED CARROTS WITH ITALIAN PARSLEY

dairy
ADAPTED FROM David Bouley

5 *tablespoons unsalted butter*
1 *pound of carrots, scraped and sliced thin*
Pinch of nutmeg
Pinch of cinnamon
Freshly ground black pepper to taste
1 *cup water*
Juice of 1 lemon
3 *tablespoons chopped Italian parsley*

1. In a heavy saucepan, melt 1 tablespoon of the butter. Add carrots, nutmeg and cinnamon, season with pepper and toss, coating carrots with butter. Continue cooking for a couple of minutes, then add water. Simmer uncovered for about 10 minutes. Carrot slices should be tender and the water evaporated.
2. Whisk in remaining butter and lemon juice. Fold in the parsley leaves and serve.

Yield: 4–6 servings

—FLORENCE FABRICANT

CARROT AND FRUIT TSIMMES

pareve

ADAPTED FROM *The Second Avenue Deli Cookbook*

3 medium carrots, peeled and sliced into ¼-inch coins
2 bay leaves
½ orange, juice and peel, chopped into ½-inch pieces
½ lemon, juice and peel, chopped into ½-inch pieces
¼ cup honey (if you rub your measuring cup with vegetable oil, the honey will slide right out of it)
¼ cup sugar
¼ teaspoon cinnamon
2 cups mixed dried fruit (prunes, pears, apricots and apples), chopped into 1-inch pieces
½ cup raisins
½ cup water
1 teaspoon cornstarch

1. Place carrots in a large pot with bay leaves and just enough water to cover. Bring to a boil, then reduce heat and simmer for about 20 minutes until carrots are al dente.

2. Remove carrots with a slotted spoon and set aside, retaining cooking water in the pot. Add orange and lemon juices and pieces to pot and simmer for 10 minutes.

3. Add honey, sugar and cinnamon, and stir until dissolved. Return carrots to pot and simmer for 5 minutes.

4. Add dried fruit and raisins along with ½ cup water. Simmer for 10 minutes, stirring occasionally so that everything cooks evenly.

5. In a small bowl, mix cornstarch with a teaspoon of cold water and stir until fully dissolved. Add cornstarch mixture to the tsimmes, stir in and simmer for 10 more minutes, or until everything is fully cooked and liquid is almost completely dissolved. Serve hot as a side dish with chicken or beef.

Yield: 1 quart, or 8 servings

MASHED TSIMMES WITH HONEY AND VANILLA

pareve

ADAPTED FROM David Kolotkin, Prime Grill

1 cup carrots, peeled and cut into ½-inch dice
1 cup sweet potatoes, peeled and cut into ½-inch dice
1 cup dried apricots
½ cup dried peaches
¼ cup dried raisins
Peel and juice of ½ orange
1 clove

2 fresh vanilla beans
¼–½ cup honey
Salt and freshly ground black pepper to taste

1. Place cubes of carrot and sweet potato into a 3-quart saucepan. Stir in the dried fruits and raisins.

2. Juice the orange and reserve juice. Insert the clove securely into the peel and add to the vegetable-fruit mixture.

3. Cut each vanilla bean in half lengthwise and

scrape the soft contents of each bean into the saucepan. Add the outer pods to the mixture.

4. Cover the vegetable-fruit mixture with 4 cups water and simmer slowly, uncovered, for 45 minutes to 1 hour or until tender. Add additional water if necessary.

5. Place the mixture in a colander over a bowl and strain the liquid, reserving it for later use. Remove the vanilla bean pods and the orange peel with the clove. Return the vegetable-fruit mixture to the saucepan.

6. With a spoon or whisk, mash the mixture. Season with salt and pepper to taste. Stir in honey to your taste and, if desired, the juice of the halved orange. Some of the reserved cooking liquid may be added to the tsimmes to make it thinner. Mix ingredients thoroughly and cook an additional 5 minutes. Transfer to a warm dish and serve.

Yield: 5–6 servings

NOTE: *The vanilla subtly accents the flavor of the other ingredients.*

TURNIP AND CARROT TSIMMES

meat

> 2 tablespoons olive oil
> 2 pounds small white turnips, peeled and quartered
> 1 cup Chicken Stock (page 48)
> Salt and freshly ground black pepper to taste
> 2 tablespoons honey
> 1 pound carrots, peeled
> 1 tablespoon finely chopped parsley, optional

1. Heat the oil in a heavy casserole large enough to hold the turnips closely in a single layer. Add the turnips and cook over medium-high heat, tossing frequently, until they are coated with the oil, about 2 minutes. Stir in the stock and season with salt and pepper. Cover and cook over very low heat for 15 minutes, shaking the pan from time to time. Stir in the honey.

2. Slant-cut the carrots ½ inch thick. Season with salt and pepper and add them to the pan with the turnips, gently mixing them in. Continue cooking over low heat, covered, until all the vegetables are tender and lightly glazed.

3. Transfer to a serving dish, sprinkle with parsley, if desired, and serve at once.

Yield: 6–8 servings

—FLORENCE FABRICANT

ROASTED CARROTS WITH GARLIC

pareve

1½ pounds large carrots (3–4 carrots), peeled
4 cloves garlic, sliced
2 tablespoons extra-virgin olive oil
Salt and freshly ground black pepper to taste
1 tablespoon chopped fresh cilantro
1 tablespoon chopped Italian parsley

1. Preheat oven to 425 degrees.
2. Slice the carrots on an angle about ¾-inch thick. Put the carrots in a baking dish that will hold them snugly in a single layer. Add garlic, oil, salt, pepper, cilantro and parsley and toss all ingredients together to mix well.

3. Rearrange the carrots in a single layer, then put the dish in the oven and roast until the carrots are tender and beginning to brown, which takes about 40 minutes. Turn the carrots once during roasting so they cook evenly. Serve hot or at room temperature.

Yield: 4 servings

—FLORENCE FABRICANT

CANDIED CARROTS

pareve

ADAPTED FROM *The New York Times Heritage Cookbook*

3 tablespoons unsalted margarine or shortening
4 cups carrots, sliced in rounds ¼-inch thick
3 tablespoons orange juice
1½ teaspoons salt
¼ teaspoon cinnamon
4 tablespoons honey

Combine all the ingredients in a saucepan, cover and cook, stirring occasionally, over low heat for 25 minutes.

Yield: 6 servings

SAUTÉED CARROTS, TURNIPS AND SNOW PEAS

dairy

ADAPTED FROM *The Best of Craig Claiborne*

2 large carrots, about ½ pound
2 large white turnips, about ½ pound
½ pound fresh snow peas
2 tablespoons butter
Salt and freshly ground pepper to taste
1 tablespoon red wine vinegar

1. Scrape and trim the carrots. Cut the carrots crosswise into 1½-inch lengths. Cut the pieces into ¼-inch slices. Cut slices into batons about ¼ inch wide. There should be about 1½ cups.

2. Trim and scrape the turnips. Cut the turnips in half. Cut each half crosswise into ¼-inch-thick slices. Stack the slices; cut them into batons about the same size as the carrots. There should be about 2 cups.

3. Trim off and discard the tips of the snow peas. There should be about 1 cup of peas.

4. Melt the butter in a heavy skillet. Add the carrots and turnips. Cook the vegetables, stirring, for about 1 minutes. Add the snow peas and cook, stirring, for about 5 minutes until crisp-tender.

5. Add the salt and pepper and the vinegar. Cook briefly and stir well.

Yield: 4 servings

CAULIFLOWER-APPLE PUREE

dairy

1 Golden Delicious apple
1 teaspoon olive oil
Sea salt, preferably coarse, to taste
1½ pounds cauliflower, trimmed and cut into
    large chunks
3 tablespoons butter, more if desired

1. Preheat oven to 375 degrees. Slash apple in several spots and place it in a small baking dish. Sprinkle oil on top. Bake until apple is very tender and wilted, 30–40 minutes. Cool, peel and core apple. Reserve flesh.

2. Fill a large pot with water, season generously with salt and bring to a boil. Add cauliflower and cook until very tender, 5–7 minutes. Drain and transfer to a food processor. Add half the apple and 3 tablespoons of butter. Process for 3–4 minutes, occasionally scraping down sides with a spatula; puree should get smoother and silkier the longer it processes.

3. Adjust seasoning, adding more apple, butter or salt as desired; there should be just a hint of sweetness from the apple. Transfer to a serving dish and serve hot.

Yield: 4 side dish servings

—AMANDA HESSER

CAULIFLOWER WITH ALMONDS AND BROWN BUTTER

dairy

ADAPTED FROM *American Cookery*

1½ pounds cauliflower, trimmed into olive-size
  florets
6 tablespoons unsalted butter
Sea salt, preferably coarse, to taste
⅓ cup slivered almonds

1. Put some water in a large steamer and bring to a boil. Add cauliflower and steam until tender but still slightly crisp, about 5–7 minutes. Remove from steamer and pour into a large serving bowl.

2. In a small pan, melt butter with a large pinch of salt over medium-low heat. When foam has subsided and butter has simmered for a minute or two, add almonds and continue cooking until butter begins to smell nutty and toasty and almonds are golden brown. Pour nuts and butter over cauliflower and toss to coat. Season with salt and toss again. Serve.

Yield: 4 servings

—AMANDA HESSER

CAULIFLOWER WITH CINNAMON

dairy

Juice of 1 lemon
1 large head cauliflower
8 tablespoons butter
1 teaspoon ground cinnamon (or to taste)
½ teaspoon ground nutmeg (or to taste)
1 cup soft bread crumbs
½ pint heavy cream
Salt and white pepper to taste

1. Preheat oven to 375 degrees.
2. Put cold water into a large bowl and mix in the lemon juice.

3. Remove the center stalk from the cauliflower, cut the head into large, thin slices and put them in the lemon water.
4. Butter a suitable au gratin dish with 2 tablespoons of the butter. Drain the cauliflower slices, layer half of them in the bottom of the dish and sprinkle them with half of the cinnamon, nutmeg and bread crumbs. Add salt and pepper to taste.
5. Dot with half of the remaining butter and pour over half of the cream. Make a second layer using all remaining ingredients. Cover and bake for 1 hour, or until done.

Yield: 6 servings

—ROBERT FARRAR CAPON

CAULIFLOWER KUGEL

Made 2/8/13

pareve

ADAPTED FROM *Spice and Spirit: The Complete Kosher Jewish Cookbook*

1 large head cauliflower

4 cups water

Salt to taste

2 large onions, diced

4 tablespoons vegetable oil, plus oil for pan

Freshly ground pepper to taste

2 large eggs, beaten

2 tablespoons matzoh meal or wheat germ

2 tablespoons cornflake crumbs

1. Wash cauliflower and separate into large florets. Bring water to boil. Add salt and the cauliflower and simmer, uncovered, 15 minutes until tender. Drain and mash.

2. Preheat oven to 350 degrees. Sauté onions in vegetable oil in a 7-inch skillet. Cook until soft and lightly browned.

3. Combine the onions with the cauliflower and add pepper, eggs and matzoh meal. Place in a greased 9-inch-square pan or casserole. Sprinkle top with cornflake crumbs. Bake in oven for 45 minutes or until golden.

Yield: 8 servings

—JOAN NATHAN

CORN PUDDING

dairy

ADAPTED FROM *The New York Times Heritage Cookbook*

2 cups cooked whole kernel corn (one way to use leftover corn on the cob)

¼ cup chopped scallions, including green part

3 eggs, lightly beaten

2 tablespoons melted butter

2 cups milk, scalded

1½ teaspoons salt

¼ teaspoon freshly ground black pepper

1. Preheat the oven to 325 degrees.

2. Combine all the ingredients and turn into a greased 2-quart baking dish or casserole. Set in a pan with hot water extending halfway up the dish.

3. Bake 1 hour, replenishing the water if necessary.

Yield: 6 servings

BAKED CHINESE EGGPLANT WITH APRICOTS

meat

4 long purple Chinese eggplants
Salt and pepper to taste
½ teaspoon cumin
1 teaspoon sesame oil
½ pound dry apricots
3 tablespoons vegetable oil
¼ cup Chicken Stock (page 48)
Juice of 1 lemon
1 tablespoon chopped parsley

1. Preheat oven to 325 degrees.

2. Cut the eggplants lengthwise and place in a baking pan. Sprinkle with salt and pepper and cumin. Sprinkle with sesame oil. Cover the eggplants with the apricots.

3. Mix together the vegetable oil, chicken stock and lemon juice. Pour this mixture over the eggplant and bake for 1 hour. Serve sprinkled with chopped parsley.

Yield: 4 servings

—COLETTE ROSSANT

EGGPLANT NAPOLEON

pareve

ADAPTED FROM Tom Colicchio

2 medium eggplants
¼ cup extra-virgin olive oil
Salt and freshly ground pepper to taste
3 large eggs
½ cup flour
2½ cups fresh bread crumbs
1 cup peanut or vegetable oil

1. Heat oven to 350 degrees. Place 1 eggplant on a baking sheet and roast for 1 hour. Allow to cool. Slice in half lengthwise and scoop pulp into a medium mixing bowl. Add olive oil to bowl and blend well with a fork. Season to taste with salt and pepper and reserve.

2. Slice remaining eggplant into disks about ⅛ inch thick. Season to taste with salt and pepper. In a small bowl, beat eggs with a fork until blended. Dip each eggplant slice in the flour, egg and then the bread crumbs.

3. In a medium saucepan, heat vegetable oil to 350 degrees. Add eggplant in small batches and sauté until brown on both sides, about a minute each side. Remove from pan and drain on paper towels.

4. To assemble, place a slice of eggplant on each of four plates, topped by a heaping tablespoon of reserved eggplant puree. Top with another slice of eggplant and another spoonful of puree, continuing until the eggplant and puree have been evenly distributed. Finish each napoleon with a slice of eggplant; there will be a total of 4–6 layers. Serve immediately.

Yield: 4 servings

—AMANDA HESSER

COUSCOUS-STUFFED EGGPLANT

pareve

4 small eggplants, about 10 ounces each

4½ cups cooked couscous

8 plum tomatoes, diced

6 cloves roasted garlic, peeled

½ cup toasted pine nuts

⅓ cup chopped fresh coriander

1 large jalapeño pepper, stemmed, seeded and minced

1 tablespoon fresh lemon juice

2 teaspoons ground cumin

1 tablespoon salt plus more to taste

Freshly ground pepper to taste

1. Preheat oven to 400 degrees. Prick the eggplants a few times with a fork. Put them on a baking sheet and bake until soft, about 45 minutes. When cool enough to handle, cut the eggplants in half lengthwise. Scoop the flesh into a bowl carefully to avoid tearing the skins. Set the shells aside.

2. Put the remaining ingredients in the bowl with the eggplant and stir to combine. Taste and adjust seasoning if needed. Spoon the mixture into the eggplant shells, mounding it over the top. Either serve the stuffed eggplants whole or cut them in half crosswise. Place on a platter and serve.

Yield: 8 servings

—MOLLY O'NEILL

THREE COATINGS FOR EGGPLANT FRITTERS

pareve

To use any of these, it is convenient to peel the eggplant at the last minute, cut it in half lengthwise and into ¼-inch slices crosswise, and then proceed directly to the coating and frying. Use one medium-size eggplant of 1½–2 pounds. If you wish, you may salt and rinse the slices, as in Step 2 of the following recipe, but be sure to dry them as much as possible before coating.

Coating I

1 egg

1 tablespoon water

½ cup flour

1 teaspoon salt

¼ teaspoon black pepper

1 cup fine bread crumbs, seasoned or unseasoned

1. Put the egg in a large bowl, add the water and beat well.

2. Mix the flour, salt and pepper in a large paper bag, add all the eggplant slices at once and shake well.

3. Empty the bag onto a countertop and then transfer the slices to the bowl of beaten egg, leaving behind as much loose flour as possible. Turn the slices over in the egg until uniformly coated.

4. Put the bread crumbs in the paper bag, put in all

the eggplant slices again and shake well. If necessary, add more bread crumbs.

5. Empty bag again, spread slices out to let coating set for 15 minutes or more. Fry in deep, hot oil (375 degrees). Drain on paper and serve.

Coating II

2 tablespoons soy sauce
2 tablespoons dry sherry
2 tablespoons peanut oil
½ teaspoon sugar
¼ teaspoon black pepper
Cornstarch

1. Put the eggplant slices in a large bowl. Add everything but the cornstarch and mix well. Sprinkle on cornstarch and continue mixing until a thin but fairly viscous coating is achieved.

2. Deep-fry (375 degrees).

Coating III

4 tablespoons soy flour
1 teaspoon salt
¼ teaspoon ground turmeric
½ teaspoon ground cardamom (or 1 teaspoon ground coriander seed)
Cold water

1. Mix the first 4 ingredients in a bowl and stir in enough water to make a batter the consistency of half-whipped cream.

2. Dip the eggplant slices in it and deep-fry (375 degrees).

—ROBERT FARRAR CAPON

WARM EGGPLANT WITH YOGURT

dairy

4 medium-size eggplants
Coarse salt
5 tablespoons extra-virgin olive oil
3 tablespoons pine nuts
¼ teaspoon cayenne pepper
½ teaspoon paprika
4 cloves garlic
1½ cups yogurt, preferably whole milk
1 tablespoon fresh lemon juice
Freshly ground black pepper to taste
1 teaspoon finely minced cilantro leaves

1. Trim stem ends from eggplants and cut in half lengthwise. Slice into rounds ½ inch thick.

2. Put in a bowl, sprinkle generously with salt and allow to sit 30 minutes. Rinse and dry well.

3. Meanwhile, heat 1 tablespoon oil in small skillet. Add pine nuts, cayenne pepper and paprika and sauté just until nuts begin to toast. Remove from heat and set aside.

4. Mash garlic in a mortar with generous pinch coarse salt. Mix garlic with yogurt and lemon. Set aside.

5. Toss dried eggplant slices in a clean bowl with remaining oil. Heat a large nonstick skillet, add eggplant and sauté, turning slices, until golden. Arrange slices on a shallow serving dish. Season to taste with salt and black pepper. Spoon yogurt mixture over eggplant. Scatter with pine nuts in pepper oil, sprinkle with cilantro and serve.

Yield: 6 servings

—FLORENCE FABRICANT

SANDRA'S STRING BEANS WITH MINT

pareve

ADAPTED FROM *The New York Times Heritage Cookbook*

2 pounds tiny string beans, washed, trimmed
    and left whole
Boiling salted water
3 sprigs mint
½ cup olive oil
¼ clove garlic
2 teaspoons wine vinegar
Salt and freshly ground black pepper to taste

1. Cook the beans in boiling salted water to cover until crisp-tender, about 6 minutes. Drain beans and rinse with cold water briefly to stop cooking but not to cool beans down too much.
2. Place remaining ingredients in an electric blender and blend until smooth. Pour over hot, rinsed beans.

Yield: 8 servings

NOTE: *These can be served cold or at room temperature.*

STEWED GREEN BEANS WITH TOMATO AND APRICOT

pareve

8 dried apricots, quartered
2 tablespoons olive oil
1 onion, diced
½ pound trimmed green beans, in 1-inch lengths
1 pound whole peeled plum tomatoes, fresh or canned
Juice of 1 lemon
¼ teaspoon ground coriander

1. Place apricots in a small bowl and cover with boiling water. Soak until soft, 15–20 minutes. Drain and set aside.
2. In a medium saucepan over low heat, heat the olive oil and add the onions. Sauté until they begin to turn golden, about 5 minutes. Add the green beans and ½ cup water. Cover and simmer 10 minutes.
3. Add remaining ingredients. Cover and simmer until beans are soft, about 20 minutes.

Yield: 4 servings

—DIANE FORLEY

JERUSALEM ARTICHOKE FRITTERS

dairy

½ pound Jerusalem artichokes, scrubbed

1 carrot, peeled

3 shallots, thinly sliced

2 tablespoons yellow cornmeal

¼ cup flour

½ teaspoon salt

½ teaspoon baking powder

Freshly ground black pepper to taste

Tabasco to taste

2 eggs

3 tablespoons chopped chives

½ cup sour cream

1 tablespoon fresh lime juice

Peanut oil for frying

1. Heat oven to 250 degrees. Grate Jerusalem artichokes and carrot into a mixing bowl. Add shallots. Stir together cornmeal, flour, salt and baking powder and stir in, mixing well. Season with pepper and Tabasco to taste. Add eggs and mix thoroughly.

2. Combine chives, sour cream and lime juice and set aside.

3. Pour oil ½ inch deep into a large skillet. Heat over medium-high heat until sizzling. Drop mixture in by tablespoons, flattening slightly. Fry until crisp and golden brown, turning once. Transfer to oven on a baking sheet lined with paper towel while frying more. Serve with sour cream mixture.

Yield: 4 servings

—REGINA SCHRAMBLING

SAUTÉED KALE WITH PINE NUTS AND RAISINS

pareve

¼ cup raisins

2 tablespoons white wine vinegar

3 tablespoons extra-virgin olive oil

3 tablespoons pine nuts

1½ pounds fresh kale

4 cloves garlic, sliced thin

Crushed red pepper to taste

Salt to taste

1. Put the raisins in a small dish, add the vinegar and set aside.

2. Heat 1 tablespoon of the oil in a large, heavy skillet, add the pine nuts and sauté over medium heat until they are golden. Remove from the pan and set aside.

3. Rinse the kale well and shake off excess water. Cut off and discard the bottom 2 inches of the stems and coarsely chop the rest.

4. Heat the remaining oil in the skillet, add the garlic and sauté until lightly browned. Stir in the kale and cook, stirring, until the kale has wilted. Stir in the vinegar, raisins and the red pepper. Season to taste with salt. Transfer to a serving dish and scatter the pine nuts on top. Serve hot or at room temperature.

Yield: 6 servings

—FLORENCE FABRICANT

LEEK PATTIES · (KOFTA)

pareve
ADAPTED FROM Leon Alcalai

6 large leeks, white and light-green parts only, washed
    well, halved lengthwise and crosswise
2 eggs, beaten
½ cup dried bread crumbs
1 teaspoon kosher salt
Freshly ground pepper to taste
2 tablespoons canola oil
1 fresh lemon, optional

1. Put the leeks in a large saucepan, cover with water
and bring to a boil. Lower the heat and simmer until
soft, about 30 minutes. Drain well. Wrap the leeks
in a cloth and squeeze out excess moisture.

2. Coarsely chop the leeks and place in a bowl. Stir
in the eggs, bread crumbs, salt and pepper. Divide
the mixture to form 8 patties that are about ½ inch
thick and 3 inches in diameter.

3. Heat the oil in a large nonstick skillet over
medium heat. Place the patties in the skillet and
cook until browned and done, about 2 minutes per
side. Serve cold with lemon juice squeezed over
them, or serve hot without the lemon.

Yield: 4 servings

—MOLLY O'NEILL

PAN-ROASTED MUSHROOMS

dairy
ADAPTED FROM *Think Like a Chef*

4–6 tablespoons extra-virgin olive oil
2 pounds mixed wild and cultivated mushrooms,
    cleaned, trimmed and thickly sliced
Kosher salt and freshly ground black pepper to taste
1–2 shallots, peeled and finely chopped
2 garlic cloves, peeled and finely chopped
2 tablespoons unsalted butter
2 tablespoons chopped fresh thyme leaves
2 tablespoons chopped fresh tarragon (optional)

1. Heat about 1 tablespoon oil in large, heavy skillet
over medium-high heat until it shimmers. Add just
enough mushrooms to loosely cover the skillet (you
should be able to see the pan between the mushrooms). Season the mushrooms with salt and pepper. Cook for about 2 minutes, then gently turn
mushrooms over as they brown and soften.

2. Add a little shallot and garlic, some butter, and
some thyme and tarragon. Continue cooking until
the mushrooms are tender, about 2 minutes more,
then transfer to a paper towel. Wipe out skillet and
repeat the process, cooking mushrooms in small
batches.

3. Just before serving, add a bit more butter or oil to
skillet and return mushrooms to the pan. Warm over
medium heat. Season with salt and pepper and serve.

Yield: 4 servings as first course or side dish

—AMANDA HESSER

SAUTÉED PORTOBELLO MUSHROOMS

pareve

¼ ounce dried porcini mushrooms

3 tablespoons olive oil

1 clove garlic, minced

5 giant portobello mushroom caps

Coarse sea salt and freshly ground pepper to taste

1 tablespoon fresh thyme leaves

1. Rinse the dried porcini and soak them in a cup of warm water for 30 minutes. Drain them, reserving the soaking liquid, and chop them. Strain the soaking liquid through a cheesecloth or paper towels into a small bowl. Set aside.

2. Cut the stems off the portobello mushrooms. Rinse the mushrooms and chop them into 1-inch pieces.

3. Heat the oil in a large skillet and cook the garlic until it is soft. Add the dried and fresh mushrooms and season them to taste with salt and pepper. Cook them over moderate heat for 10 minutes, stirring occasionally.

4. Add the porcini soaking liquid and thyme and stir. Continue to cook for another 20 minutes or so, until the liquid has evaporated and the mushrooms are crisp. Correct seasoning and serve.

Yield: 8 servings

—MOIRA HODGSON

WILD MUSHROOMS IN SOUR CREAM · (À LA RUSSE)

dairy

1 pound wild mushroom such as pleurotes, cèpes, porcini, shiitake or Black Forest, cut into bite-size pieces

3 tablespoons butter

Salt to taste, if desired

Freshly ground pepper to taste

2 tablespoons finely chopped chives

1 tablespoon finely chopped dill

2 tablespoons finely chopped parsley

½ cup sour cream

1. Prepare mushrooms and set aside.

2. Heat butter in skillet and add mushrooms, salt and pepper. Cook, stirring often, until mushrooms give up liquid. Continue cooking until liquid evaporates. Total cooking time is about 6 minutes.

3. Add chives, dill, parsley and sour cream. Blend and bring barely to boil. Do not boil or sauce will curdle. Add salt and pepper and serve.

Yield: 4 servings

—CRAIG CLAIBORNE

WOLFGANG PUCK'S MUSHROOM AND EGGPLANT RATATOUILLE

pareve

½ teaspoon ground cumin

½ teaspoon curry powder

⅓ cup olive oil

1 clove garlic, peeled and chopped

1 medium onion, peeled and chopped

3 small Japanese eggplants, trimmed and cut into
    ½-inch cubes

15 button mushrooms, halved or quartered if large

Salt to taste

1. Place the cumin and curry powder in a small skillet over medium heat. Cook, stirring, just until toasted, about 30 seconds.

2. Heat the olive oil in a large saucepan. Add spices and remaining ingredients and cook, stirring occasionally, until vegetables are tender, about 20 minutes. Season with salt and serve.

Yield: 4 servings

—MARIAN BURROS

WILD MUSHROOM–POTATO KUGEL

pareve

ADAPTED FROM *The Gefilte Variations*

1 ounce dried porcini mushrooms

4 tablespoons extra-virgin olive oil or vegetable oil,
    plus oil for pan

3 cups thinly sliced onions

Salt and freshly ground black pepper to taste

2 teaspoons chopped garlic

4 pounds baking potatoes, peeled

4 large eggs, beaten

1. Soak mushrooms in 2 cups hot water for 1 hour until soft. Strain through a sieve lined with a paper towel or coffee filter paper; reserve soaking liquid. Rinse mushrooms, pat dry and chop coarsely.

2. Heat oil in a large, heavy skillet over medium heat. Add onions and sauté, stirring, until lightly browned,

about 15 minutes. Transfer to bowl and season with salt and pepper. In same skillet, place mushrooms, garlic and mushroom liquid. Cook over high heat, stirring occasionally, until liquid evaporates. Season to taste with salt and pepper, and remove from heat.

3. Preheat oven to 400 degrees. Generously oil bottom and sides of a heavy baking dish (like a 13-by-9-inch lasagna pan), preferably enameled cast iron.

4. Grate potatoes in a food processor using coarse grating disc, or with a hand grater. Transfer to colander, rinse well, drain, then squeeze out as much liquid as possible with your hands. Combine potatoes in a large bowl with eggs, fried onions and a generous seasoning of salt and pepper.

5. Place baking pan in oven a minute or two, just until oil is sizzling. Remove pan from oven and spread half the potato mixture into it. Spread mush-

rooms over, then add remaining potatoes, smoothing the top. Drizzle a little olive oil on top.

6. Bake about 50 minutes, until top is golden and crisp. Remove from oven and let stand until it reaches room temperature, at least 30 minutes. Reheat 15 minutes at 350 degrees before serving.

Yield: 8–10 servings

—FLORENCE FABRICANT

TURKISH OKRA CASSEROLE

pareve

¾ *pound tender, fresh okra or 1 (10-ounce) package frozen okra*

1 eggplant, about 1 pound

2 medium-size zucchini, about 1 pound total weight

2 large green peppers, about ¾ pound total weight

1 large onion, about ¾ pound

3 tomatoes, about 1½ pounds

¼ cup olive oil

2 tablespoons finely chopped garlic

¼ teaspoon dried, hot red pepper flakes

½ cup finely chopped parsley

1 bay leaf

½ teaspoon dried thyme

Salt to taste, if desired

1. If fresh okra is used, wash it and then trim off any tough stems. If frozen okra is used, let it defrost.

2. Preheat oven to 375 degrees.

3. Trim off the ends of the eggplant. Cut the unpeeled eggplant crosswise into 1-inch-thick slices. Cut the slices into strips 1 inch wide. Cut the strips into 1-inch cubes. There should be about 4 cups.

4. Trim off the ends of the zucchini. Cut the zucchini lengthwise into quarters. Cut the strips into 1-inch pieces. There should be about 3 cups.

5. Cut each green pepper in half lengthwise. Cut away and discard the cores and veins. Discard the seeds. Cut the peppers into 1-inch pieces. There should be about 2½ cups.

6. Peel the onion and cut it into 1-inch cubes. There should be about 2 cups.

7. Cut away and discard the cores of the tomatoes. Cut the tomatoes into 1-inch cubes. There should be about 4 cups.

8. Heat the oil in a large, heavy casserole and add the onion and eggplant cubes. Cook, stirring often, about 5 minutes. Add the zucchini, green peppers and tomatoes and cook, stirring occasionally, about 2 minutes.

9. Add the garlic, pepper flakes, parsley, bay leaf and thyme. Stir. Add the drained okra and salt. Place in the oven and bake 1 hour. Remove the bay leaf and serve.

Yield: 6–8 servings

NOTE: *When buying okra, choose the smallest, youngest and brightest green ones you can find. Okra must be very fresh, not browned at the edges, and should be used right away because it is rather perishable. Avoid large okra because the seeds inside can be like pebbles.*

—CRAIG CLAIBORNE AND PIERRE FRANEY

SWEET-AND-SOUR OKRA

pareve

ADAPTED FROM *Madhur Jaffrey's Indian Cooking*

1½ pounds tender, fresh okra or 2 (10-ounce)
packages frozen okra, defrosted
2 tablespoons finely chopped garlic
½ teaspoon dried, hot red pepper flakes
7 tablespoons water
2 teaspoons ground cumin seeds
1 teaspoon ground coriander
½ teaspoon ground turmeric
¼ cup corn, peanut or vegetable oil
1 teaspoon whole cumin seeds
Salt to taste, if desired
1 teaspoon sugar
4 teaspoons lemon juice

1. If fresh okra is used, trim off any tough stems. If frozen okra is used, let it defrost. Cut each pod crosswise into ¾-inch lengths.

2. Put the garlic, pepper flakes and 3 tablespoons of the water into the container of an electric blender. Blend as thoroughly as possible. Empty the mixture into a small bowl and add the ground cumin, coriander and turmeric. Blend well.

3. Heat the oil in a 9-inch skillet and add the whole cumin seeds. Cook briefly until the seeds start to sizzle and add the spice paste. Cook, stirring, about 1 minute.

4. Add the okra, salt, sugar, lemon juice and remaining 4 tablespoons of water. Stir to blend. Bring to a simmer, cover closely and cook over very low heat about 10 minutes.

Yield: 4–6 servings

—CRAIG CLAIBORNE AND PIERRE FRANEY

ROASTED ONIONS

pareve

ADAPTED FROM *The Food of Southern Italy*

6 Spanish onions, all uniformly about 3 inches in
diameter
Extra-virgin olive oil
Salt and freshly ground black pepper to taste
⅓ cup balsamic or red wine vinegar

1. Preheat the oven to 375 degrees.

2. Place the onions in a small round ovenproof non-

glass baking pan that can also be used on a stove burner. Leave the outer brown skins on the onions, rub them gently with plenty of olive oil and sprinkle with salt and pepper.

3. Put the onions in the oven and bake for 1–1½ hours, or until the onions are soft but not mushy. Remove them to a serving platter and cut them in half vertically, leaving the outer brown skin in place.

4. To deglaze the roasting pan, place it on a stove burner over medium-low heat and pour in the vinegar. Scrape the pan well with a wooden spoon to dislodge all of the "caramel," and let the vinegar alcohol burn off for about 4 minutes. Push aside any large pieces of outer onion skin that may be left in the pan.

5. Use a pastry brush to brush the sauce over the open faces of the onion. Serve at once or set aside and serve at room temperature.

Yield: 6–8 servings

—JUDITH BARRETT

BRANDIED ONIONS

dairy, pareve

   2 pounds yellow onions, peeled, sliced and separated into rings
   2 tablespoons unsalted butter or olive oil
   1 (28-ounce) can tomatoes, drained and chopped
   ¼ cup brandy
   1 scant teaspoon salt
   ¾ teaspoon black pepper

1. In a large skillet over medium-low heat, cook onions in butter until golden, about 15 minutes, stirring often.

2. Stir in ¼ cup water, tomatoes, brandy, salt and pepper, and simmer 25 minutes. Serve warm or at room temperature.

Yield: 6 servings

—AMANDA HESSER

PARSNIPS ROASTED WITH GARLIC

pareve

   1½ pounds parsnips, peeled
   4 cloves garlic, sliced
   2 tablespoons extra-virgin olive oil
   Juice of 1 lemon
   Salt and freshly ground black pepper to taste
   1 tablespoon chopped Italian parsley

1. Preheat oven to 425 degrees.

2. Slice parsnips on an angle about an inch thick.

Put in a baking dish that will hold them snugly in a single layer. Add garlic, oil, lemon juice, salt, pepper and parsley. Toss ingredients to mix well.

3. Rearrange parsnips in a single layer, put in oven and roast until parsnips are tender and beginning to brown, about 40 minutes. Turn parsnips once during roasting so they cook evenly. Serve hot or at room temperature.

Yield: 4 servings

—FLORENCE FABRICANT

PARSNIPS AND POMEGRANATES

dairy

8 parsnips
3 tablespoons unsalted butter
1 cup orange juice
⅔ cup pomegranate seeds (see Note, page 583)
2 tablespoons chives, finely chopped
½ teaspoon salt or to taste, optional

1. After trimming the tops and tips of the parsnips, drop them into salted water, bring to a boil and cook until tender, about 15–20 minutes.
2. When the parsnips are tender, drain and slip off the skins under cold running water.

3. Cut parsnips into 2-inch lengths and then into about ½-inch strips.
4. In a large heavy skillet, melt the butter over medium-high heat. When it has foamed, add the parsnips, shaking to coat evenly, and continue to cook for about 8 minutes or until they start to color. Turn occasionally.
5. Pour in the orange juice and the pomegranate seeds. Turn up the heat and cook, letting the orange juice evaporate, about 2 minutes.
6. Add salt, if desired, and the chopped chives. Stir to blend.

Yield: 8 servings

—JOANNA PRUESS

ROAST PARSNIPS WITH CARROTS AND POTATOES

pareve

1 pound parsnips
1 pound Yukon Gold potatoes
4 whole carrots
1 tablespoon sage leaves
2 tablespoons olive oil
Coarse sea salt and freshly ground pepper to taste

1. Preheat the oven to 400 degrees. Cut the parsnips, potatoes and carrots into 1½-inch pieces. Put them with the sage leaves in a baking dish and sprinkle with the oil. Toss thoroughly so all the pieces are coated. Sprinkle with salt and pepper.
2. Roast for about 30 minutes, turning occasionally. The vegetables should be golden brown and tender.

Yield: 4 servings

—MOIRA HODGSON

PEAS WITH ARTICHOKES AND FAVA BEANS

pareve

2½ pounds fava beans
1½ pounds peas
4 medium artichokes
2–3 tablespoons extra-virgin olive oil
1 tablespoon snipped basil, mint or chives

1. Shell and skin the fava beans. Shell the peas. Tear off the outer leaves of the artichokes and cut the remaining leaves off about an inch and a half from the base. With a spoon, scrape out the choke from the bottom. Trim the dark green parts of the bottom and stem. Lightly rub the artichokes with some olive oil. This will help prevent them from turning brown.

2. Heat the olive oil in a large skillet. Cut the artichokes in one-inch chunks and add them to the oil. Stew them gently until they are almost tender and lightly browned, then add the fava beans. Cook for a couple of minutes, then add the peas. Season with salt and pepper and cook until the peas are tender. Sprinkle with basil, mint or chives and serve.

Yield: 4 servings

—MOIRA HODGSON

SWEET PEPPERS MIDDLE EASTERN-STYLE

pareve

ADAPTED FROM *The Best of Craig Claiborne*

3–4 large sweet green or red peppers, preferably a
    combination of both, about 1 pound
½ teaspoon ground cumin
1 tablespoon lemon juice
2 tablespoons olive oil
¼ teaspoon finely chopped garlic
⅛ teaspoon cayenne pepper
¼ teaspoon paprika
2 tablespoons chopped parsley
Salt and freshly ground black pepper to taste

1. Preheat the broiler or use a charcoal grill. Put the peppers under the broiler or on the grill and cook, turning often, until the skin is shriveled and partly blackened. Remove. Put the peppers in a paper bag and let stand until cool enough to handle. Peel off the skins.

2. Split the peppers in half. Remove and discard the stems and seeds. Place the halves on a flat surface. Cut into strips or cut them into fairly large, bite-size pieces. There should be about 1½ cups.

3. Put the pieces in a mixing bowl and add all the remaining ingredients. Toss to blend. Serve at room temperature.

Yield: About 4 servings

MASHED POTATOES MEDITERRANEAN-STYLE

pareve

2 pounds boiling potatoes, scrubbed, peeled and
    quartered
2 cloves garlic, minced
3 tablespoons olive oil
Salt to taste
Freshly ground black pepper to taste
Pinch of dried thyme

1. Cover potatoes with water in a heavy saucepan, bring to a boil and simmer until the potatoes are tender, about 20 minutes. Drain potatoes, reserving about one-half cup of the cooking liquid.

2. While the potatoes are simmering, sauté the garlic in the olive oil over low heat until the garlic is tender and barely beginning to brown.

3. Mash or rice the potatoes. Add enough of the cooking liquid to make them smooth and creamy-textured. Stir in the olive oil and garlic.

4. Season to taste with salt and pepper and stir in the thyme.

Yield: 4–6 servings

—FLORENCE FABRICANT

SORREL MASHED POTATOES

dairy

1 pound russet or Yukon Gold potatoes
4 ounces sorrel, stems removed
2 tablespoons unsalted butter
½ cup heavy cream
Coarse salt and freshly ground pepper to taste

1. Peel the potatoes and steam or boil them until they are tender.

2. Meanwhile, wash the sorrel and cut the leaves into thin strips, using a stainless steel knife. Heat the butter in a frying pan and add the sorrel. Stir over low heat for a couple of minutes, until it has wilted. Add the cream and heat through.

3. Mash the potatoes. Stir in the sorrel puree and season to taste with salt and pepper.

Yield: 4 servings

—MOIRA HODGSON

BAKED POTATOES, PLAIN AND STUFFED

pareve, dairy, meat

4 baking potatoes, 6 ounces each
1 teaspoon olive oil
Salt and freshly ground pepper to taste
Stuffing, optional (see recipes below)

1. Preheat the oven to 450 degrees. Prick the potatoes several times with a fork and coat lightly with olive oil. Place directly in the oven and bake until tender, about 1 hour. Split the potatoes lengthwise, fluff with a fork and season with salt and pepper.

2. Spoon the stuffing into the potatoes and serve immediately.

Yield: 4 servings

Scallion and Yogurt-Cheese Stuffing

dairy

1½ cups plain lowfat yogurt
8 scallions, finely chopped
1 teaspoon salt
Freshly ground pepper to taste

1. Place the yogurt in a paper-towel-lined sieve and let stand until the liquid drips out, several hours or overnight.

2. Transfer to a bowl and stir in the scallions, salt and pepper.

Yield: 4 servings

Smoked Salmon and Scallion Stuffing

dairy

4 thin slices smoked salmon
1 recipe Scallion and Yogurt-Cheese Stuffing
  (see recipe above)

1. Cut the salmon slices in half lengthwise and cut across into thin slices.
2. Fill the potatoes with the scallion and yogurt-cheese stuffing and pile the salmon on top. Serve.

Yield: 4 servings

Curried-Spinach Stuffing with Caramelized Onions

dairy

¾ cup plain low-fat yogurt
2 teaspoons olive oil
1 small onion, peeled and diced
2 teaspoons curry powder
6 cups coarsely chopped spinach
1 teaspoon salt
Freshly ground pepper to taste
1 medium onion, peeled, halved lengthwise and thinly
  sliced

1. Place the yogurt in a paper-towel-lined sieve and let stand until the liquid drips out, several hours or overnight.
2. Heat 1 teaspoon of olive oil in a medium non-stick skillet over medium heat. Add the diced onion and cook until translucent, about 3 minutes. Lower the heat, stir in the curry powder and cook, stirring, for 3 minutes more. Add the spinach and sauté for 3 to 4 minutes.

3. Place the mixture in a blender and add the salt, pepper and yogurt. Blend until smooth. Place in a small saucepan and set aside.
4. Heat the remaining oil in a medium-heavy skillet over medium heat. Add the sliced onion and cook, stirring often, until caramelized, about 30 minutes. Warm the spinach mixture. Fill the potatoes with the spinach stuffing and pile the caramelized onions on top. Serve.

Yield: 4 servings

Hearty Portobello Stuffing

meat

2 teaspoons olive oil
1 small onion, peeled and finely chopped
4 medium portobello mushrooms, stemmed and cut
  into ½-inch dice
¼ cup red wine
¼ cup Beef Broth (page 49), homemade or low-
  sodium canned
½ teaspoon salt plus more to taste
Freshly ground pepper to taste
1 tablespoon coarsely chopped Italian parsley

1. Heat the oil in a large nonstick skillet over medium-low heat. Add the onion and cook for 2 minutes. Add the mushrooms and cook, stirring often, until the onions are soft and the mushrooms have released their juices, about 8 minutes.
2. Stir in the wine and broth, increase the heat to medium and cook until syrupy, about 5 minutes. Stir in the salt, pepper and parsley.

Yield: 4 servings

—MOLLY O'NEILL

ALAN KING'S ROASTED GARLIC POTATOES

meat

6 large old boiling potatoes, peeled and cut in quarters
Salted water, for boiling
1 tablespoon Schmaltz (page 413)
1 tablespoon light vegetable oil
1 head of garlic, peeled, with cloves lightly crushed
Salt and freshly ground black pepper to taste

1. Place potatoes in salted water to cover and bring to a boil for 2 minutes. Drain thoroughly and cool.
2. Preheat oven to 400 degrees.
3. Spread film of schmaltz and oil over the bottom of a heavy baking pan in which potatoes fit in a single layer. Add crushed garlic cloves.

4. Roast in preheated oven for about 45 minutes or until potatoes are golden brown and tender. Remove garlic cloves if they begin to turn dark brown. Shake pan or turn potatoes several times during roasting. Add a little more fat or oil if pan seems dry.
5. Sprinkle potatoes with salt and pepper and stir to distribute seasonings evenly.

Yield: 4 servings

NOTE: *Make these potatoes when roasting meat or chicken, basting them as they begin to brown with the juices that accumulate in the roasting pan. Old potatoes are preferred because they have little water and a high proportion of starch.*

—MIMI SHERATON

OVEN-BAKED POTATO PATTIES • (KEFTES)

pareve
ADAPTED FROM The Kosher Cooking School

2 pounds boiling potatoes, peeled
3 tablespoons cooking oil
½ cup finely chopped onion
½ cup coarsely ground walnuts
½ cup bread crumbs
2 eggs
¼ teaspoon ground nutmeg
Pinch of ground cardamom
Pinch of ground coriander
Salt and freshly ground black pepper to taste

1. Boil potatoes until tender and then drain well. Mash in a bowl.

2. While potatoes are boiling, heat oil in a skillet and sauté onions until lightly browned.
3. Combine mashed potatoes and onion, then set aside until cooled to room temperature.
4. Heat oven to 375 degrees. Grease a baking sheet.
5. To the mashed-potato mixture, add walnuts, bread crumbs, eggs, nutmeg, cardamom, coriander, salt and pepper. Using about ¼ cup of the potato mixture for each, form flattened oval patties and place them on the baking sheet. Bake patties for about 10 minutes per side, until browned.

Yield: 16–18 patties

NOTE: *For a dairy meal, plain yogurt mixed with chopped fresh mint is an excellent accompaniment.*

—FLORENCE FABRICANT

HANA ELBAUM'S STOVE-TOP POTATO KUGEL

pareve

3 large eggs
6 large Idaho potatoes, peeled and grated
Salt and freshly ground black pepper to taste
Vegetable oil

1. In a large bowl, beat eggs just until blended. Add potatoes. Season generously with salt and pepper. Mix well.

2. Oil the interior of a straight-sided 3- to 4-quart saucepan and place over medium-high heat. When oil is hot, add potato mixture. Smooth surface with a spatula.

3. Cover and reduce heat to low. Cook until mixture is set, potatoes are tender and edges of mixture turn firm and golden, about 1 hour. (Halfway through, the oil at the edge of the kugel should be sizzling. If not, raise temperature.)

4. Run a knife around edge of pot. Reverse pot over a plate and remove kugel. Return kugel to pot with uncooked side at bottom.

5. Place pot over medium-low heat. Cook uncovered until bottom browns, 10–15 minutes. Transfer kugel to a serving plate and cut into wedges. Serve hot.

Yield: 8–10 servings

—ALEX WITCHEL

BOULEY FAMILY POTATO AND PRUNE GRATIN

dairy
ADAPTED FROM David Bouley's mother,
Terry Dezso

4 medium-size baking potatoes
1 shallot, peeled
2 cloves garlic, peeled
1 small leek, about 3 ounces, cleaned
½ tablespoon olive oil
½ tablespoon unsalted butter
¼ teaspoon thyme
¼ teaspoon marjoram
15 pitted prunes
Salt and pepper to taste
¾ cup heavy cream
½ cup half-and-half
Nutmeg

1. Preheat oven to 350 degrees.

2. Peel and wash the potatoes. Use the slicing blade of a food processor to slice into thin slices.

3. Dice the shallot, garlic and leek. Gently sauté them in the olive oil and butter until soft. Add thyme and marjoram. Set aside.

4. Place prunes between two layers of plastic wrap and tap with a plate to flatten to ¼ inch thick.

5. Cover bottom of an ovenproof dish measuring 8 inches square and 2 inches deep with potato slices. Season with salt and pepper, then spread one-quarter of leek mixture over potatoes. Add another layer of potatoes and one of the leek mixture. Next, cover with half the prunes. Add another layer of potatoes and another of the leek mixture, then the rest of prunes. Top with a layer of potatoes and the remaining leek mixture.

6. Combine cream and half-and-half in a bowl, and season with salt and pepper and a touch of nutmeg. Pour evenly to barely cover the top. Bake until very tender, 45 minutes to 1 hour. Let cool at least 10 minutes.

Yield: 4–6 servings

—DENA KLEIMAN

POTATO KNISHES

meat, pareve

ADAPTED FROM *New York Cookbook*

Dough

pareve

2 cups all-purpose flour
1 teaspoon baking powder
½ teaspoon salt
2 tablespoons vegetable oil
2 eggs, lightly beaten

1. Combine the flour, baking powder and salt in a large bowl. Make a well in the center and add the oil, eggs and 2 tablespoons water. Gradually mix. Add up to 2 tablespoons more water if necessary. Knead the dough until it forms a rough ball.
2. Knead the dough on a lightly floured surface until smooth, about 6 minutes. Place in a lightly oiled bowl, cover and refrigerate for 1 hour. Preheat the oven to 350 degrees.

Filling

meat, pareve

1 tablespoon melted schmaltz or vegetable oil
2 cups finely chopped onions
2 cups plain mashed potatoes
Salt and freshly ground black pepper, to taste

1. Combine the schmaltz or vegetable oil, onions, potatoes, salt, and pepper in a bowl.
2. Divide the dough into thirds. On a floured surface, roll out one piece of the dough into a thin rectangle about 10 inches long. Spread about ⅔ cup of the filling along one long end, about 1 inch from the edge. Roll up like a jelly roll and pinch the edges closed. Repeat with the remaining pieces of dough and filling. Arrange the rolls on baking sheets. Bake until browned, about 40 minutes. Slice the knishes and serve.

Yield: about 2 dozen

—DANIEL B. SCHNEIDER

POTATO-PARSNIP GRATIN BAKED IN CIDER

meat

1 medium onion, peeled and diced

3 medium baking potatoes, peeled and thinly sliced
crosswise

2 teaspoons salt

Freshly ground pepper to taste

3 small parsnips, peeled and thinly sliced crosswise

1½ tablespoons chopped fresh thyme

1½ cups Chicken Broth (page 48), homemade or
low-sodium canned

½ cup apple cider

2 teaspoons chopped Italian parsley

1. Preheat the oven to 400 degrees. Layer the onion in a deep pie plate. Layer half the potatoes over the onions and season with 1 teaspoon of salt and pepper to taste. Top with the parsnips and the remaining potatoes. Sprinkle with the remaining salt, pepper and 1 tablespoon of thyme.

2. Combine the chicken broth and cider and pour over the potatoes. Cover with foil and bake for 30 minutes. Uncover and bake for 30 minutes more, basting. Sprinkle with the parsley and the remaining thyme and serve.

Yield: 4 servings

—MOLLY O'NEILL

STIR-FRIED SNOW PEAS

pareve

ADAPTED FROM *Kosher Cuisine*

1 pound small young snow peas

2 tablespoons vegetable oil or peanut oil

½ teaspoon sugar

1½ teaspoons kosher salt, approximately

1½ teaspoons soy sauce, approximately

1. Pinch off both ends of snow peas. If snow peas are more mature, there may be strings on one or both sides of the vegetable; pull them off and discard them.

2. Rinse and drain the snow peas.

3. Heat oil in a wok or a large skillet over high heat until hot. Add snow peas, stir until they are well-coated with the oil. Reduce heat to medium.

4. Add sugar, salt and soy sauce and continue stirring until the snow peas are tender, about 1 minute. Season to taste. Transfer to a warm serving dish.

Yield: 4 servings

NOTE: *If snow peas are large, and perhaps not so fresh, after Step 3 add 1 tablespoon of water to the snow peas, cover the wok or skillet and cook over medium heat for less than 1 minute. Uncover, stir in sugar, salt and soy sauce, season to taste and transfer to a warm serving dish.*

—CRAIG CLAIBORNE

BRAISED RED RADISHES WITH HONEY

dairy

2–3 bunches radishes, trimmed (about 1 pound when trimmed)

1 tablespoon unsalted butter

1 medium shallot, minced

½ cup Vegetable Stock (page 51), canned or fresh

1 tablespoon honey

Salt

1 tablespoon minced fresh parsley leaves

1. Halve radishes lengthwise from stem to root end.

2. Melt the butter in a large sauté pan. Add the shallot and sauté over medium heat until softened, about 2 minutes. Add radishes and stir; cook until well coated with butter, about 1 minute.

3. Add stock and honey to pan, cover and cook until radishes are tender but not soft, about 10 minutes. Remove cover, season with salt to taste and simmer until any remaining juices in pan reduce to a glaze, about 1 minute. Garnish with parsley and serve immediately.

Yield: 4 servings

NOTE: *For meat meal, substitute unsalted margarine for butter and, if desired, chicken broth for vegetable stock.*

—JACK BISHOP

SORREL PUREE

dairy

5 pounds fresh sorrel, stems removed

1 cup Crème Fraîche (page 431)

Salt to taste, if desired

Freshly ground pepper to taste

1. Rinse the sorrel well. Do not dry.

2. In a large pot over high heat, steam the sorrel, covered, for 3 minutes, or until the leaves are wilted.

3. Add the crème fraîche and beat until the sorrel is smooth and creamy. Season with salt and pepper. Keep warm until ready to serve.

Yield: 10 servings

—BRYAN MILLER

SPINACH WITH RAISINS AND PINE NUTS

pareve

ADAPTED FROM 7 Portes, Barcelona

2 pounds young, tender spinach
Salt to taste
2 tablespoons olive oil
1 garlic clove, peeled and halved
⅓ cup dark raisins
⅓ cup pine nuts, lightly toasted

1. Carefully wash the spinach in several changes of water. Remove and discard the stems and, if necessary, remove any thick center ribs. Chop coarsely and set aside.

2. Bring a large pot of water to a boil over high heat. Salt the water, add the spinach and cook just until wilted and tender, about 1 minute. Drain thoroughly and set aside.

3. In a large skillet, heat the oil over high heat until hot. Add the garlic and cook until golden, just to flavor the oil, 1–2 minutes. Do not allow the garlic to brown or burn. Discard the garlic. In the same skillet over moderate heat, sauté the raisins and pine nuts until coated with oil and warmed through, 1–2 minutes. Add the spinach, taste for seasoning and sauté until the flavors are blended, 3–4 minutes. Serve warm or at room temperature.

Yield: 4–6 servings

—PATRICIA WELLS

SPINACH PATTIES · (KEFTES)

pareve

ADAPTED FROM Alayne Zatulov

2 tablespoons olive oil plus oil as needed for
  frying
½ cup chopped onion
2 cloves garlic, well minced
1½ cups packed, cooked chopped spinach, very well
  drained (see Note below)
1 egg
1 egg yolk
Juice of ½ lemon
¼ teaspoon grated lemon rind
Pinch of nutmeg

½ cup bread crumbs
Salt and freshly ground black pepper to taste

1. Heat 2 tablespoons of olive oil in a medium-size skillet. Add onion, sauté until tender but not brown, and then add garlic and sauté a few minutes longer.

2. In the container of a food processor, combine onion and garlic with spinach, egg, egg yolk, lemon juice and rind, nutmeg and bread crumbs and process until blended. Season with salt and pepper.

3. Pour olive oil to the depth of about ½ inch in a heavy skillet and heat. Form spinach mixture into patties, using a heaping tablespoon of the mixture for each patty. Fry until brown on one side, turn and brown the other side. Drain patties on absorbent paper.

Yield: 12 small keftes

NOTE: *Use 1 pound of cooked spinach, about 20 ounces of fresh spinach or 1½ packages of frozen spinach.*

—FLORENCE FABRICANT

CREAMED SPINACH

dairy

ADAPTED FROM *The New York Times Menu Cook Book*

3 pounds fresh spinach
¼ cup butter
¼ cup all-purpose flour
1 tablespoon grated onion
2 cups milk
1 teaspoon salt
¼ teaspoon freshly ground black pepper
Hard-cooked eggs, optional

1. Wash the spinach several times in cold water to remove all sand; discard any tough stems. Place the spinach in a kettle with only the water that clings to the leaves; cover. Cook until spinach is wilted, then drain and chop very fine.

2. Heat the butter in a skillet. Add the flour and onion and cook, stirring, until brown. Gradually add the milk, stirring constantly until thickened and smooth.

3. Add the spinach, salt and pepper; simmer for several minutes. If desired, garnish with chopped egg whites and riced egg yolks.

Yield: 4–6 servings

NOTE: *At meat meals, substitute ¼ cup margarine for the butter and 2 cups of chicken stock for the milk. For a flavorful variation, add 1½ teaspoons of grated nutmeg in Step 3.*

PERSIAN SPINACH, POTATOES AND PEAS

dairy

1 pound tiny new potatoes
12 ounces whole onion or 11 ounces ready-cut (2¼–2½ cups)
2 teaspoons olive oil
2 cloves garlic

1 (10-ounce) package fresh spinach or 1 pound loose spinach
1 cup frozen peas
⅛ teaspoon nutmeg
1 cup nonfat plain yogurt
⅛ teaspoon salt
Freshly ground black pepper to taste

1. Scrub potatoes and put in a pot with water to cover. Cover pot and cook until fork-tender, about 20 minutes, depending on size.

2. Chop whole onion. Sauté onion in a nonstick pan in very hot oil over medium-high heat until it begins to soften and brown.

3. Mince garlic and add to onion as it cooks.

4. Wash spinach; remove tough stems and cook spinach in covered pot in the water clinging to it until it wilts, 4–5 minutes, stirring once or twice.

5. Stir peas into onion mixture and cook 2–3 minutes.

6. When spinach is cooked, drain it, thoroughly pressing the water out. Cut up and add to cooked onion, along with nutmeg and yogurt.

7. When potatoes are cooked, drain and cut into bite-size pieces and stir into spinach mixture. Season with salt and pepper and serve.

Yield: 2 servings

—MARIAN BURROS

SPAGHETTI SQUASH WITH EGGPLANT AND SESAME SEEDS

dairy

ADAPTED FROM *Taste of Israel*

1 large eggplant, left unpeeled, trimmed and cut lengthwise into 8 slices

3 teaspoons kosher salt

1 medium-size spaghetti squash

3 tablespoons olive oil

2 tablespoons unsalted butter

3 cloves garlic, peeled and minced

½ cup sesame seeds, lightly toasted

1 cup freshly grated Parmesan cheese

1. Preheat the oven to 350 degrees. Place the eggplant slices on paper towels and sprinkle with 2 teaspoons of salt. Set aside to drain.

2. Cut the spaghetti squash in half lengthwise and scrape out the seeds and fibers. Place cut side down on a baking sheet and bake until tender, about 45 minutes. Scrape the squash flesh out with a fork and set aside.

3. Raise the oven temperature to 450 degrees. Pat the eggplant dry and brush on both sides with the olive oil. Place on a large baking sheet (or divide between 2 sheets) and bake until tender, about 15 minutes.

4. While the eggplant is baking, melt the butter in a large skillet over medium heat. Add the garlic and sauté for 1 minute. Stir in the spaghetti squash and 1 teaspoon of salt and cook until heated through. Turn the heat very low.

5. Coat the eggplant slices on both sides with the sesame seeds. Place a heaping teaspoon of the Parmesan cheese in the center of each slice and roll them up individually.

6. Stir the remaining cheese into the squash. Divide the squash among 4 plates and top with 2 eggplant rolls each. Serve immediately.

Yield: 4 servings

—MOLLY O'NEILL

ACORN SQUASH WITH SPICED BULGUR

pareve

6 medium-size acorn squashes
1 teaspoon sesame oil
1½ cups bulgur wheat
2 cups water
½ teaspoon ground ginger
½ teaspoon ground cinnamon
¼ teaspoon white pepper
½ teaspoon salt
2 tablespoons raisins
2 tablespoons toasted pine nuts

1. Cut the bottom off each squash so that it will sit straight. Slice off the top, clean the seeds from the squash and prick the inside evenly with a fork. Place the squash in a shallow baking dish and add water to come halfway up the sides of the squash.

2. Place the sesame oil in a skillet over medium heat and warm. Add the bulgur wheat and cook, stirring frequently, until toasted, about 4 minutes. Add 1 cup of the water and stir. Add the ginger, cinnamon, pepper and salt and stir. Reduce heat and add remaining water by the quarter cup until the grain is soft, about 10 minutes. Remove from heat and stir in the raisins and pine nuts.

3. Preheat oven to 400 degrees.

4. Divide the grain mixture evenly among the squashes and cover the baking dish tightly with foil. Bake 1 hour, until the squashes are soft.

Yield: 6 servings

—MOLLY O'NEILL

EDDA SERVI MACHLIN'S BAKED SQUASH PUDDING

pareve

3–4 pounds butternut squash (zucchini or yellow
    squash can be substituted)
1 cup water
½ cup finely chopped onion
1 tablespoon chopped Italian parsley
4 tablespoons olive oil plus oil for greasing pan
    and sprinkling
Salt and freshly ground black pepper to taste
1 small garlic clove, minced
1 tablespoon shredded fresh basil

3 eggs, slightly beaten
Bread crumbs, either packaged or homemade

1. Preheat oven to 350 degrees.

2. Clean and peel squash. Cut in half and remove seeds and fibers. Chop coarsely and place in a saucepan with water, onion, parsley, oil, salt, pepper, garlic and basil. Bring to a boil and cook over medium-high heat 10 minutes, stirring frequently. Add a few tablespoons water if needed, but keep squash rather dry.

3. Remove from heat and mash coarsely; do not use a food processor.

4. Add eggs and mix well.

5. Grease a 9-by-13-inch baking pan and sprinkle with bread crumbs. Pour in squash mixture, flatten with a rubber spatula and sprinkle top with bread crumbs and a little additional oil.

6. Bake 45 minutes or until well puffed and lightly browned.

Yield: 8 servings

—GAIL FORMAN

SUGAR SNAP PEAS WITH SUN-DRIED TOMATOES

pareve

2 tablespoons extra-virgin olive oil
2 cloves garlic, minced (green part removed)
6 sun-dried tomatoes, chopped
3 portobello mushroom caps, sliced
Coarse sea salt and freshly ground pepper to taste
1 pound sugar snap peas

1. Heat the oil in a large frying pan or wok. Add the garlic, tomatoes and mushrooms, salt and pepper and sauté, stirring frequently, for about 10 minutes.

2. When the mushrooms are beginning to get crisp, add the sugar snap peas and sauté for about 3 minutes, or until lightly cooked but still crunchy. Correct seasoning and serve.

Yield: 4 servings

—MOIRA HODGSON

SWEET POTATOES ROASTED WITH ROSEMARY AND GARLIC

pareve

2 pounds sweet potatoes, peeled, cut diagonally in
   ½-inch slices
3 large cloves garlic, peeled and thickly sliced
2 tablespoons olive oil
1½ teaspoons dried rosemary
Kosher salt and freshly ground pepper to taste

1. Set oven at 375 degrees.

2. In a medium bowl, combine the sliced sweet potatoes with the garlic and oil. Crush the rosemary in your fingers and sprinkle it over the potatoes. Add the salt and pepper. Toss the potatoes until they are coated with the oil.

3. In a roasting pan, spread the potatoes in one layer. Bake 35–40 minutes. Serve warm or at room temperature.

Yield: 6 servings

—DANA JACOBI

SWEET POTATO FRITTERS

pareve
ADAPTED FROM *Iron Pots and Wooden Spoons*

6 medium-size sweet potatoes
1½ teaspoons salt
1 teaspoon freshly ground black pepper
1 cup flour
2 eggs
2 tablespoons water
Oil for deep frying
6 scallions, minced

1. Place the sweet potatoes in a large pot, add 1 teaspoon of salt, cover with cold water and bring to a boil. Boil for 10–15 minutes until the potatoes are tender. Drain and cool.

2. Combine remaining ½ teaspoon of salt with the pepper and flour in a small bowl and set aside. Beat eggs lightly with the water. Cut the sweet potatoes into ¼-inch slices.

3. Place oil for deep frying in a heavy skillet and heat it to 350 degrees. Dip the sweet potato slices in the egg and then in the flour mixture and fry in small batches. Serve hot, topped with minced scallions.

Yield: 6 servings

NOTE: *These fritters are also a fine accompaniment with before-dinner drinks.*

—MOLLY O'NEILL

GLAZED SWEET POTATOES WITH WALNUTS

dairy
ADAPTED FROM *The New York Times Menu Cook Book*

6 sweet potatoes, boiled or baked
1½ cups dark brown sugar
3 tablespoons water
3 tablespoons butter
1 teaspoon grated lemon rind
½ cup walnut halves or chopped walnuts

1. Preheat oven to 350 degrees.
2. Peel the potatoes and halve them. Place in a baking dish.

3. Combine the sugar, water, butter and lemon rind in a saucepan. Bring the mixture to a boil and pour it over the sweet potatoes.

4. Bake for 10–15 minutes, basting several times during cooking. Remove from the oven and sprinkle with the nuts.

Yield: 6–8 servings

NOTE: *Unsalted margarine may be substituted for butter. For a honeyed flavor, ½ cup of the brown sugar may be replaced with ½ cup honey.*

SWEET-POTATO SOUFFLÉ

dairy

1½ pounds sweet potatoes
⅓ cup heavy cream
3 egg yolks
4 egg whites, beaten until stiff
⅛ teaspoon nutmeg
2 teaspoons brown sugar
1 teaspoon butter for greasing dish

1. Preheat oven to 400 degrees.
2. Prick the sweet potatoes and place in a baking dish. Put in oven and bake for 45 minutes to 1 hour, or until soft. Remove from oven, slice in half and scoop flesh into a bowl. Using a wire whisk or electric mixer, whip until smooth. Measure 1¾ cups. Reserve any remaining potatoes for another use.
3. Lower oven temperature to 350 degrees.
4. In a bowl blend the sweet potatoes and cream. Add the egg yolks, nutmeg and brown sugar, mixing well. Fold in the beaten egg whites.
5. Place the mixture in a buttered 1-quart soufflé or baking dish and bake for 35–40 minutes, or until a knife inserted in the center comes out clean.

Yield: 4 servings

—BRYAN MILLER

WILTED SWISS CHARD

pareve

1 bunch Swiss chard or other greens, like kale or escarole
2 tablespoons extra-virgin olive oil
2 garlic cloves, finely minced
2 tablespoons balsamic vinegar
Salt and freshly ground black pepper to taste

1. Rinse and drain the Swiss chard or other greens and chop coarsely.
2. Heat the oil in a large, heavy skillet over medium heat, add the garlic and sauté a few seconds. Add the Swiss chard. Increase the heat to medium-high and stir-fry just until the Swiss chard has wilted, about 5 minutes.
3. Stir in the vinegar and season to taste with salt and pepper. Serve at once.

Yield: 4 servings

—FLORENCE FABRICANT

SWISS CHARD WITH SCALLIONS

pareve, dairy

2 large bunches Swiss chard, with stems, washed
6 tablespoons butter or olive oil, or to taste
2 bunches scallions, cut into ¼-inch lengths
Salt and black pepper, to taste

1. Cut the chard into large pieces, plunge it into boiling water and cook it until the stems are just tender.

2. Drain, shock under cold water and drain again. Squeeze out as much water as possible. Put the chard on a board and chop it up with a large knife.

3. Melt the butter or olive oil in a deep pot. Add the scallions and cook them over moderate heat until just tender. Add the chopped chard, toss well, season to taste and serve.

Yield: 6 servings

—ROBERT FARRAR CAPON

CHARLIE TROTTER'S ROASTED TOMATOES STUFFED WITH COUSCOUS, CHANTERELLES AND PINE NUTS

pareve

9 small ripe tomatoes
2 tablespoons olive oil
8 garlic cloves
8 sprigs thyme
8 sprigs tarragon, plus 1 teaspoon minced
8 bay leaves
8 basil leaves
1 cup cooked couscous
8 chanterelle mushrooms, quartered and sautéed
1 tablespoon toasted pine nuts
1 tablespoon peeled and finely diced cucumber
1 tablespoon corn kernels, sautéed
1 teaspoon chopped chives, plus 16 whole chives
1 teaspoon chopped mint

1. Preheat oven to 325 degrees. Peel tomatoes. Mince 1 tomato and set aside. Cut a ¾-inch slice from the bottom of the others, reserving these pieces to serve as lids. Scoop out seeds and center flesh. Rub the insides with 1 tablespoon of olive oil; place a garlic clove, a sprig of thyme, a sprig of tarragon, a bay leaf and a basil leaf into each. Put the lids on and bake until they begin to soften, but still maintain their shape, 10–12 minutes. Remove from oven and discard garlic and herbs.

2. In a double boiler, warm the couscous. Add the minced tomato, chanterelles, pine nuts, cucumber and corn and stir. Add 1 tablespoon of oil, the chopped chives, the minced tarragon and mint and stir. Spoon into the tomatoes, reheat in the oven and serve 2 to a plate garnished with whole chives.

Yield: 4 servings

—MOLLY O'NEILL

ROASTED-TOMATO-AND-EGGPLANT CASSEROLE

meat

3 pounds plum tomatoes
  (about 12–14), halved
Salt for seasoning, plus 1 teaspoon
Freshly ground black pepper for seasoning, plus
  ¼ teaspoon
3 medium eggplants (about 3 pounds), cut into
  ½-inch slices
3 tablespoons olive oil
3 large red onions (about 3 pounds),
  halved and sliced
3 large yellow onions (about 3 pounds),
  halved and sliced
6 cloves garlic, chopped
½ cup white wine
2 cups homemade or low-sodium Chicken Stock
  (page 48)
1¼ teaspoons chopped fresh rosemary
1¼ teaspoons chopped fresh thyme

1. Preheat oven to 300 degrees. Season the cut sides of the tomatoes lightly with salt and pepper and place cut sides down on a lightly oiled baking sheet. Bake until the tomatoes are very lightly browned and collapsed, about 3 hours. Set aside.

2. Raise the oven temperature to 450 degrees. Sprinkle the eggplant slices lightly with salt and transfer them to a large colander to drain for 30 minutes. Wipe the slices dry with paper towels and place them in a single layer on 1 or more lightly oiled baking sheet. Roast the eggplant slices, turning once, until they are soft and lightly browned, about 20 minutes. Set aside.

3. Meanwhile, in a large, heavy-bottomed kettle, heat the 3 tablespoons of olive oil over medium heat and add the red and yellow onions and garlic. Cook, stirring frequently, until the onions are very soft and lightly caramelized, about 25 minutes. (Lower the heat if the bottom of the pan begins to scorch.) Add the wine, stock, herbs and 1 teaspoon salt and ¼ teaspoon pepper. Raise the heat to high and continue to cook until the mixture thickens slightly, about 5 minutes.

4. Lower the oven to 400 degrees. Spread a thin layer of the onion mixture in the bottom of a 13-by-9-inch baking pan. Top with half the eggplant slices, half the tomatoes and half of the remaining onions. Top with the remaining eggplant slices, tomatoes and onions.

5. Bake until bubbly and lightly browned, about 35–40 minutes. Let stand for 10 minutes before serving.

Yield: 6 servings

—MOLLY O'NEILL

SIMPLE ROAST TURNIPS OR RUTABAGAS

pareve

1½ pounds turnips (about 8–10 small or 5–6
   medium) or rutabagas (1 medium)
2 tablespoons olive oil
Salt and freshly ground black pepper to taste
2 tablespoons extra-virgin olive oil
1 teaspoon minced garlic
¼ cup roughly chopped fresh parsley
Juice of ½ lemon
½ teaspoon ground coriander

1. Heat the oven to 425 degrees. Peel the turnips or
rutabagas and cut them into large chunks. Place in a
roasting pan, add the olive oil and salt and pepper to
taste and toss to coat.

2. Place the pan in the oven and roast, stirring
or shaking the pan every 10 minutes, until the vegetables are tender but not mushy, about 35 to
40 minutes.

3. Remove the vegetables from the oven and place
them in a large bowl. Add the olive oil, garlic, parsley, lemon juice and coriander and toss well. Adjust
the seasonings to taste and serve while hot.

Yield: 4 servings

—JOHN WILLOUGHBY AND
CHRIS SCHLESINGER

MASHED YELLOW TURNIPS WITH CRISPY SHALLOTS

dairy

ADAPTED FROM *The Union Square Cafe Cookbook*

◆   **MASHED TURNIPS**   ◆

dairy

2 large yellow turnips (rutabagas), about 4 pounds
2 teaspoons kosher salt
1 cup milk
½ teaspoon freshly ground black pepper

1. Peel the turnips to remove their waxy skins and cut
them into generous 1-inch chunks. Put them in a
saucepan with water to cover and 1 teaspoon of salt.
Bring to a boil and simmer, covered, until the turnips
are easily pierced by a paring knife, about 35 minutes.

2. In a separate saucepan, heat the milk and the
remaining 6 tablespoons of butter over low heat
until the butter has melted and the milk just begins
to simmer.

3. Drain the turnips and puree (in several batches, if
necessary) in a food processor. With the motor running, add the melted butter and milk in a steady
stream. The turnips should be very smooth.

4. Return the turnip puree to the saucepan, season
with 1 teaspoon salt and the pepper and reheat, stirring, over medium flame. Serve piping hot, sprinkled
generously with crispy shallots.

Yield: 4–6 servings

◆ CRISPY SHALLOTS ◆

dairy

1½ cups light vegetable or olive oil
9 tablespoons butter
5–6 shallots, peeled and sliced into thin rings

1. In a saucepan, heat the oil with 3 tablespoons of butter over medium-low heat until it begins to bubble. Reduce the heat to low, add the shallots and cook them until they are a rich golden brown, 30–40 minutes. Stir the shallots occasionally while they are cooking to make sure they brown evenly.

2. Remove the shallots from the oil with a slotted spoon and drain them on paper towels.

NOTE: *Once the shallots have dried and crisped, in about 15 minutes, they can be stored in a cool place, covered, for several days. Serve the shallots at room temperature.*

—MOIRA HODGSON

ORANGE-GLAZED YELLOW TURNIPS

dairy, pareve
ADAPTED FROM *The New York Times Heritage Cookbook*

2 medium-size yellow turnips, peeled and sliced
    ¼ inch thick
Boiling salted water
1 cup brown sugar
½ cup orange juice
1 teaspoon grated orange rind
2 tablespoons butter or unsalted margarine

1. Preheat oven to 350 degrees.

2. Barely cover the yellow turnips with boiling salted water and boil 5 minutes. Drain turnips and place in shallow baking dish.

3. Combine the brown sugar, orange juice, orange rind and butter or margarine in a pan. Heat to melt the butter or margarine and stir to dissolve sugar. Pour over the turnips and bake, basting frequently, 45–60 minutes, until the turnip slices are tender.

Yield: 6 servings

SADIE BELL HERBIN'S CANDIED YAMS

pareve, dairy

5 medium sweet potatoes (about 3 pounds)
1 cup white sugar
1 cup brown sugar
½ teaspoon ginger
½ teaspoon nutmeg
½ teaspoon allspice
½ teaspoon cinnamon, optional
½ stick butter, optional
2 cups water

1. Boil sweet potatoes until soft when pierced with a fork. Peel and cut into ½-inch slices along the length or width.

2. Mix together sugars and spices.

3. Line a quart-size casserole dish with a layer of potatoes. Evenly sprinkle some of the sugar mixture and, if desired, dot with butter and continue to alternate layers.

4. Pour water over potatoes. Bake for 45 minutes at 300 degrees or until a syrup forms.

Yield: 6 servings

—YANNICK RICE LAMB

TRIESTINE PAN-COOKED ZUCCHINI WITH EGG AND CINNAMON

pareve

ADAPTED FROM *La Terra Fortunata*

3 tablespoons extra-virgin olive oil

2¼ pounds small zucchini, ends trimmed off, cut
   lengthwise into very thin strips, then crosswise into
   1½-inch-long pieces

Sea salt to taste

2 tablespoons chopped flat-leaf parsley

1 large egg

1 teaspoon ground cinnamon, more to taste

1. In a large sauté pan, heat oil over medium-high heat. Add zucchini and season with salt. Sauté for 30 seconds, then add the parsley. Stir and continue sautéing until zucchini is soft but not mushy (taste to see if it is seasoned enough; if not, add more salt).

2. Break the egg into the pan and stir in all the ingredients vigorously. The egg should break into tiny bits as it cooks. Remove the pan from the heat and dust the zucchini with the cinnamon, adding more to taste. Transfer to a platter and serve.

Yield: 6 servings

—AMANDA HESSER

WOLFGANG PUCK'S VEGETABLE CAKES WITH RED PEPPER COULIS

dairy

1 cup diced celery

1 cup diced carrots

1 cup diced onion

1 medium-size tomato, seeded and diced

1 cup fresh peas

3 tablespoons chopped fresh basil

1 teaspoon ground cumin

½ teaspoon turmeric

1/8 teaspoon red pepper flakes

1 pound baking potatoes, baked until tender
  and peeled

3 large egg whites

3 tablespoons nonfat milk

1 cup dried bread crumbs

Spray of olive oil

Red Pepper Coulis (see recipe below)

1. In a large nonstick skillet, slowly sauté celery, carrots, onion and tomato until they are tender. Partly cover the pan and, if the tomatoes are not sufficiently juicy, add a dash of water to keep from burning. Transfer to a large mixing bowl and add the peas, basil, cumin, turmeric and red pepper flakes. Stir and set aside to cool.

2. In another bowl, mash the potatoes.

3. In small bowl, whisk together egg whites and milk. Stir into mashed potatoes until smooth. Add remaining vegetable mixture and combine well. Form into twelve 2-ounce patties. Put bread crumbs in shallow pan and lightly coat both sides of patties.

4. Spray a large skillet with olive oil spray and sauté the patties over medium heat until brown, about 5 minutes each side. Serve with red pepper coulis.

Yield: 6 servings

◆ RED PEPPER COULIS ◆

pareve

1/2 pound red peppers, cored, seeded and diced

1 medium-size tomato, seeded and diced

1/2 large onion, diced

1 3/4 cups tomato juice

1/4 cup chopped basil

1/8 teaspoon thyme

1. In a medium-size skillet, combine red pepper, tomato, onion and tomato juice and cook until tender. Stir in the basil and thyme. Puree in a blender until smooth. Return to skillet and cook over low heat until mixture is reduced to about 1 1/2 cups.

Yield: 6 servings

—MOLLY O'NEILL

BALKAN MIXED VEGETABLE STEW ◆ (GHIVETCH)

pareve, dairy

1 cup olive oil

3 large onions, peeled and sliced

1 large green pepper, seeded and sliced

1 small head cabbage, cored and shredded

1 small or 1/2 medium head cauliflower,
  broken into flowerets

4 large potatoes, peeled and cut into 1/2-inch cubes

4 carrots, scraped and diced

1 eggplant, cubed

2 zucchini, cubed

1 white turnip, cubed

1 large knob celery, cubed, if available

1 parsnip, peeled and sliced, if available

1–2 parsley roots, peeled and sliced, if available

3 leeks, well washed and sliced

1/2 pound okra, sliced

¼ pound string beans, cut into 1-inch pieces

1 pound fresh white beans, if available

3 tomatoes, peeled and seeded if fresh, well drained
  if canned

1 head of garlic, cloves separated but not peeled

⅔ cup minced parsley

Salt and pepper to taste

1 cup sour grapes, or 1 pear or 2 sour plums

½ cup white wine, optional

Sour cream or yogurt as garnish, optional

Minced fresh dill as garnish, optional

1. Preheat oven to 350 degrees.

2. Heat ½ cup olive oil in a 5-quart Dutch oven, add sliced onion and sauté until golden brown. Add all vegetables, garlic and parsley and mix gently with a wooden spoon to completely stir in oil and onions. Sprinkle lightly with salt and pepper.

3. Remove seeds from grapes or peel and seed pear or plums. Add to vegetables. Stir in remaining olive oil and wine if you use it. Cover pot and cook over moderate heat until juices seep out of vegetables and come to a boil.

4. Place in oven and bake for 1–2 hours, or until all vegetables are tender and juices have just about evaporated. If mixture is too dry too soon, add a little water, but that should not be necessary.

5. Check for seasoning and serve hot or at room temperature. Pick out garlic cloves as you serve the stew. Sour cream or yogurt, mixed with dill, may be served on the side at a dairy meal.

—MIMI SHERATON

VEGETARIAN CHOLENT

pareve

ADAPTED FROM *Spice and Spirit: The Complete Kosher Jewish Cookbook*

½ cup white northern beans

½ cup kidney beans

½ cup lima beans

2 tablespoons vegetable oil

3 large onions, diced

3 cloves garlic

½ cup barley

Salt and freshly ground pepper to taste

3 large potatoes, peeled and cut in chunks (about 2
  pounds)

1 (15-ounce) can tomato sauce

1. Put beans in large bowl and cover with cold water. Soak overnight. Before cooking, drain beans and discard stones and dried-out beans.

2. Heat oil in a 4-quart pot and sauté onions and garlic until onions are translucent, 5–7 minutes. Add barley and beans to onions. Cover with water by at least 2 inches, add salt and pepper, bring to a boil and cook 30 minutes over low heat. Add potatoes and tomato sauce and cook 30 minutes more.

3. Place cholent in a crock pot or slow cooker overnight or in a 200-degree oven for 8 hours or overnight.

Yield: 8–10 servings

—JOAN NATHAN

LATKES AND OTHER VEGETABLE PANCAKES

CARROT AND PARSNIP LATKES

pareve

ADAPTED FROM the New Prospect Café, Brooklyn, in
Jewish Cooking in America

2 medium carrots
5 small parsnips (about 1 pound)
¼ cup all-purpose flour
2 large eggs, beaten
1 teaspoon minced chives or scallions (green part only)
1 teaspoon chopped parsley
Salt to taste
Freshly ground pepper to taste

Peanut oil for frying

1. Grate carrots and parsnips coarsely. Toss with flour. Add the eggs, chives, parsley, salt and pepper. Mix until moistened thoroughly.
2. Heat ¼ inch of peanut oil in a sauté pan until it is barely smoking. Drop in the batter by tablespoons and flatten. Fry on both sides until brown. Drain on paper towels and serve.

Yield: 16–18 (2-inch) pancakes

—JOAN NATHAN

JERUSALEM ARTICHOKE PANCAKES

pareve

1 medium-size carrot, peeled
1 shallot, peeled
1 teaspoon minced fresh parsley
Dash of Tabasco
2 tablespoons flour
2 extra-large eggs
½ teaspoon salt
Freshly ground black pepper to taste
½ pound Jerusalem artichokes (sunchokes), scrubbed well
6 tablespoons peanut oil

1. Heat the oven to 300 degrees.
2. Cut the carrot into chunks about as long as the Jerusalem artichokes. Using a mandoline or the second-largest holes on a 4-sided grater, finely shred the carrot lengthwise into a mixing bowl. Grate or mince the shallot and add to the bowl. Add the parsley, Tabasco, flour and eggs and mix well. Season with salt and pepper and mix again.
3. Just before you are ready to cook, grate the Jerusalem artichokes into the bowl and mix again.
4. Measure 2 tablespoons of the oil into a large heavy skillet. Heat over medium heat until a bit of the batter sizzles when dropped into the pan. Using a soupspoon, scoop out 4 mounds of the mixture into the hot oil, flattening slightly. Fry for 3–4

minutes on each side, until the pancakes are crisp and brown outside but soft inside.

5. Transfer the cooked pancakes to an ovenproof plate lined with paper towel. Keep them warm in the oven. Repeat with the remaining batter, adding additional peanut oil as necessary between each batch. Serve hot.

Yield: 12 pancakes, or 4–6 servings as a side dish or appetizer

—REGINA SCHRAMBLING

LENTIL LEVIVOT · (LATKES)

dairy

ADAPTED FROM Celia Regev, in *The Foods of Israel Today*

According to Joan Nathan, an authority on the history of Jewish cuisine, these levivot might actually resemble the first latkes—fried pancakes made centuries ago from lentils, barley or flour. Potatoes were not commonly used until the late 17th or early 18th century, when they arrived in Europe from the Americas and became a staple of the cooking of Jews in Eastern Europe.

3 tablespoons extra-virgin olive oil
1 cup diced onion
1 cup cooked lentils (½ cup uncooked)
1 cup precooked rice (any kind will do)
¼ teaspoon cumin
⅛ teaspoon ground coriander
Salt and freshly ground pepper to taste
2 large eggs
½ cup plain yogurt
¼ cup finely chopped cilantro or parsley
⅓ cup all-purpose flour
Peanut or canola oil for frying

1. Heat oil in nonstick frying pan and sauté onion until translucent. Remove and set aside.

2. In a bowl, place lentils, rice, cumin, coriander, salt and pepper to taste, eggs, yogurt, cilantro and flour. Fold in the onion and mix well. Set aside.

3. Heat a nonstick frying pan with a film of oil. Take heaping tablespoons of the mixture and fry for a few minutes on each side. Drain on paper towel. Serve as is or with a dollop of labneh (strained yogurt), topped with a confit of onions and a sprig of cilantro.

Yield: About 20 levivot

Confit of Onions with Labneh Sauce

dairy

¼ cup extra-virgin olive oil
3 large onions, sliced in rings
2 teaspoons pomegranate molasses, optional
½ cup labneh sauce (strained yogurt) (see Note below)
¼ teaspoon ground coriander
Salt and freshly ground pepper to taste
1 bunch fresh cilantro

1. Heat oil in nonstick frying pan and add onions. Reduce heat to low and cook very slowly, adding a little water if necessary, until onions become golden brown. This may take as long as 30 minutes. The longer you cook, the more flavor in your confit.
2. Remove onions to a bowl and add pomegranate molasses, if desired, mixing well.
3. Place labneh in another bowl. Add coriander and salt and pepper to taste. Place dollop of labneh on each latke, and top it with a fresh sprig of cilantro.

Yield: 1 cup confit

NOTE: *For labneh: Place 1 cup yogurt in a sieve lined with paper towels and let stand until the liquid drips out and it reaches a thick consistency. The longer the yogurt liquid is strained, the harder the resulting labneh will be.*

—JOAN NATHAN

MUSHROOM PECAN LATKES

dairy

ADAPTED FROM Hava Volman, in
The Foods of Israel Today

3 tablespoons extra-virgin olive oil
10 ounces white mushrooms, sliced
1 teaspoon thyme
Salt and freshly ground pepper to taste
½ cup cooked wild rice
½ cup toasted chopped pecans
1 tablespoon sour cream
1 large egg
3 tablespoons matzoh meal
3 tablespoons snipped dill
¾ teaspoon lemon zest
1 teaspoon ground cardamom
½ teaspoon nutmeg
Canola or other vegetable oil for frying
Smoked salmon for garnish
Pickled ginger for garnish

1. Heat oil in nonstick frying pan and sauté mushrooms. Add thyme and salt and pepper to taste. Place in food processor and pulse just until mushrooms are chopped.
2. Place mushrooms in a mixing bowl. Add rice, pecans, sour cream, egg, matzoh meal, snipped dill, lemon zest, cardamom and nutmeg. Mix well.
3. Coat a nonstick frying pan with oil and heat. Take heaping tablespoons of the mixture and fry for a few minutes on each side. Drain on paper towels. Garnish with strips of smoked salmon and pickled ginger and serve.

Yield: About 10 latkes

—JOAN NATHAN

HEIRLOOM PEA PANCAKES

dairy

ADAPTED FROM Judson Grill

4 ounces sugar snap peas, trimmed
½ cup freshly shelled green peas
2 tablespoons milk
1 tablespoon heavy cream
1 egg, lightly beaten
¼ cup flour
½ teaspoon baking powder
⅛ teaspoon sugar
⅛ teaspoon salt
2 tablespoons butter
Salt to taste
Pepper to taste

1. Preheat oven to 450 degrees. Fill a bowl with ice water. Bring a pot of water to a boil, then lightly salt it. Add sugar snap peas to boiling water and blanch for 2 minutes. Remove with a slotted spoon and plunge immediately into ice bath. Remove sugar snap peas from ice water and reserve. Repeat procedure for the shelled peas, blanching them for 3 minutes or until tender. Reserve.

2. Puree sugar snap peas with the milk and the cream in a blender or food processor. Pour into a large mixing bowl and whisk in the egg. Sift flour, baking powder, sugar and salt into mixture and whisk to combine. Coarsely puree reserved shelled peas in food processor, then fold into batter.

3. In a large ovenproof skillet over medium-high heat, melt ½ tablespoon butter. Drop tablespoonfuls of batter into pan. When edges are lightly browned, place pan in oven and bake for 1½ minutes. Remove from oven and flip pancakes over gently with a spatula. Cook until bottoms are lightly browned; return to oven for another minute. Transfer to a plate lined with paper towels. Sprinkle with salt and pepper to taste. Repeat process until all batter is used.

Yield: About 14 pancakes

—MELISSA CLARK

FLORENCE FABRICANT'S POTATO LATKES

pareve, dairy

4 large Idaho potatoes (about 2¼ pounds)
⅔ cup coarsely chopped onion
1 teaspoon lemon juice
2 eggs, lightly beaten
¼ cup matzoh meal
1 teaspoon salt or to taste
Freshly ground black pepper to taste

Vegetable oil for frying
Fresh applesauce or sour cream, optional

1. Scrub potatoes but do not peel them. Cut away any nicks or bruises, dice into ½-inch cubes and place in a bowl of cold water.

2. Dry half the potato pieces and place them, along with half the onion and half the lemon juice, in a food processor fitted with a steel blade. Process with the on-off or pulse control, stopping the machine and scraping the sides of the bowl from time to time until the potatoes are a uniformly medium-fine texture. Alternatively, a fine shredding disk may be used, or the potatoes may be grated by hand. To drain the grated potatoes, transfer them to a fine sieve placed over a bowl. Repeat the entire process for the remaining potato pieces.

3. Press the potatoes in the sieve to extract as much moisture as possible. Reserve this liquid and transfer the potatoes to a large mixing bowl. Add the eggs, matzoh meal and salt and pepper to the potatoes. Pour out the reserved potato liquid and add any

thick white starch that has accumulated in the bottom of the bowl to the batter.

4. Heat oil to a depth of about ¼ inch in 1 or 2 large, heavy skillets, preferably cast iron. Form pancakes using a heaping tablespoon of batter for each, flattening them with the back of the spoon as the batter is added to the skillet. Fry, turning once, until golden brown, adding more oil as needed. Drain on absorbent paper before serving. Pancakes may be kept warm in a 250-degree oven. Serve them with applesauce or, at a dairy meal, with sour cream.

Yield: 24–30 (4-inch) pancakes, serving 6–8

—FLORENCE FABRICANT

LOW-FAT POTATO LATKES

pareve, dairy

3 pounds Yukon Gold potatoes
1 medium onion
⅓ cup matzoh meal or unbleached white flour
½ teaspoon baking powder
1 cup egg substitute, or 2 eggs plus 4 whites
3 tablespoons chopped parsley
Kosher salt and freshly ground black pepper to taste
Olive oil spray
Nonfat sour cream at a dairy meal, optional
Applesauce, optional

1. Place a large nonstick baking sheet in oven and preheat to 450 degrees. Peel potatoes and onion and coarsely grate. Squeeze handfuls of grated vegetables tightly to wring out as much liquid as possible.

2. Transfer vegetables to mixing bowl and stir in matzoh meal, baking powder, egg substitute, parsley

and plenty of salt and pepper. Latkes should be highly seasoned.

3. Spray a baking sheet with oil. Spoon small mounds of potato mixture onto the sheet to form pancakes 2½ inches in diameter. Leave 1 inch between each.

4. Bake-fry latkes until bottoms are golden brown, 8–10 minutes. Spray tops of latkes with oil. Turn them, and cook until tops are golden brown. Repeat with remaining dough. Serve at once with sour cream or applesauce.

Yield: 50–60 small latkes; 8–10 servings

NOTE: *These latkes are "bake fried," just enough to crisp and brown them. Olive oil is traditional, but you may use vegetable oil. Yukon Gold potatoes, which have a more buttery flavor than Idahos, give the latkes a rich taste. Bake-frying works better with smaller pieces of food—they crisp better—so form the latkes in small discs.*

—STEVEN RAICHLEN

POTATO PANCAKES WITH CELERY ROOT

dairy

ADAPTED FROM *Vegetables in the French Style*

2 large potatoes
1 small celery root (about 3½ ounces)
Coarse sea salt and freshly ground pepper to taste
4 tablespoons butter
1 tablespoon peanut oil
1 medium onion, preferably white
Pale heart at the center of a head of celery and a few
  of its leaves
¼ cup Crème Fraîche (page 431) or whipped
  heavy cream
Pinch of freshly grated nutmeg

1. Peel the potatoes and celery root and wipe them clean. Grate them finely. Mix and season with salt and pepper.
2. With your hands, divide the grated vegetables into 8 balls and flatten each into a pancake about ⅝-inch thick.
3. Heat the butter and oil in a large skillet over medium heat. Add the pancakes and cook until lightly browned on one side, then turn them over. Press them with a spatula to help hold them together. Cook for a total of 15–20 minutes, turning occasionally.
4. Meanwhile, peel the onion and cut it into thin slices. Salt lightly and put the slices in a strainer to let the salt draw out some of the onion's liquid. Pluck some of the palest leaves from the celery heart and set them aside.
5. When the pancakes are cooked, arrange them, overlapping, around the edge of an ovenproof platter. Spread some crème fraîche or whipped cream on each pancake, then sprinkle with nutmeg and top with thinly sliced onion.
6. Put the platter under the broiler or in a very hot oven for a couple of minutes. Before serving, put the sliced celery heart and leaves in the center of the platter. Serve immediately.

Yield: 4 servings

—MOIRA HODGSON

POTATO-ZUCCHINI PANCAKES

pareve, dairy

1 medium zucchini, about ½ pound
1 large Idaho potato, about 10 ounces
3 tablespoons very finely minced scallions
1 tablespoon finely minced fresh dill
1 egg, lightly beaten
3 tablespoons flour
Salt to taste
Freshly ground black pepper to taste
Vegetable oil for frying
Freshly grated Parmesan cheese, plain yogurt or sour
  cream, optional

1. Scrub the zucchini, trim off the ends, cut in quarters lengthwise and then in ½-inch slices. Place in a food processor fitted with a metal blade and process with the on-off or pulse control until uniformly grated to a medium-fine texture. Or the zucchini may be grated by hand on a metal grater. Place it in a fine sieve, press out as much moisture as possible and transfer to a mixing bowl.

2. Scrub the potato, but do not peel. Cut away any nicks or bruises, and dice the potato into ½-inch cubes. Grate in a food processor or by hand, following the same process outlined in Step 1. Drain the grated potato in a fine sieve, pressing out as much moisture as possible, and then mix with the zucchini.

3. Add the scallions, dill, egg, flour, salt and pepper. Mix well.

4. Heat oil for frying to a depth of ¼ inch in 1 or 2 large, heavy skillets, preferably cast iron. Add the batter, a tablespoon at a time, flattening it with the back of a spoon into 3-inch rounds, or use ½ tablespoon at a time to make pancakes about 2 inches in diameter. Fry until lightly golden, turning the pancakes once. Add more oil as necessary, and stir the unused batter from time to time.

5. Drain the pancakes on absorbent paper briefly before serving.

Yield: About 16 (3-inch) pancakes or 32 (2-inch) pancakes, serving 4–6 as a first course or side dish

—FLORENCE FABRICANT

CURRIED SWEET-POTATO LATKES

dairy

ADAPTED FROM the New Prospect Café, Brooklyn, in *Jewish Cooking in America*

1 pound sweet potatoes, peeled
½ cup all-purpose flour
2 teaspoons sugar
1 teaspoon brown sugar
1 teaspoon baking powder
½ teaspoon cayenne pepper or to taste
2 teaspoons curry powder
1 teaspoon cumin
Salt to taste
Freshly ground pepper to taste
2 large eggs, beaten
½ cup milk, approximately
Peanut oil for frying

1. Grate the sweet potatoes coarsely. In a separate bowl mix the flour, sugar, brown sugar, baking powder, cayenne pepper, curry powder, cumin, salt and pepper.

2. Add the eggs and just enough milk to the dry ingredients to make a stiff batter. Add the potatoes and mix. The batter should be moist but not runny; if too stiff, add more milk.

3. Heat ¼ inch of peanut oil in a sauté pan until it is barely smoking. Drop in the batter by tablespoons and flatten. Cook several minutes on each side until golden. Drain on paper towels and serve.

Yield: 16 (3-inch) pancakes

—JOAN NATHAN

FRESH GREEN PEA PANCAKES

pareve

ADAPTED FROM *Jean-Georges: Cooking at Home with a Four-Star Chef*

8 ounces (about 1½ cups) fresh or frozen and
    thawed shelled peas
1 egg
1 tablespoon flour
Coarse sea salt and freshly ground pepper to taste
About 2 tablespoons canola, grapeseed or other
    neutral-flavored oil

1. Bring a small pot of water to a boil and blanch the peas for a minute. Drain, then run under water until cold.
2. Set ⅓ cup of the peas aside and puree the remaining peas in a blender with the egg and 2 tablespoons of water until smooth.
3. Put the puree in a bowl and beat in the flour along with a pinch of salt, pepper and the reserved whole peas.
4. Put a tablespoon of oil in a large skillet and turn the heat to medium. When the oil is hot, pour most of it out; you need just enough to coat the bottom of the pan.
5. Spoon the batter into the skillet, using a tablespoon, making pancakes about 2 inches across. Cook gently about 3 minutes on each side, taking care to cook them through before they brown too much. Add more oil as necessary and continue to cook until all the batter is used up. These are best served hot.

Yield: About 12 small pancakes

—MOIRA HODGSON

OLD JERUSALEM ZUCCHINI PANCAKES

pareve

ADAPTED FROM *The Delights of Jerusalem*

6 zucchini (3 pounds)
Salt and freshly ground pepper to taste
1 onion, peeled and diced
2 tablespoons chopped parsley
2 tablespoons chopped dill
2 large eggs
½ cup matzoh meal
1 tablespoon vegetable oil and oil for frying

1. Grate the unpeeled zucchini, place over a strainer, sprinkle with salt and drain for ½ hour. Squeeze to remove remaining liquid.
2. In a mixing bowl, place the zucchini, salt and pepper, onion, parsley, dill, eggs, matzoh meal and 1 tablespoon oil. Form into small patties.
3. In a heated skillet, pour a thin layer of vegetable oil. When sizzling, fry the pancakes for a few minutes on each side. Drain and serve.

Yield: 20 patties

—JOAN NATHAN

ALAYNE ZATULOV'S GIANT VEGETABLE LATKE

pareve

1 pound Idaho potatoes, scrubbed but unpeeled
  and shredded

½ pound carrots, scraped and shredded

1 cup shredded onion

¾ cup finely shredded celery root

1 Granny Smith apple, peeled, cored and
  coarsely shredded

2 eggs, lightly beaten

½ cup finely minced parsley

¼ cup flour

1 teaspoon dried thyme

Salt and freshly ground black pepper to taste

½ cup cooking oil

1. Combine shredded potatoes, carrots, onion, celery root and apple in a bowl. Stir in eggs, parsley, flour and thyme. Season with salt and pepper.

2. Heat half the oil until very hot in a heavy 10-inch skillet. Spread vegetable mixture into the skillet in an even layer, covering the entire surface.

3. Fry vegetable mixture undisturbed until edges begin to show color, 5–8 minutes. If it sticks to the pan, gently release it with a thin spatula.

4. When the underside is golden, slide the pancake onto a large plate. Invert another plate over it and flip it over. Add remaining oil to the skillet, and when it is hot, slide the pancake back into the skillet to brown the other side. Fry until crisp.

Yield: 8 servings

NOTE: *This pancake can be served with 12 ounces fresh mushrooms, sliced and sautéed, spooned on top.*

—FLORENCE FABRICANT

GRAINS, LEGUMES
AND PASTA

BASICALLY HUMBLE FOODS, GRAINS AND THE DRIED BEANS KNOWN AS LEGUMES ILLUSTRATE MAN'S GENIUS FOR MAKING MUCH OUT OF little. Seeking variety by way of enhanced flavor and, perhaps, to use other available ingredients that add nutrients as well as interest, cooks in all cultures created dishes of these dietary staples that have become comforting classics. Similarly, pasta, basically a grain product (except for Asian noodles made of vegetable starches), appears in myriad forms to which are added countless sauces, toppings and seasonings that vary from one culture to another.

Among the most ancient foods of the Jews, some of these legumes and grains date back to biblical times, although recipes for them today are results of the climate and culinary customs of the lands in which Jews settled. Potatoes were the primary source of calories to Eastern European Jews, but those who could afford to also used rice to enhance soup or rich gravies, or with meat as stuffing for peppers or cabbage, and on the nicely gritty buckwheat groats, kasha, most deliciously sautéed with mushrooms and onions or tossed with pasta bow ties to make the beloved dairy dish *kasha varnishkas.* Perhaps "Tex-Mex" kasha will be the new cutting-edge hit.

Barley was favored primarily for soups and a few baked dishes and stews, and Romanian Jews added their country's cornmeal porridge, *mamaliga*, to the Ashkenazic diet. Pasta dishes were generally derived from the noodles and dumplings of Germany and Lithuania, although today an Italian array is represented on Jewish menus, especially as dairy dishes such as ziti with smoked salmon, and linguine with pistachio-almond pesto, to say nothing of Chinese creations such as cold sesame noodles.

To Sephardic and Middle Eastern Jews, rice in spicy pilafs and as vegetable stuffings remain staples. Couscous, the chewy semolina grain native to North Africa, brings exotic touches to menus with hints of cinnamon and cumin, saffron or turmeric. There is even a luxurious sweet couscous, akin to rice pudding, with almonds, golden raisins, lemon and honey, accented by drifts of cool yogurt.

Among legumes, chickpeas are favorites, cooked and mashed into croquettes that are lightly fried in vegetable oil and alternate with dried fava beans to make the crunchy Middle Eastern street food, falafel. But chickpeas also get more soigné treatment, as do fava beans with hints of lemon, honey, olives or ginger. Cold boiled and seasoned chickpeas, known as *arbes* or *nahit*, are the traditional nibble at a bris, the ceremony of circumcision and naming of a baby boy and, in some Jewish cultures, are also served on the first Sabbath a week after the birth.

MUSHROOM AND BARLEY CASSEROLE

meat

ADAPTED FROM *The New York Times Menu Cook Book*

> 1 large onion, chopped
> ½ pound white mushrooms, sliced
> 5 tablespoons unsalted margarine
> 1 cup pearl barley
> 2 cups beef stock or Chicken Stock
>   (page 48)

1. Preheat the oven to 350 degrees.

2. Cook the onion and mushrooms in the margarine until onion is wilted and mushroom juices have evaporated. Add the barley and brown lightly. Pour the mixture into a greased casserole. Pour 1 cup of the stock over the barley and cover. Bring to a boil.

3. Bake the casserole, covered, for 25–30 minutes. Add the remaining stock. Continue to cook, covered, for 15 minutes or longer, until the liquid is absorbed and barley is tender.

Yield: 4 servings

NOTE: *For a dairy or pareve meal, substitute Vegetable Stock (page 51) for the chicken or beef stock.*

BARLEY RISOTTO

pareve

ADAPTED FROM Luma

FOR THE STOCK:

> 1 carrot, cut into 4 pieces
> 1 stalk celery, cut into 4 pieces
> 1 onion
> 1 clove garlic, mashed
> 5 sprigs parsley
> 1 teaspoon black peppercorns

FOR THE RISOTTO:

> ½ cup barley
> 1 teaspoon canola oil
> 3 tablespoons minced carrots
> 3 tablespoons minced onions
> 3 tablespoons minced celery

> 1 sprig rosemary
> 1 bay leaf
> 1 teaspoon salt, or to taste
> ¼ teaspoon freshly ground black pepper, or to
>   taste

1. To make the stock, place all the ingredients with 5½ cups of cold water in a medium-size saucepan. Simmer, uncovered, over medium heat for 1 hour. Strain and set aside.

2. To make the risotto, place the barley in a heavy skillet over low heat and toast—shaking the pan frequently—for 20 minutes, or until the barley turns light brown and smells nutty. Remove from the heat and set aside.

3. In a large, heavy skillet, heat the oil over medium-low heat. Add the minced carrots, onions and celery and cook, stirring, for 3 minutes, or until the onions are soft and translucent. Add the barley and stir to coat the grains. Add the rosemary, bay leaf and 1½ cups of reserved vegetable stock. Add the salt and pepper and simmer, covered, until the barley is ten-der and the liquid is absorbed, about 35 minutes. Add more stock if the risotto is too dry.

Yield: 2 main-course servings or 6 side-dish servings

—MOLLY O'NEILL

BULGUR WHEAT PILAF

dairy, pareve

2 tablespoons melted clarified butter or olive oil
½ cup broken-up uncooked noodles (preferably fine)
1 cup bulgur wheat
2 cups water
½ teaspoon salt, or to taste
Pepper to taste
4 tablespoons butter or margarine
6 tablespoons chopped fresh basil, or 2 tablespoons dried
¼ cup chopped walnuts
¾ cup canned chickpeas, drained

Put clarified butter or olive oil in a deep saucepan, add noodles and cook over medium heat, stirring constantly until golden brown. Add wheat and mix thoroughly. Add all remaining ingredients, boil, cover, reduce heat to very low and cook 20 minutes. Fluff before serving.

Yield: 4 servings

NOTE: *Use olive oil or margarine at meat meals.*

—ROBERT FARRAR CAPON

MAMALIGA • (ROMANIAN CORNMEAL)—BASIC AND DAIRY

dairy, pareve

FOR BASIC MAMALIGA:

pareve

5 cups water
Salt to taste
2 cups yellow cornmeal

1. Bring 4 cups of water to a boil in a 2-quart casserole and add salt to taste.
2. Combine cornmeal and remaining cup of cold water and add it gradually to the boiling water, stirring constantly with a wooden spoon. Cook over low heat, stirring, for 25 minutes. It will be very, very thick.
3. If possible, invert the casserole and let the mass fall out onto a round platter. If it does not unmold, serve it directly from the casserole.

dairy

¼ *cup butter*
2 *cloves garlic, finely chopped*
2 *cups crumbled salty cheese, such as feta*
1 *cup sour cream*

If the mamaliga unmolds in one piece, use a clean string and slice the cake in half to produce two layers. Cover the bottom layer with hot butter blended with garlic. Sprinkle with crumbled cheese. Add the top layer. Serve with sour cream on the top. If the mamaliga does not unmold, serve it by spoonfuls directly from the casserole, sprinkled with the garlic butter and cheese, with the sour cream on the side.

Yield: 6 or more servings

NOTE: *Basic Mamaliga can be served in place of potatoes or other starches at meals. The dairy version may also be served with a fried egg on top of the melted cheese. Other variations include omitting the sour cream or substituting onion for the garlic. For a tasty dish made with leftover mamaliga, pack it into an oiled loaf pan and refrigerate overnight. It may then be sliced, dipped in beaten egg and crumbs and fried in a little butter or oil until lightly browned.*

—CRAIG CLAIBORNE

GOLDEN COUSCOUS

meat

2 *tablespoons extra-virgin olive oil*
1 *large yellow pepper, seeded and diced*
1 *medium onion, finely chopped*
Kernels from 4 ears fresh yellow corn
Salt and freshly ground black pepper to taste
1½ *cups Chicken Stock (page 48; see also Note below)*
2 *teaspoons ground turmeric*
1 *teaspoon ground cumin*
1 *cup instant couscous*

1. Heat 1 tablespoon of the oil in a skillet, add the pepper and onion and sauté over medium heat until golden. Stir in the corn and cook briefly for a few minutes. Season to taste with salt and pepper and set aside.

2. Bring the chicken stock to a boil in a saucepan, stir in the turmeric and cumin and add 1 tablespoon of olive oil. Stir in the couscous, remove from heat, cover and let stand for 5 minutes.

3. Fluff the couscous with a fork and fold in the pepper and corn mixture. Fluff again and serve warm or at room temperature.

Yield: 4–6 servings

NOTE: *Vegetable stock or water may be substituted at a dairy or pareve meal.*

—FLORENCE FABRICANT

COUSCOUS WITH APRICOTS

dairy

½ *cup dried apricots*
Water
1 tablespoon lemon juice
1 tablespoon unsalted butter
¾ *cup instant couscous*
Freshly ground black pepper to taste

1. Cut up apricots coarsely and combine with water. Follow package directions for proper amount of water.

2. Add lemon juice and butter, stir and cover. Bring water to boil.

3. When water boils stir in couscous and continue stirring until water boils again.

4. Remove pot from heat, cover and allow to sit 2–3 minutes, until water is completely absorbed and couscous is tender. Add pepper to taste.

Yield: 3 servings

—MARIAN BURROS

BLACK OLIVE COUSCOUS

meat
ADAPTED FROM David Burke

1 cup plus 2 tablespoons Chicken Stock (page 48)
¾ *cup instant couscous*
3 tablespoons Black Olive Paste (page 418)
1 tablespoon extra-virgin olive oil
1 tablespoon finely minced carrot
1 tablespoon finely minced celery
1 tablespoon finely minced fresh coriander leaves

½ *teaspoon ground cumin*
Salt and freshly ground black pepper to taste

1. Bring stock to a boil in a saucepan. Stir in couscous. Cover and set aside about 5 minutes, or until all liquid is absorbed.

2. Fold in remaining ingredients and serve hot or at room temperature.

Yield: 4 servings

—FLORENCE FABRICANT

ZUCCHINI COUSCOUS

pareve

1 cup instant couscous
½ cup boiling water
2 tablespoons olive oil
2 cups zucchini, cut into ¼-inch dice
2 tablespoons minced fresh mint leaves
2 tablespoons minced flat-leaf parsley
¼ cup fresh lemon juice
Salt and freshly ground black pepper to taste

1. In a heatproof bowl, cover the couscous with the boiling water. Use a fork to gently separate the grains of couscous. Stir in I tablespoon of the olive oil, place in the refrigerator and continue stirring frequently with a fork until cool, about 30 minutes.

2. Meanwhile, in another bowl combine the diced zucchini, mint, parsley, lemon juice and remaining olive oil. When the couscous is cool, fold in the zucchini mixture and chill for at least 30 minutes before serving. Season to taste with salt and pepper.

Yield: 4 servings

—MOLLY O'NEILL

BASIC KASHA

pareve

1 cup kasha (buckwheat groats)
1 large egg, lightly beaten
1½ cups boiling water or stock
1 teaspoon salt, or to taste

1. Mix kasha with egg in a heavy I quart saucepan. Place over medium heat and stir with a fork for 2 or 3 minutes, until the grains are separate.

2. Add liquid and salt. Stir. Cover and cook over low heat 10–15 minutes, until the liquid is absorbed. Fine- or medium-grain kasha will cook faster than whole or coarse groats.

Yield: 3 cups

NOTE: *To reheat kasha, steam it over hot water in the top of a double boiler.*

—FLORENCE FABRICANT

KASHA VARNISHKAS

dairy

1 cup kasha (buckwheat groats)
1 egg, beaten
1 onion, chopped fine
2 cups water
½ teaspoon salt, or to taste
2 cups cooked bow-tie noodles
6 tablespoons butter, or to taste

1. Put the kasha into a deep saucepan, add the egg and mix well.

2. Set the pan over medium heat and cook, stirring constantly, until the egg is completely dried out and the grains of kasha are all separated.

3. Add the onion and stir for 30 seconds.

4. Add water and salt to taste, boil, cover, reduce heat to very low and cook 20 minutes.

5. Meanwhile, heat noodles in melted butter. When kasha is done, add noodles and butter and toss well to mix. Serve hot.

Yield: 4–6 servings

—ROBERT FARRAR CAPON

KASHA WITH MUSHROOMS

meat

1 cup whole or coarse-grain buckwheat groats (kasha)
1 egg white
2 cups diced mushrooms, preferably shiitake
1½ cups well-seasoned beef stock or Chicken Stock
  (page 48)
1½ teaspoons fresh thyme leaves
Salt and freshly ground black pepper to taste

1. Mix the groats with the egg white in a heavy 1½-quart saucepan. Place over medium heat and stir with a fork for 2–3 minutes, until the grains are separated.

2. Add the mushrooms and stock. Bring to a simmer, add the thyme, cover and cook over very low heat for 10–15 minutes, until the liquid has been absorbed.

3. Season to taste with salt and pepper and serve.

Yield: 6 servings

—FLORENCE FABRICANT

"TEX-MEX" KASHA

dairy

   1 tablespoon vegetable oil
   1 large onion, chopped
   1 stalk celery, chopped
   1 large green pepper, chopped
   1 clove garlic, minced
   1 teaspoon dried oregano
   ½ teaspoon cumin
   1 teaspoon pure mild chili powder (see Note below)
   ¾ cup buckwheat groats (kasha), preferably whole
   3 cups canned tomatoes
   Freshly ground black pepper to taste
   1 cup coarsely grated Monterey Jack cheese

1. Heat oil in medium skillet. Add onion, celery, pepper and garlic and sauté until onion is soft. Stir in oregano, cumin and chili powder, along with kasha and tomatoes. Season to taste with pepper; reduce heat and cover. Cook over low heat for about 20 minutes, until liquid has evaporated and kasha is cooked.
2. Sprinkle with cheese; cover and cook a minute or two longer until cheese melts.

Yield: 3 or 4 servings

NOTE: *Pure chili powder contains nothing but powdered dry chili; it is not blended with other spices or herbs. It can be found in many specialty food shops. If you wish to freeze the kasha, omit cheese. When ready to serve, defrost the kasha, reheat it slowly. Then follow Step 2.*

—MARIAN BURROS

FRITZIE ABADI'S SYRIAN WHITE RICE

pareve

   6 tablespoons vegetable oil
   1 cup chopped yellow onions
   1¼ teaspoons kosher salt
   2 cups long-grain rice
   3 tablespoons pine nuts

1. In a large, heavy saucepan, heat 4 tablespoons of the oil over medium heat. Add the onions and cook, stirring, until the onions just turn golden (do not let them brown), about 5 minutes. Add 4 cups of cold water and the salt and bring to a boil.
2. Add the rice, stir and cook, uncovered, until the water is level with the rice, about 10 minutes. Cover the pot, adjust the heat to low and cook until the rice is tender, about 10 minutes longer.
3. Meanwhile, heat the remaining 2 tablespoons of oil in a small skillet set over medium-high heat. When the oil just begins to bubble, add the pine nuts and cook until the nuts are golden brown. Immediately drain them, discard the oil and set them aside.
4. When the rice is done, scatter the pine nuts over the top.

Yield: 8–10 servings

—MOLLY O'NEILL

BASIC PILAF

dairy, pareve, meat

2 tablespoons butter or extra-virgin olive oil

1 medium onion, chopped

Salt and pepper to taste

1 cup white rice

1 cup chopped tomatoes (canned with work fine; use
   the juice), optional

1–1½ cups chicken, beef or vegetable stock

½ cup chopped fresh parsley

2 tablespoons fresh lemon juice

1. Put butter or oil in a large, deep skillet over medium heat. Add onion and a large pinch of salt, and cook, stirring occasionally, until onion turns translucent, 5–10 minutes. Add rice and cook, stir-ring occasionally, until rice is glossy and begins to brown, 3–5 minutes. Season with salt and pepper.

2. Add tomatoes, if desired, and stir for a minute; add stock (the smaller amount if you use tomatoes), and stir. Bring mixture to a boil, cook for a minute or two, then reduce heat to low and cover. Cook about 15 minutes, or until most of the liquid is absorbed. Turn heat to absolute minimum, and cook another 15–30 minutes; if stove is electric, turn heat off and let pan sit on burner for same amount of time. Stir in parsley and lemon juice, and serve.

Yield: 4 side-dish or 2 main-course servings

NOTE: *Use olive oil with chicken or beef stock.*

—MARK BITTMAN

INDIAN-SPICED RICE • (MARSALA BHAT)

pareve

ADAPTED FROM Lavinia Abraham

1 large onion, finely sliced

4 ounces margarine

2 cups basmati rice

½ pound fresh peas

¼ cup golden raisins

1 hot green chili, finely minced

1 clove garlic, finely minced

½-inch piece fresh ginger, finely minced

½ cup chopped cashew nuts

2 ripe medium tomatoes, seeded and coarsely chopped

Salt to taste

½ teaspoon sugar

4 cups boiling water

Grated meat from ¼ fresh coconut

¼ cup blanched almond slices, toasted

1½ teaspoons chopped fresh cilantro leaves

1. In 2 ounces of margarine, sauté onions until golden brown.

2. Remove onion and add remaining margarine to pan. When it is hot return half of the onion to the pan with rice, peas, raisins, chili, garlic, ginger and cashews. Sauté over low heat, stirring constantly, for about 1 minute.

3. Add tomatoes, salt to taste, sugar and boiling water; raise heat and bring to boil. Cook until about ½ cup of liquid remains in pan. Lower heat, cover and simmer until rice is cooked.

4. Sprinkle with grated coconut, toasted almonds, remaining onion and cilantro.

Yield: 10 servings

— MARIAN BURROS

BASMATI RICE WITH COCONUT MILK AND GINGER

meat

    2 cups basmati rice
    1½ cups Coconut Milk (page 430)
    1 cup Chicken Broth (page 48), canned or fresh
    1 teaspoon kosher salt, more to taste
    3 scallions, thinly sliced
    2 tablespoons finely chopped ginger

1. Place rice in a fine strainer and rinse with cold water until water runs clear. Transfer to a medium saucepan.

Add 1 cup water, coconut milk, chicken broth and salt. Cover and place over medium-high heat. Bring liquid to a boil, then reduce and simmer until liquid has been absorbed and rice is tender, about 15 minutes.

2. Remove from heat and stir in scallions and ginger. Add a little more coconut milk if rice is too dry. Season to taste with salt. Serve.

Yield: 4 servings

— AMANDA HESSER

PERSIAN STEAMED WHITE RICE
WITH TAHDEEG CRUST • (CHELLO)

pareve

ADAPTED FROM Frida Golsaz

    2 cups long-grain basmati rice
    7 cups water
    1 teaspoon salt, if desired
    4 tablespoons corn oil
    ½ teaspoon turmeric
    2 threads saffron, mixed with 3 tablespoons water

1. Wash and drain rice.

2. Put water in a medium-size pot (nonstick preferred) and bring to a boil.

3. Add rice and boil for 7–10 minutes, until the rice is beginning to soften yet still firm.

4. Remove from heat, drain rice.

5. Place pot back on medium heat and add oil and turmeric.

6. Heap rice on top in pyramid shape without mixing. Cover and cook 10–15 minutes with a towel placed between pot and cover.

7. When rice begins to steam, lower heat and continue to cook for 45 minutes.

8. Remove cover and let cool. When ready to serve, mix 1–2 tablespoons saffron water with ½ cup cooked rice and sprinkle mixture on top of white rice.

NOTE: *A bonus is to be found in the bottom of the pot, which yields a yellow, crispy crust called tahdeeg, considered a delicacy, and often served with a dousing of stew or gravy.*

—AVITAL LOURIA HAHN

PERSIAN RICE WITH DILL AND LIMA BEANS •
(POLLOW SHEVED BAKRALEE)

pareve

ADAPTED FROM Frida Golsaz

10 cups water
1 teaspoon salt
1½ teaspoons turmeric
2½ cups basmati rice
5 tablespoons corn oil
20 ounces lima beans, partially thawed
1 bunch fresh dill, washed, dried and chopped
5 tablespoons ground cardamom seed

1. Boil water, salt and 1 teaspoon turmeric.

2. Add rice, boil for about 10 minutes, or until half cooked and still firm.

3. Drain rice.

4. In large pot (nonstick preferred) place oil mixed with ½ teaspoon turmeric.

5. Place a layer of white rice, then a layer of beans and dill, and sprinkle with ground cardamom seed. Repeat and build up in pyramid shape without mixing.

6. Cook on medium heat, covered, with a kitchen towel between pot and cover to absorb steam.

7. When the rice begins to steam, after about 15 minutes, reduce heat to low and continue to cook for about another hour. Cool with lid half off.

—AVITAL LOURIA HAHN

PERSIAN RICE, LENTILS AND CURRANTS · (POLLOW ADDAS KESHMESH)

pareve

ADAPTED FROM Frida Golsaz

7 cups water

1 teaspoon salt

½ teaspoon turmeric

1½ cups rice

3 tablespoons corn oil

1½ cups lentils, quickly boiled in 6 cups water until half-cooked

1 cup currants

5 tablespoons ground cumin

1. Boil water with salt and turmeric.

2. Add rice and boil for 10–15 minutes, until it begins to soften but is still firm.

3. Remove from heat and drain.

4. In large pot, add oil.

5. Add a layer of rice.

6. Continue layering with half-cooked lentils, currants, cumin and rice in a pyramid shape.

7. Cook on medium heat, covered, with a kitchen towel between lid and pot, for about 10–15 minutes until rice begins to steam.

8. Reduce heat and continue steaming for about 45 minutes. Cool with lid half off.

Yield: 6 servings

—AVITAL LOURIA HAHN

VEGGIE BURGERS

pareve

ADAPTED FROM Joan Swensen

½ cup brown lentils

½ cup barley

½ cup brown rice

2 tablespoons olive oil

1⅓ cups minced carrots

¾ cup minced onion

¾ cup minced celery

2 tablespoons toasted or dry-roasted sunflower seeds

1 teaspoon oregano

1½ teaspoons salt

Freshly ground black pepper to taste

1 teaspoon minced thyme

1 tablespoon dried basil

1½ teaspoons minced garlic

2 large eggs

½ cup flour

2 tablespoons canola or vegetable oil

1. The day before serving, in a large (4- to 6-quart) saucepan over medium-low heat, bring 4 cups of water to a simmer. Add lentils. Cover and simmer 15 minutes. Add barley. Cover and simmer 15 minutes more. Add brown rice. Cover and simmer

20 minutes, or until the water is absorbed and the rice is al dente. Do not let the pan burn dry. (If necessary, stir in a small amount of water.) Remove from heat and set aside.

2. In a medium sauté pan over medium-low heat, combine the olive oil, carrots, onion and celery. Sauté until the vegetables are tender, about 10 minutes. Add sunflower seeds, oregano, salt, pepper, thyme, basil and garlic. Sauté a minute or two. Remove from heat.

3. Combine grains and vegetables in a large covered container and refrigerate overnight.

4. On the day of serving, add eggs and flour to the grain mixture. Mix well. With an ice cream scoop or by hand, form balls 3½–4 inches in diameter. Flatten into disks about ¾ inch thick.

5. In a large sauté pan or skillet over medium-high heat, warm the canola oil. Add the burgers and cook until golden brown, 3–4 minutes a side. Serve immediately.

Yield: 10 burgers

—DONNA ST. GEORGE

CHICKPEAS IN GINGER SAUCE

pareve

ADAPTED FROM *Classic Indian Cooking*

4 cups cooked or canned chickpeas, with 1 cup of their liquid
¼ cup neutral oil, like canola
2 cups chopped onion
2 tablespoons minced ginger
2 teaspoons minced garlic
2 teaspoons ground coriander
½ teaspoon ground cardamom
½ teaspoon mango powder, or 1½ teaspoons lemon juice
¼ teaspoon cayenne pepper
¼ teaspoon black pepper
1 medium tomato, chopped
Salt to taste
1 medium onion, thinly sliced
1 green chili, seeded, stemmed and shredded

1. Drain chickpeas, reserving liquid. Put oil in large skillet and turn heat to medium-high. Add chopped onions; cook 5 minutes, or until they turn light brown, stirring occasionally. Add ginger and garlic, reduce heat to medium and cook 2 minutes, stirring.

2. Add coriander, cardamom, mango powder (but not lemon juice), cayenne and black pepper. Stir; then add tomato. Cook until tomato becomes saucy and begins to separate from the oil, about 5 minutes. Add the reserved chickpea liquid, the lemon juice if you are using it, salt and ½ cup water.

3. Cover and turn heat to low; simmer about 10 minutes, or until mixture is thickened. Add chickpeas, cover and cook 10 minutes longer. Taste and adjust seasoning. Serve, passing sliced onion and chili at the table.

Yield: 4 servings

—MARK BITTMAN

CHICKPEAS WITH SORREL

pareve
ADAPTED FROM *How to Eat*

1 tablespoons olive oil
1 small onion, chopped
2 cloves garlic, finely sliced
Large pinch ground cumin
½ dried red chili pepper, crumbled
Kosher salt
⅔ cup or large handful shredded sorrel leaves
    (stems removed)
1 (15-ounce) can chickpeas, drained

1. In a medium pan, heat olive oil over medium heat. Add onion, garlic and cumin and stir. Sprinkle chili pepper on top and season with salt. Cook until onion is soft but not brown, about 3 to 5 minutes. Lower heat if necessary.
2. Stir in sorrel, then chickpeas; cook until chickpeas are warm. Taste and adjust seasoning. Serve.

Yield: 3 servings

—AMANDA HESSER

WARM CHICKPEAS WITH LEMON AND OLIVES

pareve

2 cups warm cooked chickpeas, rinsed and warmed
    briefly if canned ones are used
2 tablespoons chopped sweet onion
1 clove garlic, finely minced
12 pitted green olives, coarsely chopped
1 tablespoon finely chopped fresh cilantro
1 tablespoon chopped lemon peel
Juice of 1½ lemons

4 tablespoons extra-virgin olive oil
Salt and freshly ground black pepper to taste

1. Put the chickpeas in a bowl. Fold in the onion, garlic, olives, cilantro and lemon peel.
2. Mix the lemon juice with the oil. Pour over the chickpeas, season with salt and pepper and serve.

Yield: 4 servings

—FLORENCE FABRICANT

FAVA BEANS WITH HONEY, LIME AND THYME

dairy

ADAPTED FROM David Bouley

25–30 fava bean pods (see Note)
3 quarts water
Salt to taste
2 teaspoons honey
3 sprigs fresh thyme, leaves removed from stems
Juice of 1 lime
1 teaspoon unsalted butter

1. Shell beans from pods. Bring 3 quarts of well-salted water to a boil, add beans and blanch them for 2 minutes. Drain and place in a bowl of ice water for a few minutes. This loosens coats from large beans. Remove coats.

2. In a small saucepan put honey and heat for about 30 seconds. Add thyme and lime juice. Whisk in butter and simmer for a few seconds, then add beans. Reheat beans in sauce and serve.

Yield: 4–6 servings

NOTE: *1 pound of green beans or asparagus, cut in 1-inch lengths and blanched in boiling water, can be substituted for fava beans.*

—FLORENCE FABRICANT

GEORGIAN BEANS · (LOBIO)

pareve

ADAPTED FROM Jack Murphy

2 cups dry red kidney beans
1 large onion, chopped fine
2 carrots, chopped fine
1 stalk celery, chopped fine
8 pitted prunes
⅓ cup plus 1 tablespoon balsamic vinegar
3 cloves garlic
1 tablespoon tamarind paste (see Glossary, page 586)
½ teaspoon hot pepper flakes
1 teaspoon coriander seed
½ teaspoon fenugreek (see Glossary, page 585)
5 tablespoons olive oil
¼ cup fresh cilantro
¼ teaspoon salt, or to taste
Freshly ground pepper to taste

1. Soak beans overnight or cook beans for 2 minutes in plenty of water and allow to sit for 1 hour.

2. Drain water from beans and add plenty of fresh water to cover with onion, carrots and celery. Cover and simmer for about 1 hour, until beans are tender but not mushy. Drain and set aside.

3. Simmer the prunes in ⅓ cup of the vinegar for 20 minutes.

4. With food processor running, put garlic through tube. Add remaining vinegar, tamarind paste, hot pepper flakes, coriander seed, fenugreek, olive oil, prunes and vinegar and process to a paste. Add the cilantro and process to chop fine. Season with salt and pepper. Stir into warm beans.

Yield: 3 servings as a main dish

NOTE: *Jack Murphy, the executive producer for the Eurasian division, formerly the U.S.S.R. division, of the Voice of* America, *spent enough time in the Soviet Union to learn how to cook something from each republic and make substitutions when some ingredients are not available. For an ingredient common in Georgian recipes—sour plums—he cooked prunes in balsamic vinegar and added some tamarind to approximate the flavor quite closely.*

—MARIAN BURROS

SPICED LENTILS AND PUMPKIN

meat

ADAPTED FROM Susan Regis

> *1 small pumpkin, about 4 pounds*
> *1 tablespoon pareve margarine*
> *1 tablespoon sugar*
> *Salt and freshly ground pepper to taste*
> *3 tablespoons olive oil*
> *1 carrot, diced*
> *1 teaspoon chopped ginger*
> *4 shallots, minced*
> *1 leek rinsed and minced*
> *1 bay leaf*
> *1 tablespoon curry powder*
> *1 cup lentils*
> *1½ cups Chicken Broth (page 48)*
> *1 cup water*
> *2 tablespoons minced cilantro*

1. Preheat the oven to 400 degrees.
2. Cut the pumpkin into 4 wedges. Peel and remove the seeds; cut 3 of the wedges into 1-inch cubes and set aside. Cut the last quarter into 4 pieces.
3. Grease a baking sheet and place the 4 pieces on it. Sprinkle with sugar; season lightly with salt and pepper. Roast until the pumpkin is soft and caramelized, about 15–20 minutes. Reserve for garnish.
4. Put the olive oil in a heavy-bottomed saucepan over medium-low heat. Add the carrot, ginger, shallots, leek, bay leaf, pumpkin cubes and curry and cook for 5 minutes. Add the lentils, and toss to coat with oil.
5. Add the chicken broth and water and cook over medium heat until the lentils and vegetables are tender, about 20–30 minutes. Season with salt and pepper. Add the cilantro. Spoon onto 4 plates, and top with a piece of the caramelized pumpkin.

Yield: 4 servings

—MOLLY O'NEILL

BLACK-EYED PEAS WITH SPINACH

pareve

<small>ADAPTED FROM</small> Claudia Roden

1 cup dried black-eyed peas
Coarse salt and freshly ground pepper to taste
1½ pounds fresh spinach
1 large onion, finely chopped
1 clove garlic, minced
5 tablespoons olive oil

1. Cover the black-eyed peas with water and bring to a boil. Simmer gently until tender (about 30 minutes). Season to taste with salt and pepper after the peas have cooked for 20 minutes.

2. Wash the spinach and remove stems. Shred leaves and drain well.

3. Soften the onion and garlic in the olive oil and cook until soft in a large skillet. Add the spinach and sauté, stirring constantly until wilted. Season to taste and add the drained peas. Heat through, correct seasoning and serve.

Yield: 4–6 servings

<small>NOTE:</small> *This dish is good served either hot or at room temperature.*

—<small>MOIRA HODGSON</small>

UZBECKI BEANS AND RICE • (MASKITCHIRI)

meat

<small>ADAPTED FROM</small> Jack Murphy

1 cup mung dal (dried split yellow mung beans)
2 cups chopped onions
2 carrots, diced
2 tablespoons olive oil
1 large potato, peeled and diced
1 (28-ounce) can no-salt-added crushed
*   tomatoes*
2 teaspoons cumin seed
1½ teaspoons hot paprika, plus extra for garnish
½ teaspoon sweet paprika, plus extra for garnish
2 cups no-salt-added Chicken Stock (page 48),
*   canned or fresh*
1 cup long-grain rice
2 cups water
¾ teaspoon salt, or to taste
½ cup chopped cilantro

1. Soak beans overnight or cook for 2 minutes in plenty of water and allow to sit for 1 hour; drain.

2. Sauté onions and carrots in hot oil until onion begins to turn golden.

3. Add potato and cook 5 minutes.

4. Stir in the tomatoes, cumin seed, hot and sweet paprika and chicken stock. Bring to boil and add the drained beans. Cover, leaving the lid slightly askew to let steam escape. Simmer until beans are soft, 20–30 minutes, and most of liquid has been absorbed.

5. Meanwhile, bring the rice and water to a boil;

reduce heat, cover and cook 17 minutes, until rice is tender and water absorbed. Stir rice into bean mixture; add salt.

6. Garnish with cilantro and hot or sweet paprika.

Yield: 3 servings as a main dish

—MARIAN BURROS

ETHIOPIAN YELLOW PEAS WITH ONIONS • (ATERKEK ALECHA)

pareve

ADAPTED FROM Ghenet

> *1 cup vegetable oil*
> *2 cups chopped red onion*
> *2 cups yellow split peas*
> *1 teaspoon salt*
> *1 tablespoon minced garlic*
> *½ teaspoon grated ginger*
> *⅛ teaspoon ground turmeric*
> *2 jalapeños, seeded and thinly sliced*
> *6 basil leaves*

1. Pour ¼ cup oil into a heavy pot and place over medium heat. Add onion and sauté, stirring occasionally, until caramelized and golden brown. Add remaining oil and simmer over gentle heat.

2. Wash peas under running water until water runs clear. Place in pot with 6 cups water, add salt and bring to a boil. Skim foam. Cook over medium heat until half done, about 20 minutes. Strain, reserving liquid, and add peas to the onions.

3. Add minced garlic and ginger and simmer gently about 25 minutes, or until peas are tender, stirring occasionally and adding reserved water as needed to prevent sticking. Add jalapeños. Just before serving, add thin strips of basil to pan. Serve with pita or other flat bread or rice.

Yield: 6–8 servings

—ERIC ASIMOV

ALICE WATERS'S FAVA BEAN RAGOUT

pareve

ADAPTED FROM *Chez Panisse Vegetables*

3–4 pounds young fava beans
1 large clove garlic
1 small sprig rosemary
Olive oil
Coarse salt and freshly ground pepper to taste
½ lemon

1. Shell the fava beans and discard the pods. Bring a pot of water to a boil, add the favas and simmer them for 1 minute. Drain and cool them immediately in cold water. Pierce the outer skin with a thumbnail and squeeze each bean out of its skin with thumb and forefinger.

2. Peel and chop the garlic very fine. Strip the rosemary leaves off the sprig and chop them very fine.

3. Put the fava beans in a saucepan with a mixture of half water and half olive oil, enough to barely cover them. Add the garlic and rosemary and season with salt and pepper. Bring to a simmer, cover and cook until the beans are tender, about 5 minutes, more or less, depending on the beans. Add a squeeze of lemon juice and another grind or two of pepper and serve.

Yield: 4–6 servings

—MOIRA HODGSON

WHITE-BEAN CHILI

pareve

ADAPTED FROM Susan Holland Company

2½ cups white beans, like a mixture of great
    northerns, cannellini and limas
4 large yellow onions
4 carrots
4 stalks celery
3 tablespoons olive oil
2 tablespoons garlic, peeled and minced
1 jalapeño pepper
½ bunch parsley
3 quarts Vegetable Stock (page 51), canned or fresh
6 sprigs fresh thyme
1 bay leaf

1 tablespoon cumin seed
1 tablespoon black pepper, or to taste
2 tablespoons ground cumin
1 bunch cilantro
1 tablespoon fresh oregano leaves
Salt to taste

1. Soak the beans for 6 hours or overnight. Drain and reserve.

2. Peel and dice onions and carrots. Trim and dice celery.

3. Heat oil in a large pot. Add onions, carrots and celery and sauté until soft.

4. While the vegetables are cooking, peel and mince garlic. Add to pan and sauté for 2 minutes.

5. Using rubber gloves or covering hands with plastic bags, clean seeds and stem from jalapeño and dice. Chop parsley.

6. Add beans to pot and toss for 1 minute. Add jalapeño, parsley, vegetable stock, thyme, bay leaf, cumin seed and black pepper. Bring to a simmer. Add cumin. Cook slowly for 90 minutes, or until desired consistency is reached.

7. Chop cilantro and pull oregano leaves from stems. Add salt, pepper, cilantro and oregano.

8. Remove from heat and let cool slightly. Remove bay leaf.

Yield: 6 servings

—TRISH HALL

WHITE-BEAN CROQUETTES

dairy

> 3 cans cannellini beans (19 ounces each), drained
>   and rinsed
> 3 cloves garlic, peeled and chopped
> 2½ teaspoons kosher salt
> ½ teaspoon freshly ground black pepper
> 9 tablespoons plus ¾ cup dry bread crumbs
> ½ pound fresh mozzarella, cut into ¼-inch cubes,
>   about 42
> 12 sun-dried tomatoes, cut into ¼-inch pieces
> Vegetable oil for deep frying

1. Puree the beans, garlic, salt and pepper in a food processor. Stir in 9 tablespoons of bread crumbs and refrigerate several hours, until firm.

2. Form the mixture into balls, using a slightly rounded tablespoon for each one. Press one piece of mozzarella and 1 piece of tomato into the center of each and reshape into a ball. Coat with the remaining bread crumbs.

3. Working in batches, deep-fry the balls until nicely browned. It is important to keep the oil about 365 degrees. Drain on paper towels. Serve hot.

Yield: 12 servings

NOTE: *Can be prepared ahead of time and kept in a 200-degree oven. These are also excellent as an appetizer course.*

—FLORENCE FABRICANT

EGG NOODLE DOUGH

pareve

2 cups flour
Salt to taste, if desired
2 large eggs, ½ cup
1–2 tablespoons cold water

1. This dough may be made with a food processor or by hand. With a processor, combine all ingredients in container and blend thoroughly. Shape dough into a ball.

2. If done by hand, put flour on flat surface and make well in center. Add salt, eggs and half the water. Knead well for 10 minutes or longer. Add more water as necessary to make smooth dough.

3. Place dough in clean cloth and wrap neatly to enclose. Let stand 30 minutes before cutting into shape of your choice.

Yield: Slightly less than 1 pound

—CRAIG CLAIBORNE

EGG NOODLES WITH CARROTS AND LEMON

dairy
ADAPTED FROM *Cooking with the 60-Minute Gourmet*

4 carrots, trimmed and scraped, about ¼ pound
1 tablespoon butter
1 teaspoon grated lemon rind (yellow skin only)
¼ cup dry white wine
2 tablespoons fresh lemon juice
1 cup heavy cream
4 quarts water
Salt to taste, if desired
¾ pound very thin egg noodles
¼ cup freshly grated Parmesan cheese

1. Cut the carrots crosswise into 1-inch lengths. Cut the pieces lengthwise into very thin slices. Stack the slices and cut them into very thin strips. There should be about 2 cups or slightly more, loosely packed.

2. Heat the butter in a saucepan and add the carrot strips and lemon rind. Cook, stirring, about 2 minutes.

3. Add the wine and cook about 1 minute.

4. Meanwhile, bring the water to a boil in a pot and add salt to taste. Add the noodles and cook 3 minutes or until noodles are tender.

5. Drain the noodles and return them to the hot pot. Add the sauce and the cheese. Stir to blend and serve immediately.

Yield: 4 servings

NOTE: *You can substitute orzo, the rice-shaped pasta, for noodles if you like.*

POPPY SEED NOODLES

dairy

ADAPTED FROM *Cooking with Herbs & Spices*

½ pound medium noodles
Boiling salted water
3 tablespoons butter, at room temperature
1 tablespoon poppy seeds

1. Cook the noodles in boiling salted water according to package directions. Drain immediately.

2. Add the butter to the utensil in which the noodles were cooked and quickly toss the noodles in the butter. Just before serving, sprinkle with the poppy seeds.

Yield: 4–6 servings

COTTAGE CHEESE NOODLES WITH SCALLION BUTTER

dairy

ADAPTED FROM *Cooking with Herbs & Spices*

⅔ cup soft butter
1 cup creamed cottage cheese
Salt to taste, if desired
2 eggs
2½ cups sifted flour, approximately
2 bunches scallions, tops and all, chopped
Freshly grated Parmesan cheese

1. Cream ¼ cup of the butter, the cottage cheese and salt until smooth and fluffy. Add the eggs and mix well. Add the flour, mix and knead on a floured surface until smooth and nonsticky.

2. Cut in half and roll each half very thin. Dry the sheets on cooling racks or kitchen towels until just dry enough to fold without breaking. Fold and cut into any desired width. Unfold the strips and complete the drying.

3. Cook the noodles in a large quantity of boiling salted water for 10 minutes and drain.

4. While the noodles are cooking, sauté the scallions in the remaining butter until wilted. Pour over the noodles and toss gently. Serve with grated Parmesan cheese.

Yield: 6 servings

ROASTED-GARLIC NOODLE CAKE

dairy

ADAPTED FROM Allen Susser

2 heads garlic, cloves separated but not peeled
3 tablespoons olive oil
4 medium shallots, peeled and cut into thin strips
½ pound spinach fettuccine
1 pound white fettuccine
2 teaspoons salt
¾ teaspoon freshly ground white pepper
1 teaspoon dried thyme
⅛ teaspoon ground nutmeg
2 cups half-and-half
6 eggs
¼ cup freshly grated Parmesan cheese

1. Preheat oven to 350 degrees. Place garlic in a small baking dish. Drizzle with I tablespoon of the olive oil. Cover with foil and bake until garlic is very soft, about I hour. Squeeze the garlic from the skins and set aside.
2. Heat I tablespoon of the olive oil in a small skillet. Add shallots and sauté until they begin to caramelize, about 3 minutes. Set aside.

3. Cook the spinach and white fettuccines separately in salted water until tender but firm. Drain and place each in a separate large bowl. Whisk together the roasted garlic, I teaspoon of the salt, ½ teaspoon of the white pepper, thyme, nutmeg, I½ cups of the half-and-half and 4 of the eggs. Pour over the white fettuccine and mix well. Whisk together the shallots, I teaspoon salt, ¼ teaspoon white pepper, ½ cup half-and-half and 2 eggs. Pour over the spinach fettuccine and mix well.
4. Grease a 10-inch round springform pan with the remaining tablespoon olive oil. Coat the pan with the Parmesan. Place half of the white fettuccine mixture in the bottom of the pan. Top with the spinach fettuccine mixture. Cover with the remaining white fettuccine mixture. Cover the pan with aluminum foil. Bake for 45 minutes. Let rest for 5 minutes. Run a small knife around the edge of the pan to loosen. Unmold, cut into wedges and serve.

Yield: 8 servings

— MARIAN BURROS

BOHEMIAN CHEESE DUMPLINGS WITH SOUR CREAM

dairy

ADAPTED FROM *The New York Times Heritage Cookbook*

3 tablespoons milk
2 eggs
Salt to taste
2 cups flour, approximately

1 cup ricotta cheese or pot cheese
1 egg yolk
Freshly ground black pepper to taste
½ cup chopped scallions, including green part
8 cups water
2 cups sour cream
1 cup toasted, buttered bread crumbs

1. Heat the milk to lukewarm. Combine the eggs, salt and milk in a mixing bowl. Gradually add the flour, stirring. Add just enough flour to make a soft dough. Gather dough into a ball and set aside.

2. Combine the cheese, egg yolks, salt and pepper. Stir in the scallions.

3. Roll out the dough on a lightly floured board until thin. Cut dough into 4-inch squares. Place a spoonful of the cheese mixture in the center of each square and fold the dough over to make filled triangles. Pinch sides firmly to seal.

4. Bring the water to a boil in a kettle and add salt to taste. Drop in the dumplings, a few at a time, and simmer until tender, 10–15 minutes. Drain dumplings on paper towels.

5. Preheat the oven to 250 degrees.

6. Arrange dumplings in a buttered baking dish and spoon the sour cream over all. Scatter the bread cubes over the sour cream and bake until heated through but not bubbling. Serve hot.

Yield: 10 or more dumplings, 4–6 servings

POTATO AND MUSHROOM PIROGI

dairy

ADAPTED FROM Faina Merzlyak

FOR THE DUMPLINGS:

16 ounces fresh yogurt, preferably homemade, or one with a high-fat content, such as Brown Cow
1 egg, lightly beaten
1 teaspoon salt
2¼ cups flour

FOR THE FILLING:

1 large potato, about ½–¾ pound
4 tablespoons unsalted butter
1 medium-size onion, chopped
16 ounces mushrooms, trimmed and minced, 2 cups
Salt and freshly ground pepper to taste
Fried onions as garnish, optional
Sour cream as garnish, optional

1. To make the dumplings, lightly beat the yogurt, egg, and salt together in a mixer. Slowly add the flour, beating until smooth. Knead the dough on a floured surface until smooth. Add water only if needed. Form into a ball, wrap in a kitchen towel and set aside in a cool place for 2 hours.

2. For the filling, peel and quarter the potato. Cover with cold water, bring to a boil, lower heat and simmer 15–20 minutes until it offers no resistance when pricked with a fork. Drain and set aside. Slowly melt 2 tablespoons of the butter. Whip the potato with the butter until it is fluffy and creamy. Set aside.

3. Heat the remaining butter in a pan. Add the onions and sauté until they are translucent. Add the mushrooms, salt and pepper and continue to sauté until the mushrooms are tender and the moisture has evaporated, about 5 minutes. Remove from pan and let cool slightly.

4. Mix the mashed potatoes with the mushroom mixture.

5. Bring a large pot of salted water to a boil. Roll out the dough until it is ⅛ inch thick, then cut it into 3-inch rounds with a cookie cutter or the top of a glass. Put 1 heaping teaspoon of filling on one side of the circle of dough. Fold the other side over the filling so the pirogi looks like a half-moon. Press the edges together and seal with thumb and index finger.
6. Lower heat until water gently simmers. Carefully place pirogi in the water, 1 at a time, in batches of 4 to 6, for 5–7 minutes. Remove with a slotted spoon and drain on paper towels in a warm place. Serve with fried onions, Crispy Shallots (page 299), or sour cream.

Yield: 30 pirogi

—MOLLY O'NEILL

SPÄTZLE

dairy

ADAPTED FROM *Craig Claiborne's Favorites, Vol. 2*

Because spätzle (usually pronounced SHPEHT-zl in English) require no rolling or cutting, they may be the simplest, least technically demanding pasta to make. In fact, they look best when they are rather haphazard, almost misshapen. The little dumplings are dropped into boiling water until they firm up and float and are often tossed in butter afterward. But you can vary them at will. There are special spätzle-makers, but most chefs make spätzle simply by forcing the thick batter through the holes of a colander. Use a large stainless-steel colander with holes ⅛ inch to ¼ inch wide. Hold it over a pot that is half filled with boiling water, and use a large spoon, a wooden spatula or a dough scraper to push the batter through the holes.

2 cups sifted flour
3 eggs
⅔ cup milk
Salt to taste
⅛ teaspoon grated nutmeg
2 tablespoons butter

1. Place the flour in a mixing bowl. Beat the eggs and add them to the flour, stirring with a wire whisk or an electric beater. Gradually add the milk, beating or stirring constantly. Add salt and nutmeg.
2. Bring a large quantity of water to a boil in a kettle and add salt. Pour spätzle mixture into a colander and hold the colander over a pot that is half filled with boiling water. Press the mixture through the holes of the colander with a wooden spatula or large spoon. The spätzle are done when they float on top. Drain the noodles and spoon them onto a clean towel to dry briefly.
3. Heat the butter in a saucepan over medium heat until golden brown. Add the spätzle, tossing and stirring 3–5 minutes. Serve hot.

Yield: 4–6 servings

NOTE: *For Swabian Spätzle with Herbed Bread Crumbs, as made by Chef Eberhard Müller, add 4 tablespoons of dry white breadcrumbs to the melted butter, cooking them until they are golden brown. Remove from heat and add 2 teaspoons each of minced fresh parsley, chives and chervil. Then add spätzle, stir gently to coat with butter and the herbed bread crumbs. Season with salt and pepper and serve at once.*

—FLORENCE FABRICANT

BUCKWHEAT SPÄTZLE

dairy

ADAPTED FROM Sono

> ⅔ cup all-purpose flour
> ⅔ cup light buckwheat flour
> Salt and freshly ground black pepper to taste
> 1 egg, lightly beaten
> ¾ cup Vegetable Stock (page 51)
> 1 teaspoon extra-virgin olive oil
> 2 tablespoons butter

1. Whisk flours, salt and pepper in large bowl. Add egg and ¾ cup stock. Beat until well blended to make thick batter.

2. Bring 3 quarts salted water to a boil in a large pot. Add 1 teaspoon olive oil.

3. Hold a colander a few inches above the pot. With a large spoon or spatula, push about one quarter of the batter through holes into the water. Or place one quarter of the batter on a small wooden board and rest it on the edge of the pot; use a knife to scrape tiny bits into the water. When spätzle rise to top, remove with skimmer or slotted spoon to a baking sheet lined with paper towel. Continue making spätzle in batches.

4. Transfer well-drained spätzle to bowl, cover and set aside. You should have 3–3½ cups.

5. When ready to serve, melt butter in large skillet. Add spätzle and sauté a few minutes, until starting to brown.

Yield: 4 side-dish servings

—FLORENCE FABRICANT

BLACK PEPPER AND CHIVE SPÄTZLE

dairy

ADAPTED FROM Quilty's

> 5 eggs
> Grated zest of 1 lemon
> 2 teaspoons coarsely ground black pepper
> 2 tablespoons minced fresh chives
> ¼ teaspoon nutmeg
> 1 teaspoon salt
> 3¼ cups flour
> 3 tablespoons melted butter

1. In large bowl, mix eggs, lemon, pepper, chives, nutmeg and salt with 1½ cups water. Slowly beat in flour. Cover. Set aside 1 hour.

2. Bring 3 quarts salted water to a boil in a large pot.

3. Hold a colander a few inches above the pot. With a large spoon or spatula, push about one quarter of the batter through holes into the water. Or place one quarter of the dough on a small wooden board and rest it on the edge of the pot; use a knife to scrape tiny bits into water. When spätzle rise to top, remove with skimmer or slotted spoon to a baking sheet lined with paper towels. Continue making spätzle in batches.

4. Heat butter in large skillet. Add spätzle and toss until coated with butter and starting to become very lightly browned. Serve.

Yield: 5–6 cups spätzle; serves 6

—FLORENCE FABRICANT

PASTA MACEDONIA

dairy

ADAPTED FROM Johnny Nicholson

2 small onions or 1 large, coarsely chopped
¼ pound butter
1 pound mezzania or similar thin tubular pasta,
    cooked al dente and drained
16 ounces sour cream
1½ cups crumbled feta cheese
12 ripe calamata olives, pitted and sliced
½ cup finely grated Parmesan cheese
Salt and freshly ground black pepper to taste

1 pound fresh spinach, steamed
Additional feta cheese

1. Cook the onions in the butter.
2. Mix together the pasta, sour cream, onion, feta, olives and ½ cup cheese. Season with salt and freshly ground black pepper. Place in serving bowl.
3. Top with spinach and additional cheese and serve.

Yield: 4 servings as main course

—MARIAN BURROS

ITZHAK PERLMAN'S PASTA WITH TOMATO, ZUCCHINI AND CREAM SAUCE

dairy

3 tablespoons olive oil
1 clove garlic, chopped
2 medium-size zucchini, sliced ¼ inch thick
3 medium-size tomatoes, peeled, seeded and diced
1 cup tomato sauce, canned or fresh
Salt to taste
1 teaspoon sugar, optional
2 tablespoons heavy cream
1 tablespoon Parmesan cheese
1 pound of linguine or fresh egg noodles

1. Add oil to skillet. When oil is hot, add the garlic and sauté 30 seconds.
2. Add zucchini and stir-fry 2 minutes.
3. Add tomatoes and sauté for 3 minutes. Then add tomato sauce and simmer for 10 minutes. Taste first and, if necessary, add salt and sugar. (Mr. Perlman suggests adding the sugar only to counteract the acidity of the tomatoes.)
4. Just before serving, add heavy cream and Parmesan cheese; cook for 5 minutes. Serve with the pasta prepared al dente.

Yield: 3–4 servings

—JOHN ROCKWELL

PASTA WITH RED PEPPERS AND PINE NUTS

dairy

ADAPTED FROM Marcella Hazan

4 red or yellow peppers
3 tablespoons extra-virgin olive oil
4 garlic cloves, peeled
1 pound ziti, penne or fusilli
2 tablespoons unsalted butter
1 cup fresh basil leaves, snipped with scissors
½ cup toasted pine nuts
Freshly grated Parmesan cheese
Coarse salt and freshly ground pepper to taste

1. Cut the peppers into quarters and place them face down on a broiling pan lined with aluminum foil. Broil until the skins are charred and puffy. Place the peppers in a brown paper bag, seal and cool. Skin the peppers and slice them in thin strips.

2. Heat the olive oil in a skillet and add the garlic cloves and the peppers. Cook for 15 minutes, stirring frequently.

3. Meanwhile, bring 6 quarts salted water to a boil and cook the pasta until al dente. Drain and place in a heated bowl.

4. Add the butter to the peppers and stir until melted. Add to the pasta and toss. Add the basil leaves, pine nuts and 2 tablespoons cheese. Season with salt and pepper to taste and serve. Pass the rest of the cheese separately.

Yield: 4–6 servings

—MOIRA HODGSON

LINGUINE WITH PISTACHIO-ALMOND PESTO

pareve

ADAPTED FROM *The Italian Country Table*

Scant ½ cup shelled salted pistachio nuts, toasted
Scant ½ cup unblanched whole almonds, toasted
⅓ cup pine nuts, toasted
Kosher salt and freshly ground black pepper to taste
1 large clove garlic
Pinch of hot red pepper flakes
3½ tablespoons fruity extra-virgin olive oil
40 large mint leaves
1 pound linguine
1 pound cherry tomatoes, quartered

1. Coarsely chop about a quarter of the nuts. Bring 6 quarts of salted water to a boil.

2. In a mortar or a food processor, pound (or grind) garlic to a paste with hot pepper and 3 tablespoons olive oil. Work in remaining whole nuts and a little more than half the mint leaves, until mixture looks like very coarse meal. Do this in batches and season to taste. Tear up remaining mint leaves.

3. Add pasta to boiling water and cook until tender yet firm to the bite. Gently blend pesto, tomatoes and remaining ½ tablespoon oil in a deep bowl.

4. Skim off ½ cup of pasta water, then drain pasta. Add reserved pasta water to bowl with pesto. Add pasta, chopped nuts, salt and pepper and toss. Add torn mint. Toss again. Taste, adding oil, mint, salt and pepper, if needed. No cheese is used here.

Yield: 6 servings

—AMANDA HESSER

ZITI WITH SMOKED SALMON

dairy

> *5 ripe plum tomatoes, about 1 pound*
> *¾ pound ziti or any tubular pasta of your choice*
> *Salt to taste*
> *2 tablespoons olive oil*
> *1 tablespoon finely chopped garlic*
> *2 tablespoons finely chopped shallots*
> *Freshly ground pepper to taste*
> *½ cup heavy cream*
> *¼ cup pepper vodka*
> *½ pound sliced smoked salmon, cut into*
>   *1½-inch strips*
> *2 tablespoons butter*
> *½ cup coarsely chopped fresh coriander or basil*
> *Freshly grated Parmesan cheese (optional)*

1. Core the tomatoes and drop them into boiling water for 10–12 seconds. Drain immediately and peel. The skin should come off easily if you use a paring knife. Cut the tomatoes into ½-inch cubes. There should be about 2¼ cups.

2. Cook the ziti in salted water according to the package directions. The pasta should be al dente. Drain and reserve ¼ cup of the cooking liquid.

3. Meanwhile, heat the oil in a large skillet and add the garlic and shallots. Cook briefly, stirring, without browning. Add the tomatoes, salt and pepper. Cook, stirring, for 1 minute. Add the cream and vodka. Bring to a simmer and cook 1 minute.

4. Add the pasta and reserved cooking liquid to the tomato sauce. Blend well and simmer 1 minute.

5. Add the salmon, butter and coriander. Toss well and cook 1 minute. Serve with cheese if desired.

Yield: 4 servings

—PIERRE FRANEY

FETTUCCINE WITH ASPARAGUS AND SMOKED SALMON

dairy

½ pound fresh asparagus, medium thickness
Salt to taste
1 tablespoon butter
½ tablespoon minced shallots
1 cup heavy cream
4 ounces smoked salmon, sliced ¼ inch thick
Freshly ground black pepper
1 teaspoon fresh lemon juice
9–10 ounces fresh green fettuccine noodles
2 tablespoons minced fresh dill

1. Snap off the ends of the asparagus where they break naturally and peel the stalks. Cut the asparagus on a slant to pieces about an inch long.

2. Steam the asparagus until they are just barely tender and still bright green, about 3 minutes. Rinse under cold water, drain well on paper towels and set aside.

3. Bring a large pot of salted water to a boil for the pasta.

4. While the water is coming to a boil, melt the butter in a large heavy skillet. Add the shallots and sauté until soft but not brown. Stir in the cream and simmer about 5 minutes, until the cream has thickened somewhat.

5. Cut the salmon into slivers, add it to the cream and remove the skillet from the heat. Season with pepper and lemon juice. Add the asparagus.

6. When the pot of water is boiling, add the fettuccine, stir it once or twice, then cook 2–3 minutes after the water has returned to a boil. Drain well.

7. Briefly reheat the sauce. Transfer the fettuccine to a warm serving bowl, pour the sauce over it and toss. Sprinkle with dill and serve.

Yield: 4 servings

—FLORENCE FABRICANT

COLD SESAME NOODLES

pareve, meat

½ pound Chinese egg noodles, vermicelli or angel hair pasta

FOR THE DRESSING:

2 scallions, trimmed and chopped, including green
⅓ cup vegetable or Chicken Broth (page 48), canned or fresh
¼ cup smooth peanut butter, preferably sugar- and salt-free

¼ cup cider vinegar or rice wine vinegar
½ cup low-sodium soy sauce
2 teaspoons dark (roasted) sesame oil

AND SOME OR ALL OF THE FOLLOWING:

1 cucumber, peeled, seeded and cut into small pieces
1 cup sliced red radishes
1 bunch scallions, trimmed and cut in thin rounds, including more of the green
1 cup bean sprouts
1 carrot, shredded

1 cup snow peas
½ cup roughly chopped fresh coriander
¼ cup toasted sesame seeds

1. Bring a large pot of salted water to a boil. Add the noodles and boil for 3–4 minutes, until tender. Drain in a colander, then cool under running water. Shake noodles dry and transfer to a large, shallow bowl.

2. Blend all the dressing ingredients in a blender or food processor. Pour over the noodles, turning until completely mixed.

3. Add any or all of the remaining ingredients, mix well and serve. Or cover and chill; mix in the additions right before serving.

Yield: 6 servings

—SUZANNE HAMLIN

PITA POCKET PIZZAS WITH ROASTED TOMATO SAUCE

dairy

1 teaspoon olive oil
4 large mushrooms, thinly sliced
½ large onion, thinly sliced
1 clove garlic, minced
2 tablespoons plus ¼ cup chopped fresh basil
3 large pitas, split horizontally and separated
3 cups Roasted Tomato Sauce (see recipe below)
4 tablespoons freshly grated Parmesan cheese
3 ounces grated part–skim milk mozzarella cheese
Optional toppings: sun–dried chopped tomatoes, black olives, capers

1. Preheat oven to 350 degrees.

2. Heat nonstick sauté pan with olive oil. Add mushrooms, onion, garlic and 2 tablespoons basil and cook over low heat until very soft.

3. Place pita pocket halves on sheet pan with inside of pockets facing up.

4. Place 4 ounces tomato sauce on each pita and cover the pocket, leaving about a ½-inch border around edge of pita.

5. Divide the mushroom-onion mixture evenly among the pizzas and spoon on top of tomato sauce.

6. Sprinkle each with Parmesan and mozzarella cheese. Add other toppings of your choice. Garnish with remaining ¼ cup fresh basil.

7. Bake for about 10 minutes, or until cheese melts and crust is crispy. Cut each pizza into quarters and serve immediately.

Yield: 3 servings

◆ ROASTED TOMATO SAUCE ◆

pareve

6 pounds plum tomatoes, cored and quartered
1½ cups coarsely chopped celery stalks
1½ cups coarsely chopped onions
9 shallots, coarsely chopped
9 cloves garlic, minced
1½ cups coarsely chopped carrots
6 tablespoons balsamic vinegar
1 bay leaf

1½ tablespoons each of fresh thyme, oregano, basil
    and parsley leaves or 1½ teaspoons each of dried
    thyme, oregano and basil
1½ teaspoons salt or less
1 tablespoon freshly ground black pepper

1. Preheat the oven to 400 degrees.
2. Put all the ingredients in a pan and roast for about 45 minutes, or until soft.

3. When soft, remove bay leaf, transfer remaining ingredients to food processor or blender, and puree until slightly chunky.

Yield: A little over 2 quarts

NOTE: *This is also an excellent pasta sauce. It can be frozen in smaller portions, or it will keep in the refrigerator 3–4 days.*

—MARIAN BURROS

ZUCCHINI PIZZA IN A PHYLLO CRUST

dairy

ADAPTED FROM Ellen Ogden

½ cup freshly grated Parmesan cheese
¼ cup mixed, chopped fresh herbs like savory, thyme,
    parsley and basil
2 tablespoons unsalted butter, melted
2 tablespoons canola oil
½ package phyllo dough (12 sheets, defrosted
    according to package directions)
6 teaspoons wheat germ
1 medium green zucchini, thinly sliced
½ sweet red onion, chopped fine
1 medium yellow zucchini or summer squash,
    thinly sliced

1. Preheat oven to 400 degrees. Place cheese and herbs in a small bowl and set aside.
2. Combine melted butter and oil and, with a pastry brush, lightly grease a baking sheet. Place 2 sheets of

phyllo, one on top of the other, on the baking sheet. Brush lightly with the oil and butter mixture, sprinkle with 2 tablespoons of the herb-cheese mixture and 1 teaspoon of wheat germ. Repeat 5 more times, until all the sheets have been used, ending with a layer of phyllo. Brush this top sheet with the oil and butter.
3. Leaving a 1½-inch border free, sprinkle the onion on the top sheet. Place the green and yellow zucchini, in alternating rows, overlapping as necessary. Sprinkle with remaining cheese, herbs and wheat germ. Drizzle with any remaining oil and butter.
4. Bake 15–20 minutes, or until phyllo is lightly browned and the cheese has melted. Remove to cooling rack and cut into 3-inch squares.

*Yield: 3–4 servings as a light lunch or
    as appetizer*

—MARIALISA CALTA

MARIO'S EGGPLANT RAGÙ

pareve

1 pound eggplant, peeled and cut across in
 ¼-inch slices

2 tablespoons kosher salt

1 cup extra-virgin olive oil

1 pound red bell peppers, cut lengthwise in
 ⅛-inch strips

6 cloves garlic, sliced thin

2¼ pounds plum tomatoes, diced

Freshly ground black pepper to taste

12 large leaves basil, shredded

1. Sprinkle the eggplant with 1 tablespoon salt and drain in a colander for 30 minutes. Rinse, pat dry and cut in ¼-inch dice.

2. In a large skillet, heat the oil over high heat. Add the eggplant, peppers and garlic. Cook, stirring frequently, for 10 minutes. Lower the heat to medium and cover. Cook for 7 minutes, stirring occasionally. Add the tomatoes and cook, uncovered, stirring, for 5 minutes. Season with 1 tablespoon salt and pepper to taste. Stir in the basil and let sit for 5 minutes before serving with pasta or polenta.

Yield: 6 servings

—MOLLY O'NEILL

PORCINI-STYLE SHIITAKE MUSHROOM PASTA SAUCE

dairy

ADAPTED FROM *Marcella Cucina*

¾ pound fresh white mushrooms

½ pound fresh shiitake mushrooms

3 tablespoons extra-virgin olive oil

½ cup chopped onion

1½ tablespoons chopped garlic

2 tablespoons chopped flat-leaf parsley

Salt to taste

½ cup heavy cream

2 tablespoons butter

Freshly ground black pepper to taste

1 pound fresh tonnarelli, pappardelle or fettuccine

¾ cup freshly grated Parmesan cheese

1. Quickly rinse mushrooms under fast-running water. Cut white mushrooms vertically into thin slices. Remove stems from shiitakes, and slice caps thinly.

2. Put oil and onion in 12-inch sauté pan, and turn heat to medium-high. Cook onion, stirring, until it is translucent. Add garlic. Continue to cook, stirring, until garlic is aromatic but no darker than pale gold.

3. Add parsley, stir quickly, and then add all mushrooms. Add liberal pinches of salt and turn over all ingredients a few times. Cover pan, and turn heat to medium. Cook for 10–15 minutes. Uncover pan and cook a few minutes longer, until liquid released by mushrooms has evaporated.

4. Add cream, butter and liberal grindings of pepper. Increase heat to high, and cook for 3–4 minutes, stirring, to reduce cream until it has thickened to saucelike consistency. Check seasonings and remove from heat.

5. Bring a 6- to 8-quart pot of salted water to a boil. Add pasta all at once, stir and cook until tender but firm to the bite. A minute or so before pasta is done, put sauce over medium-low heat to warm it.

6. Drain pasta, place it in warm serving dish, add sauce and toss. Add cheese, toss again and serve at once.

Yield: 6 servings

—FLORENCE FABRICANT

CHICKEN RAGOUT WITH FETTUCCINE

meat

2½ tablespoons extra-virgin olive oil
½ cup finely chopped onion
½ cup finely chopped leeks
½ cup finely chopped carrots
2 large cloves garlic, minced
2 (3½-pound) frying chickens, each cut in 8 pieces
    and skinned
¼ cup dry sherry
1 cup Chicken Stock (page 48)
1 pound plum tomatoes, chopped
2 sprigs fresh rosemary or 1 teaspoon dried
2 tablespoons fresh lemon juice
1 cup shelled fresh peas
Salt to taste
Freshly ground black pepper to taste
12 ounces fresh fettuccine
2 tablespoons minced parsley

1. Heat 1 tablespoon of the oil in a heavy casserole. Add the onion, leek and carrot and sauté over low heat until soft but not brown. Add the garlic, sauté another minute or so and remove from the heat.

2. Brush a heavy nonstick skillet with a half tablespoon of oil, add the chicken and lightly brown over medium-high heat a few pieces at a time. Place the chicken pieces in the casserole as they are browned.

3. When all the chicken has been lightly browned, stir the sherry into the skillet. Cook for several minutes, scraping the skillet and pour the contents of the skillet over the chicken in the casserole. Return the casserole to the stove and place over low heat.

4. Add the chicken stock, tomatoes, rosemary and lemon juice to the casserole, cover and simmer gently for about 30 minutes. Add the peas and cook 15 minutes longer. Season the sauce to taste with salt and pepper.

5. Meanwhile, bring a large pot of salted water to a boil for the fettuccine. Cook about 2 minutes, drain well, then toss with the remaining olive oil and a tablespoon of the parsley. Season the fettuccine lightly with salt and pepper.

6. To serve, reheat the chicken ragout, then transfer it to a warm platter or serving dish and sprinkle with parsley. Place the fettuccine alongside the chicken on the platter or in a separate bowl and serve both.

Yield: 6 servings

NOTE: *The ragout also can be served over other types of pasta.*

—FLORENCE FABRICANT

DUCK RAGÙ

meat

ADAPTED FROM Paola's

1½ tablespoons extra-virgin olive oil

5 whole garlic cloves, peeled

2–3 sprigs fresh rosemary

2–3 sprigs fresh thyme

2–3 sprigs fresh marjoram

2–3 sprigs fresh sage

½ teaspoon freshly grated nutmeg

1 large carrot, peeled and finely chopped

1 large white onion, peeled and finely chopped

2–3 celery stalks, finely chopped

1 (4- to 5-pound) duck, quartered,
*   all excess fat removed*

1 bottle Cabernet or Pinot Noir

1 tablespoon tomato paste

2 cups duck stock or Chicken Broth (page 48),
*   canned or fresh*

1 (35-ounce) can Italian plum tomatoes, drained

Salt and freshly ground black pepper to taste

1. In a large sauté pan over medium heat, heat olive oil and add garlic, rosemary, thyme, marjoram, sage and nutmeg. Sauté for 1 minute, then add carrot, onion and celery. Sauté until vegetables just begin to soften, another minute or two, then add duck pieces, skin side down.

2. Raise heat to high and sear duck pieces, stirring vegetables so they do not burn. Turn duck pieces to sear other side. When duck is lightly browned, add about a cup of wine and stir gently while wine evaporates. Turn duck pieces again and add another cup of wine, repeating procedure until all wine is gone and duck is dark brown.

3. Reduce heat to medium. Add tomato paste and stock, stirring and scraping bottom of pan. Cook for a few more minutes, then remove from heat. Transfer duck pieces to a platter and allow to cool. Set aside pan of sauce.

4. When duck is cool enough to handle, remove all meat and cut into bite-size pieces. Remove sprigs of herbs and garlic cloves from sauce. Return duck meat to sauce and place over medium heat. Add plum tomatoes, breaking them with a spoon. Simmer mixture until sauce has reduced and thickened slightly, about 10 minutes. Season to taste.

Yield: 4–6 servings

NOTE: *Traditionally, this classic Tuscan stew is served over pappardelle, but any other pasta may be substituted.*

—ERIC ASIMOV

ITALIAN MEAT SAUCE

meat

4 tablespoons Italian olive oil

4 cloves garlic, peeled and thickly sliced

1 pound ground lean chuck beef

4 cups (one 35-ounce can) Italian plum tomatoes, chopped and with their canning liquid

1 large onion, peeled and studded with 5 cloves

4–5 sprigs Italian parsley

1–2 teaspoons oregano, to taste

½–1 teaspoon dried basil or about 8 large fresh basil leaves

½–1 teaspoon salt, to taste

½–1 teaspoon sugar, to taste

Several grindings of black pepper

Tomato paste, if necessary

1. Heat oil in a 2-quart, heavy-bottomed saucepan. Add garlic and fry slowly and carefully until color is light golden brown. Remove garlic and reserve. Add beef and, with a wooden spatula, break up clumps of meat and sauté slowly, stirring and breaking into smaller bits until meat loses its bright red color and just begins to turn slightly golden brown.

2. Add chopped tomatoes with their liquid, the browned garlic, the clove-studded onion and the parsley. Cover pot loosely and simmer sauce gently but steadily for 40 minutes, stirring frequently to prevent scorching. Add a little water if needed.

3. Add oregano, basil, salt, sugar and pepper and cook for 15 minutes more. If sauce is runny and thin, thicken by beating in tomato paste, a teaspoonful at a time, and simmering 5 minutes between each addition until it is thick, but do not make it dry or pasty. If you are going to store the sauce, do not thicken with tomato paste until you are reheating, or it will be inclined to scorch.

Yield: About 4 cups of sauce, enough for 2 pounds of pasta or 4–6 servings

—MIMI SHERATON

SPICED VEAL AND BEEF RAGOUT

meat

1½ pounds veal shoulder, in one piece

1½ pounds beef chuck, in one piece

2 tablespoons kosher salt

Freshly ground black pepper to taste

2 tablespoons olive oil

2 medium onions, 1 minced, 1 sliced thin

6 cloves garlic, minced

1 (1-inch) piece ginger, peeled and minced

2 teaspoons allspice

2 teaspoons cumin

4 cups canned plum tomatoes, crushed with their juice

¾ cup raisins

1. Season each piece of meat with ½ teaspoon salt and a few grinds of pepper. In a 8-quart stockpot, warm the oil over medium-high heat. Add the meats and brown on all sides, about 5 minutes for each side. Remove meat and set aside.

2. Add the minced onion, garlic, carrots and half the ginger to the pan. Lower heat to medium. Cook for 8 minutes, stirring occasionally. Stir in allspice, cumin and I teaspoon salt and cook for I minute.

3. Return the beef to the pot, add the tomatoes and cover. Simmer for 20 minutes. Add the veal and simmer for I hour. Add the remaining ginger and the sliced onion and simmer for 30 minutes. The meat should be tender enough to pull apart with a fork.

4. Remove the meat. Continue to simmer the sauce while the meat is cooling. When the meat is cool enough to handle, tear it into bite-size pieces. Return to the pot. Stir in the raisins and season with the remaining salt and pepper to taste. Simmer for 5 minutes. Serve with couscous or pasta.

Yield: 6 servings

—MOLLY O'NEILL

SALADS

To anyone who grew up in an American Ashkenazic home two generations ago, the term *salad* must seem like a joke, relegated to quarter-cut wedges of iceberg lettuce, usually with Russian dressing and sliced tomatoes and radishes—white, red and black. There were, of course, egg, chicken and tuna salads and others with potatoes or cucumbers sliced with onion in a vinegar marinade or with sour cream for a dairy meal, and pickled beets with onions and cloves, but little that suggested the pleasures of leafy greens tossed with subtle dressings of good olive oil and red wine vinegar. In fact, with winter dinners of roast meat, the closest things to salads were cold sauerkraut, and pickled tomatoes, peppers and cucumbers.

In truth, not many Americans two generations ago knew of lettuces other than iceberg, Boston and romaine, although real sophisticates were aware of Bibb lettuce and watercress and Italians long knew the pleasures of escarole and chicory. The expanded array of lettuces and other types of vegetables has gone a long way to expand our salad repertoire, and not only among Jews. Again, Sephardim and Middle Eastern Jews were way ahead with all of the cold vegetable dishes, both as appetizers and side dishes, so popular throughout the countries they lived in.

There are basically two types of salad included here: the first is the light vegetable combination that may include fruit or grain to be served as side dishes. In addition to a variety of green salads, this category includes radish and fennel salad, and black-eyed pea salad with walnuts and herbs. The second type is more substantial, made with chicken, meat or fish or copious vegetables, to be served as main courses, among them warm chicken with artichokes and spinach, duck with oranges and red onions, grilled lamb with potatoes, salmon and smashed cucumbers and a lusty Niçoise tuna salad from Alice Waters of the celebrated Chez Panisse in Berkeley.

HEARTS OF BIBB LETTUCE WITH CLEMENTINES AND CITRUS DRESSING

pareve

2 heads Bibb or Boston lettuce, leaves separated
    and washed

2 clementines

½ clove garlic, crushed and chopped

½ tablespoon lemon juice

½ tablespoon cider vinegar

2 teaspoons Dijon mustard

1 teaspoon honey

2 teaspoons chopped thyme

Coarse sea salt to taste

Freshly ground black pepper to taste

3 tablespoons extra-virgin olive oil

1 teaspoon hazelnut oil

1. Select only pale inner leaves of the lettuce; place in salad bowl. You should have 4 large handfuls. Zest clementines; reserve zest. Cut ends off clementines, cutting deeply enough to reveal flesh. Using a small paring knife, cut off remaining peel, cutting end to end in about ½-inch-wide strips. Take away the membrane, but not too much flesh. Remove each section, slicing lengthwise into the flesh, just inside the membrane. Add sections to bowl with the lettuce.

2. In a small bowl, whisk together garlic, ½ teaspoon reserved zest, lemon juice, vinegar, mustard, honey, thyme, salt and pepper. While whisking, gradually pour in olive oil, then hazelnut oil. Whisk until emulsified. Taste, and adjust seasoning.

3. To serve, pour dressing a tablespoon at a time over lettuce, tossing each time, until there is just enough to coat lightly. Serve.

Yield: 4 servings

—AMANDA HESSER

TOSSED SALAD WITH HONEY DRESSING

pareve

ADAPTED FROM *The New York Times Heritage Cookbook*

FOR THE SALAD:

1 medium-size head leaf lettuce or romaine lettuce,
    washed, drained and crisped

¼ head red cabbage, finely shredded

1 cucumber, peeled and thinly sliced

1 bunch scallions, including some green part, chopped

¼ cup finely diced celery

⅓ cup finely diced carrot

½ clove garlic, finely chopped

1 teaspoon oregano

1 tablespoon finely grated onion

Salt and finely ground black pepper
    to taste

FOR THE HONEY DRESSING:

½ cup oil

¼ cup cider vinegar

¼ cup honey

1. To prepare salad, break the lettuce into a salad bowl. Add the cabbage, cucumber, scallions, celery and carrot. Toss.

2. Sprinkle with the garlic, oregano, grated onion, salt and pepper.

3. To prepare honey dressing, combine the oil, vinegar and honey. Mix well. Pour over salad and toss.

Yield: 8 servings

ROMAINE SALAD WITH LEMON-CUMIN DRESSING

pareve

ADAPTED FROM Fritzie Abadi

¼ cup freshly squeezed lemon juice

2 teaspoons ground cumin

2 teaspoons kosher salt

A few grinds fresh black pepper

⅔ cup vegetable oil

2 large heads romaine lettuce, rinsed, dried and torn into bite-size pieces

In a small bowl, whisk together the lemon juice, cumin, salt and pepper. Very slowly whisk in the oil. Place the lettuce in a large salad bowl and toss with the dressing.

Yield: 8–10 servings

—MOLLY O'NEILL

RED SALAD

pareve

ADAPTED FROM Hank Tomashevski

FOR THE VINAIGRETTE:

1 shallot, peeled and chopped

¼ cup balsamic vinegar

1 tablespoon honey

¾ cup olive oil

Salt and freshly ground black pepper to taste

FOR THE SALAD:

1 cup cooked red beets, diced into ½-inch cubes

1 cup tomatoes, seeded and diced into ½-inch cubes

½ cup radishes, diced into ¼-inch cubes

½ cup red pepper, diced into ¼-inch pieces

About 3 cups red-leafed lettuces like red leaf, lollo rosso or red romaine, roughly chopped

1 cup red cabbage, shredded

1 cup radicchio, shredded

1. To make the vinaigrette, place the shallot, vinegar and honey in a bowl. Whisk in the oil and season with salt and pepper. Set aside.

2. For the salad, combine the beets, tomatoes, radishes and red pepper in a bowl and dress with some of the vinaigrette. Set aside.

3. Combine the lettuce, cabbage and radicchio in a bowl and toss with some of the vinaigrette, then mound it on a large platter. Sprinkle the chopped vegetables on top of the lettuce mixture and around it and serve.

Yield: 6–8 servings

NOTE: *Substitute or add any other red vegetables.*

—WILLIAM NORWICH

SALAD FOR PITA SANDWICHES

pareve

4½ cups lettuce leaves, preferably arugula, trimmed and cut into fairly large bite-size portions
2 cups thinly sliced onions, preferably red onions
1 cup thinly sliced radishes
1 cup thinly sliced, peeled cucumber
2 cored, seeded, deveined sweet red peppers, halved and thinly sliced, about 1½ cups
1 teaspoon finely minced garlic
½ teaspoon finely chopped hot, seeded red or green pepper

Freshly ground pepper to taste
2 tablespoons vinegar
4–6 tablespoons olive oil

1. Combine the lettuce, onions, radishes, cucumber, sweet pepper, garlic, hot pepper and ground pepper to taste.

2. Beat the vinegar and oil in a bowl and add it to the salad. Toss well.

Yield: Filling for 4–6 pita sandwiches

—CRAIG CLAIBORNE AND PIERRE FRANEY

MARINATED MEDITERRANEAN VEGETABLE SALAD

pareve

¾ cup extra-virgin olive oil
About ¼ cup red wine vinegar, or to taste
1 tablespoon Dijon mustard
1 clove garlic (green part removed), minced
Coarse sea salt and freshly ground pepper to taste

1 red pepper
1 yellow pepper
12 baby artichokes
2 pounds fava beans
2 pounds asparagus tips
2 tablespoons tarragon

1. Combine the oil, vinegar and mustard and mix to an emulsion. Add the garlic and salt and pepper to taste.

2. Meanwhile, preheat the broiler and cut the peppers into strips about 2 inches wide, removing the seeds. Put the peppers skin side up on a broiling rack and broil until the skins are charred and puffed. Put the pepper strips in a paper bag and close the bag. When the peppers have cooled, peel away their skins. Slice the peppers into thin strips. While they are still warm, coat them with some of the vinaigrette.

3. Meanwhile, slice the tops off the artichokes about half an inch down and remove the tough outer leaves. Steam the artichokes until they are tender (about 20 minutes). When the artichokes are cooked, cut them in quarters or slice them. Toss them in some of the vinaigrette dressing and put them on the serving platter.

4. Peel the pods from the fava beans and trim the asparagus. Steam the beans and the asparagus for about 10 minutes, or until they are tender. Peel the tough outer skins from the fava beans. Coat the beans with some vinaigrette. Arrange them on the serving platter along with the peppers and the asparagus. Pour remaining dressing over asparagus and sprinkle the vegetables with tarragon. Serve at room temperature (do not refrigerate).

Yield: 4–6 servings

—MOIRA HODGSON

AVOCADO WITH SPICED TAHINI-YOGURT DRESSING

dairy

ADAPTED FROM *Taste of Israel*

1 cup plain lowfat yogurt
⅓ cup tahini
½ teaspoon ground cumin
Pinch of ground coriander
¼ teaspoon minced garlic
1 tablespoon fresh lemon juice
½ teaspoon kosher salt
¼ teaspoon freshly ground black pepper
Pinch of cayenne pepper
3 ripe avocados
½ cup sliced almonds, toasted

1. To make the dressing, whisk together the yogurt and tahini until smooth. Stir in the cumin, coriander, garlic, lemon juice, salt, pepper and cayenne. Cover and refrigerate at least 1 hour.

2. Before serving, peel the avocados, halve lengthwise and remove the pit. Thinly slice them lengthwise and fan half an avocado onto each of 6 plates. Spoon the dressing over and sprinkle with almonds.

Yield: 6 servings

—MOLLY O'NEILL

WARM BEET AND STRING BEAN SALAD

pareve

4 medium beets
1 pound young string beans, trimmed
1 teaspoon Dijon mustard
¼ cup balsamic vinegar
½ cup walnut oil
1 small red onion, minced
1 tablespoon chives, chopped
Sea salt and freshly ground pepper to taste

1. Preheat the oven to 350 degrees. Put the beets in the oven on a rack and bake them for 1½ hours or until they are tender when pierced with a fork. When the beets are cool enough to handle, slice them into ½-inch pieces and put them in a bowl. Keep them warm.

2. Meanwhile, steam the string beans until they are tender.

3. Combine the mustard, vinegar, walnut oil, salt and pepper and mix well. Pour half the mixture onto the beets with the onions and chives and toss. Put in the center of a round serving dish.

4. Toss the beans in the remaining dressing and arrange them in a circle around the beets. Serve the salad warm or at room temperature.

Yield: 4–6 servings

—MOIRA HODGSON

COLESLAW WITH POPPY SEEDS AND SCALLIONS

pareve

1 head cabbage, about 1 pound
2 medium-size carrots, trimmed and scraped, about ⅓ pound
2 tablespoons distilled white vinegar
1 tablespoon Dijon mustard
1 teaspoon honey
Salt and freshly ground pepper to taste
½ cup vegetable oil
2 teaspoons poppy seeds
2 tablespoons finely chopped scallions

1. Cut the cabbage into quarters. Cut away and discard the core.

2. Process the cabbage in the container of a food processor to the desired degree of fineness. The cabbage could be alternately chopped with a knife on a flat surface. Place the cabbage in a mixing bowl.

3. Cut the carrots into quarter-inch rounds. Place the carrots in the container of a food processor and process, or chop the carrots to the desired degree of fineness. Combine the carrots and cabbage.

4. Place the vinegar, mustard, honey, salt, pepper and oil in a mixing bowl. Beat until smooth. Pour mixture over cabbage and carrots. Add poppy seeds and scallions. Blend well and serve.

Yield: 4 servings

—PIERRE FRANEY

TURKISH GRATED CARROT SALAD

dairy

5 cups peeled, shredded carrots

2 tablespoons extra-virgin olive oil

2 garlic cloves, crushed

Coarse salt to taste

1 cup whole-milk yogurt, preferably sheep's milk

3 tablespoons minced fresh mint

1. Put carrots in a colander. Pour boiling water over and drain well. Put in a bowl. Mix with oil.

2. Mash garlic with salt. Stir in yogurt. Fold into carrots. Garnish with mint and serve.

Yield: 6 servings

—FLORENCE FABRICANT

SPICED CARROT SALAD

pareve

ADAPTED FROM *Cooking with the 60-Minute Gourmet*

1 pound fresh carrots, about 12

3 large garlic cloves, peeled but left whole

Salt to taste

½ cup fresh lemon juice

⅛ teaspoon cinnamon

½ teaspoon cumin

½ teaspoon paprika

⅛ teaspoon cayenne pepper

¼ cup olive oil

Chopped parsley for garnish

1. Trim and scrape carrots and place them in a pot.

2. Cover the carrots with water and add the garlic and salt. Bring to a boil and cook for 10 minutes or until tender. Drain. Then cut the carrots into ½-inch-thick rounds (there should be about 2½ cups).

3. In a bowl, combine the lemon juice, cinnamon, cumin, paprika and cayenne. Blend well. Add the carrots. Mash the garlic with a fork and add to salad. Add half of the oil. Stir well.

4. Spoon out individual portions and sprinkle the remaining oil over them evenly. Garnish with parsley and serve.

Yield: 6 servings

NOTE: *Poaching the garlic gives it a much milder flavor.*

CUCUMBER SALAD WITH DILL

pareve

ADAPTED FROM *Craig Claiborne's Favorites, Vol. 4*

2–4 large cucumbers
7 tablespoons white wine vinegar
½ cup plus 1 teaspoon sugar
4 teaspoons salt
2 tablespoons chopped fresh dill

1. If the cucumbers are new and unwaxed, there is no need to peel them unless desired. Otherwise, peel them. Cut into thin slices and put in a mixing bowl. There should be 6 cups. Add 6 tablespoons vinegar, ½ cup sugar, 3 teaspoons salt and the dill. Cover and refrigerate 1 hour or longer.
2. Drain. Add the remaining 1 tablespoon vinegar, 1 teaspoon salt and 1 teaspoon sugar.

Yield: 10 or more servings

NOTE: *For a variation, substitute 1–2 cloves of garlic, mashed, for the dill.*

CUCUMBER IN SOUR CREAM

dairy

ADAPTED FROM *The New York Times Heritage Cookbook*

1 large cucumber
1 cup sour cream
1 tablespoon chopped onion
3 tablespoons cider vinegar
¼ teaspoon salt
⅛ teaspoon white pepper

1. Peel the cucumber. Run tines of fork lengthwise over cucumber and cut crosswise into thin slices.
2. Combine the remaining ingredients and pour over sliced cucumber. Marinate 30 minutes at room temperature.

Yield: 4 servings

GREEN BEANS AND PEPPER SALAD
WITH CUMIN VINAIGRETTE

pareve

1 pound green beans

1 roasted sweet red or green pepper, cored and seeded
    (see instructions for roast peppers below)

½ cup finely chopped sweet onion

1 teaspoon imported mustard, preferably Dijon

1 tablespoon red wine vinegar

Salt and freshly ground black pepper to taste

⅓ cup olive oil

¼ teaspoon ground cumin

¼ cup finely chopped parsley

1. Trim or break off the ends of the beans. Remove the strings if any.

2. Bring enough water to a boil to cover the beans when they are added. Add the beans. When the water returns to a boil, cook until the beans are tender, about 10 minutes. Drain well. Put them in a mixing bowl.

3. Put each half of the roasted pepper on a flat surface. Cut it into very thin strips about ¼-inch wide. There should be about ½ cup. Add them to the beans. Add the chopped onion.

4. Spoon the mustard, vinegar, salt and pepper to taste in a small mixing bowl. Start stirring with a wire whisk while gradually adding the oil. Add the cumin.

5. Stir and add the sauce to the bean mixture. Sprinkle with parsley and toss. Serve at room temperature.

Yield: 4–6 servings

How to Roast Green or Red Peppers

1. Place the peppers under the broiler. Cook, turning often, until blistered and slightly burned on all sides. Drop the peppers into a brown paper bag and close it tightly. This will let them steam and facilitate peeling.

2. When the peppers are cool, peel them. Remove the core and seeds.

—CRAIG CLAIBORNE AND PIERRE FRANEY

THE GOLDEN DOOR
MEDITERRANEAN MUSHROOM SALAD

pareve

1½ tablespoons raisins, preferably white
2 tablespoons olive oil
1 tablespoon finely chopped shallots or the white part
   of green onions
1 teaspoon finely chopped garlic
1 pound white mushrooms, rinsed, patted dry and cut
   into cubes
1 teaspoon chopped fresh thyme or half the amount dried
1 teaspoon herb seasoning (see recipe below), optional
½ teaspoon freshly ground pepper
¼ cup dry white wine
1 large tomato, peeled, seeded and diced
1 tablespoon fresh lemon juice
¼ cup chopped parsley
Lettuce leaves or watercress sprigs

1. Put the raisins in a small bowl and add warm water to cover. Let stand 30 minutes or until raisins are plumped. Drain.
2. In a heavy skillet heat 1 tablespoon oil and add the shallots and garlic. Cook 30 seconds, stirring.
3. Add the mushrooms, thyme, herb seasoning, if used, and pepper. Stir and cook 30 seconds.
4. Add the wine, tomato, raisins and lemon juice. Bring to a boil and cook about 30 seconds. Sprinkle with parsley and the remaining tablespoon of oil. Serve warm or cold. Serve on a bed of lettuce leaves or sprigs of watercress.

Yield: 4 servings

◆ **GOLDEN DOOR** ◆
HERB SEASONING

pareve

4 tablespoons dried thyme
2 tablespoons dried tarragon
2 tablespoons dried rosemary
2 tablespoons sea salt
1 teaspoon lemon pepper
1 teaspoon curry powder
½ teaspoon celery seeds
4 tablespoons dried basil
1 tablespoon dried lemon peel
2 teaspoons fennel seeds
1 gram saffron, optional
1 teaspoon ground coriander
2 teaspoons juniper berries

Put all the ingredients into the container of a blender or food processor and blend until fine. Use sparingly in foods.

Yield: About ¾ cup

—CRAIG CLAIBORNE

MUSHROOM SALAD WITH CURRANTS AND CORIANDER

pareve

ADAPTED FROM *You've Got It Made*

1 pound assorted mushrooms, trimmed
½ cup extra-virgin olive oil
2 large shallots, thinly sliced
2 garlic cloves, thinly sliced
1 teaspoon toasted coriander seeds
½ teaspoon coarsely cracked pepper
¼ cup currants (or raisins)
½ cup cider vinegar
Salt to taste
Minced chives

1. Bring a large pot of water to a boil. If the mushrooms are not of uniform size, cut the larger ones up so they are about the same size as the smaller ones. Put them in the boiling water and cook for 2 minutes. Drain, then rinse in cold water; drain again. Put in a serving bowl and set aside.

2. Put the olive oil in a large skillet. Turn the heat to medium-high and add the shallots and garlic. Cook for 2 minutes, then reduce the heat to medium-low. Add the coriander, pepper and currants (or raisins). Cook, stirring, for about a minute.

3. Add cider vinegar and salt to taste. Pour mixture, hot, over mushrooms, stir and cover with foil. Marinate at room temperature for 3 hours, preferably overnight.

4. Serve at room temperature, garnished with chives.

Yield: 4 servings

—MOIRA HODGSON

ORANGE-ONION SALAD

pareve

ADAPTED FROM *You've Got It Made*

4 heads romaine or red leaf lettuce or other
    salad greens
4 navel oranges, peeled and sliced into rounds
3–4 very thin slices red onion, separated into rings
4 teaspoons red wine vinegar
4 teaspoons olive oil

1. Wash and dry leaves; tear into bite-size pieces and arrange on each of 4 plates.

2. Arrange orange slices on leaves and slip onion rings in between orange slices.

3. Whisk vinegar and oil together and pour over salads.

Yield: 4 servings

NOTE: *This salad tastes best when dressed with high-quality oil and vinegar. For a variation, sprinkle the orange slices with 8 medium or large black Italian, French or Greek olives that have been pitted and cut up.*

—MARIAN BURROS

GRILLED LEMON-PARSLEY SALAD

pareve

4 lemons
¼ cup sugar
1 bunch flat-leaf parsley, well washed and dried
¼ cup extra-virgin olive oil
Salt and pepper to taste

1. Slice the ends off the lemons. Slice into thinnest possible rounds, removing the seeds. In a small bowl, combine lemon and sugar; mix well. Let sit for 2 hours.

2. Pick leaves off the stems of the parsley.

3. Grill the lemon slices over a medium-to-low fire, or place them in a single layer on a cookie sheet and broil them until slightly browned.

4. Remove, combine with parsley, olive oil and salt and pepper to taste. Toss gently, and serve.

Yield: 4 servings

—JOHN WILLOUGHBY AND
CHRIS SCHLESINGER

NEW POTATO SALAD WITH DILL

pareve

2 pounds new potatoes of uniform size, scrubbed
Salt and freshly ground black pepper to taste
⅓ cup white wine vinegar
⅔ cup extra-virgin olive oil
½ tablespoon Dijon mustard
¼ cup finely chopped scallions
2 tablespoons minced fresh dill

1. Place the potatoes in a saucepan, cover with cold water, bring to a boil, cover and reduce the heat to low. Cook until the potatoes are just tender, about 20 minutes. Drain and quarter the potatoes, taking care to keep the skins on.

2. Place the potatoes in a bowl, season lightly with salt and pepper and gently toss with 2 tablespoons of the vinegar and 1 tablespoon of the oil. Set aside until cool.

3. Mix the remaining vinegar with the mustard until well blended. Beat in the oil. Pour over the cooked potatoes and gently mix. Add the scallions and dill, season to taste with salt and pepper and serve.

Yield: 4–6 servings

—FLORENCE FABRICANT

POTATO SALAD WITH HORSERADISH-YOGURT DRESSING

dairy

¼ cup plain yogurt

2 tablespoons grated horseradish (see Note, page 414)

1 tablespoon red wine vinegar

½ cup extra-virgin olive oil

Coarse salt and freshly ground pepper to taste

6 scallions, green part included, chopped

2 pounds boiling potatoes

1 bunch watercress, leaves only

1. Combine the yogurt, horseradish, vinegar and oil. Mix thoroughly and season to taste with salt and pepper. Stir in the scallions.

2. Meanwhile, steam the potatoes until done. Drain and cut them in thick slices while they are still hot.

3. Place the potatoes in a serving bowl and toss them in the dressing. Add the watercress leaves just before serving and toss.

Yield: 4–6 servings

NOTE: *If using bottled horseradish packed in vinegar, check seasoning before you add the red wine vinegar.*

—FLORENCE FABRICANT

COLETTE ROSSANT'S RADISH AND FENNEL SALAD

pareve

1 bunch large fresh radishes

1 fennel bulb

1 tablespoon lemon juice

2 tablespoons olive oil

Salt and freshly ground pepper to taste

4 black olives for garnish

1. Trim and rinse the radishes. Discard the stems and leaves.

2. Peel the fennel bulb.

3. Thinly slice the radishes by hand or slice them, using a food processor. Cut the fennel into very fine strips or shred the fennel, using the grater of a food processor.

4. Put the lemon juice, olive oil, salt and pepper into a salad bowl and blend well. Add the radishes and fennel and toss well. Refrigerate until well chilled.

5. Divide the mixture among 4 individual salad plates and garnish each serving with a black olive.

Yield: 4 servings

—CRAIG CLAIBORNE

SPINACH ALMOND SALAD

pareve

ADAPTED FROM *You've Got It Made*

4 cups spinach leaves

¼ pound mushrooms, sliced

2 tablespoons toasted sliced almonds

2 tablespoons olive oil

2 tablespoons tarragon vinegar

½ teaspoon crushed tarragon

⅛ teaspoon nutmeg

Freshly ground black pepper to taste

1. Remove tough stems from spinach; wash and dry and tear into bite-size pieces. Place in serving bowl with mushrooms and almonds.
2. Combine remaining ingredients in saucepan and heat to boiling. Pour hot dressing over salad and toss. Serve.

Yield: 3–4 servings

—MARIAN BURROS

MIRAVAL'S SPINACH SALAD

pareve

FOR THE SALAD:

½ pound spinach leaves, stemmed, washed and dried

2 cups radicchio

½ cup jicama, cut into thin strips

½ cup sweet red pepper, cut into thin strips

½ cup sweet yellow pepper, cut into thin strips

½ cup carrots, peeled and cut into thin strips

1 tablespoon sun-dried tomato, cut into thin strips

FOR THE DRESSING:

2 tablespoons honey

1 scallion, minced

2 oyster mushrooms or 2 large white mushrooms, minced

2 cloves garlic, minced

½ teaspoon serrano chilies or other fresh chili peppers

¼ teaspoon Dijon mustard

2 teaspoons rice vinegar, with more to taste

½ teaspoon cracked black peppercorns, with more to taste

1. To make the salad, tear the spinach and radicchio into large pieces. Toss with the jicama, peppers, carrots and sun-dried tomato.
2. To make the dressing, warm the honey in a saucepan over medium heat. Add the scallion, mushrooms, garlic and chilies. Bring to a boil, then lower heat and simmer, stirring constantly, for 2–3 minutes. Stir in the mustard, remove from heat and whisk in the vinegar. Season with black pepper. Toss with salad and serve at once.

Yield: 4 servings

—MOLLY O'NEILL

CHILLED SESAME SPINACH

pareve

20 ounces crinkly leaf or 2 bunches flat leaf spinach,
    stemmed and well washed

¼ cup soy sauce

¼ cup white vinegar

3 tablespoons sesame oil

2 tablespoons sugar

2 tablespoons minced fresh ginger

1 tablespoon freshly ground white or black pepper

¼ cup sesame seeds, toasted in a sauté pan over
    medium heat and shaken frequently until fragrant
    (4–5 minutes)

1. Fill a sink or a large stockpot with ice and cold water.

2. Bring a large pot of salted water to a boil over high heat. Add the spinach (in 2 batches if necessary), leave for 5 seconds, then remove using a slotted spoon, tongs or skimmer. Immediately plunge the spinach into cold water to stop the cooking process.

3. Drain spinach, gently squeezing it between your hands, and chop roughly. Place in a medium bowl, cover and refrigerate until well chilled, about 15 minutes.

4. In a small bowl, combine the soy sauce, vinegar, sesame oil, sugar, ginger and pepper, and mix well.

5. Pour the dressing over the spinach and mix well with a fork, fluffing it to make sure it is coated with the dressing. Stir in the toasted sesame seeds.

Yield: 4 servings

NOTE: *This spinach is particularly good as an accompaniment to a strongly flavored fish like tuna, bluefish or mackerel.*

—JOHN WILLOUGHBY AND
CHRIS SCHLESINGER

EILEEN WEINBERG'S SWEET POTATO SALAD

pareve

6 sweet potatoes, scrubbed but not peeled

Fine sea salt to taste

Freshly ground black pepper to taste

1½ tablespoons lemon juice

1 teaspoon finely grated lemon zest

¾–1 cup mayonnaise

1 bunch scallions, trimmed and sliced into thin
    rounds, including most of the green

1 cup sliced celery, cut on the diagonal

1 green pepper, seeded and diced, optional

4 hard-cooked eggs, peeled and cut into small
    chunks

1. Cut the sweet potatoes in half crosswise. Put them in a large pan and add enough lightly salted water to cover them by 2 inches. Bring to a boil and boil gently for 15–20 minutes, until just tender. Drain and let rest until cool enough to handle.

2. Peel the potatoes and cut them into chunks or slices. Salt and pepper lightly. Add lemon juice and

zest to I cup mayonnaise; mix ¾ cup with the potatoes. Mix in scallions, celery and optional green
pepper.

3. Gently mix in the hard-cooked eggs. Add more

mayonnaise if desired. Adjust salt and add generous
amounts of black pepper. Chill slightly and serve.

Yield: 8 servings

—SUZANNE HAMLIN

SWEET POTATO AND CRYSTALLIZED GINGER SALAD

pareve

FOR THE DRESSING:

 ½ cup red wine vinegar
 2 tablespoons soy or other light-flavored oil
 1 tablespoon honey
 2 teaspoons soy sauce
 1 teaspoon grated fresh ginger
 Pinch of ground red pepper

FOR THE SALAD:

 1 pound sweet potatoes, peeled and cut into
  ¼-by-¼-by-2-inch pieces
 ½ cup scallions, thinly sliced
 2 tablespoons crystallized ginger, finely julienned

1. To prepare the dressing, combine the ingredients
in a small bowl, mix well and let it stand for at least
I hour.

2. For the salad, steam the sweet potatoes over boiling water just until tender when pierced with a knife,
about 6–8 minutes. Plunge them into ice water to
stop the cooking, then blot dry.

3. In a medium-size bowl, mix the sweet potatoes,
scallions and crystallized ginger, add the dressing,
toss and chill for at least I hour before serving.

Yield: 4 servings

—JOANNA PRUESS

BARRY WINE'S VEGETABLE-MATZOH "SALAD"

meat, pareve

ADAPTED FROM *Jewish Cooking in America*

 10 matzoh squares
 ¼ cup Schmaltz (page 413) or unsalted margarine

 1 red bell pepper, diced fine
 1 cucumber, diced fine
 1 bunch chives, chopped fine
 2–3 teaspoons capers (optional)
 Salt and freshly ground black pepper to taste

1. Preheat oven to 300 degrees.
2. Run a rolling pin over the matzohs to break them up into small pieces no larger than ¼ inch.
3. Toast the matzoh in oven for 10 minutes. Transfer to a bowl.
4. Heat the schmaltz or margarine in a saucepan over medium heat and add the red pepper and cucumber. Cook for 1 minute. Turn off the heat and add the chives and the capers, if desired.

5. Toss in a mixing bowl with the toasted matzohs. Add salt and pepper to taste. Serve immediately.

Yield: 8 servings

NOTE: *The chef of Quilted Giraffe, a famed Manhattan restaurant now closed, recommends his novel salad as a simple and delicious accompaniment to brisket or to roast chicken. The schmaltz gives a richer flavor for those dishes. For a lighter taste, or if serving with a fish course, use margarine.*

—JOAN NATHAN

HUMMUS, PITA AND YOGURT SALAD

dairy

3 whole wheat pitas
1¾ cups cooked chickpeas or 1 (15-ounce) can
    no-salt-added chickpeas
2 tablespoons tahini
1 clove garlic, cut up
5 tablespoons lemon juice
1 teaspoon ground cumin
Salt and freshly ground black pepper to taste
2 tablespoons chopped fresh mint
2 cups plain yogurt, whole milk or nonfat
Hot pepper flakes, optional

1. Preheat oven to 500 degrees. Cut pitas in half into two circles and dry out in oven until they are very crisp, about 3 minutes.
2. Combine chickpeas, tahini, garlic, lemon juice, cumin and 3 tablespoons water in food processor and puree. Season with salt and pepper.
3. Mix mint with yogurt. Break pitas into pieces and arrange in a flat serving dish. Sprinkle a little water on top. Top with chickpeas (hummus) mixture, then with yogurt. Sprinkle with hot pepper flakes, if desired.

Yield: 4 servings

—MARIAN BURROS

BLACK-EYED-PEA SALAD WITH HERBS, WALNUTS AND POMEGRANATES

pareve

ADAPTED FROM *Food of the Greek Islands*

1½ cups dried black-eyed peas, picked over
   and rinsed

6 tablespoons extra-virgin olive oil

3–4 tablespoons freshly squeezed lemon juice

3 tablespoons coarsely ground walnuts

1 clove garlic, minced

Salt and freshly ground black pepper to taste

½ cup coarsely chopped arugula

½ cup coarsely chopped flat-leaf parsley

½ cup torn purslane, or an additional ¼ cup each
   arugula and parsley

¼ cup pomegranate seeds

1. Place the peas in a medium saucepan, add cold water to cover by 2 inches and bring to a boil. Cook for 5 minutes. Drain. Add fresh water to just cover the peas and bring to a boil, then reduce heat to low and simmer until tender, 20–30 minutes. Drain and cool to room temperature.

2. In a small bowl, whisk together the oil, lemon juice, walnuts, garlic, salt and pepper. In a serving bowl, combine the peas, arugula, parsley and purslane. Pour the dressing over the salad and toss well. Season to taste again with salt and pepper, sprinkle with the pomegranate seeds and serve.

Yield: 4–6 servings

—MOLLY O'NEILL

TABBOULEH · (PARSLEY SALAD WITH BULGUR, MINT AND TOMATOES)

pareve

⅓ cup fine-grain bulgur

3 cups finely chopped parsley, flat leaf or curly leaf

3 tomatoes, diced small

1 red onion, diced small

1 cucumber, peeled and diced small

¼ cup finely chopped fresh mint

1 teaspoon minced garlic

⅓ cup extra-virgin olive oil

8 tablespoons lemon juice

2–4 dashes Tabasco sauce

1 head romaine lettuce

1. Rinse bulgar and place in medium-size bowl with 1 cup water. Let sit 30 minutes. Drain, squeeze with your hands and place in large bowl.

2. Add parsley, tomatoes, onion, cucumber, mint, garlic, olive oil, lemon juice and Tabasco. Toss well. Serve, using lettuce leaves as scoops.

Yield: 4 servings

—JOHN WILLOUGHBY AND
CHRIS SCHLESINGER

MED-RIM BULGUR SALAD

pareve

ADAPTED FROM *Middle Eastern Food*

1½ cups coarse bulgar
3 tablespoon olive oil
1 cup finely diced onion
⅔ cup finely chopped parsley
⅓ cup finely chopped cilantro
6 tablespoons lightly toasted pine nuts
3 tablespoons fresh lemon juice
1½ tablespoons pomegranate molasses
   (see Note, page 583)
1 tablespoon ground cumin
1½ teaspoons Mediterranean oregano
1½ teaspoons ground coriander seeds

¼ teaspoon ground allspice
Salt to taste
2 teaspoons ground sumac, if desired

1. Soak bulgar in 4 cups of boiling water for 30 minutes. Squeeze dry. Reserve.
2. Heat oil in medium skillet. Sauté onion over low heat until soft but not brown, about 8 minutes. Reserve with oil.
3. Put soaked bulgar in large bowl and add cooked onion with oil. Mix with fork. Add remaining ingredients except sumac, and mix. Chill several hours. Sprinkle with sumac before serving.

Yield: 6 servings

—ROZANNE GOLD

CHICKPEA AND OLIVE SALAD WITH FENNEL

pareve

3 cups chickpeas, freshly cooked or canned, rinsed and
   drained
1 large clove garlic, finely minced
18 European-style black olives, pitted and halved
⅔ cup finely diced fresh fennel
2 tablespoons minced scallions
2 tablespoons chopped flat-leaf parsley
⅓ cup fresh lemon juice
1 tablespoon black olive paste (available in
   fancy food shops)

5 tablespoons fruity extra-virgin olive oil
Salt to taste
Freshly ground black pepper to taste

1. Place the chickpeas in a bowl and gently mix in the garlic, olives, fennel, scallions and parsley.
2. In a separate bowl mix the lemon juice with the olive paste and olive oil. Pour over the chickpeas mixture and toss gently.
3. Season to taste with salt and pepper and mix again.

Yield: 6 servings

—FLORENCE FABRICANT

CURRIED COUSCOUS AND GRILLED ONION SALAD

dairy

1 tablespoon peanut oil

1 tablespoon curry powder

1½ cups hot Vegetable Stock, canned or fresh
   (page 51), or water

1 cup couscous

1 pound large sweet onions

1 small green pepper

3 tablespoons chopped fresh mint

3 tablespoons plain nonfat yogurt

Salt and generous grindings of fresh black pepper
   to taste

1. Mix the oil and the curry powder in a small saucepan and heat it, stirring, until the oil just begins to bubble. Stir in the stock or water and bring to a simmer.

2. Place the couscous in a bowl, pour the simmering curry broth over it, stir and cover. Set aside.

3. Preheat a grill, a heavy griddle or a large cast-iron skillet until it is very hot. Peel and slice the onions about ¼ inch thick. Grill or sear the onion slices, turning them frequently, until they are nicely browned, 5–10 minutes. It doesn't matter if they come apart into rings, but you should adjust the heat so they don't burn. Remove the seared onions to a cutting board and chop them.

4. Completely char the green pepper over an open flame or under a broiler, then place it in a paper or plastic bag for a minute or two. Remove it from the bag, peel off the charred skin, then core, seed and chop the pepper. Add the chopped pepper and onions to the couscous.

5. Fold the mint and yogurt into the salad, mixing well with a fork. Season the salad to taste with salt and enough freshly ground black pepper to make it fairly peppery.

Yield: 4 servings

—FLORENCE FABRICANT

KASHA SALAD WITH
ROASTED MUSHROOMS AND GINGER

meat, pareve

1 tablespoon canola oil

10 ounces shiitake mushrooms

1 egg white

1½ cups coarse or whole buckwheat groats (kasha)

2⅓ cups hot Chicken Stock (page 48) or Vegetable
   Stock (page 51), canned or fresh

1 tablespoon finely minced fresh ginger

3 tablespoons Chinese or Japanese sesame oil

1 tablespoon soy sauce

2 tablespoons rice vinegar

½ teaspoon Chinese chili oil, or to taste

½ cup chopped scallions

Salt to taste

1. Preheat oven to 350 degrees. Line a large baking sheet with foil and brush with the canola oil.

2. Remove and discard the stems from the mushrooms. Arrange the mushrooms, brown side down, in a single layer on the baking sheet. Turn them over, place in the oven and roast for 30 minutes.

3. Meanwhile, beat the egg white in a medium-size bowl until it is frothy. Stir in the groats, mixing them with a fork to coat the grains with the egg. Transfer the groats to a 3-quart saucepan and stir over medium heat about 2 minutes, until the grains separate and begin to toast.

4. Lower the heat, stir in the stock, cover and cook for 10 minutes. Set aside, covered, 5 minutes longer, then transfer the cooked groats to a large mixing bowl. Fold in the ginger.

5. When the mushrooms are done, slice the caps in strips about ¼ inch wide. Fold the mushrooms in with the kasha and allow the mixture to cool, about 30 minutes. Fluff with a fork.

6. Beat the sesame oil with the soy sauce and vinegar. Beat in the chili oil. Fold this dressing into the mushrooms. Fold in the scallions. Season the salad to taste with salt.

Yield: 8 servings

—FLORENCE FABRICANT

GREEN LENTILS WITH ROASTED BEETS AND PRESERVED LEMON

pareve

ADAPTED FROM Deborah Madison

FOR THE SALAD:

> 5 small beets (about 1 pound), peeled
> 1 teaspoon olive oil
> Salt to taste
> Freshly ground black pepper to taste
> 1 cup French green lentils
> 1 carrot, peeled and finely diced
> ½ small onion, finely diced
> 1 bay leaf
> 4 sprigs parsley
> 2 sprigs thyme
> 1 Preserved Lemon (page 429) or 2 teaspoons lemon zest
> ⅓ cup chopped parsley
> 2 tablespoons chopped mint sprigs for garnish

FOR THE VINAIGRETTE:

> 2 tablespoons fresh lemon juice
> 1 teaspoon lemon zest
> 1 shallot, finely chopped
> Salt and freshly ground black pepper to taste
> 5 tablespoons extra-virgin olive oil

1. Preheat the oven to 350 degrees. Reserve 1 beet for garnish and cut the remaining 4 into ½-inch cubes. Toss the cubes with 1 teaspoon of oil, season with salt and pepper and bake 30–35 minutes, stirring occasionally.

2. Meanwhile, place the lentils, carrot, onion, bay leaf, parsley, thyme and ½ teaspoon salt in a small pot and add water to cover the lentils by about three-quarters of an inch. Bring to a boil, then simmer, covered, until the lentils are tender, 20–25 minutes.

Discard the herbs, drain well and transfer to a large bowl.

3. To make the vinaigrette, combine the lemon juice, zest, shallot and ¼ teaspoon salt and let stand for 15 minutes. Whisk in the olive oil and season to taste with pepper and more salt if necessary.

4. To assemble the salad, quarter the lemon and scrape out the soft pulp. Finely chop the pulp and stir 2 teaspoons into the vinaigrette. Finely chop the lemon skin and add it, along with the vinaigrette, roasted beets, parsley and chopped mint, to the lentils. Toss and serve on a platter. Grate the reserved beet and use it for garnish with mint sprigs.

Yield: 4–6 servings

—MOLLY O'NEILL

GINGERED LENTIL AND CELERY SALAD

pareve

ADAPTED FROM Hubert Keller

1 carrot

3 ripe tomatoes, cored, peeled, seeded and minced

½ pound green lentils

1 small white onion

1 stalk celery, minced

½ red onion, minced

¼ teaspoon ginger, peeled and chopped fine

¼ cup lemon juice

1½ tablespoons soy sauce

3 tablespoons olive oil

Salt and freshly ground pepper to taste

1 cucumber, peeled, seeded and diced

1 tablespoon balsamic vinegar

½ teaspoon Dijon-style mustard

1 cup alfalfa sprouts

8 sprigs parsley

1. Bring a pot of water to a boil. Peel the carrot and cut it lengthwise into 8 strips that are ⅛ inch thick and about 5 inches long. (If it is hard to get strips that long, shorter ones can be used.) Plunge the strips into boiling water for 1 minute, cool immedi-ately under cold water, pat dry and set aside. Put the tomatoes in a fine sieve over a bowl and push them with the back of a spoon to press out excess liquid; set tomatoes aside.

2. Put the lentils and the white onion in 2 quarts of cold water over medium heat and cook gently for 45 minutes. Drain, remove the onion and let the lentils cool. When cool, put lentils in a mixing bowl with the celery, red onion, ginger, lemon juice, soy and olive oil. Mix, adjust seasoning with salt and pepper and chill.

3. Put the cucumber, vinegar and mustard in a blender; season lightly with additional salt and pepper and puree. Set aside.

4. Line the inside of a round cookie cutter 2½–3 inches in diameter with a carrot strip. Put the cookie cutter on a serving dish and use it as a mold. Spoon in the lentils and pat firmly. Gently smooth the tomatoes on top in a thin layer. Repeat with the remaining carrot strips and lentils, placing 2 rounds on each of 4 serving plates. Spoon the cucumber vinaigrette around the cakes, garnish with sprouts and parsley and serve.

Yield: 4 servings

—MOLLY O'NEILL

ORZO AND PEA SALAD WITH CITRUS DRESSING

pareve
ADAPTED FROM Neuman & Bogdonoff

1 tablespoon finely chopped carrot
1 tablespoon finely chopped celery
1 tablespoon finely chopped onion
½ cup white wine vinegar
1 cup orzo
¼ cup shelled peas
Salt to taste
Zest of 1 lemon, grated
1 tablespoon red wine vinegar
1 tablespoon lemon juice
1 tablespoon minced parsley
½ cup extra-virgin olive oil
⅓ cup julienned red pepper
⅓ cup julienned green pepper
⅓ cup julienned yellow pepper
¼ cup toasted pine nuts

Salt to taste
Freshly ground black pepper to taste

1. Combine the carrot, celery and onion with the white wine vinegar. Cook, covered, over medium heat for 3 minutes. Uncover and cook until the vinegar evaporates. Set aside.
2. Cook the orzo according to the package. Drain and cool.
3. Cook the peas in salted water until tender. Drain. Cool.
4. Combine the lemon zest, red wine vinegar, lemon juice and parsley. Whisk in the oil.
5. Toss the orzo with the carrot, celery and onion. Toss in the peppers, peas and nuts. Add the dressing, salt and pepper. Toss.

Yield: 6–10 servings

— GLENN COLLINS

FRUITED SPICED RICE SALAD

pareve
ADAPTED FROM Joyce Goldstein

1½ cups basmati rice
1 (2- to 3-inch) piece ginger, peeled and bruised
2¾ cups cold water
½ teaspoon salt
½ teaspoon freshly ground black pepper
½ teaspoon ground nutmeg
½ teaspoon ground coriander seed
¼ cup fresh lemon juice

1 medium shallot, peeled and chopped fine
2 tablespoons olive oil
½ cup currants or black raisins, plumped in hot water and drained
4 fresh ripe apricots, quartered, or 8 dried, plumped in hot water and drained
⅓ cup toasted sliced almonds

1. Combine rice, ginger and water in a large, heavy saucepan and bring to a boil. Cover, reduce heat to medium-low and simmer until tender but not soft, about 15 minutes. Drain, discard the ginger and transfer the rice to a large glass or ceramic bowl.

2. Season rice with salt, pepper, nutmeg and coriander. Add lemon juice, shallot and olive oil; toss to combine. Stir in currants and apricots. Divide among 4 bowls, garnish with toasted almonds and serve.

Yield: 4 servings

—MARIAN BURROS

WHITE BEAN SALAD WITH RED CAVIAR

dairy

ADAPTED FROM John Loring

⅓ cup extra-virgin olive oil

2 tablespoons red wine vinegar

½ teaspoon coarsely ground black pepper

¼ teaspoon salt

1 teaspoon cumin or caraway seeds

3 cups cooked or canned white beans, rinsed and drained

½ cup chopped sweet onion

½ cup finely chopped celery

½ cup (loosely packed) chopped Italian parsley

1½ cups sour cream

6 ounces red salmon caviar

1. In a small mixing bowl combine the olive oil, vinegar, pepper, salt and cumin or caraway seeds. Set aside.

2. In a medium bowl combine the beans, onion, celery and parsley. Add the olive oil mixture and mix gently but thoroughly.

3. Divide the salad among 6 serving plates or bowls. Top each with 2 tablespoons of sour cream and 1 heaping tablespoon of caviar. Serve immediately.

Yield: 6 servings

NOTE: *This salad also makes an excellent appetizer.*

—ENID NEMY

SHREDDED GREENS AND SMOKED SALMON (CHIFFONADE DE SAUMON)

dairy

ADAPTED FROM L'Aquitaine, Paris

½ cup Crème Fraîche (page 431) or sour cream

1 tablespoon lemon juice

¼ teaspoon hot paprika

1 head Boston lettuce, rinsed and dried

4 thin slices smoked salmon, cut into wide strips

1. Prepare dressing: In small bowl, combine crème fraîche or sour cream, lemon juice and paprika.

2. Stack several lettuce leaves and, using a long chef's knife, cut into fine strips, as if slicing cabbage for cole slaw. Place in large salad bowl and toss with dressing.

3. Distribute lettuce among 4 salad plates and cover each with several strips of salmon. Serve immediately.

Yield: 4 servings

NOTE: *The dressing can be made a day in advance, then refrigerated, but prepare the rest of the ingredients just before serving time.*

—PATRICIA WELLS

CHARLIE TROTTER'S ARTICHOKE AND SMOKED-SALMON SALAD

pareve

½ bunch parsley

4 artichokes, each slightly larger than a baseball

About 8 tablespoons high-quality extra-virgin olive oil, or as needed

1 carrot, peeled and chopped

1 small onion, peeled and chopped

2 stalks celery; 1 chopped, 1 in fine julienne

½ apple, chopped

1 small bulb fennel; ½ chopped, ½ in fine julienne

4 cloves garlic, peeled

2 large or 3 small bay leaves

½ teaspoon black peppercorns

1 cup haricots verts, blanched

½ red onion, peeled and sliced paper thin

3 tablespoons pitted, slivered calamata olives

2 heaping tablespoons Spanish arbequina olives or calamata olives, quartered

Salt and freshly ground black pepper to taste

Juice of ½ lemon

4 ounces smoked salmon, julienned

3–4 leaves basil, shredded

1. Place parsley in a large bowl of water. Trim artichokes of stems and leaves, leaving only smooth bottoms with prickly centers inside, and place in water.

2. Heat 3 tablespoons oil in large sauté pan over medium-low heat. Add carrot, onion, chopped celery, apple, chopped fennel and garlic. Cover and sweat until softened, about 10 minutes. Lay artichokes on top of vegetables. Cover and steam, turning 2–3 times, for 10 minutes. Add bay leaves, peppercorns and ½ cup water. Cover and simmer until very tender, 30 minutes. Cool.

3. Remove and discard the prickly center. Pat artichoke bottoms dry and cut crosswise into thin strips. Place in large bowl. Cut haricots verts into smaller pieces and add to bowl with remaining celery and fennel, red onion and olives. Toss to combine.

4. Drizzle salad with 2½–3 tablespoons oil and toss. Add a good pinch of salt and pepper and toss. Squeeze lemon juice over and toss again. Lay smoked salmon and basil over, and mix gently so fish does not break up. Divide among 4 salad plates, drizzle a little oil around each and serve.

Yield: 4 servings

—CHARLIE TROTTER

SALAD OF POTATOES, SMOKED SABLE AND EGG MIMOSA

pareve

ADAPTED FROM Michael Otsuka

4 cups Yukon Gold potatoes, cut in ¼-inch dice
6 whole cloves
2 tablespoons olive oil
4 garlic cloves
4 thyme sprigs
3 black peppercorns
2 bay leaves
4 tablespoons finely chopped shallots
6 tablespoons finely chopped Italian parsley
3 tablespoons finely chopped scallions
½ cup finely chopped celery heart
Fleur de sel or coarse salt and freshly ground
*   white pepper to taste*
1½ cups Lemon Mayonnaise (see recipe below)
1 cup smoked sable, boneless and skinless,
*   coarsely chopped*
6 eggs, hard cooked and pushed through a sieve

1. Place the potatoes, cloves, olive oil, garlic, thyme, peppercorns and bay leaves in a medium pan with water to cover. Cook until the potatoes are tender.

Remove the whole cloves, garlic, thyme, bay leaves and peppercorns.

2. In a large salad bowl, fold together the diced potatoes with the shallots, parsley, scallions and celery. Season with salt and pepper to taste. Dress with 1 cup mayonnaise, and taste; if salad is dry, add more mayonnaise.

3. Spread half the potato salad in a shallow bowl. Top with the smoked sable and then with the remaining potato salad. Cover completely with the hard-cooked egg. Press gently but firmly. Refrigerate until ready to serve.

Yield: 6 servings as appetizer or side dish

◆ **LEMON MAYONNAISE** ◆

pareve

1 egg
2 teaspoon Dijon mustard
Salt to taste
⅓ cup grapeseed oil
⅓ cup fruity olive oil
2 tablespoons white wine vinegar
1 tablespoon lemon juice

1. Place egg, mustard, salt and ¼ cup grapeseed oil in blender. Blend at high speed until completely mixed.

2. With the blender running and the center of the cover off, slowly pour in olive oil; blend completely.

Blend vinegar and lemon juice in thoroughly, then slowly add remaining oil and blend again.

Yield: About ¾ cup mayonnaise

NOTE: *This mayonnaise gives a tang to salads and to fish, poultry and vegetable dishes.*

—MARIAN BURROS

SALMON SALAD WITH VEGETABLES

pareve

ADAPTED FROM *The Best of Craig Claiborne*

1 cup fresh peas
Salt to taste
1 cup scraped and cubed carrots
½ cup diced celery
1 cup peeled and cubed turnips
1 cup freshly made Homemade Mayonnaise
  (page 415)
¼ teaspoon Tabasco sauce
½ cup thinly sliced onion
½ teaspoon Worcestershire sauce (see Note, page 582)
¼ cup finely chopped fresh dill
Freshly ground pepper to taste
1 large ripe tomato, cored, seeded, and cut into eighths
4 cups Poached Salmon, cut or broken into large
  bite-size pieces (page 120)

1. Drop the peas into cold water with salt to taste. Bring to a boil and simmer for 1–2 minutes, or until barely tender. Do not overcook. Drain and set aside.

2. Bring enough water to a boil to cover the carrots, celery and turnips when added. Add salt to taste. Add the carrots and simmer for about 3 minutes.

3. Add the celery and turnips and simmer for 1–2 minutes longer. Drain. Run under cold water to chill. Drain well on a clean towel.

4. Put the peas, turnips, celery and carrots in a large mixing bowl.

5. Add the mayonnaise, Tabasco sauce, onion, Worcestershire sauce and dill. Add salt and pepper to taste and toss.

6. Put the vegetables in mayonnaise in a serving dish. Surround it with the tomato wedges and pile the salmon on top.

Yield: 6 servings

GEOFFREY ZAKARIAN'S SALMON
WITH SMASHED CUCUMBER-DATE SALAD

pareve

1 (2½-pound) center-cut Atlantic salmon fillet,
  with skin

6 tablespoons fruity extra-virgin olive oil, preferably
  Spanish

Medium-coarse sea salt, preferably Maldon from
  England, to taste

Freshly ground black pepper to taste

2 English cucumbers, peeled and cut in 8 equal pieces

¾ cup finely sliced fennel bulb

6 Medjool dates, pitted and cut in slivers

⅓ cup coarsely chopped walnuts

2 tablespoons minced chives

2 tablespoons lemon juice

About 20 small sprigs fennel fronds

1. Place salmon on cutting board, skin side up. Cutting straight down through skin, divide fish into 6 equal portions, each about 2 by 6 inches. Turn each piece over and cut down through center lengthwise; do not cut through skin. Pieces should lie open like a book. Keeping fish flat, gently push long sides toward center seam so that each piece looks like a boneless salmon steak. Use about a teaspoon of oil to brush fish pieces lightly on both sides. Season with salt and pepper.

2. Roll cucumber pieces loosely in a clean linen napkin, and smash repeatedly with fist. Transfer to cutting board. Coarsely chop cucumber. Transfer to mixing bowl. Add fennel, dates, walnuts and chives. Toss. Set aside.

3. Heat grill or grill pan until very hot. Place fish on grill, sear briefly, less than a minute. Give each piece a quarter-turn to make crisscross markings, and turn fish over. Repeat. Fish will be barely cooked. Transfer fish to baking pan large enough to hold pieces without touching. Brush tops with a little oil. Fish can wait up to 1 hour before final cooking and serving.

4. Heat oven to 350 degrees. Shortly before serving, place pan in oven and bake 3½ minutes. Remove.

5. Toss cucumber salad with 4 tablespoons olive oil and the lemon juice. Season with salt and pepper. Divide among 6 plates. Place a fish fillet on top of salad at a slight angle on each, and brush with a little remaining oil. Drizzle rest of oil around fish and salad, and scatter with fennel sprigs.

Yield: 6 servings

—GEOFFREY ZAKARIAN

ALICE WATERS'S TUNA NIÇOISE

pareve

2 tablespoons red wine vinegar

1 tablespoon chopped chervil

1 tablespoon chopped arugula

1 clove garlic, minced

1 tablespoon diced onion

4 tablespoons extra-virgin olive oil

Freshly ground black pepper to taste

1 cup cooked green and yellow beans

4 ounces fresh grilled tuna, flaked into large pieces

8 small potatoes, cooked, peeled and sliced

4 anchovies (see Note, page 582)

6 tiny cherry tomatoes

A few basil leaves

8 niçoise olives

2 hard-cooked eggs, peeled and halved

1. Combine the vinegar, chervil, arugula, garlic, onion and olive oil. Season with pepper.

2. Using your hands, mix the beans, tuna and potatoes with the dressing and mound the mixture on a serving dish. Decorate with the anchovies, tomatoes, basil, olives and hard-cooked eggs.

Yield: 2 servings

—MARIAN BURROS

TODD ENGLISH'S TUNA TABBOULEH

pareve

1 cup bulgar

8 ounces sushi-grade tuna, ground or minced with a
   sharp knife

1 small bunch cilantro, chopped

¼ cup chopped flat-leaf parsley

Juice and zest of 1 lemon

1 tablespoon chopped fresh mint

1 teaspoon chopped fresh ginger

1 cup peeled fresh horseradish, passed through a juicer to
   make ⅓ cup horseradish juice (see Note, page 414)

½ cup full-flavored olive oil

Salt and freshly ground black pepper to taste

2 teaspoons cumin seeds, toasted

1 large seedless cucumber, peeled and cut into ribbons

1. In a casserole, boil bulgar in 4 cups water until the wheat is soft but still has some bite.

2. Drain, then spread on flat surface to cool.

3. In a large bowl, mix cooled bulgar, tuna, cilantro and parsley.

4. In another bowl, place lemon juice and zest, mint, ginger, horseradish juice and olive oil. Whisk until well blended.

5. Pour dressing over bulgar-tuna mixture. Add salt and pepper to taste and stir. Top with toasted cumin seeds and surround with cucumber.

Yield: 6 servings

—ROZANNE GOLD

TUNA, BLACK-EYED PEAS AND ARTICHOKE SALAD

pareve

ADAPTED FROM Patrick Clark

FOR THE OIL:

5 ripe tomatoes, cored and cut into large chunks
½ cup extra-virgin olive oil
Kosher salt and freshly ground pepper to taste

FOR THE SALAD:

1 cup dried black-eyed peas
½ small onion, peeled
1 small carrot, peeled and cut into large chunks
4 sprigs fresh thyme
1 bay leaf
8 cloves garlic, peeled
3½ cups water
2 teaspoons balsamic vinegar
2 teaspoons red wine vinegar
2 tablespoons extra-virgin olive oil
16 fresh baby artichokes, trimmed, tough outer leaves
    discarded
½ teaspoon kosher salt, plus more to taste
¼ teaspoon freshly ground pepper
2 tablespoons finely chopped scallions

FOR THE TUNA:

1 teaspoon olive oil
1 (8-ounce) fresh tuna steak
Kosher salt and freshly ground pepper to taste
2 tablespoons chopped Italian parsley

1. To make the oil, puree the tomatoes in a food processor. Strain through a fine-mesh sieve. Place in a medium-size saucepan and simmer over low heat until reduced to ½ cup, about 1 hour. Strain again and let cool. Gradually whisk in the olive oil. Season with salt and pepper. Set aside.

2. Meanwhile, combine the black-eyed peas, onion, carrot, thyme, bay leaf, garlic and water in a medium-size saucepan and bring to a boil. Reduce the heat and simmer until the peas are tender, about 40 minutes. Drain and remove all but the peas. Place in a large bowl and toss in the vinegars and 1 tablespoon of oil. Let cool.

3. Preheat the oven to 400 degrees. Thinly slice the artichokes, place in a roasting pan and toss with 1 tablespoon of oil. Roast until tender, about 15 minutes. When cool, toss with the peas, along with the salt, pepper and scallions. Set aside at least 30 minutes.

4. To make the tuna, heat the oil in a medium-size nonstick skillet over medium-high heat. Add the tuna and sauté until seared on both sides but still pink in the center, about 10 minutes. Let stand for 10 minutes. Slice thinly across the grain. Season with salt and pepper.

5. Shake or stir the tomato oil and drizzle it around the edge of 4 plates. Mound the salad in the center of the plates and lay the tuna over the top. Garnish with parsley and serve.

Yield: 4 servings

—MOLLY O'NEILL

WARM CHICKEN SALAD WITH ORANGE-BALSAMIC DRESSING, CRACKED OLIVES AND DATES

meat

12 cups cleaned and trimmed arugula
   leaves

2 oranges, peeled, seeded and sliced in thin
   wedges

4 boneless, skinless chicken breasts

Salt and freshly ground black pepper to taste

½ cup olive oil

½ cup orange juice

¼ cup balsamic vinegar

¼ cup Dijon mustard

2 cloves garlic, minced

2 teaspoons ground cumin

16 dates, quartered

16 green cracked olives, quartered

½ cup salted shelled pistachios, toasted and coarsely
   chopped

1. Arrange arugula on 4 large plates and top with orange slices.

2. Season chicken breasts on both sides with salt and pepper. Heat I tablespoon oil in a large skillet over medium-high heat. Add chicken. Reduce heat to medium and cook chicken for 5 minutes. Turn and cook, covered, for 4–5 minutes more, or until chicken is juicy and just cooked through. Transfer cooked chicken to a plate and cover with aluminum foil.

3. While chicken cooks, whisk together orange juice, balsamic vinegar and mustard in a small bowl; set aside.

4. Add 3 tablespoons oil to skillet used to cook chicken. Add garlic and cumin, and sauté over medium-low heat for 30 seconds. Stir in orange juice mixture, scraping up any brown bits that have stuck to bottom of skillet, and let bubble for 2 minutes. Whisk in remaining oil. Stir in dates and olives; let dressing bubble for 30 seconds. Season with salt and pepper to taste.

5. Cut each chicken breast on diagonal into thin slices. Spoon warm dressing over arugula and orange slices, and top with chicken. Sprinkle with pistachios.

Yield: 4 servings

—VICTORIA ABBOTT RICCARDI

DANIEL BOULUD'S WARM CHICKEN, ARTICHOKE AND SPINACH SALAD

meat

ADAPTED FROM *Café Boulud Cookbook*

⅔ cup plus 3 tablespoons extra-virgin olive oil

4 bone-in chicken breasts, skin removed,
    cut into small strips

Coarse sea salt and freshly ground white pepper
    to taste

6 baby artichokes, trimmed and quartered

1 clove garlic, peeled and crushed

1 sprig thyme

1 tablespoon water

2 medium shallots, peeled, trimmed, diced,
    rinsed and dried

¼ cup sherry vinegar

2 tablespoons snipped basil leaves

1 tablespoon tarragon leaves, chopped fine

4 plum tomatoes, peeled, seeded and cut
    into thin strips

8 cups baby spinach, well washed and dried

1. Center a rack in the oven and preheat the oven to 400 degrees.

2. Warm 2 tablespoons of the olive oil in a large, ovenproof sauté pan or skillet over medium-high heat. Season the chicken with salt and pepper, and when the oil is hot, slip the breasts, skin side (or what would have been skin side) down into the pan. Sear the chicken on one side until golden (3–4 minutes), then turn it over and give the other side equal treatment. Turn the breasts again and slide the pan into the oven. Roast the chicken until it is cooked through, about 12–14 minutes.

3. Meanwhile, warm 1 tablespoon of the olive oil in a sauté pan or skillet over medium-high heat. Add the strips of chicken skin and cook until they start to color lightly. Add the artichokes, garlic and thyme, season with salt and pepper, cover, and cook for 3 minutes. Lift the lid and stir in the water. Cover the pan and cook for another 3–4 minutes, until artichokes are tender. Discard the garlic and thyme. Remove the pan from the heat and keep warm.

4. When the chicken is cooked, transfer it to a cutting board and put the pan over medium heat. Add the shallots to the pan and cook, stirring, until they soften (about 2 minutes). Pour in the vinegar and scrape up whatever little bits of meat may have adhered to the pan. Reduce the vinegar by half, then whisk in the remaining ⅔ cup of olive oil and the herbs. This is the dressing for your salad. Remove the pan from the heat, correct seasoning and stir in the tomatoes.

5. Put the spinach in a large bowl and season to taste with salt and pepper. Slice the chicken breasts and put the strips, along with the artichokes and pieces of chicken skin, in the bowl. Toss the salad with the warm chicken pan juices and serve immediately.

Yield: 4 servings

—MOIRA HODGSON

DUCK SALAD WITH ORANGES AND ONIONS

meat

1 Honey-Glazed Duck (page 171)
   or plain roast duck
4 seedless oranges, peeled
1 small red onion, peeled
1 teaspoon finely minced garlic
24 imported black olives, drained
1 teaspoon ground cumin
2 tablespoons red wine vinegar
4 tablespoons pure virgin olive oil
Salt to taste, if desired
Freshly ground pepper to taste
1 tablespoon finely chopped cilantro, optional
Assorted greens such as watercress, red leaf lettuce,
   Boston lettuce and radicchio
Onion rings for garnish, optional

1. Cut the duck into serving pieces. Remove and discard the fat and bones. Cut the meat into bite-size pieces. There should be about 2 cups. Put the pieces in a mixing bowl.

2. Cut the oranges into thin slices and add them to the duck.

3. Cut the onion into thin rings and add it. Add the garlic and olives.

4. Sprinkle with cumin, vinegar, oil, salt, pepper and cilantro and toss to blend.

5. Arrange the lettuce greens neatly on a platter. Spoon the salad on top and garnish with more onion rings if desired.

Yield: 4–6 servings

—CRAIG CLAIBORNE

GRILLED LAMB AND POTATO SALAD

meat

1¼ pounds very small new potatoes
12 ounces boneless lean lamb, cut in strips
1 tablespoon olive oil
¼ cup balsamic vinegar
1 tablespoon Dijon-style mustard
1 tablespoon chopped fresh rosemary
¼ cup finely cut cornichons
2 tablespoons minced parsley
1 cup thinly sliced red onion
Freshly ground black pepper to taste

12–16 cherry tomatoes
½ head of Boston lettuce or 1 head of Bibb lettuce,
   washed, dried and leaves separated

1. Scrub potatoes and cook in water to cover in heavy-bottomed pot, covered, about 18 minutes, depending on size.

2. Grill lamb on top-of-stove grill, over charcoal grill or under broiler.

3. In serving bowl beat oil with vinegar and mustard. Stir in rosemary, cornichons, parsley and onion.

4. When potatoes are cooked, drain and cut in halves or quarters and add to dressing with grilled lamb.

5. Tuck lettuce around edges of salad and arrange tomatoes around perimeter. Serve warm.

Yield: 3 servings

—MARIAN BURROS

SALAD DRESSINGS
◆ ◆

VINAIGRETTES

pareve

WALNUT-SHALLOT VINAIGRETTE FOR BITTER GREENS

pareve

> 2 tablespoons walnut pieces
> 1/8 teaspoon salt
> 2 1/2 teaspoons fresh lemon juice
> Freshly ground black pepper to taste
> 3 tablespoons olive oil
> 2 teaspoons minced shallots

1. Using a mortar and pestle, mash walnut pieces into a paste with the salt. Add lemon juice and pepper and stir with a fork.

2. Slowly blend in olive oil and taste for balance, adding pepper and more salt if necessary. Add shallots and again taste. Use as a dressing with strongly flavored salad greens, like watercress or arugula, alone or in combination with dark green leafy lettuce.

Yield: Approximately 3/4 cup

—NANCY HARMON JENKINS

CREAMY CHICKPEA VINAIGRETTE

pareve

1½ cups cooked or canned chick peas (garbanzos),
    drained
1 large clove garlic
⅓ cup rice vinegar
2 tablespoons soy sauce
¼ cup sesame oil
¼ cup vegetable oil

1. To prepare the vinaigrette, place the chick peas, garlic, vinegar and soy sauce in the bowl of a food processor fitted with a steel chopping blade and process into a smooth puree, scraping down the work bowl as necessary.

2. With the motor running, pour the sesame and vegetable oils through the feed tube in a slow, steady stream. The vinaigrette will be creamy and thick. Scrape into a screw-top glass jar and refrigerate until needed.

Yield: About 2 cups

—JOANNA PRUESS

MOROCCAN (CHARMOULA) VINAIGRETTE

pareve
ADAPTED FROM Joyce Goldstein

1 teaspoon paprika
½ teaspoon cayenne pepper
2 teaspoons ground cumin
6 cloves garlic, minced fine
½ cup lemon juice, or part lemon juice and part red
    wine vinegar, to taste
½ cup chopped parsley
½ cup chopped fresh cilantro
1¼ cups olive oil, approximately

Salt to taste
Freshly ground pepper to taste

1. Mix paprika, cayenne pepper, cumin and garlic with the lemon juice. Add the parsley, cilantro and enough olive oil to reach a spoonable consistency.

2. Adjust tartness to suit palate, by adding lemon juice or vinegar. Add salt and pepper to taste.

Yield: About 2 cups

NOTE: *This is excellent with grilled tuna or chicken salad.*

—DENA KLEIMAN

LEMON-OLIVE VINAIGRETTE

pareve

Juice of 2 lemons
1 tablespoon Olivada (page 44)
5 tablespoons extra-virgin olive oil
Salt to taste
Freshly ground black pepper to taste
1 tablespoon finely minced Italian parsley
   leaves

1. Mix lemon juice and olivada until well blended.
Beat in olive oil.
2. Season to taste with salt and pepper and add the
parsley. Serve as a sauce for fish or cooked dried beans.

Yield: ½ cup

—FLORENCE FABRICANT

GREEN YOGURT DRESSING

dairy

1 cup unflavored yogurt
½ cup extra-virgin olive oil
3 tablespoons red wine vinegar
1 bunch parsley, flat leaf or curly leaf, well washed
   and dried
1 teaspoon cumin
1 teaspoon cinnamon
Salt and freshly ground white pepper to taste

1. Place the yogurt in a blender or food processor and
process for 10 seconds so it is completely smooth.
2. Add the oil, vinegar and parsley and blend or process until pureed. Add the cumin and cinnamon.
Mix well and season to taste with salt and white
pepper.

Yield: About 2 cups

—JOHN WILLOUGHBY AND
CHRIS SCHLESINGER

POPPY SEED DRESSING

pareve

ADAPTED FROM *The New York Times Heritage Cookbook*

½ cup sugar

1 teaspoon dry mustard

1 teaspoon paprika

¼ teaspoon salt

5 tablespoons tarragon vinegar

⅓ cup honey

1 tablespoon lemon juice

2 tablespoons onion juice or finely grated onion

1 cup vegetable oil (not olive oil)

1 tablespoon poppy seeds

1. Mix together the sugar, mustard, paprika, salt and vinegar until sugar dissolves completely.

2. Add the honey, lemon juice and onion juice or onion. Gradually beat in the oil. Chill. Add the poppy seeds just before serving.

Yield: About 1½ cups

NOTE: *This dressing complements salads containing citrus fruits.*

LIGHT FARE FOR
BRUNCH AND LUNCH

THIS CHAPTER IS MADE UP OF DAIRY DISHES AND, THEREFORE, MANY ARE STANDARDS AT FAST-DISAPPEARING KOSHER DAIRY restaurants where they share the menu with vegetable soups and fish dishes. Eggs are key ingredients, whether scrambled with smoked salmon, poached on creamed spinach, or in more stylish soufflés, or folded into a humble, savory *matzoh brei* or a noodle or challah pudding or kugel. To that traditional Ashkenazic collection, which includes puffy, crepe-wrapped cheese blintzes, are added airy latkes based on Italian ricotta or the much-missed apple pancake made famous by the bygone Manhattan restaurant Reuben's.

An elegant brunch or lunch might well center on a main course of baked asparagus and eggs, fresh corn and red pepper blini, or a Georgian cheese pie, *khachapuri,* that has a crust flavored with a little honey and coriander and a Muenster filling or an eggplant gratin with saffron-scented custard and end with coffee and French toast scented with orange juice and vanilla.

And as yet another example of a cross-cultural choice, consider the tower of bagel sandwiches layered with cream cheese, scallions and smoked salmon, or essentially the same ingredients in chef Douglas Rodriguez's lush potato and onion tortilla, brightened with salmon caviar and horseradish.

SCRAMBLED EGGS WITH SMOKED SALMON IN BRIOCHE

dairy

6 brioche
6 eggs
1/4 pound unsalted butter at room temperature
Coarse salt and freshly ground pepper to taste
1/4 pound smoked salmon, diced
1 tablespoon fresh chopped dill

1. Preheat oven to 250 degrees and heat brioche.
2. Cut tops off brioche. Scoop out insides and save them for another purpose or discard. Put brioche and tops on a baking tray in oven to keep warm.

3. Put the eggs in a blender with salt, pepper and 4 tablespoons of butter. Blend until frothy.
4. Heat the remaining butter in a thick skillet over low heat. Stir the salmon and dill into the eggs and add the mixture to the skillet. Cook very slowly, stirring until the eggs are cooked soft and not dried out.
5. Remove warmed brioche and tops from oven and fill center of each brioche with scrambled eggs. Cap each brioche with its lid. Serve immediately.

Yield: 6 servings

—MOIRA HODGSON

BAKED ASPARAGUS AND EGGS

dairy

1 pound medium-thick asparagus
1 tablespoon unsalted butter or olive oil
4 eggs
8 egg whites
1/2 cup skim milk
Pinch of salt
1/4 cup freshly grated Parmesan

1. Snap the ends off the asparagus at the point where they break naturally, then peel them. Steam the asparagus about 3 minutes, just until they are tender.

2. Preheat oven to 400 degrees.
3. Grease a 6-cup shallow baking dish with butter or oil.
4. Beat the eggs and egg whites with the milk and add the salt and cheese. Pour the mixture into the baking dish and arrange the asparagus on top. Bake 15–20 minutes, until set. Cut into portions and serve.

Yield: 4–6 servings

—FLORENCE FABRICANT

POACHED EGGS WITH CREAMED SPINACH AND SMOKED SALMON

dairy

ADAPTED FROM Ulla Wachtmeister

1 pint heavy cream
2 bags (10 ounces each) fresh spinach
2 tablespoons butter
Salt, pepper and nutmeg to taste
10 eggs
1 tablespoon white vinegar, approximately
10 slices smoked salmon
10 sprigs dill

1. Simmer cream to reduce by half.
2. Wash spinach and steam in water that clings to leaves until done, 5–7 minutes. Let drain thoroughly, pressing to remove moisture. Puree. Return to heat with butter and seasonings to taste. Stir in cream. Set aside.
3. Poach eggs in water to cover with white vinegar. Butter pan so eggs will not stick. Plunge eggs into cold water to stop cooking. Trim off uneven edges. Set aside. These can be stored up to 24 hours in cold water in the refrigerator. To serve, bring eggs to room temperature and reheat in hot, not boiling, water.
4. Reheat spinach.
5. On each plate, arrange spinach with a slice of salmon, an egg and a sprig of dill.

Yield: 10 servings

—MARIAN BURROS

BAKED MUSHROOM OMELET

dairy

ADAPTED FROM *The New York Times Heritage Cookbook*

1 pound mushrooms, white or a mixture
4 tablespoons butter, melted
8 eggs, separated
3 tablespoons flour
2 cups hot, but not boiling, milk
¼ cup dry sherry
Salt and freshly ground black pepper to taste
¼ teaspoon cayenne pepper

1. Preheat oven to 350 degrees.
2. Brush the mushrooms with a little of the butter and broil them until done. Let cool and cut them into slices.
3. Beat the egg yolks until light and lemon-colored. Beat the whites until stiff.
4. Place the flour in a mixing bowl and gradually add hot milk, stirring rapidly with a wire whisk or beater. Add 2 tablespoons of the melted butter, the egg yolks, sherry, salt, pepper, and cayenne and mix. Add the sliced mushrooms and mix.
5. Fold in the whites and pour the mixture into a greased 6-cup baking dish. Pour remaining butter over surface and bake 45 minutes.

Yield: 4 servings

POTATO AND ONION TORTILLA (OMELET) WITH SMOKED SALMON

dairy

ADAPTED FROM Douglas Rodriguez

FOR THE SALMON ROE SAUCE:

1 cup mayonnaise
½ cup sour cream
2 teaspoons fresh lime juice
1 teaspoon horseradish
2 tablespoons grated onion
3 tablespoons chopped flat-leaf parsley
4 tablespoons chopped chives
½ cup salmon roe

FOR THE TORTILLA:

3 tablespoons extra-virgin olive oil
2 medium potatoes, peeled and diced
1 large onion, diced
12 large eggs
½ cup milk
Coarse sea salt and freshly ground pepper to taste
½ pound thinly sliced smoked salmon

1. Make the sauce. Combine all the ingredients except the roe in a medium mixing bowl. Mix until well blended, then gently fold in the roe. Chill until ready to serve.

2. Make the tortilla. Heat 2 tablespoons of the olive oil in a skillet over medium-high heat. Add the potatoes and onion and sauté until tender, about 10 minutes. Remove from the heat and set aside.

3. Beat the eggs and milk together in a large bowl. Heat the remaining tablespoon of olive oil in a large nonstick frying pan. Add the egg mixture and when it starts to cook on the bottom, add the potato and onion mixture. Season to taste with salt and pepper.

4. Run a spatula along the sides of the pan, lifting up the eggs to let the uncooked egg run underneath to cook. When the tortilla is cooked except for the very top, remove it from the heat and slide it onto a plate. Flip the tortilla back into the pan, runny side down, and cook for an additional 2–3 minutes (you can also put it under a very hot broiler instead of turning it over). Slide the tortilla onto a large round serving dish and garnish with the sliced smoked salmon. Serve warm with the salmon roe sauce passed separately.

Yield: 8 servings

NOTE: *Salmon roe is available in jars or in the fish department of specialty food stores and better supermarkets.*

—MOIRA HODGSON

SWISS CHARD TART

dairy

FOR THE PASTRY:

   2 cups unbleached flour
   ½ teaspoon salt
   ½ cup water
   ½ cup extra-virgin olive oil

FOR THE FILLING:

   1 pound Swiss chard leaves (see Note below)
   Salt and pepper to taste
   3 large eggs
   1 cup freshly grated Parmesan cheese

1. Preheat the oven to 400 degrees.

2. Prepare the pastry: Combine the flour and salt in a medium-size bowl. Stir in the water, then the oil, mixing until thoroughly blended. Knead briefly. The dough will be very moist, much like a cookie dough. Press the dough into a 10½-inch metal tart tin with a removable bottom.

3. Prepare the filling: Wash and dry the green leafy portion of the chard, discarding the center white stem. Break up the leaves and chop them, in several batches, in a food processor.

4. Place the chard in a large, shallow frying pan and season with salt and pepper. Over low heat, wilt the chard and cook until most of the liquid has evaporated.

5. Combine the eggs and the cheese in a medium-size bowl and mix until thoroughly blended. Stir in the chard, mix well, then pour the vegetable mixture into the prepared tart tin.

6. Bake until the crust is golden and the chard mixture is firm and browned, about 40 minutes. Remove from the oven to cool. Serve at room temperature.

Yield: 6–8 servings

NOTE: *Spinach may be substituted for the chard.*

—PATRICIA WELLS

FRITTATA OF SMOKED SALMON AND LEEKS

pareve, dairy

   3–4 tablespoons olive oil or butter
   2 cups chopped leeks (4–6 large leeks)
   6 eggs, beaten
   ½ pound smoked salmon, diced
   1 tablespoon chopped chives
   Salt and freshly ground black pepper to taste

1. Heat 3 tablespoons of the oil in a heavy 9-inch skillet. A well-seasoned cast-iron skillet or a professional quality nonstick skillet works best. Add the leeks and cook very slowly, covered, until they are tender but not brown.

2. Meanwhile mix the eggs with the salmon and chives. Season to taste with salt and pepper. You will probably need very little salt. When the leeks are tender remove them from the skillet with a slotted spoon, leaving as much of the oil as possible in the skillet. Add the leeks to the egg mixture.

3. If necessary add additional oil to the skillet to coat it. Reheat the skillet and pour in the egg mixture, tipping the pan to fill it evenly.

4. Cook the eggs over medium heat 5–7 minutes, until they are set and golden brown on the bottom but still creamy on top. Using a spatula, loosen the frittata around the sides of the pan and, if necessary, along the bottom.

5. Place a platter larger than the skillet upside down over the skillet. Using potholders or mitts, hold both the platter and skillet tightly together and turn them over to invert the frittata onto the platter. Then quickly slide the frittata, uncooked side down, back into the skillet. Continue cooking until the underside is set, another 3 minutes or so.

6. Serve directly from the skillet or transfer the frittata to a serving platter. Serve it hot, warm or cooled to room temperature.

Yield: 4–6 servings

—FLORENCE FABRICANT

DIANE FORLEY'S ROLLED SOUFFLÉ

dairy

Nonstick baking spray
¼ pound (1 stick) butter
¾ cup all-purpose flour
⅓ cup semolina (also sold as pasta flour)
2½ cups milk
1 cup heavy cream
10 large eggs, separated into yolks and whites
⅛ teaspoon cayenne pepper
Salt and freshly ground black pepper to taste
½ cup grated Parmesan cheese
¼ teaspoon cream of tartar
1 tablespoon sugar (optional)
Spinach Filling (recipe follows)

1. Preheat oven to 375 degrees. Line a 12- by-17 inch jelly-roll pan (half-sheet pan) with parchment paper and coat with nonstick baking spray. In a large (4-quart) saucepan over medium heat, melt the butter. Using a wooden spoon, mix in the flour and semolina and stir constantly for 3 minutes. Stir in a small amount of milk to thin and smooth the mixture. Add the remaining milk and cream, beating with a whisk until smooth. Remove the pan from the heat and slowly pour in the egg yolks while whisking vigorously. Whisk for 2 minutes. Season with cayenne and salt and pepper to taste. Stir in cheese and set aside.

2. Using an electric mixer on low speed, beat the egg whites until frothy and add the cream of tartar and sugar. Increase speed to medium-high and continue to beat just until very soft peaks form when beater is lifted. Gently but thoroughly fold the whites, a third at a time, into the batter. Pour onto the parchment-lined sheet, filling pan three-quarters full. Bake 15 minutes, turn pan and bake 5 minutes, or until surface is golden brown.

3. Run a knife inside the edge of the baking pan to free souffle. Place a sheet of waxed paper or cotton cloth over the baking sheet, and invert onto a counter. Remove the pan and parchment paper. Spread the spinach filling to within an inch of the edges; lift a short end of the waxed paper or cloth until end curves, then roll soufflé into a log shape. Transfer seam side down onto a plate and serve cut into 8 slices.

Yield: 4 main-course servings

Spinach Filling

dairy

½ pound fresh spinach, stems removed
1 tablespoon butter
½ teaspoon salt plus to taste
2 tablespoons chopped fresh tarragon
4 tablespoons chopped fresh chives
4 tablespoons chopped fresh flat-leaf parsley
Freshly ground black pepper to taste

1. Wash spinach and drain but do not dry. In a large (4-quart) saucepan over low heat, melt the butter and add spinach and ½ teaspoon salt. Cover and steam until wilted, 3–5 minutes.

2. Transfer spinach and its liquid to a blender or food processor while hot. Add tarragon, chives and parsley. Puree until smooth and season with salt and pepper to taste.

Yield: About 1½ cups

—DIANE FORLEY

SOUR-CREAM SOUFFLÉ

dairy

ADAPTED FROM *The New York Times International Cookbook*

1½ cups sour cream
1 cup sifted flour
1¼ teaspoons salt
¼ teaspoon freshly ground black pepper
2 tablespoons chopped chives
½ cup grated nonprocessed Gruyère or Parmesan cheese
5 eggs, separated

1. Preheat oven to 350 degrees.

2. Mix until smooth the sour cream, flour, salt and pepper. Stir in the chives and cheese.

3. Beat the egg whites until stiff but not dry. With the same beater, in a separate bowl, beat the yolks until thick and lemon-colored. Gradually add the yolks to cream mixture, stirring constantly. Carefully fold in the egg whites.

4. Pour the mixture into four 1½-cup heatproof dishes, ungreased. Place in a shallow pan of hot water and bake until set, 30–40 minutes. Serve immediately.

Yield: 4 servings

ASPARAGUS SOUFFLÉ

dairy

2½ pounds asparagus, trimmed and peeled

2 small white potatoes (about ½ pound), peeled and
 cubed

1¼ tablespoon sesame seeds

½ cup ricotta cheese

Salt and freshly ground pepper to taste

2 teaspoons freshly grated ginger

¼ teaspoon hot pepper flakes, or to taste

2 tablespoons finely minced scallions

8 eggs, separated

1. Preheat oven to 425 degrees. Butter well and chill eight 1¼-cup soufflé dishes.

2. In separate pots, boil asparagus and potatoes in lightly salted water until soft. Drain well. Meanwhile, lightly toast sesame seeds by placing in hot nonstick fry pan. Set aside.

3. Place asparagus and potatoes in food processor or blender with ricotta. Puree slightly. Add salt, pepper, ginger, pepper flakes and scallions and puree well.

You should have about 3 cups. Transfer mixture to bowl.

4. Add yolks to mixture and blend well with wire whisk. In another bowl whisk whites until they form soft peaks. Fold one-quarter of whites into asparagus mixture, then remainder. Do not overwork mixture. Taste for seasoning.

5. Place soufflé dishes on baking sheet and fill to rim with mixture. Sprinkle sesame seeds evenly onto soufflés. Before placing in oven run thumb around rim of each to remove any overflow, which could cling and prevent soufflé from rising fully. Bake for approximately 10 minutes.

Yield: 8 servings

NOTE: *Because ricotta binds the ingredients of this soufflé instead of the traditional roux (flour, butter and milk), this version cuts the fat content of a classic soufflé. The technique, which was devised by Pierre Franey, is also employed in the recipe for the Carrot Soufflé that follows.*

—BRYAN MILLER

CARROT SOUFFLÉ

dairy

2 pounds carrots, chopped (about 4½ cups)

½ cup ricotta cheese

¼ teaspoon powdered cumin

3 tablespoons minced fresh dill

Salt and freshly ground black pepper to taste

3 eggs, separated

1. Preheat oven to 425 degrees. Butter well and chill eight 1¼-cup soufflé dishes.

2. Boil carrots in salted water until soft. Drain well.

3. Place carrots in a food processor or blender with ricotta, cumin, dill, salt and pepper. Puree well. You should have about 3 cups. Transfer to a bowl.

4. Add egg yolks to the mixture and blend well with a wire whisk. In another bowl, whisk egg whites until they form soft peaks. Fold a quarter of the whites into the carrot mixture, then the rest. Taste for seasoning.

5. Place soufflé dishes on a baking sheet and fill to the rim with mixture. Before placing in the oven, run your thumb around rim of each to remove any overflow, which could cling and prevent the souf-flés from rising fully. Bake for approximately 10 minutes.

Yield: 8 servings

NOTE: *Because ricotta binds the ingredients of this soufflé, instead of a roux (flour and butter) and milk, this version cuts the fat content of a traditional soufflé. The technique was devised by Pierre Franey.*

—BRYAN MILLER

SALMON SOUFFLÉ

dairy

½ *pound skinless, boneless fresh salmon*
2 *tablespoons butter, plus butter for greasing the soufflé dish*
2 *tablespoons finely chopped shallots*
2 *tablespoons flour*
1 *tablespoon cornstarch*
1½ *cups milk*
⅛ *teaspoon cayenne pepper*
6 *egg yolks*
2 *tablespoons Dijon-style mustard*
2 *tablespoons finely minced dill*
Salt to taste, if desired
Freshly ground pepper to taste
5 *egg whites*
Fresh Tomato Sauce (see recipe below)
¼ *cup heavy cream*

1. Put a 6-cup soufflé dish in the refrigerator.
2. Preheat the oven to 375 degrees.
3. Cut the salmon into ½-inch cubes. Put the fish in the container of a food processor or electric blender and blend thoroughly.

4. Melt 2 tablespoons of butter in a saucepan and add the shallots. Cook briefly, stirring, and add the flour, cornstarch and milk. Stir rapidly with a wire whisk. Cook until blended and smooth.

5. Stirring vigorously with the whisk, add the cayenne and egg yolks and cook until the mixture barely starts to bubble. Remove the sauce immediately from the heat. Scrape it into a mixing bowl. Beat in the mustard, dill, the ground salmon, salt and pepper. Stir to blend.

6. Beat the egg whites until stiff. Add about one-third of them to the salmon mixture and beat them in. Add the remaining whites and fold them into the mixture.

7. Generously butter the inside of the chilled soufflé dish. Pour and scrape the sauce into it.

8. Place in the oven and bake 20 minutes.

9. Meanwhile, blend the tomato sauce with the cream and bring to the boil. Serve the soufflé with the creamed tomato sauce.

Yield: 4–6 servings

Fresh Tomato Sauce

dairy

2 red, ripe tomatoes, about ¾ pound
1 tablespoon olive oil
1 teaspoon finely minced fresh garlic
Salt, if desired
Freshly ground black pepper to taste
1 tablespoon finely chopped fresh basil or 1 teaspoon dried
¼ teaspoon dried hot red pepper flakes
1 tablespoon butter

1. Drop the tomatoes into a saucepan of boiling water and let stand about 10 seconds. Drain immediately and pull away the peel. Cut away and discard the cores. Cut the tomatoes into small cubes. There should be about 1½ cups.

2. Heat the oil in a saucepan and add the garlic. Cook briefly, stirring, and add the tomatoes, salt and pepper.

3. Add the basil and pepper flakes. Swirl in the butter.

Yield: About 1¼ cups

—CRAIG CLAIBORNE AND PIERRE FRANEY

GEORGIAN CHEESE PIE • (KHACHPURI)

dairy

FOR THE DOUGH:

¾ cup milk
1½ packages active dry yeast
½ teaspoon honey
6 tablespoons butter, softened
¼ teaspoon ground coriander
1½ teaspoons salt
2 cups flour

FOR THE FILLING:

1½ pounds Muenster cheese
1 egg
2 tablespoons butter

1. Heat the milk to lukewarm.

2. Dissolve the yeast and the honey in ¼ cup of the milk. Set aside to proof for 10 minutes. Then stir in the remaining milk. Add the butter, coriander, salt and flour, mixing well.

3. Turn the dough out onto a floured board and knead until smooth and elastic, about 10 minutes. Place the dough in a greased bowl, turning to grease the top. Cover and allow to rise in a warm place until doubled in bulk, 1½–2 hours.

4. Meanwhile, prepare the filling: In a food processor or blender grate the cheese. Beat in the egg and the butter until the mixture becomes a smooth, fluffy puree. (You may have to do this in several batches.) Set aside.

5. When the dough has doubled in bulk, punch it down and then let rise again until doubled, about 45 minutes. Punch it down and divide into 6 equal pieces. Let rest for 10 minutes.

6. On a floured board roll each piece of dough out to a circle 8 inches in diameter. Grease six 4-inch cake or pie plates. Center one 8-inch round of dough in each pan.

7. Divide the cheese mixture into 6 equal parts. Spread the filling on each circle of dough, heaping it higher in the center. Then begin folding the edges of the dough in toward the center, moving in a clockwise direction, allowing each fold of dough to overlap the previous one, until the cheese mixture is completely enclosed in the pleated dough. Grasp the excess dough in the center of the pie and twist it into a topknot to seal.

8. Preheat the oven to 375 degrees. Let the pies rest for 10 minutes, then bake them for 35–40 minutes, until browned. Slip the khachpuri out of the pans and serve them immediately.

Yield: 6 servings

—DARRA GOLDSTEIN

EGGPLANT GRATIN WITH SAFFRON CUSTARD

dairy

ADAPTED FROM Deborah Madison

About ½ cup olive oil

3 cups diced onions

Salt to taste

2 large bell peppers, preferably 1 yellow and 1 red, stemmed, seeded and chopped

1 tablespoon minced garlic

½ teaspoon anise seeds, crushed with a knife

3 large tomatoes, peeled, seeded and diced

2 tablespoons tomato paste

Freshly ground pepper, preferably white, to taste

3–4 pounds eggplant, cut into slices just under ½ inch thick

⅛–¼ teaspoon saffron

1½ cups ricotta

3 eggs

¾ cup freshly grated Parmesan

1 cup plus 2 tablespoons milk or heavy cream

½ cup torn-up basil leaves

1. Preheat oven to 425 degrees. Place 3 tablespoons oil in a large, deep skillet or saucepan and turn heat to medium. Add onions and a healthy pinch of salt and cook, stirring, until translucent, 10 minutes or longer. Add peppers, garlic and anise and cook, stirring occasionally, until peppers are very tender, about 15 minutes. Add tomatoes and tomato paste. Adjust heat so mixture simmers steadily. Stir occasionally and cook until the mixture is thick and jammy, about 30 minutes. Taste and add salt and pepper as needed.

2. Lightly brush each slice of eggplant with olive oil and place the slices, in 1 layer, on 1 or more baking sheets. Bake, turning after about 20 minutes, until the eggplant is lightly browned and slightly shriveled, a total of 30–40 minutes. Turn the heat to 375 degrees.

3. Dissolve the saffron in ¼ cup hot water. Mix together the ricotta, eggs, Parmesan, milk or cream and some salt and pepper. Add saffron and its liquid. Stir basil into the tomato sauce.

4. Brush the inside of a large gratin dish or baking pan with oil. Make a layer of eggplant, then one of the tomato sauce; repeat. Top with the custard and bake for about 45 minutes or until it is nicely browned. Serve hot, warm or at room temperature.

Yield: 4 main-course or 8 side-dish servings

NOTE: *You may omit the saffron if you do not have any on hand, but the custard will lose its deep yellow color and a hint of bitterness. The eggplant may look a little dry when* it emerges from the oven, but its spongelike tendencies allow it to soak up plenty of the sauce and become tender and juicy. This dish may be served warm or at room temperature and may be served a couple of hours after cooking. To make it a more elegant entrée, serve it in individual gratin dishes or ramekins and reduce the baking time to 20 minutes or so.

—DEBORAH MADISON

FAMOUS DAIRY RESTAURANT'S VEGETABLE CUTLET WITH MUSHROOM GRAVY

dairy

ADAPTED FROM *New York Cookbook*

Vegetable Cutlets

pareve

1 pound carrots, peeled and grated

½ pound turnips, peeled and grated

1 head cauliflower, cut into small florets

1 small onion, grated

2 cloves garlic, minced

1 package (10 ounces) frozen green peas

½ pound fresh green beans, ends trimmed, cut into bite-size pieces and blanched

2 eggs

1 cup matzoh meal

½ cup unseasoned dried bread crumbs

1 teaspoon freshly ground black pepper

1 teaspoon kosher salt

3 tablespoons powdered vegetable bouillon concentrate, dissolved in 1 cup water

1. Preheat the oven to 350 degrees. Lightly grease a baking sheet.

2. Combine all of the ingredients in a large bowl and mix well with your hands. Form the mixture into eight 1-inch-thick patties. Place the cutlets 1 inch apart on the prepared baking sheet. Bake 1 hour, until lightly browned and heated through.

3. While cutlets are baking, make the gravy. Serve cutlets with the gravy.

Yield: 8 servings

Mushroom Gravy

dairy

2 tablespoons butter

1 medium onion, minced

2 pounds white mushrooms, thinly sliced

3 tablespoons powdered vegetable bouillon concentrate, dissolved in 4 cups water

¼ teaspoon freshly ground black pepper

2 teaspoons arrowroot, dissolved in ¼ cup cold water

1. Warm the butter in a large skillet over medium heat. Add the onion and cook until deep gold in color, about 5 minutes. Add the mushrooms, partially cover and cook, stirring occasionally, until the mushrooms are soft, about 10 minutes.

2. Add the dissolved bouillon mixture and the pepper and stir well. Simmer until reduced by half, 20–30 minutes.

3. Remove from the heat and whisk in the dissolved arrowroot. Return to very low heat and cook until thickened, about 3 minutes. Do not allow to boil.

Yield: Enough for 8 servings of vegetable cutlets

—MOLLY O'NEILL

JEAN-GEORGES'S NEW YEAR PORCINI TART

pareve

ADAPTED FROM Jean-Georges Vongerichten

2 cloves garlic, peeled and finely chopped
5 tablespoons olive oil
½ pound frozen puff pastry, thawed in the refrigerator
2 medium-size yellow onions, peeled and very thinly sliced
Kosher salt to taste
½ cup walnut halves
1¼ pounds fresh, whole porcini mushrooms
Freshly ground black pepper to taste

1. Combine the garlic and 3 tablespoons of the olive oil and allow to stand for at least an hour. Strain, discard the garlic solids and set the oil aside.

2. On a lightly floured surface, roll out the pastry dough to a ⅛ inch thickness. Using a 5-inch round cutter, cut 4 disks from the pastry and transfer the disks to a baking sheet lined with parchment paper. Pierce the disks' surfaces repeatedly with the tines of a fork. Refrigerate.

3. In a medium saucepan over medium heat, combine the onions, remaining 2 tablespoons of olive oil and a pinch of salt. Cook, stirring occasionally, until the onions are lightly browned and caramelized, about 15 minutes. Add the walnuts and cook, stirring, for 2 more minutes. Transfer the mixture to a food processor and process to a smooth paste. Refrigerate.

4. Bring a pot of salted water to a boil and add the porcini. Return the water to a boil and cook the porcini for 2 minutes. Drain the porcini and quickly immerse them in ice water. When cool, separate the stems from the caps. Slice the stems on the bias into ½-inch sections. Slice the caps on the bias ½ inch thick and 1 inch long.

5. Preheat the oven to 400 degrees. Remove the pastry from the refrigerator and spread a quarter of the cooled onion mixture over each disk. Top each with mushroom slices and season with salt and pepper. Brush each with the garlic oil and bake until the pastry is golden and the mushrooms are lightly browned, about 15–20 minutes. Brush the mushrooms again with garlic oil and serve immediately.

Yield: 4 servings

—MOLLY O'NEILL

LEMON PANCAKES

dairy

<small>ADAPTED FROM</small> Marian Cunningham, Bridge Creek Restaurant, Berkeley, Calif.

3 eggs, separated
¼ cup all-purpose flour
¾ cup cottage cheese
¼ cup (½ stick) butter, melted
2 tablespoons sugar
¼ teaspoon of salt
1 tablespoon grated lemon peel

1. Separate eggs and beat the egg whites until they hold stiff peaks. In another bowl, stir together the egg yolks, flour, cottage cheese, butter, sugar, salt and lemon peel until well mixed. (I use the rotary eggbeater for beating the egg whites.)

2. With a large spoon or spatula, fold whites into yolk mixture, stirring gently until there are no yellow or white streaks.

3. Heat skillet or griddle over medium heat. Grease lightly and spoon out about 3 large tablespoons of batter for each pancake. Cook slowly for about 1½ minutes, then turn pancake over and cook for about 30 seconds. Keep pancakes warm in 250-degree oven until ready to serve.

Yield: 12 (3-inch) pancakes

—MOIRA HODGSON

SOUR CREAM PANCAKES

dairy

<small>ADAPTED FROM</small> *The New York Times International Cookbook*

1 cup sifted flour
½ teaspoon salt
½ teaspoon baking soda
1¼ cups sour cream, approximately
1 egg, slightly beaten

1. Sift together the flour, salt and soda.

2. Combine the sour cream and egg. Pour into the flour mixture and stir just enough to moisten the dry ingredients. Do not beat.

3. Heat a griddle or skillet, grease if necessary and drop the batter by spoonfuls onto it. When bubbles break on the top of the cakes, turn and bake on the other side.

Yield: About 14 (5-inch) pancakes

WHOLE WHEAT MATZOH MEAL PANCAKES

dairy

ADAPTED FROM *The New York Times Heritage Cookbook*

4 eggs, separated
1 cup whole wheat matzoh meal
1 tablespoon sugar
1 cup milk
2 tablespoons melted butter
Pinch of salt
Butter or oil for frying
Sugar, honey, preserves, sour cream or yogurt for
    topping, optional

1. Beat egg yolks until frothy. Stir in matzoh meal, sugar, milk and melted butter. Set aside for about 15 minutes.

2. Beat egg whites with salt until they hold their shape but are not dry. Fold egg whites into matzoh meal mixture.

3. Heat butter or oil for frying in a large skillet. Fry the pancakes, turning once, until golden brown on both sides. Use a generous tablespoon of batter for each pancake and fry them over medium heat. Serve at once with desired topping.

Yield: 16 (3-inch) pancakes, serving 4–6

NOTE: *To serve the pancakes with a meat or pareve meal, substitute water for the milk and melted margarine or cooking oil for the melted butter. Omit optional sour cream or yogurt for topping.*

RICOTTA LATKES

dairy

ADAPTED FROM *The Jewish Holiday Cookbook*

1 (15-ounce) container ricotta cheese
4 eggs
6 tablespoons all-purpose flour
2 tablespoons butter, melted and cooled
2 tablespoons sugar
1 teaspoon vanilla extract
Butter or vegetable oil for frying
Preserves or sour cream

1. Place cheese, eggs, flour, melted butter, sugar and vanilla in the container of a food processor and process until smooth. The batter can also be mixed in a

blender, but it may have to be done in two batches.

2. Heat a heavy skillet or griddle over medium-low heat and lightly grease it with butter or oil.

3. Spoon batter by rounded tablespoons into the skillet or onto the griddle. Leave room for pancakes to spread. Allow them to cook slowly, about 6 minutes, until underside is golden and bubbles have appeared on the surface. Carefully turn them to brown the other side. Serve with preserves or sour cream.

Yield: About 30 small pancakes

NOTE: *If sugar is reduced to ½ teaspoon and vanilla is omitted, these pancakes are delicious topped with sour cream and salmon caviar.*

—FLORENCE FABRICANT

CHEESE BLINTZES

dairy

ADAPTED FROM *The New York Times Heritage Cookbook*

FOR THE FILLING:

8 ounces large-curd cottage cheese
½ teaspoon salt
1 egg, well beaten
½ teaspoon vanilla
¼ cup raisins, optional

FOR THE BATTER:

1 cup sifted flour
¼ teaspoon salt
¾ cup water or milk
2 eggs, well beaten
Butter for frying

1. To prepare filling, cream the cottage cheese with a fork. Stir in the remaining ingredients and blend well.
2. To prepare batter, sift together the flour and salt. Stir the water or milk into the beaten eggs and add gradually to flour mixture. Beat until smooth.
3. Heat a 7-inch skillet over medium heat and lightly butter it. When it is very hot, pour some batter into skillet, tilting the pan very quickly to just cover bottom surface as thin as possible, and rapidly pour back any excess into bowl. When the batter starts curling away from side of pan, it is done. Quickly shake it out onto clean dish towel or paper towels. Repeat until all crepes are done. Cover with plastic wrap or damp dish towel until you are ready to use them to prevent them from drying out.
4. Spread a spoonful of the cheese mixture in the middle of each crepe. Fold the bottom of the crepe up over the filling. Fold opposite sides of the crepe to meet in the middle. Now fold crepe over again to completely enclose the filling. Arrange filled blintzes, fold side down, on a platter to wait until all blintzes are made.
5. Place blintzes on a hot, buttered frying pan and fry until golden brown. Turn and fry on other side. Add more butter to frying pan as necessary. Serve hot with sour cream and/or jam.

Yield: 6 servings

NOTE: *Crepes freeze perfectly. Place a piece of waxed paper between each layer of crepes and arrange them in a stack. Wrap them very well in heavy-duty aluminum foil or place them in an airtight plastic container. When you want to make blintzes, remove as many of the frozen crepes as you will need and leave them out at room temperature. They will defrost in 20–30 minutes.*

PASSOVER CHEESE BLINTZES

dairy

ADAPTED FROM *The New York Times Passover Cookbook*

FOR THE BATTER:

3 large eggs
¼ cup matzoh cake meal
1½ cups water
½ teaspoon salt
Unsalted butter

FOR THE FILLING:

1 pound cottage cheese
1 large egg
½ teaspoon salt
1 teaspoon sugar
Unsalted butter for frying
Sour cream, optional
Jelly, optional

1. To make the batter: in a bowl, beat together the eggs, matzoh cake meal and water to make a thin batter. Mix in salt.

2. Place a 6-inch skillet over medium heat and brush with butter. When a drop of water froths but does not jump or sizzle, pour about 3 tablespoons batter into the skillet, spreading as thinly as possible by tilting the pan to coat the bottom. Pour any excess back into the bowl. If the batter sets in ripples as it is poured, the pan is too hot; if it slides around without setting, the pan is not hot enough. Fry until brown and carefully turn out, browned side up, onto a towel. Repeat with the remaining batter.

3. To prepare the filling: in a bowl, combine the cottage cheese, egg, salt and sugar. Spread 1 tablespoon of mixture along 1 side of each blintz. Tuck in the ends and roll up like a jelly roll. Fill all crepes before folding, so the amount of filling in each can be adjusted to fill all crepes evenly.

4. In the same skillet, place blintzes fold-side down in enough heated butter to enable them to swim lightly. Brown a few at a time over medium heat until golden brown. Turn and fry the second side until golden brown. Serve hot with sour cream or jelly, if desired.

Yield: About 10 blintzes

—JEAN HEWITT

DAVID EYRE'S BAKED PANCAKE

dairy

½ cup flour
½ cup milk
2 eggs, lightly beaten
⅛ teaspoon freshly grated nutmeg

4 tablespoons butter
2 tablespoons confectioners' sugar
Juice of ½ lemon
Choice of jams, jellies, marmalade, preserves, maple
   syrup or honey

1. Preheat the oven to 425 degrees.

2. In a mixing bowl combine flour, milk, eggs and nutmeg. Beat lightly. Leave the batter a little lumpy.

3. Melt the butter in a 12-inch skillet with a heat-proof handle. When the butter is very hot but not brown, pour in the batter. Bake 15–20 minutes or until golden brown.

4. Sprinkle the pancake with confectioners' sugar and return briefly to the oven. Sprinkle with lemon juice and serve with favorite topping.

Yield: 4–6 servings

NOTE: *This oversize pancake is one of the most popular recipes ever to appear in* The Times.

—CRAIG CLAIBORNE

REUBEN'S APPLE PANCAKE

dairy

ADAPTED FROM Reuben's

1 large Granny Smith apple
Scant ½ cup plus 1½ tablespoons sugar
½ teaspoon ground cinnamon
3 large eggs
½ cup milk
½ cup all-purpose flour
⅛ teaspoon vanilla extract
8 tablespoons unsalted butter

1. Peel and core apple and slice into moon-shaped pieces ¼ inch thick. Toss with 1½ tablespoons sugar and the cinnamon in a bowl. Cover and refrigerate for at least 24 hours, stirring occasionally.

2. When ready, preheat oven to 400 degrees. Whisk eggs and milk in a bowl until blended. Whisk in flour and vanilla until smooth.

3. Heat 2 tablespoons of butter over medium heat in a shallow 12-inch nonstick ovenproof skillet until it sizzles. Drain apples and add to the pan. Cook, stirring, until apples soften, about 5 minutes. Arrange apples evenly around pan.

4. Melt 2 more tablespoons of butter in pan. Pour in batter. Increase heat to medium-high and pull edges away from pan to allow batter to flow underneath and cook, sliding a wooden spatula under pancake to keep it from sticking.

5. When pancake begins to firm up, sprinkle with 2 tablespoons sugar. Place a cookie sheet over pan and invert the pancake onto it. Return pan to heat and add 2 tablespoons butter, swirling to coat. Slide pancake back into the pan to cook other side. Reduce heat to medium. Sprinkle top with 2 tablespoons sugar. Cook until sugar on bottom side is caramelized, about 2 minutes.

6. Using cookie sheet, flip pancake as in Step 5. Slide pancake back into pan twice more, adding 2 tablespoons butter to pan and sprinkling with 2 tablespoons sugar each time. Adjust heat so that the sugar caramelizes but pancake doesn't burn.

7. Sprinkle top lightly with sugar and bake until sugar is caramelized, about 20 minutes. Slide onto a platter and serve hot.

Yield: 2 servings

—JONATHAN REYNOLDS

FRESH CORN AND RED-PEPPER BLINI

dairy

ADAPTED FROM The Sign of the Dove

1 package active dry yeast

¼ cup lukewarm water

2 tablespoons dark brown sugar

1 cup heavy cream

1 cup finely ground yellow cornmeal

2 large eggs

½ cup all-purpose flour

2 teaspoons salt

1 teaspoon baking powder

½ cup sour cream

1 cup fresh or frozen corn kernels

1 small roasted red bell pepper, peeled, seeded and
  finely diced

Clarified butter for greasing griddle or skillet

Crème Fraîche (recipe page 431), optional

Salmon caviar, optional

Smoked Norwegian or Scotch salmon, optional

1. Combine the yeast with the lukewarm water and sugar in a small bowl.

2. Bring the cream to a boil in a small saucepan. Add to the cornmeal and whisk until smooth. Place over ice and continue beating until lukewarm. Combine the yeast mixture with the cornmeal and leave the batter to ferment in a warm, draft-free area for 2 hours. (The mixture may be refrigerated overnight at this point.)

3. When ready to serve, beat the eggs until light. Sift together the flour, salt and baking powder and stir into the eggs. Add the sour cream and mix until smooth. Combine with the cornmeal mixture (if the batter has been refrigerated and is stiff, place it over simmering water and stir until soft) and beat hard for 2 minutes. Mix in the corn and red pepper.

4. Heat the griddle or skillet until hot. Grease with a small amount of clarified butter. Ladle tablespoons of batter onto the griddle. Cook for 1 minute on the first side until lightly colored, flip and continue cooking for another 30 seconds. Serve immediately.

Yield: Between 20 and 24 (2-inch) pancakes

NOTE: *These pancakes are so flavorful that they need no accompaniments. But they become an elegant hors d'oeuvre when each is topped with a dollop of crème fraîche and a ½ teaspoon of salmon caviar. For somewhat heartier fare, place 3 pancakes on a warmed plate and cover them with 1–2 slices of Norwegian or Scotch salmon, along with a dollop of crème fraîche.*

—JOANNA PRUESS

EGYPTIAN FILLED PANCAKES · (FETEER)

dairy

This recipe requires flipping and spinning the dough in midair in a manner similar to the technique for making pizza dough. The result, however, is a translucent sheet, about 3 feet in diameter and no thicker than strudel, that is laid on an oiled marble slab, folded and filled, then crimped all around to create a dinner plate–size circle and baked.

> 3½ cups bread flour (all-purpose flour may be substituted)
>
> 1 large egg at room temperature
>
> ¼ cup vegetable oil plus oil for brushing on dough and working surface
>
> 1–1¼ cups warm water
>
> ¼ cup clarified butter (vegetable oil may be substituted)
>
> 2 tablespoons heavy cream, sour cream or Crème Fraîche (page 431)
>
> 1 cup sweet or savory filling ingredients (see Note below)
>
> Granulated sugar and confectioners' sugar, optional

1. Place flour in a large bowl and make a well in the center. Beat egg lightly with the ¼ cup vegetable oil and pour it into the well. With hands, begin working the flour into the liquid, adding about ½ cup warm water at a time, until a very soft and fairly sticky dough forms.

2. Scoop up the dough in one hand and forcefully slam it back into the bowl. Continue to lift the dough and slam it down. After 50 strokes the dough should begin to lose its stickiness so you can slam it onto a clean work surface instead of into the bowl. Slam it at least 150 times. The dough should be smooth, soft and elastic. Knead it for 5 minutes.

3. Brush the dough with oil and cover it with an inverted bowl that has been warmed in the oven or rinsed with hot water and dried. Allow the dough to rest for 1 hour.

4. Divide dough in half, reserving one-half under the bowl. Roll the other half into a circle about 15 inches in diameter, working from the center to the edges to keep the edges as thin as possible.

5. Oil a large, smooth work surface. A glass or Formica tabletop is perfect; a standard 24-inch kitchen countertop is too shallow.

6. Remove any rings from your fingers, make 2 fists and lift the dough up onto your fists. Proceed to pull and stretch the dough gently on your fists, moving the circle around from underneath, until it has about doubled in diameter and is very thin. A few small holes are of no consequence. Place the large thin circle on the oiled work surface and stretch out any edges that look particularly thick. Don't worry about small holes; pinch together any large ones. Brush dough with clarified butter or oil.

7. Preheat oven to 425 degrees.

8. Fold 2 opposite sides of the circle to the center, overlapping them a little, to form a rectangle. Brush with clarified butter or oil, spread with 1 tablespoon cream and ½ cup of the filling ingredients.

9. Fold the 2 other sides to the center, overlapping them a little, to form a square. Brush with clarified butter or oil. Shape into a circle about 12 inches in diameter by folding over and pleating 1 inch along the side edges and a little more deeply in the corners.

10. Transfer the pancake to a baking sheet, preferably black metal. Dust sweet feteer lightly with granulated sugar.

11. Repeat Steps 4–10 with remaining dough.

12. Bake feteer in the bottom third of the oven 15–20 minutes or until golden brown. Remove from oven, brush with clarified butter or oil. Dust sweet feteer with confectioners' sugar. Cut each feteer into eight sections and serve.

Yield: 2 filled pancakes, 2–16 servings

NOTE: *Depending on the filling, feteer may be served as an hors d'oeuvre, a first course or a light luncheon entrée, dessert or just a snack. Traditionally, sweet feteer may be filled with raisins, chopped nuts, coconut, jam or preserves, cinnamon sugar or just sugar, either alone or in combinations. Savory feteer calls for feta cheese and/or seasoned beaten egg. There is no reason to limit your choices to these, however. Just a few of an endless list of other possible fillings include ricotta or cottage cheese seasoned with herbs; or ratatouille, chopped mushrooms and onions and tomatoes. For sweet feteer try diced bananas seasoned with cinnamon, chopped dried apricots or prunes simmered until tender, sautéed apple slices or other fruit of your choice.*

—FLORENCE FABRICANT

MATZOH BREI

dairy

ADAPTED FROM Henrietta Goldfuss

4 matzoh squares
3 cups water
4 eggs
Salt and pepper to taste
4 tablespoons of butter

1. Break the matzoh into roughly 3-inch pieces and place in a large mixing bowl. Add water. Let soak about 20 minutes or until matzoh is completely soft. Drain in a sieve. Then, using the hands, press all the water out of the matzoh pieces.
2. Scramble eggs in another mixing bowl. Add drained matzoh. Mix well. Add ½ teaspoon salt and ¼ teaspoon pepper.

3. Heat butter in a large skillet until bubbling but not brown. Add matzoh and egg mixture. Fry over medium heat until golden brown, about 5 minutes on one side, then flip over and fry until golden brown, approximately another 5 minutes. Check seasoning and add additional salt and pepper to taste.

Yield: 4 servings

NOTE: *Some cooks prefer to pour boiling water over the matzoh and drain immediately, so that it is only slightly moistened before being tossed in the egg batter. Matzoh brei can be served in one piece or in broken pieces. The appearance does not matter. For sweetened brei you may wish to reduce or omit the black pepper and to sprinkle the matzoh brei with sugar or cinnamon sugar while it is warm. Jam is also a good accompaniment to the sweeter brei.*

—DENA KLEIMAN

NOODLE SOUFFLÉ KUGEL

dairy

<small>ADAPTED FROM</small> *The New York Times Menu Cook Book*

3 eggs, separated
½ cup melted butter
2 tablespoons sugar
1 pound creamed cottage cheese
1 cup sour cream
8 ounces medium noodles, cooked and drained
½ cup fresh bread crumbs
Butter

1. Preheat oven to 375 degrees.
2. Beat the egg yolks until light. Add the melted butter and sugar and beat until well mixed. Fold in the cottage cheese, sour cream and drained noodles.
3. Beat the egg whites until stiff and fold into the egg-yolk mixture. Place the mixture in a buttered 2-quart casserole. Sprinkle the top with the bread crumbs and dot generously with butter. Bake for 45 minutes.

Yield: 8 servings

JOAN NATHAN'S JERUSALEM KUGEL

pareve

<small>ADAPTED FROM</small> *The Jewish Holiday Kitchen*

2 teaspoons salt, or to taste
1 pound capellini spaghetti
½ cup cooking oil
¾ cup sugar
4 eggs
1½–2 teaspoons freshly ground black pepper
1 teaspoon cinnamon

1. Preheat oven to 350 degrees.
2. Place 1 teaspoon salt in about 3 quarts water and bring to a boil. Add the spaghetti and cook until al dente, about 5 minutes according to package directions. Drain well and set aside in a saucepan.

3. In a medium-size saucepan, heat the oil and ½ cup sugar. Stir constantly until sugar turns very dark, almost black, about 10 minutes. Cool.
4. Pour hot caramel into pasta immediately and mix well. Cool slightly.
5. Combine eggs, remaining salt, pepper, cinnamon and remaining ¼ cup sugar and add to pasta mixture, tossing well. Transfer to a greased tube pan and bake, uncovered, until golden brown on top—at least 1½ hours. Remove from oven, turn upside down on a serving place, unmold and serve.

Yield: 8–10 servings

—JOAN NATHAN

APRICOT NOODLE KUGEL

dairy

ADAPTED FROM *The New York Times Heritage Cookbook*

1½ cups broad noodles, cooked al dente, drained
2 eggs, lightly beaten
1 tablespoon melted butter
¼ teaspoon salt
1 cup whipped cream cheese
½ cup sour cream
¼ cup grated Cheddar cheese, optional
½ cup raisins

8 poached fresh or canned apricots, drained and diced
¼ cup slivered almonds
½ teaspoon cinnamon
½ cup sugar

1. Preheat the oven to 375 degrees.
2. Mix all ingredients together. Turn into a buttered 2-quart casserole and bake 45 minutes.

Yield: 6–8 servings

BRASSERIE ORANGE FRENCH TOAST

dairy

ADAPTED FROM Brasserie

½ cup milk
1 cup orange juice
5 eggs
6 tablespoons sugar
½ teaspoon vanilla
1 orange
2 medium-size French breads, each about 16 inches long
2 tablespoons butter (approximately)
Confectioners' sugar

1. Beat milk, orange juice, eggs, sugar and vanilla together until well blended. Strain into a large bowl. Grate the zest of the orange, taking care not to include any of the white pith, and add it to the mixture.
2. Cut breads into 1- to 1½-inch-thick slices on an angle. You should have approximately 18 slices. Do not use the ends. Briefly soak the bread slices in the egg mixture, then place them in a single layer on a tray, a large platter or a shallow baking pan. Pour any of the egg mixture not absorbed by the bread over the slices. Cover and refrigerate at least 5 hours or overnight. If possible, turn the slices once during this time.
3. Peel away all the white pith of the orange and cut the orange into slices to use as a garnish. Cover with plastic wrap and refrigerate until ready to use.
4. Melt butter in 1–2 large skillets or on a griddle. Fry the bread slices over medium-low heat until nicely browned, turning once to brown both sides. Depending on the type of skillet, you may need a little more butter.
5. Dust French toast with confectioners' sugar, garnish with orange slices and serve.

Yield: 6 servings

—FLORENCE FABRICANT

TOWER OF BAGEL SANDWICHES

dairy

4 freshly baked bagels
8 ounces cream cheese at room temperature
½ cup finely chopped scallions
¾ pound smoked salmon, preferably Norwegian

1. Place one bagel at a time on a flat surface. Hold a slicing knife parallel to the cutting surface. Cut through the bagel to make four slices of more or less equal thickness.

2. Blend the cream cheese with the scallions.

3. For each sandwich, smear 2 ounces of cream cheese on a cut surface of 4 bagel slices. Repeat until all the slices are smeared. Top each smeared surface with an equal number of salmon slices. Reassemble the bagel slices, sandwich fashion.

Yield: 4 sandwiches

—CRAIG CLAIBORNE AND PIERRE FRANEY

PEDRO DE LA CAVALLERIA'S
VERMILIONED EGGS • (HUEVOS HAMINADOS)

pareve

6 cups yellow onion skins
12 large white eggs
½ cup white vinegar
Water

1. Put half the onion skins in a large nonreactive pan. Gently place eggs on top, then top with remaining skins. Add vinegar and enough water to cover eggs and skins. Cover pan.

2. Slowly bring water to a boil. Then, reduce heat to very low. Simmer for an hour.

3. Remove eggs from pan. Tap each egg lightly with a spoon to form cracks in shell (this helps create spidery brown lines in egg white). Return eggs to water. Simmer for an additional 2 hours.

4. Remove eggs from water and allow to cool. Peel shells. Rinse in cold water. Refrigerate until serving.

Yield: 12 eggs

NOTE: *Pedro de la Cavalleria, a finance minister to the King of Aragon, was a victim of the Spanish Inquisition. The onion skins give the eggs a deep brown color, and the hours of cooking produce a creamy texture. Another version of this slow method of cooking eggs—by baking them for hours on top of a casserole—appears in the recipes for Daisy Iny's Iraqi Chicken with Rice and Eggs (Tabyeet), page 164, and Moroccan Bean and Lamb Stew (Dfina), page 227. Because of the similarity of the word hamin to Haman, these eggs are customarily served at Purim.*

—ANDREE BROOKS

TRIMMINGS, SAVORY AND SWEET

FROM SCHMALTZ TO COCONUT MILK, FROM YEMEN'S TRADITIONAL SPICE MIX, *ZHUG,* TO ITALY'S PESTO, AND FROM DILL PICKLES TO ginger-date chutney, these garnishes are the fashion accessories of cuisine. Just as jewelry or a scarf can define a dress, so can these trimmings lend style, making dishes seem traditional or contemporary, with diverse ethnic accents.

The choice of garnish can reassure by its familiarity or pleasantly surprise with its unexpectedness. Mayonnaise is the traditional dressing for chicken salad, for example, but basil-scented pesto can add new interest. Olive paste adds much to grilled tuna, just as homemade spicy ketchup does to a hamburger, and horseradish in cranberry sauce can be a sprightly wake-up call to the Thanksgiving turkey as well as to guests. Similarly, a Middle Eastern spice mix in meat loaf, a carrot and cumin confit with lamb kebobs and an onion, pomegranate and walnut sauce with cold duck or fish.

Many of these dressings, sauces and relishes can be made ahead and stored, and also are pareve, allowing for delicious and imaginative enhancing possibilities in the Jewish kitchen.

SCHMALTZ AND GRIBENES

meat

ADAPTED FROM Sammy's Roumanian

*2 pounds chicken fat and skin, trimmed of any bits of
    meat (see Note below)*
1 cup water
1 large onion, peeled and sliced very thinly
2 teaspoons salt

1. Cut the chicken skin in ¼-inch strips and dice the
fat. Place the skin and fat in a large, heavy skillet,
add the water, and simmer over medium heat for
35–45 minutes until the water has evaporated and
pure yellow fat begins to collect.
2. Add the onion to the pan and continue cooking
over medium heat until the onion is soft and golden
and chicken skin forms brown cracklings. Those
crispy bits are called gribenes; the rendered fat is the
schmaltz.
3. Strain the mixture, collecting the schmaltz in a
bowl or container. Drain the gribenes on paper towels. The fat should be a bright yellow without any
hint of brown in it. Both gribenes and schmaltz
should be stored in tightly covered containers in the
refrigerator. The schmaltz will keep for up to a
month, although it is best to use it within two
weeks. The gribenes quickly become soggy, so it is
best to use them as soon as possible after preparation, either in recipes where called for or sprinkled
with salt and eaten separately. Use schmaltz for frying and sautéing or as a spread. Gribenes is often
used as a garnish for mashed potatoes or chopped
liver or may be eaten as finger food.

*Yield: About 2 cups each of
schmaltz and gribenes*

NOTE: *Recipe may be made in smaller batches using approx-
    imate ratio of ingredients above. If desired, you can freeze
    uncooked chicken skin and fat until you have accumulated
    enough for making schmaltz and gribenes. Wrap the bits
    well in foil and freeze until ready to use. Do not keep more
    than one month because the fat never freezes completely.
    Duck and goose fat may also be prepared in this way.*

—MOLLY O'NEILL

FRESH HORSERADISH

pareve

1 pound fresh horseradish root
⅔ cup white vinegar
4–6 tablespoons dry white wine
2 teaspoons sugar
Salt to taste

1. Pare horseradish root and cut into small pieces.
Process finely in food processor (you may have to do
this in batches). Let horseradish sit in the processor
for 30 minutes before removing it to a bowl.
2. Mix the ground horseradish root with vinegar,
wine, sugar and salt to taste. The fresher the mixture
the hotter it will be. For mellower flavor, cover

tightly with plastic wrap and refrigerate for a day or two. Fresh horseradish will keep only a couple of weeks, tightly covered and refrigerated.

Yield: 2 ½ cups

NOTE: *Preparation of fresh horseradish requires care because the fumes released during the grating process may be nearly overpowering. Cut the root into small cubes and grate them in the food processor, using the knife blade and an on-off pulse motion. The lid should be removed slowly, with your face averted from the machine. As an added precaution to avoid being overcome by the fumes, you might also want to place a damp towel over your nose and mouth. Allow the freshly grated horseradish to sit in the processor for 30 minutes before using.*

—MARIAN BURROS

COLD HORSERADISH DRESSING

dairy
ADAPTED FROM *The New York Times Menu Cook Book*

¼ *cup horseradish, finely grated (see Note above)*
1 cup sour cream
1 teaspoon sugar
Pinch of salt
Pinch of freshly ground black pepper

1 teaspoon dill, finely chopped

Mix together all the ingredients except the dill. Chill, and before serving, garnish with freshly chopped dill. Serve with smoked trout or whitefish.

Yield: 1 ¼ cups

CRANBERRY AND HORSERADISH SAUCE

pareve
ADAPTED FROM *The New York Times Menu Cook Book*

4 cups cranberries
2 cups water
1 ½ cups sugar
Prepared horseradish to taste

1. Place the berries in a saucepan and add the water. Cover and cook until berries pop.
2. Add the sugar and continue cooking 15 minutes. Let cool and add the prepared horseradish. Mold, if desired, and chill. Serve with poultry or meat.

Yield: About 3 cups

HOMEMADE MAYONNAISE

pareve

2 egg yolks
1 teaspoon hot mustard
2 cups vegetable oil or olive oil
¼ cup lemon juice
½ teaspoon salt
Pinch cayenne pepper

1. In large mixing bowl whisk egg yolks and mustard until yolks begin to thicken. Slowly drizzle in 1 cup of oil while whisking vigorously.
2. Gradually whisk in one-quarter of lemon juice and continue whisking. Slowly mix in remaining oil, lemon juice, salt and pepper. Taste and adjust seasoning. Chill, covered, until needed.

Yield: 6 cups

—BRYAN MILLER

HERBED MAYONNAISE

pareve

2 egg yolks
½ teaspoon salt
Pinch of white pepper
½ teaspoon dry mustard
3 tablespoons lemon juice, or to taste
1½ cups olive oil or salad oil, or
   a combination of both
½ cup tightly packed combination of parsley leaves,
   chervil, watercress and spinach, washed and
   without stems

1. Rinse a large porcelain, glass or stainless-steel mixing bowl in hot water and dry thoroughly.
2. Drop egg yolks in the bowl, add salt, pepper, mustard and a little lemon juice and beat well.
3. Using a bottle or any narrow-necked pourer, or a teaspoon, drop oil very, very slowly into egg mixture, beating with a wire whisk between each addition. Do not add more oil until the previous addition is absorbed.
4. Add a little lemon juice from time to time to keep mixture workable.
5. When dressing has reached consistency of sour cream, add oil in a thin stream, beating as you do, until desired consistency is reached. Continue adding lemon juice to taste.
6. Blanch the greens in boiling water for 2 minutes. Drain thoroughly, puree and stir into mayonnaise.
7. Check for seasoning, and, if you plan to store mayonnaise, do so in the refrigerator for no longer than 24 hours.

Yield: 1½ cups

—MIMI SHERATON

GARLIC MAYONNAISE

pareve

ADAPTED FROM Eldorado Petit, Barcelona

3 large, fresh garlic cloves
¼ teaspoon salt
1 large egg yolk at room temperature
½ cup extra-virgin olive oil

1. Peel and halve the garlic lengthwise, then remove and discard the green, sproutlike "germ" that may run through the center of the garlic.

2. Pour hot tap water into a 1- or 2-cup mortar to warm it. Discard the water and dry the mortar.

3. Place the garlic and salt in the mortar and mash together evenly with a pestle to form a very smooth paste.

4. Add the egg yolk. Stir, pressing slowly and evenly with the pestle, to thoroughly blend the garlic and yolk.

5. Very slowly work about one-quarter of the oil, drop by drop, until the mixture is thick and smooth. Gradually whisk in the remaining oil in a slow, thin stream until the sauce is thickened to a mayonnaise consistency.

Yield: About ½ cup

—PATRICIA WELLS

SAFFRON-GARLIC MAYONNAISE • (ROUILLE)

pareve

1 teaspoon white wine vinegar
¼ teaspoon saffron threads
1½ teaspoons fresh lemon juice
1 large egg yolk
1½ teaspoons kosher salt
2 cloves garlic, peeled and minced
¾ cup corn oil

1. Place vinegar in a very small pan over medium-low heat. When vinegar is hot, remove pan from heat and add saffron. Steep 20 minutes. Add lemon juice; mix well.

2. Place egg yolk in a deep, medium mixing bowl. With a large whisk, beat about 15 seconds. Add the saffron mixture, salt and garlic and whisk 30 seconds. Then, whisking vigorously, slowly add the oil in a thin stream. Whisk until the sauce is very thick. Adjust seasonings. Transfer to a bowl, cover and refrigerate until ready to serve.

Yield: 1 cup

NOTE: *This is a classic accompaniment to Mediterranean Fish (page 100), but it also works well with poached chicken (for example, Chicken in the Pot, page 145) and with steamed vegetables.*

—AMANDA HESSER

FLEMISH SAUCE FOR POACHED SALMON OR TROUT

dairy

ADAPTED FROM *The New York Times Menu Cook Book*

¼ cup butter

2 teaspoon imported mustard, preferably Dijon

Juice of 1 lemon

Salt and freshly ground black pepper to taste

¼ teaspoon nutmeg

2 teaspoons chopped parsley

1 teaspoon chopped chives

4 egg yolks

1. In a saucepan, combine the butter, mustard, lemon juice, seasonings and herbs. Place the saucepan in a skillet containing simmering water (or use a double boiler) and stir with a wire whisk until the butter has melted.

2. Beat the egg yolks until thick and lemon-colored and stir them into the butter-mustard mixture. Continue beating vigorously over barely simmering water until the sauce thickens. Serve immediately over poached salmon or trout.

Yield: ¾–1 cup

BÉCHAMEL SAUCE

dairy

ADAPTED FROM *The Best of Craig Claiborne*

4 tablespoons butter

4 tablespoons flour

2 cups milk

Salt and freshly ground pepper to taste

1. Melt butter in a saucepan and add the flour, stirring with a wire whisk. When blended, add the milk, stirring rapidly with the whisk. Add the salt and pepper.

2. When thickened and smooth, reduce the heat and cook, stirring occasionally, for about 5 minutes.

Yield: 2 cups

BLACK OLIVE PASTE

pareve

2 cups oil-cured black olives, pitted and minced

2 cloves fresh garlic, minced

1 tablespoon lemon rind, minced

¼ teaspoon minced chili pepper

2 tablespoons fresh rosemary

¼ cup olive oil

1. In a large bowl, combine the ingredients and blend with a fork. If using a food processor, be very careful not to overprocess; a chunky texture is better. Store in a tightly sealed container in the refrigerator for up to 1 month.

2. To use the olive paste as a marinade, slather chicken, fish, beef or veal well and marinate for up to 6 hours before cooking. The mixture can also be used as a sauce by spooning over meat, poultry or fish in the last 5 minutes of cooking.

Yield: About 2½ cups

—MOLLY O'NEILL

SAUCE VERTE

pareve

1 cup chopped flat-leaf parsley

½ cup chopped chervil leaves

½ cup chopped chives

2 cloves garlic, peeled and chopped

1 shallot, peeled and chopped

½ teaspoon chopped anchovy (see Note below)

¼ cup capers

1 tablespoon fresh lemon juice

1 cup extra-virgin olive oil

Kosher salt to taste

Freshly ground black pepper to taste

1. In a blender, combine parsley, chervil, chives, garlic, shallot, anchovy, capers and lemon juice. Pulse to puree.

2. With the motor running, very slowly add the oil until it is thoroughly incorporated. Transfer to a bowl. Season to taste with salt and pepper. Cover and refrigerate until ready to serve.

Yield: 1½ cups

NOTE: *Because of the anchovy, this sauce may not be used with meat. (See Explanatory Note, page 582.)*

—AMANDA HESSER

PESTO

dairy

ADAPTED FROM *The New York Times International Cookbook*

1 cup loosely packed fresh basil leaves
½ cup pignoli (pine nuts)
2 cloves garlic, peeled
¾ cup freshly grated Parmesan cheese
½ cup olive oil

1. Place the basil, garlic and pignoli in a food processor or blender and process until well blended. Add the cheese and continue to process.
2. Gradually add the olive oil, continuing to process, until pesto has the consistency of a thick puree.

Yield: Sauce for 1 pound of spaghetti

ROASTED GARLIC BASIL PASTE

pareve

ADAPTED FROM Savoy

4 heads garlic
Olive oil
2 cups fresh basil
Kosher salt to taste
1 teaspoon lemon juice

1. Preheat oven to 350 degrees. Rub garlic heads with olive oil and wrap with aluminum foil. Bake until garlic cloves are very tender when pierced with a knife, about 50 minutes. Allow heads to cool, then squeeze softened garlic from cloves into a bowl; there should be 1 cup.
2. Using a mortar and pestle (do not use a food processor), mash basil with ½ teaspoon salt until it is a paste. Add roasted garlic 1 tablespoon at a time, and mash until fully blended. Season with lemon juice and add more salt, if desired. Spread on grilled meats or fish, or use as a sandwich spread.

Yield: About 2 cups

—MARIAN BURROS

FRITZIE ABADI'S SPICY KETCHUP

pareve

¼ cup golden raisins

1½ cups tomato puree

1 clove garlic

1 tablespoon vegetable oil

2 teaspoons lemon juice

1 teaspoon kosher salt

¾ teaspoon Aleppo pepper or cayenne pepper to taste

⅛ teaspoon ground cinnamon

1. Place the raisins in a small cup, cover with boiling water and let soak for 20 minutes. Drain the raisins and place them in the container of a blender. Add all the remaining ingredients and blend until smooth.

2. Transfer the mixture to a small saucepan and simmer until thickened, about 20 minutes. Serve warm or at room temperature with Ijeh (page 203).

Yield: About 1 cup

—MOLLY O'NEILL

SAUCE PIQUANT

pareve

ADAPTED FROM *The New York Times Menu Cook Book*

3 tablespoons hot pepper flakes

½ teaspoon cayenne pepper

¼ cup olive oil

1 teaspoon paprika

3–4 saffron shreds

Boiling water

1. Crush the pepper flakes with a mortar and pestle. Add the cayenne pepper and enough boiling water to make a paste.

2. Stir in remaining ingredients and let stand until ready to use.

Yield: ½ cup

NOTE: *An excellent sauce for spicing up couscous dishes.*

SUMAC AND ONION RELISH

pareve

4 medium onions, peeled

4 teaspoons extra-virgin olive oil

2 tablespoons ground dried sumac (*see Glossary, page 586*)

1 teaspoon salt

Pinch cayenne pepper

1. Cut onions in half from top to root end. Slice halves thinly crosswise and place in a large bowl.

2. In a small bowl, mix olive oil, sumac, salt and cayenne pepper. Pour oil mixture over onions and blend thoroughly but gently.

3. Let rest 6 hours, stirring occasionally.

Yield: 2 cups

—RICHARD W. LANGER

HARISSA—THREE VERSIONS

pareve

Here are three of the many versions of harissa, the hot pepper sauce that gives a kick to tagines and to couscous dishes. Select the one that most suits your palate and the time you have for preparation. When refrigerated, harissa will keep for weeks.

QUICK HARISSA

pareve

½ cup olive oil
1 teaspoon cayenne pepper
1 tablespoon ground cumin
2 tablespoons tomato paste
¼ cup lime juice
½ teaspoon salt

In a small bowl, combine all the ingredients and whisk until smooth.

Yield: About ¾ cup

—MOLLY O'NEILL

SLOWLY SIMMERED HARISSA

pareve

1 tablespoon small, dried, hot red peppers
1 tablespoon finely minced garlic
1 cup olive oil
1 tablespoon ground cumin
1 teaspoon freshly ground black pepper

1. Put the hot peppers into the container of a food processor or blender, or use a spice mill. Blend as finely as possible.

2. Put the ground peppers in a small saucepan and add the garlic, olive oil, cumin and black pepper. Put on the stove and stir. Bring to a boil and allow to barely simmer over low heat—use a steel heat pad such as a Flame-Tamer, if available—for 5 hours.

Yield: About 1 cup

—CRAIG CLAIBORNE AND PIERRE FRANEY

HARISSA WITH HOT SAUCE

pareve

12 hot green or red peppers
3 large cloves garlic, peeled
¼ cup olive oil
⅛ teaspoon ground cumin
Tabasco to taste, optional

1. Cut off stems of peppers. Cut away and discard veins and rest of stems. Chop peppers. There should be ½ cup.

2. Add peppers, garlic, oil and cumin to container of a blender. Blend at high speed to fine liquid. Add Tabasco to taste.

Yield: About ⅓ cup

—PIERRE FRANEY

HELBEH · (DIPPING SAUCE MADE FROM FENUGREEK SEEDS AND ZHUG)

pareve

ADAPTED FROM the Zadok family, in *The Jewish Holiday Kitchen*

2 tablespoons fenugreek seeds, ground in coffee grinder
Water
¼ teaspoon Yemenite Zhug (see recipe below)
Salt to taste
1 tablespoon lemon juice or to taste
1 grated tomato or 1 tablespoon tomato paste, optional

1. Cover the fenugreek seeds with water and let sit overnight or at least 8 hours.
2. Pour off any remaining liquid, leaving a moist paste.
3. Using a wooden spoon, whip, little by little, up to ½ cup of water into the paste. Then combine the paste with the zhug, salt, lemon juice, and, if desired, the tomato.
4. Adjust seasonings to taste. It should be very spicy.

Yield: About 1 cup

—JOAN NATHAN

• YEMENITE ZHUG • (GROUND SPICES WITH HERBS)

pareve

ADAPTED FROM the Zadok family, in *The Jewish Holiday Kitchen*

1 teaspoon black peppercorns
1 teaspoon black caraway seed
1 teaspoon whole cumin
Seeds from 3–4 cardamom pods
4 small fresh hot peppers
2 cloves of garlic, peeled, or to taste
1 cup cilantro leaves or chopped watercress

1. Using a mortar and pestle, a coffee grinder or a blender, grind all the spices.
2. Add the spices to the cilantro or watercress leaves and blend in a mortar or in a food processor. If using a standard blender, a little water may have to be added. Store well sealed.

Yield: About ¼ cup

—JOAN NATHAN

ZA'ATAR

pareve

2 tablespoons sesame seeds
2 tablespoons dried thyme leaves
2 tablespoons dried marjoram leaves
2 tablespoons ground dried sumac
½ teaspoon salt

1. Toast sesame seeds lightly in a heavy frying pan over medium heat, stirring constantly.
2. Transfer seeds to a small bowl, and add remaining ingredients. Mix well.

Yield: About ½ cup

—RICHARD W. LANGER

ONION, POMEGRANATE AND WALNUT SAUCE

pareve

ADAPTED FROM Primorski Restaurant, Brighton Beach, Brooklyn

2 tablespoons olive oil

4 cups onions, chopped fine

Fine sea salt and freshly ground black pepper to taste

2–3 teaspoons pomegranate molasses, to taste
    (see Note, page 583)

⅛ teaspoon cayenne pepper

½ cup chopped toasted walnuts

½ cup pomegranate seeds

¼ cup minced parsley, optional

1. Heat the olive oil in a skillet, add the onions, and cook over fairly high heat for about 7 minutes, stirring often, until soft, sweet and browned. Stir in the salt, pepper, pomegranate molasses and cayenne.

2. Mix in the walnuts and pomegranate seeds. Add parsley, if desired. Serve on fish or steamed vegetables.

Yield: Sauce for 6 servings of fish or vegetables

NOTE: *Onions will become sweet when the natural sugar in them is heated and caramelizes.*

—SUZANNE HAMLIN

WALNUT SAUCE

dairy

ADAPTED FROM *Recipes From Paradise*

7 ounces walnuts, broken

2 tablespoons plain dry bread crumbs

1 clove garlic, peeled

Sea salt to taste

2 tablespoons freshly grated Parmesan cheese

Pinch fresh marjoram

¾ cup fresh ricotta

4 tablespoons extra-virgin olive oil, preferably
    Ligurian

1. In a large mortar, combine walnuts, bread crumbs, garlic and salt to taste. Pound with a pestle to form a coarse-textured paste.

2. Add Parmesan and marjoram. Pound again to blend. Add ricotta, along with 2–3 teaspoons tepid water. Stir with pestle to mix. Slowly drizzle in olive oil, stirring to combine. Taste and adjust seasonings. Serve with gnocchi or pasta, or spread on small slices of country bread.

Yield: 1 cup

—AMANDA HESSER

CONFIT OF CARROT AND CUMIN

pareve

ADAPTED FROM Jo Jo

1½ pounds carrots, preferably organic, trimmed and
    peeled (about 16 pieces)
Large pinch cumin seed
¼ cup extra-virgin olive oil
1 small clove garlic, minced
Juice of 3 oranges
Zest of 1 orange
Kosher salt to taste
Cayenne pepper to taste
2 tablespoons cilantro, julienned

1. Preheat oven to 275 degrees. In a large casserole, combine carrots, cumin seed, olive oil, garlic, orange juice and zest. Season with salt and cayenne. Cover tightly with lid or aluminum foil.

2. On stove top, bring to a boil, then transfer to oven. Bake until a knife can easily be inserted into carrots, at least 2 hours. Just before serving, add cilantro.

Yield: 4 servings

NOTE: *This intensely flavored confit makes a savory garnish for poultry and meat dishes.*

—AMANDA HESSER

SMOKY EGGPLANT

pareve

ADAPTED FROM Quilty's

2 medium eggplants
Vegetable oil, for coating
2 tablespoons tahini
¼ teaspoon freshly ground cumin seed
Juice of ½ lemon
¼ cup extra-virgin olive oil
Kosher salt and freshly ground black pepper to taste

1. Rub eggplants with vegetable oil. Place directly on a hot grill or over a gas flame (this may be done on top of the stove). Char skin well on all sides, turning eggplant with tongs. Continue until eggplant is blackened and collapsed, about 20 minutes. (Eggplant may leak a small amount of liquid.) Transfer to a platter and allow to cool slightly.

2. When eggplants are cool enough to touch, peel them, removing as many seeds as possible. Place the pulp in a fine sieve and drain, pressing it lightly to remove the juices.

3. Transfer pulp to a blender and add tahini, cumin and lemon juice. Puree, adding olive oil in a steady stream while blender is running. Season to taste with salt and pepper. Serve at room temperature as a spread or on a plate under grilled meat or seafood.

Yield: About 1½ cups

—AMANDA HESSER

TOMATO JAM

pareve
ADAPTED FROM Matthew Kenney

2 tablespoons olive oil

1/4 cup minced fresh ginger

3 cloves garlic, peeled and minced

1/4 cup cider vinegar

2 cinnamon sticks

4 medium tomatoes, peeled, seeded and chopped
   (about 2 cups)

1/3 cup brown sugar

1 teaspoon ground cumin

1/4 teaspoon cayenne pepper

Pinch of ground cloves

Salt and freshly ground black pepper to taste

1/4 cup honey

1. In heavy, nonreactive saucepan (preferably non-stick), heat olive oil over medium heat. Add minced ginger and garlic, and cook, stirring, for 2 minutes.

Add vinegar and cinnamon sticks to pan and cook for about 3 minutes, until mixture is reduced by half.

2. Add tomatoes, brown sugar, cumin, cayenne and cloves. Reduce heat to very low and cook slowly, stirring occasionally, for about an hour, until all the tomato juices have evaporated.

3. Remove cinnamon sticks and discard. Season with salt and pepper. Add honey and stir over heat until jam is shiny and all liquid is evaporated, about 2 minutes.

4. Remove from heat and let mixture cool. Use at room temperature as a dip, condiment, spread or marinade. If refrigerated in covered container, jam can be stored in refrigerator for as long as a week; if frozen, for several months.

Yield: 1 1/2 cups

—SUZANNE HAMLIN

SWEET CRANBERRY-PISTACHIO CHUTNEY WITH CALIFORNIA BLACK FIGS • (KARONDA CHATNI)

pareve
ADAPTED FROM Julie Sahni

1 (12-ounce) package fresh cranberries, picked
   clean

1 orange, skin intact and seeds discarded, chopped into
   1/4-inch cubes

2 tablespoons lemon juice

2 tablespoons finely chopped shallots

1 teaspoon dry ginger powder

1 cup sugar

3/4 teaspoon coarse salt

1/2 teaspoon ground cinnamon

1 teaspoon ground cumin

1/3 teaspoon cayenne pepper

1 teaspoon mustard seeds, lightly crushed

⅓ cup shelled unsalted pistachio nuts
(preferably raw)
⅔ cup California black figs, stemmed and
chopped into ½-inch pieces, or ⅔ cup dark
raisins

1. Combine all the ingredients except the pistachios and figs in a 2½-quart microwave-proof casserole dish and cover. Cook at 100 percent power in a 650- to 700-watt microwave carousel oven for 4 minutes. Uncover and continue cooking for an additional 5 minutes, or until the chutney is boiling and the cranberries begin to burst open. Stir once during the cooking time.

2. Remove from the oven. Stir in the pistachios and figs or raisins. Replace the cover and set aside to cool completely. Spoon the chutney into sterilized jars, cover and refrigerate. Serve with grilled chicken or turkey or on toast for breakfast.

Yield: 3 cups

NOTE: *For best results, let the chutney ripen for at least a day. If refrigerated and tightly covered, it will keep for several months.*

—JULIE SAHNI

GINGER-DATE CHUTNEY

pareve

1 cup fresh dates, pitted and coarsely chopped
⅓ cup golden raisins
2 tablespoons minced fresh ginger
1–2 tablespoons minced fresh chili pepper of your
choice
2 tablespoons brown sugar
½ cup white vinegar
Salt and freshly ground black pepper to taste

1. In a small bowl, combine the dates, raisins, ginger, chili pepper, brown sugar and vinegar and mix well. Season to taste with salt and pepper.

2. This very strong chutney, which is particularly good with lamb, will keep, covered and refrigerated, for about a week.

Yield: About 1½ cups

—JOHN WILLOUGHBY AND
CHRIS SCHLESINGER

QUINCE CONDIMENT COMPOTE

pareve

2½–3 pounds ripe quinces, 4–5
1 cup port
1 cup sweet wine, such as muscat
¼ cup honey
¼ teaspoon allspice
2 tablespoons lemon juice

1. Coarsely chop the quinces, without peeling them into ½-by-¼-inch pieces. Place in a nonreactive pan with port and simmer for 45 minutes, covering the pot for the first 15 minutes. Stir occasionally.

2. Add ½ cup sweet wine and honey. Simmer 15 minutes more, until quite thick. Stir to avoid sticking.

3. Add remaining ½ cup wine, allspice and lemon juice. Stir well with a fork, mashing any chunks of fruit. Serve warm or cold with flavorful meats like brisket or roast goose. Can be refrigerated up to 3 months.

Yield: About 2 cups

—RICHARD W. LANGER

TAMATAR CHUTNEY

pareve

ADAPTED FROM *Classic Indian Cooking*

2 pounds ripe tomatoes, peeled and coarsely chopped
1 medium onion, peeled and finely chopped
1½ teaspoons finely chopped garlic
1 cup cider vinegar
¼ teaspoon ground cloves
1½ teaspoons ginger powder
½ teaspoon paprika
¼–½ teaspoon red pepper
1 cup sugar
2 teaspoons kosher salt

1. Put tomatoes, onion and garlic in heavy-bottomed enameled pan and bring to boil. Reduce heat and simmer, uncovered, until tomatoes are soft and reduced to thick puree (about 45 minutes). Stir from time to time to prevent sticking and burning.

2. Strain puree through sieve into small bowl. Discard seeds and any residue in sieve.

3. Return strained puree to pan, add remaining ingredients, and bring to boil again. Reduce heat and simmer, uncovered, for 30 minutes or until sauce turns thick and glossy and coats spoon. Stir often, especially during last few minutes, when sauce becomes thick and sticks to bottom of pan. Turn off heat and immediately pour into sterilized jars and seal. Alternatively, refrigerate in airtight plastic containers.

Yield: About 2½ cups

NOTE: *This relish will keep well for several months in the refrigerator.*

—ROBERT FARRAR CAPON

DILL PICKLES

pareve
ADAPTED FROM Wilfred Kean

2 cups cider vinegar
⅓ cup sugar
⅓ cup noniodized salt or canning salt
½ cup (packed) fresh dill
3 white onions, peeled and chopped
3 cloves garlic, peeled and thinly sliced
3½–4 pounds small Kirby cucumbers, well scrubbed
    (to fill 1-gallon jar)
1 teaspoon mustard or celery seed

1. Sterilize 1-gallon glass jar and lid by immersing in boiling water for 10 minutes. Remove from water and set aside.
2. In large enameled, glass or other nonreactive saucepan, combine 6 cups water with the cider vinegar, sugar and salt. Bring to boil, reduce heat to low and then simmer mixture while proceeding with recipe.
3. Place a third of the dill in bottom of jar. Top with a third each of the onion and garlic. Starting with smallest cucumbers, pack 1 layer horizontally over garlic. Place another layer crosswise over first. Continue until jar is two-thirds full, packing jar tightly and filling gaps with cucumbers halved lengthwise.
4. Add another third of the dill, followed by another third each of onion and garlic. Top with cucumbers, packing tightly. Top with remaining dill, onion and garlic.
5. Place jar in large plastic basin and carefully pour hot vinegar mixture (brine) into jar to fill it completely. Using a long wooden skewer, gently nudge the cucumbers deep in the jar to dislodge any air bubbles. Add more brine, if necessary, and allow to sit 5 minutes. Add more brine to fill the jar to the brim, and top with mustard seed. If using glass lid, place lid directly on jar. If using metal lid, to prevent corrosion place large piece of wax paper over top of jar before fastening lid.
6. Let mixture cool to room temperature. Remove jar from basin and wipe clean with damp sponge. Refrigerate jar at least 24 hours before eating. The pickles may be refrigerated for up to a year.

Yield: 20–25 pickles

—DULCIE LEIMBACH

PRESERVED LEMONS

pareve
ADAPTED FROM *The New York Times International Cookbook*

Lemons
Kosher salt
Olive oil

1. Cut as many lemons as desired in quarters lengthwise to within half an inch of the bottom. Sprinkle a thin layer of kosher salt in a pint or quart glass jar. Sprinkle salt inside each lemon. Press the lemons, 1 at a time, into the jar, extracting much of the juice inside the jar as they are pressed. Continue packing, adding lemons, salt, and juice.

2. Add enough olive oil to cover and seal tightly. Let stand in a cool place or refrigerate for at least 2 weeks, shaking the jar daily. Rinse each lemon well before using.

3. If desired, lemons may be flavored with cardamom and bay leaves: for 6 lemons, intersperse a total of 1 tablespoon of cardamom pods and 3 bay leaves between the layers of the lemons as you press them into the jar.

NOTE: *Traditional preserved lemons must be prepared at least 2 weeks in advance. Covered with liquid and tightly sealed, the lemons will keep for several months in a refrigerator.*

QUICK PRESERVED LEMONS

pareve

2 lemons, thinly sliced
1 tablespoon sugar
1 teaspoon kosher salt
2 cups water

Combine all of the ingredients in a small sauté pan. Simmer over medium heat until the lemons are soft, about 15 minutes. Cool the lemons in the liquid overnight and then drain, discarding the liquid.

Yield: 2 lemons

—MOLLY O'NEILL

COCONUT MILK AND COCONUT CREAM

pareve
ADAPTED FROM *The Best of Craig Claiborne*

From whole coconuts:

1. To crack 1 or more coconuts, pierce the "eyes" of each coconut with an ice pick. Drain and discard the liquid. Preheat the oven to 275 degrees.

2. Using a hammer, crack the shell of each coconut in half. Arrange the coconut halves, cracked side up, on a baking sheet. Place in the oven and bake for 15 to 20 minutes.

3. Remove the coconut halves. Pry the meat from the shells. Peel away the brown skin from the meat. Cut the meat into ½-inch cubes. Two coconuts should yield about 5 cups of cubed meat.

4. Put the coconut meat into the container of a food processor and add 4 cups of warm water. Puree thoroughly.

5. Line a colander with cheesecloth. Pour in the

coconut mixture. Bring up the ends of the cheese-cloth and squeeze to extract as much liquid as possible. The white creamlike substance that rises to the top of the liquid on standing is coconut cream. The bottom layer is coconut milk.

Yield: About 4½ cups

From dried unsweetened coconut:

1 cup dried unsweetened coconut

1. Place the coconut in a food processor or blender. Add 1¼ cups of hot tap water. Blend until the coconut is finely pulverized, about 30 seconds.
2. Pour the liquid through a fine sieve into a bowl. Press and squeeze with your fingers to extract the excess liquid. This is the coconut milk.

Yield: ¾ cup

CRÈME FRAÎCHE

dairy

1 cup heavy cream *(preferably not ultrapasturized)*
2 tablespoons buttermilk

Mix the cream and the buttermilk, which contains the required bacteria, and let the mixture sit, loosely covered, at room temperature until it thickens, anywhere from 12–36 hours. Homemade crème fraîche will keep for about 10 days in the refrigerator.

Yield: 1 cup

—MELISSA CLARK

HONEY SAUCE

dairy

ADAPTED FROM *The New York Times Menu Cook Book*

3 tablespoons butter
2 teaspoons cornstarch
⅔ cup honey
Whole almonds, optional

1. Melt the butter in a saucepan. Add the cornstarch and stir until smooth.
2. Add the honey and cook over low heat, stirring constantly, for about 5 minutes. Add almonds, if desired.
3. Serve warm or cold over ice cream or unfrosted cake.

Yield: About 1 cup

ESPRESSO, HONEY AND RICOTTA SPREAD

dairy

1½ cups whole milk ricotta
2 tablespoons very finely ground espresso
2 tablespoons honey
¼ teaspoon ground cinnamon
Pinch ground nutmeg
Milk or heavy cream

1. Combine the cheese, espresso, honey, cinnamon and nutmeg in a small bowl and stir until combined. **2.** Add milk or cream, a tablespoon at a time, until the mixture is spreadable. Use as a filling for pitted dates, or as a spread on biscotti or toasted pound cake or cinnamon bread.

Yield: About 1½ cups

—MOLLY O'NEILL

CYNTHIA ZEGER'S ASHKENAZIC HAROSETH

pareve

1 large McIntosh apple, or 2 small apples, peeled, cored and finely chopped
1 tablespoon ground cinnamon, or to taste
1 tablespoon ground ginger, or to taste
⅓ cup ground walnuts
¼ cup, approximately, sweet red Passover wine

Mix ingredients together, adding enough wine to moisten. Let ripen in refrigerator for several hours.

Yield: 2–3 cups, depending upon the size of the apples

—CRAIG CLAIBORNE AND PIERRE FRANEY

MOROCCAN HAROSETH

pareve

ADAPTED FROM *The Book of Jewish Food*

1 pound pitted dates, chopped
1½ cups sweet red Passover wine
1 teaspoon ground cinnamon
½ teaspoon ground cloves
1 cup walnuts, coarsely chopped

Put the dates in a pan with the wine and seasonings and simmer until the mixture resembles a soft paste, about 30–40 minutes, stirring occasionally. Cool. Add the walnuts and serve.

Yield: 6–8 servings

—MOLLY O'NEILL

TURKISH HAROSETH

pareve

ADAPTED FROM *Sephardic Holiday Cooking*

1 cup seedless raisins
1 pound dates, pitted
1 orange, peeled, sliced crosswise and pitted
1 apple, peeled, cored and sliced
2 tablespoons sweet wine

1. Soak raisins 30 minutes in hot water to cover. Drain.
2. Grind raisins, dates, orange and apple together. Add sweet wine to make a thick paste.
3. Cover and refrigerate until 1 hour before serving.

Yield: 3–3½ cups

HAROSETH FROM ITALY

pareve

ADAPTED FROM *The Book of Jewish Food*

3 apples, sweet or tart
2 pears
2 cups sweet wine
⅓ cup pine nuts
⅔ cup ground almonds
½ pound dates, pitted and chopped
¾ cup yellow raisins or sultanas
4 ounces prunes, pitted and chopped
½ cup sugar or ½ cup honey, or to taste
1 teaspoon cinnamon
½ teaspoon ground ginger

1. Peel and core the apples and pears and cut them into small pieces.
2. Put all the ingredients into a pan together and cook, stirring occasionally, for about 1 hour, until the fruits are very soft, adding a little water if the mixture becomes too dry.
3. Serve at room temperature.

Yield: At least 12 servings

NOTE: *This recipe is very rich and keeps well for days. For variations on this general recipe for Italian haroseth, you might want to include some of these other possible additions: chopped lemon or candied orange peel, chopped walnuts or pistachios, chopped dried figs, orange or lemon juice, nutmeg and cloves.*

ELISHEVA KAUFMAN'S HAROSETH

pareve

½ pound almonds

½–1 cup sweet Passover wine or grape juice

2 cups dried fruit, such as raisins, dates or figs

6 medium-size McIntosh apples, or combination of apples, pears and other firm fruit

½ teaspoon allspice

¼ teaspoon cinnamon

¼ teaspoon nutmeg

⅛ teaspoon cloves

1. Chop nuts either by hand or in a blender or food processor until they are fine enough to pass through a coarse sieve. Set aside.

2. Combine ½ cup of wine with dried fruit and chop fine, either by hand or in a blender or food processor, but do not puree. Set aside.

3. Peel, core and quarter apples. Chop by hand to a fine consistency, but do not puree. In a bowl, combine the apples with the dried fruit and wine mixture and gradually add nuts to achieve the consistency of a spread. If too soupy, add more nuts; if too dry, add more wine. Then add allspice, cinnamon, nutmeg and cloves. Adjust to taste. Cover and refrigerate until serving.

Yield: 12–15 servings

—MARIALISA CALTA

BREADS, ROLLS, BAGELS AND MATZOHS

BREAD IS THE METAPHOR FOR ALL FOOD AND FOR ABUNDANCE, AND IN THE JEWISH RELIGION, AS WELL AS MANY OTHERS, IT IS THE symbolic reward for righteousness. As such, it is woven into the religion, not only with the prayer—*bracha*—that must be said before each meal as a new loaf is cut, but also in the baking when a portion of the dough must be burned or sacrificed, in a ritual that translates to "separating challah," meaning the priest's portion.

No category of food so distinctly defines the various cultural influences in Jewish food. There are the round, flat, wheaty pockets that are the pita of Sephardic and Middle Eastern Jews, the shiny golden loaves of braided challah—especially favored by Ashkenazim for the Sabbath and occasions such as weddings when they are shaped in rounds to signify eternity—the moist, soured rye bread and dark pumpernickel of German Jews, spinach-filled Anatolian flat bread and Hungarian yeast bread encrusted with a cheese topping. That cheese is a rarity in Jewish breads, because they are usually made without dairy products to be pareve.

Just as pita is now in the culinary mainstream, so are the Eastern Europe classics such as the water bagel that is boiled before it is baked, and the *pletzel*, a flat round topped with poppy seeds and roasted onions, and the probable forerunner to the bialy, now made almost exclusively in large cities of the United States.

Perhaps no other bread is so rich in symbolism as the matzoh, the unleavened wafers required for Passover and a reminder of the Israelites' exodus from Egypt. Now eaten year-round and the basis not only of the fried breakfast dish *matzoh brei*, it is the source of special flours—matzoh meal and cake meal—that may be used for baking during Passover. For that holiday, special *schmura* or "watched" matzohs are made, most often mass-produced but also handmade of whole grain by Orthodox congregations who have bakeries used only for the pre-Passover period. *Watched* refers to every stage of the matzoh's production, to be sure that wheat, flour or matzoh do not ferment. Therefore the wheat fields are watched to be sure harvest precedes rain, the flour is kept dry and the baking production is stopped every eighteen minutes so boards and rolling pins can be cleaned and a new batch of dough mixed. Handmade matzohs are rolled out into rounds and tend to be deliciously grainy and thicker than commercial matzohs, and, like the rectangular versions, they are perforated before being baked so they will not buckle. Usually unsalted and neutral in flavor, matzohs can be seasoned at home as they are being refreshed in the oven.

SWEET CHALLAH

pareve

ADAPTED FROM *The Best of Craig Claiborne*

8½–9 cups flour, plus additional flour for kneading

2 packages granular yeast

2½ cups lukewarm water

½ teaspoon baking powder

½ teaspoon cinnamon

1 tablespoon salt

1 teaspoon vanilla extract

4 large eggs

¾ cup corn oil

¾ cup plus ⅛ teaspoon sugar

1 tablespoon poppy seeds or sesame seeds

1. Place 6 cups of the flour in a large mixing bowl and make a well in the center. Blend the yeast with I cup of the water and stir to dissolve. Add this to the well in the flour. Using a fork, start stirring around the well, gradually incorporating one-fourth of the flour—no more—into the yeast mixture. When approximately that amount of flour is blended into the yeast mixture, stop stirring. There is no need to remove the fork. It will be used for further stirring. Set the bowl in a warm, not too hot, place and let stand for 45–50 minutes.

2. Sprinkle the baking powder, cinnamon and salt over all. Add the vanilla, 3 of the eggs, the oil and ¾ cup of sugar. Add the remaining water and blend again, first using the fork and then the hands. Add 2 cups of the flour, kneading, and if the mixture is still too sticky, add an additional cup of flour.

3. Work the mixture well with a wooden spoon to make a very stiff dough. If necessary, add more flour. Work with the hands for about 10 minutes. When the dough doesn't stick to the hands, it is

ready. Shape the mixture into a rather coarse ball and cover. Let stand for about 20 minutes and turn it out onto a lightly floured board. Knead well, adding a little more flour to the board as necessary to prevent sticking. The kneading, which must be thorough and brisk, should take about 5 minutes. Flour a bowl well and add the ball, turning the dough to coat lightly with flour. Cover again and let stand for about 30 minutes.

4. Turn out the dough onto a flat surface once more and knead briefly. Using a knife, slash off about one-eighth of the dough at a time. As each portion is cut off, knead quickly and shape into a ball. Flour lightly. Return each piece as it is kneaded to a bowl to rest briefly. Continue until all 8 pieces are shaped and floured.

5. Take one piece of dough at a time and place it on a flat surface, rolling briskly with the hands to make a "rope" 12–15 inches in length. Continue until all the balls are shaped.

6. Align the ropes vertically side by side and touching. Start working at the top of the ropes. Gather the tops of the ropes together, one at a time, pinching down to seal well. Separate the rope down the center, 4 ropes to a side. Braid the ropes as follows: Bring the extreme outer right rope over toward the center next to the inside rope on the left. Bring the extreme outer left rope over the center next to the inside rope on the right. Continue with this procedure until the loaf is braided and each rope has been brought to the center. As the last ropes are brought over, it will be necessary to pull and stretch them a bit to get them to fit.

7. When the braiding is finished, gather the bottom ends of the ropes together and pinch them together just as at the top.

BREADS, ROLLS, BAGELS AND MATZOHS ◆ *437*

8. Meanwhile, generously oil the bottom and side of a rectangular baking pan measuring about 15½ inches by 10½ inches by 2½ inches. Carefully gather up the braided loaf, using the hands and arms to help sustain the shape.

9. Cover with a towel and let stand in a warm spot for 1 hour or slightly longer, or until the loaf is well puffed and about twice the original volume.

10. Preheat the oven to 325 degrees.

11. Beat the remaining egg with the ⅛ teaspoon of sugar and, using a pastry brush, brush the loaf all over with the egg wash and sprinkle evenly with poppy or sesame seeds.

12. Place the loaf in the oven and bake for approximately 1 hour, or until well puffed, cooked through and golden.

Yield: 1 large loaf

TUNISIAN TRIANGULAR CHALLAH · (BEJMA)

pareve

<small>ADAPTED FROM</small> *The Foods of Israel Today*

> *1½ cups lukewarm water*
> *2 scant tablespoons active dry yeast*
> *¼ cup sugar*
> *4 large eggs*
> *¼ cup vegetable oil*
> *2 teaspoons salt*
> *7 cups all-purpose unbleached flour*

1. Place 1 cup of water with the yeast and a teaspoon of the sugar in a glass bowl. Stir and let sit for about 10 minutes.

2. Add 3 of the eggs, the oil, salt, and the remaining water and sugar and slowly work in the flour, adding enough to make a soft, tacky dough. Knead for about 10 minutes or until smooth. Let the dough rise for about an hour in a greased bowl, covered.

3. Divide the dough into 9 equal rounds about the size of tennis balls. Place 3 rounds together, touching to form a triangle on a greased cookie sheet. Repeat two more times. Let rise for about a half-hour, uncovered.

4. Preheat oven to 375 degrees. Brush the dough with the additional egg, beaten, and bake for about 20 minutes or until golden.

Yield: 3 breads, or 8 servings per loaf

<small>NOTE:</small> *Unlike traditional Ashkenazic challah, this version is not braided, but composed of balls of dough arranged in a triangular fashion.*

—JOAN NATHAN

REBECCA'S CHALLAH

pareve

ADAPTED FROM *The New York Times Heritage Cookbook*

2 packages active dry yeast
8 teaspoons plus ½ cup sugar
7¾ cups flour, approximately
2¼ cups warm water
½ cup plus 1 tablespoon vegetable oil
2 tablespoons coarse salt
3 eggs
Poppy seeds (optional)

1. Place the yeast, 2 teaspoons of the sugar and 2 tablespoons of the flour in a tall tumbler. Add ¾ cup of the water and mix well. Set in a warm place, uncovered.

2. In a big bowl, place 4 cups of flour. Add 1½ cups of the water, ½ cup of the oil, ½ cup of the sugar, the salt and 2 of the eggs and mix well.

3. When the yeast mixture reaches the top of the glass, add to the batter in the bowl. Mix well and gradually add 3 more cups of the flour. Knead the mixture right in the bowl until very smooth and elastic. Cover and set in a warm place about 5 hours, or until doubled in bulk.

4. Knock dough down and add about ⅔ cup more of the flour, kneading well to give a soft but not sticky dough. Oil the top of the dough with remaining oil. Cover and let rise again until doubled in bulk, about 2½ hours.

5. Knead again. Divide dough in two. Shape into two loaves to fit greased 9-by-5-by-3-inch loaf pans and place in pans. Or braid and set on greased baking sheet. (See directions for Sweet Challah, page 439.) Cover and let rise until doubled in bulk, about 1 hour.

6. Preheat oven to 350 degrees.

7. Combine the remaining egg and remaining sugar and brush over top of the loaves. Sprinkle with poppy seeds, if desired. Bake about 45 minutes, or until done.

Yield: 2 loaves

GILDA LATZKY'S ROSH HA SHANA CHALLAH

pareve

1½ packages active dry yeast
1 tablespoon sugar
1⅓ cups lukewarm water (about 110 degrees)
¼ cup honey
A small pinch ground saffron for color, optional
3 tablespoons corn oil
2 teaspoons coarse salt

3 large eggs at room temperature
1 egg yolk
5–5½ cups all-purpose flour or bread flour
1 egg yolk mixed with 1 tablespoon water for glaze

1. Dissolve yeast and sugar in ⅓ cup of water. Set aside to proof in a warm place for about 5 minutes, until the mixture begins to froth.

2. Mix the rest of the water and the honey together

in a large bowl. Add the saffron, if desired. Stir in the corn oil, salt and the yeast mixture. Beat in the eggs and egg yolk.

3. Using a wooden spoon, stir in 3 cups of the flour and beat until well blended. Begin adding the remaining flour a half cup at a time until a soft dough is formed that leaves the sides of the bowl and can be handled.

4. Turn dough out onto a well-floured board and knead for 10 minutes. Add additional flour while kneading to make a dough that is smooth, very elastic, fairly firm but not stiff. The dough may remain a trifle sticky and so should always be worked on a lightly floured surface.

5. Place dough in an oiled bowl, turn the ball of dough in the bowl to oil all sides, cover with a clean tea towel and set aside to rise until doubled in bulk, about 1 hour.

6. Punch dough down and knead for a minute or two. Remove one-fourth of the dough and set it aside. Briefly knead the remaining dough to form a nice smooth ball 7–8 inches in diameter.

7. Line a baking sheet with parchment paper and place the ball of dough in the middle of it.

8. Cut the one-fourth portion of reserved dough into equal thirds. (If you want to observe the ritual of *challah* (see Note below), reserve a tiny piece of this dough to bake until blackened while the oven is preheating.) Knead each of the 3 pieces of dough briefly into a ball, then carefully roll each into a slender, uniform rope about ½ inch in diameter and almost 24 inches long. Braid the three ropes together and then carefully place the braid in a circle around the reserved ball of dough about halfway down from the top. Gently weave or overlap the ends of the braided circle together, pinching them to secure them and cutting off any excess bits with scissors. The surface of the dough is sticky enough that the braid adheres securely.

9. Set formed loaf aside in a draft-free area to rise, uncovered, until doubled, about 45 minutes. It is important that this bread be kept away from drafts so it rises evenly.

10. Preheat oven to 400 degrees. Gently brush bread with egg wash. Place in center of oven and bake until challah is uniformly golden brown and sounds hollow when tapped, about 40 minutes. If your oven does not seem to bake evenly or has hot spots, turn the baking sheet around once during the baking. Remove finished loaf from oven and allow to cool completely before slicing.

Yield: 1 large round loaf

NOTE: *Challah is an easy dough to mix even for inexperienced bakers. It is usually baked in a long, oval, braided shape. But for Rosh Ha Shana, the Jewish New Year, the dough is traditionally shaped into a round loaf, a circle that symbolizes the completeness of the year as well as eternity, a time without beginning or end. Shaping the round loaf for Rosh Ha Shana is also less complicated than forming the traditional braid. Sometimes challah is made in the shape of a dove or a ladder (Jacob's Ladder) for Rosh Ha Shana.*

Homemade challah has a special significance. It permits the commemoration of an ancient ceremony called challah: A small portion of the unbaked dough, the size of an olive, is torn off and burned in the oven before the bread is shaped. This represents a sacrifice, one that has been performed in the home ever since the destruction of the Temple in Jerusalem in A.D. 70. Some other customs relating to the challah are that the bread should be broken, not cut, since knives are instruments of war, and that the pieces should be passed all together on a plate, not handed from one person to another because man cannot bestow bread upon man. For Rosh Ha Shana, the first bite of bread is dipped in honey to assure a sweet New Year. Occasionally, slices of apple dipped in honey are also served, and among the Sephardim, pomegranates are customarily eaten at Rosh Ha Shana.

If there is any challah left over, it makes excellent French toast.

—FLORENCE FABRICANT

MARVIN KORMAN'S SWEET ONION ROLLS

dairy, pareve

3 packages dry yeast

3½ cups plus 3 tablespoons water, approximately

½ cup plus 1 teaspoon sugar

4 whole eggs

1 egg yolk

1½ teaspoons salt

6 tablespoons unsalted butter, approximately
  (or margarine)

5½–6 cups flour

3 large onions

2 tablespoons vegetable, corn or peanut oil

5 tablespoons poppy seeds

1. In a large bowl, dissolve the dry yeast in 1½ cups water. Add 1 teaspoon sugar to speed the proofing. Put in a warm place for 5 minutes or until mixture has proofed.

2. Meanwhile, beat together 3 whole eggs and the egg yolk. Add remaining ½ cup sugar and salt and mix.

3. In a small saucepan over a low flame, heat 3 tablespoons butter until melted. Pour the butter into a separate dish and allow to cool. Add the cooled butter to the egg mixture, stir and add this to the yeast. Add 2 cups of flour to the mixture, stirring with a wooden spoon. Add 3 more cups of flour, stirring.

4. Sprinkle a handful of the remaining flour on a large wooden board. Place the dough on the board and start kneading. Add flour to prevent the dough from sticking. The dough should be smooth and pleasantly soft.

5. Take about 1 tablespoon butter and grease the inside of a bowl whose capacity is at least twice the size of the dough. Place the dough in the bowl, turn-

ing the dough so that it is coated with butter. Cover with a cloth and put it in a warm place.

6. While waiting for the dough to rise, take the remaining 2 tablespoons butter and grease two 12-by-18-inch baking pans.

7. When the dough has doubled in size (about 1½ hours), punch it down and knead it on a floured board for about 5 minutes, adding flour as you work to achieve a firm ball of dough.

8. Divide the dough into quarters; divide each quarter into 4 pieces so that you have 16 pieces in all.

9. Shape each into a ball. Place 8 balls in each pan, leaving 3 inches between each. When placing the dough in the pan, press down with your knuckles to make a hollow in the center of each ball.

10. Cover and let rise in a warm place for 20–25 minutes, or until the balls have almost doubled in size.

11. Meanwhile, peel the onions and chop finely. You should have 2 cups. In a skillet over a medium flame, heat the oil and add the onions along with 2 tablespoons of water. Add more water if the pan gets dry. Cook until the onions are translucent, then drain and discard the liquid.

12. Preheat the oven to 400 degrees. Place an empty pan at the bottom of the oven.

13. When the rolls have doubled in size, repeat the punch-down process with your knuckles. The rolls should be about 4 inches in diameter; each indentation should be about 1½ inches in diameter. Fill the hollow of each roll with 2 tablespoons of cooked onions. Mix the remaining egg with a tablespoon of water and brush each roll with the egg mixture, sprinkling a teaspoon of poppy seeds over each.

14. Put 2 cups of cold water into the heated pan,

which will create steam. Place the rolls in the oven, turn down the heat to 375 degrees and bake for 20–25 minutes, or until the rolls are golden brown.

15. Remove them from the oven and place on racks. Let cool 15–20 minutes before serving.

Yield: 16 rolls

—ELAINE LOUIE

OLD MILWAUKEE RYE BREAD

pareve

ADAPTED FROM *The Best of Craig Claiborne*

1 recipe for Sponge for Rye Bread (see recipe below)
1 envelope granular yeast
1 cup warm water
¼ cup all-natural dark molasses
2 tablespoons caraway seeds
2 eggs
1 tablespoon salt
1 cup medium rye flour
3 tablespoons solid white shortening
5–5½ cups all-purpose flour
1 tablespoon water

1. Stir down the sponge. Dissolve the yeast in the water. Add the yeast to the sponge, stirring. Add the molasses and 1 tablespoon of the caraway seeds. Stir to blend.

2. Add 1 lightly beaten egg and salt and blend once more. Add the rye flour and blend. Add the shortening and beat to blend. Add 2 cups of the all-purpose flour and blend with a wooden spoon. Gradually add 2 more cups, kneading constantly. Add more flour, about 2 tablespoons at a time, until the dough has a proper pliable and workable consistency.

3. Turn out the dough onto a lightly floured board and knead for about 6 minutes or longer. Knead brusquely, not gently. Beat and slam the dough down on the board. Knead and beat the dough for about 10 minutes. When ready, the dough should weigh about 3½ pounds.

4. Let warm water flow into a large bowl until the bowl is heated. Drain and dry thoroughly. Grease the dough with shortening. Shape the dough into a ball and add it to the bowl. Cover tightly with plastic wrap. Set aside and let rise for 1 hour or longer, or until double in bulk.

5. There are several methods of shaping the bread before baking. If long bread tins or molds are being used, grease them. Otherwise, use a nonstick baking sheet, ungreased.

6. Divide the dough into 4 portions of equal weight. Roll each piece into a long sausage shape on a flat surface, rolling with the palm of the hand. The shapes should be about 15 inches long. Cover loosely with waxed paper and set aside to rise, about 1 hour, or until double in bulk.

7. Preheat the oven to 375 degrees.

8. Using a sharp blade, make several diagonal gashes on top of each loaf. Brush the tops with 1 egg beaten with water. Sprinkle with the remaining 1 tablespoon caraway seeds.

9. Place in the oven and bake for about 40 minutes, or until crisp-crusted and cooked through.

Yield: 4 loaves

Sponge for Rye Bread

pareve

1 package granular yeast
1½ cups warm water
2 cups medium rye flour
1 tablespoon caraway seeds

1. Combine the yeast and water in a large bowl. Stir to dissolve. Add the flour and caraway seeds and stir to blend. Cover lightly with plastic wrap.
2. Although the sponge is usable after 6 hours, it is best left to stand at room temperature for 1–3 days. Three days will give a more sour taste, which many people prefer.

Yield: Enough sponge for 2–4 loaves of rye bread

PUMPERNICKEL BREAD

dairy, pareve

ADAPTED FROM *The New York Times Large-Type Cookbook*

2 cups cold mashed potatoes
¾ cup yellow cornmeal
3½ cups lukewarm water
2 squares unsweetened chocolate, melted
¼ cup molasses
2 tablespoon salt
1 tablespoon butter or vegetable oil
2 teaspoons caraway seeds
2 packages active dry yeast
3 cups unsifted rye flour
1 cup whole bran cereal
8 cups (approximately) unsifted flour

1. In a large bowl, combine potatoes, cornmeal, 3 cups lukewarm water, chocolate, molasses, salt, butter and caraway seeds.
2. Place remaining lukewarm water in a very large bowl. Sprinkle on yeast and stir to dissolve. Stir in cornmeal mixture, rye flour and bran cereal. Beat until well mixed.
3. Stir in 3 cups regular flour to make a soft dough.
4. Turn onto a floured board and knead in enough additional flour to make a smooth and elastic dough, about 10 minutes. Place dough in a greased bowl and turn to grease the top; cover and let rise in a warm place until doubled in bulk, about 1 hour.
5. Punch down dough; let rise again 30 minutes.
6. Punch down; turn onto a lightly floured board. Divide dough into 3 equal parts, shape into loaves and place in greased 9-by-5-by-3-inch loaf plans. Cover and let rise until doubled in bulk, about 45 minutes.
7. Preheat oven to 350 degrees.
8. Bake loaves about 1 hour or until done.

Yield: 3 loaves

PRE-PASSOVER BREAD

pareve

3 cups warm liquid (can be water or liquid from
  cooked vegetables; potato water is especially good,
  but avoid strong-flavored vegetables like cabbage)
3 cakes or packages yeast or 3 tablespoons loose
  health-food store yeast
¼ cup sugar or honey
9–10 cups flour (at least 3–4 cups should be white
  or whole wheat; the rest may be rye, cornmeal,
  other flours you have on hand, or a mixture of
  these. If you don't have enough other flours, just
  use more wheat)
5 teaspoons salt
5 tablespoons vegetable oil

1. Dissolve yeast and sweetener in wrist-warm liquid.
Gradually add the flours and the salt, mixing hard.
2. Sprinkle the oil over the dough and knead in the
bowl until the oil is absorbed. If the dough is still
sticky add more wheat flour by handfuls, until it
becomes kneadable. Don't worry about quantities;
some flours are drier than others. Don't, however,
add too much extra flour at a time or you will end
up with tough, dry bread.

3. Cover the bowl with a damp cloth and set in a
warm place, such as the inside of a pilot-lit oven, to
rise until doubled, about 45 minutes. Touch the
dough lightly with finger; if a slight impression
remains, the dough has risen enough.
4. Punch it down and knead it on a board lightly
dusted with wheat flour. When it is smooth and
elastic, shape it into two loaves.
5. Place in oiled loaf pans to make standard loaves
or on oiled cookie sheets for the old-fashioned
round-loaf look. Cover with a damp towel and set
back in the warm place for a second rising. Check
after 30 minutes.
6. Bake in a preheated 400-degree oven for 30 minutes, or until browned on the outside and hollow-
sounding when tapped lightly on the bottom.

Yield: 2 loaves

NOTE: *This is typical of breads made and consumed in many
households before Passover, utilizing grains that are forbidden during the holiday and must either be consumed or discarded before Passover begins.*

—REBECCA BOROSON

HUNGARIAN YEAST BREAD
WITH CHEESE TOPPING · (TUROS LEPENY)

dairy

FOR THE DOUGH:

½ cup milk

1 packet (¼ ounce) dry yeast

1 teaspoon sugar

3 cups plus 1 teaspoon flour

½ cup unsalted butter, at room temperature

3 large egg yolks

FOR THE TOPPING:

3 cups rich fresh ricotta

¾ cup sugar

3 large eggs, lightly beaten

¼ cup sour cream

3 tablespoons chopped fresh dill

1. To make the dough, warm the milk in a small saucepan over low heat until lukewarm. Add the yeast, sugar and 1 teaspoon of the flour. Set aside until very foamy, about 8 minutes. Place the remaining 3 cups flour, the butter, yolks and yeast mixture in a large bowl and knead until smooth. Gather the dough into a ball, lightly coat with flour and return it to the bowl. Cover the bowl with plastic wrap and set in a warm place until the dough doubles in bulk, 30–60 minutes.

2. Meanwhile, to make the topping, place the cheese in a large bowl and whisk until very smooth. Whisk in the sugar, eggs and sour cream. Stir in the dill and set aside.

3. When the dough has risen, preheat the oven to 350 degrees and butter a 10-by-14-inch baking sheet. Turn the dough out onto the baking sheet and press evenly across the bottom and up the sides. Spread the topping over the dough and bake in the top part of the oven until golden, about 40 minutes. Cool on a rack, cut into squares and serve.

Yield: 16 servings

—MOLLY O'NEILL

CORN BREAD

dairy

1 tablespoon plus ¼ cup peanut or corn oil

1 cup coarse yellow cornmeal

½ cup flour

2 tablespoons sugar or honey

1 teaspoon baking powder

1 teaspoon baking soda

½ teaspoon salt

2 eggs

1 cup buttermilk

1. Heat oven to 425 degrees. Use 1 tablespoon oil to grease 9-inch square or round pan.

2. Combine dry ingredients in one bowl, whisk wet ingredients in another. Combine and stir together just until batter is moistened but not smooth. Spread into pan and bake 15–20 minutes, until toothpick inserted in center comes out clean. Cool on rack.

Yield: 8–10 servings

—REGINA SCHRAMBLING

WATER BAGELS

dairy

ADAPTED FROM *The Best of Craig Claiborne*

FOR THE BAGELS:

1 package granular yeast
2 cups warm water
¼ cup natural-flavored instant malted milk powder
2 tablespoons sugar
1 tablespoon salt
5¾ cups unsifted flour

FOR THE WATER BATH:

2 quarts water
2 tablespoons natural-flavored instant malted milk powder
1 tablespoon sugar

1. Place the yeast in a warm bowl and add the water, stirring to dissolve. Add the malted milk powder and sugar and stir until dissolved. Add the salt and flour all at once. Work the dough with the fingers and hands, kneading the mass into a stiff dough. Or use a mixer equipped with a dough hook.

2. Turn out the dough onto a lightly floured board and knead until smooth. Shape the dough into a ball and place it in an ungreased bowl. Cover with plastic wrap and let rise in a warm place until double in bulk.

3. Preheat the oven to 450 degrees.

4. Bring the ingredients for the water bath to a boil.

5. Punch down the dough and divide it into 16 equal portions. Roll each portion into a ball. Pierce the center of each dough ball with the index finger. Using the fingers, shape each portion of dough into a circle like a doughnut ring.

6. If the water is boiling, turn off the heat. When the bagels are dropped into it, the water should be just below the boiling point.

7. Drop the bagel rounds into the just-under-boiling water and let them "cook" for about 20 seconds on a side. Immediately lift the rounds from the water, using a slotted spoon.

8. Place the bagel grounds on an ungreased baking sheet and bake for about 20 minutes, or until golden brown.

Yield: 16 bagels

ONION-TOPPED BAGELS

pareve

ADAPTED FROM *The Best of Craig Claiborne*

½ cup dehydrated minced onion (see Note below),
  soaked in water and then squeezed dry
2 tablespoons oil
¼ teaspoon salt
½ egg white
Water Bagels (page 446)

1. There are two ways to prepare onion-topped bagels. The easiest is simply to sprinkle the bagels with dehydrated onions when they are removed from the water bath and are still wet. When using this method, the onions turn very brown, almost black when baked.

2. To produce a less dark onion topping, prepare the bagels in the basic recipe (page 446) until they are ready for the oven. Combine the onion, oil, salt and egg white and brush the mixture onto the bagels. Bake as indicated until golden brown.

NOTE: *Chopped fresh onions do not produce a product to taste like the commercially prepared bagels.*

PITA BREAD

pareve

ADAPTED FROM *The Best of Craig Claiborne*

1 package granular yeast
2 tablespoons plus ⅓ cup lukewarm water,
  approximately
1 teaspoon sugar
1 egg, beaten
2 cups flour
⅛ teaspoon salt
3 tablespoons oil

1. Dissolve the yeast in the 2 tablespoons of lukewarm water. Add the sugar and egg and stir well.

2. Sift together the flour and salt. Stir in the yeast mixture and 3 tablespoons of oil. Add the remaining ⅓ cup of lukewarm water and mix into a soft dough, adding a little more if needed. Cover and let rise until double in bulk.

3. Punch down the dough and form into 16 flat cakes about 4 inches in diameter. Place the cakes on an oiled baking sheet and let rise until light, or almost double in bulk.

4. Preheat the oven to 375 degrees.

5. Prick the cakes with the tines of a fork, brush with water or cooking oil and bake in the oven for 15–20 minutes, or until lightly browned. The pita should be puffed around the edges with a hollow in the center. Serve hot with appetizers.

Yield: 16 pitas

SPINACH-FILLED ANATOLIAN FLAT BREAD

dairy

ADAPTED FROM *Classic Turkish Cooking*

¼ pound unbleached bread flour (¾ cup), plus flour
 for dusting

½ teaspoon salt, plus to taste

1½ tablespoons olive oil or melted butter

3–4 cloves garlic

1 tablespoon unsalted butter

1 large onion, chopped

½ pound fresh spinach, rinsed, patted dry and
 chopped

Pinch of grated nutmeg

½ teaspoon hot red chili flakes

1 tablespoon all-purpose flour

½ cup milk

3 tablespoons grated Parmesan cheese

Freshly ground black pepper

1. Sift the bread flour and ½ teaspoon salt into a large bowl. Form a well in the center and pour in 1 tablespoon of the oil or melted butter and ¼ cup lukewarm water. Work the flour into the liquid and form a dough.

2. Knead the dough, sprinkling on a bit more flour if necessary, until it is smooth, about 5 minutes. Divide the dough into 4 parts and roll each piece into a ball, place on a lightly floured work surface and cover with a damp cloth. Allow to rest 20 minutes.

3. Meanwhile, pulverize garlic with a few generous pinches of salt.

4. Melt butter in a skillet with a cover, add onion and crushed garlic, and cook over medium heat until softened. Add spinach, nutmeg and chili flakes. Cover and cook 2–3 minutes. Stir in the flour, then the milk, and cook, stirring, until smooth. Beat in cheese and season with salt and pepper. Set aside.

5. Cut four 8-inch squares of foil or parchment paper. Heat a griddle or skillet over medium-high heat and wipe it with oil or melted butter.

6. Roll balls of dough on a floured surface into thin rounds 5–6 inches in diameter. Place one round on griddle, shift it to be sure it is not sticking and cook about a minute, until it starts to bubble and brown on the underside. Brush top with ¼ teaspoon oil or butter, then flip it over.

7. Spread one-fourth of the spinach filling on the cooked side. Allow bottom to cook about 45 seconds, until lightly browned. Lift flat bread onto a square of foil or paper, roll into a cone and wrap it up.

8. Repeat with remaining dough and filling, and serve.

Yield: 4 filled flat breads

—FLORENCE FABRICANT

ANGELINA DE LEON'S MATZOH
WITH HONEY AND PEPPER

pareve
ADAPTED FROM *The New York Times Passover Cookbook*

4 cups white flour (see Note below)
1 tablespoon freshly ground black pepper
4 large eggs, beaten
6 tablespoons honey
4 teaspoons olive oil
8 tablespoons water

1. Preheat oven to 400 degrees.
2. In a large mixing bowl, combine the flour and pepper. Mix well.
3. Mix in the eggs, honey, olive oil and just enough water to make a very dry dough. Do not overmix.
4. Divide the dough into 12 equal portions and shape into balls. On a lightly floured surface, roll each ball into a thin disk about 8 inches in diameter.

Pierce all over with fork.
5. Bake on cookie sheets for 10 minutes, or until matzohs are puffed and begin to brown. Cool on racks.

Yield: 12 (8-inch) matzohs

NOTE: *This unusual matzoh recipe, which dates from the Spanish Inquisition, survives because it was used as evidence in the trial of Angelina de Leon to prove that she was a Jew. A cautionary note: The laws governing the baking of matzoh for Passover are so stringent that doing so at home is virtually impossible. However, this recipe might be attempted at other times of the year by Jews who observe kashruth. Matzoh cake meal may be substituted for the flour, though the dough does not roll out as well. Increase the water by one-half and bake for 3 minutes longer.*

—ANDREE BROOKS

FRESHENING AND SEASONING MATZOHS

1. To freshen the flavor of matzohs, dampen them lightly on both sides by rubbing wet hands over them or running them under water. Bake in a 375 degree oven for a few minutes until dry and crisp and faintly brown around the edges. Watch carefully so they do not burn. Coarse salt can be sprinkled on the top side of each after wetting and before baking.

2. Baked matzohs can also be seasoned with garlic or onion, in which case they are delicious with soup or cheese or with various canapé spreads. Rub one side of each matzoh with a cut onion or garlic clove. Dampen the matzoh slightly, sprinkle with salt and bake for 6–7 minutes at 375 degrees.

—MIMI SHERATON

PARISIAN PLETZEL

pareve

<small>ADAPTED FROM</small> Henri Finkelsztajn, in
The Jewish Holiday Baker

1 cup lukewarm water
1 scant tablespoon active dry yeast
1 tablespoon sugar
4–5 cups all-purpose unbleached flour
2 large eggs
¼ cup plus 2 tablespoons vegetable oil
2 teaspoons salt
½ cup cold water
2 cups diced onions
¼ cup poppy seeds

1. Mix the water with the yeast and a dash of sugar in a large glass bowl. Let sit for about 10 minutes.
2. Add 4 cups of the flour, eggs, the ¼ cup oil, remaining sugar and salt. Mix well and knead for about 10 minutes or until smooth, adding more flour if necessary. Let rise, covered, for 1 hour in a greased bowl.
3. Preheat the oven to 375 degrees. Divide dough into 12 balls and roll or flatten out into rounds about 6 inches in diameter. Place on greased cookie sheets and press down centers. Brush with water and sprinkle with about ⅓ cup of onions. Brush onions with remaining vegetable oil and sprinkle with poppy seeds. Let sit for 15 minutes, uncovered.
4. Bake for 20 minutes. Then stick the pletzel under the broiler for a minute to brown the onions.

Yield: 12 pletzels

<small>NOTE:</small> *Pletzel is short for* Bialy stoker tsibele pletzel, *an onion flat bread from the city of Bialystok, Poland; the bread is known in America in a smaller version as bialy.*

—JOAN NATHAN

DESSERTS

ONE OF THE REAL COMFORTS IN LIFE TO JEWS, AS TO MANY OTH-
ERS, IS A DELICIOUS PIECE OF CAKE AND A CUP OF TEA OR COFFEE,
sometimes as dessert, but also between meals. The latter, in fact, was the basis of
much of café life in more leisurely times, as friends met midmorning or mid-
afternoon to talk and nibble on the cream-filled layer cakes, nut tortes, cinna-
mon-scented coffee cakes, fruit tarts and airy cheesecakes of Middle Europe, or
the subtly delicate Greek and Middle Eastern phyllo pastries, the flaky leaves
enfolding honeyed pistachios, almonds and dried fruits.

This is also an area where religious symbolism is expressed widely, especially for holidays. Passover is the prime example, as special cakes had to be
developed using no flour, resulting in fragrant almond macaroons, thinly layered nut tortes, and soufflé-like sponge cakes, as well as contemporary additions
such as flourless chocolate cake.

Honey, bringing the promise of a sweet year ahead, is in one form or
another served at Rosh Ha Shana whether simply as a dip for sliced tart apples
or folded into a dark, velvety honey cake like the one studded with Sephardic
delicacies of dried apricots, raisins, pistachios and walnuts.

The hanging of the evil Haman, an enemy of the Jews who was defeated by the wily Queen Esther, the Jewish wife of the Persian king, is remembered during the springtime festival of Purim. It is celebrated not only with joyous parades, costumes and masks but with various cakes. For the Ashkenazim, it is hamantaschen—Haman's pockets—triangular pastries filled with prune or apricot jam or ground, lemon-flavored poppy seeds. But Sephardim eat many sweets on that holiday and especially small honeyed fritters. Not all foods that mark Purim are sweet. Ugandan Jews exchange baskets of fish as gifts, and Tunisians eat lamb during that holiday to accompany their firecrackers. And in Morocco, couscous is on the Purim menu along with spicy fish, a springtime symbol of fertility.

Aside from such holiday symbols, there are many more traditional baked sweets favored by Eastern European and Sephardic Jews, including Hungarian strudels, Austrian Sacher and Linzer tortes, Polish babka, Bulgarian chocolate cake, French *dacquoise,* German *schnecken,* Syrian date-filled crescents, baklava and North African *bsteeyas* with dried fruits and nuts.

With the Jews having a collective sweet tooth and a taste for culinary acculturation, it's no wonder American specialties such as frothy lemon meringue pie, brownies and angel food cake have become part of the Jewish dessert menu.

In deference to kosher laws that prohibit the serving of dairy immediately after meat, some cakes and pie crusts that follow are made with pareve shortenings—oils or margarine—while others rich in butter and possibly cream are reserved for dairy meals, as are cheesecakes.

Given the lushness of traditional Jewish fruit desserts—baked apples or figs, applesauce, dried fruit compotes, and cut fresh fruits—the fusion possibilities are wide and dazzling. All manner of mousses, fruits baked or poached in wine, contemporary cold fruit soups and soufflés of honey, chocolate, prunes and even of the crushed honey and sesame confection that is halvah, bring elegant finishes to dinners, allowing that no dessert made with a dairy product be served after meat.

Homemade sherbets and ice creams are fine cool finishes to dairy meals, and are delicious based on gingersnaps, figs and pistachios, bittersweet chocolate and pineapple. The classic Eastern European noodle pudding gets a bright lift when made with apricots and Middle Eastern phyllo leaves make a delicate base for apple tart.

As with cakes and cookies, some of these confections also are symbolic on certain holidays. In December for the Festival of Lights—Hanukkah—specialties of the Ashkenazim and of the Sephardim and Middle Eastern Jews differ widely in form, but all are fried in oil to commemorate the victory of the Maccabees over the Syrian king Antiochus Epiphanes. Returning to their temple, they found only enough pure olive oil to keep the ritual eternal light burning for one day. But miraculously, the oil lasted for eight days until new supplies could be sanctified. That miracle is recalled not only in the eight-day lighting of the Hanukkah menorah, but in the eating of various fritters. For the Ashkenazim that means savory potato latkes, but to Sephardim and Middle Eastern Jews, soothingly sweet, puffy doughnuts or crullers are in order, foremost among them being the forms of the yeasty *soofganiyot* dusted with cinammon and sugar, plain or filled with jelly.

The most ardent lovers of sweets will want to try the pleasures of candies and confections such as the Rosh Ha Shana syrup dough knots that are *teiglach,* chewy nougat, nicely astringent candied orange peel, crunchy ginger brittle or sesame brittle, halvah (made with either eggplant or tahini), or luxurious chocolate-almond truffles.

FRUIT DESSERTS AND
OTHER SWEET ENDINGS

◆ ◆

SAFFRON PANNA COTTA WITH FRESH FIGS

dairy

1 packet unflavored gelatin
1¼ cups milk
1 small pinch saffron, well crushed
½ cup heavy cream
¼ cup sugar
½ teaspoon orange-flower water
1 cup plain lowfat yogurt
12 fresh figs, quartered
¼ cup orange blossom honey

1. Whisk gelatin into ¼ cup milk in a small saucepan. When gelatin is soft, stir it, then put pan over low heat just until the gelatin dissolves. Stir in saffron. Do not allow to boil.

2. Gradually stir in remaining milk along with cream and sugar. Cook, stirring frequently, until mixture barely begins to scald. Remove from heat and strain into a bowl. Whisk in orange-flower water and set aside until barely warm, about 20 minutes. Stir yogurt to smooth it, then gradually stir into milk mixture.

3. Transfer mixture to six 4-ounce ramekins or muffin tins. Cover and chill until set, at least 4 hours. Unmold onto dessert plates by running a knife around edges of molds and, if necessary, dipping bottoms in hot water for 20–30 seconds.

4. Arrange fig quarters around panna cottas, drizzle figs with honey and serve.

Yield: 6 servings

—FLORENCE FABRICANT

APRICOT MOUSSE

dairy

½ pound dried apricots
Water to cover
2 eggs

¼ teaspoon vanilla extract
1 cup milk
Juice of ½ lemon, or to taste
½ cup slivered almonds, toasted

1. Put the apricots in a saucepan and add water to cover. Simmer for ½ hour.

2. Meanwhile beat the eggs in another saucepan until thick and sticky. Add the vanilla extract and the milk. Mix thoroughly and thicken over low heat, stirring frequently, until the mixture is as thick as heavy cream. Be careful not to overcook or the custard will curdle.

3. Combine lemon juice, apricots and the custard in the jar of an electric blender and puree until smooth. Pour into a serving bowl or individual bowls and refrigerate for an hour or two before serving.

4. Just before serving, sprinkle with almonds.

Yield: 4 servings

—MOIRA HODGSON

LEMON MOUSSE WITH SLIVERED ALMONDS

dairy

5 eggs, separated
½ cup sugar
Juice and grated peel of 2 lemons
1 tablespoon unflavored gelatin
½ cup heavy cream
½ cup toasted, slivered almonds

1. Beat the egg yolks with the sugar until lemon-colored. Add the lemon juice and peel, then whisk over low heat until thick.

2. Meanwhile, dissolve the gelatin in ½ cup warm water.

3. Whip the egg whites until stiff. Whip the cream.

4. Add the gelatin to the lemon mixture and cool. Fold in the egg whites. Reserve about ¼ cup of cream for the top of the soufflé. Fold the remaining cream into the lemon mixture and pour into a 2-quart soufflé dish. Cover with remaining cream and chill until set, preferably overnight.

5. Just before serving, sprinkle with the almonds.

Yield: 4–6 servings

—MOIRA HODGSON

BITTER-CHOCOLATE ICE CREAM WITH HONEY

dairy

1 quart milk
2 ounces bitter chocolate, broken into small pieces
8 egg yolks
¾ cup sugar

1½ cups cocoa
⅓ cup honey

1. In a saucepan, add the milk and chocolate. Bring to a simmer. When the chocolate has melted, blend well and remove from the heat.

2. Place the egg yolks in a mixing bowl. Add the sugar, cocoa and honey. Blend well. Strain through a fine sieve. Let cool and refrigerate.

3. Pour the mixture into an ice-cream freezer and follow manufacturer's instructions for freezing.

Yield: About 1 1/2 quarts

—BRYAN MILLER

MOUSSE AU CHOCOLAT

dairy

> 1/2 pound semisweet chocolate
> 6 ounces butter, cut in small pieces
> 6 large eggs, separated
> 1/2 cup superfine sugar
> 1 pinch salt

1. Cut the chocolate into 1-inch pieces and place in a saucepan. Set the saucepan into a larger one with almost boiling water. Let melt over low heat. When melted, add the butter. Blend well. Remove from the heat and let cool for a few minutes.

2. Meanwhile, place the egg yolks and the sugar in a large mixing bowl. Beat well with a wire whisk for about 4 minutes, until very thick and lemon-colored.

3. Add the chocolate mixture to the yolks and blend well with a rubber spatula.

4. Beat the egg whites with salt until stiff. Do not overbeat. Fold them into the chocolate mixture. Spoon the mousse into a serving bowl and chill until ready to serve.

Yield: 6 servings

—BRYAN MILLER AND PIERRE FRANEY

TANGERINE MOUSSE

dairy

> 1 package unflavored gelatin
> 2 tablespoons orange liqueur
> 5 large eggs, separated
> 1/4 cup sugar
> 1/4 cup lemon juice
> 2/3 cup tangerine juice
> 1 cup heavy cream

1. Dissolve the gelatin in 3 tablespoons warm water and add the orange liqueur.

2. Place the egg yolks in a heavy saucepan and add the sugar, lemon juice and tangerine juice. Mix well, using a wire whisk.

3. Place the saucepan over very low heat (you may also use a double boiler) and whisk gently until the mixture has thickened enough to coat a spoon. Do not overcook. Cool and place in a large mixing bowl.

4. Whip the cream until stiff.

5. Whip the egg whites until barely stiff (not too dry).

6. Fold the cream into the egg-tangerine mixture. Gently fold in the egg whites until barely blended.

7. Place the mousse in individual bowls or glasses or in a serving bowl. Chill overnight or for at least 4 hours.

Yield: 6–8 servings

—MOIRA HODGSON

HONEY SOUFFLÉ

pareve

<small>ADAPTED FROM</small> *The Best of Craig Claiborne*

4 eggs, separated
2 tablespoons flour
¼ teaspoon nutmeg
¾ cup confectioners' sugar
2 tablespoons cream sherry or sweet red
    or white wine
½ cup honey
½ cup unsalted margarine, melted
1 teaspoon grated lemon rind
2 tablespoons finely ground almonds

1. Preheat the oven to 350 degrees.

2. Beat the egg yolks until light and creamy. Sift the flour, nutmeg and confectioners' sugar together and stir into the yolks.

3. Add the wine. Mix the honey and margarine together and add slowly to the egg mixture. Add the lemon rind and beat until smooth.

4. Beat the egg whites until stiff but not dry and fold into honey mixture. Pour into an ungreased 1½-quart soufflé dish. Sprinkle with the almonds.

5. Place dish in a shallow pan of hot water and bake 30–40 minutes.

Yield: 4 servings

FLOURLESS APRICOT AND HONEY SOUFFLÉ

dairy

Butter for soufflé dish
¼ cup light brown sugar, for sprinkling
1 cup milk
3 egg yolks
Sea salt

3 tablespoons honey
1 cup Turkish dried apricots
3 tablespoons Sauternes or other white dessert wine
5 egg whites
1 tablespoon powdered sugar
1½ tablespoons finely chopped almonds
Vanilla or almond ice cream (optional)

1. Generously butter a 1½-quart soufflé dish. Sprinkle sugar into dish, tilting so that sugar coats bottom and sides. Place in freezer.

2. In a small pan, heat milk over medium-high heat until bubbles form around edges; remove from heat and let cool slightly. Place egg yolks, pinch of salt and honey in a medium bowl and whisk until light and fluffy. Very slowly whisk a third of the milk into eggs, and then add this mixture back to pan. Stirring constantly, cook mixture over medium-low heat until it thickens enough to coat back of a spoon. Remove from heat, strain into a bowl and let cool.

3. In a small pan, combine apricots and Sauternes. Bring to a boil and stir. Shut off heat and let cool.

4. Preheat oven to 400 degrees; place baking sheet on bottom rack. In a blender or food processor, combine egg mixture and apricots; puree. Transfer to a medium bowl.

5. Remove dish from freezer. Place egg whites, a pinch of salt and powdered sugar in bowl and whisk until fairly stiff peaks form.

6. Using a rubber spatula, add about a third of the egg whites to the apricot mixture and fold until combined. Add apricot mixture to remaining egg whites in bowl. Fold together until mixed well, being careful not to overmix. Spoon this mixture into soufflé dish, leaving ½ inch on top. Sprinkle almonds on top. Place on baking sheet and bake 17 to 20 minutes, until risen and still a little wobbly when shaken. Remove from oven and serve, plunging two large spoons into center to lift out pieces. Serve with ice cream if desired.

Yield: 4 servings

—AMANDA HESSER

GINGER SOUFFLÉ CAKE

dairy

ADAPTED FROM City Grill, Atlanta

1¼ cups flour
1 teaspoon baking powder
1½ teaspoons ground ginger
1 teaspoon cinnamon
½ teaspoon ground cloves
½ teaspoon ground allspice
¼ teaspoon salt
½ pound butter, softened
1 cup light-brown sugar
2 whole eggs

½ cup buttermilk
½ cup molasses
3 teaspoons vanilla extract
3 eggs, separated
½ cup sugar
1½ cups milk

1. Whisk the flour, baking powder, ginger, cinnamon, cloves, allspice and salt in a bowl until well blended. Set aside. Use some of the butter to grease six 8-ounce soufflé dishes or charlotte molds. Preheat oven to 325 degrees.

2. Beat remaining butter with brown sugar until well

blended. Beat in whole eggs, 1 at a time. Beating at low speed, add the flour mixture alternately with the buttermilk. Stir in molasses and 2 teaspoons vanilla.

3. In a clean bowl, beat the egg whites until softly peaked. Beat in ¼ cup of the sugar and continue beating until the mixture holds peaks but is not stiff. Fold the egg white mixture into the batter. Pour the mixture into the soufflé dishes. Place in the oven and bake 45–50 minutes, until firm to the touch on top and a cake tester inserted in the center comes out clean. Remove from the oven and allow to cool almost to room temperature.

4. While the soufflés are baking, beat the remaining sugar with the egg yolks until thick and light. In a heavy saucepan, scald the milk and, whisking con-

stantly, slowly pour about half into the egg yolk mixture. Then stir the egg yolk mixture into the hot milk remaining in the saucepan. Place over medium-low heat and cook, stirring with a wooden spoon, until the custard has thickened enough to coat the spoon and steam begins to rise from it. Remove from heat, stir in the remaining teaspoon of vanilla, strain into a bowl, cover and refrigerate.

5. Unmold the soufflés by running a knife around the edges and inverting each onto a dessert plate. Spoon some of the custard around each portion and serve.

Yield: 6 individual soufflés

—FLORENCE FABRICANT

ORANGE SOUFFLÉS IN ORANGE SHELLS

dairy

ADAPTED FROM *The New York Times International Cookbook*

   6 *hostess sugar dots (cubes) or 1½ hostess sugar tablets*
   7 *very large navel oranges*
   2 *teaspoons orange juice*
   3 *tablespoons butter*
   3 *tablespoons all-purpose flour*
   ¾ *cup milk*
   3 *eggs, separated*
   6 *tablespoons granulated sugar*
   6 *tablespoons orange liqueur*

1. Rub the hostess dots or tablets all over one of the oranges until they are covered with the zest, oil, and

color of the orange skin. Place the dots in a small bowl and add the orange juice.

2. Prepare the remaining oranges for filling: Cut off a slice from ¾ inch to 1 inch off the navel end of each orange. Using a spoon, carefully scoop out the insides of the oranges, leaving the natural shell. Save the scooped-out part for another use. It will not be used in this recipe.

3. Cut off the thinnest possible slice from the stem end of each prepared orange to make a base on which the orange will stand upright. (If a hole is punctured in the bottom of an orange, it may be patched by covering it from the inside with a small slice from the top.)

4. Preheat the oven to 450 degrees.

5. Melt the butter in a saucepan and stir in the flour, using a wire whisk. When blended, add the milk, stirring rapidly with the whisk. Cook, stirring constantly, until the sauce is thickened and smooth. Remove the sauce from the heat and add the egg yolks, beating rapidly with the whisk. Return the sauce to the heat and bring just to a boil, stirring rapidly with the whisk. Do not cook for more than a split second or the sauce will curdle.

6. Remove the saucepan from the heat and stir in the granulated sugar. Add the softened hostess dots and

beat well. Let cool 20 minutes. Stir in the liqueur.

7. Place the empty orange shells on a baking sheet and bake about 5 minutes.

8. Meanwhile, beat the egg whites until stiff and stir half of them into the sauce. Fold in the remaining whites. Divide the soufflé mixture among the 6 orange shells and bake about 10 minutes, or until the soufflés are puffed and brown.

Yield: 6 servings

HOT SOUFFLÉ OF PRUNES

dairy

⅔ cup finely chopped prunes, pitted
6–7 tablespoons granulated sugar
6 egg whites
Butter for pan
Sugar for pan
Confectioners' sugar
Sweetened whipped cream, optional

1. Combine prunes with sugar.

2. Beat egg whites until stiff. Fold in prune mixture. Spoon into buttered and sugared 8- to-10-cup soufflé dish. Set in shallow pan containing 1–2 inches of hot water. Bake at 350 degrees for 40 minutes.

3. Remove from oven and sprinkle top with confectioners' sugar. Serve with sweetened whipped cream at dairy meals.

Yield: 10 servings

NOTE: *Unsalted margarine may be substituted for butter.*

—MARIAN BURROS

STRAWBERRY SOUFFLÉ WITH STRAWBERRY SAUCE

pareve

1½ pints fresh strawberries, stems removed, sliced
¾ cup sugar for strawberries
8 eggs, separated
½ cup sugar for egg whites
Strawberry Sauce (see recipe below)

1. Preheat oven to 425 degrees. Butter well and chill eight 1¼-cup soufflé dishes.
2. Place strawberries in food processor or blender. Add ¾ cup sugar. Puree well. Taste for sweetness (amount of sugar varies with sweetness of fruit). Transfer to bowl.
3. Add yolks to mixture and blend well with wire whisk. In another bowl, whisk whites while gradually adding ½ cup sugar. Whisk to soft peaks. Fold one-quarter of whites into strawberries, then remainder. Do not overwork. Taste for sweetness.
4. Place soufflé dishes on baking sheet and fill to the rim. Before placing in oven, run thumb around rim of each to remove any overflow, which could cling and prevent soufflé from rising fully. Bake for approximately 10 minutes. Add sauce before serving.

Yield: 8 servings

NOTE: *For a dairy meal, you can make a frozen soufflé by adding about 1 cup heavy cream, whipped, to strawberry mixture after folding in whites. Make a collar of aluminum foil several inches high around the rim of the soufflé dish before adding the strawberry mixture, fill to the top of the collar and freeze for several hours. Remove foil before serving.*

Strawberry Sauce

pareve

½ pint fresh strawberries, cleaned and sliced thinly
⅓ cup sugar
2 tablespoons kirsch or other fruit liqueur

Place strawberries and sugar in saucepan over medium heat. Cook, stirring occasionally, for 5 minutes. Add liqueur and keep warm until serving.

Yield: Enough for 8 individual soufflés

—BRYAN MILLER

HALVAH SOUFFLÉ

dairy
ADAPTED FROM *Taste of Israel: A Mediterranean Feast*

Softened butter and sugar to prepare soufflé dish
6 ladyfingers
7 ounces halvah
2 tablespoons cornstarch

2 tablespoons sugar
Pinch of salt
5 egg yolks
2 tablespoons brandy
1 cup milk
2 tablespoons all-purpose flour
5 egg whites

1. Preheat oven to 400 degrees. Butter inside of 5-cup soufflé dish and sprinkle with sugar. Line bottom with ladyfingers.

2. Crumble halvah and mix to smooth paste with a little water. Add cornstarch, 1 tablespoon sugar, pinch of salt, egg yolks and brandy and mix.

3. Heat milk almost to boiling, then pour into halvah mixture, beating nonstop with fork. Sift in the flour, mix gently and let cool.

4. Beat egg whites to stiff peaks with 1 tablespoon sugar. Stir a third into halvah mixture, then fold in the rest. Pour into soufflé dish and place a round, buttered piece of foil on top. Bake 25 minutes (do not open door until finished). Serve immediately.

Yield: 6 servings

—ROZANNE GOLD

COLD COFFEE WALNUT SOUFFLÉ

dairy

ADAPTED FROM *The Best of Craig Claiborne*

2 envelopes unflavored gelatin
1 cup sugar
4 tablespoons instant coffee powder
¼ teaspoon salt
4 eggs, separated
2½ cups milk
1 teaspoon vanilla
2 cups heavy cream
½ cup finely chopped walnuts

1. Combine the gelatin, ½ cup of the sugar, the coffee powder and salt in 2½-quart saucepan.

2. Beat the egg yolks with the milk. Add to the gelatin mixture. Stir over low heat until gelatin dissolves and mixture thickens slightly, about 10–12 minutes.

3. Remove from heat and add the vanilla. Chill, stirring occasionally, until mixture mounds slightly when dropped from spoon.

4. Meanwhile, prepare collars on dessert glasses or demitasse cups by binding a double strip of aluminum foil firmly around top of each glass and extending 1 inch above top rim of glass.

5. Beat the egg whites until stiff but not dry. Add remaining sugar gradually. Beat until very stiff.

6. Fold in gelatin mixture. Whip the cream and fold in with the walnuts. Spoon into prepared dessert glasses. Chill until firm.

7. To serve, remove collars. Garnish soufflés with additional chopped walnuts if desired.

Yield: 8–12 servings

PEAR SORBET

pareve

ADAPTED FROM *The Best of Craig Claiborne*

4 ripe, not too firm, unblemished pears, preferably
*   Bosc pears, about 2½ pounds, stems removed*
2½ cups sugar
2¼ cups water
1 tablespoon fresh lemon juice

1. Peel the pears. Cut the pears in half lengthwise. Using a melon ball cutter, remove the center core. Cut away the bottom center line leading from the core to the stem end.
2. Combine the sugar and water in a saucepan. Bring to a boil and simmer for 5 minutes. Add the pears and simmer, uncovered, until the pears are tender, about 15 minutes.
3. Remove from the heat and let the pears cool in the syrup. Refrigerate until thoroughly chilled.
4. Drain the pears, but save the liquid. There should be about 1⅓ cups of liquid. Put the pears into the container of a food processor and process as fine as possible. There should be about 3 cups of puree.
5. Combine the puree, cooking liquid and lemon juice in the container of an electric or hand-cranked ice-cream freezer. Freeze according to manufacturer's instructions. Serve with Strawberry Sauce (page 461), if desired.

Yield: 8–12 servings

PINEAPPLE SHERBET

pareve

ADAPTED FROM *Kosher Cuisine*

1 medium to large ripe pineapple
1¼ cups sugar
3 tablespoons freshly squeezed lemon juice
2 tablespoons kirschwasser

1. Peel the pineapple, remove the core and cut the pineapple into large pieces. Puree in a blender, in batches, until smooth.
2. Strain the batches through a mesh sieve, pushing with the back of a wooden spoon to obtain as much puree as possible. (You should have 3 cups of strained puree.)
3. Stir in the sugar, lemon juice and kirschwasser.
4. Freeze in an electric ice-cream maker, following the manufacturer's instructions. Serve the sherbet or freeze it in an airtight container.

Yield: About 1 quart, or 10 servings

NOTE: *Pineapple sherbet does not freeze very hard, so you can serve it straight from the freezer.*

—CRAIG CLAIBORNE

RHUBARB SHERBET

pareve

ADAPTED FROM Hubert's

1½ pounds fresh rhubarb
1½ cups late-harvest Riesling (see Note below)
¾ cup sugar
2 tablespoons lemon juice

1. Preheat oven to 375 degrees. Place rhubarb in 4-quart nonaluminum baking dish. Cover and bake at 375 degrees until rhubarb is soft, about 25 minutes.
2. Remove rhubarb and place with liquid in food processor or mill and puree.
3. Combine puree with wine, sugar and lemon juice. Place in ice-cream freezer and freeze according to manufacturer's instructions, or pour into large shallow dish, cover and freeze for about 1 hour or just until edges begin to harden and center is only partly frozen. Remove from freezer and beat in mixing bowl until frothy. Return to dish and cover. Refreeze for about 30 minutes, until mixture begins to harden again. Remove from freezer and beat again. Return to freezer and freeze completely, at least 2–3 hours, before serving.

Yield: 4–6 servings

NOTE: *Late-harvest Riesling is recommended because it is sweeter than the regular. If standard Riesling is used, increase the amount of sugar according to taste.*

—MARIAN BURROS

BITTERSWEET CHOCOLATE SORBET

pareve

ADAPTED FROM *Desserts by Pierre Herme*

7 ounces good quality bittersweet chocolate
1 scant cup sugar

1. Fill a large bowl, at least 4–5 quarts, with ice cubes. Have a 1- to 1½-quart metal bowl ready.
2. Place chocolate, sugar and 2 cups water in a heavy 2-quart saucepan over low heat. Cook, stirring frequently, until mixture reaches a boil (this can take 10 minutes or more). Keep stirring while the mixture bubbles furiously for 2 minutes, then pour it into the smaller bowl.
3. Set the small bowl into the large bowl and add cold water to the ice cubes, taking care that no water gets into the chocolate mixture. Allow mixture to cool, stirring from time to time, then refrigerate until very cold.
4. Freeze in an ice-cream maker according to the manufacturer's instructions. Serve at once, or pack into a container and place in the freezer for up to 1 week.

Yield: 1 pint

—FLORENCE FABRICANT

CHOCO-ORANGE ICE

pareve

ADAPTED FROM *The New York Times Large-Type Cookbook*

2 teaspoons unflavored gelatin
3½ cups plus 2 tablespoons water
2 cups sugar
Grated rind of 2 large oranges
4 ounces (squares) unsweetened chocolate
1 teaspoon vanilla
½ cup fresh orange juice

1. Soften gelatin in 2 tablespoons water.
2. Combine remaining water with sugar in a small saucepan. Heat slowly and stir until sugar is dis-

solved. Increase heat and boil rapidly 5 minutes without stirring. Remove from heat and stir in gelatin and rind. Cool to lukewarm.
3. Melt chocolate over hot but not boiling water in top of double boiler; cool slightly. Place warm chocolate in a bowl and gradually beat in warm sugar syrup with rotary beater.
4. Add vanilla and juice and pour into a freezing tray. Cover with aluminum foil and freeze until frozen around edges and mushy in middle.
5. Beat until smooth and refreeze. Remove from the freezer 15 minutes before serving.

Yield: 1 quart

FIG AND PISTACHIO ICE CREAM

dairy

ICE-CREAM BASE:

3 cups milk
¾ cup sugar
1 inch vanilla bean split or 1 teaspoon vanilla extract
3 egg yolks
1 cup heavy cream

1. In a heavy saucepan, scald the milk over medium-low heat with the sugar and vanilla bean, stirring with a wooden spoon until the sugar dissolves. (If using extract, do not add it at this stage; wait until after chilling the mixture.)

2. In a large bowl, whisk the egg yolks until they coat the whisk.
3. Slowly whisk the scalded milk mixture into the beaten yolks.
4. Steep until the mixture cools.
5. Remove the vanilla bean and scrape the seeds into the mixture.
6. Add the heavy cream, cover the bowl completely and chill.

FIG AND PISTACHIO MIXTURE:

1 cup pistachio nuts, shelled
1 pound small figs (green or black)

1. Bring a saucepan of water to a boil, add the nuts and boil for 1 minute, then rinse under cold running water. Remove and discard the outer skins and place the nuts on a paper towel.

2. Trim the stems and peel the outer skins of the figs and discard them. Quarter and then roughly chop or mash the figs. Place them in a bowl, cover tightly and chill.

3. Chop the nuts.

FOR THE ICE CREAM:

1. Churn the prepared ice-cream base in the ice-cream maker for about 5 minutes.

2. Mix the nuts with the figs and fold into the cream base. Continue to freeze according to the manufacturer's directions, then transfer to airtight containers for storage.

Yield: 8–10 servings

—CHRISTOPHER IDONE

ALMOND CRÈME BRULEE

dairy

ADAPTED FROM *The New York Times International Cookbook*

> 3 cups heavy cream
> 6 tablespoons granulated sugar
> 6 eggs yolks
> 1 teaspoon vanilla extract
> 1 teaspoon almond extract
> ½ cup blanched almonds (see Note, page 582)
> ½ cup light brown sugar

1. Preheat the oven to 300 degrees. Heat the cream gently in a saucepan over low heat or over boiling water and stir in the sugar until dissolved.

2. In a large bowl, beat the egg yolks until light in color and pour the hot cream gradually over them, stirring rapidly. Stir in the vanilla and almond extracts and strain the mixture into a 1-quart baking dish. Stir in the almonds.

3. Put the dish in a pan containing 1 inch of hot water and bake for approximately 35 minutes. It is done when a knife blade inserted in the center comes out clean. Do not overbake. Remove the dish from the water bath and cool. Cover and refrigerate for at least 3 hours or as long as 2 days.

4. When ready to serve, preheat the broiler. Place the dish on a baking sheet or on a bed of cracked ice and top the custard with a thin layer of brown sugar, using a knife to spread it evenly across the surface. Broil about 2 inches from the flame for 30 seconds to 2 minutes, until the sugar is brown and melted. Watch constantly to make sure it does not burn. Serve immediately.

Yield: 6 servings

NOTE: *If you prefer, the crème brulee can be refrigerated after it is removed from the broiler and brought to room temperature before serving.*

CHOCOLATE MACAROON DESSERT

dairy

ADAPTED FROM *The New York Times Large-Type Cookbook*

½ pound blanched almonds
¼ cup bourbon or rum
2 cups crumbled macaroons
6 tablespoons butter
½ pound confectioners' sugar
5 eggs, separated
2 squares (1 ounce each) semisweet chocolate
3 tablespoons water
½ teaspoon vanilla
18 ladyfingers
1 pint heavy cream, sweetened and whipped

1. Preheat oven to 350 degrees.
2. Scatter almonds over a baking sheet and bake 10 minutes or until toasted. Stir occasionally so to toast evenly. Let almonds cool. Reserve ⅛ cup of almonds for garnish. Chop remaining almonds.

3. Pour whiskey or rum over macaroons. Set aside.
4. Place butter in mixing bowl and beat with an electric mixer. Beat in sugar.
5. Beat egg yolks until lemon-colored and beat into butter-sugar mixture.
6. Combine chocolate and water, melt over low heat and add to butter mixture. Beat until blended. Stir in almonds and vanilla. Beat egg whites until stiff. Fold into the chocolate mixture.
7. Line bottom and sides of a 1½-quart crystal serving bowl with ladyfinger halves, split side in. Add a thin layer of crumbled macaroons and a layer of chocolate batter. Continue making alternate layers of macaroons and chocolate. Cover and refrigerate overnight.
8. Spoon whipped cream on top of cake and garnish with reserved almonds.

Yield: 10 or more servings

RICE PUDDING WITH DRIED FRUITS

dairy

5½ cups whole, low-fat or skim milk

½ cup sugar

2 teaspoons vanilla extract

¾ cup long-grain white rice

¾ cup diced (½ inch) dried fruits (raisins, apricots,
   figs, cherries)

1 cup yogurt or sour cream (optional)

1. Bring the milk, sugar and vanilla to a boil in a saucepan. Add the rice, mix well and bring the mixture back to a boil. Cover, reduce the heat to very low and simmer for about 40 minutes, until the rice is very soft. (The mixture should still be soupy; if it is not, add enough additional milk to make it soupy.)

2. Add the dried fruits to the pudding, mix and set aside until cooled to room temperature. Spoon into 6 dessert dishes and serve, if desired, with 1–2 tablespoons of yogurt or sour cream on top.

Yield: 6 servings

—JACQUES PEPIN

COUSCOUS WITH FRUITS AND NUTS

dairy

ADAPTED FROM *The New York Times Menu Cook Book*

1 cup seedless grapes

½ cup honey

1 tablespoon orange-flower water

¾ cup raisins

Rind of 1 lemon

Sugar

4 cups Buttered Couscous (see recipe below)

2 oranges, peeled and cut into sections

½ cup untoasted almonds or walnuts

1. Combine the grapes, honey and orange-flower water and set aside.

2. Cover the raisins with warm water and add the lemon rind and ¼ cup sugar.

3. Pile the cold buttered couscous in the center of a round serving tray. Sprinkle lightly with sugar. Arrange over it the honeyed grapes, the drained raisins, orange sections and almonds. Serve at room temperature.

Yield: 10 or more servings

◆ **BUTTERED COUSCOUS** ◆

dairy

2 cups couscous

½ cup water

¼ cup butter

1. Spread the couscous on a tray and sprinkle with the water. Mix lightly with the fingers to moisten all the grains.

2. Drop grains lightly into muslin-covered colander or into the top of a steamer. Do not pack solidly. Cover tightly and steam over boiling water for 20 minutes.

3. Stir the grains lightly, breaking up the lumps. Cover and steam for 20 minutes longer. Stir the butter into the grains until it is all absorbed.

Yield: About 6 cups

HANUKKAH FRITTERS • (SOOFGANIYOT)

dairy, pareve

ADAPTED FROM Corinne Klafter

¼ cup warm water
1 tablespoon sugar
2 packages dry yeast or 2 ounces fresh yeast
½ cup orange juice
¼ pound butter or margarine
5 tablespoons sugar
Dash salt
2 eggs, lightly beaten
3 cups all-purpose flour
Oil for frying

1. In a heavy pot, heat oil to 350 to 375 degrees.
2. Combine sugar with water and add yeast. To proof yeast, put in a warm, moist place or put a pot of boiling water in an enclosed space such as the oven or clean, empty dishwasher. This provides a draft-free, warm, moist place for the yeast to prove itself active.
3. While yeast proofs, heat orange juice, butter or margarine, sugar and salt in a small pan. When luke-warm, pour into bowl and add beaten eggs and proofed yeast. Stir to mix.
4. Add flour and make into a pliable dough. Knead on floured board or in bowl.
5. Grease bowl and allow dough to rise in a warm, moist place for about a half hour. Punch down.
6. Cut dough in strips or cut into circles. Place on greased, floured cookie sheet at least 1 inch apart. Return to warm, moist place to rise. (By now you should reboil water in enclosed space to provide warmth and moisture.)
7. Allow to rise for 20 minutes or longer if time allows.
8. Fry in preheated deep fat until nicely browned on both sides.
9. Drain on paper towels. Sprinkle with confectioners' sugar or cinnamon and sugar mixture. These may also be served with honey or jam or both, and may be reheated to restore freshness.

Yield: 18–24 fritters, depending on size

—NANCY ARUM

SWEET HANUKKAH FRITTERS WITH HONEY SYRUP

pareve

ADAPTED FROM Alayne Zatulov

1 cup golden raisins
¼ cup white wine
1 package active dry yeast
1 teaspoon sugar
1 cup warm water
2 cups all-purpose flour
1 egg
1 teaspoon anise seeds
¾ cup pine nuts
Corn oil or vegetable oil for frying
Confectioners' sugar or Honey Syrup
* (see recipe below)*

1. Combine raisins and wine and set aside.
2. Proof the yeast by dissolving it with sugar and water in a large bowl. When it becomes foamy, after about 5 minutes, add flour, egg and anise seeds and mix well. Cover and allow to rise for 30 minutes.
3. Add raisins and pine nuts, cover and allow dough to rise 1 hour longer.
4. Heat oil for deep frying in a skillet, wok or electric fryer. Oil should be maintained at 375 degrees.
5. Using 2 teaspoons held together, drop dollops of the batter into the hot oil. Dipping teaspoons in cold water will facilitate this. Allow fritters to brown on one side and then turn to brown other side. Do not crowd fritters in the pan. As they are done, use a slotted spoon to transfer them to absorbent paper.
6. Serve fritters while they are still warm, with honey syrup spooned over or dusted with confectioners' sugar.

Yield: About 30 small fritters; 6–8 servings

◆ HONEY SYRUP ◆

pareve

1 cup sugar
⅓ cup orange juice
1 cup honey

1. Dissolve sugar in the orange juice in a small saucepan. Heat until mixture turns clear. Simmer gently 5 minutes.
2. Add lemon juice and honey and set aside until ready to use.
3. Before using, warm gently and serve warm.

Yield: 1½ cups

—FLORENCE FABRICANT

STEVE RAICHLEN'S BAKED GREEK HANUKKAH "FRITTERS" WITH HONEYED SYRUP · (LOUKOUMADES)

pareve

FOR THE SYRUP:

1 cup sugar
¼ cup honey, preferably Greek
1 cinnamon stick
4 cloves
2 strips lemon zest
2 strips orange zest
2 tablespoons cognac or brandy

FOR THE PASTRY:

¼ cup olive oil
1 teaspoon grated lemon zest
½ teaspoon salt
½ teaspoon sugar
1 cup unbleached white flour
1 cup egg substitute, or 2 eggs plus 4 whites lightly
    beaten with fork
1 tablespoon egg substitute or 1 egg white, beaten with
    a little salt, for glaze
Cinnamon for sprinkling

1. Prepare syrup. In saucepan, combine 1¼ cups water with sugar, honey, cinnamon, cloves and lemon and orange zest, and boil until thick and syrupy, for about 4 minutes. Strain syrup into bowl and cool to room temperature. Add cognac, stir and refrigerate. Syrup can be prepared up to a day.

2. Preheat oven to 400 degrees. In heavy saucepan, combine 1 cup water with oil, lemon zest, salt and sugar and bring to boil over high heat. Remove pan from heat and sift in flour. Stir well with wooden spoon to make thick paste. Return pan to high heat and cook until dough is thick enough to come away from sides of pan in a smooth ball, about 2–4 minutes.

3. Add 1 cup egg substitute or eggs in 4 batches, beating vigorously with wooden spoon until mixture is smooth before adding next batch. Mixture should resemble soft ice cream.

4. Transfer dough to piping bag fitted with ⅜-inch round tip. Pipe 1-inch balls of dough onto nonstick baking sheet lightly sprayed with oil, leaving 1½ inches between each. (If you don't have a piping bag, use 2 spoons to drop balls of dough onto sheet.) Dip a fork in cold water, and with back of tines, smooth top of each ball. Lightly brush balls with egg glaze. Sprinkle sheet with a few drops of water.

5. Bake dough balls until puffed, firm and nicely browned for 40–50 minutes. If puffs brown too much before they are cooked through, reduce heat. Remove sheet from oven and cool for 3 minutes.

6. Using spatula, transfer hot puffs to serving bowl. Pour cold syrup on top and let soak for 3 minutes. Serve puffs with syrup in bowls. Sprinkle with cinnamon.

Yield: 32–36 puffs; 8 servings

NOTE: *For a healthier version of the traditional recipe, olive oil replaces butter in the dough and egg substitute replaces whole eggs. In addition, these loukoumades are baked instead of fried. The balls puff and crisp, though perhaps not as strikingly as the deep-fried originals. But when you douse them with cinnamon and honey syrup, you get the very essence of a Greek Hanukkah dessert.*

—STEVEN RAICHLEN

APPLE COMPOTE

pareve

ADAPTED FROM *The New York Times Menu Cook Book*

6 medium apples
3 tablespoons lemon juice
2 cups water
½ cup sugar
½ cup dry white wine
Rind of ½ lemon
1 cinnamon stick
⅓ cup currant jelly, optional

1. Peel the apples, halve and core them. Rub them immediately with lemon juice to prevent discoloration. Drop them into 1 cup of the water.

2. Combine the remaining cup of water with the sugar, wine and 1 tablespoon of the lemon juice. Add the apple halves, cover and simmer until fruit is tender but still firm. Remove the fruit, place it in a glass bowl, cover and let stand until cool.

3. Add the lemon rind and cinnamon stick to the cooking liquid. Simmer until the sauce begins to thicken. Strain it over the apples and chill. Just before serving, if desired, dot with currant jelly.

Yield: 6 servings

ELIAS SHAMMA'S MIDDLE EASTERN BAKED APPLES

dairy

ADAPTED FROM *New York Cookbook*

5 tablespoons unsalted butter, softened, plus butter
 for greasing the dish
¼ cup sugar
¼ cup honey
½ cup shelled pistachios
½ cup pine nuts
½ cup chopped walnuts
½ cup currants
½ teaspoon ground cloves
½ teaspoon ground cinnamon
1½ teaspoons rose water
6 medium-to-large Golden Delicious apples, cored
Vanilla ice cream or whipped cream, optional

1. Preheat oven to 350 degrees. Butter an 8-inch-square baking dish. Place 4 tablespoons of the butter in a food processor with the sugar and honey. Process until well combined. Add all the nuts, currants, cloves, cinnamon and rose water. Pulse until the mixture turns into a paste.

2. Stuff the center of the apples with the nut mixture. Rub the skin of each apple with the remaining tablespoon butter and sprinkle any remaining nut mixture over the apples. Bake until the apples are soft, about 30 minutes. Serve warm with vanilla ice cream or whipped cream, if desired.

Yield: 6 servings

—MOLLY O'NEILL

APPLE-RUM PUDDING TOPPED WITH MERINGUE

pareve

ADAPTED FROM *The New York Times Large-Type Cookbook*

2 cups applesauce
1 cup light brown sugar
1 cup broken pecans
1 cup seedless raisins
⅔ cup dark rum
2 teaspoons cinnamon
1 teaspoon nutmeg
⅛ teaspoon allspice
4 egg whites
½ cup granulated sugar

1. Preheat oven to 325 degrees.

2. Combine applesauce, brown sugar, pecans, raisins, rum and spices in a saucepan. Bring to a boil. Spoon into a 6-cup casserole.

3. Beat egg whites until stiff and gradually beat in granulated sugar. Pile meringue lightly on top of pudding in casserole. Bake 15–20 minutes or until meringue is a delicate brown. Serve at once.

Yield: 6 servings

APPLESAUCE WITH WINE AND VANILLA

pareve

3 pounds fragrant apples, like Gala or McIntosh
    (6–8 apples)
1 cinnamon stick or 1 teaspoon ground
    cinnamon
1 (2-inch) piece vanilla bean, cut in half
    lengthwise
2 strips lemon zest
1½ tablespoons lemon juice, or to taste
¼ cup sugar, or to taste
2 tablespoons dry white wine

1. Wash apples and cut in half. Remove stems and cores; leave skins intact. Place apples in large heavy pot with other ingredients and 2¼ cups water. Bring to boil.

2. Reduce heat, and simmer apples, covered, until soft, 20–30 minutes. Remove pan from heat and let cool slightly. Discard cinnamon stick and vanilla bean.

3. Puree apples and pan juices in blender or food processor: blender will yield a silky puree; processor, a chunkier applesauce.

Yield: About 4 cups; 8 servings

—STEVEN RAICHLEN

APPLE LATKES

pareve, dairy

ADAPTED FROM Ada Shoshan, in
The Jewish Holiday Kitchen

2 eggs, well beaten

1½ cups orange juice, yogurt or milk

2 cups all-purpose flour

1 teaspoon baking powder

Dash of salt

¼ cup sugar if using juice, ½ cup if using yogurt or
milk

3 medium-size apples peeled, cored and grated

Vegetable oil for frying

1. Mix eggs with orange juice, yogurt or milk in a bowl.

2. In a separate bowl combine flour, baking powder, salt and sugar. Add dry ingredients to the egg mixture along with grated apples. Heat a thin layer of oil in a skillet. Allowing I large tablespoon of batter per latke, or pancake, drop batter into the hot oil. Cook about 2 minutes on each side or until slightly golden. Drain on paper towels, sprinkle with confectioners' sugar and serve.

Yield: About 36 latkes

—JOAN NATHAN

SPICED APPLE CHARLOTTE

dairy, pareve

ADAPTED FROM *The New York Times International Cookbook*

4 cups finely sliced apples

¾ cup granulated sugar

¼ teaspoon salt

½ teaspoon ground cloves

¼ teaspoon grated lemon rind

½ cup orange juice

3 tablespoons medium-dry sherry

¼ cup unsalted butter or margarine, melted

3 cups soft fresh bread crumbs

1. Preheat the oven to 350 degrees.

2. Mix the apples with the sugar, salt, cloves, lemon rind, orange juice and sherry. Set aside.

3. Combine the melted butter or margarine and the bread crumbs, mixing well. Fill a greased I-quart casserole with alternating layers of bread crumbs and the apple mixture, beginning and ending with the bread crumbs.

4. Cover the pudding and bake for 30 minutes. Remove the cover and bake for about I5 minutes longer, or until the crumbs are brown and the apples are tender. Serve warm, with cream if desired.

Yield: 6 servings

HONEYED CHALLAH-APPLE PUDDING

dairy

3 tablespoons unsalted butter

3 apples, peeled, cored and coarsely chopped

2½ cups milk

¾ cup honey

1 teaspoon vanilla extract

5 cups challah torn in small pieces

4 large eggs

1 teaspoon cinnamon

2 tablespoons sugar

1. Preheat oven to 350 degrees. Place 2 tablespoons of the butter in a 9-inch square baking dish and place in the oven until the butter melts. When the butter has melted, remove the pan from the oven and use a brush to coat the bottom and sides evenly with the melted butter. Set aside.

2. While the oven is preheating and the butter melting, heat the remaining butter in a heavy skillet, add the apples and sauté over high heat until they just begin to soften and take on color, about 5 minutes. Remove from the heat and set aside.

3. Mix the milk, honey and vanilla together in a large bowl. Add the challah pieces and allow to soak about 10 minutes, until the milk is fairly well absorbed. Beat the eggs until frothy, mix them with the challah and add half the cinnamon and the sautéed apples.

4. Transfer the mixture to baking dish. Mix the remaining cinnamon with the sugar and sprinkle over the top. Bake about 45 minutes. Serve warm or at room temperature.

Yield: 8 servings

NOTE: *Unsalted margarine can be substituted for the butter and apple cider used instead of the milk.*

—FLORENCE FABRICANT

APRICOT-ALMOND CHALLAH PUDDING

dairy

1 tablespoon unsalted butter

4 cups stale challah, torn in small pieces

2 cups milk

½ cup honey

2 eggs

½ teaspoon almond extract

¼ cup sliced toasted almonds

12 ripe apricots, pitted and quartered

1. Use a little of the butter to butter a 2-quart baking dish.

2. Place the bread in a bowl. Heat the milk, add the honey and continue heating the milk just until the honey dissolves. Beat the eggs in a bowl and slowly stir in the milk mixture. Add the almond extract. Pour the milk mixture over the bread and set aside to soak for 20 minutes.

3. Spread half the bread mixture in the baking dish. Sprinkle on half the almonds. Spread the apricots in the dish, top with the remaining bread and then the remaining almonds. Dot with bits of the remaining butter.

4. Bake about 30 minutes, until the top is crusty and lightly brown.

Yield: 6 servings

NOTE: *Pieces of stale brioche may be substituted for the challah.*

—FLORENCE FABRICANT

LEBANESE APRICOT CREAM

dairy

ADAPTED FROM *The Mediterranean Kitchen*

1 pound dried apricots
4 cups water (approximately)
¾ cups sugar (approximately)
2 tablespoons cornstarch dissolved in
    ¼ cup cold water
Juice of ½ lemon
1 cup heavy cream
2 teaspoons orange-flower water
2 teaspoons grated orange zest
2 tablespoons chopped toasted unsalted pistachio nuts

1. Place the apricots in a bowl, and add the water. Allow to soak overnight. The next day, transfer the apricots and the soaking liquid to a saucepan, adding more water if necessary to cover the apricots. Bring to a boil and simmer about 30 minutes, until the apricots are very soft.

2. Transfer apricots and liquid to a food processor or food mill; puree.

3. Return the puree to the saucepan and add ½ cup of sugar, dissolved cornstarch and lemon juice. Simmer a few minutes. Adjust the sweetening to taste.

4. Transfer to a bowl or to 6 individual dishes. Cover and refrigerate.

5. Whip the cream until softly peaked. Fold in 2 tablespoons of sugar (or to taste), the orange flower water and orange zest. Whip the cream until medium stiff.

6. To serve, place a generous dollop of whipped cream on each individual serving, or spoon the apricot mixture into goblets alternately with the whipped cream. Top each serving with a sprinkling of pistachios.

Yield: 6 servings

—FLORENCE FABRICANT

BANANAS IN GINGER SYRUP

pareve

ADAPTED FROM *The Best of Craig Claiborne*

3 or 4 bananas, about 1½ pounds
½ teaspoon ginger
¼ cup sugar
⅓ cup water
2 tablespoons lemon juice

1. Peel the bananas and cut them into ¼-inch-thick rounds. There should be about 3½ cups. Arrange half of the rounds close together on a flat plate. Sprinkle lightly with half of the ginger. Cover with the remaining slices and sprinkle with remaining ginger.

2. Combine the sugar and water in a small saucepan and bring to a boil, stirring constantly until the sugar is dissolved. Add the lemon juice. Cook for 15 minutes and pour the syrup over the bananas. Let stand until cool. Chill.

Yield: 4–6 servings

SOUR CHERRY–WALNUT PUDDING WITH CHERRY SAUCE

dairy

ADAPTED FROM *The New York Times Menu Cook Book*

2 cups (1-pound can) pitted red sour cherries packed
   in water
¼ cup shortening
½ teaspoon vanilla extract
¼ teaspoon almond extract
1 egg
1½ cups sifted all-purpose flour
2 teaspoons baking powder
½ teaspoon salt
½ cup milk
½ cup chopped walnuts
Cherry Sauce (see recipe below)

1. Preheat oven to 350 degrees. Grease a glass ovenware 8-inch square pan.

2. Drain the cherries. If desired, use liquid (see Note); otherwise discard or reserve for another use.

3. Thoroughly cream together the shortening, vanilla, almond extract and sugar. Add the egg and beat well.

4. Sift together the flour, baking powder and salt. Add the creamed mixture alternately with the milk, beating until smooth after each addition. Fold in the cherries and walnuts.

5. Pour into the prepared pan. Bake 45–50 minutes. Cut into squares and serve warm with hot Sour Cherry Sauce.

Yield: 9 servings

NOTE: *For a pareve or meat meal, you can substitute the drained cherry liquid for the milk.*

SOUR CHERRY SAUCE

pareve

2 cups (1-pound can) pitted red sour cherries packed
    in syrup
¼ cup water
¼ cup white corn syrup
1 cinnamon stick
1 tablespoon lemon juice
¼ teaspoon almond extract
2 teaspoons cornstarch
1 tablespoon water

1. Drain the cherry syrup into a saucepan. Add the sugar, corn syrup, cinnamon, lemon juice and almond extract to the pan. Simmer for 10 minutes.

2. Remove cinnamon stick. Mix together the cornstarch and cold water. Add a little of the hot syrup to the cornstarch mixture and stir to dissolve all the cornstarch, return to the pan and cook over low heat, stirring, until the sauce boils. Add the cherries. Serve the sauce hot or cold.

Yield: About 2½ cups

BAKED FIGS

dairy

6 firm ripe fresh figs
1½ tablespoons butter, melted
1½ tablespoons sugar
Vanilla ice cream or 1 cup raspberries, ½ cup heavy
    cream and ¼ cup confectioners' sugar

1. Preheat oven to 375 degrees.

2. Cut the stems off figs and place figs in a buttered baking dish. Brush with butter and sprinkle with sugar. Bake 15 minutes, until bubbly and lightly caramelized.

3. With scissors or a knife, make an **X** in the top so that each fig opens like a flower.

4. Serve figs hot with ice cream or with raspberries folded into heavy cream whipped with confectioners' sugar.

Yield: 2 servings

—JONATHAN REYNOLDS

ORANGE FOAM

pareve

ADAPTED FROM *The New York Times Menu Cook Book*

   3 eggs, separated
   ½ cup sugar
   2 tablespoons cornstarch
   1 tablespoon orange liqueur
   Grated rind of 1 orange
   2 cups fresh orange juice

1. Place the egg yolks in the top part of a double boiler and beat over barely simmering water until they are lemon colored.

2. Gradually add the sugar and continue beating until fluffy. Stir in the cornstarch, the liqueur, orange rind and juice. Continue to cook and beat until the mixture has the consistency of mayonnaise. Do not allow the sauce to boil or it will curdle.

3. Beat the egg whites until stiff and fold them gently but thoroughly into the orange mixture. Pour into a glass serving bowl and refrigerate until well chilled.

Yield: 6 servings

NOTE: *People who are concerned about ingesting uncooked egg whites should not eat this dish.*

SLICED ORANGES WITH POMEGRANATE-CARAMELIZED WALNUTS

pareve

FOR THE ORANGES:

   3 Valencia oranges, scrubbed well, skin on

1. Trim ends from oranges and discard. Thinly slice the oranges crosswise. Discard seeds.
2. Lay 5 slices of orange on each of 4 plates and set aside.

◆ **POMEGRANATE-CARAMELIZED WALNUTS** ◆

pareve

   1 cup shelled walnuts, about 4 ounces
   ½ cup sugar

   Juice from 1 large or 2 small ripe pomegranates (about ½ cup) (see Note, page 583)
   Seeds from ½ small pomegranate (about ¼ cup)

1. Place walnuts in 10-inch nonstick pan over medium-high heat. After about 2½ minutes, they will begin to make popping sounds. Continue to cook, stirring and turning the nuts, until they are crisp and the edges are brown, about 2½ more minutes.
2. Sprinkle sugar evenly over nuts. Let sugar sit until it begins to melt, then start to stir. Continue to cook, stirring, until sugar completely melts, turns a dark golden caramel color and coats the nuts, about 3½ minutes.
3. Stir in the pomegranate juice. Cook, stirring vigorously, for 30 seconds. Remove nuts from heat and continue to stir for 1–2 minutes to cool.

4. Divide the warm, gooey nuts evenly over the oranges. Sprinkle with pomegranate seeds and serve.

Yield: 4 servings

NOTE: *Caramelized walnuts are a delicious snack. After cooking, spread the warm candied nuts on a lightly buttered* cookie sheet. When completely cool, they can be broken apart like peanut brittle and stored in an airtight container at room temperature for as long as 3 days.

—BARBARA KAFKA

ORANGES AND DATES IN CARDAMOM-HONEY SYRUP

pareve

4 cups water
½ cup honey
1 tablespoon orange-flower water
12 cardamom pods, crushed
4 large oranges
⅔ cup pitted dates, halved lengthwise
2 tablespoons fresh lemon juice
3 tablespoons shredded coconut
2 tablespoons shelled pistachios, coarsely chopped

1. Combine the water, honey, orange-flower water and cardamom in a medium saucepan. Bring to a boil, whisking to blend. Lower the heat slightly and simmer until reduced to 1¼ cups, about 30 minutes.
2. Meanwhile, trim the tops and bottoms off the oranges. Use a paring knife to remove the peel and pith from the fruit. Cut across into ¼-inch slices and arrange in 4 shallow bowls. Scatter with the dates. Set aside.
3. Strain the syrup through a fine-mesh sieve and stir in the lemon juice. Pour the hot syrup on the fruit. Sprinkle with the coconut and then the pistachios. Serve.

Yield: 4 servings

—MOLLY O'NEILL

WHOLE ROASTED PEACHES, ALMONDS AND PISTACHIOS

dairy

½ cup slivered pistachios
½ cup blanched almonds
8 peaches
1½ cups vanilla sugar
½ cup unsalted butter, melted

Dash of vodka, optional
Vanilla ice cream, optional

1. Preheat oven to 350 degrees. Press the slivered pistachios and almonds into the peaches. The skin of the peach will help hold the nuts in place. They should be spaced about ¼ inch apart.

2. Sprinkle half of the vanilla sugar evenly over the bottom of 9-by-13-inch baking pan (a heavy copper pan distributes the heat most evenly). Put the peaches on top of the sugar and brush them liberally with the melted butter. Sprinkle with remaining sugar. This will give the peaches a nice crust when baked. Pour ¾ cup of water into the bottom of the pan.

3. Put the pan in the oven and roast the peaches for 10–15 minutes. The roasting time will vary according to the ripeness of the peaches. As the peaches roast, you should baste them every 5 minutes or so with their juices. They are ready when they are slightly brown on top and can be pierced easily with the tip of a paring knife.

4. Put the peaches on a platter. Strain the juices through a sieve into a bowl. If you are serving adults, you might strain a little vodka into the juice to give the sauce a little pizzazz. Pour the sauce over the peaches and serve immediately. Vanilla ice cream is an excellent accompaniment at dairy meals.

Yield: 8 servings

—MOIRA HODGSON

PEARS BAKED WITH GRAPES AND WINE

pareve

ADAPTED FROM *The New York Times Menu Cook Book*

    3–4 slightly underripe table pears
    1 tablespoon lemon juice
    ¾ cup dry white wine
    ⅔ cup sugar, approximately
    1 cup white seedless grapes, or more
    2–3 tablespoons cognac, optional

1. Preheat oven to 375 degrees.

2. Cut the pears into halves and remove the cores. Place, cut side down, in a glass baking dish that contains the lemon juice and wine.

3. Bake, covered, for about 20 minutes, or until the pears are beginning to soften.

4. Turn the pears and sprinkle with the sugar. Fill with grapes. Return to the oven and cook, uncovered, until tender and glazed. Pour the cognac over the pears and serve warm or chilled. If desired, flame the cognac before pouring it over the pears.

Yield: 3–4 servings

BAKED CARAMEL PEARS

dairy
ADAPTED FROM *Chez Panisse Desserts*

3 large ripe Comice pears
3 tablespoons unsalted butter
3 tablespoons sugar
⅔ cup heavy cream
2 tablespoons chopped toasted almonds or pecans

1. Preheat oven to 375 degrees.
2. Peel, halve and core the pears. Place them, cut side up, in a flameproof baking dish large enough to hold them in a single layer.
3. Dot the pears with the butter, sprinkle with sugar and place in the oven. Bake for 20–30 minutes, basting occasionally with the juices, until the pears are tender when pierced in the thickest part with a sharp knife.
4. Remove the pears from the baking dish and transfer them to a plate. Pour any juice back into the baking dish and add any undissolved sugar from the pear cavities.
5. Set the baking dish over high heat on top of the stove, and cook, stirring constantly, until the juices become thick, bubbly and turn a light caramel color. Pour in the cream and bring to a boil. Cook until the sauce is smooth and a rich brown.
6. Transfer the pears to 6 shallow bowls; spoon caramel over each. Sprinkle with the nuts and serve.

Yield: 6 servings

—FLORENCE FABRICANT

ROASTED PINEAPPLE

pareve
ADAPTED FROM Tom Colicchio

1 ripe medium pineapple
½ cup sugar
2 teaspoons corn syrup
½ vanilla bean, split and scraped
1 cup pineapple juice

1. Preheat oven to 375 degrees. Trim pineapple and slice into 8 circles about ⅓ inch thick. Using a sharp 1-inch-diameter cutter or sharp knife, cut a circle out of the center of each.
2. Heat a sauté pan large enough to hold half the rings in a single layer until it is medium-hot. Add ¼ cup sugar, 1 teaspoon corn syrup and half the vanilla bean and heat, stirring, until sugar becomes a medium caramel color.
3. Add half the pineapple slices and half the juice and stir to melt sugar. Place pan in oven and roast about 15–18 minutes, until pineapple becomes a rich golden color. Repeat with remaining pineapple. Serve plain or with scoops of Pineapple Sherbet (page 463).

Yield: 4 servings

—MARIAN BURROS

PINEAPPLE-ORANGE AMBROSIA

pareve

ADAPTED FROM *The New York Times Menu Cook Book*

1 ripe pineapple

6 seedless oranges

½ cup confectioners' sugar

2 cups grated fresh coconut (see Note below)

⅓ cup orange liqueur, optional

1. Peel the pineapple. Discard the core and cut pineapple flesh into thin uniform slices.

2. Peel the oranges and cut into sections.

3. Place fruits in a bowl and sprinkle with sugar. Cover with the coconut. Add liqueur, if desired. Chill until ready to serve.

Yield: 6 servings

NOTE: *If fresh coconut is not available, substitute packaged unsweetened coconut.*

POMEGRANATE CREAM

dairy

1 envelope unflavored gelatin

2 tablespoons cold water

1⅓ cups pomegranate juice (approximately 3 pomegranates) (see Note, page 583, and Sources, page 584)

1 tablespoon lemon juice

½ cup sugar

⅛ teaspoon salt

1 cup heavy cream

1. Soften the gelatin in the cold water. Place it in the top of a double boiler over boiling water and stir until dissolved. Add the pomegranate juice, lemon juice, sugar and salt. Chill.

2. When the gelatin is almost set, whip the cream until stiff. Fold the cream into the gelatin mixture and turn the mixture into a mold. Chill.

3. Unmold. If desired, dessert may be decorated with additional whipped cream and sprinkled with the red-fleshed pomegranate seeds.

Yield: 4–6 servings

—CRAIG CLAIBORNE

PRUNE WHIP WITH PORT WINE

dairy

ADAPTED FROM *The New York Times*
International Cookbook

½ *pound dried prunes*
Water
⅔ *cup granulated sugar*
Lemon rind
1 cup port wine
1 cup heavy cream
3 tablespoons confectioners' sugar
Silvered blanched almonds

1. Soak the prunes overnight in water to cover. Drain. Place them in a small kettle and add the sugar, lemon rind and water to cover. Bring to a boil and cook until the prunes are tender.
2. Drain, leaving prunes in the kettle. Add the port and cook 10 minutes longer. Remove the stones and put the prunes through a sieve, or puree in an electric blender. Add a little more port if necessary to make the prunes moist; add more sugar to taste.
3. Whip the cream and mix half of it with the prunes. Sweeten the remaining cream with confectioners' sugar and use as a garnish. Top with almonds.

Yield: 6 servings

BILL YOSSES'S QUINCE COMPOTE

pareve

2 cups sugar
4 pieces star anise
4 peppercorns
3 green cardamom pods
2 cinnamon sticks
2 dried bay leaves or 1 fresh
1 whole nutmeg, quartered
4 quinces, peeled, cored and cut into eighths

1. In a pot, combine sugar and spices with 1 quart water. Bring to a boil, stirring occasionally, until sugar has dissolved. Turn off heat and let spices steep for 5 minutes.

2. Pour the liquid through a sieve set over another pot; discard the spices. Cut a round of parchment paper just small enough to fit inside the pot. Add the quinces to the liquid and place the parchment paper over the fruit to keep it submerged. Bring the liquid to a simmer. Simmer gently, over medium heat, until the quinces are tender, about 15 minutes.
3. Let cool in poaching syrup.

Yield: 4–6 servings

NOTE: *The bay leaf adds an appealing and mysterious flavor to the compote. It can be refrigerated in syrup for up to a week.*

—BILL YOSSES

RASPBERRY SABAYON

pareve

ADAPTED FROM *Holiday Eggs*

3 eggs, separated (see Note, page 479)
2 tablespoons dry Marsala or dry sherry
4 tablespoons sugar
¼ teaspoon unflavored gelatin
2 cups fresh raspberries

1. Combine egg yolks, Marsala or sherry and 3 tablespoons sugar in the top of a double boiler. Place the mixture over simmering water and whisk constantly until thick and custardy. It should leave a path if you draw a spoon through it. Remove from heat.

2. Dissolve gelatin in 2 tablespoons warm water, stir into custard and refrigerate custard.

3. Mash all but ⅓ cup raspberries in a bowl with remaining sugar.

4. Beat egg whites until stiff. Fold into cooled custard, then fold in mashed raspberries. Transfer to a serving bowl or individual goblets, and refrigerate at least 2 hours before serving. Garnish with remaining raspberries.

Yield: 4 servings

—FLORENCE FABRICANT

RHUBARB AND STRAWBERRY COMPOTE

pareve

1 (2-inch) strip of orange peel
2 pounds (10–12 slim stalks) of rhubarb
1½ cups sugar, or to taste
½–1 cup water, as needed
5 cloves
1 pint strawberries, hulled, washed and cut in half vertically
2 tablespoons orange liqueur, or to taste

1. Heat oven to 450 degrees. Place orange peel on a small piece of aluminum foil and bake for about 10 minutes, or until peel just begins to curl and turn brown around the edges. Remove from oven and reserve. Turn off oven.

2. Trim leaves from rhubarb and discard. If rhubarb is young and tender, do not peel but merely wash. If stalks are thick, peel off tough strings. Cut stalks into 1-inch lengths.

3. Place rhubarb in a heavy 1- to 1½-quart saucepan, preferably of enameled cast iron. Add 1 cup of sugar and ½ cup of water, along with orange peel and cloves. Cover tightly and bring to a gentle simmer.

4. Rhubarb should be cooked about 8 minutes after it has begun to simmer. Shake pan, or turn rhubarb gently with a wooden spatula once during cooking, but try to avoid breaking up pieces. Taste as you go along and add sugar gradually. Add more water if the mixture seems dry and in danger of scorching. Add water cautiously, however, as the rhubarb will suddenly release its own liquid when it begins to soften. Turn off heat.

5. Add strawberries and cover pot so they will soften slightly.

6. When compote is lukewarm, stir in orange liqueur to taste. Chill compote thoroughly without removing orange peel or cloves. Flavor will be best if compote is chilled for 24 hours before it is eaten. Remove orange peel and cloves before serving.

Yield: 6–8 servings

—MIMI SHERATON

STRAWBERRIES AND PINEAPPLE ALEXANDRA

dairy

ADAPTED FROM *The New York Times Menu Cook Book*

 1 ripe pineapple
 ¼ cup cognac
 ¾ cup sugar, approximately
 3 cups ripe strawberries
 ½ cup pitted canned apricots
 1 cup heavy cream, whipped and sweetened with 1
  tablespoon sugar

1. Slice, core and peel the pineapple. Cut 4 of the best slices into halves and place in a dish. Add 2 tablespoons cognac and 2 tablespoons sugar to the half-slices and chill until ready to use. Dice the remaining pineapple.

2. Reserve 1 cup of the best strawberries for garnish. Cut remaining berries into quarters and add to the diced pineapple. Sweeten to taste, mix and chill.

3. In a blender or food processor, puree the apricots. Remove puree to a saucepan, add ¼ cup sugar and cook over moderate heat, stirring until the sugar is completely dissolved. Add the remaining cognac and chill.

4. To serve, pile the diced fruits in the center of a serving plate and surround with the 8 half-slices of pineapple. Cover the center with whipped cream and garnish with the reserved strawberries. Coat the pineapple slices with the apricot sauce.

Yield: 8 servings

HUNGARIAN APPLE SOUP

dairy

ADAPTED FROM *The New York Times International Cookbook*

1 pound firm, ripe apples
2 whole cloves
¼ teaspoon ground cinnamon
Juice of ½ lemon
⅓ cup granulated sugar
½ cup dry white wine
2 cups milk
½ cup heavy cream
2 tablespoons all-purpose flour

1. Peel, core and quarter the apples and place in a saucepan. Add water to cover, the cloves, cinnamon, lemon juice and sugar. Simmer until tender. Put through a sieve or food mill. Return to a boil.
2. Add the wine and milk, stirring constantly. Remove from the heat. Blend the cream with the flour and stir into the soup. Return the soup to a boil and simmer 5 minutes. Chill.

Yield: 4–6 servings

SYRIAN COLD ROSE-WATER SOUP WITH APRICOTS AND PISTACHIOS · (MISH MOSH)

pareve

ADAPTED FROM Fritzie Abadi

1 cup shelled pistachios
1¼ cups sugar
1¼ pounds (about 3½ cups) dried apricots, thinly sliced
3 teaspoons rose water

1. Bring a small saucepan half full of water to a boil and add the pistachios. Boil for 1 minute and drain immediately. Place the pistachios between layers of paper towels and gently roll them to remove the skins. Coarsely chop the pistachios and set aside.

2. Place the sugar and 1 cup of water in a saucepan set over high heat. Cook, stirring constantly, until the mixture boils. Set aside to cool for 10 minutes.
3. In a large bowl, combine the apricots, pistachios, sugar water, 2 teaspoons of the rose water and 6 cups cold water. Cover the bowl and chill the soup at least 8 hours or overnight. Just before serving, stir in the remaining teaspoon of rose water.

Yield: 8–10 servings

—MOLLY O'NEILL

PERSIAN FRUIT MÉLANGE

pareve

ADAPTED FROM *The Best of Craig Claiborne*

1 honeydew melon

1 cantaloupe

1 pint strawberries, stemmed

2 tablespoons slivered almonds

¼ cup chopped, skinless pistachios

1 cup seedless grapes

2 tablespoons rose water

1½ cups orange juice, sweetened to taste

½ cup kirsch, optional

1. Split the honeydew melon and the cantaloupe in half and scoop out the seeds. Using a melon ball cutter, scoop out the flesh of both melons into a serving bowl.

2. Rinse the berries under cold running water and pat dry. Add them to the bowl. Add the remaining ingredients and mix gently but thoroughly.

Yield: 8 servings

NOTE: *Rose water is a clear, highly aromatic flavoring that smells strongly of roses. It is much used in Middle Eastern cookery, particularly desserts, such as this Persian fruit mélange.*

ANISE FRUIT COMPOTE

pareve

ADAPTED FROM *The New York Times Menu Cook Book*

1 cup sugar

1½ cups water

¼ teaspoon aniseeds

⅛ teaspoon salt

½ cup fresh orange sections

½ cup fresh grapefruit sections

½ cup seeded fresh grape halves

½ cup diced fresh pears

½ cup diced unpeeled raw apples

½ cup diced fresh pineapple

Combine the sugar, water, aniseeds and salt in a saucepan. Mix well, bring to a boil, and cook for 3–4 minutes. Strain over the mixed fruit, chill and serve.

Yield: 6 servings

NEW YEAR'S EVE FRUIT COMPOTE FOR A CROWD

pareve

ADAPTED FROM *The Best of Craig Claiborne*

4 pounds mixed dried fruit, including,
    preferably, equal amounts of prunes, pears,
    peaches and apples
3 (17-ounce) jars of Kadota figs in syrup
2 pounds (drained weight) fresh or canned dark
    sweet pitted cherries, about 4 cups
Sugar to taste
1 cup or more cognac
4–6 bananas, peeled and sliced
2 cups fresh berries, such a blueberries, strawberries
    or raspberries

1. If the dried fruit has pits, cut away and remove them. Cut all the fruit in half and add to a kettle or casserole. Add water to cover and bring to a boil. Simmer for 20 minutes. Let cool.
2. Pour the fruit and the cooking liquid into a mixing bowl. Cut the figs in half and add them along with their syrup to the fruit in the bowl. Add the cherries and sugar to taste. Add the cognac to taste.
3. Cover closely and refrigerate for at least 24 hours to ripen. When ready to serve, add the sliced bananas and berries. Add more sugar and cognac, if desired.

Yield: 30 servings

NOTE: *For best flavor, cooked fruit must ripen in refrigerator for at least 24 hours.*

WINTER FRUIT SALAD WITH FRESH AND DRIED FRUITS

pareve

1¼ cup sugar
3 star anise
1 plump vanilla bean, split in half lengthwise
2 (2-inch-long) pieces lemon zest (peeled with a
    vegetable peeler), preferably Meyer lemons
3 firm Bosc pears
1 firm tart apple
8 dried Turkish apricots, cut in half
4 dried figs, quartered

1. Fill a medium saucepan with 5 cups water. Add the sugar, star anise, vanilla bean and lemon zest. Bring to a boil and cook until all the sugar is dissolved. Then shut off the heat. Meanwhile, peel and core pears and apple. Slice thinly lengthwise and place in a large heatproof bowl. Add apricots and figs. Pour hot sugar syrup on top, making sure all the fruit is covered. Cover bowl with plastic wrap; poke a few holes in plastic. Chill overnight in refrigerator.
2. The next morning or when ready to serve, use a slotted spoon to ladle fruit into a serving bowl and serve.

Yield: 6 servings

NOTE: *Medjool dates can be used in place of the apricots. As the liquid cools, the dried fruit plumps and the pears and apples soften and become infused with vanilla and star anise and touched with the perfume from the lemon peel.*

—AMANDA HESSER

POACHED DRIED FRUIT WITH
CORNMEAL CRUMBLE AND PINE NUTS

dairy

FOR THE CRUMBLE:

½ cup yellow cornmeal

2 tablespoons sugar

½ teaspoon ground cinnamon

¼ teaspoon kosher salt

4 tablespoons cold unsalted butter, cut into ½-inch
  pieces

FOR THE FRUIT:

1 (375-ml.) bottle late-harvest Riesling

½ cup dried Calimyrna figs

1 cup dried apricots

½ cup pitted prunes

¼ cup pine nuts, toasted

½ cup Crème Fraîche (page 431)

TO MAKE THE CRUMBLE:

1. Preheat the oven to 350 degrees.

2. Combine the cornmeal, sugar, cinnamon and salt
in a bowl.

3. Rub in the butter until the pieces are no larger
than peas. Spread them on a baking sheet and bake
until browned and somewhat dried, about 25 minutes, stirring twice. Let cool.

FOR THE FRUIT:

1. Simmer the wine in a medium saucepan. Add the figs
and simmer 10 minutes. Add the apricots and prunes
and simmer until fruit is soft, about 10 minutes longer.

2. Divide the fruit among 4 bowls and spoon in the
wine.

3. Sprinkle with the crumb mixture and the pine
nuts. Top with crème fraîche and serve.

Yield: 4 servings

—MOLLY O'NEILL

ALMOND FLAN WITH RICOTTA AND ORANGES

dairy

1⅓ cups slivered almonds

1 container part-skim ricotta (15 ounces)

6 extra-large eggs

¾ cup sugar

Grated zest of 2 large navel oranges

¼ cup dark rum

1 teaspoon vanilla

½ teaspoon freshly grated nutmeg

Butter to grease baking pan

1. Heat the oven to 300 degrees.

2. Spread the almonds onto a baking sheet and toast
until just brown, about 3–5 minutes. Remove and
cool, then raise the oven temperature to 325 degrees.

3. Place the almonds in a blender or food processor and grind into a fine meal. Transfer to a large mixing bowl and add the ricotta, eggs, sugar, orange zest, rum, vanilla and nutmeg. Blend well.

4. Butter a deep 10-inch glass pie plate and spoon in the ricotta mixture. Bake until lightly browned on the edges and set in the center, about 30–35 minutes. Cool completely before serving in wedges.

Yield: 6–8 servings

—REGINA SCHRAMBLING

PIES AND TARTS

◆ ◆

CHEZ PANISSE ALMOND TART

dairy

1 cup flour
1 tablespoon sugar
½ cup butter, slightly softened
1 tablespoon water
6 drops almond extract
½ teaspoon vanilla extract
1 cup unblanched sliced almonds
¾ cup sugar
¾ cup heavy cream
Salt to taste
1 teaspoon orange-flavored liqueur

1. Mix flour with sugar and cut in butter until mixture is fine.

2. Mix in water 3 drops of the almond extract and vanilla extract to form a dough.

3. Line the bottom of a 9-inch tart pan with wax paper.

4. Press the dough down evenly in the tart pan's bottom and sides and chill for 1 hour or freeze. If frozen, defrost before baking.

5. Bake at 400 degrees for 10 minutes. Press down any crust that puffs up.

6. Mix together the almonds, sugar, cream, salt, almond extract and liqueur. Allow to stand in warm place for 20 minutes, until sugar dissolves. Pour into shell.

7. Bake at 400 degrees 40–50 minutes, until top is golden brown and caramelized. Keep turning tart so that top will caramelize evenly. Serve at room temperature.

Yield: 1 (9-inch) tart

—MARIAN BURROS

APPLE TART IN PHYLLO

dairy

ADAPTED FROM *Eating Well Is the Best Revenge*

5 apples, 3½–4 pounds, peeled, cored, quartered and thinly sliced

½ pound dried cranberries and/or dried cherries

1 cup coarsely chopped pecans

2 teaspoons cinnamon

2 tablespoons lemon juice

6 tablespoons sugar

4 teaspoons grated lemon rind

½ cup finely cut cyrstalized ginger

2 tablespoons flour

16 sheets Phyllo (see Note, page 583)

3 tablespoons unsalted butter

1 tablespoon canola or corn oil

1. Heat oven to 400 degrees.

2. Combine apples, dried fruits, pecans, cinnamon, lemon juice, sugar, lemon rind, crystalized ginger and flour in a bowl and mix well.

3. Unwrap phyllo and cover with wax paper and damp towel. Keep covered when not in use to prevent drying out.

4. Heat butter and add oil.

5. Using some of the butter mixture, lightly grease a baking pan, about 12 inches by 18 inches. (The pan can be as large as the sheets of phyllo, and brands differ in size. If they are too large for the pan, trim them.)

6. Arrange 1 sheet of phyllo on bottom of pan and brush lightly with butter mixture. Repeat, buttering between sheets, using 8 sheets in all.

7. Spread apple filling evenly over phyllo and top with another sheet, brushing lightly with butter. Repeat, butter each sheet, using 8 sheets in all, brushing the top sheet with butter. Cut phyllo all the way through into 12 rectangles.

8. Bake in lower third of oven for 25 minutes; reduce heat to 350 degrees and continue baking 25 minutes longer, until top is brown. Cool. Serve at room temperature.

Yield: 12 servings

NOTE: *This recipe can be prepared a day or two ahead and refrigerated. To serve, return to room temperature and reheat at 350 degrees to warm, about 15–20 minutes.*

If phyllo is purchased frozen, allow the package to defrost in the refrigerator overnight or for several hours at room temperature.

—MARIAN BURROS

FLORENCE FABRICANT'S SAUTÉED-APPLE PIE

dairy

4 tablespoons unsalted butter

5 pounds apples, peeled, cored and sliced ½ inch thick

¾ cup plus 1 tablespoon sugar

1 teaspoon cinnamon

Pastry for 2-crust 10-inch pie

Flour for rolling dough

1 tablespoon heavy cream

1. Melt butter over medium-high heat in large skillet, preferably not nonstick. (Apples will not caramelize as well in nonstick pan.) Add apples, sprinkle with ¾ cup sugar, and sauté, turning apples, about 10 minutes, until tender and lightly caramelized. Fold in cinnamon. If you do not have a skillet large enough to hold all the apples, do this step in two stages or in two skillets. Spread cooked apples on a platter to cool.

2. Preheat oven to 400 degrees. Divide pastry into two unequal halves; roll out larger portion on lightly floured board, and line pie pan. Spoon in cooled apples. Roll out remaining pastry, and cover pan; seal and crimp edges. Cut several decorative slits in top. Alternatively, top pastry can be cut in strips and used to make lattice.

3. Brush pastry with cream, and dust with remaining sugar. Bake about 40 minutes, until pastry is golden. Cool briefly, then serve.

Yield: 8–12 servings

APRICOT TARTS

dairy

ADAPTED FROM *New Food Fast*

½ cup blanched whole almonds

4 small apricots

4 ounces (1 stick) butter, at room temperature

½ cup superfine sugar

2 large eggs

1 teaspoon vanilla extract

⅓ cup all-purpose flour

Lightly sweetened whipped cream, for garnish

1. Preheat oven to 400 degrees.

2. Using a food processor, chop almonds until finely ground; do not allow to become a paste. Transfer to a bowl and set aside. Cut a small cross into stem end of each apricot and remove pit; set apricots aside.

3. In bowl of food processor, combine butter and sugar and process until smooth. Add eggs, vanilla, flour and ground almonds. Process until just combined.

4. Divide almond mixture among four 1-cup pudding or soufflé dishes. Press an apricot, cut side up, into center of batter; a portion of the fruit will remain above the batter.

5. Bake until tarts are puffed and golden, 15–20 minutes. Garnish each with a dollop of whipped cream. Serve immediately.

Yield: 4 servings

NOTE: *Small plums can be substituted for the apricots.*

—TODD PURDUM

DOUBLE-CRUSTED CARROT AND GINGER TART

dairy, pareve

ADAPTED FROM *Cucina Ebraica*

> 2¼ cups all-purpose flour, plus additional for
>   rolling dough
> 2 cups sugar
> Pinch of salt
> 14 tablespoons (1¾ sticks) chilled unsalted butter,
>   diced (margarine can be substituted)
> 2 eggs
> 1 teaspoon vanilla extract
> 1 teaspoon fresh lemon juice
> 2 pounds carrots, peeled and coarsely grated
>   (7–8 cups)
> 6 tablespoons finely chopped crystallized ginger

1. In a bowl or the container of a food processor, combine flour, ½ cup sugar and the salt. If using a food processor, whirl ingredients briefly to blend them; add butter, pulse until mixture is crumbly and transfer to a mixing bowl. By hand, cut in the butter with a pastry blender or two knives to make a crumbly mixture.

2. Beat 1 egg with the vanilla, lemon juice and 1 tablespoon cold water. Sprinkle this mixture over the flour mixture and stir and toss lightly with a fork until the mixture can be gathered together to form a ball of dough. You may have to add a little more water. Divide dough into 2 slightly unequal portions, flatten each into a disk, wrap in plastic and refrigerate at least 1 hour.

3. Combine carrots and remaining sugar in a heavy saucepan. Stir in a couple of tablespoons of water. Place over medium-low heat and cook, stirring occasionally, until the mixture is thick and jamlike. You may have to add a little more water to prevent the carrots from scorching. Stir in the ginger and remove from heat.

4. Preheat oven to 375 degrees. On a lightly floured board, roll out the larger portion of pastry and fit it into a 9-inch pie pan. Spoon in the carrot filling. Roll out the smaller disk of dough, and place it over the filling. Trim edges. Beat remaining egg with 2 tablespoons water and brush some of this egg wash on the edges of the pastry. Press the two layers together and turn them under to form a slight rim. Crimp rim with your fingertips, or press with the tines of a fork to make a pattern. Cut a Star of David in the center of the tart and brush the surface of the pastry with remaining egg wash. Tart can also be finished with a lattice crust on top.

5. Bake until golden brown, about 25 minutes. Transfer to a rack, and cool fully.

Yield: 6–8 servings

—FLORENCE FABRICANT

LEMON CURD TART WITH CANDIED ALMOND TOPPING

dairy

FOR THE CURD:

6 eggs
1½ cups sugar
1 tablespoon grated lemon zest
1 cup fresh lemon juice
4 tablespoons unsalted butter, cut into small pieces

FOR THE CRUST:

⅓ cup slivered almonds
2½ tablespoons sugar
1 tablespoon grated lemon zest
¾ cup all-purpose flour, plus additional for rolling
½ teaspoon kosher salt
6 tablespoons unsalted butter, cut into small pieces
1 egg yolk
1 tablespoon water
¼ teaspoon almond extract

FOR THE TOPPING:

Butter for greasing baking sheet
¾ cup sugar
1 tablespoon grated lemon zest
1 cup sliced almonds
2 egg whites, whisked until frothy
Confectioners' sugar

1. To make the curd, place the eggs and the sugar in a medium-size nonreactive saucepan and whisk until thickened and light in color. Whisk in the lemon zest and juice. Place over low heat and cook, whisking constantly, until thick, about 10 minutes; do not boil. Remove from heat and whisk in the butter. Let cool. Refrigerate until cold.

2. To make the crust, place the almonds, sugar and zest in a food processor and process until ground. Add the flour and salt and pulse just to combine. Add the butter and pulse until the mixture resembles coarse meal. Whisk together the egg yolk, water and almond extract. Add to the flour mixture and process just until the mixture starts to come together. Press into a bowl, flatten, wrap in plastic and refrigerate for 30 minutes.

3. Preheat the oven to 350 degrees. Roll out the dough and fit into a 10-inch quiche dish. Line with foil and fill with pie weights or dried beans. Bake for 20 minutes. Remove the foil and weights and bake until the crust is lightly browned, about 5 minutes longer. Cool.

4. To make the topping, lower the oven temperature to 300 degrees. Lightly butter a baking sheet. Combine the sugar and zest in a bowl. Toss the almonds in the egg whites, drain and toss them in the sugar. Spread out on the baking sheet and bake until the almonds are dried, about 30 minutes, stirring twice. Let cool.

5. Spoon the lemon curd into the pastry shell and top with the sugared almonds. Refrigerate until ready to serve. Before serving, sift a little confectioners' sugar over the top and cut tart into wedges.

Yield: 8 servings

—MOLLY O'NEILL

LEMON MERINGUE PIE

dairy

4 tablespoons cornstarch
¼ teaspoon salt
1 cup plus 6 tablespoons sugar
1½ cups water
3 eggs, separated
2 tablespoons butter
1½ teaspoons grated lemon rind
5 tablespoons lemon juice
1 (9-inch) baked Pie Pastry (see recipe below)

1. Preheat oven to 325 degrees.
2. Mix the cornstarch, salt and ½ cup of the sugar in the top of a double boiler. Gradually add the water, stirring. Place over boiling water and cook, stirring constantly, until the mixture thickens. Cover and cook 10 minutes, stirring occasionally. Do not remove from the heat.
3. Beat the egg yolks in a mixing bowl and add ½ cup of sugar. Stir a small amount of the hot mixture into the egg yolks. Immediately pour the egg-yolk mixture into the remaining hot mixture over boiling water; blend thoroughly. Cook 2 minutes longer, stirring constantly. Remove from the heat and add the butter, lemon rind and lemon juice. Cool to room temperature without stirring.
4. Turn the filling into the baked pie shell. Beat the egg whites until stiff but not dry. Gradually beat in the remaining 6 tablespoons of sugar. Spread the meringue over the filling, being sure to extend it over the edge of the crust.

5. Bake until delicately browned, about 15–20 minutes. Cool at room temperature. Serve as soon as it is cool.

Yield: 6–8 servings

Pie Pastry

dairy

1½ cups flour
Salt to taste
10 tablespoons very cold butter, cut into small pieces
1 egg yolk
3 tablespoons ice water, approximately

1. Put the flour, salt to taste and butter into the container of a food processor. Start processing and add the yolk through the funnel. Gradually add the water. Add only enough so that the pastry comes away from the side of the container and can be gathered into a ball.
2. If a food processor is not used, place flour and salt in a mixing bowl. Add the butter and cut it in with 2 knives or a pastry blender until mixture looks likes coarse oatmeal. Beat the yolk and water together and add the mixture, stirring quickly with a fork.
3. Preheat oven to 425 degrees. Roll out the pastry and use it to line a 9-inch pie shell. Prick the bottom and sides of the pastry generously with a fork. Bake 12–15 minutes. Let cool.

Yield: Pastry for a 1-crust pie

—CRAIG CLAIBORNE AND PIERRE FRANEY

ORANGE, DATE AND CARDAMOM TART

dairy

ADAPTED FROM *Spice*

½ cup confectioners' sugar

¾ cup flour

5½ tablespoons chilled unsalted butter, cut into cubes

2 large egg yolks

½ vanilla bean, split

4 large eggs

¾ cup plus 2 tablespoons extra-fine granulated sugar

Zest of 2 oranges

¼ cup fresh orange juice

Seeds from 4 green cardamom pods, ground

⅓ cup heavy cream

18 fresh pitted dates, halved lengthwise

1. Sift together powdered sugar and flour and place in food processor. Add butter and pulse until mixture resembles fine bread crumbs. Add egg yolks and scrape in pulp from vanilla bean. Blend until dough just comes together in a soft ball. Wrap in plastic film and refrigerate overnight.

2. In a medium bowl combine eggs and sugar and whisk until pale and creamy. Add orange zest, juice, cardamom and cream. Mix well and refrigerate overnight.

3. Lightly dust a work surface with flour and roll dough into 10-inch circle. Fold into quarters to transfer to a 9½-inch nonstick tart pan. Unfold and fit snugly into pan, trimming and patching as necessary. Refrigerate 30 minutes.

4. Preheat oven to 325 degrees. Prick tart shell all over with a fork and bake just until dry and golden, about 15 minutes.

5. Strain egg mixture through a fine sieve. Place tart shell on baking sheet and arrange dates inside. Gently pour in egg mixture.

6. If edges of the tart shell are already browned, cover with strips of foil to prevent burning. Bake until custard is lightly browned and set, about 30 minutes. Allow to cool at least 3 hours before removing from pan.

Yield: 1 (9½-inch) tart; 8 servings

— R. W. APPLE, JR.

MARIE-CLAUDE GRACIA'S PRUNE CUSTARD TART

dairy

1 pound dried prunes, pitted

3 tablespoons cognac

1 teaspoon unsalted butter for the baking dish

1 teaspoon unbleached all-purpose flour for the baking dish

5 tablespoons sugar

3 large eggs

3 tablespoons unbleached all-purpose flour

2 cups whole milk

1. Two days before preparing the flan, toss the prunes with cognac, cover securely and set aside to macerate. (If time is limited, you can skip this step and simply toss the prunes with the spirits, although the 2-day maceration will offer a richer, more flavorful dessert.)

2. Preheat the oven to 375 degrees.

3. Butter and flour a 10½-inch straight-sided ceramic baking dish.

4. Add 1 tablespoon of sugar to the cerated prunes and toss. Place them on the bottom of the prepared baking dish, forming a single, tight layer that thoroughly covers the bottom of the dish.

5. Place the eggs and 3 tablespoons of sugar in a large bowl and, using a whisk or electric mixer, beat until well blended. Add the flour and mix well. Add the milk and mix well. Pour the batter into the prepared baking dish and bake until bubbly and brown, about 45 minutes.

6. Sprinkle with the remaining tablespoon of sugar and allow to cool. Serve at room temperature. This is just as delicious the next day.

Yield: 8–10 servings

—PATRICIA WELLS

DRIED FRUIT AND NUT BSTEEYAS

dairy

ADAPTED FROM *Julian Clauss-Ehlers*

FOR THE FRUIT:

> ¼ cup dates in ⅛-inch dice
> ¼ cup apricots in ⅛-inch dice
> ¼ cup raisins
> ¼ cup brandy

Mix all ingredients in ¼ cup of warm water and leave to macerate and rehydrate for at least 4 hours.

FOR THE NUTS:

> 2 tablespoons sugar
> 1 tablespoon unsalted butter
> 1 tablespoon each sliced almonds, whole pistachios, pine nuts, walnut halves

Lightly grease a baking sheet and set aside. In a skillet, melt sugar over medium heat and cook, swirling the pan until it reaches a dark caramel color. Add butter, then nuts, and stir until nuts are covered with caramel and butter, about 5 minutes. Spread mixture on baking sheet to cool.

FOR THE ALMOND CREAM:

> 4 tablespoons unsalted butter, softened
> 4½ tablespoons sugar
> 1 egg yolk
> 4½ tablespoons almond flour
> ½ teaspoon ground cinnamon
> ½ teaspoon ground ginger

Beat butter and sugar together in a bowl until smooth, add egg yolk, mix well, then stir in flour, cinnamon and ginger.

> 6 sheets phyllo dough (see Note, page 583)
> 4 tablespoons unsalted butter, melted

Confectioners' sugar
Ground cinnamon
Ginger ice cream, optional

1. Preheat oven to 375 degrees. Line a baking sheet with parchment and set aside.

2. Cut phyllo sheets in half and work with three pieces at a time, keeping the remaining sheets covered with plastic wrap so they don't dry out. Brush one piece with melted butter, place another half sheet on top at a 45-degree angle and brush with more butter. Place third in opposite direction at a 45-degree angle and brush with butter. Carefully lifting sheets, slide a 4-inch saucer under phyllo. Spread one eighth of almond cream in phyllo center, sprinkle almond cream with one fourth of nuts and one fourth of fruit, then cover with another one eighth of cream. Fold phyllo flaps over center, creating a disk-shaped pie. Brush with butter. Repeat to make three more bsteeyas. Place on baking sheet.

3. Bake until golden brown, about 15 minutes, turning over after 7 minutes. Remove from oven. Dust with a little sugar and cinnamon. Serve with ginger ice cream, if desired.

Yield: 4 servings

—JONATHAN REYNOLDS

PEAR AND GINGER TART

pareve, dairy

ADAPTED FROM *The Best of Craig Claiborne*

Tart pastry for 10-inch pan
8 ripe but firm Comice or Anjou pears, about
    3 pounds
2/3 cup sugar
3/4 teaspoon ground ginger
1/2 cup water
6 tablespoons apricot preserves
Whipped cream, optional

1. Preheat the oven to 425 degrees. Roll out the dough to a thickness of 1/8 inch. Fit it into a 10-inch metal quiche pan with removable bottom. Trim the edges. Line the pastry with wax paper and add dried beans to cover the bottom. Bake for 10 minutes, remove wax paper and beans and bake for 2 minutes longer. Let cool before filling.

2. Reheat the oven to 425 degrees.

3. Peel 6 of the pears and cut each of them into eighths. Cut away and discard the cores.

4. Place the pear wedges in a saucepan and add the sugar, ginger and water. Cover and cook until tender but still firm, 8–10 minutes. Turn wedges so they cook evenly. Chill thoroughly. Drain but reserve 4 tablespoons of liquid.

5. Arrange the pear wedges close together in the pastry shell.

6. Peel and quarter the remaining 2 pears. Scoop out and discard the cores. Cut the quarters into thin slices. Arrange the slices symmetrically over the cooked pears.

7. Combine the apricot preserves with the reserved pear liquid. Bring to a boil and strain. Brush tart with half of the apricot mixture. Bake for 30 minutes.

8. Remove from the oven and brush with remaining sauce. Let stand until warm. Serve with whipped cream, if desired.

Yield: 8–10 servings

SPAGO'S PLUM ALMOND TARTS WITH PLUM COMPOTE

dairy

ADAPTED FROM *Spago Desserts*

FOR THE CRUST:

6 tablespoons whole unblanched almonds,
    toasted and cooled (see Note, page 582)
2 cups all-purpose flour
¾ cup cold unsalted butter, cut into small pieces
½ cup sugar
1 egg
¼ teaspoon grated lemon zest
½ teaspoon kosher salt

FOR THE FILLING:

¾ cup whole blanched almonds
½ cup plus 5 teaspoons sugar
2 eggs, beaten
1 teaspoon grated lemon zest
1½ pounds ripe plums
¼ cup sliced almonds

FOR THE COMPOTE:

1 vanilla bean, split lengthwise
2 pounds plums, pitted and cut into thin slices
½ cup sugar

1. To make the crust, place the almonds in a food processor and pulse until coarsely ground. Place in a bowl and toss with the flour. Use an electric mixer to beat the butter and sugar until light and fluffy, scraping down the sides of the bowl as necessary. Add the egg, lemon zest and salt. Add the flour mixture and begin mixing on low speed; then raise the speed just until the flour is incorporated.

2. Turn the dough out on a lightly floured surface and gently knead into a ball. Flatten, wrap in plastic and refrigerate for 2 hours.

3. Line 2 baking sheets with parchment paper. Divide the dough into 8 equal pieces. On a lightly floured surface, roll 1 piece into a 5½-inch circle (the dough breaks easily but can be pressed back together). Use a 5-inch-round cup, plate or cardboard as a guide to cut the dough into a 5-inch circle. With a wide spatula, transfer to 1 of the baking sheets. Repeat with the remaining dough, placing the circles 2 inches apart. Refrigerate 30 minutes.

4. Preheat the oven to 350 degrees. Bake the crusts until lightly golden, about 10–12 minutes. Set aside to cool.

5. To make the filling, place the whole almonds and 1 teaspoon of sugar in a food processor and pulse until ground. Place in a bowl and stir in the ½ cup of sugar, eggs and lemon zest. Set aside.

6. Halve and pit the plums. Cut each half into 5–6 thin wedges. Spread the filling over the crusts, leaving a ½-inch border. Arrange the plums in a circular pattern over the filling. Sprinkle with ½ teaspoon of sugar and a few sliced almonds over each tart. Bake until the plums are lightly caramelized, about 20 minutes.

7. Meanwhile, to make the compote, scrape the seeds from the vanilla bean. Place the pod and seeds in a small saucepan with the plums and sugar. Cook over low heat, stirring often, until the compote is thick, about 20 minutes. Keep warm.

8. To serve, place a warm tart on each of 8 plates and surround with the warm compote.

Yield: 8 servings

—MOLLY O'NEILL

VENETIAN RICE-PUDDING TART • (TORTA TURCHESCA)

dairy

ADAPTED FROM *The Mediterranean Kitchen*

FOR THE CRUST:

1⅓ cups all-purpose flour
4 teaspoons sugar
¾ teaspoons grated lemon zest
11 tablespoons cold unsalted butter, cut into chunks
4 teaspoons water
¾ teaspoon vanilla extract

FOR THE PUDDING:

¼ cup golden raisins
2¾ cups whole milk
½ cup Arborio rice
½ cup heavy cream
⅓ cup sugar
¼ cup chopped pitted dates
2 teaspoons grated orange zest
½ teaspoon cinnamon
4 large egg yolks
½ teaspoon rose water
¾ teaspoon vanilla extract

1. To make the crust: Pulse flour, sugar and zest in a food processor. Add butter and pulse until the mixture resembles coarse meal. Add water and vanilla and pulse to combine. Gather the dough into a ball. (Add a teaspoon or two of water if it seems dry.) Flatten the ball into a disk, wrap in plastic and refrigerate 1 hour or overnight.

2. Preheat oven to 425 degrees. Unwrap the dough and place it between 2 new sheets of plastic. Roll the dough out to an 11-inch circle. Remove the top sheet of plastic and invert the dough over a 9-inch tart pan. Remove the second sheet of plastic and ease the dough into the bottom and up the sides of the pan. Trim the dough off the sides. Line the tart shell with foil and fill with dry beans or pie weights. Bake for 15 minutes. Remove the weights and foil and bake until golden, about 10 minutes more. Cool on a wire rack.

3. To make the filling: Soak the raisins in boiling water to cover for 30 minutes. Drain and set aside. In a saucepan, combine 2 cups of the milk and the rice. Bring to a simmer, adjust the heat, cover and simmer until the rice is tender, about 15 minutes. Stir in remaining milk, raisins, cream, sugar, dates, zest and cinnamon. Raise heat to medium. Stirring occasionally, return mixture to a simmer and immediately remove from heat.

4. Preheat the oven to 350 degrees. In a bowl, whisk together the yolks, rose water and vanilla. Gradually stir in ½ cup of the warm rice, then stir the mixture back into the pan containing the rest of the rice. Spoon the filling into the tart shell and smooth the top. Bake until lightly browned, 25–30 minutes. Cool 10 minutes before serving warm with whipped cream.

Yield: 8 servings

—MOLLY O'NEILL

GRAHAM-CRACKER CRUST

dairy

1 cup graham-cracker crumbs
3 tablespoons sugar
3 tablespoons melted butter
Salt to taste

1. Preheat the oven to 400 degrees.
2. Combine all the ingredients in a bowl and blend well.

3. Press the mixture evenly onto the bottom and sides of a buttered 8-inch pie plate. Bake 5 minutes.
4. Remove the crust from the oven and let cool. Chill.

Yield: 1 (8-inch) crust

—CRAIG CLAIBORNE

CREAM CHEESE PASTRY

dairy

¾ cup cold sweet butter
4 ounces cream cheese
1½ cups flour
¼ teaspoon salt

1. Cut butter and cream cheese into small pieces and place in a bowl. Mix with flour and salt, using a pastry blender or fingertips until the ingredients are the

consistency of coarse meal. Continue to mix until they can be gathered into a ball. This step may also be done in a food processor. Using the steel blade, process the ingredients by turning the machine rapidly on and off about 6 times. Then let it run for about 15 seconds, until a ball of dough forms.
2. Wrap dough in plastic and refrigerate at least 1 hour or overnight.

—FLORENCE FABRICANT

NO-FAIL PIE CRUST

pareve

ADAPTED FROM *The New York Times Menu Cook Book*

3 cups flour
1 teaspoon salt
1 teaspoon baking powder
1 cup plus 2 tablespoons shortening
1 egg
⅓ cup water
1 tablespoon vinegar

1. Sift the flour, salt and baking powder into a bowl. With a pastry blender or the finger tips, blend the shortening into the flour until mixture resembles coarse oatmeal.

2. Beat the egg, water and vinegar together and stir into the flour mixture. The dough may be used immediately or kept refrigerated 2 days.

Yield: Enough for 3 pie shells or 1 large (10-inch) 2-crust pie

ALMOND SHORT PASTRY

dairy

ADAPTED FROM *The New York Times Menu Cook Book*

½ cup almond paste
3 raw egg yolks
1¼ cups sifted all-purpose flour
⅔ cup ground unblanched almonds
⅓ cup sugar
½ teaspoon salt
1 teaspoon grated lemon rind
½ cup butter, softened
Pinch of ground cloves
¼ teaspoon ground cinnamon
2 hard-cooked egg yolks, sieved

1. Cream the almond paste with the raw egg yolks.

2. Mix the flour and ground almonds together in a bowl. Make a well in the center and in it place the sugar, salt, lemon rind, butter, spices, hard-cooked egg yolks and the almond-paste mixture.

3. With the fingertips gradually work the ingredients together to form a ball of dough. Chill until firm.

Yield: Pastry for 9- or 10-inch flan ring

NANCY SILVERTON'S PASTRIES

dairy

ADAPTED FROM *Desserts*

Sweet Pastry

2¾ cups flour
½ cup granulated sugar
8 ounces unsalted butter
2 egg yolks
¼ cup heavy cream

1. Sift flour into a large bowl or the work bowl of a food processor. Stir in the sugar. Cut the butter into ½-inch cubes and toss with the flour mixture until the cubes are coated.

2. By hand, crumble the butter into the flour by working it with your fingertips until the mixture resembles coarse meal, or process it by pulsing in a food processor until the cornmeal consistency is achieved.

3. Whisk together the egg yolks and cream. If using a food processor, add the egg yolk and cream mixture through the feed tube, processing only until the dough comes together to form a ball. Otherwise, dribble the egg-cream liquid onto the flour mixture and mix lightly until the dough can be gathered into a ball. You may have to add another tablespoon or two of cream.

4. Turn the dough onto a lightly floured surface and, with the heel of your hand, lightly push the dough away from you little by little on the surface. This technique, known as fraisage, is not necessary if the dough has been mixed in a food processor.

5. Divide the dough into 2 flat balls, wrap in plastic wrap and refrigerate 2 hours before using.

6. Roll out dough to a circle 2 inches larger than your pan, making it ⅛- to ¼-inch thick. Line pan, carefully pressing the dough into the corners and trim the edge. Chill for 1 hour.

7. Preheat oven to 350 degrees.

8. Completely line the bottom and sides of the pan with parchment paper, aluminum foil or flat coffee filters and weight with dry beans or pastry weights. Make sure the pan is completely covered with the weights and that they are pressed into the corners.

9. Bake for 25 minutes. If the pastry is not completely golden brown, remove paper and weights, return pastry to oven and continue baking another 5–10 minutes. Cool, then add filling of your choice and continue baking, or use with an unbaked filling.

Yield: 2 (9-inch or 10-inch) pie or tart shells

Lemon or Orange Pastry

dairy

1. To make lemon or orange pastry, first scald 6 tablespoons of the heavy cream with ¼ cup finely chopped orange or lemon zest, remove from heat, cover and stand for 30 minutes.

2. Strain the cream, adding enough additional cream to make the ¼ cup listed among the ingredients above. Return 1 tablespoon of the zest to the cream and chill the cream, then proceed with the recipe.

Ginger Pastry

dairy

2 ounces fresh gingerroot
½ cup heavy cream
1 egg yolk
1 tablespoon molasses
2 cups flour
2 tablespoons ground ginger

5 ounces unsalted butter (1¼ sticks)
¼ cup plus 1 tablespoon dark brown sugar, packed

1. Peel gingerroot, slice into ¼-inch-thick rounds, place in a small saucepan and cover with water. Bring to a boil and boil 30 seconds. Drain.
2. In a small saucepan scald the blanched gingerroot and cream. Remove from heat, cover and let stand 30 minutes. Strain, discarding the ginger. Chill.
3. Whisk the egg yolk and molasses into the cream.

Sift the flour and ground ginger together. Now, follow the directions in the Sweet Pastry recipe, above, using the brown sugar in place of the granulated sugar.

Yield: Pastry for a 10-inch or 12-inch tart

NOTE: *Ms. Silverton recommends baking the pastry completely, not partly, before adding fillings that require further baking. An additional 25–30 minutes at 350 degrees, filled, does not cause the finished crust to overbake.*

—FLORENCE FABRICANT

COOKIES

♦ ♦

ZABAR'S BLACK-AND-WHITE COOKIES

dairy

ADAPTED FROM *New York Cookbook*

FOR THE COOKIES:

   1¾ cups granulated sugar
   1 cup (2 sticks) unsalted butter, softened
   4 large eggs
   1 cup milk
   ½ teaspoon vanilla extract
   ¼ teaspoon lemon extract
   2½ cups cake flour
   2½ cups all-purpose flour
   1 teaspoon baking powder
   ½ teaspoon salt

FOR THE FROSTING:

   4 cups confectioners' sugar
   ⅓–½ cup boiling water
   1 ounce bittersweet chocolate, chopped

1. Preheat the oven to 375 degrees.
2. Butter 2 baking sheets and set aside. Combine sugar and butter in a bowl and beat until fluffy. Add the eggs, milk and extracts. Mix until smooth.
3. Combine the flours, baking powder and salt in a bowl and mix. Add the dry ingredients to the wet in batches, stirring until combined. Drop soup spoonfuls of the dough 2 inches apart on the baking sheets. Bake until the edges begin to brown, 20–30 minutes. Cool.
4. To make frosting, place the confectioners' sugar in a large bowl. Gradually add some boiling water, stirring until mixture is thick and spreadable. Place half the frosting in the top of a double boiler set over simmering water; add the chocolate. Warm, stirring until chocolate is melted and the frosting is smooth. Remove from heat.
5. Brush half the cookie with the chocolate and the other half with the white frosting.

Yield: About 24 cookies

—MOLLY O'NEILL

SISTER SADIE'S KICHEL

pareve

ADAPTED FROM *Gottlieb's Bakery—100 Years of Recipes*

3 eggs
½ teaspoon salt
¼ teaspoon black pepper
1 tablespoon bourbon
1½–1¾ cups unbleached all-purpose flour, plus
    extra for dusting
2 tablespoons vegetable oil
½ cup granulated sugar

1. Beat eggs, salt, pepper and bourbon together in a mixing bowl until smooth. Gradually add flour, beating until dough is soft and sticky but well mixed.
2. Turn dough out onto a heavily floured cloth.

Flour dough liberally. Shape into a 10-by-14-inch rectangle, and let rest for 10 minutes. Heat oven to 400 degrees and brush a large baking sheet with oil.
3. Roll dough out once more as thin as possible, using additional flour, just enough to keep dough from sticking. Carefully transfer to baking sheet. (It may help to fold dough while transferring, then unfold on baking sheet.) Brush off excess flour and brush with oil. Sprinkle liberally with sugar and cut into 2-inch diamonds.
4. Bake until brown and curled, about 15 minutes. Watch carefully. Kichel should be dark golden brown but not burned. Allow to cool and store in an airtight container.

Yield: About 3 dozen cookies

—JOAN NATHAN

ALMOND COOKIES WITH FRUITS AND CHOCOLATE

pareve

ADAPTED FROM *The New York Times Menu Cook Book*

3 eggs, lightly beaten
½ cup sugar
½ cup sifted all-purpose flour
½ teaspoon salt
½ teaspoon cinnamon
⅛ teaspoon ground cloves
1½ cups firmly packed finely ground blanched
    almonds
1 cup semisweet chocolate bits
½ cup finely chopped mixed candied fruits
½ teaspoon grated lemon rind

1. Preheat oven to 350 degrees.
2. Beat the eggs and sugar together until thick and pale.
3. Sift together the flour, salt, cinnamon and cloves. Fold into the egg mixture.
4. Stir in the ground almonds, chocolate bits, candied fruits and lemon rind.
5. Drop batter by teaspoons onto foil-lined cookie sheets. Bake for about 12 minutes, until firm and lightly browned. Remove cookies from foil immediately and allow to cool on a rack.

Yield: About 3 dozen cookies

NOTE: *If desired, candied fruits may be sprinkled with Sabra liqueur, cognac or rum for additional flavor.*

ALMOND COOKIES FROM IRAQ • (MASSAFAN)

pareve

2½ cups ground blanched almonds

1 cup sugar

2 tablespoons rose water plus additional rose water
for shaping

1. Combine the almonds, sugar and 2 tablespoons
rose water in a bowl.

2. Pinch enough of mixture to roll into ball slightly
smaller than a walnut.

3. Using additional rose water, shape balls into stars,
pinching the points with fingers moistened with rose
water.

4. Place 1 inch apart on greased cookie sheets. Let
stand at room temperature for 3 hours.

5. Bake at 375 degrees for 10 minutes, until cookies
are set and faintly golden.

Yield: 4 dozen cookies

—MARIAN BURROS

CARDAMOM-FLAVORED ALMOND COOKIES

pareve

ADAPTED FROM *The New Jewish Holiday Cookbook*

FOR THE COOKIES:

1½ cups (about 8 ounces) whole blanched almonds

⅔ cup granulated sugar

2 large egg whites

½ teaspoon ground cardamom

FOR THE GARNISH:

¼ cup whole blanched almonds (about 21)

1. Preheat the oven to 325 degrees. In a food processor, combine the almonds and sugar and pulse
until finely ground. Add the egg whites and cardamom and continue to pulse until a thick paste is
formed. Transfer the almond paste to a bowl.

2. Place a small bowl of cold water nearby. Dip your
hands in the bowl of water and form the almond
paste into mounds, each about the diameter of a
quarter (about 21 mounds). Transfer the mounds to
baking sheets lined with parchment paper, leaving a
2-inch space between each of the mounds. Garnish
each with an almond, pressing down to flatten them
slightly. Place the mounds in the oven and bake until
they are pale and slightly firm, about 15 minutes.

3. Transfer the cookies, still on the parchment paper,
to a wire rack to cool. When the cookies are cool,
remove them from the parchment and transfer them
to a serving plate.

Yield: About 21 cookies

—MOLLY O'NEILL

ALMOND GINGER COOKIES

pareve
ADAPTED FROM *The New York Times Menu Cook Book*

1 cup vegetable shortening
1 cup sugar
½ cup molasses
1 tablespoon ground ginger
2 teaspoons ground cinnamon
2 teaspoons ground cloves
1 teaspoon baking soda
1 teaspoon salt
1 cup blanched almonds (see Note, page 582), chopped
3½ cups sifted enriched flour
Grease for baking sheet

1. Blend the shortening and sugar. Stir in the remaining ingredients.
2. Turn the dough onto a floured board and knead until smooth. Shape into thick rolls or oblongs, wrap in wax paper and chill.
3. Preheat oven to 350 degrees.
4. Cut dough crosswise into ¼-inch slices. Place slices on greased baking sheets and back for 8–10 minutes. Cool.

Yield: About 8 dozen

VIENNESE CRESCENTS

dairy
ADAPTED FROM *The Classic Art of Viennese Pastry*

9 tablespoons unsalted butter, chilled and diced
⅓ cup sugar
2½ ounces blanched ground almonds
1 cup plus 2 tablespoons flour
Confectioners' sugar

1. In a bowl, cream together the butter and sugar until smooth. Blend in the almonds.
2. Fold in the flour with a rubber spatula and gently knead dough. It is properly combined when it comes clean off the sides of the bowl.
3. Shape dough into a ball, flatten it, wrap in plastic and refrigerate it for at least 30 minutes.

4. Preheat oven to 300 degrees. Line a baking sheet with parchment.
5. Remove dough from the refrigerator, unwrap it and shape it by pulling off small cherry-size pieces. Roll each lightly between your palms into a ball, rolling each ball into a strip about 2 inches long; then shape it into a crescent by wrapping the strip around your thumb to make a horseshoe shape. Place the crescents 1 inch apart on the baking sheet.
6. Bake 30 minutes, until the bottoms of the crescents are golden but the tops have not browned.
7. Allow crescents to cool briefly on baking sheet, then dust heavily with sifted confectioners' sugar.

Yield: 2 dozen crescents

—FLORENCE FABRICANT

PINE NUT LACE COOKIES

dairy

ADAPTED FROM *In the Sweet Kitchen*

3 tablespoons dark corn syrup
6 tablespoons unsalted butter
9 tablespoons light brown sugar, packed
¼ cup plus 2 tablespoons all-purpose flour
¼ teaspoon salt
¼ cup vegetable oil
¾ cup pine nuts

1. Preheat oven to 350 degrees. Line 2 heavy baking sheets with parchment paper.
2. In small saucepan, mix corn syrup, butter and brown sugar. Place over low heat and stir until butter melts. Remove from heat. Sift flour and salt together in medium-size bowl, pour syrup mixture over and mix well.
3. Dip a teaspoon in vegetable oil. Drop teaspoons of batter on baking sheets, leaving about 3 inches between. Place 1 sheet in oven and bake 2 minutes, until cookies begin to spread. Remove sheet from oven, sprinkle each cookie with about a teaspoon pine nuts. Bake 3–5 minutes more, until cookies are lacy and bubbling.
4. Remove from oven, cool 1 minute, then transfer cookies to cooling rack with spatula. Cookies may be cooled flat or, while still warm, draped over a rolling pin to make tuiles.
5. Place second sheet of cookies in oven and repeat baking. Keep repeating until batter is finished.

Yield: About 2 dozen

—FLORENCE FABRICANT

NUT DIAMONDS

dairy

1 cup butter, softened
1 cup firmly packed light brown sugar
1 teaspoon vanilla
1 egg yolk
1¾ cups flour
½ teaspoon salt
½ teaspoon cinnamon
½ cup very finely chopped unsalted pecans or cashews
1 egg, beaten

1. Heat oven to 350 degrees. Lightly oil a 10-by-15-inch jelly-roll pan.
2. Cream together butter and sugar. Blend in vanilla and egg yolk. Combine flour, salt, cinnamon and ¼ cup nuts, and stir into sugar mixture. Press dough evenly into pan; it should be very thin. Brush top with beaten egg. Sprinkle remaining nuts evenly and press in lightly. Bake 25–30 minutes, until edges start to brown.
3. Remove from oven, run knife around edges of pan and cut into diamonds or triangles while it is hot. Cool on racks.

Yield: 5 dozen

—MARIAN BURROS

ANDREE LEVY ABRAMOFF'S DATE COOKIES • (MENENA)

dairy, pareve

> 3/4 pound pitted dates
> 1/2 pound sweet butter or margarine, softened
> 2 tablespoons sugar
> 2 cups flour, sifted
> 1/4 cup water
> 1 tablespoon orange flower water
> Confectioners' sugar

1. Soak dates in cold water for 2 hours. Drain, pat dry on paper towels, then chop fine in food processor.

2. Preheat oven to 350 degrees. Line baking sheet with foil.

3. Cream butter or margarine in food processor or electric mixer or by hand until fluffy. Add sugar and mix until incorporated. Add flour gradually, then water and orange-flower water. Mixture should be very soft but not sticky.

4. Roll lumps of dough into little balls, hollowing out as you go to make room for the filling. Stuff each with a little of date mixture, less than a teaspoon. Seal opening gently with fingers and shape into round, flattened dumpling 2 inches in diameter. Gently indent tops of each with tines of fork and arrange cookies on prepared baking sheet.

5. Bake 30–40 minutes, until lightly browned. Allow to cool, then dust with confectioners' sugar and serve.

Yield: 16 cookies

—FLORENCE FABRICANT

BAKLAVA

dairy

ADAPTED FROM Malvina Azzi

FOR THE SUGAR SYRUP:

> 1 1/2 cups granulated sugar
> 3/4 cup water
> 2 tablespoons rose water

FOR THE PASTRY:

> 1 pound unsalted butter
> 1 1/2 cups finely chopped walnuts
> 2 tablespoons rose water
> 1/2 cup granulated sugar

> 1 (16-ounce) package frozen phyllo pastry, thawed (see Note page 583)

1. To make sugar syrup, boil together sugar and water for about 2 minutes over high heat, being careful it does not burn or boil over. Just before removing from heat, stir in the rose water. Let cool slightly, then refrigerate until ready to use.

2. To make the pastry, first clarify the butter. Melt in a pan over gentle heat. Spoon off the milky froth that rises to the top and the solid residue that settles to the bottom. One pound of butter should yield about 1 1/2 cups clarified butter. Set clarified butter in a bowl over hot water to keep it liquid while you proceed.

3. Place walnuts and rose water in bowl of food processor and process in spurts until walnuts are minced. (The rose water helps keep walnuts from getting oily.) Add sugar and process briefly to mix well.

4. Preheat oven to 350 degrees.

5. Spread a sheet of plastic wrap or aluminum foil on a work surface. Open phyllo pastry and spread on the surface. Cover with a barely dampened cloth. (Phyllo dries quickly on exposure to air and should be kept covered whenever you are not working with it.)

6. Using the clarified butter and a pastry brush or clean paintbrush, butter a 10-by-14-inch baking pan liberally, bottom and sides. Place 1 sheet of phyllo pastry in bottom of pan (only half the sheet will fit). Butter surface of pastry, then fold the other half over and butter it. Proceed with the remaining sheets, buttering each one, until you have used about half the sheets in the box. The phyllo sheets should be somewhat crowded in the pan, folded up a little along the sides and at each end.

7. Distribute the walnut mixture over the pastry in an even layer.

8. Place the remaining phyllo sheets over the walnut mixture, again buttering liberally between each layer. When all the sheets have been used, cut the pastry with a sharp knife lengthwise into strips about 1 inch wide, then on the diagonal to make diamonds. Be sure to cut right down through to the bottom of the pan. Pour any remaining clarified butter over the top of the pastry.

9. Place in oven for 30 minutes, then raise temperature to 425 degrees and bake an additional 10 minutes, or until pastry is puffed and golden brown on top. Remove from oven and immediately pour cold syrup over hot pastry. Set aside to cool to room temperature before serving.

Yield: 25–30 pieces

—NANCY HARMON JENKINS

DATE-RAISIN-NUT "ROCKS"

pareve

ADAPTED FROM *The New York Times Heritage Cookbook*

1 cup light brown sugar
¾ cup shortening
2 eggs, lightly beaten
2 cups flour
1 teaspoon ground allspice
¼ teaspoon salt
¾ cup chopped dates
2 cups raisins
2 cups chopped pecans or walnuts

1 teaspoon baking soda
1 tablespoon boiling water

1. Preheat the oven to 350 degrees.

2. Cream the brown sugar and shortening together until light and fluffy. Beat in the eggs.

3. Sift the flour, allspice and salt into a bowl. Add the fruits and nuts and toss to coat. Stir into the batter.

4. Dissolve the baking soda in the boiling water and stir into the batter. Drop by teaspoonfuls onto a lightly greased baking sheet and bake about 15 minutes, or until lightly browned.

Yield: About 4 dozen cookies

ALMOND MACAROONS

pareve

ADAPTED FROM Ilana Amini

4 whites of extra-large eggs
1½ cups unblanched almonds
1½ cups granulated sugar
10 almonds, blanched and sliced in vertical quarters

1. Preheat oven to 325 degrees.

2. Combine egg whites, unblanched almonds and sugar and grind, using fine blade of meat grinder or food processor.

3. Turn mixture into top of double boiler and heat over simmering water for 8–10 minutes, stirring constantly until mixture is smooth and slightly wet, much like porridge.

4. Drop rounded teaspoonfuls onto ungreased cookie sheet, leaving 2 inches between them. Top each with slice of blanched almond.

5. Bake for about 20 minutes, or until cookies turn pale brown. Remove from pan when cool.

Yield: About 2 dozen cookies

—MIMI SHERATON

CHOCOLATE MACAROONS

pareve

ADAPTED FROM Huberts

6 ounces bittersweet chocolate
¾ cup egg whites (5–6 large eggs)
⅛ teaspoon cream of tartar
¾ cup sugar
1 egg yolk
½ cup ground blanched almonds (see Note page 582)

1. Preheat the oven to 400 degrees. Butter and flour 3 cookie sheets. Set aside.

2. Melt the chocolate in the top part of a double boiler. When done, remove from the heat.

3. Beat the egg whites with the cream of tartar until they hold a firm peak. Gradually beat in the sugar, a

¼ cup at a time, until all of it is completely incorporated. Add the egg yolk and blend.

4. Fold a third of the whipped egg whites into the chocolate using a spatula. Blend in the ground almonds. Fold in the remaining egg whites.

5. Fit a ½-inch pastry tip into a pastry bag. Scoop the cookie mixture into the bag. Press out ½-inch mounds of batter, 1-inch apart, onto the prepared cookie sheets. (You can spoon the mixture onto the sheets with a teaspoon as well.)

6. Bake the cookies for 4–5 minutes, until they puff and the edges are slightly wrinkled. Remove from the oven to cool (about 5 minutes). Remove the cookies with a spatula onto a flat plate.

Yield: About 40 macaroons

—RENA COYLE

FILLED MARZIPAN COOKIES

dairy

ADAPTED FROM *The New York Times International Cookbook*

½ *cup butter*
¼ *cup granulated sugar*
1 *egg yolk*
½ *cup plus 3 tablespoons almond paste*
1½ *cups sifted cake flour*
1 *egg white, approximately*
Raspberry jam

1. Cream the butter; add the sugar, egg, yolk, and the 3 tablespoons almond paste. Add the flour, blend well and chill.

2. Preheat the oven to 350 degrees. Grease cookie sheets.

3. Work the ½ cup of almond paste with the fingers until smooth. Add the egg white gradually, using enough to soften the paste so it can be forced through a pastry tube. Set aside.

4. Roll the chilled cookie dough on a lightly floured cloth to a thickness of ¼ inch. Cut into diamond or other shapes. Arrange the cookies 1 inch apart on the cookie sheets.

5. Force the almond cookie paste and egg white mixture through a small tube to form a 1-inch circle in the center of each cookie. Fill the circle with jam. Bake for 15 minutes.

Yield: 16–18 large diamonds

MARZIPAN "POTATOES"

dairy

ADAPTED FROM *The Russian Tea Room Cookbook*

FOR THE CHOCOLATE CAKE:

1 *cup sifted cake flour*
1 *cup sugar*
¼ *teaspoon baking powder*
½ *teaspoon baking soda*
½ *teaspoon salt*
½ *cup water*
2 *ounces unsweetened baking chocolate*
1 *egg*
¼ *cup buttermilk*
½ *teaspoon vanilla extract*

FOR THE MARZIPAN POTATOES:

5 *cups chocolate cake crumbs (recipe above)*
1 *cup finely chopped walnuts*
1 *tablespoon rum or brandy*
½ *cup apricot preserves*
2 *(8-ounce) cans of almond paste at room temperature*
½ *cup sifted cocoa*

1. Preheat oven to 350 degrees.

2. Butter and dust with flour an 8-inch diameter circular cake pan. In a large bowl, sift together flour, sugar, baking powder, baking soda and salt.

3. Bring water to boil in a saucepan. Chop the chocolate coarsely and add it to the water. Lower the heat and melt the chocolate, stirring constantly. Let it cool for several minutes.

4. Add melted chocolate to the flour. Using an electric mixer, mix for 1 minute or until it is smooth.

5. In another mixing bowl, combine egg, buttermilk and vanilla. Add to the chocolate mixture. Beat again for a minute until smooth. Pour the batter in the cake pan and bake for 30–35 minutes, or until a knife inserted in center comes out clean and the cake pulls away from the sides of the pan. Remove from heat and cool for 10 minutes. Remove from the pan; cool thoroughly on a rack.

6. When the cake is at room temperature, crumble it into pieces the size of fine bread crumbs, either by hand or using a food processor.

7. In a third bowl, combine cake crumbs, walnuts, rum and preserves. Stir with wooden spoon or your hands and blend thoroughly.

8. Form a ball with ¼ cup of the mixture. You should be able to make about 12 balls. Set aside.

9. Cut the almond paste into 12 pieces. Roll each piece into a little ball.

10. Place one ball of the almond paste between two sheets of wax paper. Roll out each to a 5-inch diameter. Wrap the rounds of almond paste around the chocolate balls. Roll the balls into a roughly oval shape, somewhat like a potato.

11. Place the ovals on a baking sheet and refrigerate for 40–60 minutes to firm up the paste. Roll each oval in cocoa, shaking off excess, and serve at room temperature. You may poke little holes in each oval with a skewer to simulate potato eyes.

Yield: 12 marzipan potatoes

—BRYAN MILLER

MAIDA HEATTER'S VIENNESE ANISE COOKIES

pareve

ADAPTED FROM *The New York Times Large-Type Cookbook*

2 eggs

1 cup sugar

1½ cups flour

¼ teaspoon baking powder

⅛ teaspoon salt

¼ teaspoon crushed anise seeds

1 teaspoon vanilla or ¼ teaspoon grated lemon rind

1. Break eggs into a measuring cup and add enough water to make ½ cup. In a small bowl, beat until thick and lemon colored. Gradually add sugar; beat until very thick, 15–20 minutes. Transfer to a large mixing bowl.

2. Sift together flour, baking powder and salt; sift, about ¼ cup at a time, over egg mixture. Fold in, along with crushed anise seed and vanilla, until well blended.

3. Cover baking sheets with baking pan liner paper (parchment paper). Drop batter from a teaspoon, or use a pastry bag with ½-inch plain round tip to make cookies about 1½ inches in diameter. Let cookies stand overnight or 8–12 hours, uncovered. A hard crust will form on top.

4. Preheat oven to 350 degrees.

5. Bake cookies 7–8 minutes. Do not bake too dry. The cookies should have a soft base and a crisp top.

6. Cool cookies on rack and store in an airtight container.

Yield: About 6 dozen cookies

NOTE: *An unusual aspect of this cookie, which helps create its texture, is that the dough rests at room temperature for a minimum of 8 hours before it is baked.*

CARROT COOKIES WITH ORANGE ICING

pareve

ADAPTED FROM *The New York Times Heritage Cookbook*

1 cup shortening
³/₄ cup granulated sugar
1 egg
1 cup mashed cooked carrots, cooled
1 teaspoon vanilla
2 cups flour
2 teaspoons baking powder
¹/₂ teaspoon salt

1. Preheat oven to 350 degrees.

2. Cream the shortening and granulated sugar together until light and fluffy. Beat in the egg. Beat in the carrots and the vanilla. Sift together the flour, baking powder and salt and stir into the batter.

3. Drop by teaspoonfuls 2 inches apart onto a greased baking sheet and bake 20 minutes, or until done.

4. Cool on a rack and then spread with Orange Icing (see recipe below).

Yield: About 30 cookies

Orange Icing

¹/₄ cup orange juice
1 tablespoon grated orange rind
Confectioners' sugar

1. Combine the orange juice, orange rind and enough confectioners' sugar to make a spreading consistency.

2. Spread over the cookies.

Yield: Frosting for about 30 cookies

LEMON-NUT WAFERS

pareve

ADAPTED FROM *The New York Times Menu Cook Book*

½ cup shortening
1 cup sugar
1 egg
1 tablespoon lemon juice
1 tablespoon grated lemon rind
2 cups sifted flour
1 teaspoon baking powder
⅛ teaspoon salt
1 cup finely chopped nuts
Grease for baking sheets

1. Preheat the oven to 350 degrees.

2. Blend the shortening and sugar. Beat in the egg, lemon juice and rind. Stir in dry ingredients and mix well. Stir in the nuts.

3. Shape the dough into rolls, wrap in wax paper and chill.

4. Slice the dough crosswise thinly, place on greased baking sheets and bake for 12–15 minutes.

Yield: About 5 dozen wafers

POPPY SEED-ORANGE COOKIES

dairy

ADAPTED FROM *Desserts*

2 sticks unsalted butter
3 tablespoons grated or finely chopped orange zest
   (from about 3 oranges)
½ cup sugar
1 egg yolk
½ teaspoon vanilla extract
2 cups minus 2 tablespoons flour
¼ cup poppy seeds

1. Use an electric mixer to cream butter with orange zest until it whitens and holds soft peaks, 3–5 minutes. Beat in sugar until well blended.

2. Whisk together egg yolk and vanilla and beat in, scraping down sides of bowl as necessary. Add flour and poppy seeds, mixing only enough to combine.

Wrap dough in plastic wrap and chill 30 minutes, or until firm.

3. Divide dough into 4 sections; work with one section at a time, keeping the remainder refrigerated. On a lightly floured surface, form each section into a solid log about 1½ inches thick. Place on a cookie sheet and put in the freezer at least 30 minutes, or until firm enough to slice. Repeat. (Dough may be wrapped and frozen for as long as 3 months; it slices most easily while frozen.)

4. Preheat oven to 325 degrees. Using a sharp knife, slice logs into ⅜-inch rounds; place them 1 inch apart on nonstick baking sheets. Bake 12–15 minutes, or until firm and evenly browned.

Yield: About 6 dozen cookies

—MARK BITTMAN

SESAME COOKIES • (BENNE WAFERS)

dairy

ADAPTED FROM *Cooking with Herbs & Spices*

½ cup sesame seeds
1 tablespoon butter
1 cup brown sugar, firmly packed
3 tablespoons all-purpose flour
1 egg, beaten
1 teaspoon vanilla
¼ teaspoon salt, if desired

1. Preheat oven to 350 degrees.
2. Put the sesame seeds in a small, heavy pan and roast in the oven until slightly brown. Remove from the oven and add the remaining ingredients.
3. Mix thoroughly and drop by teaspoonfuls onto well-buttered cookie sheets. Bake until firm, 5–8 minutes. Remove carefully from the sheets while still warm.

Yield: 30 wafers

ALMOND BISCOTTI • (MANDELBROT)

pareve

1 cup whole blanched almonds
2¾ cups flour plus flour for work surface
Pinch of salt
¾ teaspoon baking powder
½ teaspoon baking soda
4 large eggs
1 cup sugar
1 teaspoon almond extract

1. Preheat oven to 350 degrees. Spread the almonds on a baking sheet and toast, about 15 minutes.
2. Meanwhile, sift the flour, salt, baking powder and baking soda together and set aside.
3. Beat the eggs lightly just until they are blended, in a mixing bowl with a whisk or in an electric mixer. Remove 2 tablespoons of the egg mixture to a small dish and set aside. Beat the sugar into the remaining eggs until blended. Add the almond extract. Stir in the flour mixture to form a soft dough.

4. When the almonds are toasted, remove them from the oven and transfer them to a bowl. Then line the baking sheet with parchment paper.
5. Divide the dough in half and put one portion on a well-floured work surface. With floured hands, pat one portion into a 6-inch square. Scatter half the almonds on the dough and press them into the surface. Roll into a cylinder about 2 inches in diameter and 12–15 inches long. Place on the paper-lined baking sheet. Repeat with remaining dough. Brush the tops of both cylinders with the reserved egg mixture.
6. Put the cylinders in the oven and bake about 15 minutes, until golden and firm to the touch. Transfer to a cutting board and cut on an angle into slices ½-inch thick. Return the slices to the baking sheet, standing them up, and return them to the oven. Bake another 20 minutes, until the slices are crisp and dry. Allow to cool completely before storing or serving.

Yield: About 60 biscotti

—FLORENCE FABRICANT

CINCINNATI JEWISH BAKE SHOP SCHNECKEN

dairy

ADAPTED FROM *The Cincinnati Cook Book*

FOR THE DOUGH:

2 scant tablespoons or 2 packages active dry yeast
½ cup lukewarm water
½ cup sugar
2 sticks (1 cup) unsalted butter at room temperature
1 cup milk
3 large eggs
6 cups unbleached flour
1 teaspoon salt

FOR THE FILLING AND THE BOTTOM OF THE PANS:

1 stick (½ cup) unsalted butter
1½ cups dark brown sugar
¾ cup honey
1 cup blanched almonds
1 cup chopped walnuts
1 cup currants
½ teaspoon cinnamon

1. To make the dough, dissolve the yeast in the lukewarm water with a teaspoon of the sugar. Let sit for 10 minutes.
2. Place the butter in a saucepan with the milk. Stir over low heat until the butter is melted. Cool to lukewarm.

Transfer to the bowl of an electric mixer. Add the yeast, the remaining sugar and the eggs. Gradually add the flour and salt, mixing after each addition. The dough will be very sticky. Cover the mixing bowl with plastic wrap and place the dough in the refrigerator overnight.
3. The next morning, make the filling. Begin by melting the stick of butter and brush the bottom and sides of 3 muffin tins, each holding 12 muffins. Place ½ teaspoon of the brown sugar and 1 teaspoon of the honey in each tin, then add 3 almonds in the shape of a triangle.
4. Divide the dough into 3 parts, adding more flour if it is too sticky to handle. Flour a pastry board, and roll each part into a 7-by-12-inch rectangle.
5. Brush the dough with the melted butter. Sprinkle each rectangle with a third of the remaining brown sugar, walnuts, currants and cinnamon. Roll up tightly like a jelly roll.
6. Cut each roll into 12 slices about an inch wide, and place slices in the muffin tins, one of the cut sides down. Let rise, uncovered, for ½ hour. Brush the tops with the melted butter.
7. Preheat the oven to 350 degrees. Bake the schnecken for 15 minutes. Reduce the heat to 325 degrees and continue baking for 20 minutes more or until golden. Invert onto wax paper.

Yield: 36 schnecken

—JOAN NATHAN

MIMI SHERATON'S RUGELACH · (CINNAMON NUT HORNS)

dairy

ADAPTED FROM *From My Mother's Kitchen*

Cream Cheese Pastry

dairy

½ cup (¼ pound) unsalted butter, at room
    temperature
¼ pound cream cheese, at room temperature
½ cup sour cream
Pinch of salt
2 teaspoons sugar
1 large egg
About 2¾ cups flour

FOR THE FILLING:

¼ cup melted, unsalted butter
About 2 tablespoons cinnamon
About 3 tablespoons sugar
½ to ⅔ cup dried currants
2 cups chopped walnuts

1. Cream together the butter and cream cheese. Beat in the sour cream. Stir in a pinch of salt, the sugar, the egg and about 2¾ cups of flour, or just enough to make a dough that will stick together. Form a ball, cover with plastic wrap and refrigerate overnight.

2. Cut the dough into portions that are convenient to handle and roll out each between sheets of waxed paper. Brush with melted sweet butter, sprinkle generously with cinnamon, sugar, currants and nuts.

3. Cut into triangles that are about 3 inches at the base and 3½–4 inches long, tapering to a point. Roll the triangles from base to point and turn the ends in slightly to form crescents or horns.

4. Place on a lightly buttered baking sheet and chill for 1 hour.

5. Fifteen minutes before baking, preheat oven to 350 degrees. After rugelach have chilled for 1 hour, place them in the preheated oven and bake for about 25 minutes, or until golden brown.

Yield: About 30 crescents

MIMI SHERATON'S HAMANTASCHEN

dairy

ADAPTED FROM *From My Mother's Kitchen*

½ cup unsalted butter
¼ pound cream cheese
½ cup sour cream
Pinch of salt
2 teaspoons sugar

1 large egg
2¾ cups flour, approximately
1 pound prune jam (lekvar)
2 teaspoons lemon juice
1 teaspoon grated lemon rind
½ teaspoon cinnamon
⅔ cup finely chopped walnuts

1. Let butter and cream soften at room temperature. Cream them together until thoroughly blended; beat in sour cream.

2. Stir in salt, sugar and the egg.

3. Gradually beat in flour, adding just enough to make a dough that will stick together. Form a ball, wrap in waxed paper and chill overnight.

4. Before rolling out dough, prepare filling by blending prune jam with remaining ingredients. Set aside.

5. Divide dough in half; place one half in the refrigerator while you roll the first. Place a sheet of waxed paper on the counter top or pastry board and place the first half of the dough on it. Top with a second sheet of waxed paper. Using a rolling pin, roll dough between sheets of waxed paper, turning the dough over with the paper so it is rolled on both sides and lifting the sheets of paper between every 2–3 rollings. Dough should be about ⅛-inch thick.

6. Roll the second half of the dough in the same way.

7. Using a 3½- to 4-inch round cookie cutter, cut circles from the rolled-out dough. Place a well-rounded teaspoon of prune filling in the center of each circle.

8. Moisten the edges of each circle with a little cold water and shape triangles; be sure to pinch the 3 corner seams tightly closed.

9. Arrange hamantaschen on cookie sheets and place in refrigerator for 30 minutes to an hour before baking.

10. Preheat oven to 400 degrees. Bake hamantaschen for about 15 minutes, or until bottoms and tops are golden brown.

Yield: About 30 hamantaschen

NOTE: *Any favorite pie crust dough can be used for the pastry, as can coffee cake yeast dough or the flaky, rich cream cheese pastry. The standard fillings are poppy seeds or apricot jam or, best of all, lekvar, the rich dark prune jam. Because of its high butterfat content, the dough in the recipe is sticky and fragile. It should be started the night before the Hamantaschen are to be baked. Be sure to let filled Hamantaschen rest at least 30 minutes before baking or they will open.*

AUNT MARY'S KOLACHES

dairy

ADAPTED FROM *The New York Times Heritage Cookbook*

> 1 package active dry yeast
> 2 tablespoons warm water
> 1 cup milk, scalded and cooled
> ¼ cup sugar
> ½ cup melted butter
> 2 egg yolks
> 4 cups flour, approximately
> *Kolache filling (recipes below)*

1. Dissolve the yeast in the water. To the cooled milk add the sugar, ⅓ cup of the butter, the egg yolks, the dissolved yeast and 2 cups of the flour. Beat with electric mixer until mixture balls up on beaters and is smooth and shiny.

2. Beating by hand, work in remaining flour. Beat until dough is shiny and elastic, at least 5 minutes. Grease top of dough with 1 tablespoon of the remaining fat or butter. Cover and let rise in a warm place until doubled in bulk.

3. Punch dough down and let rise again. With

greased hands, turn dough out onto a greased board. Divide dough into walnut-size pieces and shape into balls. Place on greased baking sheet. Flatten slightly, cover and let rise until double in bulk.

4. Preheat the oven to 425 degrees.

5. Make a small depression in each kolache and fill with a teaspoon of desired filling. Let rise 10 minutes.

6. Bake 12–15 minutes, or until golden. Brush with remaining fat or butter.

Yield: 3 dozen

NOTE: *Each recipe for filling is more than ample for 1 recipe of the dough.*

Cottage Cheese Filling for Kolaches

dairy

1 cup cottage cheese
1 egg yolk
1/4 cup sugar
1 teaspoon vanilla
1 teaspoon instant tapioca
1 teaspoon grated lemon rind

Mix all ingredients together.

Yield: About 1 1/4 cups

Prune or Apricot Filling for Kolaches

pareve

1 pound dried prunes or apricots
1/2 cup sugar
1/2 teaspoon vanilla
1/4 teaspoon cinnamon

Place fruit in a saucepan, barely cover with water and cook until tender. Pit prunes, if used. Mash the fruit well and beat with remaining ingredients.

Yield: About 2 cups

Poppy Seed Filling for Kolaches

dairy

1/2 pound poppy seeds, ground, see Note below
1/2 cup pecans, ground, optional
1 cup water
1/2 cup milk
1/4 teaspoon salt
1 tablespoon vanilla
1/2 cup sugar
1/2 cup graham cracker crumbs or vanilla wafer crumbs
1 tablespoon grated lemon rind

Place the poppy seeds and pecans, if desired, in a saucepan, add the water and cook 20 minutes. Add the milk, salt, vanilla, sugar, crumbs and lemon rind.

Yield: About 3 1/2 cups

NOTE: *Ground poppy seeds can be bought in stores specializing in German, Viennese and Hungarian ingredients. Otherwise, poppy seeds can be ground in a coffee grinder or electric blender.*

HONEY ALMOND SQUARES

pareve

ADAPTED FROM *The New York Times Large-Type Cookbook*

3 eggs
1½ cups brown sugar
⅓ cup honey
1½ cups flour
1½ teaspoons baking powder
1 teaspoon salt
½ teaspoon cloves
¼ teaspoon nutmeg
2 tablespoons cocoa
½ cup finely ground blanched almonds
½ cup chopped blanched almonds
½ cup chopped mixed candied fruit

1½ cups confectioners' sugar
3–4 tablespoons cognac

1. Preheat oven to 350 degrees.
2. Beat eggs until foamy. Gradually beat in sugar until mixture is very thick. Beat in honey.
3. Sift in flour with baking powder, salt, cloves and nutmeg. Mix in cocoa and ground almonds.
4. Fold the mixture into egg mixture. Stir in chopped almonds and mixed fruits. Turn into greased jelly-roll pan, 15½ by 10½ inches. Bake 35 minutes.
5. Blend sugar with enough cognac to make a spreading consistency. Spread over hot cake. Cool and cut into 1- to 1½-inch squares.

Yield: 6–8 dozen squares

HONEY BROWNIES

dairy

ADAPTED FROM *The Best of Craig Claiborne*

4 tablespoons butter
4 squares (ounces) unsweetened chocolate
4 eggs
½ teaspoon salt
1 cup sugar
1 cup honey
1 teaspoon vanilla extract
1 cup plus 2 tablespoons sifted flour
1 cup chopped pecans or walnuts

1. Preheat the oven to 325 degrees.
2. Melt the butter and chocolate over low heat in a heavy saucepan.
3. Beat the eggs and salt in a mixing bowl until thick and pale yellow. Add the sugar and honey gradually, beating until the mixture is light in texture.
4. Add the melted chocolate and butter and vanilla. Stir in the flour. Add the nuts. Pour the mixture into a 9-inch-square pan and bake for 45 minutes, or until done. Cut into squares when cool.

Yield: About 16 brownies

PASSOVER BROWNIES

pareve

ADAPTED FROM *The New York Times Heritage Cookbook*

2 cups sugar

5 eggs

½ cup oil

1 cup matzoh cake meal

1 tablespoon potato starch

5 tablespoons cocoa powder

⅓ cup orange juice

⅓ cup chopped nuts

1. Preheat oven to 350 degrees.

2. Beat the sugar and eggs together well. Beat in the oil.

3. Combine the cake meal, potato starch, cocoa powder, orange juice and nuts. Stir into the batter.

4. Pour into a well-greased or wax-paper-lined 13-by-9-by-2-inch baking pan. Bake 35–45 minutes, or until done. Cut into squares while warm.

Yield: About 2 dozen brownies

CHOCOLATE SQUARES WITH WALNUTS

pareve

ADAPTED FROM *The New York Times Menu Cook Book*

2 ounces (squares) unsweetened chocolate

½ cup shortening

½ cup sugar

1 teaspoon vanilla extract

½ cup dark corn syrup

2 eggs

½ cup chopped walnuts

½ cup sifted all-purpose flour

½ teaspoon salt

Grease for pan

1. Preheat oven to 350 degrees.

2. Melt chocolate over low heat or in top of a double boiler over hot, but not boiling, water.

3. Cream together the shortening, sugar and vanilla until light and fluffy. Add syrup and beat well. Add eggs, 1 at a time, beating well after each addition.

4. Add the chocolate and walnuts to the mixture, blending well. Fold in flour and salt.

5. Pour mixture into greased 9-inch-square pan. Bake for 40 minutes or until done. Cut into squares while warm.

Yield: 20 squares

MERINGUE THREE WAYS •
(TOPPING FOR COOKIES OR SHELLS)

pareve

4 egg whites
1 cup sugar
1 teaspoon vanilla extract

1. Whisk the egg whites, sugar and vanilla together in the bowl of a heavy mixer or another metal bowl. Place over a pan of gently simmering water. Whisk constantly until the mixture is hot and the sugar is melted, about 4 minutes.

2. Remove the bowl from the pan and beat with a mixer until the meringue is completely cool, white and fluffy, about 8–10 minutes.

TO COVER A PIE:

1. Preheat the oven to 375 degrees.

2. Spread the meringue over the top of the pie, leaving it swirled with peaks. Bake until the tips of the meringue are browned, about 10 minutes.

TO MAKE COOKIES:

1. Preheat the oven to 200 degrees. Line 2 baking sheets with parchment paper.

2. Gently fold 1 cup of ground walnuts into meringue mixture, if desired.

3. Fill a pastry bag fitted with a plain 1-inch tip with the meringue. Pipe the meringue onto the parchment in 1-inch mounds. Bake until dry and crisp, about 1–2 hours.

TO MAKE MERINGUE SHELLS:

1. Preheat the oven to 200 degrees. Line a baking sheet with parchment paper. Use a glass or another round object that is 3 inches in diameter as a guide to draw 6 circles on the parchment paper.

2. Turn the paper over. Fill a pastry bag fitted with a 1-inch star or plain tube with the meringue. Starting at the inside rim of one of the circles, pipe meringue in a spiral, filling the circle.

3. Form the sides of the shell by piping 2 circles on top of each other around the rim. Repeat with the remaining circles.

4. Bake until dry and crisp, about 1–2 hours. Fill with whipped cream and fresh berries at dairy meals or with sorbet or sweetened fruit.

—MOLLY O'NEILL

MOCHA MERINGUE KISSES

pareve

4 egg whites
Pinch salt
¼ teaspoon cream of tartar
1 cup granulated sugar
1 teaspoon instant-coffee powder
2 teaspoons hot water
3 tablespoons unsweetened cocoa powder
1 teaspoon finely grated orange rind
Oil for coating wax paper

1. Preheat oven to 350 degrees.

2. In top of double boiler over simmering water, beat whites, salt, cream of tartar and sugar for 7 minutes, or until meringue is stiff enough to hold its shape.

3. Dissolve the coffee powder in the 2 teaspoons hot water and stir in the cocoa.

4. Add one-third of the coffee mixture to the meringue and beat until blended. Repeat twice more, beating after each addition.

5. Fold in orange rind.

6. Line 2 cookie sheets with lightly oiled wax paper.

7. Drop tablespoonfuls of meringue about an inch apart onto wax paper and bake 15–18 minutes, until outside is crusty and inside is still soft.

8. Remove from baking sheets and cool on cake racks. Store in tightly covered container.

Yield: 3 dozen kisses

NOTE: *You can also shape the meringue mixture into meringue patties and fill them with sorbet (pages 463–464) or with berries flavored with orange juice or liqueur.*

—MARIAN BURROS

CHOCOLATE CHEWIES

pareve

ADAPTED FROM *Gottlieb's Bakery—100 Years of Recipes*

3 cups powdered sugar
½ cup good quality unsweetened cocoa
2 tablespoons flour
3 egg whites
2 cups chopped pecans

1. Heat oven to 350 degrees, and line two cookie sheets with parchment paper. Place sugar, cocoa and flour in bowl of an electric mixer and beat until well blended. Beat in egg whites one at a time, scraping bowl as necessary. Beat at high speed for 1 minute. Stir in pecans.

2. Drop heaping tablespoons onto cookie sheets, leaving 2 inches between cookies. Bake 15 minutes on center rack, turning sheet halfway through baking time. Remove from oven. Cool, then peel cookies off parchment. Store in airtight container or freeze.

Yield: Approximately 2 dozen cookies

—JOAN NATHAN

MERINGUE CHOCOLATE NUT BARS

dairy
ADAPTED FROM *The New York Times Large-Type Cookbook*

½ cup brown sugar

⅓ cup soft butter

1⅓ cups flour

½ teaspoon baking powder

1 cup sugar

2 eggs

1 teaspoon vanilla

¾ teaspoon salt

1 cup chopped nuts

1 cup (6-ounce package) semisweet chocolate bits

1. Preheat oven to 350 degrees.

2. Cream brown sugar and butter. Sift flour and baking powder and stir into creamed mixture. Press into greased 13-by-9-by-2-inch pan. Bake 8 minutes.

3. While batter is baking, prepare topping by beating the sugar, eggs, vanilla and salt until very thick and lemon-colored. Fold in remaining ingredients gently and spread over cooked batter.

4. Bake 18–20 minutes longer. Cool and cut into bars.

Yield: 4 dozen bars

CAKES AND TORTES

◆ ◆

SPONGE CAKE

pareve
ADAPTED FROM *The New York Times International Cookbook*

6 eggs

1 tablespoon lemon juice

1 packed teaspoon grated lemon rind

1 cup sifted cake flour

¾ teaspoon salt

1 cup granulated sugar

1. Preheat oven to 325 degrees. Lightly grease and flour the bottom but not the sides of a 10-inch tube pan.

2. Break the eggs into the large bowl of an electric mixer, add the lemon juice and grated rind and beat the mixture at highest speed until soft peaks can be formed, or 12–16 minutes.

3. While the eggs are being beaten, sift together the flour and salt onto a piece of waxed paper.

4. Continue beating the eggs at highest speed (after soft peaks can be formed) and pour the sugar in a fine stream over them, taking 2½–3 minutes to add the sugar.

5. Change to lowest speed and sift the flour and salt over the surface of the mixture as the bowl turns, taking 2½–3 minutes to add all the flour. Scrape the sides of the bowl and beat at lowest speed ½ minute.

6. Pour the batter into the prepared pan and bake 50 minutes, or until a toothpick inserted in the center comes out clean.

7. Invert the cake pan and set it on a rack to cool. Prop it up if necessary so that the air can circulate between the cake and the tabletop. Let the cake cool at room temperature before removing it from the pan.

Yield: 1 (10-inch) cake

PASSOVER SPONGE CAKE

pareve
ADAPTED FROM *The New York Times Heritage Cookbook*

8 eggs, separated
1½ cups sugar
Grated rind of 2 lemons
Juice of ½ lemon
¼ cup matzoh cake flour
¾ cup potato starch
¼ teaspoon salt

1. Preheat over to 325 degrees.

2. Beat the egg whites until stiff. Beat the egg yolks with the sugar, lemon rind and lemon juice until yolks are thick and lemon-colored.

3. Sift together the matzoh cake flour, potato starch and salt. Fold the egg whites and dry ingredients alternately into the yolks. Pour the mixture into 2 ungreased 8-inch layer cake pans and bake 1 hour, or until done. Invert in pans, on a rack, and let cool completely.

Yield: 12 servings

CHOCOLATE SPONGE CAKE

dairy
ADAPTED FROM *The Best of Craig Claiborne*

6 eggs
1 cup sugar
½ cup plus 3 tablespoons flour
4 tablespoons cornstarch
6 tablespoons cocoa
3 tablespoons butter, melted

1. Preheat oven to 375 degrees.

2. Butter a round cake tin, approximately 10 inches by 2 inches. Sprinkle the inside with flour and shake the flour around until the bottom and sides are well coated. Shake out any excess flour.

3. Put the eggs into the bowl of an electric mixer. Bring about 2 quarts of water to a boil in a casserole to hold the mixing bowl. Set the bowl in the water and beat vigorously while adding the sugar. Beat constantly for about 5 minutes, or until the eggs are lukewarm.

4. Return the bowl to the electric mixer and continue beating on high speed until the mixture is thick, mousselike, and at room temperature. To test, run a spatula through the mass. If it is ready, the spatula will leave a track.

5. Meanwhile, combine the flour, cornstarch and cocoa. Sift together 2–3 times. Fold the mixture into the batter, using a wooden spoon or spatula. Fold in the butter and pour the mixture into the prepared pan. Bake for 25–30 minutes, or until the cake pulls away from the pan. Turn out cake onto a rack to cool.

Yield: 1 cake

HONEY-WALNUT SPONGE ROLL

pareve

> *½ cup cake flour*
> *½ cup finely ground walnuts*
> *¾ teaspoon baking powder*
> *Pinch of salt*
> *4 eggs, at room temperature*
> *½ cup granulated sugar*
> *Confectioners' sugar*
> *¾ cup warm honey*

1. Preheat oven to 350 degrees. Grease a 10-by-15-inch jelly-roll pan with margarine and line it with a sheet of waxed paper cut to fit the width and extending a few inches at either end. Grease the paper.

2. Sift together the flour, half the walnuts, the baking powder and salt. Set aside.

3. Beat the eggs at high speed until they become very thick and light, like softly whipped cream. Gradually beat in the granulated sugar. Fold in the flour mixture. Spread the batter in the pan and bake about 20 minutes, until puffed and golden brown. Quickly run a knife around the edges of the pan.

4. Heavily dust a clean linen towel or a large sheet of waxed paper with sifted confectioners' sugar and invert the cake, along with the pan, onto the surface. Lift the pan off and peel off the wax paper. Spread the cake with the warm honey and sprinkle with the remaining ground walnuts. Using one end of the towel or waxed paper for leverage, roll the cake up from the narrow side and transfer it to a serving platter. Allow to cool.

5. Before serving, dust the top with sifted confectioners' sugar.

Yield: 6–8 servings

—FLORENCE FABRICANT

ROSH HA SHANA HONEY CAKE WITH DRIED FRUIT AND NUTS

pareve

3 cups sifted all-purpose flour

$\frac{1}{2}$ teaspoon salt

1 teaspoon cinnamon

$\frac{1}{8}$ teaspoon ground cloves

$\frac{1}{2}$ teaspoon nutmeg

1 teaspoon baking soda

2 cups honey

$1\frac{1}{2}$ cups orange juice

$\frac{1}{2}$ cup shelled white pistachio nuts

$\frac{1}{2}$ cup shelled walnuts

$\frac{1}{2}$ cup raisins

$\frac{1}{2}$ cup dried apricots, cut in bite-size pieces

1 teaspoon unsalted margarine for greasing the baking
    pans

$\frac{1}{4}$ cup slivered almonds

1. Preheat the oven to 350 degrees.

2. In a large bowl, mix together all the dry ingredients. Set aside.

3. In another bowl, mix together the honey, orange juice and the nuts (except the almonds) and the dried fruits.

4. Add the orange juice–honey mixture to the flour. Mix well with a wooden spoon.

5. Grease two 9-by-5-inch loaf pans with the margarine. Divide the batter evenly between the two pans.

6. Sprinkle the almonds on top of the batter.

7. Reduce the oven temperature to 325 degrees and bake for 1 hour and 45 minutes, or until a skewer inserted in the center comes out dry.

8. Cool the cakes on a rack. Loosen the sides before unmolding.

Yield: 14–16 servings

—COLETTE ROSSANT

HONEY-SPICE CAKE

pareve, dairy

ADAPTED FROM *American Diabetes Association Holiday
    Cookbook*

3 eggs

$\frac{1}{4}$ cup sugar

$\frac{1}{4}$ cup unsalted margarine or butter, melted and
    cooled

$\frac{1}{2}$ cup honey

$2\frac{1}{2}$ cups all-purpose flour

1 teaspoon baking powder

1 teaspoon baking soda

1 teaspoon cinnamon

$\frac{1}{2}$ teaspoon ground nutmeg

$\frac{1}{4}$ teaspoon ground cloves

$\frac{1}{4}$ teaspoon salt, if desired

1 cup strong cold coffee

1 ripe banana, mashed (scant $\frac{1}{2}$ cup)

1. Preheat oven to 350 degrees.

2. In a large bowl, beat the eggs until thick. Gradually beat in the sugar, then the margarine and honey.

3. In a medium bowl, stir together the flour, baking powder, baking soda, cinnamon, nutmeg, cloves and salt. Gradually beat the flour mixture into the egg mixture, alternating with the coffee. Beat in the banana.

4. Pour the batter into a greased 10-inch tube pan or two 9-inch loaf pans. Bake for 45–50 minutes, or until a toothpick inserted in center comes out clean. Let cool on a wire rack for 5 minutes before removing the cake from the pan. Cool thoroughly before slicing.

Yield: 24 servings

—JANE E. BRODY

HONEY-APPLESAUCE CAKE

pareve

⅔ cup vegetable oil plus oil for pan

3 cups flour plus flour for dusting pan

2 teaspoons baking soda

¼ cup warm water

2 cups unsweetened applesauce

1 cup honey

½ cup light brown sugar

2 teaspoons cinnamon

3 tablespoons cocoa

Pinch of salt

1½ cups chopped walnuts

Confectioners' sugar

1. Preheat oven to 300 degrees. Oil and flour a 13-by-9-by-1½-inch backing pan.

2. Dissolve the baking soda in the water and set aside.

3. In a large bowl, mix the applesauce, oil, flour, honey, sugar, cinnamon, cocoa and salt. Stir in the baking soda mixture. Fold in the walnuts.

4. Bake for 1 hour. Cool on a rack. Dust with confectioners' sugar, cut into squares and serve.

Yield: 12–16 squares

—FLORENCE FABRICANT

HONEY-CHOCOLATE LAYER CAKE

dairy

ADAPTED FROM *The Best of Craig Claiborne*

  11 tablespoons butter
  1¾ cups honey
  2 eggs
  ½ cup cocoa
  1 teaspoon vanilla extract
  2½ cups sifted cake flour
  1½ teaspoons baking soda
  ½ teaspoon salt
  1 cup milk
  Honey Frosting (see recipe below)

1. Preheat the oven to 325 degrees.
2. Grease and flour 3 round 9-inch cake tins.
3. Cream the butter until soft. Beat in the honey gradually. Beat in the eggs 1 at a time. Add the vanilla.
4. Sift together the dry ingredients. Add dry ingredients to the egg mixture alternately with milk, beating constantly. Pour the batter into prepared pans and bake for 50 minutes, or until the cakes test done.

5. Turn the cake rounds onto racks to cool. Spread a little frosting between each layer and stack them. Frost the top and sides of the cake and serve cut into wedges.

Yield: 16–24 servings

Honey Frosting

pareve

  1½ cups honey
  2 egg whites
  ⅛ teaspoon salt
  ½ teaspoon vanilla extract
  1 tablespoon cognac

1. Boil the honey over medium heat to the soft-ball stage, 238 degrees on a candy thermometer.
2. Beat the egg whites and salt until stiff. Pour the hot honey into the egg whites in a thin stream, beating constantly. Add the vanilla and cognac. Beat the frosting until it is thick enough to spread.

Yield: Enough for 1 (9-inch, 3-layer) cake

PRIZE ANGEL FOOD CAKE

pareve

ADAPTED FROM *The New York Times Heritage Cookbook*

  1½ cups egg whites (9 large eggs)
  1 teaspoon cream of tartar
  ½ teaspoon salt
  1 cup granulated sugar

  1 teaspoon vanilla
  1 cup confectioners' sugar
  1 cup cake flour

1. Preheat the oven to 375 degrees. Heat a 9-inch angel food pan in the oven 5–10 minutes before using.
2. Beat the egg whites with the cream of tartar and

salt until very stiff. Gradually beat in ¾ cup of granulated sugar until mixture is very smooth and glossy.

3. Beat in the vanilla.

4. Sift together 3 times the confectioners' sugar and flour. Fold with the remaining granulated sugar into the egg white mixture.

5. Turn the batter into the prepared pan. Bake 35 minutes. Cool in the pan turned upside down.

Yield: 10 servings

"FORGET-IT" MERINGUE TORTE

dairy

ADAPTED FROM Molly Chappellet

> *Butter*
> *1½ cup egg whites (9–11 eggs) at room temperature*
> *¼ teaspoon cream of tartar*
> *3 cups plus 1 tablespoon sugar*
> *1 teaspoon vanilla extract*
> *½ teaspoon almond extract*
> *1 cup heavy cream*
> *3 packages frozen raspberries (10 ounces each)*
> *2 tablespoons kirsch, optional*

1. Preheat oven to 425 degrees. Brush the insides and stem of an angel-food cake pan with butter.

2. Add the egg whites to the container of an electric mixer and start beating on medium speed until eggs are frothy. Add the cream of tartar. Continue beating.

3. Gradually add 2½ cups of sugar, beating constantly on high speed. Add the vanilla and almond extracts. Beat until the mixture is very stiff and has a glossy sheen. Spoon and scrape the meringue into the prepared pan, packing and smoothing it down as you go. When all the meringue has been added to the pan, smooth over the top.

4. Place the pan in the oven and turn off the oven. Let the torte stay there overnight. Do not open the door until you are ready to serve the dish.

5. When the torte in the cake pan is removed, it may—and probably will—look like a disaster. Not to worry. It will be frosted with whipped cream. Push up on the removable bottom of the pan.

6. Slide a knife between the bottom of the cake and the bottom of the tin. Loosen the cake around the cylinder with a small knife. Unmold the cake onto a plate.

7. Whip the cream and sweeten it with 1 tablespoon of sugar. Smooth the whipped cream over the top and sides of the cake.

8. Chop the crust to make crumbs. Sprinkle these around the sides and top of the cake, pressing gently to make the crumbs adhere.

9. To prepare a sauce, defrost the raspberries. Put them in a bowl and add the remaining ½ cup of sugar and, if desired, the kirsch. Remove a few of the whole berries for garnish. Serve the cake sliced, with the sauce spooned over or on the side.

Yield: 12 or more servings

NOTE: *This torte, which bakes as it rests in a cooling oven, makes an elegant finish to a celebratory meal. Despite the number of steps, it is easy to prepare with an electric mixer. For a variation, serve with fresh raspberries or sweetened fresh strawberries instead of the raspberry sauce.*

—CRAIG CLAIBORNE

SOUR CREAM COFFEE CAKE

adapted from The New York Times Heritage Cookbook

FOR THE CAKE:

1 ½ cups sour cream
1 ½ teaspoons baking soda
½ cup butter at room temperature plus butter for the pan
1 ½ cups sugar
3 eggs
3 cups flour
1 ½ teaspoons baking powder
1 ½ teaspoons vanilla

FOR THE TOPPING:

½ cup sugar
1 ½ teaspoons cinnamon
⅓ cup chopped pecans or walnuts

1. Preheat oven to 350 degrees. Butter and flour a 9-inch tube pan.

2. To prepare cake, combine the sour cream and baking soda and set aside.

3. Cream the butter and sugar together until light and fluffy. Add eggs, 1 at a time, beating well.

4. Sift flour and baking powder together and add to the batter alternately with the sour cream mixture. Stir in vanilla.

5. Pour into a well-buttered and floured pan.

6. Combine the topping ingredients and sprinkle evenly over the top of the cake.

7. Bake for 1 hour and 10 minutes, or until a cake tester comes out clean. Cool before serving.

Yield: 10–12 servings

LAURA GOODENOUGH'S APPLE COFFEE CAKE

pareve, dairy

6 apples, pared, cored and sliced (3 cups)
5 tablespoons plus 2 cups sugar
5 teaspoons cinnamon
3 cups flour
3 teaspoons baking powder
1 teaspoon salt
1 cup salad oil
4 eggs
¼ cup orange juice
1 tablespoon vanilla extract
Whipped cream, optional

1. Preheat oven to 375 degrees.

2. Combine the apples, 5 tablespoons sugar and cinnamon and set aside.

3. Sift the flour, remaining sugar, baking powder and salt into a bowl. Make a well in the center and pour in the oil, eggs, orange juice and vanilla.

4. Beat with a wooden spoon until well blended.

5. Spoon one-third of the batter into a greased 9-inch or 10-inch angel-food pan. Make a ring of half the apple mixture, drained of excess moisture, on top, taking care not to have the apple mixture touching sides of pan.

6. Spoon another third of the batter over, make a ring of remaining apples and top with remaining batter.

7. Bake 1¼ hours or until done. Cover top with aluminum foil if it begins to overbrown.

8. Allow to cool to lukewarm in pan before turning onto a serving plate. Serve immediately while warm, with whipped cream if desired.

Yield: 8 servings

—JEAN HEWITT

TURKISH YOGURT CAKE WITH FLAVORED SYRUP

dairy

FOR THE CAKE:

3 eggs
1 cup sugar
1 cup whole milk yogurt
1 cup sifted all-purpose flour
1 teaspoon baking powder
1 tablespoon grated lemon rind
Whipped cream
Chopped pistachio nuts

1. Preheat oven to 400 degrees.

2. Beat eggs with sugar until thick and lemon-colored.

3. Sift flour with baking powder. Add yogurt alternately with sifted flour to egg-sugar mixture. Stir in lemon rind and beat until smooth.

4. Pour into buttered and floured 8-inch-square baking pan.

5. Bake 20–30 minutes, or until cake tests clean.

6. While cake is baking, prepare syrup.

7. Cut into diamonds while cake is still warm and in pan. Immediately pour syrup over cake. Cover and set aside until all the syrup has been absorbed. Transfer to a serving dish and chill.

8. Before serving, decorate with whipped cream and chopped pistachio nuts.

Yield: 8 pieces

Syrup

pareve

3 cups water
2½ cups sugar
1 tablespoon lemon juice or 1 tablespoon rose water

1. Mix together the water and sugar and boil gently over low heat about 15 minutes, until syrup has boiled down to about 1 cup.

2. Stir in lemon juice or rose water.

3. Pour hot syrup over warm pastry.

Yield: 1 cup

—JEAN HEWITT

MARBLED POUND CAKE

dairy

ADAPTED FROM *Spago Chocolate*

5½ ounces (11 tablespoons) unsalted butter at room
    temperature, cut in small pieces, plus butter for pan

2 cups all-purpose flour

1 teaspoon baking soda

1 teaspoon baking powder

½ teaspoon salt

1 cup sugar

2 eggs

1 cup buttermilk

1½ teaspoons vanilla extract

½ cup unsweetened cocoa, sifted

½ cup semisweet chocolate chips

4 ounces bittersweet chocolate, in bits

3 tablespoons light corn syrup

2 tablespoons brandy

FOR THE CAKE:

1. Heat oven to 350 degrees. Butter a 9-by-5-by-3-inch loaf pan.

2. Sift flour, baking soda, baking powder and salt together.

3. Beat 4 ounces butter in electric mixer until light. Gradually beat in sugar. Increase speed to high and beat until fluffy. Add eggs, 1 at a time, until just combined. On low speed, add flour mixture alternately with buttermilk, adding vanilla with the last of the buttermilk. End with flour mixture.

4. Transfer two-thirds of batter to buttered pan. Add cocoa to remaining batter, mix to blend well and fold in chocolate chips. Drop chocolate batter over batter in loaf pan and swirl gently with metal spatula or knife to marbleize. Bake until cake tester comes out clean, about 1 hour. Set on rack to cool, then remove from pan.

5. Drizzle glaze over cooled cake and allow to set about 1 hour before cutting.

FOR THE CHOCOLATE GLAZE:

1. To make glaze, combine remaining butter and bittersweet chocolate in small, heavy saucepan over very low heat until not quite fully melted. Remove from heat and stir until chocolate is completely melted. Whisk in corn syrup and brandy.

2. Strain and set aside until ready to use.

Yield: 8–12 servings

NOTE: *The cake can also be made in a 10-inch bundt pan if the batter is doubled. Increase the baking time by 30 minutes.*

—FLORENCE FABRICANT

TOASTED-ALMOND POUND CAKE WITH PAN-ROASTED STRAWBERRIES AND STRAWBERRY-RHUBARB COMPOTE

dairy

ADAPTED FROM Gotham Bar and Grill

1 cup (2 sticks) plus 1 tablespoon unsalted butter

5 large eggs

1¾ cups sugar plus more to taste

1⅓ cups almond flour

1¼ cups cake flour

1 teaspoon grated tangerine zest

2 tablespoons sliced almonds

3 pints strawberries, hulled

4 cups trimmed, sliced rhubarb

1. Preheat oven to 350 degrees. Grease and flour a loaf pan. In a small saucepan, melt butter. Set aside to cool.

2. Using an electric mixer fitted with whisk attachment, beat eggs and 1 cup sugar until thick and pale, about 3 minutes.

3. In a bowl, sift together almond flour, cake flour and zest. Fold one-third of the flour mixture into eggs until thoroughly combined. Fold in rest of flour in 2 batches. Fold in all but 2 tablespoons of the melted butter. Scrape batter into pan and sprinkle almonds on top. Brush remaining butter over almonds.

4. Bake cake until a tester inserted into the middle comes out clean, 40–45 minutes. If the top of the cake seems to be getting overly browned before the center is set, cover with foil and continue baking. Let cool on a rack before inverting.

5. Meanwhile, make the compote. In a medium saucepan, combine 1 pint of the strawberries, the rhubarb, ¾ cup sugar and ¼ cup water. Bring mixture to a simmer and cook, stirring occasionally, until fruit breaks down into a puree. Let mixture cool, then taste and add more sugar if desired.

6. Just before serving, place remaining strawberries in a large skillet and sprinkle with sugar to taste. Cook strawberries over high heat until they release their juices and sugar dissolves. Serve slices of the pound cake surrounded by strawberry-rhubarb compote and topped with strawberries.

Yield: 8 servings

—MELISSA CLARK

NEUE GALERIE'S POPPY-SEED CAKE

dairy

½ pound soft unsalted butter, plus butter for greasing pan

½ cup all-purpose flour, plus flour for pan

¾ cup finely ground blanched almonds

¾ cup dry bread crumbs

1¾ cups poppy seeds (½ pound)

9 eggs, separated and at room temperature

1⅓ cups granulated sugar

1 teaspoon grated lemon zest

2 tablespoons confectioners' sugar

1. Preheat oven to 350 degrees. Butter and flour a 10-inch springform pan. In large bowl, mix ½ cup flour with almonds, bread crumbs and poppy seeds. Set aside.

2. Place ½ pound butter in bowl of electric mixer, and beat at medium-low speed until creamy. Add egg yolks one at a time, beating after each addition. Scrape sides of bowl from time to time. When all yolks have been added, mixture may look slightly curdled. Increase speed to high and beat 2 minutes, or until butter and yolk mixture is very smooth. Set aside.

3. In clean bowl, beat whites on medium speed until softly peaked. Gradually add granulated sugar. When all sugar has been added, continue beating at high speed until whites hold peaks but are still creamy.

4. Fold whites into poppy seed mixture. Fold in yolk mixture. Fold in lemon zest. Transfer batter to pan, smooth top and bake 50 minutes to 1 hour, until cake is golden brown and a cake tester comes out clean. Cool in pan 10 minutes, remove sides of pan and continue cooling.

5. To serve, place confectioners' sugar in small strainer and dust top of cake.

Yield: 8–12 servings

NOTE: *The most important thing about making this cake is to beat the butter and egg yolks very thoroughly and to make sure they're not too cool. They have to be the same temperature and consistency as the whites or you won't be able to fold them in entirely. The cake may also be served with softly whipped cream. It is excellent with coffee or tea or with a glass of dessert wine or champagne.*

Once the butter and yolks are very smooth and satiny, beat the whites with sugar until they're firm but also satiny. Add sugar in either two stages, starting when the whites are foamy, or gradually near the end. Either way is fine. Fold in the beaten whites with the poppy seeds, flour, bread crumbs and ground almonds, then fold in the butter and yolks. A bit of lemon at the end and even a little milk make the mixture lighter.

—KURT GUTENBRUNNER

SESAME-SEED CAKE WITH SESAME-SEED FROSTING

dairy

ADAPTED FROM *The New York Times Menu Cook Book*

1½ tablespoons butter
½ cup untoasted sesame seeds
2 cups sifted all-purpose flour
½ teaspoon salt
2 teaspoons baking powder
1 cup sugar

1½ teaspoons vanilla extract
½ cup butter, softened
2 large eggs
1 cup milk
Sesame-seed Frosting (see recipe below)

1. Preheat oven to 350 degrees.

2. Melt 1½ tablespoons butter in a skillet. Add the sesame seeds. Stir and cook over low heat until

lightly browned. Set ¼ cup of the mixture aside to add to the cake batter. Reserve remaining seeds to top the frosting.

3. Sift together the flour, salt and baking powder and set aside. Gradually blend the sugar and vanilla with the softened ½ cup butter. Beat in the eggs. Mix the ¼ cup toasted sesame seeds with the flour mixture and add alternately with the milk to the butter-sugar mixture. Beat the batter for 30 seconds.

4. Turn the batter into a lightly floured and well-greased 9-inch-square pan. Bake for 35 minutes, or until a cake tester inserted into the center comes out clean. Cool in the pan for 10 minutes. Turn out onto a wire rack to finish cooling. When cold, spread with Sesame-seed Frosting. Sprinkle top with reserved toasted sesame seeds. To serve, cut into squares.

Yield: 12 squares

Sesame-seed Frosting

dairy

> 2 tablespoons butter
> 1½ cups confectioners' sugar
> 2 teaspoons milk, approximately
> ½ teaspoon vanilla extract
> 2 tablespoons toasted sesame seeds from above recipe.

1. Heat the butter until golden. Remove from the heat and blend in the confectioners' sugar, alternating with about 2 teaspoons of milk, adding as much milk as necessary to give the mixture a spreading consistency.

2. Stir in the vanilla and the toasted sesame seeds.

Yield: Enough to frost 1 (9-inch) cake

—STEPHEN KINZER

APPLE STRUDEL

dairy, pareve

ADAPTED FROM Berghoff, Chicago

> 4 large Granny Smith apples, peeled, cored and thinly sliced
> ¾ cup sugar
> ½ cup golden seedless raisins
> ½ cup chopped pecans
> 1 tablespoon ground cinnamon
> ¼ teaspoon salt
> ¼ cup fine dry bread crumbs, more for sprinkling
> 4 (16-by-22-inch) sheets phyllo (see Note, page 583)
> ¾ cup butter or margarine, melted
> Confectioners' sugar

1. In a large bowl, combine apples, sugar, raisins, pecans, cinnamon, salt and bread crumbs. Toss until mixed.

2. Heat oven to 375 degrees. Place 1 sheet phyllo on a work surface, and brush lightly with melted butter or margarine. Sprinkle with a scant tablespoon of bread crumbs. Repeat with remaining sheets of phyllo, stacking them.

3. Spoon apple mixture over phyllo to within 1½ inches of edges. Grasping long edges of phyllo, roll up jellyroll fashion. Carefully place roll on a cookie sheet, seam side down. Brush with remaining melted butter. Bake until golden, about 30 minutes. Allow to cool, then sprinkle lightly with confectioners' sugar.

Yield: 6 to 8 servings

PISTACHIO-PEAR STRUDEL

dairy

6 tablespoons unsalted butter, melted

6 Anjou pears, peeled, cored and cut into large chunks

⅓ cup honey

2 tablespoons sweet sherry

¼ teaspoon ground cinnamon

¼ teaspoon ground cardamom

⅛ teaspoon kosher salt

½ cup golden raisins

1 tablespoon cornstarch

1 tablespoon water

1 teaspoon grated lemon zest

2 teaspoons fresh lemon juice

⅓ cup coarsely chopped pistachios plus 2 tablespoons
    finely chopped

4 tablespoons sugar

4 sheets phyllo dough (see Note, page 583)

Confectioners' sugar, for garnish

1. Combine 2 tablespoons of butter, the pears, honey, sherry, cinnamon, cardamom, salt and raisins in a large saucepan. Cook over medium heat, stirring often, until the pears are soft, about 12 minutes.

2. Combine the cornstarch and water and stir until smooth. Stir into the pear mixture and cook until thickened, about 2 minutes. Place in a bowl and stir in the lemon zest, the lemon juice and the coarsely chopped pistachios. Let cool completely.

3. Preheat the oven to 350 degrees. Combine the finely chopped pistachios and the sugar. Brush a baking sheet with a little melted butter. Place 1 sheet of phyllo on a work surface so the long side is parallel to the edge of the counter, brush lightly with butter and sprinkle with one-fourth of the sugar mixture. Layer with another sheet of phyllo and repeat until you've used up the phyllo and the sugar mixture.

4. Starting 5 inches in from the long edge nearest you, spread the pear mixture down the length of the pastry in a 4-inch-wide mound, leaving a 2-inch border at each end. Fold the short ends in over the filling. Fold the side nearest you over the filling. Flip the strudel over until it's wrapped in all the pastry.

5. Slide the strudel onto the baking sheet seam side down. Cut 4 small diagonal slits in the top of the pastry. Bake until the phyllo is golden brown, about 45 minutes. Let stand until warm but not hot or serve at room temperature. Sift confectioners' sugar over the top. Cut into slices with a serrated knife and serve.

Yield: 6 servings

—MOLLY O'NEILL

POPPY-SEED STRUDEL

dairy

ADAPTED FROM *Cooking with Herbs & Spices*

2 cups ground poppy seeds
½ cup sugar
½ cup white raisins
Pinch of cinnamon
Grated rind of 1 lemon
2 leaves phyllo (see Note, page 583)
Melted butter
Dry bread crumbs

1. Preheat the oven to 400 degrees.
2. Mix together the poppy seeds, sugar, raisins, cinnamon and lemon rind.

3. Place 1 sheet of phyllo unfolded on a damp cloth so the long side is parallel to the edge of the counter, brush lightly with melted butter and sprinkle with bread crumbs.
4. Layer a second sheet of phyllo directly over the first and repeat.
5. Place the poppy seed mixture on one edge of the dough and roll the leaves slowly jelly-roll fashion. Slide the strudel onto a buttered baking pan seam side down and brush the top with butter. Cut small diagonal slits in the top of the pastry to mark portions.
6. Bake the strudel until golden brown, 25–30 minutes. Let stand until warm or at room temperature. Cut into slices with a serrated knife.

Yield: 4–6 servings

DELUXE CHEESECAKE

dairy

ADAPTED FROM *The New York Times Heritage Cookbook*

FOR THE CRUST:

1 cup flour
¼ teaspoon sugar
1 teaspoon grated lemon rind
½ cup butter
1 egg yolk, lightly beaten
¼ teaspoon vanilla

FOR THE FILLING:

5 (8-ounce) packages cream cheese
¼ teaspoon vanilla

1 teaspoon grated lemon rind
1¾ cups sugar
3 tablespoons flour
¼ teaspoon salt
5 eggs
2 egg yolks
¼ cup heavy cream

1. Preheat the oven to 400 degrees.
2. To prepare the crust, combine the flour, sugar and lemon rind. Cut in the butter until mixture is crumbly. Add the egg yolk and vanilla. Mix.
3. Pat one-third of the dough over bottom of a 9-inch springform pan with sides removed. Bake about 6 minutes, or until golden. Cool.

4. Butter the sides of the pan and attach to the bottom. Pat remaining dough around sides to a height of 2 inches.

5. Increase the oven heat to 475 degrees.

6. To prepare filling, beat the cream cheese until fluffy. Add the vanilla and lemon rind.

7. Combine the sugar, flour and salt. Gradually blend into the cheese mixture. Beat in the eggs and egg yolks, I at a time, and the cream. Beat until smooth and creamy.

8. Pour mixture into prepared pan. Bake 8–10 minutes, or until top edge is golden.

9. Reduce the oven heat to 200 degrees. Bake I hour longer, or until set. Turn off oven heat and allow cake to remain 30 minutes in the oven with the door ajar.

10. Cool cake on a rack. Chill before serving. Top with a Strawberry Glaze (recipe below) if desired.

Yield: 8 servings

Strawberry Glaze for Cheesecake

pareve

ADAPTED FROM *The New York Times Heritage Cookbook*

> 2 (1-pound) cartons frozen whole strawberries, thawed
> Cherry juice or water
> 2 tablespoons cornstarch or arrowroot

1. Drain the strawberries very well, reserving the juice. Add the cherry juice or water to it until liquid measures 2 cups. Set berries aside.

2. Slowly mix the cornstarch with the liquid in a small pan. Gradually bring the mixture to a boil, stirring, and cook 2–3 minutes, or until thick and translucent. Cool and chill. Fold in the strawberries.

Yield: 3 cups

ETHEREAL CHEESECAKE

dairy

ADAPTED FROM The Tasting Room

> 1½ cups ground almonds
> 3 tablespoons brown sugar
> ⅓ cup butter, more for pan
> 1½ pounds cream cheese, softened
> 4 egg whites
> 1 cup plus 2 tablespoons sugar
> 1 tablespoon plus ½ teaspoon vanilla
> 1 pint sour cream

1. Heat oven to 350 degrees. In a small bowl, combine almonds and brown sugar. Melt butter, then stir in. Butter bottom and sides of a 9-inch springform pan, then press nut mixture into bottom but not up sides.

2. In a small pan, warm cream cheese over low heat. When very soft, remove from heat and set aside. In a large bowl, whisk egg whites and I cup sugar until they hold soft peaks. Fold in cream cheese and I tablespoon vanilla. Pour into pan, and bake 25–30 minutes, until a toothpick inserted in center comes out only slightly moist; cake should not be brown.

3. Meanwhile, in a small bowl whisk together sour cream, remaining sugar and vanilla. When cake comes out of oven, increase setting to 450 degrees, and carefully spread mixture over cake. Return it to oven for 5 minutes. Do not overcook or it will crack or turn brown. Remove and let cool in pan. Chill in refrigerator. To serve, run a knife along edge of pan and remove sides of pan. Cut into wedges and serve.

Yield: 8 servings

NOTE: *In this unusual variation of cheesecake, the cream cheese mixture is folded into meringue, rather than whole eggs, so that when it is baked it becomes a kind of cream cheese soufflé. At The Tasting Room, the cake is often served with dried apricots poached in a sweet white wine. But the cheesecake is so exceptional that no embellishments are necessary.*

—AMANDA HESSER

POLISH PARISIAN CHEESECAKE

dairy

ADAPTED FROM Henri Finkelsztajn, in *The Jewish Holiday Baker*

FOR THE CRUST:

⅓ cup cold unsalted butter
¼ cup sugar
Dash salt
1⅓ cups all-purpose unbleached flour
2 tablespoons iced water

FOR THE FILLING:

½ cup raisins
½ cup milk
3 packages (7½ ounces each) farmer cheese
½ cup flour
5 eggs, separated
⅔ cup sugar
2 tablespoons lemon juice
Grated rind of 1 lemon
1 teaspoon vanilla
Dash salt
½ cup slivered almonds

1. To make the pie crust, use a food processor fitted with a steel blade to combine the butter and sugar. Then add the salt, flour and then the ice water until a ball is formed, adding more flour if too sticky. Refrigerate for an hour or so.

2. Place the raisins in the milk, and let sit for an hour.

3. Preheat the oven to 350 degrees. Butter a 9-inch springform pan, and press the crust into the sides and bottom.

4. Drain the raisins, reserving the milk. Add the milk to the cheese, flour, egg yolks, sugar, lemon juice and rind, vanilla and salt in a food processor, and mix. Fold in the raisins.

5. Beat the egg whites until stiff peaks form, and fold into the cheese mixture. Pour into the pan, and sprinkle with the almonds. Bake in the center of the oven for 40 minutes or until a toothpick comes out clean when placed in the center. Cool in the pan for about 15 minutes before removing.

Yield: 12 servings

NOTE: *This cheesecake, studded with raisins and topped with almonds, has a lighter texture than most versions because the recipe calls for farmer cheese, rather than cream cheese, and for beaten egg whites.*

—JOAN NATHAN

PASSOVER CHEESECAKE

dairy

ADAPTED FROM *The New York Times Heritage Cookbook*

1 cup matzoh meal

1 teaspoon cinnamon

1¼ cups sugar

¼ cup butter

4 eggs, well beaten

1½ tablespoons lemon juice

⅛ teaspoon salt

1 cup milk

3 cups creamed cottage cheese

2 tablespoons potato starch

2 teaspoons grated lemon rind

1. Preheat the oven to 350 degrees.

2. Combine the matzoh meal, cinnamon, ¼ cup of the sugar and the butter. Press into bottom and sides of ungreased 9-inch springform pan.

3. Gradually beat the remaining sugar into the eggs. Beat in the lemon juice, salt, milk, cottage cheese and potato starch.

4. Stir in the lemon rind and pour into the prepared crust. Bake 1 hour.

5. Shut oven heat off, leave door ajar and let cake cool down to room temperature in the oven. Chill thoroughly. Remove pan sides.

Yield: 10–12 servings

GINGER CHEESECAKE

dairy

ADAPTED FROM The Chelsea Baking Company

FOR THE CRUST:

¾ pound pecans, ground

2 tablespoons brown sugar

1 egg white, beaten until frothy

1 teaspoon ground ginger

1 teaspoon finely grated lemon rind

FOR THE FILLING:

2 pounds cream cheese, softened

¾ cup sugar

4 eggs, lightly beaten

½ cup heavy cream

1 teaspoon vanilla extract

1 cup minced ginger preserves

2 teaspoons ground ginger

1 tablespoon finely grated fresh ginger

1 ounce candied ginger, minced

1. Preheat the oven to 300 degrees.

2. Butter a 9-inch springform pan.

3. To make the crust, in a large bowl, mix all the ingredients. Press the mixture into the bottom and sides of the pan.

4. To make the filling, in a bowl, beat the cream cheese and sugar until the mixture is smooth and light. Add the eggs, cream, vanilla, ginger preserves, ground ginger and fresh ginger and mix well. Pour the filling into the mold.

5. Bake the cheesecake for 1 hour and 40 minutes. Turn off the heat and leave the cheesecake in the oven to cool for 1 hour. Chill.

6. To serve, remove the outside rim from the springform pan. Sprinkle the cheesecake with the candied ginger.

Yield: 12 servings

NOTE: *The cheesecake can be frozen. Defrost before serving.*

—MARIAN BURROS

CHOCOLATE BROWNIE CHEESECAKE

dairy

ADAPTED FROM *Maida Heatter's Book of Great American Desserts*

Butter for greasing cake pan
2 pounds cream cheese at room temperature
1 teaspoon pure vanilla extract
⅛ teaspoon salt, optional
1½ cups sugar
4 large eggs
3 large Maida Heatter's Brownies (see recipe below), frozen or partly frozen
¼ cup graham cracker crumbs, optional

1. Preheat the oven to 350 degrees. Arrange a rack one-third of the way up from the bottom of the oven.

2. Generously butter a round cake pan 8 inches in diameter and 3 inches deep, including the rim.

3. Place the cream cheese in the bowl of an electric mixer and beat until it is uniformly smooth. Scrape the bottom and sides as you mix. Add the vanilla, salt and sugar and beat until it is thoroughly and evenly blended without lumps.

4. Start beating on moderate speed and add the eggs, 1 at a time, beating briefly after each addition. Do not beat more than necessary. Remove the bowl from the mixer.

5. Pour enough of this batter into the prepared pan to make a layer about ½ inch thick.

6. Cut the brownies into ½-inch cubes and fold these into the remaining batter, taking care not to break up or crumble the cold cubes. Pour the batter into the pan and smooth over the top.

7. Place the pan in a larger pan and pour hot water into the larger pan. The water should be about 1½ inches deep.

8. Place the pans in the oven and bake about 1½ hours. The cake will rise about ¼ inch above the rim of the pan while baking. Remove the cake pan from the water and place it on a rack to cool. When it cools, it will sink to the original level. Let stand 2–3 hours. Refrigerate until cold. Unmold. If desired, you may sprinkle the cake with graham-cracker crumbs.

Yield: 10 servings

❖ **MAIDA HEATTER'S BROWNIES** ❖

dairy

Butter for greasing the liner of a pan
1 cup sifted flour
3 tablespoons unsweetened cocoa powder (see Note below)

8 tablespoons unsalted butter

2 squares (2 ounces) unsweetened chocolate

1 teaspoon powdered espresso coffee

½ teaspoon pure vanilla extract

¼ teaspoon almond extract

⅛ teaspoon salt, if desired

1 cup sugar

2 large eggs

1 cup walnuts, broken into quarters

1. Preheat the oven to 350 degrees. Arrange a rack one-third of the way up from the bottom of the oven.

2. Prepare a liner for an 8-inch-square pan. To do this, invert the pan and center a 12-inch square of aluminum foil (shiny side down) over the bottom of the pan. Press down all around to shape the foil to the dimensions of the pan. Carefully remove the foil, turn the pan over and place the foil in the pan. Press all around to make the foil fit the inside of the pan. Butter the inside of the foil. Set aside.

3. Stift together the flour and cocoa. Set aside.

4. Put the 8 tablespoons of butter and the chocolate in a 2½- to 3-quart saucepan. Heat while stirring until the two ingredients are melted and blended.

Add the coffee, vanilla, almond extract and salt. Stir. Add the sugar and stir. Add the eggs, I at a time, beating well after each addition. Add the flour mixture and stir. Add the nuts and blend well.

5. Pour the mixture into the foil-lined pan and smooth over the top. Place in the oven and bake 23–25 minutes until a cake tester or toothpick inserted in the center of the cake comes out clean.

6. Remove the cake to a rack and let cool. Place the pan in the freezer and let stand until the cake is quite firm. Cover with a rack and invert the pan onto the rack. Remove the pan and peel off the foil. Cover with a second rack or a cookie sheet and invert the cake, leaving it right side up.

7. Cut the cake into quarters (or brownies) while it is still totally or partly frozen. Use three-quarters of the brownies in preparing a cheesecake (see recipe page 544). Put the remainder to another use. Keep the brownies to be used in making the cake in the freezer until ready to use.

Yield: 4 large brownies, or
12–16 small brownies

NOTE: *Maida Heatter prefers Dutch-processed cocoa powder.*

—CRAIG CLAIBORNE AND PIERRE FRANEY

BABKA

dairy

ADAPTED FROM *The New York Times*
Large-Type Cookbook

1 package active dry yeast

¼ cup lukewarm milk

¼ cup lukewarm water

¼ cup sugar

¼ cup butter

3 eggs

2½ cups flour

¼ teaspoon salt

¼ cup candied fruits

¼ cup raisins

Rum Glaze, optional (recipe below)

1. Dissolve yeast in milk and water. Add ½ teaspoon sugar, stir and set aside in a warm place.

2. Combine butter, remaining sugar, eggs, flour and salt in a large bowl. When yeast mixture bubbles, beat into flour mixture until smooth. Clean sides of the bowl. Cover with a damp cloth and let rise in a warm place until doubled in bulk, about 1 hour.

3. Stir in fruits and raisins and turn onto a lightly floured board. Knead 1–2 minutes.

4. Put dough in a greased 2-quart mold or bundt pan. Cover; let rise until doubled in bulk, about 45 minutes.

5. Preheat oven to 375 degrees. Bake 35 minutes or until golden brown and done. Remove from pan immediately and, if desired, brush with Rum Glaze.

Rum Glaze

Mix ½ cup sugar with 2 tablespoons water and 2 tablespoons light rum in small saucepan. Bring to a boil and boil briskly 1 minute.

Yield: 6–8 servings

MINA PACHTER'S GESUNDHEITS KUCHEN

dairy

ADAPTED FROM *In Memory's Kitchen*

> 6 large eggs, separated
> 1 cup sugar
> 1 cup unsalted butter, melted and cooled
> ¼ cup ground almonds
> ½ teaspoon almond extract
> 2½ cups sifted all-purpose flour
> 2 teaspoons baking powder
> ½ teaspoon salt
> Grated rind of 1 lemon
> 1 cup milk
> Confectioners' sugar

1. Preheat the oven to 350 degrees. Grease and lightly flour a tube pan.

2. Beat the yolks well. Add the sugar, beating well again. Add the cooled butter, almonds and almond extract and mix well.

3. Fold in the flour, baking powder, salt, lemon rind and milk.

4. Beat the egg whites until stiff but not dry and fold in.

5. Pour into the greased pan and bake for 45 minutes, or until a toothpick inserted into the middle of the cake comes out clean. Cool in the pan for 10 minutes, then turn out and cool completely. Sprinkle the top with confectioners' sugar.

Yield: 8 servings

NOTE: *Originally written in German by women at Terezin (Theresienstadt), the ghetto and concentration camp in what was then Czechoslovakia,* In Memory's Kitchen *is a record of the lives these starving women left behind. Mina Pachter, who died in the camp on Yom Kippur in 1944, entrusted the recipes to a friend who survived the war. The Gesundheits Kuchen, or "good health cakes," traditionally were taken to the mothers of newborn babies.*

—JOAN NATHAN

MRS. DAVIS'S APPLE CAKE

dairy

ADAPTED FROM *The New York Times Large-Type Cookbook*

FOR THE CAKE:

2 cups flour
½ cup sugar
1 tablespoon baking powder
Dash of salt
½ cup soft butter
1 egg

FOR THE FILLING:

5 tart apples
½ cup sugar
Juice of *½* lemon
¼ cup raisins
½ teaspoon cinnamon

1. Sift flour, sugar, baking powder and salt into a mixing bowl. Add butter and egg. Knead until dough is firm and shapes easily into a ball. Wrap in wax paper; refrigerate 1 hour.
2. Meanwhile, peel apples and cut into small pieces. Add sugar, lemon juice, raisins and cinnamon and let mixture steep until dough is ready.
3. Preheat oven to 350 degrees.
4. Butter a 9-inch springform pan. Divide the dough into thirds. Roll out one-third of dough and line bottom of form. Roll out another one-third of dough and line inside of form halfway to top, pressing along bottom rim to seal bottom and sides.
5. Drain fruit mixture and pour into pastry-lined pan. Roll out remaining dough and use a pastry cutter to make long strips. Place strips crisscross on top of filling. Bake until golden brown, 45–55 minutes.

Yield: 6 servings

PASSOVER APPLE CAKE

pareve

ADAPTED FROM *The New York Times Heritage Cookbook*

¾ cup matzoh cake flour
¾ cup potato cake flour
2*⅓* cups sugar
5 eggs, separated
1 cup orange juice
2 tablespoons grated orange rind
½ teaspoon salt

4 apples, peeled, cored and sliced
2 teaspoons cinnamon

1. Preheat oven to 325 degrees. Grease a 13-by-9-by-2-inch baking dish.
2. Sift the matzoh cake flour and potato flour together into a bowl. Add 1½ cups of the sugar. Make a well in the center and drop in the egg yolks. Add the orange juice and orange rind. Beat until smooth.
3. In a separate bowl, beat the egg whites with the

salt until stiff. Gradually beat in ½ cup of the sugar and continue beating until stiff. Fold into batter and turn into greased baking dish.

4. Arrange the apple slices over top. Combine the remaining sugar with the cinnamon and sprinkle over apples. Bake 1 hour, or until done.

Yield: 8–10 servings

APPLE NUT TORTE

pareve, dairy

<small>ADAPTED FROM</small> *The New York Times International Cookbook*

1 egg
¾ cup granulated sugar
½ cup all-purpose flour
1 teaspoon baking powder
½ teaspoon salt
1 cup chopped, peeled, cored apples, preferably on the tart side
½ cup chopped walnuts
1 teaspoon vanilla extract
Sweetened whipped cream, optional

1. Preheat the oven to 350 degrees.

2. Beat the egg with an electric beater until light and lemon-colored. Gradually beat in the sugar.

3. Sift together the flour, baking powder and salt and fold into the egg mixture. Stir in the apples, walnuts and vanilla.

4. Butter the inside of an 8-inch-square pan and pour in the batter. Bake 35–40 minutes. Serve warm, with a sweetened whipped cream at dairy meals, if desired.

Yield: 6 or more servings

GITTA'S APPLE SQUARES

pareve

<small>ADAPTED FROM</small> Gitta Friedenson

FOR THE DOUGH:

½ pound (2 sticks) unsalted margarine
2 large eggs
½ cup sugar
2 cups flour, or more as needed
1 teaspoon baking powder

FOR THE FILLING:

⅔ cup apricot marmalade
½ cup chopped walnuts
5 Granny Smith apples, peeled, cored and thinly sliced
1½ teaspoons cinnamon
4 tablespoons confectioners' sugar

1. Prepare dough: In the bowl of an electric mixer, combine margarine, eggs and sugar. Mix until blended. Add flour and baking powder and mix until smooth. Dough should be very soft but not sticky; if necessary, gradually add up to ½ cup flour. Cover and refrigerate 1 hour.

2. Preheat oven to 350 degrees. Divide dough in two. Lightly oil a 7-by-11-inch glass baking pan. On a lightly floured surface, roll out half the dough to fit into bottom of pan. Spread marmalade evenly over dough in pan. Sprinkle with walnuts. Toss apples with cinnamon, and spread evenly over walnuts.

3. Roll out remaining dough to about 8 by 12 inches, so that it will blanket apples. Place dough in pan, tucking in edges. Bake until surface is golden brown and bottom is light brown, 45 minutes to 1 hour. (If surface browns too quickly, cover with foil.) Remove from oven. Through a sieve, dust 2 tablespoons confectioners' sugar over hot tart. Allow tart to cool.

4. Cut tart into 24 squares. Sprinkle with remaining sugar and serve warm.

Yield: 24 servings

NOTE: *Use a glass dish so you can check how brown the bottom gets. Do not serve it too hot, because it falls apart.*

— ALEX WITCHEL

DATE TORTE

pareve, dairy

ADAPTED FROM *The New York Times International Cookbook*

2 cups sifted dry bread crumbs
½ cup sifted all-purpose flour
Dash of salt
1 teaspoon baking powder
4 eggs, separated
2 cups honey
2 cups chopped, pitted dates
1 cup chopped walnuts
2 teaspoons vanilla extract
Whipped cream, optional

1. Preheat the oven to 375 degrees. Grease a cake pan (13 by 9 by 2 inches).

2. Sift together the bread crumbs, flour, salt, and baking powder. Set aside.

3. Beat the egg yolks lightly. Add the honey and mix thoroughly. Add the dates, walnuts, vanilla and sifted dry ingredients. Mix well.

4. Beat the egg whites until stiff peaks are formed. Fold gently into the batter.

5. Pour into the prepared pan. Bake for 25–30 minutes, until the cake rebounds to the touch when pressed gently in the center. Remove the cake from the oven, cut into squares and serve hot. Whipped cream may be served at dairy meals.

Yield: 18–24 servings

SPICED FIG TORTE

pareve, dairy

ADAPTED FROM *The New York Times International Cookbook*

¾ cup grated blanched almonds

¼ cup candied orange peel, finely minced

¾ cup dried figs, finely minced

½ cup sifted dry white bread or matzoh crumbs

½ teaspoon cinnamon

¼ teaspoon each nutmeg, allspice and cloves

½ teaspoon baking powder

1 tablespoon cognac

5 eggs, separated

1 cup less 2 tablespoons granulated sugar

Confectioners' sugar

Whipped cream, optional

1. Preheat oven to 325 degrees. Grease the bottom of a 9-inch springform pan.

2. Mix the almonds, peel, figs and crumbs. Mix the spices and baking powder and add to the almond mixture. Add the cognac and mix with the fingers.

3. Beat the egg yolks until foamy. Gradually add the sugar and beat until thick. Add the almond mixture and mix well.

4. Beat the egg whites until stiff but not dry. Fold into the batter until no white shows.

5. Turn the batter into the prepared pan and bake 1 hour. Invert the pan on a rack, cool and remove the sides of the pan. Sprinkle the top of the cake with confectioners' sugar. Serve with whipped cream, at dairy meals, if desired.

Yield: 12 servings

PASSOVER CARROT-ALMOND CAKE

pareve

Cooking oil

2 tablespoons matzoh meal

6 eggs, separated

⅔ cup plus 1 tablespoon sugar

⅓ cup honey

1 tablespoon lemon juice

2 cups finely grated carrots

1½ cups finely ground almonds

½ cup Passover cake meal

Pinch of salt

1 teaspoon cinnamon

1. Preheat oven to 350 degrees. Heavily oil an 8-cup tube pan or bundt pan. Dust with matzoh meal.

2. Beat egg yolks until thick. Add ⅔ cup sugar and continue beating until pale yellow and very creamy. Beat in the honey. Stir in the lemon juice.

3. Fold in the carrots and almonds.

4. Mix cake meal with salt and cinnamon and mix into batter until just combined.

5. Beat egg whites until they hold peaks but are not dry. Gently fold beaten egg whites into the batter. Transfer batter to the baking pan and bake 1 hour and 15 minutes, until nicely browned and springy to the touch.

6. Place on a rack and allow to cool completely in the pan. Run a knife or a thin spatula around the edges to loosen the cake, then invert onto a serving plate. Dust with a tablespoon of granulated sugar before serving.

Yield: 8–12 servings

—FLORENCE FABRICANT

ORANGE ALMOND CAKE

pareve, dairy

¾ cup fresh orange juice
3 tablespoons grated orange rind
1 tablespoon orange flower water
1 cup finely ground dried homemade bread crumbs
1 cup finely ground almonds
2 eggs, separated
¾ cup sugar
½ teaspoon salt
2 egg whites
2 teaspoons unsalted margarine or unsalted butter
Confectioners' sugar or whipped cream, for garnish

1. Preheat the oven to 350 degrees. In a large bowl, combine the orange juice, orange rind, orange flower water, ¾ cup of the bread crumbs and the almonds.

2. In a separate bowl, beat the egg yolks with ¼ cup of the sugar and the salt and gently fold into the orange juice mixture.

3. In another bowl, beat the 4 egg whites with the remaining sugar until they form stiff peaks, then fold into the orange juice mixture.

4. Lightly grease an 8-by-8-inch square cake pan with the margarine or butter and dust it with the remaining bread crumbs. Pour in the cake batter and bake until done, about 40–60 minutes. Set aside to cool. Serve sprinkled with powdered sugar or with a dollop of whipped cream.

Yield: 6 servings

NOTE: *If serving at a meat meal, use margarine and omit whipped-cream garnish.*

—MOLLY O'NEILL

PRUNE TORTE

dairy

ADAPTED FROM *The New York Times International Cookbook*

1½ cups cooked prunes, drained
1 cup brown sugar, packed
½ cup granulated sugar
¾ cup butter
3 eggs
⅓ cup milk
2½ cups sifted all-purpose flour
2 teaspoons baking powder
½ teaspoon salt
½ teaspoon soda
1 teaspoon cinnamon
1 cup coarsely chopped walnuts
Whipped cream

1. Preheat oven to 375 degrees.

2. Pit the prunes and cut into small pieces.

3. Cream the sugars and butter together thoroughly. Blend in the eggs and milk.

4. Sift together the flour, baking powder, salt, soda and cinnamon. Blend into the creamed mixture. Stir in the prunes and walnuts. Spread the mixture in the bottoms of 2 greased 9-inch layer cake pans.

5. Bake 30 minutes and cool.

6. Put the layers together with whipped cream and spread cream over the top. Cut into wedges and serve.

Yield: 10–12 servings

LINZER TORTE

dairy

ADAPTED FROM Richard Stoltzman

1 cup flour
2 tablespoons cocoa
½ teaspoon cinnamon
¼ teaspoon ground cloves
½ pound salted butter, softened
½ cup plus 1 tablespoon sugar
2 egg yolks
2 cups ground almonds
1 cup raspberry preserves
1 egg white

1 tablespoon water
Confectioners' sugar

1. Mix the flour, cocoa, cinnamon and cloves together in a bowl and set aside.

2. Cream the butter and beat in the ½ cup sugar. Beat in the egg yolks. Gradually blend in the almonds and the flour mixture to make a thick batter.

3. Using about half the batter, spread an even layer, ⅛–¼ inch thick, in the bottom of an 8- or 9-inch round baking pan with a removable bottom. Spread the jam over the batter to within ½ inch of the edge, taking care not to break the layer of batter.

4. Spoon the remaining batter into a pastry bag fitted with a large tube, ½ inch in diameter. Pipe 3–5 parallel lines of batter straight across the layer of jam from one edge to the other. Give the pan a quarter turn and pipe 3–5 more parallel lines across the pastry from edge to edge. Pipe the remaining batter around the edge. Any excess batter can be used to form round cookies on a baking sheet. Fill with jam and bake.

5. Refrigerate for 1 hour.

6. Preheat the oven to 300 degrees.

7. Beat the egg white with the remaining sugar and the water until frothy. Brush this mixture over the pastry strips and the edge. Place the linzer torte in the oven and bake for 1 hour. Allow to cool completely.

8. Before serving, sift confectioners' sugar over the top. Remove the sides of the pan and serve.

Yield: 8 servings

—FLORENCE FABRICANT

SACHER TORTE

dairy

ADAPTED FROM Joyce Goldstein

FOR THE TORTE:

> 8 egg yolks
> 10 egg whites
> ⅛ teaspoon salt
> ¾ cup sugar
> 7 ounces semisweet chocolate
> 1 stick (½ cup) unsalted butter
> 1 teaspoon vanilla extract
> 1 cup flour

FOR THE FILLING:

> *Apricot preserves*

1. Preheat oven to 350 degrees. Grease the bottom of three 9-inch or 10-inch pans (foil pans are good). Line the bottoms with waxed paper and grease the paper.

2. When separating the eggs, reserve 2 extra yolks

for the frosting. Add salt to egg whites and beat until peaks just begin to firm. Add the sugar a little at a time, beating constantly. Beat a few more minutes till stiff and glossy.

3. Meanwhile, melt the chocolate and butter over hot water. Cool a little and add vanilla. Then add this to the yolks, stirring with a wire whisk. It will be thick.

4. Add a third of the whites to the chocolate mixture and stir well. Pour onto the remaining whites and sift in flour. Fold altogether with whisk, being careful not to overmix but not leaving any white lumps showing.

5. Pour into pans and bake for 25–30 minutes. Turn onto rack and peel off the paper.

6. Prepare Chocolate Frosting (recipe below).

7. When cake is cool, spread apricot preserves between layers and spread frosting over the cake, smoothing sides with spatula. Chill well. Serve cake at almost room temperature.

Yield: 12–16 servings

◆ CHOCOLATE FROSTING ◆

dairy

3 ounces unsweetened chocolate

1 cup heavy cream

1 tablespoon corn syrup

1 cup sugar

2 egg yolks

1 teaspoon vanilla extract

1. Combine chocolate, cream, corn syrup and sugar in a small heavy pan and heat, stirring until sugar is dissolved and the chocolate is melted. Raise heat to medium and cook to 224–226 degrees Fahrenheit on a candy thermometer (soft ball).

2. Using a small wire whisk, beat the hot mixture into the egg yolks. Cool and stir in vanilla.

Yield: Enough to frost 3 (9- or 10-inch) layers

—MOIRA HODGSON

FRESH GINGER CAKE

pareve

ADAPTED FROM *Room for Dessert*

1 cup mild molasses

1 cup sugar

1 cup peanut oil

2½ cups flour

1 teaspoon ground cinnamon

½ teaspoon ground cloves

½ teaspoon ground black pepper

2 teaspoons baking soda

4 ounces fresh ginger, peeled, sliced and finely chopped

2 eggs at room temperature

1. Position rack in center of oven. Preheat to 350 degrees. Line a 9-inch round cake pan with 3-inch sides, or a 9½-inch springform pan, with a circle of fine parchment paper.

2. Mix together the molasses, sugar and oil. In another bowl, sift together flour, cinnamon, cloves and black pepper.

3. In a small saucepan, bring 1 cup water to a boil. Stir in baking soda, then mix hot water into molasses mixture. Stir in ginger.

4. Gradually whisk the dry ingredients into batter. Add eggs and continue mixing until everything is thoroughly combined. Pour the batter into prepared cake pan and bake for about 1 hour, until top of cake springs back lightly when pressed or until a toothpick inserted into center comes out clean. If the top of cake browns too quickly before cake is done, drape a piece of foil over it and continue baking.

5. Cool cake for at least 30 minutes. Run a knife around edge of cake to loosen it from pan. Invert cake onto a cooling rack and peel off parchment paper.

Yield: 10 servings

—AMANDA HESSER

LEMON CHIFFON CAKE

pareve

ADAPTED FROM *The New York Times Menu Cook Book*

2 cups sifted cake flour

1½ cups sugar

3 teaspoons baking powder

1 teaspoon salt

½ cup vegetable oil (not olive)

5 egg yolks

2 tablespoons grated lemon rind

¼ cup lemon juice

½ cup water

½ teaspoon cream of tartar

1 cup egg whites

1. Preheat oven to 325 degrees.

2. Sift together the flour, sugar, baking powder and salt.

3. Make a well in the center of the dry ingredients and add the oil, egg yolks, lemon rind, juice and water. Beat with a wooden spoon until very smooth.

4. Add cream of tartar to egg whites; beat until stiff. Gently fold egg-yolk mixture into the egg whites.

5. Turn into an ungreased 10-inch pan. Bake for 55 minutes; increase heat to 350 degrees and bake for about 10 minutes longer. Invert pan on rack to cool.

Yield: 12 servings

ORANGE AND OLIVE OIL CAKE

dairy, pareve

1 teaspoon butter or unsalted margarine for pan

1½ cups flour plus flour for pan

½ teaspoon baking powder

¼ teaspoon baking soda

Pinch of salt

2 eggs

1¾ cup sugar

Grated zest and juice of 2 oranges
    (⅔ cup juice)

⅔ cup extra-virgin olive oil

Confectioners' sugar

Orange sorbet

1. Preheat oven to 375 degrees. Grease and flour a 10-inch springform pan.

2. Whisk flour with baking powder, baking soda and salt and set aside. Beat eggs, then gradually beat in sugar and continue beating until thick. Mix orange zest, juice and olive oil together. Add to egg mixture in thirds, alternating and ending with flour mixture.

3. Spread batter in pan and bake about 50 minutes, until cake tester comes out clean. Cool on rack 15 minutes and remove sides of pan. Continue cooling, then dust with confectioners' sugar and serve with orange sorbet.

Yield: 8 servings

—FLORENCE FABRICANT

WARM HONEYED PEAR CAKE

dairy

   7 tablespoons unsalted butter

   4–5 ripe pears, peeled, cored and sliced fairly
     thick

   2 tablespoons fresh lemon juice

   1⅓ cups flour

   ¼ cup sugar

   2 teaspoons baking powder

   Pinch of salt

   1 egg

   ½ cup milk

   ½ cup honey, warmed

1. Preheat oven to 350 degrees. Butter a 10-inch springform pan, using about ½ tablespoon of butter.
2. Toss the pears with the lemon juice and set aside.
3. Sift the flour with 3 tablespoons of the sugar, the baking powder and salt into a bowl. Cut in 5 tablespoons of the butter until the mixture resembles coarse meal. (This step may be done in a food processor, first blending the dry ingredients, then pulsing in the butter.)
4. Beat the egg and the milk together and lightly stir into the butter-and-flour mixture until a soft, sticky dough forms.
5. Spread the dough in the baking pan and sprinkle with the remaining tablespoon of sugar. Arrange the pears on top and drizzle with about a ⅓ cup of the honey. Dot with remaining butter.
6. Bake 50 minutes to an hour, until nicely browned.
7. Remove from the oven and serve while still warm, first removing the sides of the pan and drizzling the top with the remaining honey.

Yield: 6–8 servings

—FLORENCE FABRICANT

PRUNE LAYER CAKE

dairy

ADAPTED FROM *The New York Times Heritage Cookbook*

FOR THE CAKE LAYERS:

   1 cup granulated sugar

   10 tablespoons butter

   3 eggs

   3 tablespoons sour cream

   2 cups flour

   ½ teaspoon nutmeg

   1 teaspoon cinnamon

   1 teaspoon baking soda

   2 cups cooked, drained, pitted and quartered
     prunes

FOR THE FILLING:

   1 cup sour cream

   1 cup granulated sugar

   5 egg yolks

   ½ cup chopped walnuts

FOR THE ICING:

¾ cup light brown sugar

¼ cup butter

6 tablespoons heavy cream

1½ cups confectioners' sugar

1. Preheat the oven to 350 degrees

2. To prepare cake layers, cream the sugar and butter together until very light and fluffy. Beat in the eggs, 1 at a time, very well. Stir in the sour cream.

3. Sift together the flour, nutmeg, cinnamon and baking soda and fold in the batter. Fold in the prunes and turn into 2 greased and floured 9-inch layer pans. Bake about 35 minutes, or until done.

Cool in the pans 10 minutes before turning onto a rack to finish cooling.

4. To prepare filling, place the sour cream, granulated sugar and egg yolks in the top of a double broiler and heat, but do not boil, over hot water, stirring occasionally, until mixture thickens. Do this slowly. It takes about 20 minutes. When thickened, stir in the walnuts. Cool and chill.

5. To prepare icing, place the brown sugar, butter and cream in a small saucepan and bring to a rolling boil. Remove from the heat and stir in the confectioners' sugar.

6. Spread the filling between the layers and frost.

Yield: 10 servings

MARY JURIK'S SLOVAK PRUNE
AND APRICOT UPSIDE-DOWN CAKE

dairy

ADAPTED FROM *The New York Times Heritage Cookbook*

½ pound pitted prunes

½ pound dried apricots

¼ cup soft butter

½ cup light brown sugar

½ teaspoon grated lemon rind

5 tablespoons unsalted margarine or shortening

⅔ cup granulated sugar

1 egg

2¼ cups flour

4 teaspoons baking powder

½ teaspoon salt

1 cup milk

Whipped cream, optional

1. Preheat the oven to 350 degrees.

2. Cover the prunes and apricots with water and simmer gently until tender, about 20 minutes. Cool. Drain, halve the prunes. Drain the apricots.

3. Cream the butter and brown sugar together until smooth. Stir in the lemon rind and spread mixture in the bottom of a greased 8 inch-square pan.

4. Arrange the apricots and prune halves slightly overlapping in neat rows on top of the butter-sugar mixture.

5. Cream the margarine or shortening and granulated sugar together. Beat in the egg. Sift the flour with the baking powder and salt and add alternately with the milk to the creamed mixture.

6. Spoon the batter carefully over the fruit and bake 50 minutes, or until done. Turn upside down onto a warm plate and serve, if desired, with whipped cream.

Yield: 8 servings

ISABELLE D'ORNANO'S BULGARIAN CHOCOLATE CAKE

dairy

6 ounces best-quality bittersweet chocolate (preferably
  Lindt or Tobler brand)
6 ounces milk chocolate
¾ cup sugar
¾ cup butter, cut into tablespoons, at room
  temperature
5 eggs, separated
2 tablespoons cake flour
Whipped cream, optional

1. Preheat the oven to 350 degrees.
2. Break the two types of chocolate into bite-size pieces. Melt the chocolate in a large saucepan over very low heat, or on top of a double boiler.
3. When the chocolate is melted, stir in the sugar and the butter. Remove from the heat and add the egg yolks to the mixture.

4. Beat the egg whites until they become frothy and white. Sprinkle the flour over them and beat until stiff but not dry.
5. Add one-third of the egg-white mixture to the batter and mix thoroughly. Then gently fold in remaining whites. Do not overmix, but be sure the mixture is well blended.
6. Butter a large, 8-inch springform pan and fill with the batter. Bake for 35–40 minutes, or until the top of the cake is firm and springy.
7. Cool before unmolding. The cake is best served a day or two after baking. Refrigerate until about 1 hour before serving. Serve with sweetened whipped cream, if desired.

Yield: 8–10 servings

—PATRICIA WELLS

ORANGE-CHOCOLATE DACQUOISE

dairy

FOR THE MERINGUE LAYERS:

6 extra-large egg whites (1 scant cup), at room
  temperature
Pinch of cream of tartar
½ cup sugar
1⅓ cups (6 ounces) ground almonds

FOR THE CHOCOLATE-DIPPED ORANGES:

1 navel orange
3 ounces imported bittersweet chocolate
1 teaspoon vegetable oil

FOR THE ORANGE-CHOCOLATE BUTTERCREAM:

6 extra-large egg whites (1 scant cup), at room
  temperature
1½ cups superfine sugar (or processed regular
  sugar)

1 pound unsalted butter, cut into pieces, at room
temperature

6 ounces imported bittersweet chocolate plus chocolate
left over from dipping the orange pieces

1 tablespoon water

1 tablespoon orange extract

Zest of 1 orange, minced

2 tablespoons orange liqueur

½ teaspoon salt

1. To make the meringue layers, preheat the oven to 250 degrees. Generously butter and flour 2 cookie sheets. Shake extra flour from sheets. Trace 3 circles about 8 inches in diameter on them.

2. Place egg whites in a large bowl, add cream of tartar and beat until soft peaks form. Gradually add ¼ cup sugar and beat until egg whites are stiff. Add another ¼ cup sugar to the ground almonds and, reserving ⅓ cup of the mixture, fold the rest into the egg whites.

3. Fill a pastry bag fitted with a plain (No. 3) tip with the egg-white mixture and pipe circles following the patterns on the cookie sheets, working from the outside toward the center. Smooth any missed spaces with a spatula. Pipe or spoon extra mixture in dollops on cookie sheets.

4. Bake the meringues in the middle of the oven, rotating for even cooking, for 55–75 minutes, until firm to the touch and lightly colored. Remove from the oven and run a long, thin-bladed knife or spatula carefully under the meringues. If they are not firm, return to oven and check again in 5-minute increments. Once firm, transfer them to cake racks. They will become crisper when cooled.

5. For the orange segments, remove and mince the orange zest. Set aside. Remove as much pith as possible and carefully separate the fruit into segments without breaking the membranes.

6. Melt the chocolate in a double boiler and stir in the vegetable oil. Allow the mixture to cool slightly, then dip each orange segment halfway into the chocolate, letting extra chocolate drip back into the pan. Place the segments on wax paper to harden. Once hardened, cover lightly with plastic wrap and refrigerate until needed.

7. To prepare the buttercream, place egg whites in a large metal mixing bowl and set over (not touching) boiling water. Using a wire whisk, beat, while gradually adding sugar, until the mixture is slightly thickened and reaches 105 degrees on an instant-read or candy thermometer.

8. Immediately remove bowl from the heat and begin beating the mixture with an electric mixer. Continue to beat while gradually adding pieces of butter. Beat until the mixture reaches room temperature and thickens to the consistency of stiff filling, about 10–15 minutes. (The buttercream will look ugly and you will think that it won't come together. Keep beating. It will!)

9. Meanwhile, add the 6 ounces of chocolate and tablespoon of water to the double boiler used for the garnish. Let it all melt, then add the orange extract, zest, orange liqueur and salt and stir to blend. Stir in ½ cup of the buttercream and beat until chocolate is smooth. Scrape the mixture into the bowl of buttercream and mix well. Refrigerate for 10–20 minutes.

10. To assemble the dacquoise, save the best meringue for the top. Put a small amount of buttercream in the center of a dessert plate, or a cardboard circle on a turntable, and place a meringue over it. Spread a generous quarter of the filling over this, making it a little thicker toward the outside.

11. Gently place the second meringue on top, pushing down lightly, and spread another fourth of the filling. Add the final meringue layer and cover the top and sides of the dacquoise with another fourth of the buttercream.

12. Crumble the reserved pieces of meringue and combine them with the sugar-nut mixture. Pat this around the sides of the dacquoise. Arrange the chocolate-dipped orange segments on top like spokes of a wheel and pipe the remaining buttercream through a pastry bag fitted with a star tip, making rosettes on the outside edge. Refrigerate, uncovered, until an hour before serving.

Yield: 8–12 servings

NOTE: *In dry weather, the meringues may be made the night before and left out in a cool, dry spot. If it is humid, do not attempt this.*

—JOANNA PRUESS

FLOURLESS CHOCOLATE CAKE WITH ORANGES

dairy

½ cup orange juice

1⅓ cups sugar

6 ounces unsweetened chocolate

6 ounces bittersweet chocolate

9 tablespoons butter at room temperature

5 eggs

8 navel oranges

¼ cup orange liqueur

Confectioners' sugar

1. Preheat the oven to 325 degrees. Butter an 11-by-17-inch baking sheet with ½-inch sides, line with parchment paper and butter the paper.

2. Bring the orange juice to a boil in a medium-size saucepan and add 1 cup of the sugar. Remove from the heat. Break up the chocolate and add it, stirring until the chocolate has melted and the mixture is smooth. Add the softened butter a little at a time, stir well and set aside.

3. Beat the eggs with the remaining sugar for 12 minutes, until very thick and light. Gently fold a third of the eggs into the chocolate mixture. Fold in the rest.

4. Spread the batter into the prepared pan and bake until set, about 15 minutes. The surface of the cake will have dulled somewhat and have become firmer to the touch. Allow to cool completely in the pan.

5. Meanwhile, remove all the skin and pith from the oranges, separate the sections and toss with the liqueur. Refrigerate.

6. Run a knife around the edge of the cake in the pan. Place a large flat baking sheet over the cooled cake, invert, then lift off the baking pan. Peel the parchment paper off the cake.

7. To serve, preheat the oven to 150 degrees. Cut large squares of the cake and, using a wide spatula, place each on an ovenproof plate. Place in the oven to warm for about 5 minutes. Arrange the orange sections and a little of their syrup in a decorative pattern on the cake or around it, sift a little confectioners' sugar over the top and serve.

Yield: 6–8 servings

—FLORENCE FABRICANT

BESSIE FEFFER'S SEVEN-LAYER CAKE FOR PASSOVER

dairy, pareve

ADAPTED FROM *The New York Times Passover Cookbook*

½ pound fine-quality semisweet chocolate, Elite
    brand, if possible
1 tablespoon unsalted butter or pareve margarine
8 ounces orange marmalade
2 large eggs
2 tablespoons brandy
1 cup white wine, semisweet
8 matzohs, preferably round
Chopped walnuts

1. In the top of a double boiler, melt the chocolate, butter or margarine and the marmalade over simmering water.

2. Add the eggs and beat with a wire whisk until the mixture is as thick as sour cream. Add the brandy and remove the pan from the heat.

3. Continue beating until the mixture again attains the consistency of sour cream.

4. Pour the wine into a large, shallow dish. Dip the matzohs, 1 at a time, in the wine just to moisten but not to soak. Place the moistened matzoh on a cake plate and coat with a layer of the chocolate mixture. Top with another moistened matzoh and more chocolate until all are used. Use the remaining chocolate to frost the sides. Decorate with nuts and let set at room temperature. Cut with a serrated knife.

Yield: 6–8 servings

—JEAN HEWITT

CHOCOLATE-AND-ALMOND CAKE • (TORTA DI MANDORLE E CIOCCOLATA)

pareve

ADAPTED FROM *The Book of Jewish Food*

1½ cups blanched almonds, sliced
7 ounces unsweetened chocolate
1¼ cups granulated sugar
2 tablespoons margarine
3 tablespoons matzo meal
7 large egg whites

1. Preheat the oven to 350 degrees. In a food processor, combine the almonds and chocolate and process until finely ground. Add the sugar and continue

to process until fully incorporated. Transfer to a bowl and set aside.

2. Grease a 9-inch springform pan and dust with matzo meal. Using an electric mixer, beat the egg whites until stiff. In three batches, fold the egg whites into the chocolate mixture. Scrape the mixture into the springform pan. Place the pan in the oven and bake until a toothpick inserted in the center of the cake comes out clean, about 45 minutes.

3. Remove from the oven and set aside to cool. Slice and serve at room temperature.

Yield: 8 servings

—MOLLY O'NEILL

BITTERSWEET CHOCOLATE DACQUOISE
WITH HALVAH CREAM

dairy

FOR THE COCOA MERINGUE:

1½ cups confectioners' sugar, more to dust
  cake
⅓ cup plus 1 tablespoon unsweetened cocoa
  powder
6 large egg whites
⅛ teaspoon cream of tartar
¾ cup plus 2 tablespoons sugar

FOR THE BITTERSWEET CHOCOLATE GANACHE:

4 ounces bittersweet chocolate, chopped
1 cup heavy cream

FOR THE HALVAH CREAM:

2 cups milk
½ cup tahini (sesame paste)
7 tablespoons honey
⅓ cup cornstarch
2 large egg yolks
1½ cups crumbled halvah
1½ cups heavy cream

1. For the meringue, preheat oven to 250 degrees. Line 2 baking sheets with parchment paper; use a marker to trace three 8-inch circles onto paper. Turn paper marked side down.
2. In a large bowl, sift together confectioners' sugar and cocoa powder; set aside. In the bowl of an electric mixer, whip egg whites until foamy. Add the cream of tartar and a tablespoon of the granulated sugar; whip until soft peaks form. With mixer run-

ning, gradually pour in rest of granulated sugar and whip until very stiff peaks form. Fold a third of the egg whites into the sugar and cocoa mixture. Fold in remaining whites.
3. Transfer mixture to a pastry bag fitted with a large plain tip or to a large resealable plastic bag with a corner cut off. Starting just within the circles marked on parchment paper, pipe rounds of batter, working inward in a spiral. Bake for 2 hours, then turn off oven; allow meringue to dry in oven until oven has cooled completely, at least 4 hours longer.
4. For ganache, place chocolate in a bowl. In a saucepan, bring cream to a boil. Pour it over chocolate and let sit for 3 minutes. Starting in center, whisk well to combine. Refrigerate, covered, until thickened but still pourable, 1–2 hours.
5. For halvah cream, pour milk into a saucepan and bring to a simmer. Meanwhile, in a large heatproof bowl, whisk together tahini, honey, cornstarch and egg yolks. Pour a little bit of hot milk into tahini mixture, whisking constantly. Continue to whisk, and add rest of milk to bowl. Pour mixture back into saucepan and bring to a boil, whisking constantly. Boil, whisking, for 2–3 minutes until very thick. Transfer to a bowl, and whisk in half of crumbled halvah. Cover bowl with plastic wrap, and refrigerate until chilled, at least 1 hour.
6. Whip heavy cream just until it is thick enough to hold soft peaks. Gently fold cream and the remaining crumbled halvah into chilled tahini mixture.
7. To assemble, set aside nicest meringue disk for top layer. Place 1 meringue layer in an 8-inch springform pan. Spread half of halvah cream over

meringue. Place another round of meringue over cream. Pour ganache onto meringue in an even layer. Spread ganache with remaining halvah cream. Top with last round of meringue. Freeze for 1–2 hours.

8. Before serving, run a knife around edge of pan, then unmold dacquoise. Sift a thin layer of powdered sugar over top. To slice, use a serrated knife dipped in hot water. Wipe dry between cuts.

Yield: 8 servings

—BILL YOSSES

WARM CHOCOLATE CAKES WITH COFFEE CREAM

dairy

ADAPTED FROM Da Fiori restaurant, Venice

FOR THE COFFEE CREAM:

1¾ cups strong black coffee
1¾ cups whole milk
1 vanilla bean
8 large egg yolks
1 cup minus 2 tablespoons sugar
1½ cups cake flour

FOR THE CAKES:

9 tablespoons unsalted butter plus more for greasing
3 tablespoons cake flour plus more for dusting
11 ounces bittersweet chocolate, chopped
3 tablespoons dark rum
½ cup sugar
6 large eggs, separated
Powdered sugar for dusting the cakes

1. To make the coffee cream, in a large saucepan, combine the coffee and milk and bring just to a boil. Remove from heat, add the vanilla, cover and cool for 15 minutes. Meanwhile, in a large bowl, whisk together the yolks and sugar until thick and light-colored. Whisk in the flour. Remove and discard the vanilla bean and very slowly whisk the hot milk and coffee into the flour mixture.

2. Return the mixture to the saucepan and cook over medium heat, stirring constantly, until the custard thickens and coats the back of a spoon, about 15 minutes. Immediately remove from heat and strain through a fine-mesh sieve.

3. To make the cakes, preheat the oven to 400 degrees. Butter and flour ten ⅔-cup ceramic ramekins.

4. In the top of a double boiler set over barely simmering water, combine the chocolate, butter and rum and cook, stirring, until the chocolate melts and the mixture is completely smooth. Set aside. In a large bowl, combine the sugar and egg yolks and whisk until thick and light-colored. In the bowl of an electric mixer, beat the egg whites until stiff but not dry. Gently fold the egg whites into the yolk mixture. Fold in the chocolate and then the flour. Spoon the mixture into the ramekins, filling each two-thirds full. Bake until the cakes have risen and the tops just begin to crack, about 10–15 minutes. (The centers will still be slightly gooey.)

5. Remove the cakes from the oven and immediately

unmold them by inverting them onto dessert plates (run a thin-bladed knife around the edges of the ramekins if they stick). If necessary, rewarm cream in the top of a double boiler set over simmering water. Sprinkle the cakes with powdered sugar and spoon coffee cream around them.

Yield: 10 servings

—MOLLY O'NEILL

CHOCOLATE BLACK PEPPER CAKE

dairy

6 tablespoons unsalted butter plus more for pan

10 ounces best-quality bittersweet chocolate, chopped

¼ cup sugar

¼ cup honey

½ teaspoon kosher salt

5 eggs, separated

½ cup ground almonds

⅓ cup flour

2 teaspoons coarsely ground black pepper

½ teaspoon allspice

¼ teaspoon cinnamon

Pinch cayenne pepper

Pinch salt

Powdered sugar, for sprinkling

Unsweetened whipped cream, for garnish

1. Preheat oven to 375 degrees. Butter a 9-inch springform pan. In a double boiler, melt butter and chocolate, stirring constantly, just until chocolate is melted. Remove from heat. Stir in sugar, honey and salt, then egg yolks. Transfer to a large mixing bowl. Whisk in the ground almonds, flour, black pepper, allspice, cinnamon and cayenne, just until combined. Do not overmix.

2. In a large bowl, whisk egg whites with a pinch of salt until they hold stiff peaks. Using a rubber spatula, fold three-fourths of the egg whites into chocolate mixture. Pour chocolate mixture into remaining egg whites and fold gently, just until there are no clumps of egg white. Pour into prepared pan. Bake until firm and springy, 30–35 minutes.

3. Remove cake from oven; cool completely on a baking rack. Remove sides from pan, sprinkle lightly with powdered sugar and serve slices with whipped cream.

Yield: 8 servings

—AMANDA HESSER

MOCHA CAKE WITH RAISINS

pareve

<small>ADAPTED FROM</small> *The New York Times Menu Cook Book*

2 cups strong coffee

2 cups granulated sugar

2 tablespoons cocoa

1 cup seedless raisins, cut up

½ cup shortening

½ teaspoon vanilla extract

2 eggs

2 cups sifted all-purpose flour

½ teaspoon salt

2 teaspoons baking powder

½ teaspoon baking soda

1 teaspoon ground cinnamon

1 teaspoon ground nutmeg

½ teaspoon ground cloves

Confectioners' sugar

Grease for pan

1. Preheat oven to 350 degrees.

2. Combine the coffee, 1 cup granulated sugar, the cocoa and raisins in a saucepan. Bring to a boil and simmer for 10–15 minutes. Cool.

3. Cream the shortening and add remaining granulated sugar, gradually creaming until light and fluffy. Add vanilla. Add eggs separately, beating well after each addition.

4. Mix and sift the remaining ingredients, except the confectioners' sugar and stir in. Spoon into a greased and floured 10-by-10-by-2-inch pan. Bake for 1 hour. Remove from oven and cool to room temperature.

5. When cake is cool, place paper doily on top. Sift confectioners' sugar onto doily. Lift doily off carefully. Or sprinkle confectioners' sugar through a fine-mesh strainer over top of cake. Cut cake into squares to serve.

Yield: 8–10 servings

BELLE'S HEIRLOOM MOCHA PUDDING-CAKE

dairy

¼ cup white sugar

1 cup sifted all-purpose flour

2 teaspoons baking powder

⅛ teaspoon salt

1 square unsweetened chocolate

2 tablespoons unsalted butter

½ cup milk

1 teaspoon vanilla extract

½ cup white sugar

½ cup dark brown sugar

4 tablespoons cocoa

1 cup cold double-strength coffee

1. Preheat the oven to 350 degrees.

2. Mix and sift together the first 4 ingredients.

3. In the top of a double boiler, melt chocolate and butter together over hot, but not boiling, water. Add to the flour mixture and blend well.

4. Combine milk and vanilla, add to flour mixture and blend well. Pour the batter into a greased 9-inch-square pan.

5. Combine the brown and white sugars with the cocoa. Sprinkle the mixture over the batter.

6. Pour cold coffee slowly over the sugar-cocoa mixture, covering it uniformly.

7. Bake for 40 minutes and remove from oven.

Spoon portions out and serve warm or cold. Top with ice cream or whipped cream, if desired.

Yield: 6 servings

NOTE: *The sugar-cocoa-coffee mixture settles at the bottom of the pan during baking, forming a rich mocha sauce.*

—JEAN HEWITT

ALMOND CAKE

dairy

½ pound butter

⅓ cup sugar

6 ounces almond paste

3 eggs

¼ teaspoon orange-flower water

¼ cup flour

⅓ teaspoon baking powder

1 cup apricot preserves for glaze, approximately

1. Preheat oven to 350 degrees.

2. Grease and flour a 3- to 4-cup mold suitable for baking.

3. Using an electric mixer, cream butter, sugar and almond paste together until light. Add eggs and

orange-flower water and beat on high speed for 2–3 minutes. Add the flour and baking powder and mix only until combined. Do not overmix.

4. Bake for 30–40 minutes, or until cake tester comes out clean from the center.

5. Cool for 15 minutes in the pan and turn out while still slightly warm.

6. Heat the apricot preserves until boiling. Strain the preserves and brush the clear glaze over the top and sides of the cake. Let the cake absorb the glaze, then brush it again. This cake freezes well and will keep for at least 5 days if wrapped tightly and stored in a cool place.

Yield: 6–8 servings

—MOIRA HODGSON

SOAKED NUT CAKE · (TISH PISHTI)

pareve

ADAPTED FROM *Light Jewish Holiday Desserts*

FOR THE CAKE:

1 cup sliced almonds
¾ cup matzo meal
1 cup granulated sugar
1 teaspoon grated orange zest
2 teaspoons ground cinnamon
4 large whole eggs
6 large egg whites

FOR THE ORANGE SOAKING SYRUP:

3 cups orange juice
¼ cups granulated sugar

FOR THE GARNISH:

3 tablespoons sliced almonds

1. To make the cake, preheat the oven to 350 degrees. In a food processor, combine ¾ cup of the almonds with the matzo meal, ½ cup of the sugar, zest and cinnamon and pulse until the nuts are ground. Add the whole eggs to the food processor and continue to pulse until they are fully incorporated. Carefully transfer the almond mixture to a large bowl and stir in the remaining ¼ cup almonds.

2. Using an electric mixer, beat the egg whites and the remaining ½ cup sugar until they are stiff. Set aside.

3. Fold the egg whites into the almond mixture until just combined. Scrape the batter into a greased 9-by-13-inch baking pan, place in the oven and bake until a toothpick inserted in the center of the cake comes out clean, about 25 minutes.

4. Meanwhile, make the syrup. In a medium saucepan over high heat, combine the orange juice and sugar and bring the mixture to a boil. (The sugar will dissolve.) Set aside.

5. Remove the cake from the oven, turn it out onto a cutting board and cut into 24 squares. Return the squares to the pan. Pour one-half of the syrup over the cake squares and set them aside to soak for 10 minutes. Turn the squares over and pour over the remaining syrup. Garnish each square with 3 almond slices to form a Y-shaped pattern. Cover the squares and set aside at room temperature to soak for 3 hours. Serve at room temperature.

Yield: 24 cake squares

—MOLLY O'NEILL

MANDELTORTE WITH LEMON FILLING

pareve

ADAPTED FROM *The New York Times Cookbook*

6 eggs, separated

1 cup sugar, sifted

3 tablespoons lemon juice

1 teaspoon grated lemon peel

½ teaspoon almond extract

1 teaspoon cinnamon

1 cup blanched, grated almonds
 (about ½ pound)

½ cup fine dry bread or matzoh
 crumbs

½ teaspoon salt

Lemon Filling (see recipe below)

1. Preheat oven to 350 degrees.

2. Grease two 8-inch layer pans. Line the bottoms with waxed paper and grease the paper.

3. Beat the egg yolks until light. Gradually add the sugar and continue to beat until creamy. Beat in the lemon juice, peel, almond extract and cinnamon. Thoroughly fold in the almonds and crumbs.

4. Beat the egg whites and salt together until stiff but not dry. Fold into the batter until no egg white shows.

5. Pour the batter into the prepared pans and bake until the top is firm to the touch about 40 minutes.

6. Invert the pans on a rack, cool and then remove the cakes. When thoroughly cool, remove the paper and layer the cakes together with lemon filling. Frost with any desired white icing and decorate with whole almonds.

Lemon Filling

pareve

2½ tablespoons lemon juice

6 tablespoons orange juice

⅓ cup water

½ cup sugar

2 tablespoons flour

⅛ teaspoon salt

3 egg yolks

½ teaspoon grated lemon rind

Combine the ingredients in the top of a double boiler. Cook, stirring, over simmering water until thick. Cool.

Yield: 12 servings

MARZIPAN CAKE

dairy

ADAPTED FROM *The New York Times International Cookbook*

2 whole eggs
3 egg yolks
¼ cup almond paste
2 tablespoons milk
½ teaspoon vanilla extract
1 cup sifted all-purpose flour
1 teaspoon baking powder
¼ teaspoon salt
1 cup granulated sugar
⅓ cup melted butter
Frosting

1. Place the eggs and egg yolks in the bowl of an electric mixer and stand the bowl in warm water.
2. Preheat the oven to 350 degrees. Grease a 9-by-9-by-1¾-inch baking pan.

3. Blend the almond paste with the milk and vanilla. Sift together the flour, baking powder and salt.
4. Remove the bowl with the eggs from the water and beat the eggs on moderately high speed, adding the sugar gradually, until the mixture stands in stiff peaks. Add about ½ cup to the almond paste mixture, then add this mixture to the rest of the eggs and blend.
5. Fold in the dry ingredients, one-quarter at a time. Cool the butter, add it to the batter and fold in lightly and quickly. Turn the batter into the prepared pan.
6. Bake for 30–35 minutes, or until the cake begins to shrink from sides of pan and rebounds when touched gently in the center.
7. Frost with a standard vanilla butter frosting.

Yield: 9–12 servings

HAZELNUT ROLL

dairy

8 eggs, separated
1½ cups sugar
1 teaspoon vanilla extract or 1 tablespoon rum
1 tablespoon sugar
1½ cups unblanched hazelnuts, shelled and coarsely grated
Butter, for pan
Flour, for pan

Confectioners' sugar
2 cups heavy sweet cream
2 teaspoons rum or 1 teaspoon vanilla to taste
2 teaspoons quick-dissolving sugar, or to taste

1. Preheat oven to 350 degrees.
2. Beat yolks with 1½ cups sugar and vanilla or rum until mixture is pale yellow and thick enough to form a ribbon when poured from a spoon.
3. Beat egg whites and as they begin to thicken add 1 tablespoon sugar; beat until whites stand in stiff

but glossy peaks. Turn into a large wide bowl unless they are already in one.

4. Stir 2–3 tablespoons of the beaten whites into the yolk mixture. Pour yolk mixture over whites and sprinkle with grated nuts. Using a rubber spatula, fold mixtures together gently but thoroughly. There should be no trace of whites or nuts showing.

5. Spread onto an 11-inch-by-16-inch jelly-roll pan covered with a buttered and floured sheet of paper. Bake about 1 hour, or until cake springs back when you press it down with your finger. Cool in pan.

6. Cover with a slightly damp towel and chill for several hours or overnight.

7. Place 2 large overlapping pieces of wax paper (the seam should run lengthwise on a pastry board) and sprinkle with confectioners' sugar. Turn cake over onto sugar and peel off wax paper carefully.

8. Whip cream until stiff, flavoring with rum or vanilla and sugar.

9. Spread with whipped cream flavored with vanilla or rum. Roll cake gently, jelly-roll style, using the wax paper to lift it. Wrap paper snugly around roll and chill 1–2 hours before serving.

10. Sprinkle more sugar on top of roll before lifting it onto serving board or platter.

Yield: About 8 servings

NOTE: *Mousse Au Chocolat (page 456) is an excellent alternative to whipped cream.*

—MIMI SHERATON

MARCELLA HAZAN'S WALNUT CAKE

dairy

ADAPTED FROM *Essentials of Classic Italian Cooking*

7 *tablespoons butter at room temperature plus more*
  for greasing pan
1 *cup flour*
½ *pound walnuts*
⅔ *cup sugar*
1 *egg*
2 *tablespoons rum*
Grated zest of 1½ lemons
1½ *teaspoons baking powder*

1. Place a rack in the upper third of the oven and preheat to 325 degrees. Butter and flour an 8-inch springform pan. Spread the walnuts on a baking sheet and place in the middle of the oven. After 5 minutes, take the walnuts out of the oven and increase the heat to 350 degrees. Let walnuts cool completely.

2. Place the walnuts in a food processor with 1 tablespoon sugar and grind, using the pulse button, to fine granules but not to powder. Pour into a bowl and reserve.

3. Place the butter in the processor with the remaining sugar and process until creamy. Add the egg, rum, lemon zest and baking powder and pulse until mixture is uniform. Transfer to a mixing bowl.

4. Fold the ground walnuts into the butter mixture with a spatula. Sift the flour in small amounts over the batter and fold together. When all the flour is incorporated, pour the batter into the cake pan, leveling it off with the spatula.

5. Bake in the upper third of the oven. After 45 minutes, test the center of the cake with a toothpick. If it comes out dry, the cake is done. If not, bake roughly 10 minutes longer. Remove from the oven and remove the sides of the pan. After cake has cooled somewhat, invert it onto a plate and carefully lift off pan base.

Invert once more onto a serving plate. The cake's flavor improves the next day. It may be served with unsweetened whipped cream, but it's delicious alone.

Yield: 8 servings

—AMANDA HESSER

ITALIAN PASSOVER WALNUT CAKE • (TORTA DI NOCI PER PESACH)

pareve

ADAPTED FROM *The Classic Dolci of the Italian Jews*

2 tablespoons margarine
3 tablespoons matzo meal
6 large eggs, separated
⅛ teaspoon salt
1½ cups granulated sugar
2½ cups coarsely ground walnuts
½ teaspoon orange zest
1 teaspoon honey
½ teaspoon vanilla extract
½ teaspoon ground cinnamon
¼ teaspoon ground cloves
Sugar for sprinkling

1. Preheat the oven to 325 degrees. Grease a 10-inch springform pan with the margarine, dust with the matzo meal and shake out any excess.

2. Using an electric mixer, beat the egg whites and salt until they are stiff. Transfer to a bowl and set aside.

3. In a large mixing bowl, whisk the egg yolks and sugar vigorously until the mixture is thick and lemon-colored. Then mix in the walnuts, zest, honey, vanilla, cinnamon and cloves until fully incorporated. In 3 batches, fold the egg whites into the nut mixture.

4. Scrape the batter into the springform pan and bake until a toothpick inserted in the center of the cake comes out clean, about 1 hour.

5. Remove the cake from the oven and set aside to cool. Unmold the cake and transfer to a cake platter. Sprinkle with sugar. Slice and serve.

Yield: 8 servings

—MOLLY O'NEILL

CONFECTIONS AND NUTS

◆ ◆

CANDIED ORANGE PEEL

pareve

3 navel oranges, unblemished
1½ cup sugar
2 whole cloves

1. With a channel knife, make long continuous strips of orange peel. Place them in a saucepan filled with water and bring it to a boil. Simmer for 10 minutes.
2. Pour the peels into a strainer, then fill the saucepan with water and repeat ther blanching process another 2 times. Place ½ cup of water in the saucepan along with 1¼ cups of sugar, the cloves and peels.
3. Bring all to a boil, then simmer and let the peels cook for 2 minutes. Remove the peels with a slotted spoon and make a single layer on a sheet of wax paper or aluminum foil. Let the peels cool and air-dry them for several hours.
4. Toss the candied peels with the remaining sugar, just to coat them. (If you roll them in the sugar while they are still warm, the sugar will crystallize and coat them with too much sugar.) Keep any extra peel to serve with coffee or store in an airtight container.

Yield: 2 cups

NOTE: *If you don't have a channel knife, just cut the fruit in half and scoop out the pulp and membrance. Then slice the peel into thin ¼-inch strips and begin the cooking process. Grapefruit and limes may also be candied in this method.*

— RENA COYLE

NOUGAT

pareve

ADAPTED FROM *The New York Times International Cookbook*

2½ cup shelled almonds
½ cup pistachios
1 cup sugar
½ cup water
3 tablespoons light corn syrup

½ teaspoon salt
2 egg whites at room temperature
½ cup honey
1 teaspoon vanilla extract

1. Blanch the almonds and, while soft, cut lengthwise into slivers. Brown lightly in a 350-degree oven, stirring often.

2. Blanch the pistachios and let dry by spreading out on paper towels. (To blanch the nuts, cover with boiling water, let stand 5 minutes, drain and slip off the skins.)

3. In a 1-quart saucepan combine the sugar, water, half the corn syrup and the salt. Cook together, stirring, until the sugar dissolves. Cook to 290 degrees (syrup forms a brittle ball in cold water). Remove from the heat.

4. In a large bowl, beat the egg whites until stiff but not dry. Add the cooked syrup gradually, while beating.

5. Boil together the honey and remaining corn syrup to 290 degrees. Add gradually, while beating, to the egg-white mixture. Add the almonds and pistachios.

6. Stand the bowl of mixture on a rack in a pan of boiling water and steam, stirring occasionally, until a spoonful of the candy, cooled, is not sticky to the touch, or about 1½ hours. Add the vanilla.

7. Line an 11-by-7-inch pan with parchment paper, turn the nougat into the pan and cover with wafer paper. Place a pan of the same size on top of the candy and press with a heavy weight. Let stand overnight or longer.

8. Turn the candy out of the pan and cut into 1½-by-½-inch bars. Wrap immediately in freezer wrap or waxed paper. Store in a covered tin box in a cool place.

Yield: About 1¾ pounds

GINGER BRITTLE

pareve, dairy

¾ *cup sugar*
¾ *cup finely chopped crystalized ginger*
Butter or shortening for greasing pan

1. Pour the sugar into a small, heavy saucepan set over medium heat. Watch the pan constantly throughout the entire cooking process. When the sugar begins to melt, stir occasionally with a fork.

2. Add the ginger and cook, stirring occasionally, until all the sugar is melted (the crystalized ginger will not melt) and the mixture is a deep amber color.

3. Immediately remove from the heat and pour the mixture onto a buttered or greased sheet pan. Let cool and harden, about 30 minutes. Chop the brittle coarsely with a large knife. Eat plain, or serve over ice cream.

Yield: About 1 cup

—MOLLY O'NEILL

SESAME SEED BRITTLE

pareve, dairy

ADAPTED FROM *Cooking with Herbs & Spices*

1½ *cups sugar*
½ *cup honey*
2 *tablespoons water*
1 *teaspoon lemon juice*
¼ *teaspoon cinnamon*
1 *cup (⅓ pound) sesame seeds*
Butter or shortening for greasing pan

1. Cook the sugar, honey, water and lemon juice in a saucepan over low heat, stirring constantly, until the sugar is dissolved.

2. Continue cooking over low heat, without stirring, until the mixture reaches 300 degrees on a candy thermometer (a brittle, hard thread will form when a few drops are tested in cold water), about 20 minutes.

3. Remove from the heat and stir in the cinnamon and sesame seeds. Pour the brittle in a thin layer onto a buttered or greased cookie sheet. Loosen with a knife blade before the candy hardens. When cold, break the brittle into pieces.

Yield: About 1½ pounds

HALVAH

pareve

ADAPTED FROM *From My Grandmother's Kitchen: A Sephardic Cookbook*

2 *cups sugar*
1 *cup water*
1¾ *cups sesame paste (tahini)*
1 *teaspoon pure vanilla extract*
2 *egg whites*
1 *cup shelled pistachios, preferably unsalted*

1. Combine the sugar and water in a saucepan and bring to a boil. Cook to the hard-ball stage (a few drops of the syrup, when dropped into a small basin of cold water, will form a firm ball that will not flatten on removal) or to a temperature of 234 degrees. Set aside.

2. Put the sesame paste with its oil in the container of an electric mixer. Add the vanilla and blend thoroughly.

3. Beat the egg whites until they are stiff and fold them into the sesame paste. When thoroughly blended, gradually add ¾ cup of the syrup, stirring. When completely blended fold in the nuts and the remaining syrup.

4. Pour and scrape the mixture into a loaf pan. Smooth over the top. Cover closely and refrigerate 3 days before unmolding. This halvah will keep for 6 months in the refrigerator.

Yield: 1 loaf

—CRAIG CLAIBORNE

EGGPLANT HALVAH

dairy

Juice of 1½ lemons
1 cup sugar
1½ cups water
1 large eggplant, about 2 pounds
¼ pound salted butter
1 teaspoon ground (preferably freshly pounded)
 cardamom
½ cup pistachios (or walnuts)
Clotted Cream (see recipe below)

1. Put the lemon juice in a large bowl.
2. Boil the sugar with 1 cup of water and set aside.
3. Peel the eggplant, cut it into dice and toss the pieces in the bowl with the lemon juice.
4. Melt the butter in a deep saucepan, empty the bowl into the saucepan, add ½ cup water and cook over medium heat, covered, stirring frequently, until the eggplant is soft (about 20 minutes). Add a little more water if it threatens to brown.
5. Mash the eggplant as thoroughly as possible in the pot, add the sugar syrup and cook, uncovered, stirring constantly, until it has the consistency of very thick oatmeal. Remove from the heat and stir in the cardamom.

6. Sprinkle the pistachios over the bottom of a 9-by-9-inch-deep baking dish, add the eggplant and, when cool, top with clotted cream. Refrigerate thoroughly, (at least 6 hours), divide into squares and serve.

Yield: 9 servings

◆ CLOTTED CREAM ◆

dairy

1 pint heavy cream
1 tablespoon sugar
⅛ teaspoon salt

1. Put the cream in a heavy saucepan, place it over high heat and boil it down by half, stirring frequently. (To make measuring easy, put a pencil mark on a wooden spoon handle to show the depth when you began. Then check the progress every 4 minutes or so.)
2. When it is reduced, add the sugar and salt, stir well, cool a little and pour over the eggplant mixture.

Yield: 1 cup

—ROBERT FARRAR CAPON

HONEY BALLS · (TEIGLACH)

pareve

<small>ADAPTED FROM</small> *From My Mother's Kitchen*

3 eggs, lightly beaten

3 tablespoons vegetable oil, preferably peanut

2–2½ cups flour, as needed

¼ teaspoon salt

1 scant teaspoon baking powder

3 pounds dark honey

1½ cups sugar

2 teaspoons powdered ginger

2 teaspoons lemon juice

Grated rind of 1 orange

2 cups coarsely chopped walnuts or hazelnuts

1. Preheat the oven to 375 degrees. Grease a shallow jelly-roll pan with vegetable oil.

2. Combine the eggs and oil. Sift together 2 cups flour with the salt and baking powder. Mix the eggs and oil and dry ingredients together, adding enough flour to give you a dough that is soft and workable but one that will not stick to your hands. Knead the dough several times on a lightly floured board until it is smooth and supple. Let rest, lightly covered, for 10 minutes.

3. Working with convenient amounts of dough, form long, thin rolls about ⅓ inch in diameter. Twist the rolls to form a rope effect. Cut into pieces ⅓–½ inch in length. Arrange pieces in a single layer on the oiled pan and bake for about 20–25 minutes, or until the teiglach turn a rich golden brown.

4. When the teiglach are brown, boil the honey with the sugar and ginger for 10 minutes, using a heavy saucepan so it does not burn. Add the baked teiglach and the lemon juice, orange rind and nuts; mix well.

5. Pour teiglach and honey onto a marble slab or a board that has been wet with cold water and shape into a single cake or into balls about 2½ inches in diameter.

Yield: About 5 dozen teiglach

<small>NOTE:</small> *If you prefer teiglach that remain softer in a more gooey syrup, do not shape them into a cake or into balls. Instead, pour the teiglach-nut-honey mixture from saucepan into wide jars and keep covered. When ready to serve, spoon teiglach and syrup onto plates as a small dessert.*

—MIMI SHERATON

VICKY NAHMAD'S EGYPTIAN MATZOH CONFECTION

pareve

FOR THE SUGAR SYRUP:

1¼ cups water
1 cup sugar
Few drops lemon juice
1 teaspoon cinnamon

Simmer the water, sugar and lemon for 10 minutes;
add cinnamon and cool.

FOR THE MATZOHS:

8 sheets plain matzoh
3 eggs
1 cup vegetable oil
Sugar and cinnamon mixture, optional

1. Break each matzoh into 6 equal pieces. If matzoh
crumbles, put a damp cloth on it to soften.
2. Heat oil in pan.
3. Beat eggs thoroughly; dip matzoh into eggs and
fry in hot oil until golden brown. Drain on paper
towels.
4. Dip hot matzohs in cold syrup and sprinkle, if
desired, with a mixture of sugar and cinnamon.

Yield: 48 pieces

NOTE: *Matzoh served in a sweetened syrup is an elaborate
version of the Ashkenazic matzoh brei.*

—MARIAN BURROS

CHOCOLATE-ALMOND TRUFFLES

pareve

ADAPTED FROM *Kosher Cuisine*

1 cup shelled almonds, unblanched
¼ pound imported unsweetened semisweet chocolate,
    broken into small pieces
2 egg yolks at room temperature
½ cup sugar
1¼ tablespoons imported dark rum
1 egg white at room temperature
3 tablespoons imported unsweetened cocoa powder

1. Preheat oven to 350 degrees.
2. Put almonds in baking dish in one layer. Place in

oven and bake 10 minutes or until nicely roasted. Let
cool. Put almonds and chocolate in food processor
and process with steel blade until coarsely chopped.
3. Add egg yolks, sugar and rum and blend until
mixture is medium-fine and moist enough to shape.
If mixture is too dry and does not hold together,
add a teaspoon of egg white and process again.
4. Scoop up 1 teaspoon of the mixture and roll
between palms into marble-size balls. After each is
rolled, dip it into cocoa until coated.

Yield: About 4 dozen

—CRAIG CLAIBORNE

SPICED AND ROASTED HAZELNUTS

pareve

ADAPTED FROM The Heathman Hotel

2 pounds skinned hazelnuts

¼ cup honey

1 teaspoon chili powder

1 teaspoon freshly ground white pepper

1 tablespoon salt

1. Preheat oven to 350 degrees. Put the hazelnuts on a cookie sheet and roast until they are golden, 10 minutes. Put them in a large glass or ceramic bowl and reserve the baking sheet.

2. Meanwhile, put the honey, chili powder and white pepper in a heavy-bottom skillet and stir to combine. Heat the spice mixture over medium heat until it begins to liquefy, about 2 minutes.

3. Drizzle the spice mixture over the nuts. Add the salt and stir until all the nuts are well coated. Spread the coated nuts on the cookie sheet and roast them in the oven for another 10 minutes, until they begin to darken slightly. Take the tray out of the oven and stir until cool, 30 minutes. Store in airtight containers.

Yield: 6–8 cups

—MOLLY O'NEILL

GINGERED ALMONDS

pareve

1 tablespoon kosher salt

4 tablespoons finely chopped ginger

2 tablespoons coriander seeds, coarsely ground with a mortar and pestle

1 teaspoon freshly ground black pepper

2 egg whites

1 tablespoon honey

5 bay leaves

5 cups almonds, skin on

1. Preheat oven to 300 degrees. Line 2 baking sheets with parchment paper. In a small bowl combine salt, ginger, coriander and pepper. Set aside. In a large bowl, whisk egg whites until frothy. Whisk in honey, then spices. Using a rubber spatula, fold in bay leaves and almonds.

2. Spread almond mixture in a single layer on baking sheets. Bake, stirring nuts and rotating baking sheets once or twice, until almonds are dry and crisp. Remove bay leaves. Serve immediately or spread out on baking racks covered with parchment to cool. Keep in an airtight container for up to a week.

Yield: 5 cups

—AMANDA HESSER

AFTERWORD

◆

A Glimpse of the Past

In a "Food and the Public Health" column on February 23, 1896, *The New York Times* published an article entitled "The Shoket, and Kosher and Trefa Dishes—Where to Buy Meats," which was probably the first lengthy discussion of Jewish food preparation and religious practices to appear in the pages of the paper. The perspective of the author, Juliet Corson, while thoroughly cordial to "the wonderful Hebrew Scripture," reflects the intellectual atmosphere of the late nineteenth century, when many Christian scholars generally believed that the dietary laws of the Torah were borrowed from other cultures, a view no longer widely held.

Although the article may seem like a quaint curiosity to contemporary readers, the proposed dinner menu that followed the main text—perhaps surprisingly—could still be served today, although only if modified to conform to the laws of kashruth, with which the writer was apparently unfamiliar. Because the combining of dairy and meat ingredients is prohibited, butter may not be used in preparation of the roast chicken, and a pareve product must be used in place of the dairy ingredients in the recipes for biscuits, potato salad, spinach and cake if they are to be served at a meal with poultry or meat. In the lemon tart recipe, a pareve fat should be substituted for suet. In addition, foods prepared in advance may be served warm on Saturday only if they have been placed on a *blech* (a metal plate that separates the heat from the container) and kept on a heat source that has been maintained prior to the start of Shabbos on Friday evening. That would preclude most soups and gravies, because of the evaporation from such lengthy contact with heat. However, fresh fruits and nuts may be prepared on the Sabbath, because they do not require cooking.

With these caveats in mind, below are the recipes as they appeared in *The Times* of

1896, preceded by Juliet Corson's introductory sentence. We hope you will agree that they provide a fascinating glimpse into a bygone moment of *Times* food coverage.

—LINDA AMSTER

As our Christian readers may like to try some genuine Hebrew cookery, we give a seasonable menu, which is both economical and savory:

Frimsel Soup.

Brown   Stew,   with   Quenelles.

Cold Roast fowl.   Salad of Potatoes.

Spinach, rewarmed.

Biscuits, Apples, Oranges, Raisins, Nuts, Wine.

FRIMSEL SOUP.—Make this soup on Friday. Put into a saucepan five pounds of beef brisket, a knuckle of veal, four quarts of water, one root each of parsley and celery, with the leaves attached, one onion, and a teaspoonful of mixed ginger, mace, saffron, and pepper, tied in a bit of cloth; boil for three hours slowly, skimming off any scum that may rise; take up the meat, strain the soup, and put it in a earthen pot to stand over night. Just before dinner the next day take off all the fat, put it in a saucepan over the fire, add four ounces of frimsels or vermicelli, and boil it up; serve it as soon as the vermicelli is tender.

BROWN STEW WITH QUENELLES.—Cut one pound of veal and three pounds of beef in small pieces and fry them with an onion sliced; then add one quart of cold water, season the stew with pepper, salt, ginger, mace, and a tablespoonful of mushroom catsup; thicken with a tablespoonful of flour, and add a tablespoonful of vinegar; make some little balls of finely chopped cold meat or poultry, highly seasoned and boiled with an egg; drop them into the stew, and let it cook slowly for about three-quarters of an hour until the meat is quite tender. Cook this stew on Friday and warm it on the Sabbath.

COLD ROAST FOWL.—Put a koshered chicken into the dripping pan, dust it with flour, ginger, and salt pour over a little salad oil or melted butter, and baste it frequently while roasting. When it is nearly done take it out of the oven, remove all the fat, put a little water in the pan, baste the chicken with it, and cook it ten minutes longer. If you want to stuff the chicken, use the following forcemeat: Mix half a pound of bread crumbs, a tablespoonful of chopped parsley, a teaspoonful of mixed thyme, marjoram, pepper, and ginger, a teaspoonful of salt, a little cayenne, and one egg; some persons like the addition of a little chopped onion. The chicken must be cooked on Friday, and used cold for the Sabbath day, with hot gravy.

SALAD OF POTATOES.—Slice some cold boiled potatoes; mix them with a tablespoonful each of chopped parsley and onion, and serve them with the following dressing: Mix one tablespoonful of cream, two of oil, one teaspoonful each of salt and mustard, and three table-spoonfuls of vinegar: stir until smooth, and use.

SPINACH, REWARMED.—Pick four quarts of spinach, wash it in six waters, put it into a saucepan with a tablespoonful of salt, and cook it, uncovered, until tender; drain and chop it; add to it two tablespoon-fuls of flour, one onion chopped, one ounce of butter, and season it with salt, pepper, and nutmeg. The next day add a pint of gravy to it, and warm it over the fire.

BISCUITS.—Warm two ounces of butter in three-quarters of a pint of milk; mix it with a pound of flour, and beat it with a rolling pin for five minutes; knead it very smooth, roll it out thin, cut it in small rounds, prick each with a fork several times, and bake in a moderate oven until brown, about six minutes. The fruit and nuts for dessert are of course to be prepared on Friday, and have only to be set upon the table at the proper time. The extra recipes for sweets will prove acceptable for the children's dinner and for plain desserts. The butter cakes are excellent for luncheons and teas.

STEWED APPLES.—Pare two dozen small apples; take out the cores without breaking them, putting each one into cold water as soon as it is done; when all are ready, weigh them, and to each pound of apples allow half a pound of white sugar; make this into a syrup, using a pint of cold water to each half-pound of sugar, and skimming the syrup until it boils; then add the rind of one lemon grated and the apples, and stew them until they are clear, but do not break them. Take them up on a dish, strain the syrup over them, and use them cold. Any other fruit in season may be stewed in the same way.

BUTTER CAKES.—Mix together one pound of brown sugar, one pound of butter, two eggs, one lemon rind, grated, one ounce of cinnamon, two ounces of rice flour or corn starch, and a pound and a half of wheat flour; make a stiff paste, roll out thin, cut out with a biscuit cut-ter, and bake in a hot oven for about ten minutes.

LEMON TARTS.—Line a deep pie plate with good pastry, making a rim at the edges; fill it with the following ingredients—the grated rind and juice of two lemons, two ounces each of blanched and pounded almonds, chopped suet, and grated bread crumbs, four ounces of fine sugar, and six eggs, the whites and yolks of which have been beaten separately; bake the tart about half an hour in a quick oven.

—JULIET CORSON.
Founder of the New York Cooking School.

EXPLANATORY NOTES

ADVISORY NOTE: COOKING WITH ANCHOVIES AND WITH WORCESTERSHIRE SAUCE

According to the Shulchan Aruch (the Jewish Code of Law), fish and meat may neither be cooked together nor eaten together with the same utensils. Fish and meat courses may be served at the same meal, however, as long as separate plates and utensils are used for the separate courses. To further separate the courses at a meal where meat is served, observant Jews traditionally eat bread or drink something between the soup, fish, meat and salad courses. Because Worcestershire sauce contains anchovies, it may not be used in a course where meat is served. But it may be consumed at another course of the meal, as long as the strictures are observed. In the few meat recipes where Worcestershire sauce was an ingredient, I followed the guidance of Gilda Angel, using an equal amount of tamari to approximate the savory character of Worcestershire sauce. That substitution is noted below the recipe.

BLANCHING AND TOASTING NUTS

To blanch nuts: Blanching removes the skin from shelled nuts. To blanch nuts, plunge the shelled nuts into boiling water for 1 minute (or pour boiling water over nuts and let stand for a few minutes).

Drain and transfer to a clean towel, wrapping the towel around the nuts. Then rub gently and the skin will slip off. For hazelnuts, which have a tougher skin,

add 1 tablespoon baking soda for every cup of water that you use for blanching. You can also remove the skins from shelled hazelnuts, walnuts, peanuts and pistachios by toasting.

To toast nuts: Place shelled nuts in a single layer in a dry skillet and cook, shaking pan often, over medium-low heat until nuts are fragrant and slightly browned, 2–3 minutes. Remove from heat and stir until nuts cool slightly. Or spread on baking sheet and toast in 200-degree oven until fragrant, 5–15 minutes depending on size of nuts. Toasted nuts turn rancid more quickly than raw nuts, so use them within a few days.

KOSHERING LIVER

According to kashruth, liver must be broiled over a fire before it is cooked so that the fire will draw out all of the blood. Beef liver must be cut open and placed cut side down over a fire. Chicken liver may be broiled whole.

Here is the method used by Gilda Angel for koshering beef liver or chicken livers:

1. Place liver in a pan lined completely with aluminum foil. Place a rack (used only for koshering livers) in the pan.
2. Rinse liver, salt on all sides and place on rack.
3. Place pan under broiler and broil liver until browned on all sides, turning liver with a forked utensil that is used only for koshering liver.

4. Discard foil and any accumulated blood or liquid. After this process, the liver may be used in other dishes.

MUSTARD OIL

Because mustard oil is quite pungent, you may wish to use it very sparingly.

POMEGRANATES

The word *pomegranate* comes from the Latin *pomum grana-tum*, or "apple of many seeds." Because of its hundreds of seeds, the pomegranate repeatedly appears in Jewish texts as a symbol of fertility, relating to the first commandment of the Torah, "to be fruitful and multiply." The flavor, as André Gide described it, is tart and somewhat lemony, "like the juice of unripe raspberries."

For the seeds: Cut the pomegranate in half horizontally. Then cut each piece in half to produce quarters. Bend each quarter back on itself, so that the seed sacs loosen. Use your fingers or a demitasse spoon to pluck out the seeds. *Beware: pomegranate juice stains like a red dye.*

For the juice: Crush the seeds by hand or in a blender, juice extractor or food processor. Transfer to a mesh strainer and press down hard with the back of a spoon to get out as much juice as possible. One pomegranate will yield a ½–1 cup of juice.

For the molasses: Use 1 teaspoon sugar to each ½ cup fresh pomegranate juice, and boil until the syrupy brown liquid resembles blackstrap molasses. Bottled unsweetened pomegranate juice and molasses are available, usually in health-food stores and at Middle Eastern food sources like those listed on page 584. Cortas and Knudsen are reliable brands.

PHYLLO

If possible, use fresh phyllo leaves from a bakery that makes the dough. If you use frozen phyllo, thaw it in its original wrapper overnight in the refrigerator and let stand unopened at room temperature for 2 hours before using. (If thawed at room temperature, phyllo sheets may stick together.) Remove dough from its wrapper at the last possible moment, after all other ingredients are assembled and ready to use. Work with one leaf at a time, keeping the rest covered with plastic wrap or a damp cotton towel. If the leaves are especially delicate, you can use a spray bottle to spritz them with oil (or butter, in a dairy recipe) instead of brushing it on. To repair torn phyllo, layer an extra scrap of dough over the tears wherever needed and the pastry will bake up beautifully.

SELECTED SOURCES FOR INGREDIENTS

Many of the ingredients in the recipes may be found in stores that sell Mediterranean, Middle Eastern or specialty foods. Below is a list of sources that have been mentioned in *The New York Times*.

* Adriana's Caravan, 78 Grand Central Terminal, New York, NY 10017; (212) 972-8804, (800) 316-0820 (www.adrianascaravan.com).
* Batmanglij's advieh combination: Mage Publishers, 1032 29th Street NW, Washington, DC 20007; (800) 962-0922.
* Dean & DeLuca, 560 Broadway, New York, NY 10012; (212) 226-6800 (www.deandeluca. com).
  Festival of Food, 41B Main Street, Port Washington, NY 11050; (516) 883-6037.
  International Taste, 150 Seventh Avenue, Brooklyn, NY 11215; (718) 768-7217.
* Kalustyan's, 123 Lexington Avenue, New York, NY 10016; (212) 685-3451 (www.kalustyans. com).
  Likitsakos Market, 1174 Lexington Avenue, New York, NY 10028; (212) 535-4300.
  Natura, 615 Ninth Avenue, New York, NY 10036; (212) 397-4700.
* Sahadi Importing Company, 187 Atlantic Avenue, Brooklyn, NY; (718) 624-4550 (www. sahadis.com).
* The Spice House, 1941 Central Avenue, Evanston, IL 60201; (847) 328-3711 (www. thespicehouse.com).
* Sultan's Delight, P.O. Box 090302, Brooklyn, NY 11209; (800) 852-5046 (www. sultansdelight.com).
  Whole Foods Market 2421 Broadway, New York, NY 10024; (212) 874-4000 (www. wholefoods.com).

*Items available by mail order.

GLOSSARY OF SOME OF THE INGREDIENTS AND TERMS IN THIS BOOK

ALEPPO PEPPER: A red pepper from Syria with a mild, rich heat. A mixture of equal parts of sweet paprika and cayenne pepper rubbed with a few drops of olive oil may be substituted.

CHOLENT: The Ashkenazic word for a stew that is traditionally made with meat, potatoes, barley and beans, and cooked in advance, to be eaten on the Sabbath. The Middle Eastern equivalent is *dfina.*

FENUGREEK: A plant related to clover. The seeds need slow heating to bring out their full flavor, but overheating makes them bitter. Their aroma resembles that of celery and the flavor is sweetish and slightly bitter.

FLEUR DE SEL: Salt from France that is obtained through solar evaporation, raked naturally into crystals and hand-harvested. It has a very pure flavor and bright white color.

GUNDI: Dumplings made from chickpeas that may be served in chicken soup or eaten separately.

HALVAH: A grainy confection most commonly made from ground sesame seeds, sweetened with honey or sugar syrup and pressed into a cake. Sometimes it is garnished with pistachios or almonds or flavored with chocolate.

HARISSA: A fiery hot paste made of red chili peppers that are traditionally soaked and then pounded with coriander, caraway, garlic and salt and moistened with olive oil. A staple of Tunisian cuisine.

HELBEH: A hot red-pepper sauce made from fenugreek seeds and zhug.

HERBES DE PROVENCE: A combination of herbs from the French region of Provence that is used in stews, roasts and vegetable dishes. Its composition varies, but it usually contains a few of the following: thyme, tarragon, basil, savory, cracked fennel, marjoram and lavender.

HUMMUS: A dip made from pureed chickpeas, tahini, garlic and lemon juice.

KASHA: Buckwheat groats.

KEFTES: Patties, either fried or baked.

KREPLACH: Small triangular egg-noodle pockets filled with minced meat or chicken that are either fried or boiled in water or soup. They are traditionally added to chicken soup, but may also be boiled and then fried in schmaltz as an accompaniment to meat. A version filled with cheese can be served as a main dish at dairy meals.

KUGEL: A pudding, either sweet or savory.

LABNEH: A sauce or cheese made by straining yogurt. The longer it is strained, the harder it becomes.

MAMALIGA: A cornmeal dish similar to a porridge, Romanian in origin, that may be served plain or as a base for sauces or other ingredients.

MARZIPAN: A sweet, rich paste of ground almonds and sugar, sometimes with a touch of bitter almonds.

PIROGI: Small pastries with either savory or sweet fillings that are either baked or fried. They can be made with a variety of doughs, depending which suits the filling best.

POLO: A dish made with rice. Similar to pilaf.

ROSE WATER: The distilled essence of rose petals.

SOUR SALT (CITRIC ACID): A white substance of either granular or small crystal chunks that should be used sparingly. When dissolved, it imparts a distinctive tart flavor.

SUMAC: A spice made from the dried, powdered berry of the Middle Eastern sumac variety. It is a major component of Za'atar. Sumac has a very nice, fruity-tart flavor that is not quite as overpowering as lemon. It imparts a deep red color that makes a very attractive garnish.

TAGINE: A traditional Moroccan slowly simmered stew that is cooked in tagine, a special earthenware pot with a distinctive, high, conical cover.

TAHINI: A thick paste made of ground untoasted sesame seeds, used alone or as an ingredient in dips, spreads or sauces.

TAMARIND: The pulp of pods from the tree of the same name. It has a lingering, strong sour flavor and is an ingredient of Worcestershire sauce. When combined with sugar, it imparts a sweet-and-sour flavor.

TSIMMES: A stew, traditionally prepared with root vegetables and dried fruits and/or other sweetening agents and often with the addition of meat.

ZA'ATAR: An herb mixture of powdered sumac, roasted sesame seeds, salt and wild thyme and/or hyssop (a biblical herb similar in taste to wild marjoram).

ZHUG: An extremely hot and spicy Yemenite paste of peppers, cilantro, garlic and spices.

SUGGESTED HOLIDAY DISHES:
TRADITIONAL AND CONTEMPORARY

The following list of recipe suggestions for selected Jewish holidays is not intended to be comprehensive, but simply to present examples of some foods that are either appropriate to or associated with those occasions—either symbolically, historically, customarily or, in the case of Passover, through laws of kashruth. Many of the dishes are appropriate for more than one holiday, of course, as are a multitude of recipes in this book that do not appear below.

THE SABBATH

Delicious dishes for Erer Shabbos—and others made ahead to be served on the weekly day of rest.

Chopped Liver
Mimi Sheraton's Chopped Mushrooms, Eggs and
    Onions (Vegetarian Chopped Liver)
Potato and Mushroom Pirogi
Mushroom and Kasha Pastries
Mimi Sheraton's Classic Chicken Soup
Persian Chicken Soup with Gundi
Kurdish Chicken Soup with Kubbeh
Beef and Barley Soup
Wild Mushroom Soup
Wallsé's Goulash Soup
Lentil Soup with Lamb Meatballs
Uzbeki Lamb, Vegetable and Noodle Soup
Roast Chicken with Green Olives and Cilantro

Roast Chicken with Lemon and Rosemary
Roast Chicken with Spiced Apples and Onions
Daisy Iny's Iraqi Chicken With Rice and Eggs
    (Tabyeet)
Czech Stuffed Chicken
Circassian Chicken with Walnut Sauce
Mimi Sheraton's Chicken Fricassee with Meatballs
Onion-Smothered Chicken
Chicken with Okra
Classic Braised Brisket of Beef
Pot Roast with Curried Tomato Sauce
Goulash
Cholent Brisket
Cholent with Pastrami
Vegetarian Cholent
Spiced Beef Tongue
Spoon Lamb
Moroccan Bean and Lamb Stew (Dfina)
Charles Michener's Potted Veal
Armenian Artichoke Hearts with Onions and Potatoes
Red Cabbage Stewed with Fruits and Wine
Roast Parsnips with Carrots and Potatoes
Alan King's Roasted Garlic Potatoes
Bouley Family Potato and Prune Gratin
Balkan Mixed Vegetable Stew (Ghivetch)
The Golden Door's Mediterranean Mushroom Salad
Pineapple-Orange Ambrosia
Orange Foam

Prune Whip with Port Wine
Winter Fruit Salad with Fresh and Dried Fruits
Poached Dried Fruit with Cornmeal Crumble and
Pine Nuts
Pear and Raisin Charlotte
Sister Sadie's Kichel
Babka
Lemon Chiffon Cake
Chocolate Sponge Cake
Walnut Cake
Rebecca's Challah
Marvin Korman's Sweet Onion Rolls

ROSH HA SHANA

To symbolize the New Year—and the continuity of the annual cycle: foods that are round—circular-shaped challahs, couscous, black-eyed peas. To symbolize the sweet year: brightly colored foods and dishes prepared with honey—especially apples dipped in honey. To evoke mitzvot, or good deeds: pomegranates, said to contain 613 seeds—equal to the number of commandments in the Torah. To symbolize fertility and abundance: seeds. To symbolize Rosh Ha Shana (literally, "head of the year") and Israel as a leader among nations: the head of either a fish or a lamb.

Arctic Char with Carrots and Honey
Red Snapper Crusted in Sesame Seeds
Poached Whiting (Merluzzo in Bianco)
Roast Chicken Brushed with Honey and Cumin
Sweet Rice with Orange Peel, Chicken, Saffron and
Carrots (Shirin Polo)
Chicken Breasts with Fresh Figs
Turkey and Apricot Tagine
Honey-Glazed Duck
Rosh Ha Shana Pot Roast with Onion Confit
Braised Pot Roast with Pomegranates
Sweet Meatballs for Couscous
Lamb Shanks Braised with Apricots and North
African Spices
Golden Couscous

Couscous with Lamb and Seven Vegetables
Tuna, Black-Eyed Peas and Artichoke Salad
Syrian Veal with Black-Eyed Peas
Moroccan Artichokes with Oranges and Saffron
Beets in Orange Sauce
Honeyed Carrots
Carrot and Fruit Tsimmes
Leek Patties (Kofta)
Candied Sweet Potatoes
Sweet Potato Soufflé
Tossed Salad with Honey Dressing
Turkish Grated Carrot Salad
Sweet Potato and Crystallized Ginger Salad
Apple Compote
Anise Fruit Compote
Oranges and Dates in Cardamom-Honey Syrup
Bill Yosses's Quince Compote
Honey Soufflé
Maida Heatter's Viennese Anise Cookies
Carrot Cookies with Orange Icing
Honey Brownies
Honey-Chocolate Layer Cake with Honey Frosting
Honeyed Apple Cake
Rosh Ha Shana Honey Cake with Dried Fruits and
Nuts
Warm Honeyed Pear Cake
Sesame Seed Cookies (Benne Wafers)
Sesame-seed Cake with Sesame-seed Frosting
Sesame Seed Brittle
Honey Balls (Teiglach)
Gilda Latzky's Rosh Ha Shana Challah

YOM KIPPUR

To precede the fasting on the Day of Atonement: foods that are filling, but light on salt and spices.

Chicken Soup with Kreplach Filled with Chicken
Chicken in the Pot
Chicken Soup with Tiny Veal Balls

Yemenite High Holiday Soup Stew
Colette Rossant's Mushroom Consommé
Mushroom-Barley Soup
Simple Roast Chicken
Daisy Iny's Iraqi Chicken with Rice and Eggs
    (Tabyeet)
Hana Elbaum's Stove-Top Potato Kugel
Persian Steamed White Rice (Chello)
Kasha with Mushrooms
Braised Carrots with Italian Parsley
Simple Roast Turnips or Rutabagas
Persian Fruit Mélange
Sponge Cake

To break the fast: an array of tempting light, brunch-like foods that can be served without further cooking or preparation upon return from day-long services.

Asparagus Mimosa
Cold Zucchini Terrine with Raw Tomato-Basil Sauce
Savory Herring
Herring Salad with Beets and Apples
Matjes Herring in Sherry Sauce
Le Bernardin's Fresh and Smoked Salmon Spread
Salmon Marinated in Wine and Herbs
Gravlax: Classic, Citrus or Moroccan-Spiced
Hummas, Pita and Yogurt Salad
Cold Salmon Mousse with Mustard-Dill Sauce
Smoked Salmon Terrine with Spinach
Smoked Fish Spread
Rosemary-Lemon Bean Puree
Chilled Cod Tomato
Baked "Poached" Whole Salmon with Two Sauces
Chilled Whole Cod in Tuna-Mayonnaise (Cod
    Tonnato)
Fried Whitings
Salad of Potatoes, Smoked Sable and Egg Mimosa
Cucumber Salad with Dill
The Golden Door's Mediterranean Mushroom Salad
New Potato Salad with Dill

Noodle Soufflé Kugel
Apricot Noodle Kugel
Tower of Bagel Sandwiches
Spiced Apple Charlotte
Laura Goodenough's Apple Coffee Cake
Ethereal Cheesecake
Fresh Ginger Cake
Mimi Sheraton's Rugelach (Cinnamon Nut Horns)
Cincinnati Jewish Bake Shop Schnecken
Viennese Crescents

SUKKOTH

To celebrate the harvest: stuffed vegetables and casseroles, like tsimmes or tagines, that are easy to carry to the Sukkoth. And, of course, an abundance of seasonal fruits and vegetables.

Beef-Stuffed Grape Leaves with Apricots (Yerba)
Grape Leaves Stuffed with Lamb and Figs
Baked Tomatoes Stuffed with Salmon, Garlic and Crepes
Trout Filled with Spinach, Mushrooms, Prunes and
    Nuts
Miraval's Chicken with Couscous in a Pumpkin "Pot"
Roast Chicken with Pomegranate Glaze and Fresh
    Mint
Roasted Cornish Hens with Bulgur Stuffing
Turkey Pilaf in a Phyllo "Turban"
Sweet-and-Sour Stuffed Cabbage (Ashkenazic Style)
Stuffed Cabbage with Spiced Beef and Apricots
    (Sephardic Style)
Peppers Stuffed with Saffron Rice and Beef
Tsimmes with Beef Cheeks, Dried Apricots,
    Cranberries and Root Vegetables
Lamb Tagine with Dried Figs and Almonds
Sweet Peppers Stuffed with Lamb and Minted
    Couscous
Lamb-Stuffed Artichokes, Syrian-Style
Braised Veal with Curry
Acorn Squash with Spiced Bulgur
Cabbage Strudel

Cauliflower with Cinnamon
Roasted Onions
Balkan Mixed Vegetable Stew (Ghivetch)
Roasted Tomato-and-Eggplant Casserole
Wolfgang Puck's Mushroom and Eggplant Ratatouille
Gaston LeNotre's Baked Apples Stuffed with Beets,
    Pine Nuts and Currants
Stuffed Artichokes
Couscous-Stuffed Eggplant
Spinach with Raisins and Pine Nuts
Turkish Okra Casserole
Turnip and Carrot Tsimmes
Hungarian Apple Soup
Elias Shamma's Middle Eastern Baked Apples
Almond Cookies with Fruits and Chocolate
Pear and Raisin Charlotte
Poached Dried Fruit with Cornmeal Crumble and
    Pine Nuts
Couscous with Fruit and Nuts
Dried Fruit and Nut Bsteeyas
Baklava
Fresh Ginger Cake

Fresh Green Pea Pancakes
Curried Sweet-Potato Latkes
Old Jerusalem Zucchini Pancakes
Alayne Zatulov's Giant Vegetable Latkes
Apple Latkes
Ricotta Latkes
Eggplant Fritters Coated Three Ways
Jerusalem Artichoke Fritters
Yogurt Cheese (Laban)
Khachpuri (Georgian Cheese Pie)
Fritzie Abadi's Syrian Small Fried Meat Patties (Ijeh)
Duck With Olives in Sherry Sauce
Roasted Cornish Hen with Grapes
Sweetbreads Dusted with Cloves
Easy Brisket in Sweet-and-Sour Sauce
Apple Sauce with Wine and Vanilla
Hanukkah Fritters (Soofganiyot)
Sweet Hanukkah Fritters with Honey Syrup
Steve Raichlen's Baked Greek Hanukkah "Fritters"
    with Honeyed Syrup
Polish Parisian Cheesecake
Orange and Olive Oil Cake

HANUKKAH

To commemorate the victory of the Maccabees over the Syrians and the miracle of the oil, which burned for eight nights, instead of one: foods fried in oil, particularly pancakes and fritters. Richly flavored goose and duck and fine meats. And cheese to honor Judith, who is said to have saved Judea by feeding the Assyrian General, Holofernes, salty cheese, then slaying him after he fell into a stupor from drinking wine to slake his thirst.

All manner of latkes:
    Jerusalem Artichoke Pancakes
    Carrot and Parsnip Latkes
    Lentil Levivot with Confit of Onions
    Mushroom Pecan Latkes
    Potato Latkes: Classic or Low-Fat
    Potato Pancakes with Celery Root

PURIM

To celebrate the saving of the Jews of Persia by Queen Esther, who risked her life to disclose to her husband, the king, the plot of his Prime Minister, Haman: Hamantaschen and other foods made with poppy seeds (Haman, pronounced "Hamohn" in Hebrew, sounds similar to "mohn," the German word for "poppy seeds") and Huevos Haminados; to include as Shalach Manot (Gifts to One Another): sweets like marzipan, halvah and cookies or, as in Uganda, fish. Meals featuring sumptuous meat dishes and meat-filled pastries. Or, because according to legend Esther subsisted on a vegetarian diet rather than eat non-kosher meat in the palace: dishes with grains and legumes—particularly chickpeas.

Dried Chickpeas (Arbes)
Hummus: Classic, or Spiced Gingered, or Warm
Moshe's Falafel as a Canapé

Pedro de la Cavalleria's Vermilioned Eggs (Huevos Haminados)
Turkish Split-Pea Soup with Mint and Paprika
Mark Bittman's Vegetarian Mushroom Barley Soup
Chickpeas in Ginger Sauce
Chickpea and Olive Salad with Fennel
Curried Couscous and Grilled Onion Salad
Bouley's Fava Beans with Honey, Lime and Thyme
Kasha Varnishkas
Poppy Seed Noodles
Frontière's Grouper with Za'atar and Tomato
Baked Whole Fish with Tahini Marinade
Venetian-Style Pompano with Raisins and Pine Nuts
Baked Fish with Almond Stuffing
Baked Flounder with Moroccan Spices
Alain Ducasse's Rib-Eye Steaks with Peppered Cranberry Marmalade and Swiss Chard
Crown Roast of Lamb with Mushroom–Pine Nut Stuffing
Shoulder of Lamb Braised in Chianti
Wolfgang Puck's Lamb Chops with Lamb's Lettuce
Paul Prudhomme's Veal Roast with Mango Sauce
Famous Dairy Restaurant's Vegetable Cutlet with Mushroom Gravy
Wolfgang Puck's Vegetable Cakes with Red Pepper Coulis
White-Bean Croquettes
Persian Rice, Lentils and Currants
Mimi Sheraton's Hamantaschen
Honey-Spice Cake
Poppy Seed–Orange Cookies
Poppy-Seed Strudel
Neue Galerie's Poppy-Seed Cake
Halvah Soufflé
Filled Marzipan Cookies
Marzipan Potatoes
Zabar's Black-and-White Cookies
Cardamom-Flavored Almond Cookies
Pine Nut Lace Cookies
Almond Cookies from Iraq (Massafan)

Andree Levy Abramoff's Date Cookies (Menena)
Marzipan Cake
Chocolate Chewies
Chocolate Macaroons
Chocolate-Almond Truffles
Nougat
Halvah

SHAVOUT

To commemorate the giving of the Ten Commandments and the Torah to Moses at Mount Sinai, which was preceded by a day in which the Israelites abstained from meat, and to symbolize the "Land flowing with milk and honey": dairy products. To celebrate the beginning of the spring wheat harvest: breads and other dishes made from grains. And, of course, an abundance of seasonal harvest fruits and vegetables.

Mimi Sheraton's Cold Beet Borscht
Cheese Blintzes
Bohemian Cheese Dumplings with Sour Cream
Sour Cream Soufflé
Carrot Soufflé
Sour Cream Pancakes
Baked Asparagus and Eggs
Baked Mushroom Omelet
Wild Mushrooms in Sour Cream (à la Russe)
Salmon in Phyllo with Spinach and Cheese
Barley Risotto
Mushroom and Barley Casserole
Tabbouleh
Baked Chinese Eggplant with Apricots
Eggplant Gratin with Saffron Custard
Bulgur Wheat Pilaf
Black-Eyed Pea Salad with Herbs, Walnuts and Pomegranates
Kasha Salad with Roasted Mushrooms and Ginger
Fresh Corn and Red-Pepper Blini
Corn and Pudding
Mamaliga

Med-Rim Bulgar Salad
Cold Sour Cherry Soup
Lebanese Apricot Cream
Baked Figs
Almond Flan with Ricotta and Oranges
Saffron Panna Cotta with Fresh Figs
Pomegranate Cream
Fig and Pistachio Ice Cream
Deluxe Cheesecake
Ginger Cheesecake
Turkish Yogurt Cake with Flavored Syrup
Sour-Cream Coffee Cake
Spiced Fig Torte
Date Torte
Mimi Sheraton's Rugelach (Cinnamon Nut Horns)
Hungarian Yeast Bread with Cheese Topping (Turos
    Lepeny)
Tunisian Triangular Challah (Bejma)

Passover*

To commemorate the liberation of the Israelites from slavery in Egypt: Matzoh—the bread of affliction that the fleeing slaves took with them, unleavened because they could not wait for it to rise—and a wide array of dishes made from matzoh; haroseth, a fruit mixture that symbolizes the mortar used to build the pyramids; pungent herbs or horseradish that represent the bitterness of slavery. To celebrate spring and renewal: green vegetables, green herbs, young lamb or veal.

Cynthia Zeger's Ashkenazic Haroseth
Elisheva Kaufman's Haroseth
Moroccan Haroseth
Turkish Haroseth
Haroseth from Italy
Simplified Odessa-Style Gefilite Fish
Baked Gefilte Fish Loaf
Carpe à la Juive
Joyce Goldstein's Pickled Salmon
Multi-Layered Vegetable Terrine
Mushroom-Stuffed Eggs
Polish Sour Cream and Mushroom Dip
Hana Elbaum's Chicken Soup with Flanken
Garlic Soup
Colette Rossant's Mushroom Consommé
Sorrel and Potato Soup
Fish in Rhubarb Sauce
Aquavit's Oven-Steamed Chilean or Black Sea Bass
    with Warm Citrus-Beet Juice
Czech Carp with Black Prune-Raisin Sauce
Cod with Sweet-and-Sour Tomato Sauce
Baked Fresh Cod with Onions in a Potato Crust
Le Bernardin's Halibut in Borscht with Warm
    Chive-Horseradish Sauce
Salmon with Sorrel Sauce
Argentine Roast Chicken with Vegetables and
    Chimichurri Sauce
Chicken Paprikash
Braised Chicken with Sweet Peppers
Sweet-and-Sour Pot Roast
Braised Short Ribs in Porcini-Prune Sauce

*Note: The only foods that are *hametz*—universally forbidden by biblical law at Passover—are fermented or leavened wheat, rye, oats, spelt and barley, and their related products. After that, the rules are defined by each community. Jews who observe Ashkenazic rabbinical tradition will not eat any grains, including corn and rice, or any legumes and many seeds during Passover. Depending on local traditions, Sephardic Jews and Middle Eastern Jews may or may not exclude some or all of these foods from their Passover menus and may use ingredients in their Passover dishes that observant Jews in other communities will not eat during the holiday. Given such complexities, some recipes noted above as appropriate for Passover may be acceptable to one community of Jews, but not to another. It is the ultimate responsibility of the reader to ascertain if a particular recipe meets the Passover dietary standards that he or she observes.

Tsimmes with Meatballs

Matzoh Meat Pie (Megina)

Syrian Meatballs (Kofte) with Cherries

Armenian Artichoke Hearts

Asparagus and Mushrooms

Brussels Sprouts and Carrots with Almonds

Cauliflower-Apple Puree

Sautéed Portobello Mushrooms

Brandied Onions

Sweet Potato Soufflé

Claudia Roden's Prune Tsimmes

Mashed Yellow Turnips with Crispy Shallots

Turnip and Carrot Tsimmes

Triestine Pan-Cooked Zucchini with Egg and
    Cinnamon

Orange-Onion Salad

Red Salad

Grilled Lemon-Parsley Salad

Barry Wine's Vegetable-Matzoh "Salad"

Geoffrey Zakarian's Salmon with Smashed
    Cucumber-Date Salad

Bouley's Warm Chicken, Artichoke and Spinach Salad

Whole Wheat Matzoh Meal Pancakes

Passover Cheese Blintzes

Matzoh Brei

Baked Caramel Pears

Strawberries and Pineapple Alexandra

Rhubarb and Srawberry Compote

Almond Macaroons

Passover Sponge Cake

Passover Cheesecake

Ethereal Cheesecake

Flourless Apricot and Honey Soufflé

Passover Carrot-Almond Cake

Flourless Chocolate Cake with Oranges

Chocolate-and-Almond Cake

Orange-Chocolate Dacquoise

Hazelnut Roll

Italian Passover Walnut Cake (Torta di Noci Per
    Pesach)

Bessie Feffer's Seven-Layer Cake for Passover

Soaked Nut Cake (Tish Pishti)

Vicky Nahmad's Egyptian Matzoh Confection

Angelina de Leon's Matzoh with Honey and Pepper

Apple Horseradish

Cranberry and Horseradish Sauce

BIBLIOGRAPHY

Algren, Nelson. *America Eats*. Iowa City: University of Iowa Press, 1992.

Amster, Linda, ed. *The New York Times Passover Cookbook*. New York: William Morrow/HarperCollins, 1999.

Angel, Gilda. *Sephardic Holiday Cooking: Recipes and Traditions*. Mount Vernon, N.Y.: Decalogue Books, 1996.

Basan, Ghillie. *Classic Turkish Cooking*. New York: St. Martin's Press, 1997.

Batmanglij, Najmieh. *The New Food of Life*. Washington, D.C.: Mage Publishers, 1992.

Beard, James. *James Beard's American Cookery*. Boston: Little, Brown, 1972.

Bergin, Mary, and Judy Gethers. *Spago Chocolate*. New York: Random House, 1999.

Berl, Christine. *The Classic Art of Viennese Pastry*. New York: Van Nostrand Reinhold, 1998.

Blonder, Ellen, and Annabel Low. *Every Grain of Rice*. New York: Clarkson Potter, 1998.

Boulud, Daniel, and Dorie Greenspan. *Cafe Boulud Cookbook*. New York: Scribners, 1999.

Brennan, Georgeanne. *Holiday Eggs*. New York: Smithmark, 1999.

Burros, Marian. *Eating Well Is the Best Revenge*. New York: Simon & Schuster, 1995.

———. *Keep It Simple*. New York: William Morrow/HarperCollins, 1981.

———. *Pure and Simple*. New York: William Morrow/HarperCollins, 1978.

———. *You've Got It Made*. New York: William Morrow/HarperCollins, 1984.

Casas, Penelope. *The Foods and Wines of Spain*. New York: Alfred A. Knopf, 1991.

Claiborne, Craig. *Cooking with Herbs & Spices*. New York: Harper & Row, 1970.

———. *Craig Claiborne's Favorites from The New York Times*. New York: Quadrangle/New York Times Book Co., 1975.

———. *The New York Times Cook Book*. New York: Harper & Row, 1990.

———. *The New York Times International Cookbook*. New York: Harper & Row, 1971.

———. *The New York Times Menu Cook Book*. New York: Harper & Row, 1966.

Child, Julia. *The Way to Cook*. New York: Alfred A. Knopf, 1989.

Clark, Ann. *Fabulous Fish*. New York: New American Library, 1987.

Cohen, Jayne. *The Gefilte Variations*. New York: Scribners, 2000.

Colicchio, Tom, with Catherine Young, Lori Silverbush and Sean Fri. *Think Like a Chef*. New York: Clarkson Potter Publishers, 2000.

Cooperative Society of the Children's Hospital of Cincinnati. *The Cincinnati Cook Book*. Cincinnati:

Cincinnati Children's Hospital Medial Center, 1966.

Daley, Regan. *In the Sweet Kitchen: The Definitive Baker's Companion*. New York: Regan Daley/Artisan, 2001.

Darden, Norma Jean, and Carole Darden. *Spoonbread and Strawberry Wine*. Garden City, N.Y.: Anchor Press, 1978.

DeSilva, Cara, ed. *In Memory's Kitchen: A Legacy from the Women of Terezin*. Northvale, N.J.: J. Aronson, Inc., 1996.

Ducasse, Alain, with Linda Dannenberg. *Ducasse: Flavors of France*. New York: Artisan, 1998.

Eisenberg, Penny Wantuck. *Light Jewish Holiday Desserts*. New York: William Morrow/HarperCollins, 1999.

Franey, Pierre. *The 60-Minute Gourmet*. New York: Times Books/Random House, 1979.

Ganor, Avi, and Ron Maiberg. *Taste of Israel: A Mediterranean Feast*. London: Prion, 1990.

Goldstein, Darra. *À la Russe*. New York: Random House, 1993.

———. *The Winter Vegetarian*. New York: HarperPerennial, 2000.

Goldstein, Joyce. *Back to Square One*. New York: William Morrow/HarperCollins, 1992.

———. *Cucina Ebraica: Flavors of the Italian Jewish Kitchen*. San Francisco: Chronicle Books, 1998.

———. *Kitchen Conversations*. New York: William Morrow Avon/HarperCollins, 1999.

———. *Mediterranean the Beautiful Cookbook: Authentic Recipes from the Mediterranean Lands*. San Francisco: Collins Publishers, 1994.

———. *The Mediterranean Kitchen*. New York: William Morrow/HarperCollins, 1989.

Gottlieb, Isser. *Gottlieb's Bakery—100 Years of Recipes*. Memphis: Wimmer, 1984.

Greene, Gloria Kaufer. *The New Jewish Holiday Cookbook: An International Collection of Recipes and Customs*. New York: Times Books/Random House, 1999.

Greenspan, Dorie. *Desserts by Pierre Herme*. Boston: Little, Brown, 1998.

Harris, Jessica B. *Iron Pots and Wooden Spoons*. New York: Stewart Tabori & Chang, 1989.

Hay, Donna. *New Food Fast*. Sydney: Murdoch Books, 1999.

Hazan, Marcella. *Essentials of Classic Italian Cooking*. New York: Alfred A. Knopf, 1993.

———. *Marcella Cucina*. New York: HarperCollins Publishers, 1997.

Heatter, Maida. *Maida Heatter's Best Dessert Book Ever*. New York: Random House, 1990.

———. *Maida Heatter's Book of Great American Desserts*. New York: Alfred A. Knopf, 1985.

Hewitt, Jean. *The New York Times Heritage Cookbook*. New York: G. P. Putnam's Sons, 1972.

———. *The New York Times Large-Type Cookbook*. New York: Golden Press, 1968.

Hushaw, Glenda et al. *Asparagus, All Ways—Always*. Stockton, Calif.: Stockton Asparagus Festival, Celestial Arts, 1986.

Iny, Daisy. *The Best of Baghdad Cooking*. New York: Saturday Review Press/E. F. Dutton, 1976.

Kasper, Lynne Rossetto. *The Italian Country Table*. New York: Scribners, 1999.

Kirschenbaum, Levana. *Levana's Table: Kosher Cooking for Everyone*. New York: Stewart Tabori & Chang, 2002.

Kouki, Mohamed. *Cuisine et Patisserie Tunisiennes*. Le Patrimoine Tunisien, 1997.

Lassalle, George. *East of Orphanides: My Middle Eastern Food*. London: Kyle Cathie, 1991.

Lawson, Nigella, and Arthur Boehm, eds. *How to Eat*. New York: John Wiley, 2000.

Lebewohl, Sharon. *The 2nd Ave. Deli Cookbook: Recipes and Memories From Abe Lebewohl's Legendary Kitchen*. New York: Villard, 1999.

Lebovitz, David. *Room for Dessert*. New York: HarperCollins, 1999.

Le Coze, Maguy, and Eric Ripert. *Le Bernardin Cookbook: Four-Star Simplicity*. New York: Doubleday, 1998.

Levi, Zion, and Hani Agabria. *The Yemenite Cookbook.* New York: Seaver Books, 1987.

Levy, Faye. *1,000 Jewish Recipes.* New York: Hungry Minds, 2000.

Lorain, Michel, and Jean-Michel Lorain. *La Cuisine: Une Passion de Pere en Fils.* Paris: Robert Laffont, 1987.

Lubavitch Women's Cookbook Organization of Brooklyn. *Spice and Spirit: The Complete Kosher Jewish Cookbook.* Brooklyn, N.Y.: Lubavitch Women's Cookbook Publications, 1990.

Machlin, Edda Servi. *The Classic Dolci of the Italian Jews.* Croton-on-Hudson, N.Y.: Giro Press, 1999.

Manfield, Christine. *Spice.* New York: Viking, 1999.

Marks, Copeland. *The Varied Kitchens of India: Cuisines of the Anglo-Indians of Calcutta, Bengalis, Jews of Calcutta, Kashmiris, Parsis, and Tibetans of Darjeeling.* New York: M. Evans, 1986.

Meyer, Danny, and Michael Romano. *The Union Square Cafe Cookbook.* New York: HarperCollins, 1994.

Miner, Viviane Alchech, with Linda Krim. *From My Grandmother's Kitchen: A Sephardic Cookbook.* Gainesville, Fa.: Triad Pub. Co., 1984.

Moosewood Collective. *Sundays at Moosewood Restaurant.* New York: Fireside/Simon & Schuster, 1990.

Nash, Helen. *Kosher Cuisine.* New York: Random House, 1984.

Nathan, Joan. *The Foods of Israel Today.* New York: Alfred A. Knopf, 2001.

———. *Jewish Cooking in America.* New York: Alfred A. Knopf, 1998.

———. *The Jewish Holiday Baker.* New York: Schocken Books, 1997.

———. *The Jewish Holiday Kitchen*, Rev. and Exp. New York: Schocken Books, 1988.

O'Neill, Molly. *New York Cookbook.* New York: Workman Publishing, 1992.

Pappas, Lou Seibert. *The Working Cook.* White Hall, Va.: Betterway Publications, 1991.

Peterson, James. *Fish & Shellfish.* New York: William Morrow/HarperCollins, 1996.

Plotkin, Fred. *La Terra Fortunata.* New York: Broadway Books, 2001.

———. *Recipes From Paradise.* Boston: Little, Brown, 1997.

Puck, Wolfgang. *The Wolfgang Puck Cookbook.* New York: Random House, 1986.

———. *Wolfgang Puck's Modern French Cooking for the American Kitchen.* New York: Houghton Mifflin, 1998.

Riely, Elizabeth. *A Feast of Fruits.* New York: Macmillan/Simon & Schuster, 1993.

Roden, Claudia. *The Book of Jewish Food: An Odyssey from Samarkand to New York.* New York: Alfred A. Knopf, 1996.

———. *Mediterranean Cookery.* New York: Alfred A. Knopf, 1987.

———. *The New Book of Middle Eastern Food.* New York: Alfred A. Knopf, 2000.

Rojas-Lombardi, Felipe. *The Art of South American Cooking.* New York: HarperCollins Publishers, 1991.

Sahni, Julie. *Classic Indian Cooking.* New York: William Morrow/HarperCollins, 1980.

———. *Classic Indian Vegetarian and Grain Cooking.* New York: William Morrow/HarperCollins, 1985.

Sheraton, Mimi. *From My Mother's Kitchen: Recipes and Reminiscences.* New York: HarperCollins, 1991.

———. *The Whole World Loves Chicken Soup: Recipes and Lore to Comfort Body and Soul.* New York: Warner Books, 1995.

Shere, Lindsey Remolif. *Chez Panisse Desserts.* New York: Random House, 1994.

Silverton, Nancy, with Heidi Yorkshire. *Desserts.* New York: Harper & Row, 1986.

Soltner, Andre, with Seymour Britchky. *The Lutèce Cookbook.* New York: Alfred A. Knopf, 1995.

Stavroulakis, Nicholas. *The Cookbook of the Jews of Greece.* Northvale, N.J.: Jason Aronson, Inc., 1996.

Stewart-Gordon, Faith, and Nika Hazelton. *The Russian Tea Room Cookbook.* New York: Richard Marek Publishers, 1981.

Torres, Jacques. *Dessert Circus*. New York: William Morrow/HarperCollins, 1998.

Valero, Rena. *The Delights of Jerusalem*. Jerusalem: Steimatzky, 1985.

Verge, Roger. *Vegetables in the French Style*. New York: Artisan Books, 1994.

Veyrat, Marc. *Fou de Saveurs*. Paris: Hachette, 1994.

Vongerichten, Jean-Georges, and Mark Bittman. *Jean-Georges: Cooking at Home with a Four-Star Chef*. New York: Broadway Books, 1998.

Waters, Alice. *Chez Panisse Vegetables*. New York: HarperCollins, 1996.

Weir, Joanne. *Joanne Weir's More Cooking in the Wine Country*. New York: Simon & Schuster, 2001.

Whitman, Joan, ed. *The Best of Craig Claiborne*. New York: Times Books/Random House, 1999.

INDEX

nougat, 572–573

nuts. *See* confections and nuts; *specific nuts*

Odessa-style gefilte fish, 5

okra
    casserole, Turkish, 276
    lamb with, 228
    sweet-and-sour, 277

olivada (olive dip), 44–45

olives
    black
        couscous, 317
        paste, 418
    chicken salad with dates and
        orange-balsamic dressing,
        381
    dip (olivada), 44–45
    salad, chickpeas and, with fennel,
        369

omelets
    baked mushroom, 390
    potato and onion with smoked
        salmon, 391

onion(s)
    brandied, 278
    confit, 182–183, 304–305
    orange-onion salad, 361
    pomegranate and walnut sauce,
        424
    potato omelet and, with smoked
        salmon, 391
    roasted, 277–278
    rolls, Marvin Korman's, 441–442
    salad, couscous and grilled onion,
        curried, 370

orange(s)
    almond flan with ricotta and,
        490–491
    balsamic dressing, chicken salad
        with cracked olives and
        dates and, 381
    cake
        almond, 551
        flourless chocolate, 560
        olive oil, 555
    chocolate dacquoise, 558–560
    dates and
        in cardamom-honey syrup, 480
        cardamom tart, 497
    foam, 479
    French toast, Brasserie's, 410
    icing, carrot cookies with, 515
    onion salad, 361
    pastry, Nancy Silverton's, 504
    peel, candied, 572
    pineapple ambrosia with, 483
    poppy seed-orange cookies, 516
    sliced, with pomegranate-
        caramelized walnuts,
        479–480
    soufflé, in orange shells, 459–460

orzo, salad, pea and, with citrus
    dressing, 373

pancakes. *See also* vegetable latkes and
    pancakes
    apple, 405
    baked, David Eyre's, 404–405
    filled, Egyptian (feteer), 407–408
    lemon, 401
    sour cream, 401
    whole wheat matzoh meal, 402

panna cotta, saffron, with fresh figs,
    454

Parisian pletzel, 450

parsley, tabbouleh (parsley salad with
    bulgur, mint and tomatoes),
    368

parsnips
    carrot and, latkes, 303
    gratin with potato baked in cider,
        287
    pomegranates and, 279
    roasted
        with carrots and potatoes, 279
        with garlic, 278

Passover
    brownies, 523
    cakes
        apple cake, 547–548
        carrot-almond, 550–551
        Italian walnut (torta di noci per
            Pesach), 571
        seven-layer cake, Bessie Feffer's,
            561
        sponge cake, 527
    cheese blintzes, 404
    cheesecake, 543
    menu suggestions, 592–593

pasta. *See also* egg noodles; noodles
    cold sesame noodles, 342–343
    fettuccine with asparagus and
        smoked salmon, 342
    linguine with pistachio-almond
        pesto, 340–341
    Macedonia, 339
    with red peppers and pine nuts, 340
    with tomato, zucchini and cream
        sauce, Itzhak Perlman's,
        339
    ziti with smoked salmon, 341

pasta sauce. *See also* trimmings
    chicken ragout with fettuccine, 346
    duck ragù, 347
    eggplant ragù, Mario's, 345
    Italian meat sauce, 348
    pesto, 419
    porcini-style shiitake mushroom
        sauce, 345–346
    spiced veal and beef ragù, 348–349

pastrami salmon, 124

pastries (savory). *See also* crusts and
    pastries

beef-filled, 30
    mushroom and kasha, 29

pato a la Sevillana (duck with olives in
    sherry sauce), 172–173

peaches, whole roasted, with almonds
    and pistachios, 480–481

pear(s)
    baked
        caramel, 482
        with grapes and wine, 481
    cake, honeyed, 556
    and ginger tart, 499
    pistachio-pear strudel, 539
    sorbet, 463

peas
    with artichokes and fava beans, 280
    black-eyed peas
        with herbs, walnuts and
            pomegranates salad, 368
        salad, tuna with artichoke and,
            380
        with spinach, 329
    fresh green, pancakes, 310
    Persian spinach, potatoes and,
        290–291
    salad, orzo and pea, with citrus
        dressing, 373
    snow peas
        sautéed, with carrots and turnips,
            265
        stir-fried, 287
    sugar snap peas
        pancakes, heirloom, 306
        with sun-dried tomatoes, 293
    yellow peas with onions, 330

peppered cranberry marmalade, rib-
    eye steaks with Swiss chard
    and, 192–193

peppers. *See* red peppers; stuffed
    peppers, sweet peppers;
    yellow peppers

Persian carrot soup with mint, cold,
    82

Persian chicken breasts, roast, 151

Persian chicken soup with gundi
    (chickpea dumplings),
    53–54

Persian fruit mélange, 488

Persian rice. *See* rice

Persian spinach, with potatoes and
    peas, 290–291

peshe en saltsa (fish in rhubarb sauce),
    101

pesto sauce
    basic recipe, 419
    pistachio-almond, linguine with,
        340–341

phyllo
    apple tart in, 492
    baklava, 510–511
    bsteeyas, dried fruit and nut,
        498–499

pudding
  apple-rum, topped with meringue,
    473
  apricot-almond challah, 475–476
  baked squash, Edda Servi Machlin's,
    292–293
  corn, 267
  honeyed challah-apple, 475
  mocha pudding-cake, Belle's
    heirloom, 565–566
  rice
    with dried fruits, 468
    tart, Venetian, (torta Turchesca),
      501
  sour cherry-walnut, with cherry
    sauce, 477–478
pumpernickel bread, 443
pumpkin, spiced lentils and, 328
Purim, menu suggestions, 590–591

quail, honey-mustard, 179
quince compote
  Bill Yosses's, 484
  condiment, 428

rack of lamb. See also lamb
  hot and spicy rubbed, 214–215
  Syrian spiced, 214
radishes
  braised with honey, 288
  canapes, 42
  salad, fennel and, Colette Rossant's,
    363
ragù
  chicken ragout with fettuccine,
    346
  duck, 347
  eggplant, Mario's, 345
raspberry sabayon, 485
ratatouille
  baked fish with, 94–95
  mushroom and eggplant, Wolfgang
    Puck's, 275
red cabbage. See also cabbage
  Alsatian style, 258
  stewed, with fruits and wine, 258
red caviar. See caviar
red lentil soup, Turkish (ezo gelin), 70.
    See also lentil(s)
red-onion compote, tuna steaks with,
    134. See also onion(s)
red peppers. See also sweet peppers;
    yellow peppers
  and corn blini, 406
  coulis, vegetable cakes with,
    Wolfgang Puck's, 300–301
  pasta with pine nuts and, 340
  relish, fish in hazelnut crust with,
    98–99
  roasting of, 359
red radish. See radishes
red salad, 353–354

red snapper. See also snapper
  baked, with almond stuffing, 92–93
  crusted in sesame seeds, 99–100
  fillets with thyme and yellow
    pepper, 118–119
  grilled with tamari and avocado,
    120
  whole, on bed of fennel with
    mashed Jerusalem
    artichoke-potatoes, 92
relishes. See trimmings
rhubarb
  sauce, fish in (peshe en saltsa), 101
  sherbet, 464
  strawberry and, compote, 485–486
rib-eye steaks, with peppered
    cranberry marmalade and
    Swiss chard, 192–193
rice
  basmati
    with coconut milk and ginger,
      322
    Indian-spiced (marsala bhat),
      321–322
    Persian steamed, with tahdeeg
      crust (chello), 322–323
    Persian with dill and lima beans
      (pollow sheved bakralee),
      323
    Persian, with lentils and currants
      (pollow addas keshmesh),
      324
  pilaf, basic, 321
  pudding
    with dried fruits, 468
    tart, Venetian (torta Turchesca),
      501
  salad, fruited spiced, 373–374
  stuffing
    for chicken, 145
    grape leaves, 11
  Syrian white, Fritzie Abadi's, 320
  Uzbecki beans and (maskitchiri),
    329–330
ricotta
  almond flan with, and oranges,
    490–491
  espresso, honey and ricotta spread,
    432
  Hungarian yeast bread with cheese
    topping (turos lepeny), 445
  latkes, 402
risotto, barley, 314–315
roasted-garlic
  basil paste, 419
  noodle cake, 335
roasted tomato sauce, pita pocket
    pizzas with, 343–344
roast fish. See fish
rolled soufflé, 393–394
rolls. See breads, rolls, bagels and
    matzohs

romaine lettuce
  with lemon-cumin dressing, 353
  tossed salad with honey dressing,
    352–353
Romanian cornmeal (mamaliga), basic
    and dairy, 315–316
rose-water soup, Syrian cold, with
    apricots and pistachios
    (mish mosh), 487
Rosh Ha Shana
  honey cake, with dried fruit and
    nuts, 529
  menu suggestions, 588
rouille (safron-garlic mayonnaise), 416
roulades, with smoked salmon or
    caviar, 26–27
rugelach, cinnamon nut horns, Mimi
    Sheraton's, 519
rum glaze, babka, 546
rutabagas, roasted, 298
rye bread, Old Milwaukee, 442–443

sabayon, raspberry, 485
Sabbath, menu suggestion, 587–588
sable, smoked, salad, potatoes and egg
    mimosa, 376–377
Sacher torte, 553–554
saffron custard, eggplant gratin with,
    398–399
saffron panna cotta, with fresh figs,
    454
safron-garlic mayonnaise (rouille), 416
salad
  artichoke and smoked-salmon,
    Charlie Trotter's, 375–376
  avocado with spiced tahini-yogurt
    dressing, 355
  bean, with red caviar, 374
  beef, boiled, salad vinaigrette, 189
  beet and string bean, warm, 356
  Bibb lettuce hearts with clementines
    and citrus dressing, 352
  black-eyed-pea, with herbs, walnuts
    and pomegranates, 368
  bulgur, Med-rim, 369
  carrot, 357
  chicken, 381–382
  chickpea and olive, with fennel, 369
  coleslaw with poppy seeds and
    scallions, 356
  couscous, curried, grilled onion
    and, 370
  cucumber, 358
  duck, with oranges and onions, 383
  green beans and pepper, with
    cumin vinaigrette, 359
  hummus, pita and yogurt, 367
  kasha, with roasted mushrooms and
    ginger, 370–371
  lamb, grilled with potato, 383–384
  lemon-parsley, grilled, 362
  lentil, 371–372